Bureaucracy and the Policy Process

Bureaucracy and the Policy Process

Keeping the Promises

Dennis D. Riley
and Bryan E. Brophy-Baermann

ROWMAN & LITTLEFIELD PUBLISHERS, INC.
Lanham • Boulder • New York • Toronto • Oxford

ROWMAN & LITTLEFIELD PUBLISHERS, INC.

Published in the United States of America
by Rowman & Littlefield Publishers, Inc.
A wholly owned subsidiary of The Rowman & Littlefield Publishing Group, Inc.
4501 Forbes Boulevard, Suite 200, Lanham, Maryland 20706
www.rowmanlittlefield.com

P.O. Box 317 Oxford OX2 9RU, UK

British Library Cataloguing in Publication Information Available

Library of Congress Cataloging-in-Publication Data

Riley, Dennis D.
    Bureaucracy and the policy process : keeping the promises / Dennis D. Riley
and Bryan E. Brophy-Baermann.
        p.   cm.
    Includes bibliographical references and index.
    ISBN 0-7425-3810-9 (cloth : alk. paper) — ISBN 0-7425-3811-7 (pbk. : alk. paper)
    1. Bureaucracy—United States.   2. Administrative agencies—United States.
3. United States—Politics and government.   I. Brophy-Baermann, Bryan E.   II. Title.
JK421.R518 2006
352.6'3'092273—dc22

                                                                    2005016518

Printed in the United States of America

∞™ The paper used in this publication meets the minimum requirements of American
National Standard for Information Sciences—Permanence of Paper for Printed Library
Materials, ANSI/NISO Z39.48–1992.

Contents

Preface

This book is about bureaucrats as policy makers. Its goals are two, to explain to you why and how bureaucrats have become policy makers and to lay out the forces both inside and outside bureaucracy that influence how bureaucrats choose to play their roles in the policy process.

Chapter 1 is devoted to a consideration of that first goal. It starts with a look at why bureaucracy is indispensable to modern government and then goes on to sketch out how bureaucracy plays the role in policy making that only it can play. Then, before heading on to chapters 2–10 and the discussion of the forces that affect what bureaucrats do and how they do it, the first chapter stops to remind us that we are a society committed to the idea of creating self-government and that fitting bureaucracy into a system of self-government is anything but an easy task.

Both the processes and the outcomes of bureaucratic policy making are dictated in part by the internal dynamics of bureaucracy itself. Those dynamics, in turn, are dictated by the individuals who make up bureaucracy—one organization at a time, but bureaucracy—and the structured environment in which they work. Chapter 2 looks at the individuals who do the work of bureaucracy. Though each bureaucrat really is an individual, there are two identifiable sets of folks in any bureaucracy, the men and women who specialize in the various subject matters that a particular bureaucracy must master if it is to make sense of the questions to be addressed and the men and women who manage the work of all those specialists. Each set comes to a definition of its role in the policy process—including an idea of how to make that role compatible with the values that underlie self-government—and then the two sets work in a somewhat uneasy relationship to try to do what they believe they have been hired to do. Chapter 3 looks at the structured environment in which these two sets of people try to do their respective jobs and how that environment affects what each can accomplish.

Important as these internal dynamics may be, however, external forces are every bit as important in determining what bureaucracy will do and how it will do it. Chapters 4–9 discuss those external forces. Political scientists have long speculated about what makes some agencies—the basic building blocks of bureaucracy—more powerful than others, and chapter 4 addresses that question, arguing that it is primarily the complexity and the controversy associated with the subject matter an agency must deal with that determines the extent to which it is likely to face political pressure and how effectively it can "stand up to" that pressure. Chapters 5 and 6 deal with the most pervasive of external influences on federal government agencies, the President of the United States and the U.S. Congress respectively. The President, it turns out, has only minimal influence on most agencies most of the time, but he does try—and occasionally succeeds—in changing the course of some agencies some of the time. Congress, on the other hand, is a constant in the environment of every agency. For any given agency it isn't the whole Congress, of course. It is a set of congressional committees and subcommittees, but their influence is felt and felt often. Chapter 7 explores the relationships between agencies and the public, or, more properly, between agencies and the various groups that claim to be, or at least to represent, the public. Backed by clientele groups, professional associations, and the occasional independent expert, and opposed by critics, most agencies work their way through the political briar patch without so much as a thought about some abstraction known as the general public. Chapters 8 and 9 take a look at how the legal system serves as an external influence on bureaucratic policy making. All bureaucrats are sworn to uphold the law and the Constitution, and chapter 8 is devoted to understanding how that obligation has been defined. Chapter 9 looks at the questions involved in judicial review of administrative action, in particular at the questions of when such review is available and the ground rules that apply when citizens challenge administrative decisions in court. Finally, chapter 10 pulls all of this together in an analysis of policy making at the Environmental Protection Agency.

Finally, this book is not a typical academic collaboration. It started as Dennis Riley's book, grounded in a course he teaches. Slowly but surely, however, it became Dennis Riley and Bryan Brophy-Baermann's book. As Dennis worked on it, he came to rely more and more on Bryan's insights, examples, and remarkable ability to see relationships between things that don't seem to be related on the surface. That led to Dennis asking Bryan—now a full-fledged scholar of environmental policy—to draft a concluding chapter pulling the emerging book's themes together in an analysis of the Environmental Protection Agency. Then came more discussion, more collaboration, and eventually the decision to make the cover and the title page of the book reflect its construction. In the final product you have in your hand, the collaboration worked out more or less as follows. Bryan did chapter 10—the Environmental Protection Agency: Our Better Angels or Promise Breakers—on his own. Dennis did chapter 4—Some Agencies Are More Powerful Than Others: Expertise, Politics, and Agency Power—on his own. For the other chapters, most of the sentence crafting was done by Dennis. It is simply not possible to attribute the research and analysis to either one of us. We did it together.

So, that's it. We hope you have as much fun reading this book as we had writing it. We also hope you learn as much as we did.

Dennis D. Riley and Bryan E. Brophy-Baermann

Acknowledgments

I don't remember when I first heard the statement "It's not what you know, it's who you know." I don't remember when I first heard it, but you can bet that the Dodgers were still in Brooklyn, the Giants in New York, the Twins in Washington—as the Senators—and the St. Louis Browns were about halfway between their glory year and their move to Baltimore.

I got it. Or at least I thought I did. But I've discovered over a thirty-five-year career in college teaching that I had gotten the cynical surface meaning that most folks intend to convey, but that I hadn't gotten the real meaning that lay beneath that surface. Namely, what will bring you joy and pain, what will bring you triumph and failure, in other words what will make you human, is not the knowledge you accumulate, but the people you meet. I have met some marvelous people these past thirty-five years, and those marvelous people made me who I am, and, therefore, made this book what it is. I want to thank them.

First, I have to thank Ed Stillings. Ed got me interested in political science at Willamette University in the early 1960s and gently steered me toward a career as a college professor. He was also the role model for every day I have spent in this profession. I am forever in his debt. I also have to thank Roscoe Martin, who got me excited about the issues that animate this book during my year at Syracuse University. And I have to thank Jack Walker, who guided me through my time at the University of Michigan with a hand just firm enough to make sure I got it all done, and just gentle enough to make sure I learned to relax and enjoy it.

Second, I want to thank the scholars who attacked the questions examined in this book before me and upon whose work I have tried to build. So thanks to Emmette Redford and Frederick Mosher, to Herbert Kaufman and Francis Rourke, to Dwight Waldo and Victor Thompson, to Hugh Heclo and, though he might not recognize his influence in this book, to Ted Lowi, whose *The End of Liberalism* has been part of everything I have taught and written since I encountered it in my first year as a faculty member at Gonzaga University clear back in 1970.

Third, I want to thank some folks here at the University of Wisconsin, Stevens Point. Mark Cates, John Morser, Richard Christofferson, and I were once considered the four horsemen of the Political Science Department at UWSP. Now I ride alone, but my three retired colleagues will always be my colleagues. They kept this job fun against overwhelming odds. I also want to thank three younger colleagues: John Blakeman, who provides a great sounding board for anything about the courts; Michelle Brophy-Baermann, who has steered a hundred great students my way and whose personal friendship has been a joy these past seven years; and especially Bryan Brophy-Baermann, who has been not just a colleague and now co-author, but the kind of friend who comes along only once or twice in a lifetime. Finally, I'd like to thank Judy Nygaard and Rita Koch. Judy is our program assistant and Rita our work-study student. Both seem to think that no demand is too silly or too much, and both seem to think that creating an atmosphere of mutual respect and cooperation is the way to organize a workplace.

Fourth, I want to thank the students who have made this the greatest job in the world. Over and over, year after year, they keep enrolling in my courses, asking tough questions, writing great exams, and putting up with my sometimes bizarre sense of humor. From Bill Ehmann, Roy Koegen, and John Timm in my first class at Gonzaga University in the fall of 1969, to Colleen Adams, Tami Bauer, Andy Bloeser, Matt Clinton, Will Kramer, Craig Johnson, and Wes Kornowske in the classes I am teaching thirty-five years later, I have always been surrounded by real human beings who want to help me teach and learn.

Fifth, I want to thank the people who made this book happen. There are other books with pedigrees as strange as this one, but probably not many. It was originally signed by Richard Meade of Burnham, Inc., a small Chicago publisher. Burnham, alas, went bankrupt and I figured that was the end of the book. But Mary Lynch of the White Oak Group was given the responsibility of liquidating the company's assets, and she decided that a contract for a nowhere-near-finished book—several of them I suspect—was an asset and signed the redoubtable Tamra Phelps to try to make the sale. She did, or at least she put together a package of materials that convinced Rowman & Littlefield to buy the contract, and the book was alive again. At R&L, Jennifer Knerr, Renee Legatt, and Alden Perkins are unmatched at the care and feeding of the academic author. Finally, an anonymous reviewer for Rowman provided the impetus to completely rewrite chapter 4, improving it immeasurably.

Sixth, thanks to my family. I'm not at all sure who I would be without my wife Pam, my daughters Emily, Annie, and Helena, my son-in-law Scott, my granddaughter Sophie, or my grandson Aiden. But I do know this. Whoever I would be, that man would be so much poorer than I am.

Finally, the acknowledgments page of any book I write must include thanks to Jeff Olen and Jane Cullen. Jeff was a colleague and close friend who convinced me I could write and propped me up when I met with nothing but failure in the early 1980s. Jane Cullen was the acquisitions editor at Temple University Press and a friend of Jeff's. Together they conspired to make me a published author, and in 1987 they finally succeeded, when Temple published *Controlling the Federal Bureaucracy*. Without Jeff and without Jane there would have been no first book, no second book, no books at all.

DDR

A dozen years ago, no one would have predicted that I would be a collaborator on a book about bureaucracy. The specializations I was working on then were international relations and terrorism. My analytic focus was on general trends over long periods of time. I enjoyed (and still do) American politics, but couldn't abide the detailed machinations of the bureaucracy, that "fourth" branch few instructors cover in their introductory courses on American politics. Overall, my training, the general pressure of the profession itself to specialize, and my inclinations would not have allowed the thought. Then life happened. The path from there to here was full of volatility and unpredictability, and a number of people deserve to be acknowledged for helping me get to this now happy place. I owe them a great deal of thanks.

First, I would like to thank two of my professors: Doug Madsen and John Conybeare. They have both been instrumental to my successes (I'll take the blame for all of the failures) in political science. Madsen drew me into the field and got me thinking about the fundamentals of power and conflict to the point where it was almost an obsession. Conybeare helped me focus, and refocus, as I wound my way through my dissertation. Without him I might never have settled on a definition of terrorism, set deadlines for completing my degree, nor been a part of something publishable so early in my career.

Second, I too would like to thank John Morser and Richard Christofferson, two of my former colleagues at UWSP. They played important roles in bringing me to UWSP not once but twice, encouraging me all along the way, and supporting me right up to the present. Morser was a constant reminder about the need for casting a critical eye on all things political. And Christofferson is a key link in the chain of causation from terrorism to the bureaucracy: he taught the environmental policy course at UWSP, and when he retired he suggested I take over, since I had been teaching in international environmental politics. Domestic environmental policy making was a different world to me, but his encouragement and advice led me to overcome my hesitancy and plunge into those bureaucratic machinations. Moreover, I would like to thank my co-author and colleague, Dennis Riley. He too has been a constant source of encouragement, support, and friendship. I have come to rely on his advice, trust his judgment, and take his criticisms because of the great deal of respect I have for him and his expertise. He was patient with me—writing has never flowed as easily for me as it does for him. He never pestered, always believed, and that finally got me to focus (again).

Third, I would like to acknowledge the yeomen efforts of the scholars whose work I have tried to digest and build upon. Thanks, and congratulations on a job well done, go especially to Michael Kraft and Norman Vig, Lawrence Rothenberg, Jacqueline Vaughn Switzer, and Paul Portney. I must note, too, that these scholars' efforts, as well as my own, rest on the tremendous work done by those in government, in the media, and in independent interest groups: they produce the documents, reports, data, and make them as public as possible—often challenging the political status quo to do so. Thanks!

Fourth, I would like to thank the wide variety of students at UWSP who have taken my course in environmental policy making. From freshmen to seniors, from political science majors to students from the College of Natural Resources who had never taken a political science class before, this varied group made me work extra hard to make the mundane interesting, to tie the theoretical to the practical, to make environmental issues relevant but not unsolvable, to emphasize the importance of democratic citizenship and political processes.

Finally, I would like to thank my wife and colleague, Michelle, and my kids, Belamy and Miya. I cannot overstate how much they have influenced who I am, what I care about, and the kind of work I produce. Without their love and support, and their tolerance for my sitting at the computer for another ten hours on another Saturday, I would not be where I am today: this now happy place.

BEB

1

Promises, Promises: The Why and How of Bureaucracy

According to the U.S. Bureau of the Census, nearly 20 million people work for the just over 87,000 units of government currently operating in the United States. It doesn't seem terribly likely that any of those 20 million individuals hung out around Fourteenth and Independence in Washington, D.C., hoping for a glimpse of some of the GS 14s, 15s, or 16s who called the Department of Agriculture building their working home, carpooled with friends out to Silver Spring, Maryland, in the hope of getting autographs from some of the rising stars at the National Oceanic and Atmospheric Administration, or responded to the ever-present inquiry of friends and family about what they intended to do when they "grew up" with an enthusiastic: "be a government bureaucrat."

But bureaucrats they are, and the fact that they are raises a question or two. There is, of course, the question of why they chose such a career. But that is an individual question that—fortunately—I don't have to answer for anyone but myself. The other question, however, does require an answer. Namely, why were there 20 million careers as bureaucrats available for these people to pursue? In other words, why did we as a society create an entity we call "the bureaucracy" and make it big enough to absorb nearly one in every six Americans in the workforce? (Yes, I have slipped the words bureaucracy and bureaucrat into these first two paragraphs without defining them. You will have a pretty good working knowledge of both by the end of the next section of the chapter and know all you need to know about both to handle the rest of the book by the end of the chapter itself.)

KEEPING THE PROMISES: THE WHY OF BUREAUCRACY

To get a handle on the why of bureaucracy, you have to focus on the fact that what government does is make and keep—or at least try to keep—promises. Consider, for a moment, the words of the preamble to the U.S. Constitution: "We the people of the United States, in order to form a more perfect union, establish justice, insure domestic tranquility, provide for the common defense,

1

promote the general welfare, and secure the blessings of liberty to ourselves and our posterity, do ordain and establish this Constitution for the United States of America."

A government is being created "in order to" keep what is obviously a very impressive set of promises, and the document that follows that preamble not only establishes the institutions that will constitute that government but grants those institutions the powers presumed to be necessary for them to go about the tasks set out in that remarkable sentence. It seems clear enough that in order to keep the fundamental promises of the preamble, government has to make and try to keep other promises. At various times in our history we have been convinced that the general welfare required that we promise fledgling—then eventually aging—American industries protection from foreign competition, the railroads vast and valuable tracts of land if they would lay track and run trains across the continent, and the general public air they could breathe, water they could drink, meat they could eat, and medicines they could take, all with considerable confidence that they could breathe, drink, chew, and swallow in safety.

As we move from the eighteenth-century promise that American industry would be protected from European competition by high tariffs to the twentieth-century promises of clean air and water or safe food and drugs, it becomes increasingly clear that the task of keeping promises is far different from the task of making them. First of all, keeping promises requires a substantial amount of technical knowledge about the subject at hand. Second, keeping promises requires a lot of bodies.

Think a bit about the promise of workplace safety. What would it take to move from promise to reality?

To begin with, somebody is going to have to be able to identify the risks present in a particular place of work. It would be difficult enough to recognize the immediate safety threats posed by certain kinds of equipment and machinery, but that would be relatively easy compared to seeing the dangers in many work routines and processes. That, in turn, would be nothing compared to assessing the risks associated with exposure to an almost unbelievable array of chemicals used in various industrial processes around the country. The expertise to do all of this exists, but none of us has all of it and only a few of us have any of it.

Finding out what constitutes a threat to the health and safety of workers is only the beginning, of course. We also have to figure out ways to eliminate those hazards. That, too, requires specialized knowledge most of us just haven't got.

Finally, once we have what we consider a reasonable idea of what threatens the health and safety of America's industrial workforce and what to do about those threats, we've got to do it. That is, we've got to go out to thousands of work sites around the country and identify the specific threats, suggest the corrective actions, and make sure that those actions are taken. Specialized knowledge is still needed, but now we also need bodies. Lots of bodies.

It will surprise absolutely none of you to be told that the level of specialized knowledge and the number of bodies needed to keep the promise of workplace safety—a promise embodied in the Occupational Safety and Health Act of 1970—are not to be found in the Congress, the Oval Office, or the Supreme Court chambers. That government created directly by the Constitution can make the promise of workplace safety. Such a promise, after all, is a value judgment. Any of us is capable of deciding that industrial workers need and deserve protection—or that they don't—and casting a vote to provide or deny that protection. But the constitutional government can't keep the promise, because it lacks the needed expertise and the needed bodies.

Again, to no one's surprise, the constitutional government is well aware that it lacks the bodies and the knowledge to keep the promise of workplace safety, just as it knows it lacks the bodies and the knowledge to keep the promise of safe skies, or protection for the collective bargaining rights of millions of American workers. That government is also aware that promises don't mean much without some sort of effort to keep them. So the promise of workplace safety was accompanied by the creation of the Occupational Safety and Health Administration, the promise of safe skies came complete with the creation of the Federal Aviation Administration, and the promise of protection for workers' rights brought with it the National Labor Relations Board. In short, every time the constitutional government decides that the general welfare, the domestic tranquility, the common defense, or the pursuit of justice or liberty requires that it promise us something more specific, it has to create another organization, that is, a collection of people who bring with them the needed specialized knowledge to deal with the questions raised by the effort to keep this particular promise. The result of all this promise making, then, is a set of such organizations—created one promise at a time—that we lump together and call bureaucracy. The men and women engaged in keeping those promises are the ones we call bureaucrats.

The existence of a large and complex bureaucracy is driven by necessity, that is, by the need for knowledge and bodies. So is much of the power that bureaucracy exercises. But not all of bureaucracy's power derives from the constitutional government's lack of knowledge and bodies. Some of it comes from that constitutional government's lack of political will.

Take, for example, California's July 2002 legislation aimed at curbing the emission of greenhouse gases from the tailpipes of automobiles and light trucks. The law calls for the "maximum feasible reduction" in such emissions, but does so by instructing the California Air Resources Board—a body appointed by the governor—to develop a plan by 2005 to accomplish that objective. There is no statement of how much reduction the board is to seek, or how it is to seek that reduction. There are several avenues closed off—limits on vehicle weight, taxes on miles traveled, and lower speed limits, to name three—but that's it. Give us a plan by 2005 to be put in place by 2009. The legislature reserved for itself the right to review the plan, but did not require of itself another vote to approve that plan.[1]

Clearly, much of the California legislature's vagueness was driven by its own lack of knowledge on exactly how to reduce greenhouse gas emissions. But just as clearly, it could have answered more of the tough political questions than it did, and was just afraid to do it. California is hardly alone. Legislation that shifts tough political decisions from the legislative branch to the bureaucracy can be found at every level of government. In fairness, it can be hard to tell where to draw the line between legitimate necessity and political fear, but such a line exists—and legislatures cross it routinely, even as they complain mightily how the bureaucrats to whom they pass the buck act when the buck ends up in their hands.

GATHERING AND USING INFORMATION: THE HOW OF BUREAUCRACY

Since we create bureaucracy because we need lots of people who know lots of highly specialized things, it should be obvious that bureaucracy's role in the policy process will center around those people and how they use what they know. Before we talk more specifically about what bureaucrats do and how they do it, however, we need to take a look at a couple of preliminaries.

First, I have rather blithely used knowledge and information interchangeably. There is a difference, though they are very closely intertwined. Very roughly, information refers to things we believe we have discovered about the world we live in, while knowledge, again very roughly, refers to the ability to make sense out of the things we believe we have discovered about the world we live in. That is, knowledge refers to the ability to look at a new piece of information, to connect it to other pieces of information, to determine what it means, and perhaps most important of all, to decide what, if anything, we ought to do about what we now know. To use the phrase I nearly gagged on during the summer of 2002, information refers to the "dots" and knowledge to the ability to "connect the dots." When that knowledge becomes more and more removed from what ordinary people know, we begin to refer to it as expertise, a word I'll use quite often in this book, since much of what bureaucrats know really is pretty far removed from what the rest of us know.

Information isn't worth much without knowledge, of course, but neither is knowledge worth much without information. If our goal is to protect spotted owls, it won't do us much good to know how many breeding pairs of owls are needed to sustain the species or precisely what sort of habitat they need to thrive, if we don't have any idea how many breeding pairs are out there or what sort of habitat they live in. Nor would it do us the slightest bit of good to know how many owls are out there and where and how they are living if we don't know how many pairs we need to keep the species going and what sort of habitat they need in order to do it. Without both information and knowledge—expertise—bureaucracy simply can't do what it is supposed to do.

It can't do what it is supposed to do without bodies, too, of course, and that's the second of my preliminaries. The bodies and the information/knowledge come together in integrated packages called human beings. That means that from here on we can focus all of our attention on the information/knowledge part of the bureaucratic package, secure in our own knowledge that only bodies can gather information and possess and use the kind of knowledge that is our concern. So it's off to the business of acquiring knowledge—and information.

Find the Experts and Get the Information

Information has to be gathered and understood before anything can be done with it. If only experts can really understand the information—indeed, in some instances even know which information to collect—we have to start with the finding of experts.

Acquiring Expertise: Hire It

The assumption of all concerned, of course, is that agencies acquire expertise when they hire the experts who make up the agency doing the hiring. These agencies, do, after all, describe jobs in terms of the skill and knowledge needed to do them—or at least in terms of the degrees and experience that are supposed to generate that skill and knowledge—and they pore over the credentials of those who would claim to have them. Sometimes I have trouble imagining the Talmud, the Koran, or the Book of Revelation getting a more careful textual analysis than did the transcripts and letters of recommendation of applicants for teaching positions in the department I chaired for twelve years. An agency's own experts may have to be supplemented by outside experts now and then—in some cases even routinely with specialized advisory committees, such as those created by the Food and Drug Administration to review new drug applications—but for the most part agencies assume that they have hired the kinds of people who know what information to collect and how to use it to keep the promises that are at the heart of the agency's existence, and they are willing to proceed on that assumption.

Acquiring Information: Research and Investigation

Some of the information gathering that bureaucrats do is essentially research, much like the research they did as undergraduate, or more likely, graduate or professional students, before joining a particular agency.

Some of that research is basic and done directly by the agency staff. Biochemists at the National Institute for Occupational Safety and Health research the effects of exposure to specific chemicals used in certain industrial processes, while epidemiologists at the Centers for Disease Control and Prevention continue to try to understand AIDS, and hydrologists at the Bureau of Reclamation investigate the impact of continued population growth in Phoenix and Tucson on the region's underground aquifer. Other basic research needed by government is conducted at universities and think tanks. Some of that research is funded by the agencies who need the information, and some is not, but either way, agency experts are going to review that information, fit it into the information they already have, and decide whether and how to use it.

Agencies are also engaged in another, closely connected type of research, research aimed at more specific and immediate questions. In the fall of 1996, for example, the Food and Drug Administration (FDA) was faced with an outbreak of food poisoning, which it eventually traced to e coli bacteria present in some fresh New England apple cider. That, in turn, led the FDA to see if it could find an alternative to pasteurization as a means of eliminating that danger while preserving that "fresh apple cider flavor," a flavor which the companies producing the cider were sure would be destroyed by applying Pasteur's century-old technique for killing germs. That same year, the National Highway Traffic Safety Administration accelerated its research into the safety of automobile airbags, and, as they do every year, the Centers for Disease Control and Prevention researchers tried to find out enough about that year's strain of flu to provide pharmaceutical companies with the information needed to produce the vaccine needed to combat it.

Vital as this basic and applied research may be, much of the information gathering engaged in by bureaucrats would fall more into the category of inspection or investigation. The Occupational Safety and Health Administration, for example, has to measure noise levels in factories, inspect construction sites, and go over the accident and illness records of hundreds of companies. The Federal Deposit Insurance Corporation has to examine the books of every national bank, just as someone at the Wage and Hour Division of the Employment Standards Administration has to look at the payroll of the Baker, Oregon, Pizza Hut if someone complains that that particular Pizza Hut isn't paying its employees the overtime it is required to pay by federal law.[2]

In short, agencies assume they have the knowledge (expertise) to make sense out of what they find. They got it when they chose the men and women they chose to do the work of that particular agency. Then these experts go out and gather the information they will need to do the other part of their jobs. They do basic research and read the results of the basic research of others, and they do more specific or applied research. They inspect and they investigate. When they are done, they know a great deal. Now it's time to talk about how they use what they know.

Using Knowledge: Advice, Rules, and Enforcement

Once they have gathered information and made sense out of it, bureaucrats use it in three ways. They share it with decision makers and with the public, usually in the form of advice. They use it as the basis for what is generally their most visible—and vilified—activity, the writing of rules. And they use it to enforce the rules they have written. Let's consider each of these in turn.

 Using Bureaucratic Knowledge I: Information and Advice

Sometimes bureaucrats simply tell us, or tell the constitutional government, what they know and leave it to us—or to the President or Congress—to figure out what to do with it. Sometimes. Most of the time, however, they tell what they know and offer at least some suggestions about what course of action is dictated by what they have just said.

Informing the Constitutional Government

When we think of bureaucrats providing information/advice to the constitutional government, we think first of men and women trying to keep the President abreast of what's going on in their particular corner of the government. The President is, after all, the chief executive, charged with the responsibility that the laws be faithfully executed. Informing the chief of what they know and what they think ought to be done is certainly part of the bureaucratic job description.

It was frequently the responsibility of President Clinton's Trade Representative, for example, to brief him on the intellectual property rights questions raised by the considerable skill the Chinese seemed to possess at bootlegging compact discs. Just before he left the job in 1997, Mickey Kantor also had to inform the President about China's penchant for making clothing and sewing in labels to make it appear that the clothing had been produced elsewhere, so it could be brought into the United States without appearing to violate "voluntary" quotas on textile imports. Though it was often lost in the crush of other news, President George W. Bush's Trade Representative spent time in 2002 offering his chief information and advice, first on international reaction to Mr. Bush's decision to impose stiff quotas on steel imports, then on Europe's considerable frustration with the substantial subsidies contained in that year's $70 billion farm bill. It is well known to all concerned that few of the information/advice sessions that bureaucrats hold with the President will rise to the level of public attention captured by that briefing about the possibility of terrorist hijackings of airliners delivered at President Bush's Texas ranch in August of 2001. Still, Immigration and Naturalization Service and Food and Drug Administration commissioners, Forest Service chiefs, Bureau of Reclamation and Bureau of Land Management directors, and, of course, the ever-present directors of the Federal Bureau of Investigation and the Central Intelligence Agency, know that they must be ready to provide the chief executive with information and advice should he or she ever decide to ask for it. It goes with the job.

Congress, too, expects bureaucrats to supply it with information and advice. In fact, if you ever end up in a key position at nearly any agency of the federal government, your odds of being asked to provide information or advice to Congress are far greater than your odds of being asked to provide either information or advice to the President of the United States. As we'll see in chapter 6, it is committees and subcommittees of the House and Senate that ask for this information and advice, and they ask for it for a wide variety of reasons. But ask they do, and they expect key bureaucrats to drop whatever else they might be doing and head over to the hill to provide answers to the committee's questions. A quarter century ago, Herbert Kaufman found that the Commissioner of the FDA and his top staff made eighty-five separate appearances before congressional committees in a single year.[3] The determination of Congress and its committees and subcommittees to ask questions of those who serve in the various agencies of government certainly hasn't diminished in the intervening years. Before President Bush decided to push for creation of a Department of Homeland Security rather than continue to fight such proposals, members of Congress grew very restive at the thought of not being able to ask questions of Tom Ridge, the President's Homeland Security Advisor. During the late spring and summer of 2002, nearly a dozen subcommittees were active in questioning all sorts of executive branch folks in the wake of revelations of potential "intelligence failures" leading up to the events of September 11, 2001. Even more than a dozen subcommittees took an immediate interest in questions arising from the accounting practices of a number of firms and their impact on corporate profits, stock prices, and the economic fate of company shareholders and employees. In short, Congress sees itself as having every bit as much of a claim on the information and advice of the bureaucracy as the President has, and it will do what it takes to assert that claim. Bureaucracy will respond.

We don't normally think of bureaucrats providing information/advice to the courts, but they do. Since, as we shall see in chapter 9, the courts play their role in our governing system by deciding specific cases, bureaucrats are normally called on to provide information without the advice, and to do it in the context of such cases. In the vast majority of instances, that information will consist of an explanation of what an agency has done and why, an explanation needed so that a judge can evaluate a citizen complaint about the action in question. There are agencies, however, which do provide information and advice to the courts in a direct way. U.S. companies who wish to merge must notify the Bureau of Competition of the Federal Trade Commission (FTC) and the Anti-trust Division of the Department of Justice of their intentions, and each agency must evaluate the proposed merger under the provisions of a variety of statutes. Back in the summer of 1997, the FTC's Bureau of Competition concluded that a proposed merger between Office Depot and Staples—at that time two of the nation's leading office supply chains—should not be permitted to go forward. At that point, the commission's job was to put the bureau's conclusion before a U.S. district court. On June 30, 1997, a U.S. district judge agreed with the FTC that the information presented to him justified an order delaying the merger and calling for a full-scale trial to determine its ultimate fate.[4]

Informing the Public

Bureaucrats are also in the business of sharing what they know with the public. We are all familiar with the National Weather Service's daily sharing of what it knows—or thinks it knows, anyway—about what we can expect from the weather, and even those of us who don't smoke have some idea of the Surgeon General's advice to smokers. But bureaucratic information sharing with the public goes far beyond these obvious examples. I was extremely glad in August of 2001 when the Food and Drug Administration blanketed the airwaves with the news that Bayer had voluntarily recalled the cholesterol-lowering drug Baycol from the market because of some very serious side effects experienced by some users of the drug. I was so glad, of course, because I had just begun taking Baycol and was having some trouble with a muscle in my leg, trouble that sounded remarkably like one of those side effects.

Then there is all the information gathered by the Federal Reserve System and shared with banks and thrift institutions, the information gathered by the Labor and Commerce Departments and shared with businesses and consumers alike, and perhaps the most extensive of all of government's information-sharing activities, those that fall under the jurisdiction of the Under Secretary of Agriculture for Research, Education, and Economics. From tornado warnings to health warnings to suggestions to improve soybean yields to the index of leading economic indicators, government is in the business of providing information and advice to the public. A good bit of it we end up using.

Using Bureaucratic Knowledge II: Writing Rules

As I said more than once in the first part of this chapter, statutes are promises. They state what we want to make happen and then they create and/or empower some agency to try to make it happen.

The Clean Air Act, for example, mandates reductions in the level of what is called fine particle pollution. It also empowers the Environmental Protection Agency (EPA) to write—and enforce, but that's for the next section of the chapter—rules spelling out how much fine particle pollution will be allowed from which particular sources. Diesel fuel contains a good deal of sulfur, making diesel engines a pervasive source of fine particle pollution throughout the country. EPA has issued rules requiring a decrease from 500 parts per million of sulfur in diesel fuel—the current level—to 15 parts per million by the year 2006. But the rules don't apply to off-road diesel vehicles—farm and construction machinery primarily—and some of them use fuel containing as much as 3,000 parts per million of sulfur. Another rule is on the way.[5]

EPA also has responsibility for keeping the promises contained in the Safe Drinking Water Act and the Food Quality Protection Act, and that, too, means writing rules. In early June 2002, while some at the agency were struggling with the process of putting together a new rule for the fuel used in off-road diesel equipment, others were trying to assess the information available to them about the pesticide atrazine and its possible impact on the health of millions of Americans who might be exposed to it through their drinking water or through eating crops grown in fields in which it was used. Presented with a study indicating serious abnormalities in frogs exposed to the chemical, an adamant response from the manufacturer saying the frog study was flawed, evidence of a higher than normal incidence of prostate cancer among the men who work in the plant producing atrazine, and a demand from the Natural Resources Defense Council that the pesticide be banned from use immediately, the EPA has to sort through what it knows and come to some conclusion about the need for a new rule.[6]

While the EPA struggles with rules about atrazine and sulfur in diesel fuel, the Occupational Safety and Health Administration worries—as it has for the better part of a decade—about the need for rules to deal with repetitive-motion injuries, the Federal Aviation Administration continues to consider new rules for fuel-tank safety on commercial airliners, and the Food and Drug Administration (FDA) wonders if some day it will end up writing rules governing the content of cigarettes. Every agency has its statutory promises to keep, and keeping those promises almost certainly means writing rules.

Using Bureaucratic Knowledge III: Enforcing the Rules

Anyone who has ever raised—or, for that matter, like all of us simply been—a teenager knows that as important as setting the rules may be, it is the decisions made in the process of enforcing those rules that have the direct and immediate impact on the lives of those who must obey them. It wasn't, after all, the decision of the FDA to set standards for the manufacture of drugs that cost the

Schering-Plough Corporation $500 million in May of 2002. It was the FDA's conclusion that the company had failed to meet those standards—repeatedly failed to meet them—that sparked the negotiations that resulted in Schering-Plough's agreement to pay the record settlement.[7]

The notion of rule enforcement encompasses an almost unbelievable array of activities, but they all have one thing in common. They start with an agency gathering information. The question at hand is always simple enough. Are the rules being followed? Sometimes the information gathering takes the form of a routine inspection, whether of a facility or a set of documents. Other times, it takes the form of what might be called an inquiry or investigation triggered by some suspicion that some folks have in fact been breaking the rules. Regardless of the form it takes, the information gathering inevitably has as its focus two questions. Are the rules being broken, and if so, what should the agency do about it?

As I noted above, the phrase "agency enforcement action" covers a remarkable variety of decisions. Consequently, there is no way we can—and no reason we should—try to catalog all of them. But it would still be useful to give you at least a representative sample.

I have already mentioned the FDA's inspections of the manufacturing facilities used by the pharmaceutical industry and its resulting $500 million settlement with Schering-Plough. The agency reached a $100 million settlement over similar issues with Abbot Laboratories in 1999 and in 2002 negotiated with Eli Lilly over compliance problems in some of its Indiana facilities. The FDA's agreement with Schering-Plough illustrates another key element in many enforcement actions, namely, an agreement by the company to submit a plan for bringing its manufacturing operations into compliance with the rules and even an agreement to hire outside consultants to monitor that compliance on a continuous basis, something the agency simply does not have the personnel to accomplish. Should the FDA conclude that a company's violations reach a certain level of seriousness, it can turn that conclusion over to its own Office of Criminal Investigation, as it did with some of its complaints against Schering-Plough.[8]

Of course the Food and Drug Administration doesn't just inspect drug company factories. It also has to approve all new prescription drugs as well as review drugs already on the market should problems with those drugs be called to their attention. Again, I already mentioned the agency's successful efforts to get Bayer to recall Baycol. This came less than a year after its successful efforts to convince British manufacturer GlaxoSmithKline to recall Lotronex, a prescription treatment for irritable bowel syndrome. Neither of these medicines was alone. More than 300 drugs had to be recalled during 2001. In a rare move, in June of 2002, the FDA allowed Lotronex back into the American market, but under a very strictly drawn marketing agreement, which would seriously limit its use, and, consequently, its profitability.[9]

Product recalls, of course, are a way of life at the National Highway Traffic Safety Administration and the Consumer Product Safety Commission. As with the FDA, most of those recalls are voluntary—carefully and sometimes forcefully negotiated, but voluntary—and, again as with the FDA, conditions for the products' continued use are sometimes part of the bargain. The Federal Aviation Administration (FAA) doesn't exactly recall airlines, but they do have the power to shut them down—the official mechanism would be a suspension of the carrier's operating certificate—and the agency has done so on very rare occasions. Its investigation of ValuJet following a crash in the Florida Everglades in the mid-1990s led it to pull that airline's certificate. The certificate was ultimately reinstated, but only after a long and careful process in which the carrier was required to demonstrate to the FAA the existence of a plan to correct the problems that had led to the suspension in the first place and the personnel, equipment, and capital to carry that plan out.

As I noted earlier, the list can go on forever, from Forest Service timber planners setting the terms of sale for particular stands of trees, through U.S. Fish and Wildlife Service wildlife biologists deciding to place a particular animal on the protected—or endangered—list, on to veterinarians at the Animal and Plant Health Inspection Service refusing to permit private labs to do the testing of deer carcasses to determine if the deer suffered from chronic wasting disease.[10] The point remains the same. Bureaucrats gather information about a specific situation and decide whether what they have discovered requires action by the agency they work for. If it does, they try to decide what sort of action will be most likely to eliminate whatever rules violation they have uncovered. Friendly chat, written warning, requirement of a plan to correct the problem, a half-billion dollar settlement, or even criminal prosecution are all in the catalog of agency enforcement actions. The question is always, which one fits?

In Summary

Bureaucracy exists because the constitutional government can't keep the promises it makes. Gathering up enough people to carry out the myriad of tasks required to keep all of those promises—carefully making sure they possess the specialized knowledge needed to figure out how to keep them—the hundreds of agencies that make up that bureaucracy set out to gather the information they need, to make sense of that information, and then to use it. So they engage in research and they review research and they do inspections and they even conduct investigations. Then they tell us what they have found. And they tell the constitutional government that represents us what they have found. Sometimes they tell us how we ought to behave based on what they have just told us. They also write rules that tell us how we must behave. Then they have to make sure we are abiding by those rules.

That is a tall order, and now we are about to make it even taller. Bureaucracy has to do all of this without losing sight of our very first promise to ourselves, the promise of self-government.

THE DILEMMA OF BUREAUCRACY: FIRST PROMISE

The promises of the Preamble reflected the earlier promise—premise, perhaps— of the Declaration of Independence: "That to secure these rights governments are instituted among men, deriving their just powers from the consent of the governed." We were going to govern ourselves. To be sure, the "governed" whose consent the new government sought included only white male property owners, and it took nearly a century before Abraham Lincoln would call it a government of, by, and for the people. Still, self-government was the goal and the promise, and our history is a history of an ever expanding commitment to the notion of government power grounded in the consent of those to be governed and an ever expanding notion of precisely whose consent must be sought if government is to be considered just.

It never really occurred to us to govern ourselves directly, of course. The idea was always self-government through representative institutions. That's what the Constitution is there to create. The question then becomes, how can we delegate the task of governing to institutions, even institutions created for that purpose, and still be said to be governing ourselves? Without doubt, better minds than mine have been wrapped around that question, but I'm convinced that we can say we have a pretty good approximation of self-government through representative institutions if we can get those institutions to be responsive, respectful of the rights of individuals, and accountable for their actions. Let's talk about each of those in turn.

Responsiveness

There is no simple definition for the notion of responsiveness, but at a minimum it has to mean that governing institutions do things the people want done and don't do things the people do not want done. There is room for the representatives to "lead"—I prefer educate, actually, but that should be no surprise—but in the end what the representative institutions do should be pretty close to what the people would have done themselves were they there to do it.

But responsiveness in the American political system—in any system of self-government in a modern society—is complicated by the fact that for any decision government must make, there will be at least two different sets of people that system finds worthy of being heard and responded to. There is always the majority. It can hardly be self-government if people aren't considered equally worthy of participation and influence; and if all are to count equally in a given situation, institutions claiming to represent the people are going to have to listen to majority interests. But we are also very concerned about the interests of those directly and substantially affected by the decision to be made.

That concern stems in part from the political calculus a representative institution is obligated to make. Those with a direct and substantial stake in a decision government is about to make will be far more motivated to take an interest in that decision, indeed, to use the outcome of that decision as a basis for future political action. In more concrete terms, Congress didn't vote for a $70 billion farm bill in the spring of 2002 because the majority of citizens was clamoring for it, but because every member knew that those in the agriculture community would be voting in the congressional elections that November and that the outcome of the farm bill vote would have a real impact on how that farm community voted in that election. Members of Congress were also betting, of course, that those of us not in the farm community would find that $70 billion vote of only passing interest.

We are also concerned with the thoughts of the directly and substantially affected because we believe that their greater stake in a particular decision entitles them to some special consideration—consideration beyond their numbers—when that decision is made. We just think it's fair. They have so much to gain or lose in a particular decision and most of the rest of us so little. Frustrated as I may be about which particular members of the agriculture community had the biggest stakes in the 2002 farm bill, I am still forced to concede that there are members of that community whose way of life depended on passing the legislation, and that seems to make my share of the bill pale by comparison.

The 2002 farm bill still may have been lousy public policy. But you can see how the political calculation, buttressed by a concern—perhaps misunderstood, certainly overstated, but a concern—for the fairness of the situation would lead a representative body to conclude that it was being properly responsive when the bill was passed.

There are groups of citizens who do not get the same sort of solicitous attention that the agriculture community gets, of course. But it remains true that in our system, for representative institutions to be responsive they have to listen to the majority and to the directly and substantially affected "minority" and balance the two sets of interests as they make decisions. The problem isn't in the two-pronged notion of responsiveness. The problem is in a system that hears only from some kinds of groups of directly and substantially affected citizens.

Respect for the Rights of Individuals

"And endowed by their creator with certain unalienable rights." If, as Jefferson goes on to say, governments are created for the purpose of securing these rights, it can't be self-government through representative institutions unless those institutions have respect for the rights of individuals. Once again, "life, liberty, and the pursuit of happiness" may have been "unalienable rights," but they were rights for a fairly small percentage of the population. But, also once again, the power of the words and their constant repetition led to a national history of the expansion of the nature of individual rights, and, more to the point, of exactly who constituted an individual entitled to those rights. The Bill of Rights—augmented a bit by the Fourteenth Amendment and its equal protection clause—is the place we look to understand our version of the rights of individuals. When we do, we see two different but distinctly complementary notions of those rights.

First, we see an effort to put areas of an individual's life off limits to government intervention. Nothing is completely off limits, of course, but we do tend to give individuals pretty wide latitude when it comes to religious belief and practice, speech, and association—the key ingredients in the First Amendment. And though it raises a red flag or two in some quarters, most of us agree that there is something called privacy and that Americans are entitled to it.

Second, and more to the point in terms of our look at bureaucracy and its role in policy making, when we speak of individual rights we are speaking of protection from arbitrary government action. We tell government it cannot search anywhere it wishes, any time it wishes, or take anything it feels to be evidence of a crime. We tell it not to coerce confessions, put people on trial without benefit of counsel, punish in cruel and unusual ways, or put people in jail unless those people have been convicted of some specified crime by an impartial jury. And we tell government that it must accord all citizens equal protection of the laws and that if it takes any action that might deprive any citizen of his or her life, liberty, or property, it must guarantee that citizen due process of law.

Individuals have rights, and a representative government has to respect those rights. It has to do its best to stay out of people lives, and when it has to intervene in those lives, whether to accuse someone of murder or instruct someone not to build a septic system that close to a lake, that government has to play by a carefully crafted set of rules, a set of rules designed to equalize what without those rules would be a decidedly unequal battle.

Accountability

Finally, if we are to get self-government through representative institutions, those institutions must be accountable to the people. At a minimum, with respect to any government decision, we must be able to find out what decision was made and who made it. We also have to be able to discipline the decision maker or makers in question if we are unhappy with the decision that was made. We hope to achieve accountability in three interrelated ways.

First, and most obvious in a system of representative institutions, we try to hold government accountable politically. In simple terms, we have elections and those elections are supposed to represent our collective retrospective judgment on the performance of government since the last election. That kind of direct political accountability is impossible in bureaucracy, of course, so we have to look for substitutes in the influence of representative institutions—and of the public itself—on bureaucratic decision making.

Second, we try to hold government accountable through the law. With respect to bureaucracy, that means three different things. To begin with, there is an entire body of law called administrative law that tells bureaucrats how they ought to make decisions. Those rules and procedures are supposed to embody the notions of responsiveness and respect for the rights of individuals that we want to put at the center of our governing system, so in a sense they provide both legal and political accountability. Beyond administrative law, there is judicial review of bureaucratic decision making. A citizen unhappy with anything done by any agency can mount a court challenge to that action. There are all kinds of rules governing those challenges, including some that in effect rule out the challenge itself, but the presumption is that agency actions are subject to review in the courts and that review is a mechanism for accountability. Finally, citizens can sue the government for monetary damages for actions that government has taken.

Last of all, we expect government to hold itself accountable. That is, we expect individual bureaucrats to be ethical public servants, committed to the notions of responsiveness and respect for individual rights and willing to hold themselves to the highest possible standards of responsible behavior.

But Don't Forget Effectiveness

Government—including bureaucracy—must be responsive, respectful of the rights of individuals, and accountable if we are to meet the first promise of self-government. But the Preamble makes some substantive promises about the common defense and the general welfare, and the constitutional government has made subsequent substantive promises about clean air and clean water and safe food. As we've said numerous times in this chapter, that constitutional government has also moved to create and empower organizations composed of individuals possessed of the specialized knowledge we assume is necessary to keep those substantive promises. We don't want those organizations to lose sight of their original purpose, keeping substantive promises by applying their knowledge and bodies to the questions at hand. In other words, while bureaucracy is being responsive, respectful of individual rights, and accountable, it is also supposed to be effective. That is, it is supposed to keep the promises it was established to keep.

Ultimately, as I suggested above, effectiveness means keeping the promise in question. But no agency can be sure when it makes a particular decision whether that decision is going to be effective in that ultimate sense. So if effectiveness is going to be one of the guideposts for bureaucratic decision making—and for our evaluation of that decision making—bureaucrats, as well as those of us who watch them, are going to need a working definition for the concept. Given the fact that our need for bureaucracy centers on the knowledge bureaucrats bring to their tasks, that working definition of effectiveness is also going to have to center on knowledge. In other words, bureaucrats and citizens alike are going to have to define effectiveness as the application of the best available expert knowledge to the decision at hand. Ironically, our look at bureaucracy is going to show that agencies relying on what they defined as the best available expert knowledge have frequently produced policies that were anything but effective in the ultimate sense of keeping the underlying promise a particular policy and the agency that adopted it were supposed to be keeping. Still, we have no choice but to use that working definition of effectiveness, all the while realizing that agencies can easily, and will often, think they are applying the best available specialized knowledge when they are not.

The Dilemma of Bureaucracy Becomes Real: Juggling Responsiveness, Rights, and Effectiveness

I have used this metaphor for a long time, but the fact that our youngest daughter married a juggler has given me a new appreciation for it. Juggling three balls takes some practice—I've watched Scott try to teach it—but this is much tougher than most three-ball juggling acts. The balls aren't uniform sizes and shapes, and there are all sorts of other people—the Congress, the President, the Courts, and the people themselves—standing onstage with the juggler and occasionally reaching in, grabbing one of the balls, reshaping it, and tossing it back into the act.

Start with the ball marked responsiveness. It is, remember, actually two balls merged into one, and the two halves are not always equal in weight. Worse yet, the juggler can't always be sure which half is going to be heavier when he or she goes onstage. As we shall see later, the responsiveness to the directly and substantially affected citizenry will normally be the heavier half, but events can change that. When a man named Arthur Levitt was the chief juggler at the Securities and Exchange Commission, he found that the half of the responsiveness ball marked accounting industry and friends was much heavier than the half marked

investors, employees, and pension holders. A couple of years and some spectac-
ular accounting-driven business collapses later, the halves had changed relative
weights, much to the frustration of the new chief juggler—Harvey Pitt—who
had once represented the folks in the accounting industry half. Most important,
of course, the relative weights of the two halves faced by each juggler were determined not by the jugglers—each, after all, would have preferred the opposite
weighting—but outside actors. In the case of Mr. Levitt it was members of the
Congress, and in the case of Mr. Pitt it was both members of Congress (some of
the same ones, by the way) and the President who reached into the SEC chief's
juggling act and changed the responsiveness ball.

The balls marked respect for individual rights and effectiveness are somewhat
more uniform and predictable, but they are still subject to outside influence
and redefinition. The courts are always ready to step in and reshape the ball
marked respect for individual rights, as they did in a landmark case requiring the
New York City Welfare Department to hold the hearing at which a recipient could
challenge a decision to terminate welfare benefits *before* and not after the benefits
were actually revoked.[11] There are even groups ready to challenge an agency's
definition of the ball marked effectiveness, that is, to say that an agency has not
brought the best available expert knowledge to bear on a particular decision. As
I noted earlier, the Natural Resources Defense Council (NRDC) has challenged
the Environmental Protection Agency's lack of action on the pesticide atrazine.
In the words of Jennifer Sass, one of the council's senior scientists, "I think that
the EPA has missed the boat on the cancer assessment completely, because they
did not have available important information about its links to cancer."[12] NRDC
will first ask EPA to redefine the effectiveness ball in this case, but if that fails,
they will almost certainly ask the courts to reach in and force the agency to do it.

If you are getting a little weary of the juggling metaphor, please hang in there.
Its real point is about to become clear. Even when nobody jumps onstage and
grabs one of the balls, changes it, and throws it back in, responsiveness, respect
for the rights of individuals, and effectiveness can bang into one another, making
it very tough for the juggler to keep them all in the air. Yet keeping them all in
the air is exactly what we want that juggler to do.

Sometimes it is easy enough for the juggler to see the collision coming. It is
hard to imagine any homeland security or immigration specialist being unaware
that a proposal for a national identity card to be required for any transaction involving air travel, car or truck rental, purchase of fertilizer or diesel fuel, or just
upon the demand of any law enforcement officer, would, no matter how effective
it might be in eliminating threats to our security and our borders, bump smack
into our belief in the rights of individuals. For that matter, it would bump smack
into the intensely held preferences against such a card that would develop in
a number of minority communities in the United States. In other cases a juggler might be caught quite off guard by the collision between two balls, as the
city of New York was when the U.S. Supreme Court told it that its policy of
post-termination hearings for recipients "kicked off" the welfare rolls violated
the due process rights of those individual recipients, whatever its merits in conserving government resources and speeding up the process of reducing welfare
fraud.[13]

Whether they see any particular collision coming or not, all of our bureaucratic jugglers are well aware that such collisions are going to happen and that sometimes they are going to have to let one or even two balls hit the stage because the other has to be kept up. The strongly held preferences of southern whites aside, African Americans had to be given the right to vote and that right had to be enforced. That ball had to stay in the air whatever happened to the others.

But, over the long haul, we don't want any of our bureaucratic jugglers to decide that one of those balls is so much more important than the other two that it must never be allowed to drop. If effectiveness becomes the only goal, then self-government has no further meaning. If responsiveness is the only goal, we may wander into policies that simply don't work, and we will surely wander into policies that violate the rights of individuals. If the rights of individuals become the only goal, we are just as certain to trample on the sincerely held beliefs of a majority of citizens and may well produce less effective policies in the bargain.

In Summary

We create bureaucracy because only through a large set of organizations, each composed of lots of men and women in possession of a wide range of specialized knowledge, can we possibly begin to do all of the things our representative institutions have decided we want to get done. So that bureaucracy sets out committed to the goal of effectiveness, that is, committed to the idea that by gathering information and applying the best available expert knowledge to that information, it will ultimately make decisions that keep the promises the constitutional government has made. But long before any substantive promises were made, the first promise of self-government through representative institutions was made, and that means finding ways to make sure that those governing institutions—including the bureaucracy the representative institutions found it necessary to create—are responsive, respectful of individual rights, and accountable.

In the end, then, we create a set of organizations and tell each to take great care to be effective, but to do it without sacrificing responsiveness and respect for the rights of individuals. Then we try to make sure they do all of this by having their performance monitored by the directly representative institutions of the constitutional government—the President and Congress—as well as by the public—in some of its guises—and by the legal system that is also part of that constitutional government. This book is going to be about that set of organizations, the people who work there, and how they try to make the decisions they are supposed to make in the environment in which they are supposed to make them.

SUMMARY AND CONCLUSION

Bureaucracy exists because the institutions we created to govern ourselves more than 200 years ago can make promises to us—promises they are convinced we want made, of course—but they can't keep those promises. They don't have the

bodies or the knowledge that would be required. Given the reasons for its existence, it comes as no surprise that bureaucracy tries to keep the promises it was
created to keep by gathering information and then sharing that information with
us and with the constitutional government, and applying the knowledge it possesses to that information to write and enforce rules that will make the promises
contained in statutes something more than promises.

In playing its role in our governing system, bureaucracy is expected to focus
on its knowledge and use that knowledge to produce effective policies—policies
grounded in knowledge that eventually keep the promises they were aimed at
keeping—but, likewise, bureaucracy is expected to pay attention to the fact that
we are striving for self-government, and that means responsiveness, respect for
the rights of individuals, and accountability. So bureaucrats must take account of
how the public—defined as the majority and defined as the directly affected and
maybe even defined as a balance between the two—will react to their decisions.
They must also take account of how those decisions might affect the rights of
individual citizens. And they have to be prepared to answer for their decisions,
answer to the President, the Congress, and the public, and answer to the law and
the courts.

It may be that "no man can serve two masters." But we expect bureaucrats
to serve many more. And we expect them to do it well. This book is about how
they try to do it.

NOTES

1. Danny Hakim, "California Is Moving to Guide U.S. Policy on Pollution," *New York
Times* (electronic edition), July 3, 2002.

2. I am not picking on Baker, Oregon, or its Pizza Hut. I used Baker for the fun of it. I
had a couple of fraternity brothers from Baker forty years ago and I thought I would plug
their hometown. However, as recently as the spring of 1997 there were some very serious
charges leveled at Pizza Hut, the multinational corporation, and those charges did involve
cheating their employees out of legitimately earned wages.

3. Herbert Kaufman, *The Administrative Behavior of Federal Bureau Chiefs*
(Washington, D.C.: Brookings Institution, 1981), 48.

4. National Public Radio, *Morning Edition*, July 1, 1997.

5. Andrew C. Revkin, "E.P.A. and Budget Office to Work Jointly on Diesel Soot Rules,"
New York Times (electronic edition), June 8, 2002.

6. John H. Cushman Jr., "New Study Adds to Debate on E.P.A. Rules for Pesticide,"
New York Times (electronic edition), June 2, 2002.

7. Melody Petersen, "Drug Maker to Pay $500 Million Fine for Factory Lapses,"
New York Times (electronic edition), May 18, 2002.

8. Petersen, "Drug Maker to Pay $500 Million." Also see Melody Petersen and Reed
Abelson, "Drug Makers and F.D.A. Fighting Hard Over Quality," *New York Times* (electronic edition), May 17, 2002.

9. Denise Grady, "U.S. Lets Drug Tied to Deaths Back on Market," *New York Times*
(electronic edition), June 8, 2002.

10. I didn't make any of these up, even the last one. Chronic wasting disease has been
discovered in the deer herd here in Wisconsin and it has state hunters and wildlife managers scared. Deer have been shot out of season, but APHIS believes it cannot trust many

privately operated labs to perform the tests necessary to discover whether a particular deer was infected, so the tests must be done at state and federal labs, which are overwhelmed by the volume of testing they must now do.

11. *Goldberg v. Kelly* 397 U.S. 254 (1970).
12. Cushman, "New Study Adds to Debate."
13. *Goldberg v. Kelly*.

2

The Individual Bureaucrat

Somebody Has to Do All That Work

As I noted just a moment ago, organizations don't gather, interpret, and use information. Individuals do. In effect, then, the admonitions to be effective and to be responsive and respectful of individual rights, along with the warning that they will be held accountable for their actions, are not the marching orders for some dark, anonymous entity we call bureaucracy. Rather they are the goals, expectations, values, maybe ultimately the hopes we have for these individual men and women who make up the specific organizations that in turn make up our bureaucracy. This chapter is about how those individual men and women interpret and apply those goals, values, expectations, and hopes as they gather, analyze, and most important, use information in the process of keeping the promises they have been hired to try to keep.

There are actually two very different sets of individual bureaucrats engaged in interpreting the mandates handed them by the constitutional government, so we need to start by identifying those two groups and exploring the most important differences between them. Then we will briefly review the mandate these two sets of people are interpreting, and take a look at the two very different interpretations they come to.

A TALE OF TWO BUREAUCRATIC CITIES

Don't worry. I won't put you through anything like the juggling metaphor. But sometimes it does appear that the two sets of bureaucrats I am about to talk about inhabit different cities. Sometimes it almost seems like they inhabit different planets. And how exactly do the denizens of these two different cities or planets differ from one another in terms of how and why they get their jobs, how long they expect to stay, and where they place their loyalties?

The City of the Policy Specialists

Bureaucracy exists because the constitutional government doesn't have the expertise it needs to answer some of the questions it has to answer, and part of that bureaucracy's mandate is to hire men and women who can answer those questions. It is only logical, then, that one of the sets of people we would be talking about would be the policy specialists: the folks with the training and background to handle the technical questions that arise in keeping a particular promise. It is for precisely that reason that policy specialists, no matter where they work or what they do, share three characteristics.

First, policy specialists come to their jobs because of what they know. The process of hiring them is a complex one, but it always revolves around their knowledge and experience as expressed in and judged by their professional credentials.

Second, policy specialists expect to stick around. What they are hired to do is a job, but they expect the subject matter they have studied to provide a career. More to the point, perhaps, most of them expect that career to be a career in government—indeed, for many if not most, a career in the particular piece of the government that has provided them with their first job.

Finally, policy specialists identify with—maybe better, attach their loyalty to—an agency or even a subunit within that agency rather than to a broader entity like a department, or the government itself. A specialist in marine biology may in some sense work for the Department of Commerce, but in his or her mind, the job is not with the Commerce Department, or even with the National Oceanic and Atmospheric Administration. It is with the National Marine Fisheries Service. In fact, there is a good chance that in the mind of that marine biologist, the job is with some outfit whose name doesn't appear in *The United States Government Manual*, but whose activities center on "habitat conservation operations" and is formally a part of the National Marine Fisheries Service.

The City of the Political Executives

Bureaucracy is told to hire the policy specialists to handle the technical questions associated with keeping the promises that bureaucracy is created to keep. But the constitutional government is bound and determined to hold that bureaucracy responsible, and since the men and women who make up that constitutional government can't become part of the bureaucracy themselves, it is inevitable that some group of people will be sent in their place to put their stamp on its operations. Enter the political executives. Once again, the very circumstances of the group's creation mean that the members of this particular group will share three characteristics.

First, unlike the policy specialists who are chosen for what they know, political executives are chosen for what they believe. More properly, they are chosen for the correspondence between what they believe and the beliefs of the members of the constitutional government instrumental in their choice. This is not to say that what political executives know has no impact on their selection. They have to know something about the subjects they will be dealing with. Former Senator John Ashcroft would not have been chosen to head the Food and Drug Administration. But neither would he have been chosen to head the Justice Department had Al Gore been selected President of the United States in 2000. There is a wide variety of jobs in this category called political executive, and the mix between

knowledge and beliefs that will go into the final selection of someone for a particular job will vary from one job to another. But for most of these jobs, beliefs,
beliefs about the "right" direction for the policies this person will be involved in
making, will be a crucial factor in the selection.

Second, again unlike the policy specialists, the political executives expect to
be around for a fairly short period of time. Some may hope to come back at a
higher level in the same policy field. Others may hope to move from one field to
another, just up the ladder. Still others may hope to cash in on this position later
on with something lucrative in the private sector. All still have that one thing
in common. They know they won't be in this particular job for more than a few
short years.

Finally, and in stark contrast to the policy specialists, the political executives
attach their loyalties primarily to the departments in which they work, or even
to the chief executive who nominated them for the position. This will be less
true, of course, for those at the bottom of the political executive chain. The chief
of the U.S. Forest Service is a political executive, but he or she is nearly always
from within the service (or a closely related agency), has scientific credentials, and
identifies as strongly with the service as with the U.S. Department of Agriculture
or the President of the United States. Still, the bulk of the political executives see
themselves as representatives of the constitutional government, and that means
first loyalty must be to the officers of that government.

THE MANDATE REVISITED

As we saw in chapter 1, the mandate that these two sets of bureaucrats are
expected to interpret and apply is complex, sometimes even seemingly contradictory. No more images of jugglers, but I think it is worth our time to take a quick
look back at this mandate before we go on to see its very different interpretations
in the cities of the policy specialist and the political executive.

It starts, of course, with the goal of effectiveness. Bureaucracy exists to
bring specialized knowledge to bear on complex problems and produce solutions that work to solve those problems. As we also saw earlier, we can never
be sure a decision or policy will be effective—solve the problem and keep the
promise—at the time at which that decision is made or policy put in place.
Consequently, effectiveness has to be given a working definition—and given bureaucracy's reason for existence, that working definition has to center on the
use of the best available information by the best available experts. As we shall
see in a moment, political executives tend to put a somewhat different twist on
the notion of best available knowledge than do the policy specialists. Nonetheless, in bureaucracy everything has to account for, probably even start with,
some version of using the best available knowledge to solve the problems at
hand.

Then comes the goal of responsiveness. Bureaucracy is supposed to listen
to the people, and it is supposed to heed what it hears. Most of that listening, of course, is to the elected representatives of the people, but sometimes the

people—some of them anyway—speak directly, and bureaucracy is supposed to be listening.

On the surface it may seem that bureaucrats spend little time and energy on questions that involve the rights of individuals. In fact, it may seem that we expect little of them in this area. But, as we shall see later on, a good bit of administrative law is aimed at making sure that bureaucrats do respect and protect the rights of individuals. They may not factor individual rights into their decisions in a direct way, but those rights do help to structure the decision-making systems in which bureaucrats operate.

Finally, we turn to the goal of accountability. Accountability, remember, is a two-dimensional animal. First, it is internal, that is, bureaucrats are expected to behave in an ethical manner. In that sense it is just like effectiveness, responsiveness, and respect for the rights of individuals in that it is something bureaucrats are expected to build into their own decision-making processes. But accountability is also external, and in its external manifestation it is different from effectiveness, responsiveness, and respect for individual rights in one very important way. Namely, accountability is imposed on bureaucracy, imposed from the outside and after the fact. In simpler terms, a decision is reached, somebody is unhappy, and a bureaucrat and the agency he or she works for is called upon to explain and defend that decision before politicians, judges, or both. Accountability may happen differently than effectiveness or responsiveness, but we are no less committed to making sure that it happens, so bureaucrats have to be no less prepared to decide exactly what it means and no less willing to live within the boundaries that it creates for their work.

So there it is. Four goals or expectations that bureaucrats must take account of as they play their role in the policy-making process. Three they are expected to factor into their own decision-making process, and the fourth they are expected to be prepared to "endure" in the name of self-government. Now it's time to see how the two very different sets of bureaucrats we met in the first section of this chapter interpret and apply those goals or expectations as they do their respective jobs.

EFFECTIVENESS, RESPONSIVENESS, RESPECT FOR INDIVIDUAL RIGHTS, AND ACCOUNTABILITY IN THE CITY OF POLICY SPECIALISTS

Before we tour the city of policy specialists, two quick reminders. First, remember who these people are. They are men and women who got their jobs because of their specialized backgrounds, they expect to make careers out of what they do, and their loyalties lie with some fairly small subunit of the bureaucracy and the narrow piece of some broader promise that has been assigned to that particular subunit. Second, remember that while all four of these goals or expectations will be present in the mind of every policy specialist as he or she makes decisions, there is a good bit of room for maneuver in deciding exactly what each of these goals means, as well as in deciding how much emphasis to place on each. That, after all, is why we are exploring the views of these policy specialists—and later on those of the political executives. They have the chance to define and redefine these values, and they take it.

Effectiveness and the Policy Specialists: Faith in What They Know

It can't be a surprise to any of you that policy specialists place their primary emphasis on the goal of effectiveness and are happy indeed to adopt an operational definition of effectiveness that stresses the use of the best available knowledge in the making of public policy. Emphasizing effectiveness, and in particular adopting that working definition for it, taps into the two most powerful motivating forces we know of, self-interest and true belief.

The self-interest part of the policy specialists' motivation is pretty transparent. We need bureaucracy itself for the knowledge it possesses, but it possesses that knowledge through the individuals it hires, so for those individuals to stress any decision-making factor other than knowledge is to undermine their own power and legitimacy as well as that of the organizations they work for. To be sure, other factors have to be considered. But knowledge has to be at the very center of what bureaucrats stress or they are cutting their own throats.

But important as it is, self-interest is rarely the sum total of what anybody is about. Most people, especially those who seek the kind of specialized knowledge needed by bureaucracy and, maybe more to the point, seek to use it in the context of government, need to believe in what they are doing, at least on some level. Policy specialists believe in knowledge. Their own knowledge. And they believe in it deeply. They have two pretty good reasons to do so.

We Train Them That Way

Not all of the policy specialists we are talking about have PhDs in biochemistry and speak in an incomprehensible insider's language. But they do have specialized credentials of some sort. Undergraduate degrees, graduate degrees, professional degrees, advanced certifications, whatever the name of the piece of paper used to signify it, the community of policy specialists is composed of people who have taken a lot of time to study a particular subject. And even if that subject is public administration and the presumed specialty is personnel administration or budgeting or some other "housekeeping" activity, the holders of these specialized credentials were taught to believe in what they know. It is worth exploring this process of preparing policy specialists a little further, and the best guidebook for such an exploration was prepared by Frederick C. Mosher more than two decades ago.[1]

Since you are a university student—one who might just become a policy specialist one of these days—you are quite well aware that society long ago delegated to the university system the job of preparing such specialists, indeed of preparing anyone deemed to be in need of expert knowledge in order to do his or her job. Universities house the process of preparing subject-matter experts, but we don't actually control it. We have long since surrendered that control to associations that represent the profession—or set of subject-matter experts— in question. Though we never actually handed over some equivalent of higher education's sword, subject-matter experts took control of the preparation of the next generation aspiring to join their happy band in two interrelated ways.

First, as Mosher pointed out, all of the traditional professions, and virtually all of the collections of subject-matter experts who see themselves individually as professionals and collectively as a profession, set up bodies to accredit the university programs that produce that next generation of experts.[2] As a veteran of several terms on our campus Curriculum Committee, I can testify to the commitment and determination with which at least this university seeks that accreditation. With the question of "whether they come from accredited schools" at the top of the list of criteria for hiring entry-level professionals, most universities feel they have no real choice.[3] How can they expect to attract good students to what is pretty clearly a career-oriented program when those students won't be able to compete with others when they finally enter the job market? For that matter, how can a university expect to attract and keep qualified faculty if the program it wants those faculty for is not accredited?

In addition to their role in accrediting academic programs, groups of subject-matter experts assert their control over the preparation of the next generation of such experts through the men and women who teach in those programs and their own identification with the profession they have chosen and/or the subject matter they teach. It is a real compliment here at UWSP to be called a good teacher. It is almost certainly a bigger compliment to be called a good biologist, a good forester, a good soil chemist, or a good speech pathologist. These faculty members quite literally embody the profession and the knowledge—and the attitudes—they want to impart and that has to enhance the hold that that profession and its knowledge and attitudes have gained over the students.

It is hardly surprising that groups of subject-matter experts would seek control over the preparation of new experts, and no more surprising that universities would let them have it. The very notion of expertise, after all, is highly specialized knowledge that no one else has, and how else is someone going to get that specialized knowledge except from those who have it? Once apprenticeship was no longer a practical way to learn something, specialized education controlled by the masters of a subject was destined to take its place, and once universities decided to sell higher education as the passport to certain kinds of jobs—better-paying and more prestigious ones—the die was unquestionably cast on the question of who was tail and who was dog in the professional program/larger university relationship.

This pattern of professional control over most aspects of professional education may not be surprising, but it is important. First of all, there can be no doubt that the kind of preparation process from which most professionals emerge has the effect of separating the professionals from the larger society. Again to rely on Frederick Mosher, "Much of professional education and practice is still so focused on substance and science as to obscure the larger meaning of the profession in the society."[4] With a code of ethics that speaks about public service but often keeps the public at arm's length, a language that unites the profession but definitely divides it from the public at large, and a set of skills that by definition the rest of us haven't got, the profession becomes a group unto itself, *for* us, but not at all *with* or *of* us. Second, this kind of tightly controlled professional education is bound to convince people that "There are *correct* ways of solving problems and doing things."[5] More to the point, of course, it is the profession which has identified those *correct* ways of doing things, and it seems a fairly short jump from there to Mosher's conclusion that these professionals enter their jobs believing that "Politics is . . . carried on by subject-matter amateurs. Politics is to the professions as ambiguity to truth, expediency to rightness, heresy to true belief."[6] It may be a short jump horizontally, but as we'll see shortly, it is a huge leap vertically. There are walls called responsiveness, respect for individual rights, and accountability that mean that not all bureaucrats are prone to see politics as ambiguity, expedience, or heresy, and that even those who do face serious obstacles to acting on that vision.

I don't mean to suggest that everyone emerges from a professional program with exactly the same attitude toward every question that will cross his or her desk in a lifetime of work. Far from it. Foresters don't march in lockstep any more than do economists, biochemists, astrophysicists, or child psychiatrists. But people do come out of those programs believing in their own knowledge and the contribution that knowledge can make to answering the questions that arise in the process of trying to keep specific promises made to the American public by the constitutional government. Armed with such a belief, policy specialists could not possibly do anything but make effectiveness the centerpiece of their value structure and define it in terms of following the policy path laid out by their own specialized knowledge.

The Job Reinforces Their Faith

That powerful belief that one's knowledge really is the key to making effective policy decisions is reinforced by three interrelated characteristics of the job of the policy specialist.

First of all, most people tend to establish what we might almost call a "relationship" with their jobs. They want to feel comfortable—happy if they are lucky—and motivated to do what has to be done, and if possible to do it well. Organizational and professional goals can provide some of that comfort and motivation, but only some. Both tend to be the product of committees forced to compromise and seek bland—occasionally almost empty—phrases to capture "what this agency or profession is really about." But the work routines and processes that make up the day-to-day content of a job are a very different business. This is where a policy specialist can use the skills and knowledge gained from all that education. This is where salmon are studied, owls are counted, mergers are evaluated for their impact on competition, econometric models combed for evidence of inflationary trends, or the latest research on benzene added to what we already know about that dangerous liquid as we try to protect oil refinery workers from its devastating effects. When I make this point with my own students, I tell them that when it's ten minutes before class, it isn't "The Wisconsin Idea"—quality education for the whole state—or some long forgotten discussion in graduate school about the role and importance of political science as a discipline, or even my desire to help them get a great job that brings me down to class ready and anxious to go. It's the fact that I love putting together my lectures and I dearly love to deliver them. It is show time and I enjoy the process of writing, editing, directing, and most of all performing. In short, at virtually every stage of a policy specialist's career, he or she is going to find that the real source of fun and motivation in the job is found in the job itself, in the routines and processes of the day, and that means it is found in the process of using the specialized knowledge that brought that person to this job in the first place.

Second, policy specialists find that they do their work in fairly narrowly defined organizational units. More to the point, they find that these narrowly defined units are composed of people who share their specialty—or at least a closely related specialty—and that the unit is defined in terms of goals that mesh very neatly with those specialties. It is, in other words, an environment in which shared knowledge is emphasized and relied on. Consequently, the policy specialist can develop an organizational loyalty without compromising that abiding faith in his or her knowledge. Indeed, that faith will be reinforced by the other specialists and their loyalty to the subunit of which all are a part.

Finally, policy specialists are almost always in their specialty for the long haul, so they will have some concern for the career ladder that is present in that specialty. Movement up the career ladder in any subject-matter specialty is heavily dependent on demonstrating a mastery of that specialty, and commitment to the shared knowledge of that particular profession or specialized subfield is the easiest way to show that one is a good forester, economist, budget analyst, or whatever. Nowhere is this more clearly demonstrated than in academic life, where movement up the ranks requires that one demonstrate that he or she is a good biologist, a good chemist, a good musicologist, or a good geologist, and demonstrating same requires recognition from other biologists, chemists, musicologists, or geologists, in particular practitioners of those specialties from other universities. In plain English, ya gotta publish. Actually, former students of mine who have moved into government careers in specialized fields like forestry or wildlife management tell me that this is increasingly true in their work as well. To be sure, the career ladder does place other demands on new professionals. There is always the "go along" or "fit in" factor, and the specialist who wishes someday to "manage" other specialists may well have to demonstrate other skills and talents besides those of the professional devoted to his or her knowledge and its uses. But, as I have argued elsewhere, even when it comes to this move to the administrative career ladder, knowledge and performance-based credentials within one's subject-matter specialty tend to dominate the selection process.[7] The best bet for grabbing hold of the next rung on virtually any professional ladder is to show what a good professional you are, and demonstrating your mastery of and commitment to the profession's shared pool of knowledge is the most visible way of showing you are a "real pro."

In Summary

Defining it "on the ground" as relying on the best available knowledge—generally their own—policy specialists attach themselves first and foremost to the goal of effectiveness. In part they are doing it as a means of protecting their power. Bureaucracy exists because we need its expertise; its expertise comes in the form of individual policy specialists, so those specialists have to emphasize the value of expertise. Self-interest rules. But policy specialists are doing something else when they emphasize the goal of effectiveness as defined in terms of reliance on their knowledge. With my hat off to Billy Joel, they are "keepin' the faith." Trained to believe deeply in the value of their knowledge—and in the fact that very few folks share that knowledge—and immersed in routines that rely on that knowledge and surrounded by some of those very few who do share it, these policy specialists really do believe that what they are doing is not just a matter of self-interest. It is a matter of doing things right to advance a—maybe even *the*—public interest, a job entrusted to them by that public's very own representatives.

Responsiveness and the Policy Specialists: It Is the People's Government, After All

As I hinted in that previous section, I don't really agree with Frederick Mosher's characterization of policy specialists as believers that politics represents only "ambiguity, expediency, and heresy." There are certainly days on which they might use those words, but I'm convinced that the vast majority of policy specialists believe that politics also represents self-government, and self-government cannot and should not be ignored. Therefore, politics cannot and should not be ignored.

Policy specialists cannot ignore politics, of course, because the resources those specialists need to use the knowledge they have so much faith in are in the hands of the people's representatives—politicians, one and all—and those resources will be allocated through a distinctly political process. For a policy specialist to say that politics has no place in the bureaucratic decision-making process is to deny reality. They might as well make a place for it. If not, it will make its own.

But I am convinced that policy specialists also believe they should not ignore politics. Politics—through politicians, of course—is the process by which we govern ourselves, so to say that politics *ought* to have no place in the bureaucratic decision-making process is to deny self-government itself. These policy specialists are part and parcel of the American culture, including its political culture, and that means that self-government is a goal they have long since come to accept.

Important as it is, this conviction by policy specialists that they cannot and should not ignore politics—in other words, that they should commit themselves to the goal of responsiveness—still leaves open two very important questions. Whom should they be responsive to, and how are they to fit responsiveness into a decision-making framework grounded in specialized knowledge as the key to effectiveness? Let's take them in reverse order.

Effectiveness and Responsiveness: Peaceful Coexistence

Responsiveness can't be allowed to overwhelm effectiveness. As we said in the previous section, for policy specialists to let that happen would be to surrender power and break faith with themselves and their colleagues. That just isn't acceptable. But responsiveness has entered the picture and that brings with it the realization that all decisions are now going to be a blend of knowledge and politics.

That's clear enough, but two questions remain. What will be the relative mix between knowledge and politics, and what kind of politics are we talking about? Let's consider each of those in turn, and, once more, let's do it in reverse order.

In a sense, there are two very different kinds of politics in this country. One is generally open and frequently partisan. Issues involved in this kind of politics attract attention from the President, the leaders and much of the membership of Congress, a good portion of the mass media, and even a substantial fraction of the public. Few issues are subject to this kind of politics on a constant basis, but there are some—welfare, gun control, abortion, taxes, and a few more—that will be in this political world whenever they leave the back burner long enough for any kind of consideration. But there is a second kind of politics. This one is generally closed and often not partisan at all. It rarely attracts attention from the President or the leaders of Congress but rather is the province of committees and subcommittees of the House and Senate, interest-group representatives, experts in a particular subject matter, and agencies of the executive branch. Any issue can explode out of its closed niche, of course. Summer 2002 was the summer of accounting rules policy. Few had heard much about it the previous summer. Still, some issues generally find themselves on a political radar screen scanned only by a few, and most of the people interested in these issues take great comfort from that lack of visibility.

Now, what about our other question? Every decision is part knowledge and part politics, but some end up being heavy on the knowledge and light on the politics, while others end up being just the reverse. The mix is hardly random, but we'll save our discussion of the patterns for a later chapter. At this point all we need to remember is the fact that the mix can vary from one decision-making situation to another.

Policy specialists know all of this, of course. They know it and they know its implications for their activities, and particularly for their efforts to define responsiveness in such a way that it does not overwhelm their primary commitment to effectiveness. If the mix between knowledge and politics leans more toward knowledge, and if the politics that does enter the mix is the closed politics of congressional committees, interest groups, policy experts, and themselves, then effectiveness and responsiveness really can coexist peacefully, with the former taking the lead role and the latter on display for all to see.

The policy specialists' desire to see knowledge as the heavier of the two ingredients in the knowledge/politics cocktail is self-explanatory, but what about the desire for a more closed politics? In the open kind of politics, recall, the President, party leaders in both houses of Congress, and the mass media are all going to be involved, all claiming to be articulating the true desires of the public at large. Even the most generous proponent of self-government isn't going to argue that that combination is designed to bring specialized knowledge to bear on the question at hand. But if the politics of a decision-making process can be confined to congressional committees, interest-group representatives, recognized policy experts, and the policy specialists themselves, knowledge can play a role in the process, or at least it can be made to appear as if knowledge has played a role. All of the participants have a definite stake in the policies in question, and all have some experience with the issues as well as some knowledge about them. Politics can never represent pure knowledge. That's the policy specialist's job. But politics has to be allowed to play a role, and this kind of politics is going to feel like the best approximation of knowledge that the world of politics can produce.

So what does all of this add up to? Policy specialists, remember, have to decide to whom they are going to be responsive. That decision is going to be substantially affected by the goal of guaranteeing peaceful coexistence between effectiveness and responsiveness. That, in turn, is going to mean trying to define responsiveness in such a way that they produce a decision-making environment in which knowledge gets more emphasis than politics and in which the politics that does enter is the closed politics that is—or at least appears to be—the politics of the informed. Not all agencies succeed. The deck is stacked in favor of some and against others. But they all try. So on to the process of defining responsiveness by deciding to whom to be responsive.

So, Who You Gonna Listen To, Anyway?

At first glance, of course, this is an easy question. If, as I have argued throughout this chapter, policy specialists really do believe in responsiveness, they are going to feel obligated to listen to the constitutional government and to the people who are that government's—and the bureaucracy's—ultimate masters. But if we take another look, especially a look from the perspective of the policy specialist, two factors complicate the question immensely.

First of all, to listen one must be able to hear. To listen to the President, for example, a policy specialist has to hear something from the President, which in turn, of course, means that the President has to say something. And it has to be something at least coherent and directive enough that a response is possible. The same is true, obviously, for the Congress, the courts, and most of all for the people. Can the people or the constitutional government be heard in any sort of coherent way?

Second, ours is a government grounded in the notions of separation of powers and checks and balances. The institutions of the constitutional government may not agree with each other on any given policy question and, consequently, may well be sending mixed messages to the policy specialists, if indeed messages are being sent at all. Then, recall, there are at a minimum two very different sets of people who might lay claim to the right to instruct the policy specialists, and there is a good chance they will be pointing those specialists in different directions. At least there is a good chance they will, if both are pointing at all.

So, in the end, policy specialists have to come up with a working definition of responsiveness. That working definition can't be allowed to compromise their working definition of effectiveness without undermining the very purpose and ethos of bureaucracy. Not only that, that working definition of responsiveness has to be carved out in a real-life government in which there may be contradictory messages—or no messages at all—and in which, as we shall see later, they can be held accountable for not being responsive even if they sincerely believe that they were. But a definition they must have, and they do.

Responsiveness to the President

The President is the chief executive, so he or she has a clear and legitimate claim on responsiveness from the policy specialists. But the President is very definitely an amateur on most of the questions that would come before the policy specialists, and amateurs aren't supposed to be the ones to answer these questions. Too much responsiveness to the chief really could compromise the goal of effectiveness. But no responsiveness to the chief means exactly that, no responsiveness to a duly elected representative of the people. That doesn't compromise a major value. It ignores one.

Fortunately—from a policy specialist's perspective, anyway—the horns of that particular dilemma are very frequently far enough apart to step between them without much trouble. We will explore this more, adding in the President's perspective, in chapter 5. At this point all we need note is this. Most policy specialists can feel confident that the President will almost never speak to any of the questions on that specialist's agenda. It's easy enough to see how that specialist can come to the conclusion that he or she can't reasonably be accused of failing to be responsive to something that was never said!

But what if the President does speak? Things get trickier, of course, but separation of powers may come to the rescue in the form of a communication from Congress that seems to point in the opposite direction from the one that came from the chief. Or "the public" might be expressing its own views on the subject at hand. Then there is always the question of whether this particular presidential directive came from the President or from someone else trying to use the chief to advance his or her own agenda. The dilemma is a whole lot more real now, but there is still some distance between the horns. It just requires a bit more footwork to stay there.

More than a quarter-century ago, Thomas Cronin, one of his generation's leading scholars of the presidency, quite nicely captured the policy specialists' attitudes toward responding to the chief's views. "There is a great residual of respect toward the presidency both in Washington and in the federal agencies throughout the country. But this respect for what the President can do is predicated on the fact that the Presidential voice can be heard and believed as authentic. . . . Otherwise, federal civil servants feel that they must protect their 'rational' and 'professional' interests from White House interference."[8]

Responsiveness to the Congress

No title of chief executive, but Article I makes it pretty clear that Congress has the constitutional right to hand out the legal authority and the money, and that puts responsiveness to Congress on the same plane as responsiveness to the President. It is inescapable and it's right.

Responding to Congress as a body would pose most of the same problems as responding to the President. Most members of Congress know no more than the President about most of the questions facing any particular policy specialist. So, once more, too much responsiveness to the body could compromise effectiveness, and no responsiveness would walk all over a critical value in our system of self-government.

Once again, the horns of the dilemma are far enough apart that there is little chance of ending up impaled on either one. We will spend a good bit of time on the relationship between Congress and the agencies of the federal bureaucracy in a later chapter, but the key to escaping the dilemma is simple enough. Congress as a body has very little, if any, contact with most agencies. Rather it is committees and subcommittees of each chamber that hand out whatever instructions those agencies may get from the Congress. We will go into the details more in chapter 6. Suffice it to say here that these committees and subcommittees have more interest in, more experience with, and more expertise about the issues that face a given agency's policy specialists than can be found in the White House or in the Congress as a body. And they will speak to "their" agencies loud and clear.

Consequently, from the point of view of the policy specialist, being responsive to Congress almost always means being responsive to a handful of committees familiar with the issues, capable of grasping those issues at least at the level of informed laypersons, and more than willing to offer their views on the questions at hand. Responding to these committees can easily be seen as an effort to strike a balance between effectiveness and responsiveness rather than as a compromise of the principal value of effectiveness. After all, Congress has a legitimate claim to instruct bureaucracy, and it has delegated the right to stake that claim to these committees. The committees are only too happy to exercise that right, and they exercise it in language familiar to the policy specialists. It's obviously not pure knowledge driving the policy process, but it may be as close as they can hope to get. And they have to be responsive to someone.

Responsiveness to the Courts

Responsiveness to the courts is a very different business. While the President and Congress can provide instructions to bureaucracy at any time they wish in any way they wish, courts can only instruct in the context of a particular case, that is, a particular dispute brought by some citizen or group of citizens against a particular bureaucratic action. There is no general expectation that agencies will keep in touch with the courts, providing a "heads up" whenever new policy directions are about to be explored, or informing them of issues soon to be confronted. The contact is case by case. It is true that agencies are expected to try to stay within the law and the Constitution as currently defined by the courts, but that's very different from what Congress—and to a lesser extent the President—expect. In effect, then, the relationship between policy specialists and the courts is less one of responsiveness than of accountability.

Responsiveness to the Public

From the perspective of the policy specialist, responsiveness to the public probably looks very much like responsiveness to the Congress. The public in its entirety could only be thought of as uninterested, uninformed, and uninvolved.

Responding to its wishes could, once again, easily constitute a threat to the value of effectiveness. Of course, the public's very lack of interest, information, and involvement means that it is unlikely that any policy specialist would ever be trapped between instructions from that undifferentiated public and his or her considered professional judgment.

But there is another public—there are two or three more actually, but that's for chapter 7—and that public can and will be listened to. In the forms we will talk about in that later chapter, this public is somebody with interest, information, expertise, and commitment and, once again, like the congressional committees and subcommittees, becomes someone to whom policy specialists feel they can be responsive without abandoning their first commitment to effectiveness. So, responsive they are.

In Summary

Policy specialists will be responsive. Politicians will demand it, and given the mechanisms of accountability we will discuss in this book, they can make that demand stick. Policy specialists will also demand it of themselves. It is part of their obligation to the ultimate goal of self-government. But responsiveness policy-specialist style has to fit with effectiveness, and that means coming up with a working definition of responsiveness that makes plenty of room for—or at least appears to make plenty of room for—knowledge. That means that responsiveness to the President will come only when the chief speaks in a clear, direct, and forceful voice. That won't be all that often. Congress as a body won't speak clearly or directly all that often either, but the committees and subcommittees of the House and Senate most definitely will speak in clear, direct, and forceful terms to the agencies under their purview. The policy specialists who populate those agencies will listen and they will respond. The vocabulary will be familiar and passably expert, and the men and women doing the talking will be the same. The same will be true when we turn to the public. The general public—if there is such a thing—will remain silent, but groups of people—frequently claiming to represent a general public interest rather than their own narrow interests—will speak clearly and directly, and, once again, the people and the vocabulary will be familiar and able to pass at least the test of informed amateur, if not that of fellow professional. The courts have the right to demand responsiveness, but the vehicle for demanding it—a specific case filed by a citizen or group of citizens and challenging an agency action—makes the court/policy specialist relationship unique, and we will discuss it in a framework structured by the notion of accountability rather than that of responsiveness.

So, a working definition of responsiveness does in fact emerge in the city of the policy specialist. It keeps the President—and by extension his or her representatives—and the general public at a respectable distance, and focuses instead on listening to congressional committees and subcommittees, interest groups, professional associations, think-tank representatives, and even some folks best called critics. As we shall see in later chapters, not all policy specialists work in agencies able to operate on this working definition of responsiveness consistently, and no policy specialist works in an agency able to operate on it all of the time. But this is the definition they will follow when they can, and they can a great deal of the time.

Individual Rights and the Policy Specialists: The Courts, Administrative Law, and a Little Sensitivity

Policy specialists have a clear sense of the importance of the rights of individuals in our scheme of self-government. But they don't see themselves as guardians of those rights in the same way they see themselves as the chief architects of effectiveness or even as experts who must be responsive to outsiders in order to preserve self-government even as they pursue the "right" answers to complex public policy problems. Consequently, they don't spend the same kind of time or energy in working toward a definition of respect for individual rights that they do in working toward definitions for effectiveness and responsiveness.

Still, individual rights cannot and should not be ignored, so they have to think about what those rights might mean in the context of their highly specialized work. Recall from chapter 1 that when we speak of individual rights we are really speaking of two different, though clearly interrelated, phenomena. First, we are talking about staying out of some aspects of people's lives. Government is not to tread on people's religious or intellectual lives or invade their privacy except in the most extreme of circumstances for the very best of reasons. Second, when we speak of individual rights we are speaking of protection from arbitrary government action. There ought to be rules that govern all citizen-government interactions and those rules ought to favor the individual, since it seems that when citizen and government must come together, absent such rules the odds are going to favor the government.

Policy specialists don't generally see themselves as likely to step into areas of people's lives protected by the First or Fourth Amendments, but they can, and more to the point, people are going to accuse them of having done so quite regularly. Those specialists do, no doubt, make guesses about what might step on the rights of individuals and try to avoid such actions. For the most part, however, they tend to act on their notions of effectiveness and responsiveness and leave this aspect of the rights of individuals to the citizens who feel aggrieved and the courts set up to hear those grievances. Again, this is not to say that policy specialists don't care about individual rights. They do. They just believe that courts are the places to decide whether or not government has deprived someone of one of his or her fundamental rights, so if the specialists are careful to avoid the most egregious violations of those rights, they can safely go ahead and do what they believe needs to be done and leave the close calls to the judges.

When it comes to procedural rights, however, policy specialists understand that they need a working definition of respect for those rights other than "wait for the courts." That working definition is found in administrative law—the topic of chapter 8—and while much of administrative law is constructed by Congress and the courts, bureaucrats, including policy specialists, produce a good bit of it themselves, and they do it in part out of a recognition that to respect the rights of individuals to be protected from arbitrary government action, they must operate within a set of rules understandable to citizen and bureaucrat alike, and that those rules must embody the notions of equal protection and due process that represent our constitutional idea of fairness.

As I implied in the title of this section, much of what policy specialists do to show their respect for the rights of individuals is to wait for the courts to tell them when they have crossed the line in terms of a fundamental right, and contribute to and live within the procedural protections for individuals contained in the body of administrative law. That's much of what they do, but not all of it. Policy specialists do think about the rights of individuals and do make an effort to protect or at least not threaten those rights, by recognizing them and factoring them into their decision-making processes. In the end, however, the rights of individuals are simply much harder for policy specialists to define and focus on than effectiveness and responsiveness, so the courts and administrative law become the primary vehicles for protecting those rights.

Accountability and the Policy Specialists: Living With an 800-Pound Gorilla

As we noted at the beginning of the chapter, accountability is both an internal and an external phenomenon. Let's start with the internal. Policy specialists are expected to behave in an ethical manner. There are actually three separate, though generally complementary, codes of ethics to which these specialists are presumed to owe at least some loyalty. First, policy specialists are public servants and that means loyalty to the public service code of ethics. Embodied in statutes and executive orders, the public service code of ethics generally focuses on being responsive to duly constituted authority, treating all citizens equally, and avoiding the use of public office for private gain. Second, we find professional codes of ethics. All policy specialists by definition have a subject-matter specialty, and subject-matter specialties have associations with codes of ethics. Such codes are often long and written in the specialized language of that particular profession, but most can be reduced to something far simpler—as Jack Ward Thomas, world-renowned wildlife biologist and one-time chief of the U.S. Forest Service, did for the ethical code of the National Wildlife Society in the newsletter of the Forest Service Employees for Environmental Ethics, a group of Forest Service employees who were convinced that the agency had lost its ethical moorings.[9] Finally, policy specialists are human beings, and they have their own personal codes of ethics. Now let's look to the outside.

For policy specialists—for that matter, as we'll see shortly, for political executives—external accountability really is the 800-pound gorilla of the policy process. The problem isn't so much where does this gorilla sleep. It sleeps in Congress, the White House, and the courts. In other words, it sleeps in the constitutional equivalent of wherever it wants. The problem is when does it wake up, why does it wake up, and what is it going to eat now that it is awake?

Given the fact that in extreme cases accountability can eat budgets, legal authority, positions, and in very rare instances entire agencies, it may seem strange to say that, policy specialists spend a lot more time worrying about effectiveness and responsiveness than they do about accountability. But they do. In part that is a reflection of their sincere belief that if they and their policies are effective and responsive, no one will wake up the gorilla. To some extent, they are right.

Accountability mechanisms—we'll talk about those in detail in chapters 5, 6, 7, and 9—are generally only triggered when somebody is angry, and while no group of policy specialists can keep everybody happy all the time, they can probably keep the relevant people happy most of the time by pursuing the goals of effectiveness and responsiveness as they have come to define them.

But there is another reason that policy specialists tend to work to head off the gorilla's rampage by doing business as usual. What else can they do? There is no such thing as a policy-specialist–constructed definition of accountability. It happens when outsiders say it is going to happen, and it happens pretty much on their terms. A citizen sues and the courts are asking for documents and testimony and a defense, and they will have to be provided. It's contempt if you don't. A congressional committee is angry over a decision and wants someone to come to discuss it, so someone goes to discuss it. It shouldn't happen all that often with "their own" committees, but it can, and all committees can ask and they have to be responded to. If the President jumps in and demands an explanation, he or she can be stalled for a while, especially if the request comes from a second-level aide. But if the chief persists, an explanation has to be prepared. This is not to say that policy specialists never hide information, cover their tracks, or try to escape accountability for their actions. Rather it is to say that they are rarely successful when they do. At least they are rarely successful in the long run. And they know it.

In a sense, then, the working definition of accountability is try to avoid it, but if it comes, face the music. Probably not very good advice for facing a real 800-pound gorilla—not the second half of it anyway—but for the metaphorical gorilla faced by our policy specialists, there isn't much choice.

In Summary

Policy specialists know that the mandate given to bureaucracy—and therefore to them—by the constitutional government is a complex and multi-faceted one. Likewise, they know that they must interpret and apply that mandate. To be more specific, they know they are going to have to figure out how to approach their tasks of gathering and using information in a way that reflects and advances the goals of effectiveness, responsiveness, respect for the rights of individuals, and accountability. Most believe that they have done so.

Effectiveness has to be first for the policy specialist, and it has to be defined in terms of basing policy decisions on the best available knowledge. To believe otherwise would be to undermine bureaucracy's power and challenge their own powerfully held belief in the knowledge they have acquired and the contributions that knowledge can make to keeping the promises that lie at the heart of the bureaucratic enterprise.

Responsiveness has to be second because politicians will have their due sooner or later, and self-government is grounded in the people's right to determine their own collective fate, and that means government has to listen to those people and do as they say. Bureaucracy is part of government, of course, so policy specialists, too, must listen. But they must listen in a way that doesn't do too much violence to the value of effectiveness, and there are four different sets of voices they might hear. So they sort. The President must be listened to some of the time, but only some of the time and then with considerable reluctance. He or she just "doesn't know the territory." Congressional committees and subcommittees, on the other hand, have to be heard. As we'll see in chapter 6, they can make quite a bit of noise if they feel they aren't being heard at any particular moment, and they speak often and in the right kinds of words and the right tone of voice. The same can be said for interest-group representatives, policy experts, think-tank intellectuals, and even the occasional self-styled representative of "the public interest." Along with the policy specialists and the committee and subcommittee members and staff, these interest-group representatives and policy experts, in the words of Hugh Heclo, "[have] established a common language for discussing the issues, a shared grammar for identifying the major points of contention, a mutually familiar rhetoric of argumentation."[10]

Self-government is not exclusively about responding to public sentiment. It is also about the rights of individuals, and policy specialists cannot ignore those rights. They don't. But they do leave the protection of those rights mostly to the courts and to administrative law. They supplement those two institutionalized mechanisms with a definite sympathy for individuals—when they can figure out how—but most of the time, most policy specialists feel a little out of their element in thinking and deciding about the rights of individuals. Better leave it to the experts.

Finally, policy specialists, like everyone else in government, must be prepared to be held accountable for actions they have taken. They have to hold themselves accountable by behaving in an ethical manner, and they must be prepared to be held accountable by outsiders. That external accountability might come in the form of a lawsuit, a congressional investigation, or an inquiry from the President. Whatever form it takes, it can be a harrowing experience. But there is no escape. The best strategy is avoidance—sound familiar?—and from the perspective of the policy specialist the best strategy for avoidance is to be effective and responsive.

That's the city of the policy specialist. In the real world, of course, these specialists live in a wide variety of cities and each has its own distinct terrain and climate. We'll explore those differences more as the book goes on. For now, one of the two main groups of individuals out there in bureaucracy can be seen pretty much as a set of very knowledgeable people with a pretty good idea of what it means to be effective and responsive and a desire to focus on those two goals, expecting the rights of individuals to mostly be taken care of by somebody or something else and hoping that they never really come face to face with the specter of accountability.

Now let's take a look at how bureaucracy's other major group, the political executives, sees this very same mandate.

EFFECTIVENESS, RESPONSIVENESS, RESPECT FOR INDIVIDUAL RIGHTS, AND ACCOUNTABILITY IN THE CITY OF POLITICAL EXECUTIVES

As we did with the city of policy specialists, we need to take a quick refresher course about the inhabitants before we tour the city of political executives. Specifically, we need to remember three things.

First, recall that these men and women get their jobs through an expressly and deliberately political process in which what they believe about the policy area into which they will be thrust is almost certainly more important than what they know about that policy area. Beyond that, these political executives come to their jobs expecting a fairly short stay—indeed, when compared to the policy specialists, a very short stay. Finally, while policy specialists attach their loyalties to agencies or subunits of agencies, political executives attach theirs at the department level or, quite often, to the individual who was responsible for their appointment in the first place.

Responsiveness and the Political Executives: We Represent the People's Representatives

Just as it could not have surprised you that the policy specialists focus first on effectiveness, it couldn't be much of a shock to find that political executives put their main emphasis on the value of responsiveness. They are chosen, after all, because their views on the issues that will come before them are consistent with the views of the men and women whom the people have elected to represent them. In fact, as we shall see in the next chapter, the very jobs they are sent to occupy exist in large part to bring those viewpoints to the process of policy implementation. Responsiveness has to be their top priority.

Just like policy specialists, political executives are expected to be responsive to the President, the Congress, the courts, and the people. But the process of constructing a working definition of responsiveness out of those expectations is, as we've noted over and over in this chapter, very different for the political executives than for the policy specialists. Different in two ways. One may make the task easier. The other may make it harder.

Because responsiveness is first, it doesn't have to be defined in a way that produces the fewest compromises with effectiveness. This is not to say that effectiveness doesn't matter to the political executives. As we'll see in the next section, it matters a great deal. But responsiveness is first, so there is no desire to try to construct a definition for it that keeps supposedly knowledgeable people at the center of the responsiveness equation and others out at the periphery.

But there is another level, driven by another dynamic, that may make the process a bit more tricky. Political executives can be fired for not being responsive enough—or not responsive to the right people—in a particular situation. They can be fired for other reasons as well, of course. But the point remains that a political executive may find himself or herself shown the door over a decision he or she made to be—or not to be—responsive, and being shown that exit door inevitably carries with it career implications for the person being ushered out. Policy specialists almost never face that daunting prospect.

Responsiveness to the President

Unlike the policy specialists who wish to keep the uninformed chief at arm's length, the political executives are set to embrace the President and his or her policy objectives. On one level they have to be. He or she is the one who can pull the job in a moment. On another level, of course, the political executives want to be responsive to the chief. The President, or more likely, someone with the ear of the people the President put in charge of putting together his or her administration, came up with this person's name and, as I've said over and over in this chapter, said name surfaced in large part because the person attached to that name is presumed to be in tune with the President's policy preferences in this particular subject-matter area.

This is not to say that any chief's set of political executives are minted someplace in New Jersey, each a perfect replica of the President on some set of issues. Nor do they line up each morning as if they were the cast of *Hill Street Blues* to get their orders for the day. Political executives have ideas of their own and, like policy specialists, sometimes operate in a world in which presidential ideas, let alone presidential directives, are few and far between. But the point remains that they are chosen in large part because those who choose them, whether the President or someone operating on the President's behalf, believe that these individuals will handle the jobs assigned to them with the President's views and goals in mind, and perhaps most important, will be loyal to the President and his or her viewpoints should such loyalty be needed and asked for. All of this belief and loyalty, of course, plays out against a background in which both sides know the meaning of "serving at the pleasure of the President."

Responsiveness to the Congress

Congress as a whole is no more likely to speak directly or clearly to political executives than it is to policy specialists. Committees and subcommittees, on the other hand, are no less likely to do so. But from the perspective of the political executive, the committees and subcommittees of Congress look very different than they do from the perspective of the policy specialist.

Policy specialists, remember, were attracted by the level of knowledge they found at the committee level. Committee members and staff might not be experts in the sense that the policy specialists of a given agency were specialists, but as noted earlier, many certainly deserved the title "informed layperson," and informed layperson was about the best the policy specialists could hope for. This knowledge kinship, even if it was at the level of cousins and not brothers, was so important because the policy specialists needed a definition of responsiveness—a set of legitimate people to whom to be responsive—that did as little violence as possible to their primary commitment to effectiveness, and because it gave them a plausible excuse for not worrying about what views, if any, the President might have on the issues facing them.

Political executives, of course, have no need to define responsiveness in a manner consistent with a primary goal of effectiveness and are dead set against looking for a way to eliminate the President's viewpoints from their decision calculus. So from that point of view, responding to congressional committees and subcommittees doesn't look like such a good idea.

But these committees and subcommittees have a great deal of influence in their own areas of jurisdiction. Senate committees play the lead role in the confirmation of political executives in the first place, so the groundwork may well have been laid for a certain amount of responsiveness to these committees on the part of the political executive corps, and for those who may wish to rise through the ranks of political executives, committees have memories to rival those of the elephants of legend. Beyond that, it is at the committee and subcommittee level that most legislation is crafted, that budgets are reviewed, and that investigations and oversight occur. If a political executive is going to be giving a command performance before the Congress, it will actually be before one of these committees or subcommittees. If a political executive is to be embarrassed by Congress, it will be by one of these committees or subcommittees. From that point of view, failing to respond to congressional committees and subcommittees doesn't look like such a good idea.

So, as I've said so many times, the perspective of the political executive ends up being very different from that of the policy specialist. The policy specialist concludes that committees and subcommittees are someone they want to hear from. They probably couldn't avoid it anyway, but being responsive to these committees and subcommittees allows the policy specialists to accomplish some very important goals. The political executives know that they, too, might feel the pressure from these committees and subcommittees should they fail to be responsive, but choosing to be responsive wouldn't advance the goals of these men and women. Indeed, it might threaten the important goal of being responsive to the President.

In the end, then, political executives will have to be responsive to the committees and subcommittees of the Congress. But just how responsive they will have to be will depend. For the most part it will depend on three things.

First it will depend on the organizational level at which the political executive operates. The Executive Director for Supervision, in the Office of Thrift Supervision of the Treasury Department, will almost certainly pay more attention to the desires of the Financial Institutions and Consumer Credit subcommittee of the House Banking and Financial Services Committee than will the secretary of the treasury, or his or her deputy or assistant secretaries. This latter group is far more likely to feel itself part of the Presidential team than is the Office of Thrift Supervision's director. From the opposite side, the Financial Institutions and Consumer Credit subcommittee is far more likely to apply pressure to the director than to the treasury secretary.

Second, how responsive a particular political executive will be to a congressional committee or subcommittee will be affected by the directness and clarity of the President's views on the policies that a political executive is involved in making and implementing. The more the President has said about a set of issues, the less likely a political executive is to be highly responsive to a congressional subcommittee moving in some other direction from that of the chief. It isn't inevitable, of course, that a subcommittee would be diverging from the President's views, but if that subcommittee is in tune with the President, the political executive can race over to the hill, his or her cup filled to the brim with responsiveness.

Finally, responsiveness to congressional committees and subcommittees by a particular political executive will be affected by that political executive's own views and perceptions. There is some room for maneuver, and political executives use it. Presidential directives, as we said in talking about the policy specialists, can be vague or even non-existent. In such a situation some political executives will choose to be very responsive to the committees and subcommittees. Others, however, will choose to pursue their own policy agendas, sometimes trying to put what appears to be the President's stamp on those policy agendas, even if the chief has never really endorsed them in so many words.

Responsiveness to the Courts

When it comes to being responsive to the courts, we find policy specialists and political executives in precisely the same situation, saying and doing precisely the same things. Because courts become involved in bureaucratic policy making only upon the specific request of a citizen or group of citizens to review a particular decision, political executives, like policy specialists, go about their business and hope that the courts receive few such requests concerning their decisions. Accountability, not responsiveness.

Responsiveness to the People

Political executives might be expected to be far less frightened by the idea of being responsive to something they might call the general public and far less attracted to the idea of being responsive to the narrowly defined knowledgeable publics than are the policy specialists. After all, they represent the views of a President elected by that so-called general public, and they have no need or desire to define responsiveness in a way that includes those with knowledge of the subject and excludes everybody else the way that policy specialists do. But two things get in the way of that expectation of ours.

First, the general public doesn't speak to political executives much more clearly or directly than it speaks to the policy specialists. The President is our only nationally elected official, but our national elections speak directly and forcefully to only a tiny handful of major issues, and even then those elections are not exactly models of clarity. So while political executives might well want to be highly responsive to some articulated national interest, they may wait a long time before hearing that interest. Or, more likely, rather than hearing from the general public, they will hear from what Herbert Kaufman described long ago as "self selected, interested parties, [all claiming] to speak for 'it.' "[11]

Second, those narrowly defined segments of the public so popular with the policy specialists have a lot more say at the White House than might appear on the surface. In the first place, they have a great deal of influence on the selection of political executives. (We'll talk about that later, in chapter 5.) And presidents soon learn that these special publics—or special interest groups—have tremendous influence in Congress, especially with the committees and subcommittees that political executives are so often forced to work with. Finally, Presidents learn quickly, if they didn't know before, that these special publics are very often the only people who seem to care about these narrower issues, so if there is any political opportunity or any political danger in them, it lies with these groups. Political executives ignore these narrow publics at the President's peril. Consequently, of course, that means political executives ignore these narrow publics at their own peril.

In Summary

By definition, the political executive is obligated to be responsive to the same constellation of forces as the policy specialist. The President, the Congress, the courts, and the people all have the right to expect political executives to listen and to heed what they hear.

For the political executive, unlike the policy specialist, responsiveness is the first priority and it all starts with responsiveness to the President. Directly or indirectly, the chief gave this political executive the job and the chief can take it away. And, directly or indirectly, every political executive owes the broader loyalty of person, party, or ideology that is at the heart of the selection process. Congress inevitably comes next, and just as inevitably that means a decision by the political executive as to how responsive he or she is going to be to the demands of congressional committees and subcommittees. Like the policy specialists, the political executives see the dangers in not being responsive to these committees, but where policy specialists see in the committees a set of fellow experts—almost, anyway—capable of helping them create the kind of political environment they so very much want to create, political executives see in these very same committees a possible threat to implementing the policies of their chief. So political executives listen to congressional committees, but exactly how much they listen varies from one political executive to another, depending on the executive's position in the administration, the clarity of the President's views on the subject at hand, and even the executive's own preferences and career hopes. The courts must be listened to, but only when they speak, and since they only speak in the formal context of a case initiated by some citizen complaint, political executives, like policy specialists, see heeding the courts as more a matter of accountability than responsiveness.

Finally, the people are out there, and the whole notion of self-government tells us—and the political executives, remember, are part of us—that the people must be heard. But the general public says little, while special publics say much. Political executives are probably tempted on occasion to refer to broad general mandates from the election of the man or woman who put those executives in office as justification for pursuing the general public interest. But the temptation must generally be resisted, since the mandates are too broad and the power of the special publics too great, for political executives to act much differently from the policy specialists. They may have a little more desire and a little more opportunity to represent a broader notion of the public interest than do policy specialists, but only very rarely are they able to indulge the desire or take the opportunity.

Effectiveness and the Political Executives: They, Too, Have Faith in What They Know

Just as policy specialists realize that this is the people's government and responsiveness must be part of their decision-making calculus, political executives realize that they are working in bureaucracy, and even if they were sent to that bureaucracy in the name of responsiveness, they cannot ignore the goal of effectiveness. Bureaucracy exists to apply knowledge and bodies to the process of promise keeping, and these political executives have to fit themselves into that essential bureaucratic framework.

But, of course, the knowledge possessed by the political executive is very different from the knowledge possessed by the policy specialist, and it is the knowledge of the latter that is presumed to be the knowledge directly connected to keeping the promises at hand. In plainer language, if the promise is aviation safety, the knowledge we need would seem to be that of the aircraft engineer, the flight instructor, the air traffic controller, and the aircraft mechanic. But that is almost certainly not the knowledge possessed by most political executives, even political executives headed for jobs in organizations charged with keeping the promise of aviation safety.

Therein lies the dilemma for every political executive. Effectiveness must be considered a primary goal, and the application of the best available knowledge is bureaucracy's working definition of effectiveness. The best available *technical* knowledge is clearly in the hands of the policy specialists, and even the political executive who is trained in the field of the policy specialists of his or her organization is going to be outgunned by those specialists in *technical* terms. What the political executive needs, of course, is another type of knowledge, a type that he or she possesses but policy specialists don't possess, and that can plausibly be seen as necessary to accomplishing the goal of effectiveness. Enter the knowledge, skills, and most especially the vocabulary of management.

What political executives know that policy specialists do not know is how to "get things done." They know how to see "the big picture." They know how to coordinate. They bring business sense, real-world experience, and common sense, all badly needed to complement the technical knowledge of the specialists, a group that seems in their eyes almost akin to a cloistered order, brilliant and useful in their own way but woefully unprepared to "run this place." I know that sounds like, maybe even is, something of a caricature of the men and women who enter the ranks of the political executives. Still, caricatures are only recognizable because they strongly resemble their subject, just exaggerating one or two features. One of the most coveted—or at least most lucrative—degrees one can earn is an MBA, and the presumption is that once you have earned one you are ready to do some administering (managing) in businesses that make cars and businesses that make cholesterol medication. You aren't supposed to have to know all that much about either of the products to do the job.

So political executives have their knowledge base. Now they can lay claim to a role in producing effectiveness by asserting that what they know really is vital to achieving that central bureaucratic goal. But, as we said with the policy specialists, self-interest is almost never enough to sustain a group of people as they try to carve out a role in any important institution or process. In the immortal words of left-handed relief pitcher Tug McGraw during the New York Mets' improbable run to the 1973 National League Championship, "Ya Gotta' Believe!" For precisely the same reasons that policy specialists believe in their knowledge, political executives believe in theirs.

We Train Them That Way

Political executives, like policy specialists, are trained in our universities, indeed, often in the very same programs. This means that, in terms of initial training anyway, there may well be a great deal of similarity between the two groups, particularly in terms of the commitment to the knowledge gained and its importance to answering the questions this area of policy is likely to pose. But there are two big differences in the training of the two groups.

First, the ranks of political executives will have a far higher percentage of folks sporting the initials JD, or MBA, on their vitae. That, in turn, means a far higher percentage of folks who have at least been exposed to the management vocabulary and the idea that there is a type of knowledge that can be applied to a wide range of specific subject matters.

Second, with the exception of the lower-level political executives who have been tapped out of the ranks of an agency's own policy specialists, most political executives have received their on-the-job training in institutions imbued with the view that management is a separate specialty vital to the organization's ability to accomplish its goals. Beyond that, they have almost certainly worked in jobs labeled management and have very possibly attended seminars and training sessions reinforcing the centrality of management to organizational success. In fact, even those political executives who have emerged from the ranks of policy specialists are almost certainly veterans of management training.

Please don't read this as an indictment of the notions of management, coordination, leadership, and the like. All are real. All are valuable. The point, remember, is this. Political executives need to be able to lay claim to knowledge that policy specialists don't have. That knowledge has to somehow be relevant to accomplishing organizational goals, and it has to be knowledge they can believe in. The knowledge of management is the most logical candidate. The political executives probably got some of it as they passed through the university system and a whole lot more of it in the world of their work. Society respects it enough that it is taught as a separate specialty in some of the best graduate schools in the country. And, as we shall see in a moment, managing is what they seem to do in their jobs. Seems like something they can believe in.

The Job Reinforces It

Just as policy specialists come to their jobs firmly believing that they know a great deal about their specialty and that what they know is essential to making sound and workable public policy, political executives come to their jobs believing that they know a great deal about managing, and that managing is every bit as essential to making sound and workable public policy as is the technical knowledge of the specialists. Maybe even a little bit more essential. And just as the tasks, the work environment, and the career ladder of the policy specialist reinforce that conviction, the tasks, the work environment, and the career ladder of the political executive reinforce his or her view that leadership and management make things work.

Start with the job itself. Managers manage. They review budgets and read reports, or at least they review summaries of budgets and summaries of reports.

They attend meetings, meetings with the policy specialists whose work they are supposedly overseeing, and meetings with other political executives who are supposed to be overseeing their work. The political executive's day is filled with management tasks conducted in management language, no less than the policy specialist's day is filled with technical tasks conducted in technical language. Why would we expect political executives to be any less convinced that their knowledge, their tasks, their language are any less important to organizational success than the knowledge, tasks, and language of the policy specialists?

The work environment reinforces the political executive's faith in his or her knowledge in a couple of interconnected ways. First, the atmosphere in which managing takes place is characterized by a good bit of deference. Some of it is personal. Every political executive has some sort of staff, and that staff is likely to be deferential, in part to protect job prospects but often out of the kind of loyalty that was instrumental in the staff person's selection in the first place. Then, of course, all but the top echelon of political executives will automatically show deference to the men and women in positions above them for precisely the same reasons. Then we have to add in the deference that seems to be accorded to people because of the positions they occupy. I have been amazed more than once at the deference my faculty colleagues—a group of men and women prone to a freewheeling egalitarianism in their relationships with other faculty—will show to campus and especially University of Wisconsin System administrators, even if those administrators have no administrative track record and mediocre credentials in their previous lives as fellow academics. I suspect that on the rare occasions in which they interact at all, we would find precisely the same sort of deference shown by policy specialists to political executives.

It is important to note that this deference to campus administrators has absolutely no impact on how faculty do their main jobs of teaching and research, and I am convinced that the same would be true for any set of policy specialists and any set of political executives anywhere in the rest of government. Still, deference there is, so the question is, is all this deference important? Sure. If everywhere you go in your job and everyone you encounter in your job is showing deference to those who manage—even when the deference is like that of faculty to key administrators and has no effect on how the job is eventually done—how can you not come to believe that managing really is vital and that managers, therefore, really do contribute a great deal to the organization by doing what they do? Managing.

The political executive's work environment reinforces the importance apparently attached to management in a darker, more frightening way as well. When things go drastically wrong at some agency, "mismanagement" is often the first charge leveled, and the first—or at least second—heads to roll are quite often those of managers. Consider the case of Kathleen Kearney.[12] By all accounts a highly competent juvenile court judge and strong advocate for children trapped in the state's child welfare system, she agreed to take the job of Secretary of the Department of Children and Families in her home state of Florida after Jeb Bush's victory in that state's 1998 gubernatorial race. The story is long and sad, and though it probably deserves to be told, this isn't the place to tell it. But, in an article of fewer than 1,500 words detailing Judge Kearney's resignation, the word management is used no fewer than four times. Perhaps even more telling than the number of times some variant of management is used is the fact that it is used with equal fervor by both sides to the debate. The judge's leading critic in the legislature referred to her as "a good judge but not a good manager of a state agency," while her leading supporter in the legislature referred to her as "caught up in a system that has really had a management structure that's been broken for some time." Judge Kearney herself referred to a few isolated incidents of mismanagement, and Janet Reno, hoping to become Governor Bush's Democratic challenger in the fall of 2002, called on the governor to find an experienced child welfare manager to succeed the judge. In short, management—of the bad variety—was the reason an agency could not do its job, and management—of the good variety—was going to put that agency back on track. Again, how could someone in that work environment not begin to believe in the power and importance of his or her management knowledge and skills?

Finally comes the career ladder. In one sense, political executives view the career ladder very differently than do policy specialists. The latter are quite often like college professors, that is, people who mostly want to keep doing what they are doing and get paid more for it each year. Oh some want the dizzying heights of administration, but most are content to do the things they love and maybe to manage a handful of their colleagues if it means a few extra bucks. Political executives, by definition, have higher ambitions. Most don't want to stay put in the same agency niche, getting an adequate raise each year and performing the tasks they enjoy. They want to move up the ladder in the more conventional, almost business-oriented sense of moving from one job to another, each with a better title and more people ostensibly under one's domain. Not all of those jobs will be in the government. There are universities, foundations, public relations firms, indeed, enterprises of all sorts who might be interested in the talents of experienced government managers. The point is that the specialty now is managing, and that's a career ladder all its own.

But, though the political executive's ladder may be more of a conventional ladder, the best climbing outfit is the same as the climbing outfit for the policy specialist. Show your mastery of, and commitment to, the shared body of knowledge and skills that "we" possess and that "our" job is grounded in. For political executives that means showing that they know how to manage and understand why—believe might be more accurate—managing really is central to making policy work. That task, of course, is made so much easier by real faith in what they know, what they say, and what they do. The faith, in turn, is reinforced by its importance to moving up the system. Self-interest and true belief really do have a chicken and egg relationship in many aspects of human affairs.

In Summary

Political executives need to commit themselves to the goal of effectiveness, and effectiveness has to be defined in terms of knowledge. But it can't be the technical knowledge of the policy specialists that political executives consider the exclusive coin of the effectiveness realm. That would leave them broke, or at least pretty poor relative to the policy specialists. So they focus on the notion of management. The political executives know management. They know how to coordinate, to lead, to make things happen, and after all, isn't making things happen the real bottom line? Their definition of effectiveness works every bit as well for the political executives as the policy specialists' definition works for them. Most political executives have some sort of management-oriented education or at least work background before they come to the job, and the job itself provides them with tasks, an environment, and a career ladder that all strongly reinforce the idea of a body of knowledge and a set of skills that can be called management and that are essential to the success of any organization. And if all of that isn't enough to convince them that management is the key to getting important things accomplished, they can reassure themselves by thinking of President George W. Bush, who declared that he would have to veto any bill creating a Department of Homeland Security that did not include a pretty sweeping exemption from traditional civil service law. His reasoning: "It is important that we have the managerial flexibility to get the job done right."[13]

Individual Rights and the Political Executives: The Courts, Administrative Law, and a Little Sensitivity Redux

As far as the rights of individuals are concerned, political executives are in very much the same boat as the policy specialists. It is true that more of the political executives are lawyers, and it is true that more of them work in proximity to the lawyers that provide the official legal advice to the agencies and departments that make up the bureaucracy. Still, more often than not, political executives view individual rights through lenses very much like those of the policy specialists.

When it comes to the fundamental rights guaranteed in the first ten amendments to the U.S. Constitution, it is best to leave things to the courts. It is good to keep those rights in mind when making decisions, and it is even better to ask agency or department counsel when in doubt about the individual rights implications of a decision about to be made. Richard Nixon's second Agriculture Secretary, Earl Butz, didn't ask department counsel and ended up finding his name on a famous administrative law case. In *Butz v. Economu*, the Supreme Court told him he was obligated by law—Section 1983 of the Civil Rights Act of 1871—to ask his lawyer.[14] But, in the end, it can be extremely difficult to predict when a citizen will believe that his or her rights have been violated, and not much easier to predict when the courts will agree. When it comes to procedural rights, once more, administrative law is the key, and political executives, perhaps even more often than policy specialists, contribute to the writing and interpretation of that law and, again perhaps more often than policy specialists, find it an important ingredient in their decision-making environment.

There is one major difference between the vantage point of the political executive and that of the policy specialist when it comes to individual rights, however. Political executives are more likely to be the targets of citizen complaints that rights have been violated than are policy specialists. When the owner of a Pocatello, Idaho, plumbing supply shop thought an Occupational Safety and Health Administration inspection violated his Fourth Amendment rights, he did not sue the inspector who wanted to go into his back room. He sued F. Ray

Marshall, the Secretary of Labor.[15] But, with the exception of certain suits filed under the Tort Claims Act or Section 1983 of the Civil Rights Act of 1871, the "real" defendant is the political executive's unit. Consequently, except for those few Tort and Section 1983 actions, and the "pain in the neck" factor involved in finding one's name on a lawsuit, political executives really do find themselves in the same position as the policy specialists and really can take the same basic approach to the goal of respecting the rights of individuals. Make a serious effort not to threaten the rights of individuals, focus on responsiveness and effectiveness, and trust the courts and administrative law to do the rest.

Accountability and the Political Executives: Same Gorilla, but Closer to Home

Once again, accountability is both an internal and an external phenomenon, and the internal side of accountability is to be found in the application of ethical codes to the decisions an individual bureaucrat is called upon to make. Political executives, like policy specialists, are subject to three such ethical codes—a public service code, a professional code, and a personal code—and, once again like the policy specialists, the political executives merge the three together into a general notion of the right thing to do and try to do it.

From the perspective of the political executive, external accountability is pretty much the same 800-pound gorilla that it is from the perspective of the policy specialist. It still sleeps in the same three spots and still has the annoying habit of waking up—sometimes quite unexpectedly—and demanding to be fed. There is, however, one major difference between the gorilla the political executive sees and the gorilla the policy specialist sees. It is much closer.

If the President is unhappy with policy decisions made at a particular agency, the first phone call isn't going to go to the specialists who worked on the policy. It will go to the political executive deemed "responsible." If some congressional committee wants its pound of bureaucratic flesh, it, too, will look first to the "responsible" executive. In part that is the price to be paid for the emphasis on management as distinct specialty and essential activity, but in part it happens because political executives really do play a key role in the policy-making process. Whatever the reason, political executives know that when the accountability gorilla wakes, they are the ones it is going to see first, and that almost certainly means they are the ones it is going to go after first. Add to this the possibility of an "accountability crossfire"—normally the President and some congressional committee shooting at each other over some decision made in the executive branch—and you can see how political executives would feel far more vulnerable than policy specialists when it comes to accountability.

More vulnerable or not, the political executive's strategy for approaching the goal of accountability is the same as that of the policy specialist: pursue responsiveness and effectiveness, in the hope of avoiding accountability—defined in terms of serious outside interventions from the President, Congress, or the courts—and in the hope of achieving the real goals of accountability, a responsive and effective bureaucracy that respects the rights of individuals. If that fails, then face the music, and hope no one decides to sing "Hit the Road, Jack."

In Summary

Like the policy specialists, the political executives know that the bureaucratic decision-making process is supposed to be guided by the values of effectiveness, responsiveness, and respect for individual rights, and that they will be held accountable for how well they apply those values in their corner of that bureaucracy. Again, like the policy specialists, these political executives know that they must give concrete meaning to those values if they are going to apply them as they make decisions. So they do.

Responsiveness must be the first priority of any political executive. After all, he or she was sent into the bureaucracy to make sure that the views of the public—or at least the public's representatives—are heard and taken into account as policy is formulated and implemented. The President gets first call on the political executive's loyalty, but the President doesn't always exercise that option, and even when he or she does, Congress—through its committees—is constantly reminding those political executives that Article I of the Constitution means that it, too, has the right to be heard. These can be rough moments for the political executive corps, but, as I said, if the chief has spoken clearly and directly, the chief has first call. If there is no presidential direction, the political executive can try to figure out what that direction might be, figure out what the political executive himself or herself would want it to be, or just be responsive to whoever is claiming to represent the public interest as defined in the legislative branch. The courts are more a matter of accountability, but the public can be a bit of a problem, since, like the policy specialists, the political executives realize there are multiple publics. But, unlike the policy specialists, the political executives often have some vague notion that there is a general public interest they ought to be protecting. It turns out that the problem is less pressing than it might appear on the surface, since the President is quite often more than willing to be responsive to the same narrow publics that have so much say in the congressional committees, and that usually settles the issue.

The goal of effectiveness can't be ignored by political executives, of course, so they must find a way to argue—and believe their own argument—that they have a type of knowledge that the specialists don't have and that is essential to successful policy implementation. Management is their salvation. They may have studied it, they have almost certainly practiced it, and when they get to their jobs, they are surrounded by it. And everybody seems to think it is important. At least everybody they talk to does. So they manage, and that is their contribution to effectiveness.

The rights of individuals are important, but the political executives, again much like the policy specialists, feel compelled to get by with as much sensitivity to individual rights as they can figure out how to apply, and a lot of reliance on the courts and the rules and procedures we call administrative law.

Finally, political executives must hold themselves accountable by behaving ethically and must be prepared to be held accountable by others for what they do. In fact, in a personal sense, they must be far better prepared to be held accountable than must policy specialists, since they are far more likely to feel the heat when one of the key players in the constitutional government begins to demand accountability. Personal vulnerability may change the ulcer potential of account-ability mechanisms, but not the strategy for being prepared. Be responsive, be effective, be careful about rights, and if accountability happens, it happens. There is always another job somewhere.

And that's the city of the political executive. On the surface it's very much like the city of the policy specialist, inhabited by men and women who sincerely believe that they have figured out how to be effective, responsive, and respectful of the rights of individuals, and convinced that by pursuing those goals in the way they define them they will be accountable to the people and their constitutional government without ever having to face the unpleasant prospect of actually being "held" accountable. Underneath that surface, of course, the city of the political executives is very different from the city of the policy specialists, as different as are the inhabitants themselves. You know what the differences are. In the next chapter, we'll explore what difference those differences make.

SUMMARY AND CONCLUSION

Organizations are more than the sum total of the individuals who work there. But take those individuals away and you don't have much left. That's why we started our consideration of the organizational forces that affect the process of bureaucratic promise keeping with an examination of the individuals who make bureaucracy go.

We found two sets of individuals in bureaucracy. The men and women of one group are chosen for their subject-matter expertise, are around for the long haul, and each attaches a fierce and abiding loyalty to the small piece of the organization in which he or she engages in the daily routines of the job. The men and women of the second group are chosen for their positions on the issues they will confront in their respective jobs, fully expect to be short-term players at least in the positions they are being chosen for at the moment, and each attaches his or her loyalties to the bureaucratic abstractions we call departments and/or to the people who deemed him or her worthy of inclusion in this select group.

Despite these obvious and enormous differences, each group has to interpret and apply the very same mandate from the people and its government. Policy specialists and political executives alike must decide what it means to be effec-tive, responsive, respectful of individual rights, and accountable and then have to apply their respective definitions—definitions which, to no one's surprise, are very different—to the decisions they have to make.

For obvious reasons, policy specialists focus first on effectiveness, defining that central bureaucratic notion in terms of the application of the best available expert knowledge. Since they believe that they possess that knowledge, they apply it. But they apply it in a context in which they recognize the importance of the goal of responsiveness, and they quickly conclude that they must come up with a definition of responsiveness that doesn't represent too big a compromise with the primary goal of effectiveness. That can be found by focusing attention on those participants in the policy process who seem to be the best informed about the issues at hand, so congressional committees and subcommittees and interest groups, professional associations, and independent subject matter experts become a kind of circle of the informed to whom a policy specialist can be responsive without doing damage to his or her first commitment to the application of the best available expertise. Respect for individual rights has to be factored in, but most of that factoring is done by responding to the courts when they speak to questions involving those rights and by building procedural protections into the rules under which they operate. To adapt a famous bumper sticker, accountability happens. Policy specialists hope they are being accountable by being responsive and effective, but when it comes to being held accountable, that comes from outside, and it just has to be lived with when it does.

Political executives are coming from a very different perspective, of course, but they face the same challenge. They, too, must define effectiveness in terms of the application of the best available knowledge, but it clearly cannot be the subject-matter expertise of the policy specialists. The expert knowledge of the manager, however, is quite another matter. This they can lay claim to, they can believe in it themselves, and it turns out that there is a great deal of respect for the knowledge of the manager among precisely the set of people that political executives wish to please. So they can apply their management expertise secure in the belief that they are pursuing the goal of effectiveness when they do. Responsiveness is the primary goal of the political executive, of course, and the first duty is to be responsive to the President. If the chief has a position and communicates it, the political executive is expected to do whatever he or she can to make sure that position prevails. They can't always be successful, since the committees and subcommittees of Congress and the various segments of the public also believe that they have a legitimate claim on the political executive's loyalty, and they will press that claim vigorously. Again, first loyalty goes to the chief, if the chief has asked for it, but often as not the President has articulated no particular position on an issue or is willing to compromise a bit with the political reality represented by the committees, subcommittees, and interest groups, so political executives can and do listen and accommodate to those non-executive-branch players.

Like the policy specialist, the political executive makes an effort not to trample on the rights of individuals, but mostly leaves the questions of such rights to the courts and to the procedural protections of administrative law. If accountability happens, it happens most frequently to political executives. Still, their belief is pretty much that of the policy specialists. Be effective and responsive and that should mean they are being accountable. If the constitutional government concludes otherwise, then accountability will happen.

If you take these individuals away, you may not have much, but you do have something. That something is organizational structure. That's where we go next.

NOTES

1. Frederick C. Mosher, *Democracy and the Public Service*, 2nd ed. (New York: Oxford University Press, 1982), ch. 5.

2. Mosher, *Democracy and the Public Service*, 137–41.

3. Mosher, *Democracy and the Public Service*, 140.

4. Mosher, *Democracy and the Public Service*, 118.

5. Mosher, *Democracy and the Public Service*, 118.

6. Mosher, *Democracy and the Public Service*, 119.

7. Dennis D. Riley, *Public Personnel Administration*, 2nd ed. (New York: Longman, 2002), 309–11.

8. Thomas E. Cronin, "Presidents as Chief Executives," in *The Presidency Reappraised*, ed. Rexford G. Tugwell and Thomas E. Cronin (New York: Praeger, 1974), 241.

9. For a fuller description of these professional ethical codes and in particular a look at Jack Ward Thomas's condensed version of the Wildlife Society code, see Riley, *Public Personnel Administration*, 109–10.

10. Hugh Heclo, "Issue Networks and the Executive Establishment," in *The New American Political System*, ed. Anthony King (Washington, D.C.: American Enterprise Institute, 1978), 117.

11. Herbert Kaufman, *The Administrative Behavior of Federal Bureau Chiefs* (Washington, D.C.: Brookings Institution, 1981), 51.

12. This story has been reported in the Florida press and even in the national press. I am relying here on Dana Canedy, "Under Fire, Florida Chief of Child Welfare Resigns," *New York Times* (electronic edition), August 14, 2002.

13. Quoted in Spencer Ackerman, "Home Office," *New Republic*, August 19 and 26, 2002, 10.

14. *Butz v. Economu* 438 U.S. 478 (1978).

15. *Marshall v. Barlow's Inc.* 436 U.S. 307 (1978).

3

Structure

We've Got to Get Organized

Individuals are clearly an essential ingredient in organizations. Structure is just as clearly an essential ingredient in organizations. Take away either one, and things just don't seem to work.

All the right people with all the right skills can show up at 4 Yawkey Way, but if they don't put on the uniforms, bring out the balls, bats, and gloves, step out between the white lines, post the results in the American League standings, and most of all, play under long-since agreed-upon rules, we don't have a Red Sox/Yankees game. Of course, we can put a rule book at home plate, scatter uniforms, bats, balls, and gloves around the infield and outfield, and even cram 40,000 screaming New Englanders into Fenway Park, and it's still not a Red Sox/Yankees game unless we also have the right people with the right skills. You have to have the people and you have to have the structure.

So the next question, of course, is: what do we mean by structure? Turns out we mean two closely connected things.

Structure starts with rules. Structure, after all, is what is supposed to bring order to the activities of the individuals who make up an organization, and sooner or later, order comes from rules.

Organizations have rules about all sorts of things. The Suffolk County New York Sheriff's Department, for example, once had a rule prohibiting its deputies from wearing their hair down over the collar of their uniform shirts.[1] The Maricopa County, Arizona, Assessor's Office was equally interested in the hair length of its male employees; the city of Columbus, Georgia, demanded that all of its officers wear an American flag patch on their uniform shirts and jackets; and Philadelphia, Pennsylvania, demanded that all of its employees reside within the city limits.[2]

Those, of course, were all rules from the quirky world of personnel administration—I wrote a book about that world once—and organizations have all sorts of other rules as well. But our inquiry is into the impact of organizational forces—defined in terms of the individuals who make up the organization and the structure of that organization—and that means we are really interested in only one organizational rule. Who makes the rules? Who has the authority to commit the organization to a specific course of action? In more concrete terms, who gets to say that a particular species of bird is endangered, a particular labor practice unfair, or a particular food additive unsafe? This question is particularly important, of course, when there is some disagreement within the organization about what course of action is "the right one." If we return to the question of whether a particular bird species should be classified as endangered under the law, it would be distinctly possible that some within the U.S. Fish and Wildlife Service might be convinced that this species should be so classified, while others might be equally convinced that it should not. Fish and Wildlife hasn't done its job until that final decision is made, and that means that someone has to be given the right to make it. Consequently, bureaucracy's most important rule is the rule that says this is the person—the position, but we'll get to that shortly—with the right to decide.

Bureaucracy does indeed have a rule to dictate who gets to decide. It is called the principle of hierarchy. But to apply such an important rule, of course, bureaucracy has to write it down, and in the process of that writing down we find the second meaning of the notion of organizational structure, what we might best call the paper structure. It takes the federal government the better part of 800 pages to describe its paper structure, with all of those pages devoted to providing the answers to three basic questions.

First comes the question of which organizational unit will be responsible for the conduct of which government activities. As we said in the first chapter, each promise the constitutional government makes sets in motion a set of activities. We want safe skies and that means we must be certain that aircraft are well designed and maintained, pilots skilled and healthy, and the airspace controlled by knowledgeable men and women. The activities involved in making sure these things are true have to be performed by individuals, but the constitutional government cannot assign those activities directly to those individuals. In the first place, that constitutional government has no idea who those individuals might be. Beyond that—and probably more important overall—the conduct of these activities requires the exercise of government authority, and in a "government of laws not men," such authority can only be assigned to institutions and then exercised by individuals who occupy specific positions within those institutions. It cannot be assigned directly to those individuals. So, whenever it makes a promise, the constitutional government has to find or create some institutional home for the activities required to keep that promise.

Second comes the question of the relationship of these organizational units to each other and/or to the broader government. Of the 638 pages of the government manual actually devoted to talking about the specific activities of specific federal government agencies, 250 are devoted to discussing the work of "Independent Establishments and Government Corporations," while 385 are devoted to "Departments."[3] In the latter case, of course, that means these pages will indicate the department—a kind of government holding company—to which a particular organizational unit has been assigned, and equally important, will indicate how these units will be grouped in terms of that department's authority structure. Consider a fairly small and organizationally simple department like the Department of the Interior. One of its best-known constituent units is the Bureau of

Land Management. One of its least known is the Minerals Management Service. Both are under the organizational purview of an Assistant Secretary of the Interior for Land and Minerals Management.[4] (If this doesn't mean much yet, don't worry. It will.) If we go back to the "Independent Establishments, etc.," that occupy pages 496 to 747, we are in a very different land, a land without departments and assistant secretaries. Instead, each unit somehow stands alone. The list of these independent units is long and includes such luminaries as the Central Intelligence Agency, the Environmental Protection Agency, the Federal Trade Commission, and the Federal Reserve System. Of course, it also includes the Panama Canal Commission, Pension Benefit Guaranty Corporation, the United States International Development Cooperation Agency, and the Railroad Retirement Board. One thing is true of all of them. They are not linked together with anybody else in the overall scheme of government. They take their marching orders directly from the President and the Congress, though the ones we call independent regulatory commissions are supposed to march to their very own drummer, sort of.

Finally comes the question of who—which position in the overall scheme of things governmental—has the authority to make which decisions. You may think that question has already been answered by answering the other two, and in a sense it has. The activities involved in making sure that our air transportation system is safe have been assigned to the Federal Aviation Administration and the general authority to conduct those activities is granted under "Subtitle VII, Aviation Programs, of title 49, United States Code."[5] But if the FAA should decide that a new rule governing the design of fuel tanks on commercial aircraft is needed to make good on its promise of safe air travel, is the signature of the agency's administrator good enough? Or does it require the signature of the Secretary of Transportation? Congress has to make that determination, and it is not automatic that the decision will be to give the authority to the FAA administrator. Rules on highway traffic safety are developed in the National Highway Traffic Safety Administration, but the Secretary of Transportation has to go along, just as rules on mine safety originate in the Mine Safety and Health Administration, but without the OK of the Secretary of Labor, they do not take effect. In short, Congress can create all sorts of organizational units and group them together into departments or leave them out on their own. It still has to decide exactly whose signature is necessary to make a decision from that unit binding on the American people.

The essence of the structure of any organization is its rule for deciding who gets to commit that organization to a particular course of action. The organizations I am calling bureaucracy have such a rule. It is called hierarchy and it will be discussed in gory detail in the next section of the chapter. Applying that rule to the various organizations created by the myriad of promises made by the constitutional government results in an intricate network of units, some linked together with other units and others allowed to stand alone, and each given some authority to make the decisions needed to keep the promises that brought that unit into existence in the first place. The principle of hierarchy and the complex paper structure that principle generates have a significant impact on the decisions reached by the individual men and women who perform the day-to-day tasks associated with keeping the constitutional government's promises. It's almost time to try to see how. First, however, we need to say a little more about what we mean by hierarchy.

THE PRINCIPLE OF HIERARCHY

Hierarchy, remember, is an authority principle. It tells us who has the *right* to make a particular decision or set of decisions, including the *right* to tell other people in the organization what they ought to be doing. We need to begin our investigation of hierarchy by addressing three questions. First up, obviously, we need to get a better handle on exactly what the principle of hierarchy means. Second, we need to address the question of why hierarchy. There are, after all, a number of other possible authority principles we might have chosen, so why did we settle on hierarchy? Finally, this authority principle of ours is being imposed on organizations driven by another principle, the principle of specialization. Bureaucracy exists, remember, because we have concluded that we need to bring the knowledge and expertise of highly specialized individuals to bear on complex questions. Now all of a sudden we are going to lay an authority principle called hierarchy over the top of organizations composed of thousands and thousands of men and women trying to use their knowledge to solve problems that in their minds require the application of that knowledge.

What Is Hierarchy?

The principle of hierarchy tells us two things about authority within a particular organization. First, it tells us that there is one single place in the organization—one person or group of people—with the right to make any decision in that organization. Second, it tells us that this person or group delegates that authority to others in the organization, but that such delegation is always both partial and conditional. We need to take a more careful look at both of those.

First of all, the idea of hierarchy is based on the notion that there is one central figure—even if that central figure is a group—that has "final" authority over everything that happens inside a particular organization. That doesn't mean, of course, that that person or group actually makes every decision in the organization. But it does mean that that person or group would have the right to make every decision, or in more practical terms, the right to review and overrule any decision made by any individual in that organization.

Second, because that central authority figure can't—and frankly, probably wouldn't want to—make every decision in the organization, authority is parceled out to others in the organization. But that authority is always handed out in such a way that it is said to be partial and conditional. It is partial in the sense that it applies only to a part of the organization, and conditional in the sense that it is always subject to appeal.

Though part of me has hated them ever since I saw my first one almost four decades ago, the easiest way to pull together all of the components of the principle of hierarchy is to look at an organization chart. So in figure 3.1 you will find the

U.S. Department of the Interior

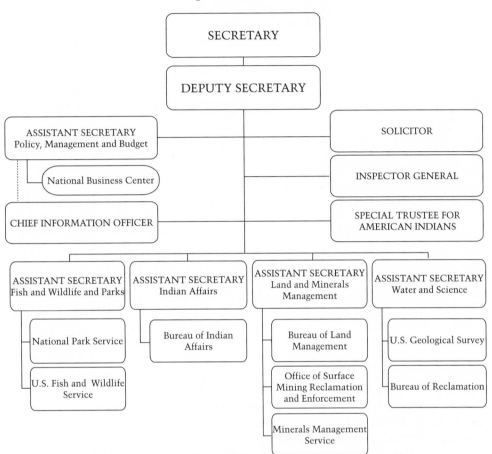

Figure 3.1.   U.S. Department of the Interior Organizational Chart.

Department of the Interior as it appears in two dimensions on the DOI website (www.doi.gov).

The Secretary of the Interior is the central figure who represents the "final authority," though that particular water is a bit muddy since the Secretary does have to take direction from the President and Congress. For now, give the Secretary that "coveted" title of final authority. We'll get to the complexities of using that authority later in the book.

Now take a look down at any of the five boxes with an Assistant Secretary trapped inside. He or she has authority over only the boxes directly below. The Assistant Secretary for Water and Science has authority over the U.S. Geological Survey and the Bureau of Reclamation. The Assistant Secretary for Fish and Wildlife and Parks has authority over the National Park Service and the U.S. Fish and Wildlife Service. And on it would go. That, of course, is what we mean by partial authority. To put it in more concrete terms, if the men and women at the

Park Service have some sort of dispute with the people at the Fish and Wildlife Service, the Assistant Secretary for Fish and Wildlife and Parks is the one to settle the fight. If, on the other hand, the Park Service should lock horns with the Bureau of Land Management or the Bureau of Reclamation, those fights would have to go up to the Secretary.

The authority of the Assistant Secretary for Land and Minerals Management isn't just partial. It is also conditional. If the Bureau of Land Management and the Office of Surface Mining Reclamation and Enforcement have a problem with one another, the Assistant Secretary has the right to tell both of them what to do. But they have the right to appeal to the Secretary. Of course, exercising that right can be dangerous. The Assistant Secretary may be more than a little miffed by an appeal "over his or her head," and there is even the possibility of retaliation. One of my last acts as department chair back in 1997 was to involve the university's two top administrators in a battle I was having with the Dean over the salary for an incoming faculty person. The Dean and I have been friends for a long time. We play softball together. But he was still angry and he even used the phrase "going over my head." In the end, he didn't retaliate, but I used to work for a Dean who would have. Every bureaucrat has to weigh the possibility that an appeal to the next level of the organization will be greeted with considerable anger and frustration. And it may not work. Despite what I thought was a compelling case, my new colleague did not get the salary I recommended. Still, all this cautioning aside, appeals are possible, and that means authority in a hierarchical system is conditional.

Why Hierarchy?

We normally think of the need for some sort of authority principle as a product of the internal disagreement that seems to occur almost as a matter of course in any organizational setting. But internal organizational disagreement tells us only part of the story of hierarchy as bureaucratic authority principle. Two reasons.

First of all, disagreement demands an authority principle for its resolution, but it doesn't demand any particular authority principle. Internal disagreements within the Interior Department could, after all, be resolved by a vote of its 80,000-plus employees, or maybe more likely of the portion of that 80,000 interested in and knowledgeable about the issues at the heart of the disagreement. But to resolve such disagreements within the Interior Department by a vote of some or all of its employees/members is to imply that that department belongs to those folks, and it doesn't. It belongs to us.

But we can't exercise the control that is implied by that ownership one Interior Department employee at a time. All we can do is give our instructions to the constitutional government and have that government relay those instructions to the department. But the constitutional government can't instruct those employees one at a time any more than we can, so it has to find a way to instruct a manageable number of those 80,000—multiplied by the total number of departments and independent entities that constitutional government has created—and send them into the executive branch armed with those instructions and the authority to tell the rest of the people who make up that executive branch what the instructions are and to make sure those instructions are followed. The 4,500 or so men and women we call political executives constitute that manageable number, and the principle of hierarchy is their source of the authority to relay and enforce the instructions that are supposedly coming from us to the constitutional government to the political executives and ultimately to the entire bureaucracy.

Second, and on a directly related note, even if the Interior Department's entire crew of 80,000 or its much smaller crew of men and women interested in and knowledgeable about a particular question were to be in complete harmony on the "right" answer to that question, the decision would not be theirs alone to make. It is not just our organization when it is characterized by internal disagreement. It is our organization, period.

In the end it comes down to ownership and control, or more properly, to the fact that the principle of hierarchy seems to be the authority principle most consistent with the ideas of ownership and control. All of these specialized organizations that we lump together and call bureaucracy are supposed to belong to the people. We own them and we are supposed to be able to control them, and the only way we can possibly do that is indirectly through our control of the constitutional government and its control of all of these specialized organizations.

As we will see throughout the rest of this book, the chain from citizen to constitutional government, to top bureaucrat, to middle bureaucrat, to bottom bureaucrat can be pretty hard to see. But it is supposed to be there, and more to the point, it is our belief that it is supposed to be there that leads us to the conclusion that hierarchy must be the authority principle we impose on the bureaucracy we create to keep the promises we make to ourselves.

But What About Specialization?

The desire for the control that is supposed to come with our ownership of our own government may demand the imposition of the principle of hierarchy on bureaucracy, but as I've said repeatedly, bureaucracy exists because the government we created in our constitution does not have, and could not possibly have, the numbers of people and the *specialized knowledge* to do what that constitutionally created government has concluded we want done. In short, we need to impose hierarchy on organizations that need to use specialized knowledge. As Victor Thompson pointed out more than forty years ago, these two principles are at odds with one another, creating the potential for enormous organizational conflict.[6] Given what we saw in the last chapter—a bureaucracy populated by two very different sets of individuals—policy specialists hired for their specialized knowledge, expecting to stay around for a while, and intensely loyal to a small and specialized subunit of bureaucracy, and political executives hired for what they believe, knowing they will not be around for long, and just as intensely loyal to a President, a party, or a patron—there can be little doubt that that potential for conflict will be realized.

Still, we have no choice. We have to organize bureaucracy on the basis of the principle of specialization because gathering and using knowledge is the purpose of bureaucracy, and gathering and using knowledge is the province of subject-matter specialists. We have to organize bureaucracy on the principle of hierarchy because that bureaucracy does not belong to those who populate it but to us, and we have to have some way to control what we own. To abandon one is to give up on government that can solve problems. To abandon the other is to give up on government that is ours. Uneasy and not so peaceful coexistence is about all we can hope for.

THE IMPACT OF HIERARCHY

There can be no doubt that hierarchy leaves its mark on the decisions that bureaucracy makes and the ways in which it makes them. In part it leaves its mark as Victor Thompson pointed out, by granting the authority to make organizational decisions to people who by definition cannot have the technical knowledge that almost certainly ought to be brought to bear on those decisions.[7] In part it leaves its mark by its impact on the organizational communication system. And in part it leaves its mark by exposing such organizations to all of the problems that can so easily occur when one person and his or her ideas dominate an organization's decision making. Let's take a look at each of these in turn. Then we can see if in combination they have any impact on bureaucracy's ability to be effective, responsive, respectful of the rights of individuals, and accountable.

Hierarchy and Organizational Communication: Sometimes the Emperor Is Naked

It may well be that in the world outside bureaucracy, bad news does indeed travel fast. But inside bureaucracy, it hardly travels at all. Bad news—defined as any news an organization's top officials would rather not believe to be true—is likely to run into some pretty formidable roadblocks on its difficult path up the ladder in a hierarchically structured organization. Let's look first at the question of why these roadblocks are consistently placed in the way of information moving up the bureaucratic chain. Then we can consider the question of how the road is actually blocked.

Information can only be detoured on its way up the bureaucratic system by people who are part of that system, so our look at the question of why these roadblocks exist, of course, is a look at what might motivate someone in a government organization to keep a piece of bad news from moving unimpeded from one level of that organization to another. Four such motivations come easily to mind.

First comes fear. The fear involved, of course, stems in large part from the fact that the bureaucratic equivalent of shooting the messenger is far from dead. The individual who keeps a particular piece of bad news from reaching the desk of a particular official is a subordinate of that official, depending on him or her, as subordinates always do, for raises, promotions, perks, status, recommendations for employment outside of government, or in many cases for the very power that he or she is able to wield inside this particular organization. In its extreme form, this fear can be a major contributor to what Jack Gonzales and John Rothchild called "the McNaughton factor," named after former Harvard law professor John McNaughton, who served as special assistant to Defense Secretary

Robert McNamara during the mid-1960s.[8] McNaughton, it seems, had private doubts about the conduct, even about the very wisdom, of the war in Vietnam. He would express those doubts to close friends and associates, but whenever those same arguments were made by others in front of McNamara, McNaughton would tear them apart. As David Halberstam put it in his best-selling *The Best and the Brightest*, McNaughton knew that "his power existed only as long as he had Robert McNamara's complete confidence, and as long as everyone in government believed that when he spoke he spoke not for John McNaughton, but for Bob McNamara."[9]

Not everyone who blocks information from reaching a key member of the hierarchy occupies the position of special assistant, nor do they all depend totally on the favor of the boss to survive in their particular organization. But the farther up the system information has to go, the more likely it is that it will have to pass through the hands of someone very fearful of the reaction of the person next in line to receive it and with strong motivation to act on that fear by seeing to it that that particular piece of information gets sidetracked if not just plain buried. It is no accident that of all the insightful phrases turned in an illustrious career by political scientist Aaron Wildavsky the one that found its way into the language was the title of his 1979 classic *Speaking Truth to Power*.[10] It passed into the language, of course, precisely because the act of speaking truth to power is known to be so very difficult.

Strange as it may sound at first, bad news can be deflected as much out of loyalty as out of fear. David Halberstam concluded that loyalty played every bit as large a role in John McNaughton's behavior as did fear.[11] Remember, the men and women guarding the information flow to a particular political executive were very likely picked by that particular executive, and loyalty was one of the criteria in the selection. It shouldn't be so surprising that that loyalty would surface when a piece of information that would challenge long-standing positions or current policies advocated by that executive hit the desk of such a handpicked subordinate. It is even less surprising when you also recall that much of the information flowing in bureaucracy originates with policy specialists, a group that the political executives tend to see as representing their own narrow agency interests and unable to see the bigger picture that they—the political executives and their teams—see ever so clearly.

Fear and loyalty often meet, of course, at a place called ambition. A substantial number of those in mid-level bureaucratic positions, or especially in special assistant or other staff positions, hope—indeed expect—to be something other than mid-level bureaucrats or special assistants. Even if they don't anticipate marrying a senator along the way, a good many wouldn't mind a career path like that of Elizabeth Hanford Dole, who went from her low-level job in the Nixon administration, on through higher jobs in the Reagan and Bush administrations, to a short but high-profile run for the presidency, to her current seat in the U.S. Senate from North Carolina.[12]

Beyond fear and loyalty, there is the ever present deference to authority that characterizes most interactions in bureaucracy. This deference is particularly acute, of course, in formal interactions, most especially in the most formal of such interactions, memos and meetings, the very interactions in which organizational communication is supposed to take place. I was already a tenured full professor and an elected department chair when I first had to deliver a piece of what I knew he would consider very bad news to the chancellor of this university many years ago. My hands shook as I spoke. He couldn't fire me, even as chair, and I certainly wasn't loyal to him. But he was the top dog and it made me uneasy to confront him with information I knew he didn't want to hear.

Finally, whether inside bureaucracy or out, people just don't like to deliver unpleasant news to other people. After all these years, I still don't like to tell my wife I don't want to go to a movie she really wants to see, just as she isn't terribly excited about telling me that a certain couple is coming over for dinner on Friday. To put it back into a bureaucratic context, supervisors generally have to do formal appraisals of the work of their subordinates. Those supervisors are so bothered by the possibility of having to deliver bad news in these appraisals that their concern now has its very own name in the literature of public personnel administration. It is called Performance Appraisal Discomfort.[13]

Important as it is to understand why some of the men and women of bureaucracy would try to keep information from reaching their bosses, even more is revealed about the impact of hierarchy on organizational communications when we consider the question of how that information finds itself disappearing into some special netherland of derailed communications. As it turns out, it can happen in any or all of three ways.

First of all, subordinates can lie. A story circulated in Washington after J. Edgar Hoover's death to the effect that his second in command had once been upbraided quite thoroughly for giving Hoover a report concluding that Martin Luther King Jr. was not a Communist. That number two man is said to have returned to his office, thought about his job, his wife and his kids, and his mortgage, and decided to write a report that concluded that Dr. King was indeed a Communist. That kind of lying may not be common, but lying by omission—hiding something, especially a judgment or conclusion—is very much a common occurrence. Let's return to John McNaughton for a moment. McNaughton was a Harvard law professor before joining the Defense Department and, at least according to David Halberstam, had no desire at all to return to that job when his days at DOD were over. At a 1966 meeting at which he decided to take another major step in escalating the Vietnam War by bombing the oil depots at Haiphong in North Vietnam, President Lyndon Johnson tried to obtain a consensus for his decision by asking each individual around the table for a final comment. McNaughton had made his opposition to such a course of action clear enough in private, but his response to the President's inquiry was a simple, "I have nothing to add, sir."[14] Secretary McNamara had already said yes to the bombing.

Important as lies of omission may be, few will find their way into books by highly respected journalists. For that matter, not all that many will ever even see the light of day. But there is another equally effective method for omitting bad news from the flow of information to key players in the hierarchy, and this one doesn't rely on anybody lying by omission. Well, to be more accurate, nobody has to go through what John McNaughton almost certainly went through in that moment just before he said, "I have nothing to add, sir." Jack Gonzales and John

Rothchild call this method "Tell Me on My Own Terms," though it might just as easily be referred to as the original version of "Don't Ask, Don't Tell."[15]

Once again, as did Gonzales and Rothchild, we can rely on David Halberstam and his careful analysis of our involvement in Vietnam. Consider just two incidents involving Secretary of Defense Robert McNamara. Early in the escalation, McNamara visited Vietnam, and as part of the briefing process he got a pessimistic assessment of the situation from a civilian employee by the name of Rufus Phillips. Later in the day, when the Secretary met with the military commander in the region that Mr. Phillips had described as increasingly under Viet Cong influence, he asked if the commander agreed with his civilian counterpart. He said he did. Then why no report? asked McNamara. The major's answer: the guidelines for his reports asked only for his assessment of the military situation, so that is what he reported.[16] Around a year later, McNamara got another assessment of the situation—this time of the entire war effort—from the CIA's third in command, a man named Desmond Fitzgerald. This one challenged not only the course of action but McNamara's entire style of making decisions by quantifying every possible variable. Fitzgerald, who had been briefing McNamara every week prior to this meeting, was never invited back.[17]

Lest you think that "Tell Me on My Own Terms" disappeared with Robert McNamara and his team, think about 2002 and the Bush administration planning for a possible war with Iraq. Parker Borg spent thirty years in the U.S. State Department, capping his career as deputy chief of counterterrorism. In an interview done by senior correspondent Robert Dreyfuss of *The American Prospect*, Borg gave a former insider's take on the debate—or lack thereof—involving the prospect of such a war. "When [Near East Affairs] meets, there is no debate. How vocal would you be about commenting on Middle East policy with the vice president's daughter there?"[18] Elizabeth Cheney, it seems, served as Deputy Assistant Secretary of State for Near East Affairs, and she and Under Secretary of State John Bolton, who often attended these meetings, were both outspoken proponents of military action against Iraq. So convinced was Secretary of Defense Donald Rumsfeld that he had to get the right information, he created "a parallel, *ad hoc* intelligence operation, in the office of Under Secretary of Defense for Policy Douglas J. Feith, [which] collects information from the [Iraqi] exiles and scouts other raw intelligence for useful tidbits to make the case for preemptive war."[19] As McNamara learned from his experience with Desmond Fitzgerald, sometimes asking the right questions isn't enough. You have to ask the right people.

Meetings have been mentioned twice already in this section, so this is as good a place as any to indicate that both of the methods for derailing information discussed so far tend to be exaggerated in the setting of a meeting. At its heart, the reason doesn't seem all that much more complicated than what adults observe when a bunch of kids want to do something—sort of—but nobody wants to go first for fear the others will chicken out. In a meeting conducted by an official identified with a position—try the daughter of a high-profile vice president who has taken the same position—and attended by another even higher-ranking official identified with the same position, nobody is likely to volunteer opposition to that position. And neither of those officials is likely to ask them to. I'm sure you got the reference in the title of this section, but in case you don't remember, there is an old children's story about the Emperor and his new clothes. The Emperor, of course, turns out to be naked, having been sold a bill of goods by the tailor. It was not, as you recall, the tailor or any of the Emperor's ministers or royal court who informed him of his nakedness. It was a little kid. But there almost never seem to be bureaucratic equivalents of little kids at these meetings. Instead we get the silent men and women at the Near East Affairs meetings, or the six-word assents of men like John McNaughton, not about to state what he really thought in a room full of people who had already staked out the position they were pretty sure the chief was going to take by the end of the session.

Finally, the last and almost certainly the most pervasive and the most effective of the roadblocks to bad news is the ability of hierarchically structured organizations to put a very different face on information that would make its top officials unhappy as that information moves upward, one organizational layer at a time. As information moves upward in a hierarchically structured organization, it passes from the hands of the specialists who collected and analyzed it to the hands of the political executives who have the authority to act on it. Along the way, it passes through the hands of others. Some will be specialists who have moved into lower-level administrative positions, some will be lower-level political executives, and some will be members of the staffs of upper-level executives. At each succeeding level, the information will be delivered to someone with less specialized knowledge about the subject at hand, less time to digest the information, and a greater sensitivity to the question of whether this particular information constitutes "bad news" from the point of view of the person at the next level.

A great deal of information is communicated upward in bureaucracy in the form of reports and memos, and the lesser expertise, greater time pressures, and increased concern over the reaction the information is likely to generate from its next recipient combine to mean that at each succeeding level more and more of the attention given to the document will be given to the summaries, conclusions, and recommendations. But it is in precisely these sections of any document that it is easiest to give that document a facelift. Don't alter the data or the tables. Nobody really understands them at this level anyway. Just "soften" the conclusions or recommendations. Make them more palatable to the next level. If you think that "is very likely to become" might raise a flag for the boss, how about "has the definite potential to become"? It's almost the same thing, yet it doesn't convey quite the same sense of urgency. Then if the next level is still a little unsure, the concerned folks at that level can just drop the word "definite." To the person doing the rewrite, these minor changes could hardly compare to lying to the boss. In fact, the person doing the rewrite isn't even holding anything back. The data and tables are intact. They are just being interpreted from a slightly different viewpoint.

In the fall of 2002, some of my departmental colleagues decided that a report I had written for the university had too much of an "in your face" quality and needed toning down. They gave it that toning down. But the tables went forward exactly as I had constructed them. It was the narrative, and especially the final paragraph of that narrative, that needed to be made more palatable to our new

Vice Chancellor for Academic Affairs. Palatable, by the way, was the word used by one of my senior colleagues when he demanded the rewrite.

An even better example would be found in the Department of Transportation and the tragedy of ValuJet Flight 592. Flight 592 went down in the Florida Everglades in May 1996. Less than one month before that crash, the DOT had released a report touting the wonders of the "Low-Cost Airline Service Revolution."[20] The report focused on the economic benefits—$6.3 billion worth—to the traveling public, and assured us that the so-called "start-up" airlines were as safe as the established lines whose names and commercials we all remembered. In the aftermath of that crash, we began to learn a great deal about that report, about ValuJet, and about the Department of Transportation.

First of all, on May 2, about halfway between the DOT report and the crash, an analyst in the Accident Investigation Office of the Federal Aviation Administration produced a second report. Very short, it simply took the original safety data about the start-up airlines and analyzed them a little differently from the way they had originally been analyzed by the same FAA experts earlier. Specifically, this report separated Southwest Airlines—an outfit that had been in business since 1971—from the other "start-ups." The results were interesting. With Southwest out, the safety records of these airlines were definitely not comparable to those of the established carriers. Then the FAA analyst, Bob Matthews, separated out ValuJet, and the results were astounding. Its record was terrifying. On every indicator possible, the airline's record was far worse than that of anybody else.

All of this information had been available inside the FAA and the Department of Transportation before. Much more was available. But it had never gotten very far up the ladder. Reports that included all the sets of tables—with and without Southwest, with and without ValuJet—had been constructed and even circulated. As those reports went around, however, those in charge of constructing the April 23 report—the one to be titled "Low-Cost Airline Service Revolution"—looked at the "whole start-up" tables, saw what they wanted in those tables, and constructed their report. No one contradicted that report until Bob Matthews, and what he did was construct the new, more direct report and send it on up, complete with a handwritten note attached saying that "Southwest so dominates the data for the low-cost group that this finding [of an accident rate comparable to the high-cost airlines] is not transferable to low-cost carriers in general."[21]

It is hard to be sure exactly what the people at the top of DOT made of Bob Matthews's report. What we do know is that Transportation Secretary Federico Peña got a copy and continued to assert that the safety record of the start-ups was comparable to that of the established airlines. He did it on national television. The day after the crash of Flight 592.

Bad news doesn't move very well inside hierarchically structured organizations. People are afraid to let it move. People are too loyal to their bosses to let it move. People tend to be deferential to those who exercise authority even when they are neither afraid nor loyal. People just don't like to give other people bad news no matter what the relationship between them. So subordinates sometimes lie outright and more frequently lie by not telling all they know. Bosses shape their questions so that bad news can be filtered out without anybody feeling as if they have lied and, if that fails, are careful to ask questions only of people they can trust to give them what they want. Most of all, as information moves up the hierarchical ladder, the people on the receiving end are less and less prepared to make sense of it and more and more dependent on the interpretations given that information by the last person to handle it. And the last person to handle it can sometimes make just a small change that will make it news that is a little less bad in the eyes of the person who gets it. Whatever the reasons, whatever the means, people who have to exercise authority in bureaucracy have to do so with a less than accurate picture of what is going on "down below."

Separating Authority from Knowledge

As I noted earlier in the chapter, Victor Thompson argued as far back as 1962 that as a result of the effort to fit specialization into the hierarchical framework, "There is a growing gap between the right to decide, which is authority, and the power to do, which is specialized ability."[22] I prefer to think of it in terms of a gap between authority, which an individual possesses because he or she is appointed to a particular position in the organization, and knowledge which an individual possesses because he or she has specialized in a particular field of study and then been appointed to a position in the organization that demands that particular expertise. Either way, it is pretty clear that imposing the principle of hierarchy on an organization whose reason for existence is the collection of information and the application of specialized knowledge in the use of that information is going to result in a situation in which the men and women with the right to make decisions will not be the men and women with the knowledge that should be a central ingredient in the making of those decisions.

Let's visit once more with one of the Interior Department's assistant secretaries. Would any one individual, no matter what his or her professional training and experience, be prepared to handle the technical side of the questions that would emerge from the activities of the Fish and Wildlife Service and the National Park Service? Or how about the Bureau of Land Management, the Minerals Management Service, and the Office of Surface Mining Reclamation and Enforcement? You can go just about anyplace else in government and find the same predicament for the men and women who have been assigned the role of political executive and taken with it the authority to decide a myriad of public policy questions.

The escape from this predicament is supposed to be the delegation of authority, either in the formal sense of handing the authority over to a subordinate, or more likely in the informal sense of becoming more or less a rubber stamp for the organization's experts. Political executives use that escape hatch some of the time, of course, but they don't use it all that often. The reasons are partly personal and partly organizational/philosophical.

Let's start with a quick look at the personal side. People don't usually reach these sorts of positions if they lack self-confidence or just plain don't like to decide things. Most of them are used to giving orders in one context or another and to having people take those orders seriously. The man who was chancellor of this university when I signed on and who later became governor of Wisconsin, Lee Sherman Dreyfuss, used to tell the story of the day he looked in the mirror and decided that he had been born to lead. The faculty generally snickered when he said it, but he meant it. Now add to that sort of personal confidence the role of boss. Bosses are supposed to be leaders, decision makers, believers that the buck has to stop somewhere and their office is as good a place as any for it to finally come to rest. Delegating authority won't come all that easily to someone who thinks that he or she is particularly adept at exercising it and who is in a position that is defined in terms of the decisions its occupant is expected to make.

Important as these personal dimensions may be in the decision not to delegate much authority to an organization's specialists, organizational/philosophical dimensions may well be even more important. Three of them would seem likely to play a significant role in the tendency of political executives to hang onto authority even in the face of their own lack of technical knowledge of the issues they are about to decide.

First, and clearly connected to the notion of the role of boss as decision maker, remember that political executives come to their jobs with knowledge that they believe is key to effective organizational decision making, namely, the knowledge of how to manage. So while they may lack some technical knowledge about a particular question, they know how to get things done, how to organize so there are concrete results, and so on. Policy specialists may believe authority should be delegated their way so that their knowledge can get its proper organizational due, but political executives are reluctant to hand over too much authority because they believe that their knowledge deserves its proper due every bit as much as does the knowledge of those policy specialists.

On a related note, political executives are more than a little suspicious of the policy specialists and their knowledge. These policy specialists are indeed hired for what they know, but as we said in the last chapter, they are fiercely loyal to their professions and to the organizational subunits they work in, and in the eyes of most political executives that makes them narrow minded, stubborn, and probably a bit self-serving. With a little appropriate adaptation, you could probably get most political executives to subscribe to Hubert Humphrey's lament that "Every once in a while one gets the view down here in Washington that the respective departments are members of the United Nations, and that each has a separate sovereignty."[23] From that perspective, handing over authority that was given to you—your position, but you get to exercise it—to a bunch of uncooperative specialists doesn't seem very appealing somehow.

Finally, recall the connection between hierarchy and the public's ownership of its own government. These political executives see themselves as having been sent by the winner of the last election to do the bidding of those who made that individual the winner. They can't just abandon that role. The knowledge of the policy specialists deserves respect. But the people's right to govern themselves deserves even more respect, and these political executives can convince themselves rather easily that the people's ability to govern themselves depends to a very real degree on their willingness to exercise the authority they have been given.

Specialization and hierarchy are on a collision course, and when they do collide, authority goes one way and knowledge another. There is really no practical way to bring the two back together by giving the knowledge to the one with the authority. When Federico Peña was pressed into service as Bill Clinton's Energy Secretary, one energy consultant referred to the process of preparing him for the task as akin to "going from grade school into a graduate course in one month."[24] But going the other way, delegating authority, has its problems as well. Political executives aren't personally anxious to do it. They are bosses, with all that means in their minds, and they are confident people, with all that implies. More to the point, to delegate very much authority to policy specialists is to hand that authority to individuals the political executives often perceive as narrow minded and self-interested. And most of all, much delegation to policy specialists flies in the face of the reasons the political executives are where they are in the first place. They are there to bring their management expertise to bear on policy questions, and most of all to make sure that the people's views can ultimately prevail. In the eyes of those political executives, that is a pretty important mandate, and they are not about to abandon it simply because someone tells them they lack the necessary expert knowledge to understand the questions they have been put there to decide.

Absolute Power May Not Corrupt Absolutely, but . . .

But it can corrupt, and when it does it can also be corrupted. The power exercised by political executives in most contexts is hardly absolute, of course, but it is substantial—more substantial in some organizations than in others, but always substantial—and it can corrupt and it can be corrupted.

First of all, from the time James Madison told us that "ambition must be made to counteract ambition" if we were to be safe from tyranny, we have known that if one viewpoint—one person or group's viewpoint, really—comes to dominate an organization and that viewpoint becomes warped in some way, so does the organization itself. Its policies are bound to follow. Once J. Edgar Hoover decided that the strictures of the Fourth Amendment didn't apply to the FBI, the rest of the bureau followed along. Breaking and entering became a standard investigative technique and wiretaps routine. The Mafia was defined out of existence, and the American Communist Party was said to be a significant internal threat. How much damage an organization headed by someone who does go off the deep end like J. Edgar Hoover can do depends in part, of course, on the mission of that particular agency. Hoover couldn't have harmed as many people or trampled on as many of our basic values had he been put in charge of the Bureau of Land Management, any more than Allen Dulles could have turned the Forest Service into the kind of rogue elephant he was able to make out of the CIA in the 1950s.

But no matter what an organization's mission, as it becomes more and more controlled by its hierarchy, the combination of fear and loyalty we were talking about earlier in the chapter comes to pervade the organization, and the almost inevitable result is what comes perilously close to complete control of the flow of communication from inside the organization to those outside that organization, that is, to us. The efforts by political executives to keep things inside the organization are pervasive enough—and effective enough—that we are all still a bit startled when someone does "blow the whistle," and we have seen the need to try to protect those who do.[25] We need to protect them, of course, because we need to know what they know. Without what they know, we can never be aware of problems we need to fix, or agencies gone haywire. The American public and its representatives might well have let J. Edgar Hoover and his FBI continue on the path Hoover took the bureau in the 1950s and 1960s. But they might not have. We'll never know, precisely because Hoover's FBI was so tightly controlled that we did not know exactly what it was up to.

It is a little iffy to hold up J. Edgar Hoover's FBI or Allen Dulles's CIA and say See, that's where bureaucracy ends up. Rarely does an agency head lose his or her democratic compass that completely. But the more thoroughly the principle of hierarchy establishes itself in a particular organization, the easier it will be for Hoover or Dulles writ small to take some other organization to places it ought not to go. And most of all, the more thoroughly the principle of hierarchy establishes itself in a particular organization, the less we as citizens will know about what is happening inside that organization. We need to know. As Sixth Circuit Justice Damon J. Keith put it for a unanimous panel of his colleagues who had just told the U.S. Department of Justice that it could not hold deportation hearings in secret just because it believed the subjects of those hearings had ties to terrorism, "Democracies die behind closed doors."[26]

Hierarchy, Political Executives, and the Bureaucratic Mandate

We want a bureaucracy that is capable of effectiveness. In the long run, we define effectiveness in terms of success, that is, of actually solving the problems that policies are aimed at solving. But bureaucracy has to make decisions in the short run, and we have to make judgments about those decisions in the short run, so both bureaucrats and those they work for—that's us, recall—have to have some sort of working definition of effectiveness that can be applied as decisions are being made. That working definition has to center on the application of the best available specialized knowledge of the subject at hand or the whole idea of bureaucracy is called into question. Why gather together a group of specialists if their specialization is to be ignored?

Hierarchy, alas, seems to fly in the face of that working definition of effectiveness. Two ways. First, of course, it does so by granting the right to make decisions to people who, by definition, do not possess that specialized knowledge that effectiveness presumably demands. Second, it does so by keeping those with the right to make decisions from getting the information and opinions that would seem to be vital to making those decisions in a reasoned and informed manner.

To be sure, we have to give some credence to the arguments of the political executives that they bring to bear some other knowledge—the knowledge of management—that is badly needed in any effective organization. As we shall see when we discuss the impact of specialization in the next section of the chapter, we must also give some credence to the political executives' contention that the knowledge that policy specialists so want to have at the center of the bureaucratic decision-making process is a knowledge that is narrow, confined by professional norms and organizational loyalties, and in the end, not exactly the pure specialization its practitioners make it out to be.

Still, in the end, there is good reason to conclude that the imposition of hierarchy on organizations devoted to the process of gathering and using specialized information does pose real problems for the ability of those organizations to work toward the goal of effectiveness. Specialized knowledge simply cannot get its due in a truly hierarchical organization.

But effectiveness is not the only goal we have for bureaucracy, and a price may have to be paid in terms of reliance on specialized knowledge in order to accomplish those other goals. That is certainly what the political executives would have us believe, and it is true, even if not to the extent that they would claim.

In slightly more straightforward terms, the principle of hierarchy—operating through the decisions made by political executives—almost certainly does sometimes rein in specialists whose decisions might well have been out of step with the desires of citizens, or even violated the rights of some of those citizens. Likewise, hierarchy does create something that approximates a chain of command, and that, in turn, creates something that approximates a chain of accountability. Hierarchy can, and does, help us to realize the other goals we have for bureaucracy. And it often does so precisely by preventing policy specialists from "doing their thing." Sometimes.

But other times the principle of hierarchy—again operating through the decisions made by political executives—can thwart responsiveness, violate the rights of individual citizens, and create anything but an accountable organization. Again, no one can argue the general case about bureaucracy by citing J. Edgar Hoover's FBI. But neither can that FBI be considered completely irrelevant to the understanding of bureaucracy. In the extreme case, an organization can become so isolated from the rest of government, so immune to the normal mechanisms of external influence, that it really can go its own way, arrogant, unresponsive, and quite thoroughly unaccountable. In less than extreme cases, it can make that journey part way, and whenever any organization heads down that path, hierarchy must take some of the responsibility for the trip. After all, it is hierarchy that tends to create a climate of deference that can easily become a climate of fear and loyalty, a climate that will almost certainly stifle the flow of information inside the organization and the flow of communication from inside to outside. And an organization that cannot move information inside and cannot—or will not—communicate with the outside is responsive and accountable only to those who occupy its positions of authority, in other words, to its own hierarchy.

In short, the impact of hierarchy on bureaucracy's ability to pursue the mandate we have given it is decidedly mixed. Political executives—the embodiment of the principle of hierarchy—do have a specialized knowledge that is useful in policy making and they do represent, however imperfectly, the notions of responsiveness and accountability. However, as the embodiment of the principle of hierarchy, they also help to create an organization in which specialized knowledge will often get less respect than it deserves, and (more to the point) will almost inevitably create an organization in which any information—and especially any opinions—those political executives would rather not hear won't be spoken in their presence. In addition, they will almost certainly work very hard to create an organization in which all communication with the outside will hew to the "company line."

THE IMPACT OF SPECIALIZATION

Now it's time to talk about specialization and how it affects bureaucratic policy making. Specialization didn't exactly make the definition of organizational structure that we started the chapter with, but in a sense it didn't need to. Specialization is, after all, the essence of bureaucracy, its reason to exist and the primary source of its role and power. In a very real sense, in other words, organizational structure is imposed on specialization, or more properly, on specialists as they go about their business, the business of applying what they know to the problems they see. There would be no organizational structure without it.

What I want to do in this discussion is lead you through two examples of policy making in two very different organizations, the Federal Housing Administration and the Bureau of Reclamation. Though their specific missions—guaranteeing loans so that the nation's housing stock might be increased and improved versus "making a desert bloom"—couldn't be much farther apart, each operated in a remarkably similar way. The similarities were driven by certain aspects of the very notion of specialization, or perhaps better, by how that notion is interpreted and applied by individual specialists.

Surrounding the City: The Federal Housing Administration Guarantees Suburbanization

The Federal Housing Administration (FHA) was created in the 1930s as part of Franklin D. Roosevelt's New Deal. Its job was to help make housing more affordable—and to get the housing industry back on its feet again—by guaranteeing mortgages. The economy wouldn't let the agency get too far in the late 1930s, and World War II wouldn't let it get anywhere in the first half of the 1940s. But the nation's postwar housing needs meant that the FHA could, and would, become a major force in the American housing market from 1946 on.

The agency was staffed from the very beginning by real estate people and mortgage bankers, and as Harold Seidman pointed out in 1970, "the values and prejudices" of those original FHA professionals became the driving force in its policies.[27] In concrete terms, the FHA committed itself to sound banking principles as the guide for its mortgage guarantee policies. In effect, then, it committed itself to a definition of agency success that would rest exclusively on "the number of loans made and the repayment record."[28] Once the FHA was committed to such a definition of success, it was also committed to a search for the least risky loans, and as anyone in the real estate or mortgage banking professions could/would have told you—and as what systematic data that existed would have confirmed—the least risky housing loans are those made on newly constructed, single-family, owner-occupied homes. So, beginning in the late 1930s, accelerating in the late 1940s, and continuing well into the early 1970s, that is where the FHA put just over $110 billion in loan guarantees.

In the twenty-five years between the end of World War II and 1970, an FHA mortgage guarantee was prized by buyers and lenders alike. Lenders, of course, got out from under the only really frightening part of being a lender—the risk of not being repaid—because the federal government would pay if the borrower could not. Buyers were just as happy, because FHA mortgages had a lower interest rate and a lower down-payment requirement. So the FHA had plenty of lenders ready to make the loans the agency would guarantee, and the lenders had plenty of borrowers anxious to get the money and buy homes of their own. What we needed, of course, were the homes.

If you want to build several billion dollars' worth of single-family homes each year for who knows how long, you are going to need a lot of land to build them on. If you want those homes to be within the price range of middle-income Americans, you need a lot of cheap land to build them on. There wasn't much land available inside our large or even medium-sized cities, and what land there was certainly wasn't cheap. There was existing housing stock that could have been renovated, but it wasn't new, and much of it wasn't single family, so the FHA had no interest in it. There was, however, as we all know, plenty of cheap land available just outside our cities, and more and more of that land became available as more and more people took the money and converted farm land into land for single-family housing. With the help and inspiration of the Levitt brothers—and lots of other people—we created the American suburb, and FHA loan guarantees played an important role in that creation.

The Desert Really Did Bloom: The Bureau of Reclamation and Western Agriculture

In 1902, Congress authorized the Secretary of the Interior to administer a program designed to provide water for irrigation in the seventeen western states. The Secretary was to be assisted in this endeavor by the Reclamation Service, a unit created within the U.S. Geological Survey.[29] By 1907, the Service was split off from the Survey, and in 1923 given its present name, the Bureau of Reclamation. Long before 1923, however, it began to acquire its present status within the Interior Department.

The law itself was in part the brainchild of President Theodore Roosevelt, who wanted to see the American West opened up for agricultural development. Its chief sponsor in the House of Representatives was Democrat Francis G. Newlands of Nevada, who succeeded in including in the statute both a residency requirement and an acreage limitation in order to "guard against land monopoly and to hold this land in small tracts for the people of the entire country, to give each only the amount of land that will be necessary for the support of a family."[30] But Representative—then Senator—Newlands's vision of a region of small family farms ran smack into the Reclamation Service's—later Bureau of Reclamation's—vision of its role and mission. Mr. Newlands's vision didn't survive the resulting crash.

The Reclamation Service, you see, had a very clear idea of what it wanted to do. It wanted to see as much land as possible cultivated, and it wanted to see that result as quickly as possible. Beyond that, it wanted to keep the price of the food grown on this reclamation land as close as possible to the price of food grown in the rest of the country. In a sparsely populated region like the interior West of the early part of the twentieth century, small family farms didn't seem to be the way to accomplish any of these goals. As we moved into the agricultural depression of the 1920s and 1930s, the hope of cultivating lots of land in owner-worked plots consisting of no more than 160 acres for each family member living on the farm seemed dim indeed. Who had the money to buy such plots?

Believing firmly that their goals of cultivating as much land as possible as quickly as possible and keeping the resulting food prices competitive represented the most reasonable interpretation of their mandate, and believing just as firmly that those goals could never be accomplished within the strict letter of Representative Newlands's law, the Reclamation Service acted. First of all, the residency requirement that Newlands had hoped would guarantee family farms was phrased in a rather awkward way. Specifically, it required that those who purchased water from the Reclamation Service "live in the neighborhood" of the farm to be irrigated. So the service defined "in the neighborhood" as within a fifty-mile radius of the land to be worked. Nobody traveled fifty miles to work in the Colorado, Arizona, or even California of that era, so the service's definition of neighborhood effectively ended the residency requirement. It didn't take long for a variant of tenant farming to take hold. Beyond that, the service also ignored the acreage limitations, selling water to irrigate as much land as a farmer could cultivate.

Then in 1926, the Reclamation Act was amended, and those amendments gave the newly named Bureau of Reclamation a good deal of what it needed to complete the substitution of its vision of reclamation policy for that of Representative Newlands. Specifically, the 1926 law failed to restate the residency requirement in any form, and the bureau responded by dropping the fifty-mile radius requirement. Now the irrigated land needn't be owned by a local banker or merchant. It could be owned by a banker or merchant from anywhere in the country. Or, for that matter, it could be owned by a railroad. In addition, the 1926 amendments permitted the bureau to sign what were called recordable contracts with reclamation farmers. In those contracts, the bureau agreed to sell water to irrigate as much land as the farmer owned, and the farmer agreed to sell the excess land ten years later at the "dry land price," that is, the price without the irrigation rights. Contracts were signed covering millions of acres.

Finally, Representative Newlands's original Reclamation Act had included a requirement that the reclamation farmers pay the government back for the costs of the irrigation projects. But there was no specific provision to set up a payback system, and the Reclamation Service simply ignored the whole idea. In 1939, the Bureau of Reclamation convinced the Congress to adopt a payback system, one in which farmers got a ten-year "development period" before payments were due, forty years to pay back the costs, and an interest rate of 0 percent. Not only that, the bureau was authorized to charge up to 80 percent of the cost of each dam constructed to "other users." Mostly those other users were hydroelectric power customers, though boaters and other recreational users of the lakes created by the dams ended up paying some fraction of the costs as well.

Specialization, Policy Specialists, and the Bureaucratic Mandate: Tunnel Vision and the Law of Unintended Consequences

Just over a quarter-century ago, Hugh Heclo observed that "It is not difficult to imagine situations in which policies make excellent sense within the cloisters of expert issue watchers and yet are nonsense or worse seen from the viewpoint of ordinary people, the kinds of people [these experts] rarely meet."[31] Just a few years earlier, Frederick C. Mosher had concluded that the perspective of most specialists on the issues they confront can best be likened to that of "a submariner [looking] through a periscope whose direction and focus are fixed."[32] I guess I prefer the more pedestrian metaphor of tunnel vision, maybe because I talk about this in class a lot and wonder exactly how to pronounce submariner. In any event, if we revisit the FHA and its single-minded pursuit of the lowest possible default rate on the loans it guaranteed, and the Bureau of Reclamation and its dedication to cultivating as much land as possible as quickly as possible with the prices of the resulting food comparable to prices paid to farmers outside the seventeen so-called reclamation land states, with Heclo and Mosher in mind, we can begin to grasp the impact of specialization—of largely unchecked power in the hands of policy specialists—on our efforts to create a bureaucracy that is effective, responsive, respectful of the rights of individuals, and accountable. Let's proceed one agency at a time.

Of Energy Dependence and Redlining: The FHA and Suburbanization

The FHA's grounding in its real estate/banker culture made its subsequent commitment to a goal of the lowest possible default rate an almost automatic consequence. As Harold Seidman pointed out, most other government loan and insurance programs end up with exactly the same perspective, namely, the perspective of a banker—that is, someone who really wants to loan money, to someone absolutely guaranteed to pay it back with appropriate interest.[33] Franklin D. Roosevelt came to exactly the same conclusion when he was asked to support a proposal to consolidate all federal loan programs under the Treasury Department. "That won't work. If they put them in the Treasury, not one of them will ever make a loan to anybody for any purpose. *There are too many glass eyed bankers in the Treasury.*"[34] From the FHA perspective, then, the lowest possible default rate was the only reasonable standard by which to judge their performance, and judged by that standard that performance was a clear and unmistakable success. An incredible amount of housing had been built, middle-income Americans owned their own homes in numbers that no one could have anticipated before World War II, and all of it had been done with the help of policies clearly grounded in sound banking principles.

But what if we take the suggestions of Professors Heclo and Mosher? What if we move outside the cloister of experts? What if we unfreeze the periscope? It is, as you no doubt expected, a very different world.

The creation of suburbia certainly meant that a good many families who could not have owned their own homes in the cities they left behind could own their own homes in the suburbs they left those cities for. However, whatever they may have become as they matured, in their early years these suburbs were called bedroom communities, and they were called bedroom communities for a reason. Everybody went back to the cities to work or shop or do much of anything else besides sleep. That meant we had to get people back and forth from city to suburb, and since we very much wanted to do that primarily by private automobile—in many parts of the country no rail alternative even existed—we needed roads. But, as we soon began to see, roads meant congestion, pollution, more than a little ugliness, and eventually, a type and level of energy dependence that sent shock waves through the economy in the mid and late 1970s. The hole in the ozone layer we wouldn't discover for a while yet.

The FHA policy of putting its loan guarantee money behind new, single-family, owner-occupied housing had a second effect. It made the federal government a partner in the practice of racial discrimination in the American housing market, helping to perpetuate segregated residential patterns and to exacerbate the housing problems of middle- and lower-class blacks in nearly all of the nation's cities.

First of all, even those blacks able to afford the kind of housing that existed in the FHA-preferred suburbs faced tremendous social and psychological, not to mention legal, barriers to joining the outward movement. Twenty years after Jackie Robinson played his first game for the Brooklyn Dodgers, the Detroit Tigers' outstanding young power-hitting left-fielder Willie Horton couldn't use his 1968 World Series check as down payment on the house he wanted in a Detroit suburb. For some reason, the owners decided not to accept his offer. We appreciate the first World Championship since 1945, but it would be best if you lived somewhere else. Even for blacks with the money, it was stay in the cities. But that meant older housing stock to choose from, and there was no FHA money to back up loans for renovation and restoration. There was money to be borrowed, but at higher interest rates with bigger down-payment requirements.

Maybe more to the point for most blacks, there was no FHA money for rental housing. Consequently, those who would buy and fix rental property, whether white or black, had to pay the higher interest rates and come up with the higher down payments, so they had to charge higher rents. And this was only true, of course, if they could get the money for such renovations. Increasingly lenders put their money where it was safer—in every sense—that is, into the FHA-subsidized suburbs. The final blow came when we learned that in the 1960s, and to a much greater extent in the 1970s, the FHA had condoned—even occasionally participated in—the practice that has come to be known as redlining. Literally drawing red lines on city maps, mortgage bankers and insurance company executives—with the cooperation of FHA officials—made the decision not to lend money or insure properties within those lines, leaving large sections of America's cities to die.[35]

I am certainly not suggesting that there was an FHA staff meeting at which there was unanimous agreement on a motion to try to create a sprawling, ugly city, choking on its own exhaust, or one to condemn blacks to several generations of living in substandard housing in what remained of our big cities. I used the phrase unintended consequences in the title of this section precisely because the problems that unchecked specialist power create really are the products of decisions aimed at accomplishing other purposes. There were FHA staff meetings, and at those meetings the agency committed itself to the continued implementation of what that staff considered its incredibly successful policy of putting its—our—loan guarantee money behind newly constructed, owner-occupied, single-family housing. After all, as Harold Seidman pointed out, these policies make perfectly good sense "if a remarkably low default rate were the sole criterion of program effectiveness."[36] Frederick Mosher's point, of course, was that through the frozen periscope created by the banker/real estate subculture of the FHA it was.

But what about Hugh Heclo's observation that policies which "make excellent sense within the cloisters of expert issue watchers . . . are nonsense or worse seen from the viewpoint of ordinary people"?[37] I don't know for sure that a New York journalist and architecture critic and a government commission count as ordinary people, but they certainly count as non-experts from the FHA's point of view, and both did in fact find the agency's policies to be nonsense or worse.

In 1964, I paid $1.95 for a book called *The Death and Life of Great American Cities*, by Jane Jacobs. I read it for a class in Urban Planning. She gave the following assessment of the first quarter-century of FHA loan guarantee policies: "The cataclysmic use of money for suburban sprawl, and the concomitant starvation of all those parts of cities that planning orthodoxy stamped as slums, was what our wise men wanted for us; they put in a lot of effort, one way and another, to get it. We got it."[38] When Ms. Jacobs asked a New York City official why he wasn't backing a proposal to preserve a neighborhood of mixed uses, he cited good planning principles, but then just looked at her and said, "The question is academic anyhow. We couldn't get FHA approval on loans with mixed uses like that."[39]

Four years later came the National Commission on Urban Problems (the Douglas Commission) which concluded that "the main weakness of the FHA from a social point of view has not been what it has done but what it has failed to do—in its relative neglect of the inner cities and of the poor, and especially Negro poor."[40]

Once again, the point is not that the FHA was peopled by covert racists out to perpetuate housing discrimination, or by men and women secretly advancing the agenda of the oil companies, automobile manufacturers, and road builders. The FHA was peopled by bankers and real estate executives and folks who had never worked in either of those industries but who soon absorbed the agency culture and set to work to accomplish the mission of achieving the lowest possible default rate on the loans it guaranteed. They succeeded. They didn't see what else happened, because they didn't look. Their frozen periscopes wouldn't let them.

The Desert Bloomed, but at What Cost?

Just as the FHA fixed on its target and sailed right for it, so did the Bureau of Reclamation and its predecessor, the Reclamation Service. If your goals are lots of land cultivated quickly and keeping the prices of the food grown on that land competitive with the prices of food grown elsewhere, every decision the bureau made over the first seventy-five years of its existence makes perfectly good sense.

By the time the first reclamation law was passed, there were already some large farming operations in existence, and more than a few were absentee operations. There seemed no compelling reason to force these people out of business or reduce the value of their land, and ignoring residency requirements and acreage limitations was not only a way to leave well enough alone, but it had the added effect of bringing lots of land into cultivation quickly. Once the projects were completed—the dams built, the canals, ditches, and pumps in place—it seemed a little silly to bureau personnel to let land lie idle while they waited for someone to come along to buy 160 acres of it and get going. This became a particularly acute problem in the 1920s and 1930s, when so few people could pay even the dry land price for what was available. If wealthy easterners, the Southern Pacific Railroad, or a local farmer who already owned a thousand acres had the money to put another thousand or two into cultivation, why quibble? Wasn't it better to see the water used and the land produce than to stick to the letter of the law—a law they felt was badly thought out anyway—and waste the resources of "their" land?

Recall from earlier in the chapter the 1926 amendment to the reclamation statute that empowered the bureau to enter into recordable contracts with farmers under which the farmer would irrigate all the land he owned if he agreed to sell the "excess" land after ten years. As I noted then, the Reclamation Bureau signed contracts covering millions of acres, but not one of these contracts was ever enforced. Once again, it just didn't seem to make much sense to the bureau's leadership. A farmer cannot sell excess land when there are no buyers, and to deny the water at that point would be to pull land out of production. If the number one goal is land in production, a policy that would pull it out just couldn't make any sense.

Finally, the decision to lay as much of the cost of each dam on hydroelectric customers and recreational users was just a way to meet another of the bureau's key goals. Reclamation land farmers have to recover the costs of their water, so the more of a reclamation project's cost that can be passed on to somebody else, the lower the price of the food produced on reclamation land. Besides, the bureau reasoning went, hydroelectric customers do benefit, it is only a few extra pennies per kilowatt hour, and even with these costs added, it was difficult to find cheaper electricity anywhere in the country.

But if you unfreeze your periscope, or better yet, come to the surface, the bureau's policies begin to take on a very different character. Viewed from virtually any perspective but the bureau's, these policies would certainly seem to deserve Heclo's description of "nonsense or worse." Once more, I'm not sure if David Brower, the man who guided the Sierra Club through its formative years, or Gaylord Nelson (D-WI), founder of Earth Day and a man who spent so long in the environmental movement that he was once known as a conservationist, or George Miller (D-CA) who once chaired the House Interior Committee, qualify as ordinary people, but I am sure they would be seen by the Bureau of Reclamation as outsiders who just didn't get it. And once more, and more to the point, all three of these men did see the Bureau of Reclamation policies as "nonsense or worse."

As is so often the case, it is best to start by trying to follow the money. When California Democrat George Miller did that back in 1979, he characterized reclamation policies as "the biggest Western stage coach robbery of the public since Jesse James."[41] Though Representative Miller may not be much of a historian of nineteenth-century outlaws—Jesse generally stuck to trains and banks and never got much farther west than he was that day in Northfield, Minnesota—Miller was discouragingly accurate in his assessment of the bureau's policies. By the way, Miller never forgot what he learned back in his 1979 look at the Bureau of Reclamation. In 1992, in his second year as chair of what was then the House Interior Committee (now Resources Committee), he managed to engineer a significant change in water policy, at least as it applied in his home state of California.[42] But most of the bureau's policies survived George Miller's assault, so let's get back to the money.

The first thing you'll notice about the money is the amount. California's Westlands District is one of the largest and richest—both agriculturally and economically—in the reclamation farming system, and subsidies for farms in that region generally run in the neighborhood of $1,540 per acre. That's for farms with an average size of more than 2,000 acres. The subsidy comes in the form of cheap and abundant water, of course, water that costs the bureau around $21 an acre foot to deliver, but costs the farmer only $7 per acre foot to purchase. For projects built in the high-interest days of the 1970s and 1980s, the interest-free status of the required project payback can be worth more than an additional $500 an acre.

The second thing you are bound to notice about the money is the direction. It flows up the income scale, not down. The average federal taxpayer has less income than the average reclamation land farmer, particularly when you remember how much of the federal budget is being funded by the payroll tax through "IOU's" from the Treasury to the Social Security Trust Funds. This upward flow is the case even if you accept the argument that the largest of these average farmers—Southern Pacific Land Co., Southern Pacific Transportation Co., Tenneco Oil Co., etc.— make sure that every dime of that subsidy finds its way back to their shareholders, and that their shareholders really are the pensioners and small investors they used to feature in their many ads. Even the true family operations tend to generate incomes above those of most taxpayers. A farm as small as 320 acres, if located in the Westlands District, should produce a profit of close to $50,000, and a 640-acre farm in Oregon's magnificent Columbia River Basin would bring in just under $200,000 in net income in a typical year.

If you take your eyes off the money and put them on the land, it's an equally discouraging sight.[43] In California's San Joaquin Valley, years of irrigation on land that has an almost impenetrable layer of clay not far below the surface has made some acreage unusable, scarred by a residue of salt and chemicals that looks for all the world like a light dusting of snow. By the time it reaches Mexico, the Colorado River has been tapped so often that its flow is more like a trickle, and the condition of the water is so bad that one of Mexico's most important agricultural regions suffered tremendous economic loss. And the American government agrees to do something about it only in situations like the energy crisis of 1973, when OPEC member Mexico began to threaten retaliation in the form of a cutoff of natural gas supplies. The long-term problem is anything but solved. Even far away from the Colorado, the waste of water is staggering, as evidenced by rice fields not more than ten miles from my hometown of Lodi, California, a town that, in an average year, receives not much more than an inch of rain between the first of May and the first of October. At $7 an acre foot, the Feather River and the American River are enough of a bargain to make it profitable to grow rice even where it doesn't rain.

Finally, if you turn your eyes to the Midwest and the Southeast, to those places where people farm without the help of the Bureau of Reclamation, you'll see farmers who have to compete with these large subsidized agricultural operations with far fewer subsidies of their own. This is not to say no subsidies, of course, especially after the more than $70 billion farm bill of the summer of 2002, but it is to say far fewer. A lot of potatoes are grown here in central Wisconsin. A lot of potatoes are grown in Idaho. Both sets of potatoes are grown on land that has to be irrigated. Here in Wisconsin, the farmer pays the full cost of the irrigation projects. In Idaho, he or she does not. Much of what is grown on reclamation land—especially reclamation land in California—can't be grown in the rest of the country, at least not year round. But, back in 1979, when Congress was engaged in a full-scale war over reclamation policy, Wisconsin's Democratic Senator and well-known environmentalist Gaylord Nelson found that 45 percent of the land receiving subsidized water from the Bureau of Reclamation was being used to grow corn, cotton, and grain, crops grown by farmers in other parts of the country without the subsidies. In that same debate, Senator Nelson cited General Accounting Office estimates that subsidies for a 640-acre reclamation land farm would range anywhere from $20,000 to $100,000 per year, while the same sized farm elsewhere would probably average about $500 per year. All that has changed in the intervening twenty years are the numbers. They're bigger.

An inverse redistribution of income, very likely irreversible environmental damage, and a rather striking departure from the premise of equal treatment for citizens in more or less the same circumstances seems like quite an indictment of a set of policies and the organization that played the lead role in designing and implementing them. But it is an indictment that only an outsider could see. The insiders saw, instead, a set of policies that met their professional goals and, as time went on, came to meet with almost unanimous approval within the narrow confines of the political system that had grown up around the policies and the agency that designed them. Once more, as with the FHA and its impact on the fate of our large cities and the goal of racial justice, there was no Bureau of Reclamation meeting at which it was decided to make the rich richer, ruin the rivers and destroy the land, anger Mexico, and stick it to midwestern farmers in the process. Rather, there was meeting after meeting at which the bureau staff congratulated itself on the success of its policies. The desert had been made to bloom, and they were the ones who had done it, just exactly as they had set out to do all those years ago.

In Summary

Turn them loose, and the specialists will take their expert knowledge, adopt specific agency and program goals, and pursue policies that will move toward those goals. To be sure, these policies have to pass political muster. But they have to pass political muster within a very narrowly defined political universe, and in any case, that universe is a story for subsequent chapters. Our focus now is on expert knowledge and specifically and narrowly defined agency goals, and if you'll permit one more return to Frederick Mosher's submarine imagery, the course charted by these experts will be pretty much dead straight ahead. To knock them off that course, you will have to fix some other image in their periscope. No easy task, to be sure.

What they cannot see, however, others can. As we noted earlier, Jane Jacobs could see the impact of FHA policies on the shape of the city, just as the Douglas Commission could see the impact of those policies on the fate of urban blacks as they sought decent and affordable housing in those cities. Likewise, California Representative George Miller saw the environmental and economic impact of Bureau of Reclamation policies in 1992, just as Wisconsin Senator Gaylord Nelson—and Representative Miller, for that matter—saw them in 1979. And David Brower, the first paid Executive Director of the Sierra Club, saw them as far back as the 1950s and fought them continuously during the decade he held that job and long after.[44] Brower lost most of those fights, though he and the Sierra Club did manage to prevent the building of dams in the Grand Canyon. What they never were able to do—for that matter, what Gaylord Nelson and George Miller were never really able to do—was change bureau policies and the thinking that lay behind them.[45] That had to await President Bill Clinton's decision to appoint Dan Beard, a former aide to Representative George Miller, to head the bureau, and even then, the change was slight and definitely reversible.[46]

One final time, policy specialists don't pursue policies that many of the rest of us find "nonsense or worse" because they are evil. They pursue those policies because they believe in them. They believe in them because their perspective on the problems these policies are designed to solve is so very narrow.

THE PAPER STRUCTURE

Now it is time to turn our attention to the paper structure of bureaucracy, that is, to the actual organizations that the constitutional government creates to carry out its various promises. As we said at the beginning of the chapter, the paper structure is built by answering three basic questions.

First, which unit of the government will be responsible for the conduct of which activities? Once we decide that miners disabled by pneumoconiosis—black lung disease—are entitled to benefits provided by the federal government, some unit of that government has to be assigned the task of letting miners know the benefits are now available and how to apply for them, has to determine which miners really are disabled by the disease, and has to get them their money.

Second, and obviously intimately connected to the first question, comes the question of the relationship among governmental units. Specifically, will a particular unit be set out on its own, or will it be part of a larger conglomerate? Should we make the unit that will handle benefits to miners disabled by black lung an independent commission answerable directly to the President and Congress à la the Securities and Exchange Commission, the Interstate Commerce Commission, or the Federal Trade Commission? Or should we make it a constituent unit in one of the departments of the government as we did with the Occupational Safety and Health Administration, the Bureau of Land Management, or the Forest Service? If we go with the latter answer, of course, we have to ask ourselves which department.

Finally comes the question of who will have final authority over decisions made about a particular government function. Who will have the ultimate say as the chosen governmental unit tries to take the constitutional government's general direction to compensate disabled miners and make it happen by establishing specific criteria for disability, setting up the educational programs to let miners know they might be eligible, monitoring the system for fraud, and making sure that checks are actually written and delivered? The answer will depend, of course, on the answer to the second question above. If we decide to have an independent commission handle compensating black lung victims, then the commission will decide. But if we decide on the other alternative and put the unit within an existing department, we still have to decide if authority over these—and other—questions should reside with someone called a program administrator, an agency head, an assistant secretary, or the secretary himself or herself.

By the way, in case you are interested, we do in fact have a program for compensating black lung victims while they are alive and their families when they die. We assigned responsibility for that program to a unit called the Office of Workers' Compensation Programs, and that office is a piece of the Department of Labor. Final authority over the program rests with the individual who carries the title Deputy Assistant Secretary for Workers' Compensation Programs, though he or she gets lots of help from the Deputy Director for same, and almost certainly has to consult with the Labor Department's Associate Solicitor for Black Lung Benefits.[47]

As we noted a moment ago, the questions concerning which unit will be responsible for a particular set of functions and how that unit will relate to "the rest of the government" are intimately connected. In fact, it is pretty much impossible to answer one and not answer the other, particularly when, as is so often the case, the answer to the first question is to assign a set of functions to an existing governmental unit. Its relationship to the rest of the government is already established. Consequently, it makes sense for us to lump those two questions together and simply ask where a particular set of functions should be placed. Then we can consider the question of who—which position—gets final authority over that unit's decisions.

The Impact of Program Location Decisions: It's a Matter of Attitude

Back in 1963, on the occasion of its fiftieth anniversary, the Department of Labor published its first official history. Delightfully titled *The Anvil and the Plow*, this history opened with the following observation: "In fifty years an institution, just as a person, takes on a character and develops attitudes which distinguish it from all others. The Department of Labor is no exception."[48] The fact that each institution is unique, of course, is why it makes so very much difference which of those institutions is assigned a particular set of tasks. No two institutions would approach those tasks in exactly the same way. To be sure, no two institutions would approach any set of tasks in completely different ways. Performing any set of tasks requires assigning those tasks to policy specialists, and those specialists will leave the mark of their expertise on the performance of those tasks, regardless of their institutional home. Still, the homogenizing influence of the power of specialization notwithstanding, any institution will leave its unique mark on decisions made by people working there.

The Labor Department's assertion that every institution "develops attitudes which distinguish it from all others" has been confirmed by countless scholars and practitioners alike. Harold Seidman, a man who spent time in both roles, titled a chapter in his highly respected *Politics, Position, and Power* "The Executive Establishment: Culture and Personality," and that chapter, complete with that title, lasted through all four editions of the book.[49] He was joined by Steven Kelman, who wrote about the distinctive culture of the Occupational Safety and Health Administration; Suzanne Weaver, who examined the attitudes and policies of the Anti-trust Division of the Department of Justice; and Morton Halperin, who tried to guide us through the complex culture of the Department of State.[50]

Since an institution's attitudes distinguish it from "all" other institutions, cataloging those attitudes, understanding their origins and impacts, and then comparing one institution to even a handful of others would be an almost impossible task. Fortunately, it is a task we need not attempt. For our purposes, we simply need to identify the three major sources of these distinctive institutional attitudes and then take a look at a couple of examples in which we can compare two government units that might have been home to a particular function to see if we can find any impact of the ultimate choice of organizational home on the conduct of that function.

Strictly speaking, of course, institutions don't have attitudes. People have attitudes. But when a bunch of people are gathered together into something called an institution, and when those people exhibit very similar attitudes toward their common enterprise, it doesn't seem such a stretch to refer to institutional rather than individual attitudes. In fact, it just may be that for a very high percentage of the men and women working in an institution, there wouldn't really be much point in trying to distinguish between individual and institutional attitudes. They would be one and the same.

In any case, as I noted above, I think there are three major sources for these institutional attitudes. First, there is what might be called a professional source. Much of what is done in any institution is done by its policy specialists, and they will bring to their jobs, and therefore to the institution, a set of attitudes about what ought to be done and why. Second, the distinctive attitude of any institution that is part of the government will be shaped by politics, specifically by the politics of the particular programs/functions assigned to that institution. Finally, an institution's attitudes will be in part a product of the personal—as distinct from, even if distinctly related to, the professional—attitudes of the men and women who work there. When I refer to personal attitudes in this context, I am referring to attitudes directly connected to the issues a particular institution has been told to address. If that's not clear yet, it soon will be. We need to flesh each of these sources out some, so let's start on the professional side of institutional attitudes.

Professionals Believe

Enough ink has been spilled in this chapter and the previous one about the belief policy specialists have in their knowledge and in the contribution that knowledge can—and should—make to the making of policy decisions. Nowhere does that belief stand in starker relief than in the Occupational Safety and Health Administration (OSHA), and nowhere are the professional/specialist origins of that belief better expressed than in this conclusion from Steven Kelman:

> The evidence suggests that the most important factor explaining OSHA decisions on the content of regulations has been the pro-protection values of agency officials, derived from the ideology of the safety and health professional and the organizational mission of OSHA.
>
> Most OSHA officials either come from the occupational safety and health professions (safety engineering or industrial hygiene) or take courses in these fields after going to work for the agencies. Members of these professions share a body of knowledge. Like members of many professions, they also tend to share certain values or orientations which comprise a professional ideology. For occupational safety and health professionals, these are pro-protection values. They tend to believe that workers ought to be protected from hazards to life and limb and that larger reductions of risk are preferable to smaller reductions (without much consideration of cost).[51]

Kelman goes on to note that the professional ideology of the safety community of which OSHA's safety specialists are a part takes on a kind of moral tone when it tells that safety community that "needless destruction of life and health is a moral evil," or that "failure to take necessary precautions against predictable accidents involves moral responsibility for those accidents."[52] Kelman further observes that these safety professionals take that moral exhortation to heart, as exhibited in their choice of language to describe such accidents. As he puts it, "I have frequently been struck by hearing safety professionals utter expressions such as 'We killed ten workers when that scaffold collapsed' rather than saying, impersonally, 'Ten workers were killed.' "[53]

The choice between redesigning work processes or replacing equipment, on the one hand, and relying on personal protective equipment—ear muffs, respirators, and the like—on the other, is one of the most important decisions OSHA has to make, both in terms of safety itself and in terms of the economics of safety. The distinctive attitudes of OSHA are quite clearly on display, according to Kelman, every time that choice must be made. Recognizing that "Nearly every textbook on safety engineering or industrial hygiene is replete with warnings against reliance on personal protective equipment," Kelman concludes that within OSHA's institutional culture "personal protective equipment is visualized as a paste-over, a Band-Aid—indeed a sort of industrial Potemkin village, a pleasing façade masking actual failure. As much as it may be unpleasant to the workers, personal protective equipment is insulting to the engineer."[54]

OSHA may be the best example of the impact of professional values on an institution's distinctive attitudes, but it is a far cry from the only one. Robert Katzmann shows us the lawyer attitudes of the Federal Trade Commission's Bureau of Competition, as well as the economist attitudes of the FTC's Bureau of Economics, and then shows how those attitudes clashed time after time as the commissioners themselves had to make the final decision on a variety of anti-trust questions.[55] Suzanne Weaver, too, looked at lawyer attitudes toward anti-trust policy in an institution—the Anti-trust Division of the Department of

Justice—in which those attitudes have no opposition. Her finding: "The Antitrust Division described so far is an organization slowly but inexorably extending the reach of the antitrust laws through an ongoing series of *opportunistically chosen prosecutions*" (italics mine).[56] Finally, I have watched the seeds of some of these distinctive attitudes being sown here on my own campus as I have taught public administration to future wildlife managers, foresters, soil conservation specialists, and even the occasional biologist or chemist planning for a career in his or her own specialty's role in the field of resource policy.

Politics Counts

Now let's turn to the role of politics in shaping these distinctive institutional attitudes. Politics enters in three distinct but decidedly interrelated ways, namely, through the groups of citizens with access to the institution, through the members and staffs of the committees and subcommittees of Congress with jurisdiction over that institution, and finally, through the corps of political executives sent to provide central guidance to the institution and its policy specialists. Each of these will be discussed in far greater detail in subsequent chapters, but we need to take at least a quick look at them now, in order to understand the impact of a decision by the constitutional government to place responsibility for a program or function in one organization rather than another.

Every unit of the government has a set of people directly affected by the policies it makes, and those people are going to try to organize and present their views on those policies to that unit's leaders. As we will see in chapter 7, some of these groups are what political scientists have long called interest groups or clientele groups, while others are professional associations—groups of people with some sort of shared professional interests in this particular unit and its policies—and still others might well deserve the name critics. The point remains the same. Every agency of government has a constellation of groups interested in what it is up to and hoping to influence its decisions, and it is extremely unlikely that any two agencies would face the same—or even a very similar—constellation. In choosing between two agencies as home for a particular program or function, then, the constitutional government is also choosing which of two constellations of groups will have some impact on how that program is run or that function carried out.

The committees and subcommittees of Congress have long been recognized as the primary focal points of congressional activity, particularly congressional activity concerning bureaucracy. Subcommittees have considerable power over agency budgets, conduct the oversight of agency activities, and play the central role in writing the legislation those agencies must administer. Indeed, except in the rare case like the creation of the Department of Homeland Security in the fall of 2002, committees and subcommittees play the lead role in deciding the very question we are talking about, where we are going to put a particular program or function. A good deal more will be said about this in chapter 6, but the members of these committees are quick to use their power over agencies to move policy in the direction those members want to see it go, and agencies are generally responsive to such committee prodding. Again, we'll say more about why in chapter 6. Finally, it is important to note the connections—information connections, campaign finance connections, and voting connections—between the members of these committees and the groups talked about in the previous paragraph. Just as it was choosing between different constellations of groups when choosing one agency home over another for a particular program or function, the constitutional government is choosing between two different sets of committees when it does so. Given the different constituency and interest-group connections we find in different committees and subcommittees of the Congress, the choice of one set of committees and subcommittees over another is always going to leave its mark on program administration.

Last among the political forces that shape a government unit's distinctive attitudes we find the political executives sent to represent the constitutional government and its interest in exercising control over the promise keeping process. Though these men and women are, in some sense anyway, a presidential team, as we will see in chapter 5, there are a great many constraints on the President's selections for that team. Chief among them in this context would be the unspoken rule that the President must make sure that the men and women sent to lead a particular unit will "fit in" with the culture of that unit. If you will permit me to borrow once more from Harold Seidman, "As one descends the hierarchical scale, the distinctive departmental colorations come into focus even more sharply. Under Secretaries and Assistant Secretaries are less likely than Secretaries to be generalists or people with broad political background. Subcabinet appointments tend to mirror the diverse clientele groups, dependencies such as defense contractors, construction companies, educational institutions, and professional organizations which constitute an agency's constituency."[57] The reasons for this appointment pattern will be explored in depth in chapter 5, but its importance should be clear enough by now. The people chosen to fill the role of political executive in a particular unit will almost certainly be familiar with and sympathetic to the distinctive attitudes of that unit. So, once again, a choice between two agencies is a choice between two sets of political executives, and those two sets of political executives are likely to be very different in attitude, outlook, and approach when it comes to looking at a particular program or function assigned to the agency they have been sent to lead.

I'm sure you have seen the interconnections here, but just to put them right on the surface, each agency has its own little political world—a world of groups, committees and subcommittees, and political executives—each connected to the other and each reflecting similar, though clearly not identical, attitudes toward the issues they are dealing with. In the words of Hugh Heclo, "Whether in Congress or the executive branch or somewhere outside, the 'movers and shakers' in energy policy (as in health insurance, welfare reform, strategic arms limitation, occupational safety, and a host of other policy areas) tend to share an analytic repertoire for coping with the issues. Like experienced party politicians of earlier times, policy politicians in the knowledge networks may not agree; but they understand each other's way of looking at the world and arguing about policy choices."[58] The choice of one agency over another is really the choice of one entire political or policy system over another, and it is a choice that matters.

They Are People Too

Now it's time to add in the personal dimension that guides the shaping of an agency or department's distinctive attitudes. It is hard to imagine the person who sought a career in government for the exciting lure of the life of the civil servant. People are drawn to government service by issues, programs, and problems— issues, programs, and problems that touch some sort of personal nerve. Quite frequently, of course, that turns out to mean that people with similar personal nerves to be touched end up in the same agencies and departments. The Agriculture Department is drawn mostly from people with farm, or at least small-town, backgrounds, while the Interior Department is predominantly western in its origins. Westerners tend to distrust easterners, especially those with any connection to banks or railroads, and to take a view of resources as something to be used, not to be "locked up." Over the years, both of these feelings have left their marks on a variety of Interior Department land management policies. In a similar vein, small-town and rural people tend to distrust big-city folks and to take seriously the notion of agriculture as a "way of life," not a sector of the economy. Their ideas, too, rub off on the policies they pursue. As Harold Seidman pointed out, other departments, too, have recruitment patterns that produce a certain amount of homogeneity within those departments, though Interior and Agriculture are the most clearly linked to a particular regional and social recruitment base.[59] Common background and shared values may even be born of tragedy, as Steven Kelman found when he learned of the substantial number of OSHA safety professionals who had lost a relative in an industrial accident.[60] It is hard to imagine how a shared event of such magnitude could fail to become a force in shaping the attitudes of a set of people toward the jobs they had chosen.

There can be no doubt that the 2002 decision to create the Department of Homeland Security will prove fertile ground for public administration scholars interested in the impact of organizational home on program administration. Never before have so many specialized organizations been told to pack up and move to a new organizational home. But it is far too early to tell what, if any, impact the move will have on the performance of these various units because the department itself is brand new and doesn't have any distinctive attitudes to which the newly moved agencies, bureaus, and offices will have to adapt. So we'll have to look back a bit for examples of how decisions by the constitutional government to put programs and government functions in one organizational location rather than another left their mark on the administration of those programs or the performance of those functions. To do that, let's talk about mining—mining on the surface and mining deep below.

In the wake of the energy crisis of 1973, the United States decided it needed to rely more on its own energy sources, in particular coal. But we didn't want to rely too heavily on the high-sulfur coal from the deep-shaft mines of the Appalachian region, so we began to consider more strip mining in the western part of the country. The fledgling environmental movement was determined that these strip miners not be turned loose without regulation from the federal government, and in the end, they prevailed. But who would do the regulating? It would be done, of course, by people with some expertise in that kind of mining, but where would they do it? That is, where would they and their programmatic responsibilities be lodged?

It was pretty much agreed right away that a new agency would have to be created. No existing agency had the needed experts or a mission close enough to this one to be ready for the job. Besides, a new agency almost always means more recognition and status for a new activity. But there were two possible homes for this new agency, and they couldn't have been much more different.

First, of course, was the Environmental Protection Agency (EPA). The purpose of regulation, after all, was environmental. We wanted to make sure that all this new strip mining did not destroy the western landscape and make the land unusable for anything else. Created in 1970, EPA was new, but there was no doubt that its central job was enforcing environmental legislation—the Clean Air and Water Acts primarily—and that its early staff and leadership, including Russell Train, the highly respected former president of the Conservation Foundation who had moved over from the Interior Department, were committed to the goal of environmental protection. EPA was overseen by congressional committees with ties to the increasingly active environmental organizations, and those groups were busy gaining access to the agency itself. In short, while one would hardly compare this political system growing up around the Environmental Protection Agency with the long established systems surrounding the Forest Service, the Bureau of Reclamation, or the Bureau of Land Management, that political system was establishing itself and it definitely exhibited its own distinctive attitudes already.

In stark contrast to the EPA was the Department of Interior. Its claims were two. First, it was the home of the federal government's lead agency on mining matters, the Bureau of Mines. Second, this strip mining was going to take place in the West, and the Interior Department's relationship to the West was known to everyone in Congress as well as to the President. The department had an obvious presence in every western state, and through its Bureau of Land Management was the West's most prominent landlord, managing much of the land that would be strip mined. Of course, as noted before, the Interior Department isn't just in the West, it is of the West, and its attitudes are distinctly western. Use the resources. Develop the land. Western land user groups have had access to the department's decision makers for decades, the committees and subcommittees with jurisdiction over the department are almost the exclusive province of western legislators, and the men and women selected for positions as political executives in the department are almost to an individual products of that western culture and cleared by the western land user groups that have power in the department and in the committees that oversee it. The political system that had grown up around the Interior Department—its agencies mostly, but they could come together as a system around the department if need be—was powerful and very much interested in becoming the political system that would control strip-mine regulation in "their" home region.

Interior won, and the results of that victory were pretty predictable. In that crucial first decade, rules were slow in coming and enforcement was slower yet. Resources—coal, not too far below the surface—were used, the economy was developed, jobs were created, and in the eyes of the Department and its political system anyway, the damage was minimal. Would EPA have done it differently? Yes. How much differently? No one really knows.[61]

Not all of our coal, of course, is on the surface, easily scooped up by giant shovels that look for all the world like the dinosaurs that we presume roamed that region an age or two ago. Some of it is down deep and can only be brought to the surface by a combination of human and machine, with a heavy emphasis on the human. Men—and in the last couple of decades, women—have to go deep beneath the surface and "dig" the coal and transport it up top. It is a dangerous business. The air is terrible, black lung seems to be the long-term fate of almost everyone, and for most of the history of American coal mining, there wasn't a miner alive who didn't know someone who had died deep under the earth. In fact, though I cannot for the life of me find the book in which I read it, between 1865 and 1965, one hundred men per month went down into an American coal mine and did not come up alive. That's a statistic you just never forget.

We passed coal-mine safety laws in the early part of the twentieth century and strengthened them a couple of times later on. Responsibility for the enforcement of those laws was assigned to the Interior Department's Bureau of Mines, which created a subunit called the Office of Safety Inspection to take on the task. It did. But the unit was weak—it's statutory authority included the right to post notices at mine entrances about safety problems—and it was anything but aggressive in exercising its enforcement responsibilities. Then, during Thanksgiving week in 1968, an explosion and fire at Consolidated No. 9 in Farmington, West Virginia, convinced the Congress that something had to be done. A tough new safety law was passed, but enforcement stayed with the Office of Safety Inspection at the Bureau of Mines.

Then, in 1977, Congress decided the time had come to create a new mine safety enforcement agency, and the Mine Safety and Health Administration was born. Office of Safety Inspection (OSI) personnel were inevitably to be a key part of the new agency, but Congress was convinced of the need for more vigorous enforcement, and that meant a move from the Interior Department to the Department of Labor. All of a sudden—well, as all of a sudden as anything gets in American government—mine safety enforcement was taking place not in a department whose primary concern was resource development and use but in one whose primary concern was with workers. The Labor Department can hardly be considered exclusively a worker-oriented organization, but compared to Interior it was dedicated to the health and safety of the American workforce. With the Mine Safety and Health Administration (MSHA) modeled after OSHA and operating in the same home department, there was bound to be a change, and there was. To be fair, not long after arriving at their new home, many of the Office of Safety Inspection veterans became aggressive advocates of mine safety, using the tools that Congress had placed at the new agency's disposal. Chief among these new tools was the power to conduct warrantless inspections, a power upheld by the Supreme Court and exercised by the agency often enough to convince mine owners that they had better get used to the idea of inspections at any time. The shift of responsibility from OSI to MSHA brought results, this time results that could be measured in lives saved and injuries prevented.[62]

Who Has Final Authority?

Now we need to consider the question of where to place the final authority over a particular program and the day-to-day decisions needed to implement that program. It is a question that can be every bit as important as the question of the organizational home of the program itself, but the impact on the decisions made in the program of the answer to the question of where to put final authority over those decisions can be far harder to predict, or even to analyze after the fact. Three reasons.

First, as we noted earlier in the chapter, scholars, administrators, and politicians have all long been acquainted with the distinctive attitudes/cultures of the various agencies and departments of the government. So when the constitutional government decided that regulation of strip mining ought to be done by a new agency called the Office of Surface Mining and Reclamation and Enforcement, and further, that that new agency ought to be located in the Interior Department and not at the Environmental Protection Agency, everyone involved knew that a choice was being made to lighten the regulatory hand that would be guiding the industry. The attitude/culture of any particular agency or department is pretty well entrenched and will leave its mark on everyone there, from the policy specialists to the political executives. To be sure, not everyone at any agency or department will approach every question in exactly the same way. Not even all Annapolis graduates are equally steeped in "the Navy way." Still there will be a lot more similarity of outlook and viewpoint within any agency or department than between any two agencies or departments, so it is bound to be harder to be certain what impact, or how much impact, the decision to assign final authority to an assistant secretary rather than to a bureau chief will ultimately have than to decide what difference it will make to assign a new program to one department or the other.

Second, we very often find substantial differences between the attitudes and actions of people who end up occupying the very same offices. We see it at the cabinet level in particular, of course, and we expect it. We elect a new President, but we get a new administration. Even within the departmental expectations we discussed earlier, there remains considerable leeway. Ronald Reagan's two Secretaries of Interior were both westerners, as were those of his predecessor, Jimmy Carter, and his successor once removed, Bill Clinton. But other than regional origin, it is pretty difficult to find much in common between Cecil Andrus and Bruce Babbitt—appointed by Carter and Clinton, respectively—and James Watt and Manuel Lujan—appointed by Reagan. Such differences may be lessened as we move down toward the subcabinet and the bureaus themselves, but they definitely do not disappear. Jimmy Carter's choice to head the Occupational Safety and Health Administration was Eula Bingham, a highly respected occupational safety and health expert from the academic community. She pushed aggressively for greater worker safety. When President Reagan came to office, Bingham was succeeded by Thorne Auchter, a former construction company executive whose company had been cited for numerous safety violations by the agency he was now to head. One of Mr. Auchter's first actions was to order OSHA to conduct cost benefit studies on all new regulations, even those involving the possibility of workplace-induced cancer. The staff was startled, since the agency had just been sued over its decision under Bingham not to conduct such analyses when cancer was involved—on the grounds that the law did not require such analyses—and had won the suit in the U.S. Supreme Court.[63] As anyone familiar with cost benefit analysis knows, it slows down the process of regulation and quite often works to the benefit of the regulated industry.

Third, even though political executives are frequently reluctant to delegate authority, they do it, and when they do, of course, then it is exercised not by the person occupying the position to which the constitutional government assigned it but to the person occupying the position to which that authority was delegated. In simpler terms, we can't be sure of the impact of assigning authority over a set of decisions to the Assistant Secretary of Interior for Land and Minerals Management rather than to the Director of the Bureau of Land Management (BLM) if the Assistant Secretary is going to have that authority exercised by the Director anyway. We can be even less sure of the impact if we find out that the Director prefers to have said authority exercised by the heads of the various BLM field offices. Recall how we described hierarchy in the early part of this chapter. In theory, final authority is the right to make a decision, but as a practical matter it is often exercised as the right to review and reverse a decision made below.

So it is reasonable to say that the differences in viewpoint between different levels within the same organization will be muted somewhat by the distinctive attitudes/culture that help to define that organization. Likewise, it is reasonable to say that two individuals, chosen at different times to occupy the same organizational position, might well approach their duties and use their authority in very different ways to pursue very different ends. Finally, it is also reasonable to say that in any given organizational setting, authority may well be exercised at a level different from the one it was assigned to by the constitutional government.

And there is one more thing it is reasonable to say. Within the parameters established by the power of organizational attitudes/cultures, and taking account of the differences in outlook that can accompany a change in the occupant of a particular office and the necessity of delegating authority down the organizational ladder, the men and women who occupy the position of Cabinet Secretary are going to approach the questions they must face differently from those who occupy the position of Deputy Secretary or Under Secretary. Those who occupy the position of Deputy Secretary or Under Secretary, in turn, are going to approach those questions differently from those who occupy the position of Assistant Secretary, who are going to approach them differently from those who occupy the position of Bureau Chief, who are almost certainly going to approach them differently from those who occupy the top civil service positions in a particular agency. The difference will be found mostly in things we will talk about in the rest of the book. To preview that, all policy decisions are based on knowledge and politics. What changes is the relative proportion between the two and the type of politics that prevails. As you move up the organizational ladder, the mix becomes more political, and the politics taken into account tends to change from the traditional agency/department politics as interpreted by policy specialists and the lowest level of political executives to politics as interpreted by the President and his supporters.

Despite all this complexity and uncertainty, there can be little doubt that decisions about who will exercise formal authority matter, and no doubt at all that those involved in making public policy—and especially those involved in trying to influence them—are well aware of that impact. Consider the Army Corps of Engineers, the Environmental Protection Agency, the National Association of Homebuilders, the Natural Resources Defense Council, and the issue of wetlands development/protection.

Authority over wetlands development is shared by the Corps and EPA. It has been long conceded that the Corps' jurisdiction over rivers that flow from state to state and their tributaries included jurisdiction over the wetlands associated with those tributaries, even if those wetlands were wholly within the boundaries of a single state. But wetlands do exist that are not really connected to the tributaries of our great rivers, and the Corps finally decided that they, too, needed protection, so it developed what is called the "migratory bird rule." Under that rule, the Corps— and EPA, which followed along—asserted their authority over any wetlands that were used by migratory birds on the theory that such birds were an important ingredient in interstate commerce.

In January 2001, the U.S. Supreme Court invalidated the migratory bird rule in the case of *Solid Waste Agency of Northern Cook County v. Corps of Engineers*.[64] Nothing much changed, as the Corps, the EPA, and even the Justice Department lawyers assigned to defend those two organizations in federal court interpreted the Court ruling to apply only to wetlands that had been given protection under the migratory bird rule. But developers, property rights advocates such as the Pacific Legal Foundation, and a vocal group of House and Senate members representing western states argued that the Court decision had actually limited the jurisdiction of the Corps and the EPA to waters that are navigable themselves or directly adjacent to waters that are navigable. On January 10, 2003, the Army Corps of Engineers and the Environmental Protection Agency invited public comment on new rules to govern wetlands development.

And what does all of this have to do with the constitutional government assigning authority and how that affects policy choices? First, at the same time that they invited public comment on wetlands development rules, a directive went out to field staff instructing them to "seek formal project-specific HQ approval prior to asserting jurisdiction over isolated non-navigable intrastate waters."[65] Both agencies, it turns out, had left a great deal of authority in field-office hands, letting them interpret the migratory bird rule—and several others—in terms of projects in their part of the country. The authority had been lodged with the Corps "HQ" but had been exercised locally. Now it would be exercised centrally as the new rules would be developed. Second, for a full two years after the Supreme Court decision, the attitudes/cultures of the Corps and EPA—hardly rabidly pro-environment, but clearly less pro-development than the home builders and property rights advocates thought they should be—had prevailed, and business went on as much as usual as it could, given the Court's ruling. Third, one wouldn't necessarily have to agree with Daniel Rosenberg of the Natural Resources Defense Council, that "Once again, the White House has tuned out the science and is only listening to the siren song of developers and mining companies," to conclude that the political executives at the top of the EPA and the Army Corps were looking at the issues through a different lens than did their counterparts in the Clinton administration just three years earlier.[66] Finally, there can't be much question that the authority to approve specific projects will be exercised differently by "HQ" than it would have been by the field offices, and it doesn't seem too much of a stretch to conclude that the differences will lean in the direction defined by President Bush and those whose opinions he values.

In Summary

The paper structure matters because it is the paper structure that tells us who is empowered to decide a particular question, and who decides a question has a tremendous impact on what is decided. So when the constitutional government chooses to locate a program in one agency rather than another, place an agency in one department rather than another, or give authority over a given set of decisions to an Assistant Secretary rather than a Bureau Chief, it is not engaged in a low-stakes exercise that only a professor of public administration could possibly find interesting. Rather it is making a high-stakes choice, interesting to a wide range of people inside the government and out and almost certain to leave a lasting imprint on the decisions reached in that area of public policy.

Specifically, when the constitutional government chooses one organizational home over another, it chooses one distinctive set of attitudes, one institutional culture, over another. Those distinctive cultures are born of a combination of professional viewpoints, political reality, and personal values that often become so tightly woven together that not even an insider can really tell where one leaves off and the other begins. What insiders—and even us outsiders—can tell, however, is this: an institutional culture will leave its mark on everything that institution does. Strip mining will be regulated differently in the Interior Department than in the Environmental Protection Agency, even if the law is the same and even if the primary burden of writing and enforcing the regulations falls to more or less the same set of professionals.

When the constitutional government hands authority to one organizational official as opposed to another, the outcome is likely to be less clear-cut and easily understood. Institutional cultures are hardly monolithic, but they do have some sort of hold on almost everyone who works in that institution, especially those who stick around for a while. That impact will tend to mute the differences in outlook among the various levels of the organization. Beyond that, the differences in outlook that might be found between an Assistant Secretary and a Bureau Chief might well pale by comparison with those found between an Assistant Secretary in one administration and his or her successor in the next. That, of course, makes using the choice of which position to assign authority to a less useful tool for those who hope to influence the administration of a particular statute. Finally, though it may often be reluctantly done, authority is delegated, and when it is, the choice between granting authority to one level of an organization rather than another loses some of its impact.

Still, keeping all of these caveats in mind, it does matter where authority is lodged. The farther up the organizational ladder authority is placed, the greater the impact of politics on the resulting decisions, and the more the politics that does come to bear on those decisions will be the politics of the President and his or her winning coalition. Just as strip mining will be regulated differently in Interior than at EPA, permits to develop wetlands will be more likely to be granted by the headquarters staff at EPA and the Army Corps of Engineers than at the field level of either organization.

SUMMARY AND CONCLUSION

With a thousand apologies to Duke Ellington, it don't mean a thing if it ain't got that structure. Groups of people become organizations because of structure, and structure is bound to have a significant impact on what those groups of people do.

Structure starts with authority, that is, with the right to commit the organization to a course of action. We chose the authority principle known as hierarchy because the bureaucracy we are creating is supposed to belong to us, and hierarchy, with its—for lack of a better term—chain-of-command-style decision-making system seemed most consistent with the notion of public ownership and control over such a large and complex system. We would elect the members of the constitutional government, and they would select the political executives that would make up the hierarchy, and they would direct the actions of the organizations they were asked to lead. Somehow our goals and preferences would end up as the guideposts for all of this.

Hierarchy may indeed be consistent with the notion of public ownership and control, but it still brings with it some serious consequences. First, as we saw, such an authority structure tends to make it nearly impossible for any news to travel toward those in authority unless the men and women below think these authority figures will like what they hear. Fear, loyalty, deference, and human nature seem to combine to provide a real incentive to sanitize information as it moves from one organizational level to another, and lying, the careful selection of questions or even of those to be questioned, and the ever present tendency to just make one small change before this goes forward offer ample means to make that sanitizing happen. Second, because the authority structure we call hierarchy is being imposed on an organization composed of individuals who are in that organization to use some specialized knowledge and skill that they possess to solve some problem that the organization was created to solve, there is an inevitable separation of the technical knowledge essential to attacking that problem from the ultimate authority to decide how the problem will be attacked. Finally, just as imposing the principle of hierarchy seems to induce those at the bottom or in the middle of organizations to clean up information before it gets to the top, it seems to induce those at the top to clean up information before it gets out to the public. In fact, of course, it seems to provide them with plenty of inducement to simply keep that information secret altogether. Combined with the fact that a tightly hierarchical organization can often take on the negative characteristics of a leader loose from his or her moorings, this tendency to stop the flow of information from bureaucracy to public creates a dangerous kind of organizational irresponsibility that can threaten many of our most important values.

Dangerous as unchecked hierarchy may be, however, unchecked specialization is not much better. Policy specialists tend to define goals in narrow and professionally acceptable terms and pursue them with a single-mindedness that really does tend to remind you of a submarine guided by a periscope frozen in place. They may, indeed most often do, accomplish those narrowly defined goals, but the reason that they put blinders on milk horses is to make sure they can see only straight ahead and not be distracted by anything to either side; and to shift metaphors in mid-stream on you, most policy specialists will work like powerful milk horses, going straight ahead and being proud of their accomplishments. So we get an FHA that defines success in terms of the lowest possible default rate and makes whatever decisions are necessary to get there, never seeing, never even being capable of looking to see, that cities are deteriorating, energy dependence and environmental degradation are growing, and blacks are being frozen out of the new suburbs and condemned to living in substandard housing back in the cities or paying far higher interest rates to fix up what they can get. And we get a Bureau of Reclamation that wants to cultivate as much of the West as possible as quickly as possible with food prices competitive with the rest of farm country, a goal that justifies—in the bureau's mind—tenant farming, an inverse redistribution of income, imperiling land and rivers, infuriating another nation, and an incredible waste of natural resources.

But structure isn't just a matter of hierarchy and specialization. It is also a matter of the paper structure of bureaucracy, that is, of where we locate programs and who has final authority over those programs. The organizational location of a program—or the departmental home of an agency—is so important, as we saw, because every organization really is unique. Every organization has its own tradition, values, attitudes, and culture, and any program assigned to a particular organization will find that organization's imprint on it. Likewise, authority can be assigned to positions at various levels of an organization, and though the impact of one assignment of authority as opposed to another will be harder to gauge, it will still be felt.

NOTES

1. *Kelley v. Johnson* 425 U.S. 238 (1976).
2. *Jacobs v. Kuenes* 541 F2d 222 (9th Cir. 1976); *Leonard v. City of Columbus* 705 F2d 1299 (1983); *McCarthy v. Philadelphia Civil Service Commission* 424 U.S. 645 (1976).
3. These numbers are for the 1998/99 edition of *The United States Government Manual* (Washington, D.C.: U.S. Government Printing Office, 1998).
4. *The United States Government Manual,* 310.
5. *The United States Government Manual,* 421.
6. Victor A. Thompson, *Modern Organization* (New York: Alfred A. Knopf, 1961). This is the theme of Thompson's entire work, but see especially ch. 5.
7. Thompson, *Modern Organization,* chs. 3 and 4.
8. Jack Gonzales and John Rothchild, "The Shriver Prescription: How the Government Can Find Out What It's Doing," in *The Culture of Bureaucracy,* ed. Charles Peters and Michael Nelson (New York: Holt, Rinehart and Winston, 1979), 118–27.
9. David Halberstam, *The Best and the Brightest* (New York: Random House, 1969), 365–366.

10. Aaron Wildavsky, *Speaking Truth to Power* (Boston: Little, Brown, 1979).

11. Halberstam, *The Best and the Brightest*, 366.

12. Carl Hulse, "New Senators Take Seats After Facing Bush in 2000," *New York Times* (electronic edition), December 30, 2002.

13. Wanda J. Smith, K. Vernard Harrington, and Jeffrey D. Houghton, "Predictors of Performance Appraisal Discomfort," *Public Personnel Management* 29 (Spring 2000), 21–32.

14. Halberstam, *The Best and the Brightest*, 368.

15. Gonzales and Rothchild, "The Shriver Prescription," 123–124.

16. Halberstam, *The Best and the Brightest*, 284.

17. Halberstam, *The Best and the Brightest*, 348–349.

18. Robert Dreyfuss, "The Pentagon Muzzles the CIA," *American Prospect*, December 16, 2002, 26.

19. Dreyfuss, "The Pentagon Muzzles the CIA."

20. Michael Fumento, "Flight From Reality," *New Republic*, October 7, 1996, 20.

21. Fumento, "Flight From Reality," 21.

22. Thompson, *Modern Organization*, 6.

23. Hubert Humphrey, speech before the National Housing Policy Forum, February 14, 1967, quoted in Harold Seidman and Robert Gilmour, *Politics, Position, and Power*, 4th ed. (New York: Oxford University Press, 1986), 171.

24. Hanna Rosin, "Educating Feddie," *New Republic*, February 3, 1997, 12.

25. For a brief discussion of those efforts, see Dennis D. Riley, *Public Personnel Administration*, 2nd ed. (New York: Longman, 2002), 115–116.

26. Quoted in Adam Liptak, "Court Backs Open Deportation Hearings in Terror Cases," *New York Times* (electronic edition), August 27, 2002.

27. Harold Seidman, *Politics, Position, and Power: The Dynamics of Federal Organization* (New York: Oxford University Press, 1970), 119.

28. Seidman, *Politics, Position, and Power*.

29. Unless otherwise noted, all of the information in this section of the chapter concerning the Bureau of Reclamation and its policies comes from "Senate Water-use Bill Pits Big Firms Against Small Farms," *Congressional Quarterly Weekly Report* 37, no. 39 (September 29, 1979), 2121–2133, or from my forty years of observing agriculture in the region I still sometimes call home.

30. "Senate Water-use Bill Pits Big Firms Against Small Farms," 2123.

31. Hugh Heclo, "Issue Networks and the Executive Establishment," in *The New American Political System*, ed. Anthony King (Washington, D.C.: American Enterprise Institute, 1978), 123.

32. Frederick C. Mosher, *Democracy and the Public Service*, 2nd ed. (New York: Oxford University Press, 1982), 118.

33. Seidman, *Politics, Position, and Power*, 119.

34. Seidman, *Politics, Position, and Power*.

35. Seidman, *Politics, Position, and Power*.

36. Seidman, *Politics, Position, and Power*.

37. Heclo, "Issue Networks and the Executive Establishment," 123.

38. Jane Jacobs, *The Death and Life of Great American Cities* (New York: Vintage Books, 1961), 310.

39. Jacobs, *The Death and Life of Great American Cities*, 305.

40. National Commission on Urban Problems, "Building the American City," report to the Congress and the President, December 12, 1968, 100.

41. "Senate Water-use Bill Pits Big Firms Against Small Farms," 2125.

42. Michael Barone and Grant Ujifusa, *The Almanac of American Politics 1996* (Washington, D.C.: National Journal, 1995), 111.

43. Marc Reisner, *Cadillac Desert* (New York: Penguin Books, 1986); see especially 7–11.

44. Reisner, *Cadillac Desert*, 293–299.

45. Reisner, *Cadillac Desert*; see especially ch. 11, 393–451.

46. Barone and Ujifusa, *The Almanac of American Politics*, 111.

47. *The United States Government Manual*; see 383 for a brief description of the Office of Workers' Compensation and 367–369 for the job titles of the men and women who run it.

48. Quoted in Seidman, *Politics, Position, and Power*, 108.

49. Seidman, *Politics, Position, and Power*, 109.

50. Steven Kelman, "Occupational Safety and Health Administration," and Suzanne Weaver, "Antitrust Division of the Department of Justice," in *The Politics of Regulation*, ed. James Q. Wilson (New York: Basic Books, 1980), 236–266 and 123–151, respectively. Also see Morton Halperin, *Bureaucratic Politics and Foreign Policy* (Washington, D.C.: Brookings Institution, 1974).

51. Kelman, "Occupational Safety and Health Administration," 250.

52. Kelman, "Occupational Safety and Health Administration," 251.

53. Kelman, "Occupational Safety and Health Administration," 251.

54. Kelman, "Occupational Safety and Health Administration," 252.

55. Robert A. Katzmann, "The Federal Trade Commission," in *The Politics of Regulation*, ed. Wilson, 152–187.

56. Weaver, "The Antitrust Division of the Justice Department," 146.

57. Seidman, *Politics, Position, and Power*, 104.

58. Heclo, "Issue Networks and the Executive Establishment," 117.

59. Seidman, *Politics, Position, and Power*, 111–116.

60. Kelman, "Occupational Safety and Health Administration," 251.

61. I am indebted for much of this analysis to my friend and colleague of twenty-five years, Professor Emeritus Richard D. Christofferson. Chris understands surface-mining policy as a professional. He taught environmental policy for three decades. He understands surface-mining policy as a person. He was born and raised in western South Dakota and his brothers were still ranching in the area near Wyoming when the strip-mine boom that followed the oil embargo of 1973 began.

62. Florence Heffron, *The Administrative Regulatory Process* (New York: Longman, 1983), 377.

63. *American Textile Manufacturers Institute v. Donovan* 101 S.Ct. 2478 (1981).

64. *Solid Waste Agency of Northern Cook County v. Army Corps of Engineers* 531 U.S. 159 (2001).

65. Douglas Jehl, "U.S. Plan Could Ease Limits on Wetlands Development," *New York Times* (electronic edition), January 11, 2003.

66. Jehl, "U.S. Plan Could Ease Limits on Wetlands Development."

4

Some Agencies Are More Powerful
Than Others

Expertise, Politics, and Agency Power

Students of politics have been interested in bureaucratic power for well over a century. Much of that interest has centered on questions of whether such power could ever be tamed, that is, of whether bureaucracy could ever be made compatible with the ethos of democracy.[1] But almost as much has been centered on the more pragmatic question of why some bureaus or agencies seem to be so much more powerful than others.[2] Since this book is about the role bureaucracy plays in the policy process and the forces that influence how it plays that role, we need to consider that question of why some bureaucratic units are able to exercise far more power in that process than others are. There is no definitive answer to the question, of course, but the road map for analyzing it was laid out for us a long time ago by Professor Francis Rourke, and what I want to do with the next few pages is to provide you with the pocket version of that map.

The ability to exercise power seems to depend on two things. First, of course, it depends on possession of the resources that define power in a particular context. But in every situation in which someone hopes to exercise power, that someone will face constraints on his or her ability to do so. In some contexts these constraints will simply serve as a check on the efforts of an individual or agency to use its resources to influence a particular policy decision, while in others the constraints will effectively block an individual or agency from gathering the necessary resources to exercise power at all. Either way, power is exercised to the extent that resources can overcome constraints, so agency power can best be seen in that context—that is, it can best be mapped by looking at the major sources of that power as well as the primary constraints on its exercise.

In what was "its time"—from the late 1960s to the early 1990s—Francis Rourke's vision of the sources of bureaucratic power pretty much dominated the intellectual landscape for scholars of public administration.[3] In a very real sense it still does, as evidenced by the fact that in what is now probably the leading text on bureaucratic politics, Kenneth Meier bases his discussion of the sources of bureau power directly on Rourke's earlier analysis.[4] Professor Rourke's description of the constraints on bureaucratic power, however, didn't exactly achieve the same dominant status. That no doubt happened in part because he devoted a single chapter of twenty pages to the question of constraints as opposed to the three chapters of nearly one hundred pages that he had devoted to the question of the resources needed for the exercise of bureaucratic power. Beyond that, *Bureaucracy, Politics, and Public Policy* appeared in the same year—1969—that Emmette Redford published *Democracy in the Administrative State*, pulling together the work of a generation of scholars of public administration around the idea of overhead democracy as the key to holding bureaucracy in check, and most of the attention of the discipline was focused on Redford and his work.[5] So, though we may need an additional guide or two for our journey into the land of constraints on bureaucratic power, it is a journey we must take to understand the contours of that power and the reasons why some agencies are so much more powerful than others—that was the question we started this discussion with—so let's go. It makes more sense to start with the resources an agency needs to exercise power, of course, so that is where we should begin.

SOURCES OF AGENCY POWER

Bureaucratic power, according to Rourke, is derived in part from sources internal to bureaucracy—knowledge, cohesion, and leadership—and in part from sources outside of bureaucracy, that is, from the support of outsiders with power of their own. Let's start our pocket version of the Rourke bureaucratic power atlas with a look inside bureaucracy itself.

Power from the Inside: Knowledge, Cohesion, and Leadership

In the interests of historical accuracy, Rourke speaks of Varieties of Bureaucratic Expertise, Organizational Esprit, and Administrative Statecraft, but I don't think that Professor Kenneth Meier's decision to switch to Knowledge, Cohesion, and Leadership does much violence to the concepts themselves, so I think it makes sense for us to follow his lead. The words are just easier to use.

Knowledge

Given what you read in the first three chapters, it can hardly surprise you that knowledge would be the number one internal source for an agency's power. Agencies exist to gather information, apply specialized knowledge to that information, and then try to accomplish specific goals by sharing that information and by writing and enforcing rules. Logically enough, then, an agency would rely on its knowledge as a major part of its effort to influence policy decisions in its areas of responsibility.

Relying on their knowledge is logical enough, but it doesn't always work. More properly, since our concern is with the question of why some agencies are more powerful than others, relying on their knowledge works a whole lot better as a means of exercising influence over policy decisions for some agencies than it does for others. As he so often does, Francis Rourke provides us with the reason why some agencies can cash in on their expert knowledge so much more easily than others in a single, delightfully understated, sentence: "All administrative agencies have some degree of expertise in the functions they perform, but not all bureaucratic skills exact equal deference from the community."[6] In other words, it isn't so much the possession of expert knowledge but the reaction to—respect for—that knowledge that gives an agency power.

We will explore this point in much more detail later in the chapter in the context of a scheme for classifying policy areas and the agencies that operate within them. At this point, suffice it to say that the motto of the Lodi Union High School class of 1961 should have been changed from Knowledge Is Power to Knowledge Can Be a Source of Power in Situations in Which Other Folks Figure They Need to Rely on That Knowledge. Maybe not. I'm not sure the makeshift stage in the middle of the football field would have held a banner that long.

Cohesion

Whether the label is cohesion (Meier), or organizational esprit (Rourke), both men are talking about a notion with two distinct components. As Meier himself puts it, "The reader should be aware that while cohesion is defined as commitment to the organization and that this commitment is a source of power, one cause of both is the performance of a function that excites the community."[7]

Performing a function that excites and unites the staff of an agency and at the same time excites the public—even a reasonably large segment of the public—would seem to be a key ingredient in the recipe for agency power. Both Meier and Rourke cite the examples of the Peace Corps and the Marine Corps, and one could certainly include NASA, at least NASA from its creation until the end of the lunar missions. But as a source of agency power, cohesion has some serious drawbacks.

First of all, it is something that can be hard to sustain for the long haul. Maybe the Marine Corps has managed to do so, though it has the distinct advantage of being a branch of the armed services, and for that matter, the branch most likely to be glorified in the popular media. Is there a picture from any other branch as famous as that of the men hoisting the flag on Iwo Jima? But the Peace Corps is hardly in the position it was four decades ago, and NASA can't reasonably be said to be a cohesive unit performing a function everybody rallies around.

Second, and maybe more to the point, cohesion/esprit is said to depend "to a large extent upon the development of an appropriate ideology or sense of mission on the part of an administrative agency both as a method of binding outside supporters to the agency and as a technique for intensifying the loyalty of the organization's employees to its purposes."[8] As I have argued elsewhere, organizational goals are rarely the source of the kind of motivation and unity that Rourke was describing.[9]

To begin with, such goals are often vague, or even contradictory, the product of endless committees and task forces unable to be much more specific than is the U.S. Fish and Wildlife Service when it says that it exists "to conserve, protect, and enhance fish and wildlife and their habitats for the continuing benefit of the American people."[10] I doubt that anyone at USFWS quarrels with that goal. But I also doubt that any dozen people at USFWS agree on its precise meaning or how it helps them to decide what to do about salmon in the Pacific Northwest. How exactly, then, can it bring them together?

Much more to the point, as Victor Thompson pointed out more than forty years ago, every agency employs people whose primary commitment is to the goals and even more to the work routines of their professions, not to the goals of the agency that employs them. After a series of decisions made during the past two academic years, I am most definitely one of them. I still love teaching and I still love writing, but it is all I can do not to hate this institution. A more appropriate example might be found in the work of Robert Katzmann in his study of attorneys employed at the Bureau of Competition of the Federal Trade Commission (FTC).[11] To shorten the story quite a bit: Katzmann found that a decade-long effort by FTC leadership to change anti-trust policy as implemented by the Bureau of Competition floundered on the shoals of the attorneys' powerful attachment to their own vision of what they saw as the real work—and, therefore, the real goal—of the lawyer. They wanted to go to court and they wanted to win. Lest you think that only college professors and lawyers could be so narrow minded, Katzmann found exactly the same mind-set at the FTC's Bureau of Economics, only this time it was the mind-set of a group of economists, bound and determined that a potential prosecution against natural gas companies for deliberately underreporting reserves not go forward because it might cloud the debate over deregulation of the natural gas industry. Even enforcing the law as it existed could not take precedence over their commitment to the superiority of free markets.[12]

Finally, we have to ask ourselves whether internal cohesion is a source of power or a product of power. It would seem pretty obvious that the successful exercise of power would excite an agency's staff and, more than likely anyway, get that staff to overlook the kinds of disagreements and frustrations that would soon become magnified if that agency began to lose its ability to influence the direction of policy in its particular corner of the governmental world. I don't want to rely too heavily on analogies to the world of sport, but winning teams are often pretty cohesive aggregations, and over and over one hears that players, managers, owners, and even fans ignore all sorts of difficulties as long as the winning continues. That doesn't mean that cohesion is not a source of power. It is. It is also a product of power. I'm not sure if we are in the land of chickens and eggs exactly, but we are surely in a land in which the relationship between power and cohesion is at least a two-way street, if not a circle.

Leadership

As you might have guessed if you remember much of the discussion of the City of the Political Executives from chapter 2, I tend to be a little skeptical about the men and women who occupy those leadership positions, indeed, even about the notion of administrative leadership in general. Still, even I have to concede that it does matter who occupies the top positions at an agency or bureau, and it even matters who occupies the positions in the departmental hierarchy above those agencies and bureaus. Leadership can make a difference.

Leadership may be one of those things that we can only recognize and not define, but it is hard to find a better description of leadership at the agency level than that of the highly respected NASA Administrator James E. Webb.

> [H]e has to represent within the endeavor the outside environmental factors—the Federal Government, the President and the administration in all its facets, the Congress, and the national public; he has to make sure that the endeavor's goals and activities are responsive to the requirements and desires of the environment under conditions of rapid change and uncertainty.
>
> At the same time, the executive represents the entire endeavor as against the environment. He has the ultimate responsibility for securing from the environment the support necessary for gaining and sustaining momentum, for safeguarding against dysfunctional forces seeking control and influence, for—in short— keeping the endeavor viable and on course toward its goals.
>
> The executive can do none of these inside or outside tasks alone. He must bind his associates to his objectives and to his team, even though they may hardly understand all the forces that are at work.[13]

A leader, in other words, is part spokesperson or symbol and part manager, and as Mr. Webb goes on to say, playing one of those roles may get in the way of playing the other often enough to cause some real problems for an organization and for its leader.

Beyond that, as Francis Rourke points out, leadership is situational, that is, "dependent on factors in the environment other than the leader himself."[14] For example, President Kennedy's brother-in-law, R. Sargent Shriver, was considered a masterful leader while he was in charge of the Peace Corps, but he got very different marks when he took over the leadership of the much less respected Office of Economic Opportunity. After briefly discussing these two radically different assessments of Mr. Shriver the leader, Rourke once again exercises his masterful penchant for understatement when he concludes, "But the presumption is strong that Shriver was no less able a leader in the Office of Economic Opportunity than he was in the Peace Corps."[15]

Finally, of course, there is the simple—and simultaneously complex—fact that for somebody to lead, somebody has to agree to follow. Since leading an agency is both an internal and an external enterprise, some of the somebodies that have to follow are inside the organization the leader "heads" and some are outside. To make things tougher yet, most of the insiders are career bureaucrats with deep attachments to their own specialties and their own particular jobs, and most of the outsiders have independent power of their own and their own agendas for the agency's operations. As Francis Rourke himself put it, "It is in this refractory environment that administrative statecraft must be carried on in the public service, and what is perhaps most remarkable is not that many fail, but that some succeed."[16]

So, does all of this mean that leadership isn't much of a resource for increasing agency power? No. It means that the task of leading any given agency is immense, and only every once in a while will someone be put in charge who can handle all of the various demands. So it means that the impact of leadership on agency power will be marginal. That is, a good leader will marshal the other resources in such a way that the agency's power grows a little, and a bad leader will fail to marshal those resources and the agency's power will shrink a little. In short, no leader is going to take an agency with no other resources and turn it into a powerhouse, and no leader is going to take an agency with all of the other resources and turn it into a bad joke. But, within the limits imposed by the possession—or lack thereof—of those other resources, leadership can add or subtract from an agency's power, and since the game of policy making is often played at the margins, a marginal increase or decrease in power can sometimes determine the outcome of a particular battle in that never-ending game.

The Advantage of Always Being on Duty

Woody Allen, comedian, writer, director, actor, and even occasionally essayist, once said that 90 percent of life is just showing up. Bureaucrats show up, every day, to work on the same policy questions they and their agencies have been working on in one way or another ever since anybody can remember. More accurately, they come to work every day and work in the same policy area with a somewhat shifting set of specific questions, but with the same general sets of issues and concerns that plagued their agencies before and will plague them again. There is rarely anyone in the constitutional government who can match a given agency for sticking to the subject, and that sticking to it can eventually become a source of power. Consider this observation from Francis Rourke: "The sustained attention that bureaucrats can devote to specific problems gives them a decided advantage over political officials who deal with a wide variety of problems and confront each issue of public policy only at sporadic intervals."[17]

As we will see in the rest of this chapter and in the next three chapters, we don't want to make too much of the advantage of just showing up. People with political power can still win a confrontation with an agency even if they can't "outexpert" that agency. Nonetheless, being the ones always working in a policy area gives a myriad of subtle opportunities to shape policy and it is the agencies that are the ones always working on their questions.

Power from the Outside: Clientele, Congress, and the Chief(?)

Knowledge, cohesion, and leadership can give an agency a considerable amount of power, but no agency could, would, or even should be content to let its position in the policy-making system rest on that particular three-legged stool. No agency could or would be content because all agencies know that the resources necessary to accomplish their objectives are in the hands of the constitutional government and that the processes for obtaining those resources—money, positions, and legal authority—are expressly and overtly political. To enter the policy-making business without external support, in short, would be something of a suicide mission. But I also said that no agency should be content to operate without external support, and that may be a little less obvious on its surface. Remember, however, that we are trying to create a system of self-government through representative institutions. No agency can ever truly become a representative institution, but it can link itself with such institutions, and maybe even more important, it can link itself with the people those institutions are supposed to represent, and in the process make its exercise of power much more legitimate in the eyes of those people and their representatives.

So, for reasons both practical and philosophical, agencies seek outside support for just about everything they do. In fact, they seek outside support for their very existence. And where do they look? To absolutely no one's surprise, they look to the people, the Congress, and the President, though not necessarily in that order. Because the next three chapters concern the relationships between executive branch agencies and the President, the Congress, and the people, the discussion in this section will be mercifully short.

Power From the People

Political power in this country ultimately belongs to the people, though as with pigs in George Orwell's *Animal Farm*, some people are decidedly more equal than others when it comes to holding and using that people power. From the perspective of any given agency, the people who are going to hold and use power the vast majority of the time will be "the people who directly benefit or suffer from the programs that the bureau administers."[18] When such people organize, we call them clientele groups, and they are inevitably the cornerstone of outside support for an agency. As we will see in chapter 7, they are frequently joined by other groups of consistent supporters drawn from the realm of professional associations and individual policy experts. Still, without a strong and supportive clientele, an agency is going to be fighting an uphill battle as it tries to play the key role its people believe it ought to be playing in the policy process.

There is, of course, another set of people that might provide their support to an executive branch agency, namely the people that Rourke refers to as "the public at large" and that I will be calling the general public when we get to chapter 7.[19] It won't surprise you a bit to learn that Francis Rourke is less than sanguine about the chances for any one agency to capture the interest and attention of that "public at large," let alone garner its support for any but the briefest time. Kenneth Meier's brief discussion of the ups and downs of public support for NASA more than justifies his conclusion that "An agency dependent on the whim of public opinion is in a precarious position."[20] As you will see in chapter 7, I see no reason at all to disagree with the positions taken by Rourke and by Meier. The general public simply doesn't see most agencies through the prism of self-interest that moves clientele groups to become consistent backers of "their" particular agency.

Power From the People's Representatives

Again, there is a chapter—chapter 6—devoted to the relationship between executive branch agencies and the Congress, so very little needs to be said here. Congress passes laws and OKs the spending of money, and since most agencies are created by law, get their powers and their program responsibilities by law, and for that matter get their money by law, there would be absolutely no way for agencies to avoid some relationship with Congress. But, as we have known for a very long time, the relationship between agencies and Congress is really a series of relationships between a particular agency and a set of committees or subcommittees of the House and Senate, so it is that relationship that we explore in chapter 6. Meantime, suffice it to say here that it is the conventional wisdom among students of public administration that no agency would try to function in the world of policy making without at least trying to gain the support of one or more committees or subcommittees of the Congress.[21]

Power From the Chief and His—Someday Her—Teams

As we noted in the previous chapter, when it comes to those agencies that are collected together into the various cabinet departments, every official reports to somebody who reports to somebody who reports to somebody who reports to the President—or more properly, who would be expected to report to the President if the chief ever turned out to be interested enough to try to find out what that particular official was up to. The organizations in the other half of the U.S. Government Manual—the ones known as Independent Establishments and Government Corporations—have a somewhat less clear-cut relationship to the President, but presumably they would welcome his support or that of his inner circle.

One study of presidential support for agencies found that agencies seeking new legislative authority were successful more than 75 percent of the time if the proposal had presidential backing.[22] But as we'll see in the next chapter, most agencies are a little wary of seeking presidential backing—the President, after all, is an amateur whose time and attention are in limited supply—and Presidents involve themselves in the details of agency policy making much less often than the title Chief Executive might imply.

The President is not alone in the executive branch, of course. There is a White House Staff, the rest of the Executive Office of the President, and an army of political executives, and their support could be useful to an agency trying to flex its policy-making muscles. But, again as we'll see in the next chapter, with the exception of the Office of Management and Budget, most of these individuals and aggregations don't have all that much impact on what happens at most agencies. Consequently, they can't provide much in the way of support to those agencies.

In Summary

Agencies derive their power from both internal and external sources. We need them because of their expertise, so agency power has to start with knowledge, but because we feel that we need the expertise of some agencies a whole lot more than we need the expertise of others, knowledge cannot be an equal opportunity agency power source. Cohesion and leadership can provide some power, but mostly at the margins—that is, mostly they can add to power that comes from elsewhere. Agencies also derive power from outside themselves. Public— read clientele 90 percent of the time—support is a crucial source of power, as is support from key legislative committees. Support from those in the rest of the executive branch, especially support from the Chief Executive, can be useful, but it can also be tough to come by, and as I hinted in the previous chapter and will return to in the next, support from the chief and his inner circle may come at a price that an agency will pay only if it concludes it really has to.

CONSTRAINTS ON AGENCY POWER

No matter what combination of these resources an agency gathers up, there are going to be constraints on how the resulting power can be exercised. Like the resources that give power, the constraints can be found both inside and outside bureaucracy itself. Beyond that, these constraints can operate in either—or both— of two ways. First, they can operate in the context of a clash of wills. An agency attempts to use its power resources to get its way, and roadblocks are set up by others who want a different outcome. Every bit as important, however, constraints can operate to prevent an agency from gathering the necessary resources of power. There isn't much conflict or confrontation because an agency doesn't have the ammunition to start a fight, or in some cases, even to fight back when attacked. As we did with the resources that give an agency power, let's start with the internal constraints and then move to those imposed from the outside.

Internal Constraints: Ethics, Competition, and Representativeness

As I noted a couple of pages ago, Francis Rourke devoted only a single chapter to the question of restraints on bureaucracy, but in that chapter he makes at least the outlines of a case for the existence of three internal constraints. All three clearly exist, but one wonders just how much impact any of them really has on the day-to-day exercise of power by the various agencies of the executive branch.

Ethics

I am convinced that if asked, most of the men and women at any given agency would consider themselves to be ethical public servants striving to do the right thing. But as I have argued elsewhere, the ethical codes to which bureaucrats subscribe do not always provide the clearest of guideposts, and even when they do, those guideposts must be interpreted in the context of the agency they work for and the decisions to be made.[23] That context, unfortunately, can include directives that conflict with the individual's sense of what is the right thing to do. At that point, as Professor Albert Hirschmann pointed out more than three decades ago, the individual has but three choices: "Exit, Voice, or Loyalty."[24] These would, of course, be precisely the situations in which we would hope that ethics would provide some sort of constraint on the exercise of agency power, but the legitimacy of directives from duly constituted authority in a hierarchically structured environment, plus the personal fear that comes from years of watching the fate of others who have raised ethical complaints about such directives, tend to make loyalty the option most individuals feel they ought to/have to choose. It is probably true that a general sense of ethics will permeate an agency enough to keep it from abusing power routinely, but it is almost certainly also true that that general sense of ethics leaves an awful lot of room for the exercise of agency power, or as Herman Finer put it more than sixty years ago: "Reliance on an official's conscience may be reliance on an official's accomplice."[25]

Competition

Turf battles between agencies are the stuff of legend. As a retired Army colonel I once taught with said, "If we fought the Russians as ferociously as we fought the Navy, the Berlin Wall would have come down twenty years earlier." So we know that agencies do contest one another, and given the number of interagency task forces aimed at securing greater agency cooperation, it would appear that a good many of those contests are seen as significant by the upper-level administrators who create such task forces. If the men and women at the top of the hierarchy feel the need to force agency cooperation—which means reduce agency conflict in most instances—it seems a pretty safe bet that the agency conflict that is present is preventing one or both of those agencies from doing what those top officials believe needs to be done. In other words, there can't be much doubt that at least inside the executive branch there are a good many people who believe that agencies do compete with one another and that that competition does constrain the agencies in question.

Still, three questions remain. First, how widespread is such competition? Do most agencies have serious competitors out there, or is this kind of battle confined to a handful of visible agencies and conflicts, such as the recent and continuing struggle between the Central Intelligence Agency and the Office of the Secretary of Defense over their respective roles in gathering human intelligence for use in "battlefield" operations.[26] Second, even where agencies can be found to be in competition, does that competition involve an entire agency with all of its staff and its core mission, or does such competition usually take place at the margins of agency power, a result of the gray areas where responsibilities might overlap? Finally comes the central question: Does competition between agencies really amount to a significant constraint on the exercise of agency power much of the time?

Representativeness

At least since Andrew Jackson argued that the American people would be better served by a government that looked and sounded like the people it served, we have believed to one degree or another that "a bureaucracy which mirrors a society in its social, economic, and cultural composition will be much more sensitive to the needs of citizens of that society, and much less likely to be arbitrary or abusive when it is exercising power over 'its own kind' of people."[27] Though I have always had a great deal of sympathy with Jackson's dismantling of the old elitist traditions of government staffing of the first six Presidents, and I silently applauded Bill Clinton's vow of a government that looks more like America, I tend to doubt very strongly that a more representative bureaucracy would be that much more responsive to the population or constitute that much of a check on agency power.

The reason: it is just hard to figure how such a representative bureaucracy could be put in place. Two barriers to its creation spring readily to mind. First, agencies are, by definition, places where individuals with a great deal of special-ized knowledge use that knowledge to deal with complex issues. We can try to make sure that the pool of specialized people able to handle these issues is "rep-resentative" at least in racial, ethnic, and gender terms, and it is good that we do. But we can't make that pool representative in any other sense. The men and women we hire for a particular agency need the specific knowledge in question, and as we saw in chapter 2, the process of acquiring it is going to change them fundamentally. They are going to act like specialists. It's their job. Beyond that, as Harold Seidman pointed out long ago, agencies tend to exhibit "distinctive colorations," these colorations are well known, and they have an impact on who seeks—and who gains—employment in particular agencies or bureaus.[28] As one of my students once put it on an exam, "It's a whole lot easier to imagine a career at the Agriculture Department if you grew up with cow(bleep) on your boots." We may see it most clearly in the agencies of the Agriculture or Interior Departments, but Steven Kelman found that a surprisingly high percentage of safety inspectors at the Occupational Safety and Health Administration had relatives who had been killed or seriously injured in industrial accidents.[29]

External Constraints: Politics and the Law

Bureaucracy is, of course, a creature of the constitutional government, deriving its personnel, its money, its authority, and even its very existence from that gov-ernment. Since politics is the fuel that drives the engine of that government, there can be no doubt that politics, whether in the form of a legislative com-mittee, an organized interest group, a set of political executives sent to do the President's bidding, or the President himself, can and will act as a constraint on agency power. Important as politics may be in constraining the power of execu-tive branch agencies, the law should never be underestimated as a check on what those agencies can do. There is a whole body of law called administrative law that spells out decision-making rules and procedures for the various agencies as they go about their jobs, and in theory anyway, most important agency decisions are subject to legal challenge. Indeed, most of the men and women who have writ-ten about the need to limit bureaucratic power in order to preserve our vision of self-government have put far more faith in these external constraints than in any of the internal constraints we just discussed. In keeping with the organization of the rest of the book, let's start with the political constraints.

Political Constraints: The Impact of Power and Powerlessness

A couple of pages back, I said that agencies seek political power from those outsiders who have it. That meant cultivating clientele support, working cooper-atively with congressional subcommittees, and even, on occasion anyway, allying themselves with the political executives sent to represent the President's views or on even rarer occasions with the President himself. We know that some agencies are far more successful in cultivating the kind of outside support that translates into power than are others, but that's a subject for later in the chapter. Here we are interested in external constraints on agency power, and though it may sound strange at first, agencies that find themselves successful in the hunt for political power are subject to political constraints, just as are those who come home from that hunt empty handed.

Consider first the constraints on the agencies that cannot create the kind of power base that every bureaucrat knows is essential to success. Such constraints are obvious, of course. Agencies without any source of power can be buffeted about by politicians who do have such power. In effect, political constraints operate to prevent an agency from getting power in the first place. I'll have more to say about that shortly.

But if you consider the fate of those agencies successful in the great power hunt, you will still find constraints on the exercise of the power they have managed to acquire. Sometimes it will be the result of someone else with power stepping up to fight. The Federal Communications Commission had its media and congressional allies on board when it voted to relax the rules for television station and newspaper ownership, but a broad coalition of groups stepped up and used their power, and in the end, the only vote that counted, that from the White House through the Solicitor General, pulled the plug on the relaxed rules by refusing to authorize an appeal of a Third Circuit Court ruling setting them aside.[30]

Other times, however, the constraints will simply be those inherent in the relationships that have been created by the search for power. In simpler terms, the support from clientele groups, legislative subcommittees, or anyone else for that matter, does not come free. The price is some say in what agencies do, and that say, in a very real sense, places constraints on the power an agency can wield. In the extreme case, an agency can seem—maybe even become—little more than the servant of its supporters, exercising little if any independent power. This seems to be what happened to a number of the so-called independent regulatory commissions—a topic to be discussed in chapter 7—and at least according to Aaron Wildavsky, the poster child for this sort of dependence was the old Grazing Service, an agency of the Interior Department that could do only what the "stockmen and those who spoke for them in Congress" would agree to.[31] But even short of the extreme case, there can be no doubt that supporters expect something in return for their support and that that something is influence over agency decisions.

Whether for the "captive" agency or the influenced agency, the goal of responsiveness seems to justify such influence, of course, and as we'll see in chapters 6 and 7, if the support comes from sources that are knowledgeable enough about the issues at hand that responding to them does not feel too much like a compromise of the agency's primary commitment to its knowledge as the key element in the policy process, it is likely that allowing supporters to have a say in agency decision making won't feel much like a constraint on agency power. It will feel instead like a reasonable way to fit expert policy making into a framework of self-government.

Legal Constraints: Administrative Law and the Courts

Neither administrative law—the rules and procedures that tell agencies how they must make decisions and that we hope embody our most important values—nor the courts have gotten much in the way of attention in most discussions of the constraints on agency power. Rourke, for example, doesn't mention administrative law at all, and gives the courts only two pages, while Meier devotes just over five pages to what he calls judicial controls on agency power, again with almost no mention of the rules that guide those agencies as they make decisions.[32] The fact that chapter 8 is devoted to a discussion of administrative law and chapter 9 to a discussion of judicial review of administrative decision making should indicate that I think both topics need a whole lot more discussion in a book about agency policy making than they have gotten in the past. Mercifully, because each gets its own chapter later, all that needs to be said here is that the law and the courts constrain agency power, not so much by keeping an agency from gathering up the resources necessary to exercise power but by serving—in the case of administrative law—as a kind of internal embodiment of values we want agencies to keep sight of, and in the case of the courts as a forum in which others with power can challenge what an agency has done.

In Summary

No agency operates free of constraints. Some of those constraints come from inside the bureaucracy. The expectation that individuals within agencies will operate in a context bounded by ethical principles is pretty well established, even though the pressure to bend those principles in the face of instructions from legitimate superiors is always present. Likewise, competition from other agencies may place some limits on an agency's power by preventing it from taking over policy territory it would like to have or even forcing it to surrender territory it would like to keep, and a representative bureaucracy might be more prone to reflect our most basic values than a "non-representative" one, if such a bureaucracy could be constructed.

Still, important as these checks may be, it is to the outside of bureaucracy that we look when we want to constrain agency power. Clientele groups and congressional subcommittees may provide an agency with power, but at the very same time they will restrict its freedom of action. Then, of course, some groups just can't get that kind of support, and their actions are even more circumscribed. But politics isn't the only source of outside control over agencies. Even though we presume that their primary concern is with questions of how agencies do what they do, the law and the courts can make a substantial difference in what they do.

Resources Meet Constraints: It's a Matter of Subject Matter

In 1964, Theodore J. Lowi published a review of Bauer, Pool, and Dexter's *American Business and Public Policy*, and ever since, political scientists have been using his public policy categories: distributive, redistributive, and regulatory.[33] Eight years later, in an article in *The Public Administration Review*, he added a fourth category—constituent—to cover those policy areas that other scholars had pointed out simply didn't fit into one of the original three.[34] With only slight alterations Lowi's classification scheme has been used by all sorts of scholars for all sorts of purposes, including the one relevant to this chapter,

Kenneth Meier's use of it to explain variations in "bureau policymaking," including variations in how much power different agencies can muster as they try to shape the policies within their own jurisdiction.[35]

Like Lowi and Meier, I believe strongly that the type of policy area in which an agency operates will have a significant impact on how much power it can exercise over decisions made in that area. Unlike Lowi and Meier, however, I don't believe that a classification scheme based on the categories of distributive, redistributive, regulatory, and constituent will help us understand that impact. For that I think we need a different scheme, and presenting that different scheme is what most of the rest of the chapter is devoted to. Before doing that, however, I feel constrained to give you at least a brief indication of why I don't think the Lowi scheme—as applied by Meier—is much help in understanding differences in agency power.

My complaints are two. First, a scheme for categorizing something has to generate at least reasonably clear boundaries between categories and some guidance as to which of the objects one is categorizing go in which categories. The regulatory, distributive, redistributive, and constituent scheme for categorizing policy areas really doesn't. Second, if we are going to use these categorizations to discuss patterns of agency power or differences in the political environments of various policy areas, there is going to have to be enough internal coherence within the specific categories to show consistency on these dimensions from one member of the category to another. Again, within at least the first three of these categories, we don't find that kind of coherence. Let me flesh out these two objections a bit.

Looking Across Categories: A Question of Boundaries

I would be the first to concede that a system for categorizing policy areas will never have the kinds of clearly defined boundaries that we would expect in a system for classifying types of wild mushrooms or butterflies. Kenneth Meier acknowledges the inevitable messiness of such schemes when he says that "Several agencies implement policies in many different policy areas simultaneously."[36] In his original work laying out the regulatory, distributive, redistributive classification scheme, Ted Lowi admits that "all governmental policies may be considered redistributive . . . or all may be thought regulatory."[37] The inevitability of messiness conceded, this scheme is simply too messy. Consider just two examples.

First, think about the categories of regulatory policy and redistributive policy. Whether we are thinking of the economic regulation that goes all the way back to the late nineteenth century, or the newer health and safety regulation, regulatory policy is always redistributive policy.

In the case of economic regulation, we find policies that not only have the effect of redistribution but redistribution was their original purpose. Our decision in 1887 to create the Interstate Commerce Commission and regulate the railroads was driven by our conviction that Mr. Rockefeller, Mr. Harriman, and Mr. Stanford and cronies were abusing the power that came with owning the only means of transportation by overcharging their customers, especially American farmers. By giving the commission control over the rates that could be charged for shipping goods, we tried to take some of the money that would have flowed to these "robber barons" and keep it in the pockets of their customers. The National Labor Relations Board (NLRB) was created by the National Labor Relations Act (the Wagner Act) to make sure that the collective bargaining rights of workers were not violated, and collective bargaining itself was a means by which workers were supposed to be able to alter the distribution of income between those workers and the business owners who employed them. Likewise, the Wage and Hour Division of the Employment Standards Administration, housed in the Department of Labor, while not an independent regulatory commission like the ICC or the NLRB, nonetheless defines its role as one of "protecting low wage incomes as provided by the minimum wage provisions of the Fair Labor Standards Act (29 U.S.C. 201); [and] safeguarding the health and welfare of workers by discouraging excessively long hours of work through enforcement of the overtime provisions of the Fair Labor Standards Act."[38]

Though less obvious on the surface, agencies engaged in health and safety regulation were also created to redistribute, albeit to redistribute power. The Occupational Safety and Health Administration exists to shift power over workplace safety from employers to workers. The Environmental Protection Agency is there to shift power over the quality of the air we breathe, the water we drink, and at least in the minds of some, ultimately over the nature of the planet we leave our grandchildren, from industry to "the public." And the Food and Drug Administration is about to celebrate its centennial as the agency responsible for shifting power from the nation's food processors to its food consumers, though if the food one wants to eat is meat, poultry, or eggs, the job falls to the Food Safety and Inspection Service of the U.S. Department of Agriculture. To be sure, power over worker safety isn't really exercised by workers any more than power over meat processors is exercised by the folks who line up to get a Big Mac for lunch. The power shifts—incompletely to be sure, but it shifts—from employers and meat processors to government officials, and those officials are expected to exercise it in such a way that workers and Big Mac buyers are better protected than they would be. None of that, however, negates the basic point, namely, that even health and safety regulation is about redistribution.

So, if the purpose of a policy is redistribution, and the principal technique for implementing that policy is regulation, which category does it belong in?

Now turn your attention to the categories of distributive and redistributive policy. According to Meier, "Redistributive policy taxes one group of people to provide benefits for another group."[39] Distributive policies, on the other hand, "use general tax revenue or other nonuser taxes to provide benefits directly to individuals."[40]

Meier tells us that there are too many distributive policies to list. He does, however, go on to provide a set of five categories of distributive policies. We don't really need to consider them all, but a quick look at one or two should suffice to illustrate the problem.

Start with the category he calls subsidy. A subsidy, it would seem, would take money from somebody to help somebody else pay for something. That's what we usually mean when we talk of taxpayers subsidizing higher education in Wisconsin. In fact, Meier's first example is the farm subsidy program, and with the 2002 legislation three years into its implementation and expected to cost more than $80 billion over its lifetime, how can we call it anything but redistribution? The $80 billion, after all, comes from the general run of American taxpayers and it goes to people in the agriculture business because the Congress and the President decided that the consequences of letting "the free market" decide how much money flowed to the agricultural sector were unacceptable, politically, economically, or maybe morally. How is that different from deciding that business owners got too much relative to their workers so collective bargaining should be put in place to level the playing field, employers would work their employees too long so overtime pay is guaranteed, or even that people shouldn't go hungry so food stamps would be provided, that is, that some people would pay taxes so other people could trade coupons for food?

Government-supported research, according to Meier, is an important category of distributive policy because "many industries are too small and too fragmented to support the research necessary for improving productivity [but government] with its great resources can easily bear the costs of such research and distribute the results to industry."[41] Likewise, the government provision of insurance benefits is vital because there are areas "where private insurance is not feasible or profitable, [so] the resources of government are sometimes used to provide the distributive benefits of insurance."[42] In both cases the resources to which he refers, of course, consist of taxes collected from all of us, soon to be devoted to advancing the interests of some of us. Meier certainly argues that this use of public resources benefits the public, and in some cases I don't dispute it. But that begs the question of what makes such policies distributive and not redistributive. Money is put into a general pool by a lot of us and spent for the direct benefit of some of us. That's exactly what we do when we fund programs for the homeless, after-school programs for at-risk kids, food stamps, or the reduced-price lunch my granddaughter got in the first grade because her mother is a single mom who couldn't make a whole lot of money as a classical violinist in a small town. I, for one, think the public benefits from every one of those programs or policies. The point here is not whether Professor Meier and I can agree on which programs are beneficial. The point is that it is pretty difficult to tell why a program that takes tax money to subsidize farmers, conduct research on behalf of a particular industry, or help some folks purchase insurance they couldn't get on their own is significantly and systematically different from a program that takes tax money and provides some people with coupons that can be exchanged for food, pays a school part of the cost of lunch for some but not all of its students, or provides a monthly stipend to a man disabled and unable to work. Yet according to the scheme Meier is using, the first three are different enough from the second three that we need two separate categories to describe them.

Once again, we are not classifying wild mushrooms. Some imprecision in drawing the boundaries between categories is inevitable, and nobody is going to die if we misclassify something. But what we have when classifying policies as regulatory, distributive, or redistributive is more than a little imprecision. What we have is no real boundaries at all. But that's not the only problem with Lowi's policy classification scheme. If we look inside each category, we discover that knowing that an agency is considered a regulatory, distributive, or redistributive agency tells us very little about how much power it is able to exercise in its corner of the policy-making world. So let's take a moment to look inside those categories to see how much they really tell us about agency power.

Looking Inside Categories: Questions of Politics and Power

In his discussion of each of the four policy types, Kenneth Meier includes a section on "the environment" of that particular policy category. He does it, as he says in the opening paragraph of the chapter, because "Variations in [these environments] affect the actions individual bureaus can take and also affect the ability of bureaus to influence the policy process."[43] If we look inside these categories, however, we see variation within each category that matches—if it doesn't exceed—the variation between the categories themselves. Again, a full discussion of each category is well beyond the scope of this chapter, but a quick glance at the remarkable variation in policy-making environments that can be found among regulatory and redistributive agencies will serve to indicate why the categories themselves tell us very little about the remarkable variations in how much power different agencies can exercise in their respective policy areas.

Political scientists have long observed that some regulatory agencies establish such close and cooperative working relationships with the industries they regulate that the agencies can reasonably be said to have become captives of those industries.[44] It is equally clear to us, however, that a good many regulatory agencies remain at odds with those they regulate. Chapter 7 explores the reasons for such differences in detail. Suffice it to say here that if an agency regulates a single industry, is engaged in primarily economic regulation (prices and services), is expected to promote the economic health of the industry as well as regulate it, and is dominated by lawyers, then closeness, cooperation, and ultimately possibly capture is the likely result. On the other hand, if an agency regulates a number of industries, is engaged in regulation that can be called health and safety regulation, has no responsibility for the economic health of the industries it regulates, and is dominated by subject-matter experts and not attorneys, then some distance and hostility between regulators and regulated is almost certain to develop. In other words, knowing that an agency is engaged in regulation tells us little about one of the most important elements of its policy-making environment, namely, what will be its relationship with its most natural ally, its clientele. Nor does knowing that an agency is in the business of regulation tell us much about how many politicians—or which ones—will pay attention to that agency and its decision making and how often those politicians will want to "interfere" in what the agency tries to do. Yet these are precisely the kinds of questions we want a policy-area classification scheme to help us answer.

If you want to put it in more concrete terms, the Office of Thrift Supervision, the National Labor Relations Board, the Securities and Exchange Commission (SEC), and the Environmental Protection Agency (EPA) are all engaged in writing rules that somebody must follow and are all considered regulatory agencies under the Lowi/Meier classification scheme. But it seems pretty obvious that the accounting industry/securities traders/business dominated under the normal political radar screen environment of the Securities and Exchange Commission would have very little in common with the high-profile industry versus environmental group environment of the Environmental Protection Agency. Likewise, would we really expect much similarity between the mostly quiet savings and loan industry dominated environment of the Office of Thrift Supervision and the all out labor-management war that would characterize the environment of the National Labor Relations Board?

In short, being a regulatory agency does little to structure that agency's policy-making environment, so being labeled a regulatory agency does little to help us understand the structure of that environment.

Things aren't so much clearer when we turn our attention to the agencies in the areas Lowi and Meier label redistributive. If we look first just at the three Department of Housing and Urban Development agencies that Meier identifies as conducting our redistributive housing programs, we see remarkable disparities. The Federal Housing Administration is rarely thought of as engaged in redistribution. As you may recall from the previous chapter, it guarantees mortgages on single-family, owner-occupied housing, and while it provided substantial subsidies for the growth of suburbia after World War II, no one really gave much thought to its role in redistributing income. More to the point, its policy-making environment is, and always has been, composed almost exclusively of institutions drawn from the housing and mortgage lending industries. Hardly the clientele we would associate with an agency busily redistributing income, except maybe income coming their way. The second of these HUD agencies, the Government National Mortgage Administration, seems just as unlikely a candidate for the redistributive label, and as an institution created to provide a government-guaranteed secondary mortgage market, its policy environment is strictly a place for the mortgage industry to flex its muscles. But the Office of Fair Housing and Equal Opportunity generates a fair bit of controversy, enough to attract far wider political attention, and as we might expect of an agency that touches on our country's racial nerve, one in which tempers have been known to flare.

An entirely different political configuration would no doubt be found around the Social Security Administration's supplemental security income program or the Health Care Financing Administration's activities in administering the Medicaid program. In effect, some things that fall in the Lowi/Meier category of redistribution are actually thought of by the public as redistributive policy—something we are leery of—and some that fall in that category are thought of by the public in entirely different terms. Hence political attention from many quarters on Medicaid, but from only the predictable insiders on mortgage guarantees or creating a secondary mortgage market. Such a difference would be telling to the agency involved.

Once more, being a redistributive agency does little to structure that agency's policy environment, and being labeled a redistributive agency does little to help us understand the structure of that environment.

In Summary

Students of bureaucratic policy making have observed and tried to explain differences in the relative power of various agencies for three-quarters of a century or more. Many of those scholars have concluded that the nature of the policy area in which an agency operates is one of the keys to those power differences.

More than forty years ago, Theodore Lowi offered a system for classifying policy areas that he felt would explain the differences in the politics of those various areas, and Randall Ripley and Kenneth Meier, among others, believed that Lowi's system could also be used to explain differences in agency power. Unfortunately, I don't think that system can really help us understand why some agencies are powerful participants in their specialized policy arenas while others are not. As I have argued in this section, I think there are two reasons to look for another policy-area classification scheme.

First, the Lowi/Meier system presents us with a set of categories that tells us that the National Labor Relations Board, one of the cornerstones of Franklin D. Roosevelt's New Deal and a clear-cut effort to redistribute power and ultimately income from business owners to their workers, is a regulatory and not a redistributive agency. Its goals are redistributive. If its policies are successful, its accomplishments are redistributive. But since its mechanisms are regulatory, it is regulatory. Likewise, the Lowi/Meier system tells us that a program designed to spend $80 billion of tax revenues to subsidize American agriculture is distributive and not redistributive. Herb Kohl (D-WI), in referring to his own effort to make sure the dairy farmers of our state remain included in the program, referred to the need to keep the "dairy safety net" in place in these difficult times of low prices.[45] Is there a more directly redistributive phrase than "safety net"?

Beyond that, if we look inside the various categories, we find agencies whose role and power in the policy process, with respect to the issues in their areas of administrative responsibility, varies tremendously. In the world of regulatory agencies, the politics of policy making ranges from the scientific-sounding clashes of environmentalists and industry that characterize EPA policy making, to the ideological rhetoric of debate at the NLRB, to the highly specialized insider talk of the SEC or the Office of Thrift Supervision. Other than writing rules that segments of society are expected to obey, what do these agencies have in common? Do the Department of Agriculture agencies that administer the distribution of that $80 billion to the nation's agriculture producers really operate in an environment that has much in common with the men and women whose job it is to run the Medicaid program? Both are redistributing income, but politically they live and work on very different planets.

Enough said. Classifying policies as regulatory, distributive, and redistributive hasn't moved us much closer to understanding why some agencies are more powerful than others. Indeed, doing so hasn't moved us much closer to understanding the difference in the politics of various policy areas. So now it's on to offering a classification scheme that I believe will do those things.

CLASSIFYING POLICY AREAS: COMPLEXITY, CONTROVERSY, AND THE POLITICS OF PUBLIC POLICY

The politics of any particular policy area are best thought of in terms of the answers to two questions. First, what is the relative mix of expertise and politics normally found in the decisions and decision-making processes in that policy area? Second, are the politics of that policy area generally open or closed? The answers to those questions, as you no doubt surmised from the title of this section of the chapter, are driven by the complexity and the controversy of the policy area in question. Before we get to that discussion, however, we need to get a better handle on what we mean by the politics/expertise mix in a policy area as well as what we mean by open and closed politics.

Any decision made in government is going to be based in part on calculations grounded in expert knowledge of the subject at hand, and in part on calculations grounded in the politics of that subject. The question remains, however, how much of each will enter the formula? Will it be mostly expertise tempered with a little politics to make the decision palatable? Or will it be mostly politics with a little expertise spread on as a kind of veneer to make it respectable? Or will it be sort of a 50/50 mix of the two? To be sure, we can never be all that precise about the mix. There is no decision-making litmus paper to turn red or blue to guide us. Still, if we think of a continuum from decisions that appear to be mostly grounded in expert knowledge to those that appear to be mostly grounded in politics, we can locate most policy areas on that continuum—more often than not toward one end or the other—and which end of that continuum a policy area occupies will go a long way toward defining the nature of the politics that will prevail as the decisions in that policy area get made.

If we think of the political calculations that enter into a policy decision as an assessment by decision makers of how this decision will be greeted by those who will know and care about it, then from that decision maker's perspective, the politics of the question at hand is defined by two things. First comes the number and range of people likely to know and care about decisions made in this policy area. Second comes the question of what are the keys to access—the opportunity to have one's reactions taken into account—in that particular issue area. Now it is time to take those two questions—how many folks are likely to want to be heard on a set of questions and what resources do they need to make themselves heard—and put them in the framework of open and closed politics I slipped into the opening of this discussion.

Start with thing one, that is, with the question of how many people are going to want to be counted as decisions are made in a particular policy area. The higher the number and broader the range of people who could be considered likely to know and care, of course, the more open the politics of that issue area, just as the lower the number and narrower the range, the more closed the politics. The number and range of people likely to know and care about public policy decisions in any area are never extremely high, to be sure, but it seems clear enough that for some issue areas—welfare, social security, health care, and taxes, to name a few—the number and range are going to be a lot higher than they will for others—say rules governing the accounting industry, agricultural marketing orders, or approval of the latest merger in the office equipment industry. As we will see shortly, if those who know and care about an issue area are split into opposing camps and care deeply about the issues in question, we will tend to see a more open politics even if the numbers involved are relatively small. For now, however, let's stick to the number and the range of those who are likely to react to a particular decision or set of decisions.

Now let's turn to thing two. Access to a system of open politics is almost exclusively political, that is, depends on clearly and obviously political resources, while access to a closed politics depends on a less obvious mix of political and expert resources. In somewhat more concrete terms, in some issue areas, if a politician, a citizen, or a group of citizens wants to be sure that his/her/its reaction to a particular decision about to be made gets factored into the making of that decision, the process of persuasion is grounded almost completely in political factors, that is, in the currency of American politics, money, and votes. The focus is on the next congressional committee hearing, the next budget, the next executive order, the next election, and how the money and votes available to this particular politician, citizen, or group will affect that next hearing, budget, executive order, or election, and how that effect will trickle down to this particular decision maker. In other issue areas, however, the process of persuading a decision maker to factor someone's reaction to his or her decision into the process of making it requires that in addition to demonstrating the possession of political resources, a politician, citizen, or group be able to demonstrate expert resources as well. As we will see later in this chapter and in others, separating expertise and politics is not always all that easy, even for the experts and politicians involved. At this point all we are saying is this: in some issue areas it seems that the resources needed for participation are overwhelmingly political, while in others those resources seem to be a combination of political and expert.

If thing one and thing two haven't made themselves quite as clear to you as they had hoped they would, consider one group trying to make itself heard in two different issue areas. Area one: welfare. Area two: regulations governing the accounting industry. Political clout will be needed in both areas, but expert knowledge, or at least the ability to speak the insider's language, is going to play a far larger role in gaining access to area two than to area one.

As with the expertise/politics mix, the types of politics that surround various issue areas almost certainly constitute a continuum from open to closed, but I think we will find that most issue areas tend toward one end of that continuum or the other, and in any case, as with the discussion of the expertise/politics mix, the discussion of the impact of open and closed politics on the politics of policy areas only becomes manageable if we use the admittedly oversimplified dichotomy of open and closed rather than the almost certainly more accurate notion of the continuum.

As I said earlier on, I believe that the expertise/politics mix found in a policy area's decision processes and the open or closed nature of its politics are driven by the complexity and controversy of the subject matter in that policy area. Actually, as I hinted, it is the interaction between the complexity and controversy of a policy area's subject matter, but we need to look at the independent impact of each before we put them in intellectual play together. So let's start by looking at the impact of controversy on these two defining characteristics of the politics of policy areas.

Controversy and the Politics of Public Policy Making

We've all heard the term "hot-button issues," and we all know that it was coined because some issues just generate more political heat than do others. If for some odd reason you are interested in starting a political argument, you know you would have better luck by staking out a position on gun control, welfare policy, or prayer in public schools than you would by vigorously attacking—or defending, for that matter—the latest Agricultural Marketing Service marketing order for avocados or the Office of Thrift Supervision's decision to change reporting requirements for savings and loan institutions.

Though it may seem counterintuitive at first, given the impression that many people seem to have of politicians as risk-averse folks who look for "mom and apple pie" issues that will shelter them from having to take stands on "the really important stuff," the controversy of a subject matter has so much impact on the politics of a particular policy area precisely because that controversy attracts politicians to it. Three reasons, but before we get to them, a clarifying note on controversy.

When we think of controversy in politics, we normally think of issues that attract widespread attention among a fairly broad cross section of us and on which we have definitely diverging views. Hence my suggestion that if you really do want to start a political argument, gun control, welfare, and school prayer would be good bets to get something going. But an issue can have the kind of controversy that will have a significant impact on the politics of an issue area without ever making the radar screen of most of us. All that is needed for controversy that will attract politicians and leave its mark on the policy process is two sides, each willing to engage in some sort of political combat for its own view of how the issue ought to be resolved. Most Americans have probably given only passing thought to the question of whether or not we ought to place greater restrictions on the rights of employers to hire replacement workers when their regular workers go on strike, and there is a very good chance that we have given no thought at all as to what those restrictions might be. For the leaders of the labor movement and for the men and women who run corporate America, however, feelings on that issue run high, the sides are clearly drawn, and specific policy positions are staked out. The lack of general public concern notwithstanding, that's plenty of controversy to leave its mark on labor relations policies and on the processes by which they are made.

Now let's return to those controversy-seeking politicians. As I said a moment ago, there are three reasons that politicians get interested in these issues. First of all, people become politicians—go into government or enter public service, if you prefer—for a variety of reasons, but for a great many of them, having an impact on what the government does about a certain set of issues is somewhere on that list of motivating factors. The story that Tom DeLay (R-TX) first entered politics to get even with the Environmental Protection Agency for what he considered too vigorous enforcement of its regulations against his pest control firm may well be apocryphal, but issues do bring people into politics, and controversial issues seem more likely to have sparked someone's interest in politics than do non-controversial issues. If a particular issue is what brought someone to politics in the first place, that issue is likely to remain on that individual's agenda.

Second, leaving the judges aside—they will get their due in the final section of the book—the members of the constitutional government are in a fundamental sense representatives. They clearly have some considerable leeway in deciding exactly whom they will represent, but representatives they are, they know it, and they know that people most want representation on the issues they care the most about, and in a good many cases those issues are tinged with controversy.

Finally, and probably most important of all, the more controversial an issue area the more it presents politicians with opportunities and dangers. Any issue with a proven track record of moving votes and campaign dollars is an issue that politicians cannot afford to ignore. In the best of circumstances, it gives them a chance to latch onto something that might be used to advance a career. In the worst of circumstances, it forces them to fend off something that might destroy a career. Whether trying to move a career forward or keep it alive, the results are the same. The politician has to make sure that he or she has some impact on the decisions to be reached in this kind of policy area, and that means paying attention to what the policy specialists working in that area are up to and trying to exercise some influence over the decisions those specialists reach.

So, stereotypes of issue-evading politicians notwithstanding, controversy does bring politicians to an issue area, and that inevitably means a more open politics in that area. A lot of politicians, representing numerous and competing interests— including their own—will mean a large and varied group demanding that their preferences be taken into account, and a politics in which political resources will trump expert resources in a fairly open and unashamed way when it comes to deciding which voices will actually be heard.

As I noted earlier, some issues are highly controversial even though there isn't widespread public interest in them. Most union-management issues stir bitter debate in union halls and corporate boardrooms, but little concern at all among the vast numbers of Americans who have never entered either sanctuary. The same might be said of a good many environmental issues, that is that they stir incredible emotions in the environmental community and among the business owners or land users frustrated by that environmental community's demands, even as a great many of us remain blissfully unaware of most of the confrontations over this wilderness trail, that threatened species, or the long-term possibility that such and such will happen if we don't mend our ways. Does the politics of such issues deserve to be called open? Clearly such areas do not normally attract lots of politicians and lots of groups. Numbers and variety are not there. But the debate is shrill, and decision makers know there is no escape from the need to take account of the reactions of those engaged in it.

Beyond that, the politics of such issues are never all that far from being opened up. In such situations, with two sides battling it out over something each considers high stakes, there is always a strong temptation for the side that perceives itself to be losing to try to expand the conflict, that is, to call for reinforcements, even if those reinforcements come from way outside the normal confines of the arena. Consider the tremendous amount of energy expended in response to the Federal Communications Commission decision in early June of 2003 to liberalize its media ownership rules. There had been plenty of insider debate, with some general media attention as befits an issue that involves the media itself, but once the decision was made, the reaction was swift and loud and, more to the point in this context, it came from some unusual quarters. It doesn't seem too likely that the National Rifle Association, the National Organization for Women, the Consumer's Union, and the United States Conference of Catholic

Bishops would have considered themselves insiders on a debate about media ownership. It doesn't seem too likely they would have considered themselves candidates for cooperation on a public policy issue. Yet they were part of an "unusually broad coalition" that weighed in on the issue in Congress after the FCC decision.[46] It may close again, but the politics of that issue opened, and it was controversy—a long-standing battle among media insiders, some of whom sought outside help when they lost at the commission—that opened it.[47]

A high level of controversy in an issue area will also tend to tip the expertise/politics mix toward politics. It will have that impact in two interrelated ways. First, of course, by bringing more politicians into the mix, controversy is going to push the decision-making system more toward political factors and forces. Politicians come to these issue areas, after all, as representatives and as advocates, that is, as people with a cause to push—even if the cause is their own careers—and they are going to play to their strengths. Their strengths, obviously, lie in politics, so they are going to push hard to emphasize political concerns rather than expert ones. The not-very-well-hidden secret of American policy making lies in the fact that politics can almost always prevail if the politicians are determined enough to make it happen. In an appearance on NBC's *Meet the Press* in June 2003, retired General Wesley Clark informed us that Vice President Dick Cheney made a number of visits to CIA headquarters in Langley, Virginia, during late 2001 and 2002 to see how the intelligence gathering was going on the threat posed to the United States by Iraq.[48] That sounds like a politician pretty determined to make sure that politics—the reaction of the VP and those he represented to the decisions to be reached—would get the fullest possible consideration. At least in the eyes of many, he was quite successful.

Second, and as I said distinctly interrelated, is the tendency of politicians to shift the rhetoric or terms of debate from the expert to the political. Politicians will learn some of the specialized language of any policy area they spend much time working on. Former Vice President Al Gore, for example, is said to have first won his reputation for intellectual firepower by becoming fluent in the jargon-filled and decidedly esoteric language of national defense strategy. But when it comes to the highly controversial and attention-getting issues, politicians will tend to stick with the kind of language that will play to the constituencies they are choosing to represent on this particular issue, and that is not going to be the language of that issue area's experts. By framing the terms of the debate, they can at least partially frame the debate itself, and that, in turn, can have a real impact on the kinds of arguments that will be considered relevant to that debate. The expertise/politics mix is bound to be different—more politics, less expertise—as a result of that shift. Consider President George W. Bush's 2005 offensive to change the Social Security System. Words like crisis, or exhausted and bankrupt, are not the terms in which actuaries discuss the long-term fiscal health of that program. But the President did, and the debate shifted. (For those of you who pay close attention to environmental issues and are used to lots of references to "science" in those debates, hang in there. We'll see how that factors in a bit later in the chapter.)

Some issue areas, as we've said, aren't characterized by much in the way of public controversy. Consequently, these are generally not the kinds of issues that drew people to politics or that provide opportunities or present dangers for the political careers of the vast majority of the men and women of the constitutional government. So they leave them alone. To be sure, these issues do attract the attention of a few politicians and a fraction of the citizenry. We'll get to that in the next three chapters. What is important here is the fact that these issues don't attract widespread attention in the political community and, therefore, can be said to have closed political systems. The numbers of participants in these systems are small, the range is narrow, and the currency of the system mixes political resources with expert resources in proportions that not even the insiders can always calculate. Again, as we will see in the next three chapters, politics enters into the mix to a degree that is rarely admitted and not always understood by system insiders. But for now it is fair to say that when an issue area is not surrounded by controversy, its politics are going to be closed both in terms of the number and range of participants and in terms of what it takes—or at least appears to take—to become an insider and to argue one's case once inside.

A lack of controversy will also have its effect on the expertise/politics mix, of course. Obviously any group of policy insiders that believes that expertise is currency on a par with politics in its deliberations is going to be convinced that in its little corner of the world the expertise/politics mix is definitely weighted in favor of expertise. With a lack of controversy preventing a great deal of outside scrutiny of their activities, they are generally able to convince themselves that the outside world shares that assessment. As long as they can continue to escape that outside scrutiny, belief can become reality and the expertise/politics mix "really will" tip in favor of expertise.

Other things being equal, issue areas that are characterized by a great deal of controversy are also characterized by open politics and a reduced emphasis on expertise. A relatively large and varied set of citizens and politicians will demand to have their views taken into account as decisions are made about such questions, and they will amass and use the political resources necessary to make their demands felt. On the opposite end of the spectrum, again other things being equal, there are issue areas that are characterized by very little controversy, and as a result, by a closed politics and an increased emphasis on expertise. A relatively small and homogeneous set of citizens and politicians will demand to have their views taken into account as decisions are made about such questions, and they will amass and use the political and expert resources to make their demands felt.

But other things are not always equal. Indeed, as I said at the beginning of this chapter, the contours of the political environment of any particular agency are going to be a product of two aspects of the issues with which that agency must deal. We've talked about controversy. It's time to talk about complexity.

Complexity and the Politics of Public Policy Making

Just as issues and issue areas vary dramatically in terms of the controversy that surrounds them, they vary in terms of the extent to which we as citizens view them as the primary province of experts, that is, as issues that can be addressed only by people who, in the words of Francis Rourke, are in "possession of a highly technical body of knowledge that the layman cannot readily master."[49] Since we see ourselves as laymen with respect to these issues, we prefer to stay out of the game. How many of us would really feel comfortable trying to answer the question of whether we need new fuel-tank safety regulations for commercial airliners? How about deciding if the alternatives to pasteurization offered by some New England cider producers would "protect the public health" while preserving that great "fresh cider taste"? Or maybe setting the rules for the review of applications to market new medications in the United States?

The list could go on. The point is this. Some issues just seem to most of us to be beyond our grasp, and when we come to that conclusion we tend to shy away from them. When most of us shy away from an issue, the politics of that issue ends up closed and the mix between expertise and politics normally found in resolving the questions surrounding the issue tends to emphasize expertise. The reasons are simple enough. If most citizens and most politicians don't want to become involved with a particular issue area, the resulting politics will be confined to those who do, and that will be a fairly small and fairly narrow segment of the population who will, as we saw when we discussed the impact of a lack of controversy, emphasize expertise—or what they think of as expertise—in their internal deliberations and especially in whatever relations they may have with the outside political world.

In sharp contrast to the issues we tend to feel might be a little beyond our comprehension, however, are those we strongly believe are matters not of expertise but of common sense and moral values. We might be quite unwilling to take on fuel-tank safety or drug approval processes, but we would be more than ready to take on welfare reform, rules for the possession and use of firearms, or guidelines for religious expression in public schools. No experts need apply. Indeed, could most of us agree on what would constitute expertise on issues like welfare reform, gun control, and religious expression in public schools, let alone on who possessed that expertise?

If an issue is widely perceived as one that can be handled by applying common sense and moral values, the politics of that issue is likely to be wide open. By definition, no citizen or politician would feel he or she didn't know enough to become involved. Interest—more properly the lack of interest—would be the only barrier to their involvement. Not surprisingly, the expertise/politics mix would emphasize politics. Those citizens and politicians who became involved in arguing these issues would insist on arguing them in the rhetoric of common sense and moral values—their own version of same, but common sense and moral values—and no amount of effort by experts to shift to a rhetoric of expertise would work. After all, by definition, no experts are needed. Maybe no experts even exist. It is hard for me to imagine what sorts of credentials would be expected of the group of experts gathered together to discuss much tighter controls on assault weapons, but it is easy for me to imagine the response to their expert ruminations among gun control advocates and gun control opponents alike.

Again, as I pointed out at the start of this section on how the complexity of an issue affects the politics of a particular policy area: as a people, we *see* some issues as pretty much out of our league. The choice of words here is deliberate, and it is important to remember as we complete the chapter that we are dealing with people's perceptions. In the words of Francis Rourke quoted earlier in the chapter,

"All administrative agencies have some expertise in the functions they perform, but not all bureaucratic skills exact equal deference from the community."[50] I've never met a chemist who ever faced an angry student who wanted to know how he could possibly have gotten a D in organic chemistry when organic chemistry is nothing but common sense. I have, however, met an exceptionally talented and well-trained sociologist who heard that assertion from a student of his about that student's grade in social psychology. Woody's reply? "How does it feel to get a D in common sense?" Lest you think that only college students would act this way, I will never forget the spectacle of two senators at a committee hearing on the balanced budget amendment lecturing two of the nation's most prominent economists on why their opposition to the amendment didn't make sense. The point is this. It is not the training, background, or credentials of the people who claim to be experts in a subject. It is us and whether or not we give any credence to the claim.

We see issues differently. Some we see as pretty much beyond the understanding of the uninitiated. Others we see as pretty much within the grasp of anyone willing to think about them for a minute or two. As a former student of mine once put it, "People are always saying it doesn't take a rocket scientist to [whatever]. Nobody ever says it doesn't take a political scientist to." Alas, no one seems to think it takes a political scientist to do much of anything.

All other things being equal, if we think an issue does require a rocket scientist—or whatever type of expert we recognize as appropriate for the issue at hand—then we will be far more likely, of course, to defer to experts, and that means that the expertise/politics mix will lean a bit more toward expertise, and in turn, that the politics that will enter into decision making will be closed. If, on the other hand, all other things being equal, we think of an issue as within the range of everybody's understanding, we will have little respect for experts, and that will mean an expertise/politics mix with a bigger dose of politics and a strong tendency toward open politics, since no one will feel intimidated by the subject matter at hand and any of us can believe that his or her opinion is informed and ought to count just as much as anyone else's.

But, and you knew this was coming, all other things are not equal. There is controversy to consider. Of course, we already considered it. That's why it is finally time to put both complexity and controversy into the mix together.

Controversy and Complexity Interact

Before we look at how controversy and complexity interact, let's take a minute to summarize the independent impact of each.

Some issues generate a lot of controversy. Some don't. Controversy brings with it citizens and politicians demanding that their preferences on the issue in question be taken into account by agency decision makers. The result is a political system with a large and varied set of participants who get their seats at the table mostly with political resources, a rhetoric that is generally more political than expert and a decision-making system that takes account of both expert knowledge and political clout but tends to emphasize the latter at the expense of the former more often than not. The lack of controversy has pretty much the opposite effect, that is, leads toward a political system with a narrow and homogeneous set of participants, a rhetoric that is generally more expert than political, and a decision-making system that takes into account both expert knowledge and political clout but emphasizes the former as strongly as it can.

Likewise, some issues are seen as complex matters best left to experts. Some are not. Complexity seems to reduce the number and narrow the range of citizens and politicians anxious to weigh in on an issue, resulting in a political system with a limited set of participants who get their seats at the table with a combination of expert and political resources, a rhetoric that is decidedly expert, and a decision-making system that does take account of both expert knowledge and political clout but makes a concerted effort to convince itself and the outside world that it is expertise that really dominates the system. A lack of complexity—maybe better, a perception that an issue is one of values and common sense—will increase the number and broaden the range of citizens and politicians who want to make their views felt, leading to a political system with a large number and broad range of participants, a rhetoric that is decidedly political—even though its specific terms are often those more likely found in moral arguments—and a decision-making system that will pay mostly lip service to expert knowledge while emphasizing politics, again, politics couched in the language of moral argument.

So, finally, how do they interact? To no one's surprise, they can interact in one of two ways. They can reinforce each other, or they can run counter to each other.

Controversy and Complexity in Concert

As we've noted repeatedly, if an issue is surrounded by controversy, its politics will be open. There will be a number of participants representing a variety of often conflicting viewpoints, the rhetoric of debate will contain a heavy dose of the political, and the expertise/politics mix in the decision-making system will emphasize politics. That is precisely what will happen, of course, if an issue is perceived as one lacking in complexity, that is, a matter of common sense and moral values. So if an issue is both, that is, steeped in controversy and seen as the province of any of us, there will be two powerful forces pushing toward an open system with politics as its driving force. Citizens and politicians will insist on being heard—and responded to—and the debate will be conducted in political terms and the decision-making system organized around political concerns. Should an agency's policy specialists attempt to regain control by trying to shift the rhetoric of the debate to their own specialized language or asserting the need for their expertise, they would almost certainly be greeted with a response that would border on incredulity. This issue is, after all, a matter of common sense and moral values. Expertise is an alien idea, and conclusions are simply opinions, and all opinions are created equal.

This is almost certainly the kind of political environment that faces those who work in policy areas like welfare, corrections, civil rights, or education. Education policy makers can never be entirely certain when they will find themselves in a debate over creationism, intelligent design, bilingualism, etc., but they can be pretty certain that when they do, those who have forced the debate will demand that it take place in their language, not the language of "the educationists," and that no pile of studies done by education school faculties from around the country will be given so much as a cursory look by the men and women who have demanded that their views on education take precedence over those of the policy makers. Likewise, civil rights policy makers might well want to debate the issues involved in job discrimination in carefully framed terms, drawing on an extensive body of research by sociologists and psychologists, and an equally extensive body of court decisions, but they would almost certainly be forced to defend their policies in very different terms on what must sometimes seem almost like foreign turf.

At the opposite end of the spectrum would be an issue low in controversy but high in complexity. With little controversy, most citizens would show no interest and most politicians would follow suit. There would be interested citizens and politicians, of course, and they would want to have their opinions count, so they would become part of the closed politics that would inevitably surround such an issue. They would gladly learn the language and agree that only experts— they are now magically included in that special group—should be involved in making decisions in this little corner of the world. The perception that this was an issue suitable only for expert resolution, of course, would reinforce that tendency toward closed politics, debate conducted in the arcane language of a particular policy specialty, and a decision-making system that puts experts first, or at least does a good job of appearing to put experts first.

Hugh Heclo perfectly captured the dynamic of such policy-making systems twenty-five years ago when he argued that, on a wide range of issues, policy makers had "established a common language for discussing the issues, a mutually familiar rhetoric of argumentation . . . [that became a shared] analytic repertoire for coping with the issues."[51] So powerful was this common language, grammar, and repertoire, according to Heclo, that even in the face of real policy disagreement, there was understanding and mutual respect.[52]

Those who regulate airline safety or the New York Stock Exchange almost certainly find themselves in this sort of political environment. The majority of us may fly, and the majority of us may own stock, but the vast majority of us don't really feel that we understand the business of regulating either flying or exchanging stocks, and it takes something extraordinary to get us to even pay attention to the activities of the men and women who are engaged in that regulating. There may be an occasional battle royal inside the closed political system that regulates airlines, or in the system that regulates the stock exchange. But the battle will be conducted in the language of the expert, the participants will be drastically limited, and most of the public and most of our representatives will be only dimly aware that the battle ever took place, let alone of who won.

Controversy and Complexity at Odds

Again, with issues surrounded by controversy, we expect to find an open political system, one with numerous participants, a rhetoric with more than a hint of politics, and a decision-making system that emphasizes politics every bit as much as it does expertise. But what if such an issue is also generally seen as highly complex? What if there is substantial disagreement among us as to what we ought to do about an issue, but fairly widespread agreement that the path to the answer probably goes through some data and concepts that most of us just don't quite get?

If we enter an area like environmental policy making, we see precisely what happens when controversy and complexity "can't play nicely together." Consider the Environmental Protection Agency and its efforts to regulate the use of a widely used pesticide called Atrazine. Atrazine's manufacturer, Syngenta AG, based in Switzerland, wants rules that will permit the continued widespread use of the pesticide. So do a lot of the farmers who use it to kill weeds in cornfields, and even the homeowners who want to use it to kill weeds in their lawns. A number of environmental interest groups want it banned because of the harm they believe it does to the ground, the groundwater, and even to animals, including us. There is plenty of controversy, but nobody thinks the decision about Atrazine is one to be made by applying common sense and moral values. How, for example, applying common sense and moral values, would you evaluate the results of the studies of Dr. Tyrone B. Hayes, who found serious abnormalities in male frogs exposed to Atrazine, or those of Atrazine's manufacturer purporting to show that Dr. Hayes's research is really inconclusive and ought not to be the definitive word on the subject? How would you factor in the high incidence of prostate cancer among workers in the factory producing Atrazine, the complaints of the chief of the environmental bureau of the New York State Office of the Attorney General, or the charges of "junk science" leveled by the Natural Resources Defense Council—or the similar countercharges fired back by Syngenta AG?[53]

You can substitute off-road diesel rules, snowmobile pollution rules, smokestack emission rules, and a host of other critical decisions that have faced the EPA in the last decade or will face it in the next, and you would find precisely the same kind of situation. Plenty of controversy and a recognition that expert knowledge has to play a key role in sorting out the issue. Indeed, you can substitute policy areas within the purview of the Forest Service, Soil Conservation Service, Park Service, Occupational Safety and Health Administration, and a host of other agency names for those that face the Environmental Protection Agency and find, once more, issues of great controversy and immense complexity.

What sort of political environment can such agencies expect as they deal with one issue like this after another? Controversy would normally lead to an open environment with an emphasis on politics more than on expertise, while complexity would normally lead to the opposite. The environment can't be both open and closed, both political and expert. Or can it?

By definition, with a high level of controversy there will be at least two sets of citizens with opposite viewpoints determined to make those viewpoints felt. Consequently, there will be politicians to represent those viewpoints and they will want to shift the terms of debate and the nature of the decision-making process from the expert to the political. But science—broadly conceived in this context—is stubborn and most of these issues cannot be discussed in a vocabulary that disregards that science. In such environments we will almost certainly see two things going on simultaneously.

First of all, we will see what might be called "dueling experts." Syngenta AG could not simply assert its political power. It could not say we have economic clout, we contribute to campaigns, American farmers have considerable political influence themselves, and we are just going to bury you politically. Nor could it make an appeal to common sense or moral values. It had to produce "science" to counter Dr. Hayes's "science." There may be times when the "dueling experts" can reasonably be accused of molding the "science" in question to fit the positions they want to take. The point remains the same. The debate will be strongly flavored by the rhetoric of expertise even if the experts themselves have trouble drawing the line between their expert opinions and their deeply held beliefs.

Second, politics, in the form of strongly held preferences grounded in some unknown combination of self-interest and true belief, will find its way into the decision-making calculus. Sometimes it will be camouflaged in the exchanges between the experts, but many times it will be pretty plain to all concerned, even if not exactly openly admitted by the participants. Take the EPA again, only this time shift from Atrazine to the broader—and possibly even more frightening—question of climate change.

In May 2002, the State Department, with White House approval, submitted a climate report to the United Nations. The report cited a good bit of data to suggest that climate change was a serious problem and we were contributing a great deal to that change. About a month later, the President dismissed the report as "put out by the bureaucracy," and a new version was done and circulated.[54] That second version stressed the lack of scientific certainty about climate change. That wasn't quite enough for the President and his people, however, so, for the first time in six years, the Environmental Protection Agency's 2002 version of its annual report on air pollution did not include a chapter on global warming.[55] The White House must have liked the result. A relatively long section on the risks from rising global temperatures that was included in the EPA-prepared draft of a special study on the state of the environment, commissioned by then Administrator Christine Todd Whitman back in 2001, was pulled by the White House and replaced by what *New York Times* environmental reporters Andrew Revkin and Katharine Seelye described as "a few noncommittal paragraphs."[56]

In the end, agencies who must face a set of issues steeped in controversy and yet seen by most of us as highly complex face a political environment that can only be described as complicated and volatile. Expertise and politics mix—sometimes in ways that seem reminiscent of the mixing of oil and water—and policy decisions get hammered out. Though the EPA's 2003 state of the environment report isn't exactly a policy decision, it almost certainly gives us some insight into policy decisions yet to come with respect to the problem of global warming, and more to the point, provides a prototypical example of the interplay of expertise and politics as a decision gets made in a political environment created by high levels of controversy combined with high levels of complexity. So let's consider it just a bit further.

The section of the draft report that so offended the White House had included references to two earlier studies, one from 1999 "showing that global temperatures had risen sharply in the previous decade compared with the last 1,000 years . . . [and another] about the likely human contribution to warming from a

2001 report on climate by the National Research Council."[57] In their place, the White House included a reference to a more recent study—one financed in part by the American Petroleum Institute—that questioned both findings. The President and his people did not, in other words, assert their election mandate, the economic importance to American industry of permitting it to continue doing business as usual, or the glories of unfettered capitalism. They felt constrained to come back with some sort of science at least connected to the issues involved. They would have felt no such pressure on a report dealing with affirmative action, the success of the Welfare Reform Act of 1996, family planning efforts in Africa, or the importance of faith-based initiatives.

And what was the reaction outside the White House? Jeremy Symons, a climate policy expert for the National Wildlife Federation, was straightforward and straightforwardly critical. His comment: "Political staff are becoming increasingly bold in forcing agency officials to endorse *junk science*"[58] (italics mine). But in many ways it is the response of the EPA professionals in charge of the preparation of the study that is the most interesting. Rather than accept the White House version of the climate change section of the report complete with its reference to the American Petroleum Institute funded study, they proposed the elimination of the whole section. Their reasoning, according to Andrew Revkin and Katharine Seelye: they wanted to "avoid criticism that they were selectively filtering science to suit policy."[59] To the policy specialists at any agency, there may not be any more devastating charge.

As it turns out, in policy areas characterized by high controversy and high complexity, there is no relatively consistent bottom line as there is in areas characterized by high controversy and low complexity or low controversy and high complexity. It is the expertise of the policy specialists at the agencies working on these high-controversy/high-complexity issues—and that of their fellow experts on the outside—that raises these issues in the first place, and it is their expertise that frames the terms of the debate. But once the issues themselves are raised, politics comes into play and comes into play in the most forceful ways. Politicians entering these issue areas must accommodate to the experts for whom these issues are the stuff of their professional lives—something they would not have to do if they were entering an issue of high controversy and low complexity— but to accommodate is not to surrender. The politicians will leave their mark. The experts will leave theirs. The resulting baby may not look much like either parent.

Just as we find issues that are characterized by high controversy and high complexity, we find issues that exhibit low controversy and low complexity. It is hard to imagine much in the way of controversy about the question of the need to feed the men and women stationed on America's military bases around the world. Their families, too. So, headquartered at 1300 "E" Avenue in Fort Lee, Virginia, complete with a Director and two Executive Directors, is the Defense Commissary Agency.[60] There probably wouldn't be too many Americans who would quarrel with DeCa's—that's what it calls itself in its publications—mission of "providing an efficient and effective worldwide system of commissaries for reselling groceries and household supplies at low, practical prices (consistent with quality) to members of the military services, their families, and other authorized patrons."[61] While the knowledge to accomplish that worthy goal would probably not be subsumed by the notion of common sense and moral values, it also probably wouldn't be put on a plane with the knowledge needed to operate the nation's air traffic control system, approve new prescription drugs, or guarantee an adequate supply of safe drinking water. In more straightforward terms, DeCa seems more or less like Safeway, and while running a Safeway—or a whole bunch of Safeways—requires some business sense and some experience in the grocery business, it isn't, as we say, "rocket science." At least we don't see it as such, even if the top executives at Safeway are handsomely compensated for what they know and do.

Once more, what kind of political environment will an agency like DeCa face? (Yes, there are others. Just look at the U.S. Government Manual. You'll recognize them.) Low controversy should lead to a closed political environment in which the handful of citizens and politicians who know and care about the issues at hand work together with the policy specialists at the agency to create an environment all of them believe is a place in which experts use their knowledge to make sound policy, and politics takes its proper place at the back of the bus. On the other hand, low complexity would mean an open political environment with no particular respect for expert knowledge and an emphasis on political resources as the key to resolving disputes over the proper course of policy.

The result of the clash, it turns out, is very different from the train wreck that so often occurs when high complexity collides with high controversy. First of all, of course, there will be no "dueling experts." There isn't enough controversy to spark a duel, and the only people who respect these insiders as experts are the insiders themselves. Second, there will be no headlines resulting from the clash of politics and science. In fact, except under the most extraordinary of circumstances, there will be no headlines at all. I know that DeCa exists only because I searched the Government Manual for an example I could use to discuss the political environments of agencies that deal with low-controversy/low-complexity issues. There were no *New York Times* articles about White House censorship of major DeCa reports, or quotes from outside experts attacking political leaders for forcing "junk science" on DeCa's Director and his two Executive Directors.

What there will be, it seems, is a closed political system that will operate as if it were a collection of subject-matter experts who really did deserve to be on a plane with those of the agencies everyone recognizes as composed of "rocket scientists." There is a difference, of course, and that difference comes from the fact that these experts aren't seen as such by the society as a whole. They are allowed to operate as if they were "rocket science" type experts because the issues they deal with exhibit no real controversy, not because we accept their self-designation as experts. In other words, it is our complete lack of interest in, and attention to, the issues these agencies deal with that protects them from outsiders and allows them to function in a manner that mimics the functioning of the low-controversy/high-complexity agencies they want to believe they are. Enter a scandal, however, and these agencies quickly find that their political environment was built of straw, and it doesn't take too many political wolves too many huffs and puffs to blow it down.

Controversy and Complexity: Some Complications

By speaking of issues as either high or low in controversy, and high or low in complexity, without ever directly admitting it, I have painted a picture of four types of political environments. Unfortunately, there are two things wrong with this picture.

First, as I said when I introduced the notion that political environments are largely structured by the interaction of controversy and complexity, those two dimensions of any issue probably vary along continua from very high to very low or, at the very least, have a number of gradations along the way from high to low. In other words, it's a simplified picture. But it is still a useful picture. It gives you, in a sense, a look at the four "pure" types. You can use them to think about other types.

Policy areas, for example, that are seen as high in complexity but generate moderate rather than high or low controversy will be characterized by politics somewhere in between the high-complexity/low-controversy politics we see in areas like airline safety, and the high-complexity/high-controversy politics we see in areas like environmental policy. Experts will create a rhetoric, and it will be the rhetoric of the debate. There will probably be fewer duels among them—though there will definitely be some such confrontations—and politics will play a definite role, just not as prominent a role as it plays in the high-controversy issues. Policy areas in which issues are moderate in complexity but high in controversy will likely be the same. Remember, each policy area has a politics that is unique. But if you can figure out how much controversy is associated with the issues involved in that policy area and figure out how the public tends to view the complexity of those issues, you can begin to sketch the outlines of the politics of that area. To paint the rest of the picture, you have to find out just exactly who has put themselves in that picture. That you have to do one policy area at a time.

Second, issues change. Once in a great while they change in terms of the public's perception of the complexity of the issue, but far more often, of course, they change in terms of the controversy that surrounds them. When this kind of change occurs, the politics of that policy area changes with it.

The Atomic Energy Commission quietly morphed into the Nuclear Regulatory Commission (NRC), and hardly any outsiders noticed. Some people opposed the growth of nuclear power, but that group was small and very definitely marginalized by everything from their protest tactics, the names of their organizations—the Abalone Alliance and the Clamshell Alliance were two of the most vocal—and even their image as part of what my dad's generation called "the sandals and long hair crowd." Besides, the issue of the government's role in regulating the industry was considered one of considerable complexity best left to experts. Then came Three Mile Island, and all of a sudden concerns about nuclear power were mainstream and legitimate and the Nuclear Regulatory Commission found itself in a much more open and contentious political environment in which the commission's experts were frequently involved in scientific shootouts with experts representing very different viewpoints. As the vision of the Three Mile Island containment building faded from public memory and the Reagan administration came in determined to license more plants, the NRC's political environment began to change back, though thanks to Ralph Nader's creation of something called Critical Mass, that environment never quite returned to what its insiders would no doubt have referred to as "the good old days."[62]

It appears that that very same scenario may well have played out around the Securities and Exchange Commission with the Enron and WorldCom meltdowns followed by a summer—the summer of 2002—of frantic rhetoric, some genuine efforts at reform, some actual window-dressing reforms, and a return to something that approximated business as usual by the summer of 2003.[63] If they ever thought about it, the policy specialists at the NRC might well envy those at the Securities and Exchange Commission.

POLICY AREAS AND AGENCY POWER

I can't imagine that it surprises any of you that I am about to argue that these two key differences in the politics of different policy areas have their fallout for the power of the agencies operating in those areas. Indeed, I doubt that the contours of that argument are going to surprise any of you either. That is, agencies operating in policy areas in which the expertise/politics mix tips toward expertise—or, at least, toward the insiders' view of expertise—are going to be more powerful than are agencies operating in policy areas in which the mix clearly tips toward politics, just as agencies operating in policy areas characterized by closed politics are going to find themselves better able to influence policy decisions than are those agencies operating in areas characterized by open politics. Of course, since both of these aspects of a policy area are determined by the interaction of the controversy and complexity of the policy area itself, we can go straight to the question of the relative power of agencies in the four types of policy areas discussed earlier.

Before we do, however, recall from early in the chapter that, following the lead of Francis Rourke, scholars of bureaucracy have long asserted that agencies derive power from their knowledge and from outside political support, and then face certain constraints on using that power. Much of the time such constraints come in the form of the power that can be exercised by other participants in the policy process, but other times constraints operate to prevent agencies from even acquiring power in the first place.

Controversy and Complexity in Concert: The Strongest and the Weakest

Agencies operating in policy areas characterized by a high level of perceived complexity and a low level of controversy, of course, are the strongest agencies around. They have a relatively easy time gathering the resources that translate into power, and though no agency's power is unchecked, the constraints they face often require nothing more than more or less painless compromise.

Let's start with the question of acquiring the resources of power. First, of course, by definition the expertise these agencies bring to the table gets considerable respect from the others seated at that table. That's what we mean when we say there is a high level of perceived complexity. Beyond that, with a low level of controversy, few individuals or groups will expect to be part of the decision-making system, and those that do will do so because of some long-standing interest in the issues, generally speaking an interest driven by a real stake in those issues. Such people are likely to be conversant with the vocabulary in which experts discuss these sorts of questions, and while they may have occasional policy disagreements, they are, as Heclo said, very likely to be on the same page.[64] Cultivating clientele support in such an environment should be easy enough, and since these are precisely the kinds of policy areas dominated by House and Senate subcommittees—who themselves are well acquainted with these agency clientele groups—it should be easy enough to cultivate congressional support as well. I do not mean to imply that agencies operating in low-controversy/high-complexity environments have found a bureaucratic Camelot in which no clouds ever darken their policy-making skies. Disagreements erupt, and sometimes the fights can be serious. But, to go back to Hugh Heclo once more, what united these policy participants was so strong that even in the face of real and serious disagreement, there was that sense of understanding and mutual respect that kept the conflict manageable and that convinced all of the insiders that they were better off with each other than with any possible group of outsiders.[65]

Power seems to flow to such agencies, but every bit as important is the fact that what constraints they face seem to be coming from other insiders, people with whom they feel more than comfortable trying to hash out a common position or, failing that, a compromise that gives each participant some of what it wants. Rarely, if ever, will they be stared down by powerful outsiders here for today's issue and seriously contemplating a return engagement on other issues some time in the future.

Do such agencies exist? Sure. The Federal Aviation Administration has to deal with the major air carriers, the discount carriers, the men and women who fly and maintain the planes, the private pilots, the folks who run the airports, the companies that build the planes, and a couple of key committees in the Congress. But it deals from a position of strength based on its expertise and on the closed nature of the political system within which it operates. In a very real sense, so do the Coast Guard—see the discussion of the Guard and new rules for port security in chapter 6—the Securities and Exchange Commission, the Federal Deposit Insurance Corporation, and dozens and dozens of others.

Just as there are agencies that deal from a position of strength created by functioning in a policy area characterized by a high perception of complexity and low controversy, there are agencies that deal from a position of obvious weakness because they function in policy areas characterized by a low perception of complexity and a high degree of controversy. Now the resources of power are much tougher to come by. Just as high-complexity/low-controversy agencies get considerable respect for their expertise, low-complexity/high-controversy agencies get little for theirs. What they do is a matter of common sense or moral values, and we can all lay claim to those, so an agency cannot, by definition, play the expert card. It might seem as if a policy area characterized by great controversy, controversy that opens the policy-making system to more participants, would provide fertile ground for cultivating clientele and subcommittee support, but that much controversy often has the opposite effect, making it harder to get any real and lasting support. If, for example, the National Labor Relations Board decided to cultivate a close working relationship with business groups, it would be attacked by organized labor. If it tried to create a close relationship with labor, on the other hand, it would find itself attacked by business. And, of course, the politicians—especially the members of the relevant committees of Congress—that represent business or labor would gleefully join in the attacks. Unfortunately, from the NLRB's point of view, a middle course might well end up with attacks from both sides. In any case, the point is clear. Controversy means battles among the interested, and that means that getting the interested as an agency's supporters is going to be a difficult and dangerous course.

Again, such agencies exist. Besides the NLRB, this is almost certainly what we would find at the various subdivisions of the Employment Standards Administration of the Department of Labor, or at the Department of Health and Human Services' Administration for Children and Families. Dealing from a position of vulnerability dictated by the lack of respect for their expertise and the attention that outsiders are ready to pay to their work anytime it touches a nerve, such agencies plod along hoping to leave their mark, even though they know that the policies they work on are subject to the political influence of a myriad of groups.

Controversy and Complexity at Odds

As we saw earlier, high complexity need not be accompanied by the reinforcing low controversy. Environmental policy, indeed most policies in the general areas of health and safety protection, require considerable expertise to understand but generate tremendous political heat, even if that heat is confined to battles between businesses on the one hand, and environmental or "public interest" groups on the other. The agencies that operate in such policy areas are in an ambiguous position when it comes to gathering the resources necessary for bureaucratic power. Their expertise is obvious and we agree that expertise is necessary. But the credibility of that expertise is undermined a good bit by the presence of other experts challenging their conclusions and recommendations, especially when those challenges include the ubiquitous charge of using "junk science." Beyond that, when people dig in around policy positions, they tend to discount the evidence and arguments coming from the other side and pump up the value of the evidence and arguments provided by their own side. That might seem to suggest that clientele group allies might be available, but as in the case of low-complexity/high-controversy areas, the controversy makes it virtually impossible to cultivate such support for more than the issue of the moment. In such a charged atmosphere, it is almost inevitable that the agency will run afoul of today's supporters when tomorrow's battles arise. Then, of course, there is also the problem of being too closely associated with one side and the charges that would come from the other. Ask any career professional who worked at the Environmental Protection Agency in the first part of the twenty-first century, and you will find someone who knows the sting of being labeled a tool of industry when his job is to protect the environment. And, once more, the middle of the road really can be the place where the cars hit you from both sides.

In the end, then, such agencies exist and they exercise power. As you might expect, they are more powerful than are the agencies that function in areas of low complexity and high controversy but less powerful than those that function in areas of high complexity and low controversy. Who are these agencies? The aforementioned Environmental Protection Agency, of course, but others would no doubt include the Occupational Safety and Health Administration, the Food and Drug Administration, and quite possibly the Immigration and Naturalization Service.

As I suggested in the earlier discussion of policy areas characterized by low controversy and low complexity, agencies operating in such areas are likely to exercise considerable power, but they exercise considerable power over something few people much care about. They derive not much in the way of power from respect for their expertise, of course, since such respect doesn't exist. But they are able to use their insider status and vocabulary to create the appearance of expertise, even the appearance of respect for that expertise, since no one but the insiders ever pays any attention to what is happening in such policy areas. Such "expertise" can be shredded should anyone wade in to try to do it, but in the absence of controversy, no one is likely to try. These agencies can, however, gain some clientele and other insider support, and there are almost certainly opportunities to gain support among the members of the subcommittees with legislative and/or budgetary responsibility in their respective policy areas. Should such an agency be challenged by outsiders, its clientele and congressional support wouldn't necessarily be stripped away as easily as its expertise could be ignored, so it might weather any storm such outsiders could raise. Still, there is no question that if challenged, the Defense Commissary Agency would face a very different fight than would the Federal Aviation Administration, and the difference would be primarily a product of the latter's long recognized expertise.

SUMMARY AND CONCLUSION

Every agency at every level of government has its own unique political environment. But even though each agency's environment is unique in terms of the people involved and the language they use to discuss the issues that have brought them together, there are still similarities from one agency to another, and there are still discernible patterns in terms of the numbers and range of people involved, the extent to which the language of debate is grounded more in the vocabulary of the expert or that of the politician, and perhaps most of all, the relative influence of expert knowledge and political concerns in that agency's decisions and its decision-making processes.

As we saw, the more controversy that is associated with the set of issues an agency deals with, the more open its political environment is going to be. A fairly large number of citizens and politicians will want to be heard on such issues. And they will be convinced that in a system of self-government, that desire to be heard plus the resources needed to make some political noise should be enough to make sure that they are heard.

If this particular set of issues is also seen by most of the public as a matter of common sense and moral values, this tendency toward openness will be powerfully reinforced and a distinctly political environment will be created. Issues will be debated primarily in the language of politics and morality—with a bone or two thrown to the experts—and they will be resolved that way as well.

On the other hand, if this particular set of controversial issues is seen as highly complex, that is, as issues that require a good bit of expertise to understand, we find a very different political environment. Citizens and politicians still expect their due, and when they are determined enough, they will get it. But experts cannot simply be written off as irrelevant the way they can if an issue is seen as a matter of common sense. Expert knowledge has to be countered with other expert knowledge. Of course, since the purpose of countering is to argue for a different policy outcome, the "other" expert knowledge—more properly the other expert—has to be carefully selected. Dueling experts, arguments laced with data and concepts foreign to the average citizen, and a recognition by everybody that political factors—the reaction of some people and some politicians—will play a central role in whatever the final decision might be, make for a fascinating political environment to observe. How much fun it would be to be a policy specialist in the middle of such an environment. That is a very different story.

But not all issues and issue areas are controversial. Some just don't seem to divide us at all. With no real controversy, only a handful of citizens and politicians seem to want to be part of the politics of resolving such issues, and it is a pretty narrow handful at that. They will join the policy specialists in constructing a political environment that gives every appearance of being the province of real experts. The language of debate will seem—maybe even be—extremely complex, and all of the insiders, including the interested citizens and politicians, will convince themselves and work to convince any outsiders who might happen along that without the mastery of this language and the concepts it represents, there is just no making sense of the issues at hand.

If the issue area at hand is also seen as a matter of great complexity, that is, if most of us in the public buy the insiders' assertion that only someone who masters this language and this set of concepts has anything useful to say about these issues, then those insiders will be thoroughly successful and the political environment of the agency working in this issue area will be limited to only the handful who have managed to show the required combination of political and expert resources to become insiders. They will debate policy choices in their own language, and they will believe—and we will believe—that expert knowledge has triumphed and politics has played the minimal role appropriate to such complex issues. That is, there has been enough politics to give the appearance of self-government at work without upsetting the carefully packed apple cart of the system's "expert" insiders.

If, however, this generally non-controversial issue area is not seen as the province of experts, things can be very different. They won't be necessarily. Whether a non-controversial issue is perceived as complex or not, it will start with a closed politics, and the insiders involved will make every effort to keep it that way. Their best efforts will be aimed at constructing a language as impenetrable to outsiders as is the language of any set of experts recognized as such by most of us. But complex insider language or no complex insider language, agencies dealing with issues that lack controversy, but are not really seen as complex by most of the society, operate in semi-autonomous political environments not because the broader political system feels it can't understand what these folks are up to, but because it doesn't care. The moment the broader system cares, the carefully constructed system of insider politics wrapped in expert language collapses like a house of cards.

The contours of an agency's political environment, and therefore the power that agency will wield within that environment, will be shaped largely by the controversy and the complexity of the subject matter it confronts. The important details of an agency's political environment will be filled in by the specifics of that subject matter. The political environment of the Federal Aviation Administration will be very similar to that of the Securities and Exchange Commission in terms of the closed nature of the politics that will surround policy making at each agency and in terms of the heavy emphasis on the expert knowledge of the policy specialists and the other insiders within that environment. What won't be the same, of course, will be the list of the insiders or the vocabulary they use when they discuss the issues at hand. There is, however, one individual whose name might appear on the FAA list and the SEC list. He or she might not speak the language or understand the concepts of either issue area, but the name might appear on the list at any time anyway. That individual, of course, is the President of the United States. The next chapter is devoted to a look at how the President might try to get on the list of people whose reactions these two agencies would be likely to consider as they make a particular decision, and perhaps even more important, how much success the chief executive might have should he or she make the effort.

NOTES

1. In a sense this concern had surfaced by the 1880s, as evidenced by Woodrow Wilson, "The Study of Administration," *Political Science Quarterly* (June 1887), 197–222, an effort to allay the fears of an overpowering bureaucracy by arguing that policy and administration were two different spheres of government. The debate continues on, and the list of scholars who have addressed the question in one forum or another would make a pretty good inaugural class for a Public Administration Hall of Fame. A partial list would include John Gaus, Herman Finer, Carl Friedrich, Paul Appleby, Arthur Maass, Dwight Waldo, Stephen Bailey, Frederick Mosher, Roscoe Martin, Emmette Redford, Herbert Kaufman, and Francis Rourke.

2. Many of the scholars listed in the preceding note were interested in both questions, of course, but others, such as Norton Long, James Q. Wilson, Marver Bernstein, Wallace Sayre, and especially Herbert Kaufman turned their attention more to questions of what Francis Rourke called "Differentials in Agency Power."

3. You can find that vision in chs. 2, 3, and 4 of any of the three editions of the classic, Francis E. Rourke, *Bureaucracy, Politics, and Public Policy* (Boston: Little, Brown, 1969, 1976, and 1984).

4. Kenneth J. Meier, *Politics and the Bureaucracy*, 4th ed. (New York: Harcourt College Publishers, 2000), 48–67. The debt to Rourke is stated expressly in footnote 5 on p. 48.

5. Emmette S. Redford, *Democracy in the Administrative State* (New York: Oxford University Press, 1969).

6. Rourke, *Bureaucracy, Politics, and Public Policy*, 2nd ed., 82.

7. Meier, *Politics and the Bureaucracy*, 62.

8. Rourke, *Bureaucracy, Politics, and Public Policy*, 2nd ed., 93.

9. Dennis D. Riley, *Public Personnel Administration*, 2nd ed. (New York: Longman, 2002), 285–287.

10. *The United States Government Manual 1998/99* (Washington, D.C.: U.S. Government Printing Office, 1998), 315.

11. Robert A. Katzmann, "The Federal Trade Commission," in *The Politics of Regulation*, ed. James Q. Wilson (New York: Basic Books, 1980), 162–166.

12. Katzmann, "The Federal Trade Commission," 171.

13. James E. Webb, *Space Age Management* (New York: McGraw-Hill, 1969), 128.

14. Rourke, *Bureaucracy, Politics, and Public Policy*, 2nd ed., 95.

15. Rourke, *Bureaucracy, Politics, and Public Policy*, 2nd ed., 97.

16. Rourke, *Bureaucracy, Politics, and Public Policy*, 2nd ed., 101.

17. Rourke, *Bureaucracy, Politics, and Public Policy*, 2nd ed., 15.

18. Meier, *Politics and the Bureaucracy*, 52.

19. Rourke, *Bureaucracy, Politics, and Public Policy*, 2nd ed., 44.

20. Meier, *Politics and the Bureaucracy*, 52.

21. That conventional wisdom goes back at least as far as the classic work of J. Leiper Freeman. See J. Leiper Freeman, *The Political Process: Executive Bureau–Legislative Committee Relations* (Garden City, N.Y.: Doubleday, 1955).

22. Steven A. Shull, "Presidential-Congressional Support for Agencies and for Each Other," *Journal of Politics* 40 (August 1978), 753–760.

23. Riley, *Public Personnel Administration*, 106–113.

24. Albert O. Hirschmann, *Exit, Voice, and Loyalty* (Cambridge: Harvard University Press, 1970).

25. Herman Finer, "Administrative Responsibility in Democratic Government," *Public Administration Review* 1 (Summer 1941), 336.

26. Eric Schmitt, "Pentagon Sends Its Spies to Join Fight on Terror," *New York Times* (electronic edition), January 24, 2005.

27. Rourke, *Bureaucracy, Politics, and Public Policy*, 2nd ed., 180.

28. Harold Seidman, *Politics, Position, and Power*, 3rd ed. (New York: Oxford University Press, 1980), ch. 6.

29. Steven Kelman, "Occupational Safety and Health Administration," in *The Politics of Regulation*, ed. Wilson, 236–266.

30. Steven Labaton, "U.S. Backs Off Relaxing Rules for Big Media," *New York Times* (electronic edition), January 28, 2005.

31. Aaron Wildavsky, *The Politics of the Budgetary Process*, 2nd ed. (Boston: Little, Brown, 1974), 172.

32. Rourke, *Bureaucracy, Politics, and Public Policy*, 173–175; Meier, *The Politics of Bureaucracy*, 138–143.

33. Theodore J. Lowi, "American Business, Public Policy, Case Studies and Political Theory," *World Politics* 16, no. 4 (July 1964).

34. Theodore J. Lowi, "Four Systems of Policy, Politics, and Choice," *Public Administration Review* 32 (July/August 1972), 298–310.

35. Meier, *The Politics of Bureaucracy*. See p. 69 for the quoted passage, and all of ch. 4, 69–102, for the comments on how these differing policy areas affect agency power.

36. Meier, *The Politics of Bureaucracy*, 70.

37. Theodore J. Lowi, "Distribution, Regulation, and Redistribution: The Functions of Government," in *Public Policies and Their Politics*, ed. Randall B. Ripley (New York: W. W. Norton, 1966), 27–40. The quote is on p. 27. This is an adaptation of Lowi's review of Bauer, Pool, and Dexter's *American Business and Public Policy*, cited in footnote 33.

38. *The United States Government Manual*, 381.

39. Meier, *Politics and the Bureaucracy*, 81.

40. Meier, *Politics and the Bureaucracy*, 88.

41. Meier, *Politics and the Bureaucracy*, 89.

42. Meier, *Politics and the Bureaucracy*, 90.

43. Meier, *Politics and the Bureaucracy*, 69.

44. See Marver H. Bernstein, *Regulating Business by Independent Commission* (Princeton, N.J.: Princeton University Press, 1955); or Louis M. Kohlmeier, *The Regulators* (New York: Harper and Row, 1969).

45. Quoted on Wisconsin Public Radio News, Friday morning, February 4, 2005.

46. Stephen Labaton, "Senate Begins Process to Reverse New F.C.C. Rules on Media," *New York Times* (electronic edition), June 20, 2003.

47. Labaton, "Senate Begins Process to Reverse New F.C.C. Rules on Media."

48. Clark appeared with Tim Russert on NBC's *Meet the Press* on June 15, 2003, and made that assertion.

49. Francis E. Rourke, *Bureaucracy, Politics, and Public Policy*, 3rd ed. (Boston: Little, Brown, 1984), 94.

50. Rourke, *Bureaucracy, Politics, and Public Policy*, 3rd ed., 92.

51. Hugh Heclo, "Issue Networks and the Executive Establishment," in *The New American Political System*, ed. Anthony King (Washington, D.C.: American Enterprise Institute, 1978), 117.

52. Heclo, "Issue Networks and the Executive Establishment."

53. You can read about this battle in a number of places. A nice short summary can be found in John H. Cushman Jr., "New Study Adds to Debate on E.P.A. Rules for Pesticide," *New York Times* (electronic edition), June 2, 2002.

54. Andrew C. Revkin, "With White House Approval, E.P.A. Pollution Report Omits Global Warming Section," *New York Times* (electronic edition), September 15, 2002.

55. Revkin, "With White House Approval, E.P.A. Pollution Report Omits Global Warming Section."

56. Andrew C. Revkin and Katharine Q. Seelye, "Report by the E.P.A. Leaves Out Data on Climate Change," *New York Times* (electronic edition), June 19, 2003.

57. Revkin and Seelye, "Report by the E.P.A. Leaves Out Data on Climate Change."

58. Revkin and Seelye, "Report by the E.P.A. Leaves Out Data on Climate Change."

59. Revkin and Seelye, "Report by the E.P.A. Leaves Out Data on Climate Change."

60. *The United States Government Manual*, 226, describes the purpose and a little about the operations of this agency.

61. *The United States Government Manual*, 226.

62. Susan J. Tolchin and Martin Tolchin, *Dismantling America: The Rush to Deregulate* (New York: Oxford University Press, 1984), ch. 6.

63. Just dig into the archives of the *New York Times*, the *Washington Post*, or even the *Wall Street Journal* from the summer of 2003 to watch the ebb and flow and then the ebb of enthusiasm for real change at the SEC.

64. Heclo, "Issue Networks and the Executive Establishment," 116–120.

65. Heclo, "Issue Networks and the Executive Establishment."

5

Bureaucracy and the Presidency

Hail to the Chief (Sort Of)

We ended the previous chapter with the suggestion that the President of the United States might want to become a force in the political environment of the Federal Aviation Administration, or of the Securities and Exchange Commission. He or she might want to become a force in the political environment of the Environmental Protection Agency, the Bureau of Reclamation, the Employment Standards Administration, and maybe even the Defense Commissary Agency. In short, the President might want to become a force in the political environment of any agency, possibly, just possibly, of every agency. After all, the opening sentence of Article II of the Constitution tells us—and tells the President—that "The executive Power shall be vested in a President of the United States of America." That would seem to give the President a pretty clear right to be part of the political environment of any agency, and probably an equally clear obligation to be part of the political environment of every agency. This chapter is about how the President goes about exercising the rights or meeting the obligations imposed by that single sentence that makes him or her the chief executive of the government of the United States of America.

Our primary mission in this chapter may be to look at how a chief executive tries to become a force in the decision-making operations of any of the agencies supposedly under his or her constitutional authority, but two additional questions spring readily to mind when we think about how a chief does it and we will need to address those two along the way. In fact, we will start with one of those additional questions. Specifically, how often does the President try to become a force in the operations of most agencies of the federal government? Then there is the additional additional question. When the President does try, how likely is it that he or she will be successful? That one we will take on as we talk about how he or she can try to exercise influence. So, it's time to see how often he or she is going to try.

NOT THAT OFTEN: MOTIVATION, RESOURCES, AND A LACK OF PRESIDENTIAL ATTENTION TO BUREAUCRACY

I guess an author isn't supposed to offer the bottom line for a section of a chapter in this first paragraph of the section, but here it is anyway. The President leaves all agencies alone some of the time, and some agencies alone all of the time. The reasons won't surprise you one bit.

Motivation, or Rather, the Lack Thereof

Exasperated by what he considered a trivial question, Lyndon Johnson once bellowed at a reporter: "Why do you come and ask me, the leader of the Western World, a chickenshit question like that?"[1] Though other Presidents would likely have chosen other language—in public, anyway—there can be no question that those other Presidents have harbored the same feelings when confronted with some of the day-to-day questions faced by the myriad of agencies they supposedly preside over. Robert Sherrill didn't record the question that elicited President Johnson's outburst, and though I will never forget the magnificent exchange between Johnson and legendary reporter Sarah McClendon over some now long forgotten issue brewing at the then Veterans Administration (VA), it was not the subject of that "chickenshit" question or the issue that had prompted Ms. McClendon's query about the VA that caused President Johnson to conclude he could not win another term, or that follows him in history books and college lectures three decades after his death. And Lyndon Johnson knew it.

Presidents, to no one's surprise, are motivated by a combination of factors, just like the rest of us. From a chief's point of view, there is always the question of reelection, or in a second term, of partisan or even ideological advantage. There is the question of the President's place in history. There are issues the chief cares deeply about. There are even issues that someone very close to the chief cares deeply about. But only rarely will the issues before any given agency touch one of those key presidential motivations. To be sure, as we noted in the previous chapter, George W. Bush decided that global warming touched something of such importance that the White House saw the role of chief executive in terms of the role of chief editor when it came to assessments of that particular problem and its presumed causes and potential solutions. But the vast majority of reports by the vast majority of agencies were issued with no assistance at all from the White House editors.

In short, Presidents ignore most of what goes on at most agencies because most of what goes on at most agencies does not touch anything the President cares deeply about. Naturally enough, this is going to mean that the motivation to become a force at most agencies just isn't going to be there. If we think in terms of our discussion of political environments from the previous chapter, it is quite likely that the President will be more interested in issues surrounded by high controversy than in those that are not. Such issues may, of course, be issues the President or someone close to him has been interested in for a long time, may affect his or her reelection, and in fact, may even affect his or her place in history. But there are only a handful of such issues, and as we shall see in the next section, a lack of motivation is not the only barrier to presidential efforts to influence agency-level decision making. There is also a question of resources.

Time, Knowledge, and Interest: How Can a President Keep Track?

The time pressures on a President are almost impossible to comprehend. Presidents practice for it, in a sense, while they campaign, but even the campaign can't compare with the job. Ceremonial duties range from meeting with the reigning Stanley Cup Champions—Wayne Gretzky once likened his meeting with the President to being photographed with Santa as a kid—to state dinners that blend ceremony with diplomacy. Congress is at work most of the year, and some of the time it is doing things the President really has a stake in. American troops are always somewhere, and sometimes they are in places where they are shooting and getting shot at. The chief's party needs help raising money, every group of any size and importance is hoping for a presidential speech or at least a brief photo op with him or her, and the White House staff is always trying to get just a few minutes so they can draft a response to this or that inquiry, brief the media on the schedule for the next several days, and respond to the latest crisis in Alabama or Afghanistan. And, oh yeah, there are all those agencies writing and enforcing all those rules. There just cannot be enough time to keep any sort of eye on more than a tiny number of them at any one time.

As obvious and important as the time problem is for a President, the knowledge problem is also a significant barrier to keeping track of what most agencies are up to. The President's knowledge problem has two interrelated dimensions. First comes the question of information. Recall from chapter 2 that the information that tends to rise through a hierarchically structured organization tends to undergo a rather thorough cleansing process on its way up. Recall also that we said the primary motivations for cleaning up this information are fear and loyalty. No one in government is more likely to inspire fear and loyalty than the President, especially fear and loyalty in those who are the last ones to have a chance to apply the scrub brush to the information coming from down below before it reaches that President.

The chief will never find it easy to get an accurate picture of what is going on in most of the rest of the government. But even if such a picture were to emerge, there would still be the second piece of the President's knowledge problem, namely knowledge. Even were he or she to get an accurate picture of Federal Aviation Administration deliberations about a new fuel-tank safety rule for jetliners, how would the President make sense out of that accurate picture? As we saw in chapter 3, there are almost certainly aspects of that picture that are actually better understood without the blinders that most experts bring to their work. But there are going to be aspects of that picture that only an expert can understand, and the President is, by definition, not an expert in the subject matter that faces any of the government's many agencies.

This lack of knowledge does nothing to undercut the President's constitutional legitimacy should he or she wish to become involved in the resolution of a particular public policy question. What that lack of knowledge does do, however, is make it so very much harder for the President to become an active participant in agency policy making. With only fragmentary and not always accurate information flowing upward, the President may not know that he or she has any real reason to want to become involved in the issue, and without the expertise to make sense out of what information does come, the chief may wonder how to intervene to advance his or her own cause. On top of all that, it turns out, whenever a President does choose to become involved in some aspect of agency policy making, there is always the question of how to respond to the charge of substituting politics for knowledge in what is supposed to be a knowledge-driven process.

The President's lack of time is painfully obvious. So is his or her lack of knowledge about so many of the issues being confronted throughout the government. Less obvious, perhaps, but no less real, is the chief's lack of interest in so much of what is going on at the majority of that government's specialized agencies. In that sense, of course, the President is not so very different from you and me. When you look at the class schedule for the next semester, how many of the classes listed there would you just skip over, sure that you would have absolutely no interest in them? I have served for several years on our University Curriculum Committee with an excellent geologist. He is an award-winning teacher, a good scholar, and a genuinely interesting man. He spends his days asking and answering questions that I am ever so confident I would not have the slightest interest in asking or answering. He may well feel the same about the questions I ask and answer all day. How could the President be any different from the rest of us in this regard?

If you will indulge me in yet another analogy, when facing the question of how often to make a serious effort to become a force in policy making at the agency level, the President is pretty much a man or woman in the Library of Congress. Look at all those books. There is no time to read more than a tiny fraction. Most of them have titles that are incomprehensible, and even if the chief were to ignore the title of any given volume, the first few pages might well leave him or her quite thoroughly lost. And some of them just don't seem to touch on anything the President is interested in. So a huge percentage of the books will simply go unread. A few will get a quick glance, even if that glance leaves the President knowing only a little more than he or she did before. A very few will get read, or at least get a good skimming. Then there will be a tiny number that will be taken off the shelf more than once.

In Summary

The range of activities engaged in by the U.S. government is astounding. Presidents choose to become involved in only a very very small handful of those activities. To begin with, every President has a set of issues he or she believes will make a difference in the next election, a set of issues he or she believes might make a difference in how his or her presidency is viewed by history, and a set of issues he or she cares about enough to want to make some difference in how they are addressed and resolved. These issues may arrive with the President on Inauguration Day—cutting taxes for Ronald Reagan and George W. Bush, health care and economic recovery for Bill Clinton—or they may arise out of events—homeland security and reform in the regulation of the accounting industry for

President Bush, Somalia and the question of "gays in the military" for President Clinton. Either way, these are the issues that will motivate presidential attention to bureaucratic activity, and once the attention barrier is broken, the chief may very well want to become a player in what that bureaucracy is doing.

But whether this set of issues grabbed the President's attention before or after he or she moved into the Oval Office, once we get outside those issues, the lack of time, knowledge, and interest erects some very substantial barriers to presidential efforts to become a force in an agency's political environment. Under normal circumstances, the President just doesn't have time to devote to the question of whether or not accounting firms ought to be able to provide both regular accounting and auditing services to the same clients. The accountants and the accounting regulators are going to argue strongly that he doesn't really understand the subtleties of the issue anyway, and in the end, how many of us really find accounting an interesting subject? To be sure, events can change the equation for the President in an instant. For George W. Bush in the summer of 2002, those barriers of time, knowledge, and interest fell as Enron, Global Crossing, and others collapsed and as accounting giant Arthur Anderson went with them. The accountants and their regulators have now gone back to business more or less as usual. So has the President.

In sum, most agencies most of the time know that they are not doing anything that will attract presidential attention. It's a comforting thought. Other agencies know that the President does have some interest in what they do, and while that interest won't be translated into anything like a consistent presidential effort to be a factor in agency decision making, they must be prepared for at least an occasional communication from the White House. As we shall see shortly, that is not always a comforting thought. Finally, every agency knows that its turn in the presidential gaze could be coming. It just depends on events, events that really are beyond that agency's control. That is never a comforting thought.

AN AGENCY-LEVEL VIEW OF THE WHITE HOUSE: SUSPICION, SUSPICION, SUSPICION

The rest of this chapter is devoted to the questions of how the President can try to become a significant force in the policy-making process and how successful those efforts are likely to be. Before we do that, however, we need to take one more detour. Specifically, we need to ask ourselves how presidential efforts at influence are going to be viewed at the agencies whose decisions he or she is trying to affect. That view, as you can see from the title of this section, is one of suspicion. Three reasons.

Plenty of Insults, and Even a Few Injuries

It is likely that every President from George Washington on offered at least an occasional criticism of the federal bureaucracy. Franklin Roosevelt was only half joking when he told Louis Brownlow, the political scientist he had commissioned to advise him on why the government he led didn't work the way he thought it should, that Brownlow's plan to consolidate all federal loan programs in the Treasury wouldn't work because "not one of them will ever make a loan to anybody for any purpose. There are too many glass-eyed bankers in the Treasury."[2] Harry Truman wasn't joking at all when he made this doleful prediction about the fate he felt was certain to befall his successor, Dwight Eisenhower: "He'll sit here and he'll say, 'Do this! Do that!' *And nothing will happen.* Poor Ike—it won't be a bit like the Army. He'll find it very frustrating."[3]

While it seems likely that most Presidents voiced plenty of criticism of the bureaucracy they had been elected to "lead," most of that criticism remained low key and rarely surfaced in any serious way until an unusually warm January day in 1981 when, in his inaugural address, Ronald Reagan informed the nation that "In this present crisis, government is not the solution to our problem; government is the problem."[4] From the point of view of a career policy specialist at any agency of the government, those were both frightening and insulting words. Frightening, of course, because if government—meaning you and all the rest of the career specialists at all the rest of the agencies—was the problem, how else to solve it but get rid of you, but insulting because as a career policy specialist you believe in what you are doing. You are using your specialized knowledge to make sense out of all of the information you gather, and you are using it to inform people, and to write and enforce rules. Now you are told—by the President of the United States, no less—that by doing your job you have created a problem, in fact, a crisis.

It became fairly clear early in his administration that President Reagan's words were not exclusively rhetorical "red meat" for his conservative supporters. Before 1981 was over, he had responded to a strike by the Professional Air Traffic Controllers Organization by ordering them back to work and firing the lot when they didn't return. He even barred most of them from ever working as federal air traffic controllers again and moved to decertify their union.[5] Important as this remarkable response to the controllers' actions might have been, it was the President's continuous efforts at deregulation of industry and the privatization of government activity that really created suspicion among federal employees. To insist on moving jobs from the public to the private sector is to say something fundamental about the former. To insist on moving *your* job from the public to the private sector just might be to say something fundamental about you.

It was tempting to the public employees of the 1980s to think of Ronald Reagan as something of an aberration rather than the wave of the future. But privatization continued apace in the Clinton-Gore administration. As Paul Light of the Brookings Institution pointed out, most of the job reductions in the federal government that occurred during Mr. Clinton's term occurred through privatization, and it was the Clinton-Gore team that introduced the National Performance Review and talked of the need for a new entrepreneurial spirit in government.[6] Then came George W. Bush and his call for a dramatic reduction in the size of the federal workforce through even more privatization as well as through the simple path of doing less.

While the Presidents of the last two and a half decades may not have been elected primarily to preside over the dismantling of the federal government, they have moved systematically to shrink its size and to have it do less. That means fewer employees, but it also means fewer activities. Federal employees can be expected to take some exception to both of those. What makes their response important in this context, of course, is their reaction to subsequent efforts at presidential leadership in their own areas of public policy. Why exactly should one take orders from a leader who has specifically and repeatedly said that your job probably doesn't need to be done at all, most certainly could be done with far less in the way of taxpayer money, and in any event, would clearly be done better were it done by someone working in "the private sector"?

It's All a Matter of Timing

Most things are, or at least are said to be, a matter of timing. What matters here, of course, is that Presidents and agencies have very different senses of timing, indeed, very different senses of time itself.

From the President's point of view, time is short. New policy initiatives have to be offered early in the term, adopted as quickly as Congress can act—if they require congressional approval, anyway—and implemented as soon as possible. At least that's the timing if the President is going to get much credit for those new proposals in time for it to do him or her much political good. The stuff for the history books can be done a little more slowly, but it is hard to believe that Harry Truman would have been as proud of the Marshall Plan if it had been planned in his administration and carried out in Ike's.

So a President would like to move things along. Most agencies see time a little differently. They see it a little differently in two senses.

First, agencies are places where expertise is supposed to drive the decision-making process. Politics will play its role, but expertise—or at least that "shared analytic repertoire for coping with the issues" that passes for expertise in the political environments that surround most agencies—must be at the center of the debate and at the center of the process by which the decision is reached.[7] Expertise, even when leavened with a certain amount of politics, still moves more slowly than the President is likely to want to move. Remember the basic point that both FDR and Harry Truman were making in the passages I quoted earlier. Bureaucracy doesn't necessarily move when the President says jump. In fact, a close aide to President Eisenhower confirmed Harry Truman's prediction that Ike would find the bureaucracy a major source of frustration. That aide told Richard Neustadt, "The President still feels that when he's decided something, that ought to be the end of it . . . and when it bounces back undone or done wrong, he tends to react with shocked surprise."[8] Often times "it bounces back undone" because the experts at the agency in question just didn't think it was time to do it.

Second, agencies—the expert policy specialists who work there, primarily—are a little reluctant to move quickly to respond to the President's leadership on an issue because they know that they will be the ones to take the bulk of the heat should something go wrong. To begin with, while the media may try to pin a policy failure—or just a negative reaction among the public—on the President who initiated the idea, the people whose lives are affected by the change can't get at the President until the next election. If then. But they can get at the agency and its experts. They can yell. They can scream. They can contact members of Congress. Beyond that, there is a very good chance that by the time a failure has to be acknowledged, of the folks involved only the career specialists will be left to take any of the heat. The President can't be there longer than eight years—OK, ten if he or she succeeds to the office more than halfway through a predecessor's term—and as we'll see shortly, the political executives who had to play the role of "point persons" on the issue have long since left government for their old jobs in industry or academe, or for even more lucrative jobs as lobbyists for businesses they came in contact with while serving in government. No agency wants to take the heat for a policy hatched elsewhere by people who won't be there to share the blame. So, once more, they tend to be a little slow in implementing policies that come from above. They will move when they feel the time is right, not when the White House does. At least that's what they will do if they can. More on that shortly.

"And He Doesn't Know the Territory"

Finally we come to what is probably the most important source of all for agency suspicion of presidential policy leadership, that is, the expert's distrust of the viewpoint of the amateur.[9] By definition, from the point of view of any agency-level policy specialist, he or she knows far more about the subject at hand than does the President of the United States. For that matter, he or she knows far more about the subject at hand than almost anybody who might be advising or representing the President. Remember back to chapter 2. The policy specialists believe in the value of responsiveness as a key element in our system of self-government. But also recall from that chapter that they feel a real push to find a definition for responsiveness that does not force too much of a compromise with their fundamental goal of using their knowledge to make the right decisions. The first response of any policy specialist is to distrust presidential recommendations, assuming them to be motivated more by the politics of the moment than by any real understanding of the substance of the issue or the information and expertise that must be brought to bear to deal with it. Again, by definition, the President just doesn't have that expertise.

In Summary

No one likes to have his or her job, let alone career, threatened, and no expert likes to hear that by doing his or her job—using that expert knowledge in the way he or she has been taught—he or she has made things worse. In our own way all of us who stake the claim to professional expertise subscribe to the physician's maxim, first do no harm. It is hard to turn around after that kind of "abuse" and follow the lead of the "abuser."

It gets even harder to follow that lead when you believe that that leader is going too far too fast. Experts move—or tell themselves that they move—when their expertise tells them it is time to move and not before. Besides, the leader in this situation will not be around to shoulder a fair share of the blame should he or she turn out to be leading in the wrong direction. Better to slow down and be a little more certain.

And it gets even harder yet to follow that lead when you are convinced that the leader in question hasn't looked at—in fact, couldn't even read—the maps of the area he or she has just wandered into. Indeed, it might be possible to endure the insults and even occasionally to move a little sooner than the expert community would normally choose to move. All policy specialists know that the caution of their own expert community can sometimes result in a form of paralysis that works against sound policy. But there is that matter of knowledge and it will not go away. The President is an amateur and that is that.

I am not suggesting that the President can never become a serious player in agency-level policy making. I am not even suggesting that all agencies search for ways to ignore every policy initiative that comes out of the White House or even out of the political executives sent by the White House to lead those agencies in presidentially defined directions. The President can, and sometimes does, become a major force in agency-level decision making. The rest of this chapter is about how he or she does it. All I am saying here is this. When the President does try to become a significant force in agency activity, he or she faces a wary bunch of policy specialists with a natural predisposition not to follow his or her lead.

HOW DOES THE PRESIDENT INFLUENCE BUREAUCRACY?

If you reflect for a moment, what I have done up to now is walk you through what I hope is a convincing, but hardly surprising, case for the proposition that the President of the United States is very very rarely an active participant in policy making at the agency level. He or she doesn't have the resources, isn't really motivated, and would meet with some considerable suspicion from the policy specialists involved in an agency's day-to-day activities if he or she did make the effort.

But does the fact that the President can never really be an active participant in policy making at the Federal Aviation Administration (FAA), the U.S. Fish and Wildlife Service (USFWS), or the Wage and Hour Division of the Employment Standards Administration preclude any influence for him or her over the decisions reached at those agencies? To put it in somewhat more concrete terms, even if the President has never met the FAA expert who is chairing the agency's task force on fuel-tank safety, has never read a single USFWS report on an endangered species, and doesn't even know that there is a Wage and Hour Division at the Employment Standards Administration, can he or she still be a force in how those disparate aggregations of individuals do their jobs? The answer is yes, but very definitely a qualified yes. That is, the President can have an impact on the activities of any agency, but there are a number of forces at work to limit that impact. Let's take a look at how the President does it, and what keeps him or her from doing even more of it.

Before we begin our detailed look at how the President tries to exercise influence over the various agencies of the government—and for that matter, our detailed look at the forces that limit that exercise of presidential influence—we need to get a general grasp on what it is that Presidents try to do. We know—and they know—that they cannot be frequent and active participants in the deliberations of all of those agencies. What they can do, however, is to try to have an impact on the organizational, budgetary, and legal environments in which agencies make their decisions. It is an indirect and imperfect route to influence, but it is a route that the President can take. It's finally time to see how.

Influencing the Organizational Environment I: A Matter of Management

It is obvious from what has been said so far that the President is in no position to manage any agency directly. But he or she does have opportunities to manage indirectly, that is, to manage through others who would bring his or her thoughts, preferences, and goals to bear on agency-level decision making. Specifically, the President has three such opportunities through the White House staff, the political executives who occupy positions in the cabinet and subcabinet, and the combination of the organizations that make up the Executive Office of the President, the numerous special presidential commissions and advisory panels, and the men and women of the Senior Executive Service, that we can, for lack of a better term, call the institutionalized presidency.

The White House Staff

Let's start closest to the President, that is, with the people who work in or very near the White House and who see themselves, in the delightful words of longtime scholar of the presidency Louis Koenig, as the President's "lengthened shadow."[10] The President's staff has grown considerably since Congress first authorized Franklin Roosevelt to hire "six administrative assistants who would be officially part of the White House but not subject to Senate confirmation."[11] Part of that growth can be attributed to the increased attention focused on the presidency in the last half-century, but some of it no doubt comes, as Koenig argues, because of the "heightened presidential interest in monitoring the departments and agencies to assure that his policies are implemented."[12] Louis Koenig penned those words during the presidency of Ronald Reagan, but there is no reason whatever to believe that Presidents George H. W. Bush, Bill Clinton, or George W. Bush would be likely to conclude that bureaucratic responsiveness has gotten dramatically better in the intervening twenty years. Unfortunately, from the President's perspective anyway, there are three rather good reasons why the White House staff is not going to provide the President with much of a way to indirectly manage the executive branch agencies he or she can't manage directly.

First of all, the group is too small. Even if we add in the men and women "on loan" from various departments and agencies and still paid by those departments and agencies, the total is almost certainly under 1,000, far too few to effectively monitor hundreds of agencies working on thousands of initiatives.

Second, the White House staff is seen as too political to be taken seriously as policy makers. They almost certainly got their jobs because they helped the President get elected or they are close to somebody who helped the President get elected, and they are pretty widely perceived as dedicated to the idea of getting him or her reelected. Even in a second term, White House staff members are going to be seen as men and women loyal to the President as person and politician, pursuing the goal of making the chief look good to the public and, if possible, to history. And, not so coincidentally, they might be pursuing the goal of making themselves attractive to some future employer. So from an agency perspective, their motives are every bit as suspect as are those of the President himself or herself, and they are seen as every bit as uninformed about the issues at hand as the chief. That's hardly a position of strength when dealing with policy specialists.

Finally, and maybe most important of all in undermining the ability of the President's staff to play the role of manager, these staff members have no independent source of power. Their power comes from the President. In more direct terms, the influence of any White House staff person comes from the fact that he or she speaks for the President of the United States. But, of course, that means that the person being spoken to has to believe that the person speaking actually does speak for the President of the United States, and as a matter of fact, very few people really do. The number of people who do speak for the President is far fewer than the number of people who claim to, so the claim is always weighed against what the bureaucrat knows about the person doing the claiming and his or her place in the President's own world. In the words of well-known observer of the presidency Thomas Cronin, "There is a great residual of respect toward the Presidency both in Washington and in the federal agencies throughout the country. But this respect for what the President can do is predicated on the fact that the Presidential voice can be heard and believed as authentic, not just through *second-level* [italics mine] staff voices. Otherwise, federal civil servants feel that they must protect their 'rational' and 'professional' interests from White House interference."[13] In effect, a small staff—small relative to the task, anyway—becomes even smaller. The result, of course, is to make it that much harder for the President to use that staff as managers and thereby to extend his presence as chief executive down to the operating level of bureaucracy.

I am not suggesting that no one on the President's staff is ever successful at carrying his or her viewpoints down to the agency level and making those viewpoints felt. Clearly it happens. But most of the time, the staff is making a very limited effort to get down to that level, and when they do, such staff members are greeted with a double dose of skepticism. First, of course, there is the normal skepticism about White House policy initiatives that we discussed earlier in the chapter. Now we have added to it skepticism over whether this person really represents the chief and his or her viewpoints.

The Political Executives

Louis Koenig is undoubtedly right that presidential staffs expand in part out of the chief's frustration with the fact that, in the words of the Eisenhower aide quoted earlier, things do "bounce back undone or done wrong."[14] But given the relatively small number of individuals on the White House staff available to try to make sure fewer things do "bounce back," the fact that they have other—more expressly political and seemingly more pressing—duties elsewhere, and most especially the realization that they range across a fairly wide range of policy areas doing what would probably be characterized by these insiders as "troubleshooting" very likely means that the White House staff is seen pretty much as the "special forces" of the President's efforts to exert some management control over the executive branch. They are vital when a crisis springs up, but day-to-day operations require an "infantry," and that means the men and women of the cabinet and subcabinet, that is, the political executives we spoke of in chapter 2. From their point of view, remember, their knowledge of and skill at management is the reason they are where they are. Unfortunately, however—again, unfortunately from the President's point of view—there are three rather substantial barriers to his or her use of these political executives as a real presidential management team.

Political Executives Are Not Always Who (What) the President Bargained For

Let's start with the possibility that the set of political executives who constitute what we so off-handedly refer to as the Reagan or Bush or Clinton or Bush administration is not really the set that Mr. Reagan, or Mr. G. H. W. Bush, or Mr. Clinton, or Mr. G. W. Bush wanted and/or expected. It did happen to every one of those Presidents, just as it happened to their predecessors and just as it will happen to their successors. It's built into every step of the process of picking these "presidential" teams.

First of all, of course, a President may very much want someone to serve in a particular post in his or her administration, and that individual may simply turn him down. Former Montana governor Marc Racicot declined the offer to serve as Attorney General of the United States even though it came from his friend and fellow former governor George W. Bush.[15] Bill Clinton and retired Admiral Bobby Ray Inman weren't exactly friends, but when the President tapped Inman for the job of Defense Secretary, the former naval officer said yes. Then he said no. And, for President Clinton, the search was on again. For the third time in a year.

It is almost certainly the case that turning a President down is never easy, and for that reason it may not happen all that often. Of course, there is a good chance that, unlike the cases of Racicot and Inman, most such refusals are kept under wraps to avoid embarrassment to the chief. So it is possible that it happens on more than the rare occasion. There is no way to know. What we do know, however, is that for whatever reasons—Racicot was said to have refused because he really wanted the Interior Secretary's job, and Inman made it very clear when he changed his answer from yes to no that he didn't want to go through the confirmation process—men and women the President taps for jobs in his or her administration choose to decline the honor. That, of course, means that the President is sending out a team of managers different from the one he or she had hoped to send. It may make a difference to the kind of managing the chief can get.

Odd as it may sound, there are even occasions on which the President ends up with a management team that is not so much missing people he or she did want, but containing people he or she didn't particularly want. It is said that Bill Clinton was more than ready to say good-bye to Federico Peña, the man who had served as Transportation Secretary during his first term, when he was reminded by departing Housing and Urban Development Secretary Henry Cisneros that if he (Cisneros) and Peña both left the cabinet, that cabinet would not have a single Hispanic. Peña's phone rang, his house came off the market, and he headed over for a stint as Secretary of Energy, a job for which he had almost no preparation.[16] After Ronald Reagan's first Environmental Protection Agency Administrator, Anne Gorsuch Burford, had resigned after being threatened with a contempt of Congress citation for refusing to answer questions at a committee hearing, the President was persuaded to seek to repair the damage that had been done by Ms. Burford's abrasive style and extremely conservative positions on environmental issues by bringing back to the agency one of its most respected former administrators, William Ruckelshaus. The President agreed, though Ruckelshaus held positions on most environmental issues far less congenial to those of Mr. Reagan than had Anne Burford. It can even happen in the world of the independent regulatory commissions, as Richard Nixon found out in 1971 when he was told that the price for continued support by the Teamsters Union was the reappointment to the National Labor Relations Board of one John Fanning, a man targeted by conservative supporters of the President as too pro-union (anti-business) to be kept on the board. Politics, in the form of a likely Teamsters endorsement in 1972, won out, and Mr. Fanning kept his job.[17]

Finally, of course, the President's team of political executives isn't always composed of the men and women he or she really wanted, because that team has to be confirmed by the United States Senate and some people just don't get confirmed. The President and the Senate have almost never been willing to let it come to a vote not to confirm a nominee, but there have been numerous instances of nominations blocked because the Senate never actually took a vote, and every bit as many instances of nominations withdrawn.

President Clinton had a particularly difficult time with the Justice Department, being forced to withdraw the nominations of Zoe Baird and Kimba Wood for the top spot, and that of Lani Guinier for the job of Assistant Attorney General for Civil Rights. Ms. Baird had employed a domestic worker who was in the country illegally and Ms. Wood had failed to pay the payroll taxes due for the services of the woman who cared for her children. Ms. Guinier's sins were more ideological. She was a tough advocate of affirmative action and had advanced some far-reaching ideas for revising the electoral system in order to guarantee more legislative seats for African Americans. President Clinton never did back down on the nomination of Bill Lan Lee for the civil rights post at the Justice Department. Senate Republicans had blocked a vote on Mr. Lee's nomination, so the President made Mr. Lee the Acting Attorney General for Civil Rights and submitted his name a second time. Confirmation troubles even stalked George W. Bush, who felt compelled to withdraw the name of his first nominee for Secretary of Labor, Ms. Linda Chavez, when it was revealed that she had for years employed at her home a woman who was in the country illegally. The fact that Ms. Chavez was nominated for Secretary of Labor and yet had almost certainly paid this woman below the minimum wage added fuel to the fire, of course. In any event, she called her own press conference and announced her withdrawal.

But even more important than nominations withdrawn or votes delayed are the nominations that never occur. Presidents certainly don't want nominations voted down. It casts a shadow on what is supposed to be one of their most important judgments—picking "a team" to run the government—and they want to avoid that. Though this may be changing in this newer, more ideological era, historically Presidents also have wanted to avoid contentious nominations. Nomination fights draw media coverage, and often worse yet, they draw the President in as he or she has to decide how much and how long to defend a nominee. It can easily become a no-win situation. So, Presidents have long consulted with key members of the Senate committees that have so much influence in the confirmation process in order to make that process go a little more smoothly. As we will see a bit later on in this chapter, that kind of consultation net is cast a little wider when the President has to fill the second- and third-level administrative jobs, as those jobs are very often seen as the province of the organized interest groups that are inevitably part of the political environments of the agencies who fall under the purview of a particular second- or third-level job. These interest groups, it turns out, have a great deal of influence not just with those agencies but with the Senate committees who play the lead role in the confirmation process. In the end, this point remains. The President might feel compelled not to nominate someone he or she—or his or her advisors—feel would be a real addition to the administration in order to avoid problems in the Senate.

Frustrating as it can be to the President not to be able to get the individual he or she wants for a particular job in the administration, it is so very much more frustrating to get exactly whom he or she wants but not get what he or she wants. The ultimate purpose of all of these men and women being asked to fill all of these jobs, remember, is to advance the President's agenda, protect the President's interests, and pursue the President's policies. People unwilling or unable to do those things don't help the President much, even if they are just the people he or she so carefully selected. Consider the short and ever-so-rocky tenure of President Bill Clinton's first Defense Secretary, Les Aspin.

When he prepared to take office in January 1993, Bill Clinton very much needed to make a certain kind of statement in his selection of a Secretary of Defense. Clinton, recall, had no real defense or foreign policy credentials and only minimal connections in the Congress. Beyond that, as a key player in the centrist Democratic Leadership Committee, Clinton very much wanted to project an image of a party committed to a role of strength on the world stage. From that perspective, Les Aspin seemed an ideal choice for the job. Aspin had served as Chair of the House Armed Services Committee for the past several years. In the process, he had gained a reputation as something of a hawk on defense and foreign policy issues, and established himself as one of Congress's leading experts on the Pentagon and its policies.

Unfortunately—for both men—the former chair's brains, knowledge, reputation, and connections notwithstanding, by the end of 1993, Bill Clinton felt compelled to fire Les Aspin. We don't need to go into all of the reasons for Mr. Clinton's decision, but a quick look at just two of the major concerns with the Secretary's performance will give you an idea of how a President can pick one thing and end up with another.

Secretary Aspin's major initiative was to be something called the "bottom up review," through which he would lead an examination of manpower and materiel capabilities and needs of all of the services in the light of the President's view of the role of our military in the modern world. By the time that "bottom up review" was six months old, it was clear that Aspin was finding out nothing new, planning nothing new, and that the services were using the exercise as an excuse to push for new weapons systems and new personnel numbers. The Secretary was not saying no. He may have had an expert's grasp of the issues as Armed Services Chair, but he didn't seem to have much of a grasp of anything in the Secretary's chair. Beyond that, Aspin, who had worked very well with the top men and women of the uniformed services while in the House, couldn't work with them at all as Secretary. Some of that came from their early battle over the issue of gays serving in the military—more on that shortly—but most of it apparently was culture clash. Les Aspin had a PhD in economics from MIT and had taught briefly at the college level. He looked the part. His appearance was often, to put it politely, rumpled, and he was known to show up as much as a half hour late for a morning meeting with high-ranking officers. Those officers simply found it harder and harder to relate to a boss who didn't seem to understand that 0800 hours did not mean 8:30 or so with a cup of coffee in your hand, and that appearance—even in the form of a clean and pressed shirt, pressed suit, and shined shoes—was a part of discipline, and discipline was central to an effective military. In the end it was simply very clear to the President that Les Aspin in the House of Representatives was very different from Les Aspin at the Pentagon.[18]

A President hopes to use a team of political executives to leave his or her stamp on the activities of the hundreds of agencies scattered throughout the executive branch. But every President soon learns that that team will not include some people he or she would very much like to have it include. Every President also learns that that team will include some individuals that he or she would just as soon not have on board. Finally, every President learns that some people just don't turn out to do the job as he or she had hoped and expected that they would. In the end, not getting everyone he or she wanted, getting "stuck" with some people he or she didn't want, and worst of all, finding that he or she would have been better off not getting some of the people that had been recruited with such high expectations does more than just frustrate a President and provide grist for the journalistic mill. It makes it just a little bit tougher for the chief to leave that stamp on the rest of the executive branch.

Loyalty to More Than One Master

Just as every President is forced to live with the unpleasant fact that the team of political executives sent to move the presidential agenda isn't exactly who or what he or she would have hoped for, every chief has to come to grips with the equally unpleasant fact that the men and women of that team of political executives are going to have to—indeed, are going to want to—be loyal to more than one master. They will think first of the President, of course. But they will also think of the Congress, the department or agencies under their purview, and especially the constituencies of those departments and agencies.

Loyalty to the President is first, and the reasons are obvious enough. To begin with, people get jobs as political executives in part because of the loyalty they have shown, loyalty either to the President or to someone in a position to influence the President's decision. On a slightly darker note, of course, the acceptance of one of these positions carries with it a generally unspoken agreement to leave the minute the President says go. Nobody really wants to be fired, even if he or she will land gently in some private-sector job or on a pile of money discreetly left behind when signing on to this stint of government service. Whether out of the normal desire to avoid the embarrassment of being fired and having to read about it in the papers, or out of a real commitment to a President and the success of his or her administration, the result is the same. The 4,000 or so political executives really do pay attention to what the President wants done and feel a strong obligation to try to do it.

But loyalty to the President inevitably ends up being tempered by loyalty to the Congress. Congress, after all, has a legitimate constitutional claim on that loyalty. It is a co-equal branch of government, and every one of those political executives takes an oath of office that in effect swears loyalty to the government, not to the President. But as important as constitutional obligation may be to most political executives, it is probably political reality that moves the bulk of them to worry about Congress's reaction to the decisions they make as they try to represent the President's interests in some corner of the executive branch. As I noted in chapter 2, Senate committees play the dominant role in the confirmation process for these political executives, and committees often lay the groundwork for future responsiveness—if not actual loyalty—from those executives during the verbal exchanges that are so central to that confirmation process. Beyond that, of course, it is in House and Senate committees that legislation is crafted, budgets are reviewed, and oversight takes place. Political executives ignore these committees at considerable peril, to the agencies they are supposed to manage and even to their own careers. As I also noted in chapter 2, this loyalty to Congress tends to be on display more the farther down we go in the ranks of the executive branch. Lower-level officials are likely to feel less like a part of the President's team, may well have more maneuvering room since they may well have not much in the way of instructions from the top, and almost certainly are more likely to find themselves in day-to-day contact with congressional committees—or at least staff members of same—than with anyone representing the White House. The President is always first. But Congress is a very definite second.

Two masters is tough enough, but the loyalties of political executives can almost never end with the President and Congress. These men and women are the managers/overseers of specific organizations—or at least pieces of organizations—and they have to exhibit some sort of loyalty to those organizational units and subunits. No large organization can be run by command, particularly not if subordinates have considerable knowledge and power of their own. So these political executives need the cooperation—or at least the neutrality—of the policy specialists if anything much is to be accomplished, and the price of that cooperation or neutrality is almost certainly going to be some loyalty to those policy specialists and their goals. Often as not, it turns out that loyalty to "their" agencies and the policy specialists who work there will play well in the congressional committees that are such an important part of the environment in which the political executives work.

Finally, political executives will find considerable pressure to be loyal to the constituencies—defined in terms of clientele groups, professional associations, and individual policy experts as you'll see in chapter 7—of the agencies or departments they are trying to manage. Some of that pressure will come from the aforementioned congressional committees and some from the careerists at the agencies and departments themselves. But a good bit of it will be self-imposed, that is, will come from the fact that with the exception of the handful of po-sitions at the top of each department, most of these political executives already have considerable loyalty to those constituencies. They have such loyalty, it turns out, because those constituencies played a significant role in their selection.

Constituency power in the selection of political executives is hardly news, so the story need not be told here in full.[19] Presidents are very responsive to the input of a department or agency's constituencies when making appointments to those departments or agencies, for what they consider two very good reasons. First comes the politics of the nomination/confirmation process. Politically, there is nothing much for a President to gain or lose in making most nominations to the ranks of the political executives, except what there is to gain or lose with the var-ious constituencies associated with the particular piece of the bureaucracy this individual is being selected to lead. This is particularly true on the confirmation end of the process, since these constituencies inevitably have close working re-lationships with the Senate committees who will hold the hearings and take the initial—and more often than not decisive—votes on these nominees. In the end there may not be all that much to gain politically by giving these constituencies exactly who they want at "their" agencies, but there is plenty to lose by trying to give them someone they don't want.

Outside of the realm of politics, Presidents still feel there are good reasons to listen and accommodate to these groups when selecting political executives. First of all, no President wants to send someone to lead an agency or group of agencies if that individual has no experience with the issues and agencies in question. Relying on an agency's constituencies would at least appear to avoid that trap. Beyond that, there really is a concern in American politics for making sure that directly affected groups have a disproportionate say over the resolution of the issues that involve them directly, and a major role in deciding who will hold the key executive positions at the agencies who work on those issues seems an excellent way to give these groups that sort of opportunity for influence over "their" issues. In short, the President and the Senate committees, the two sets of people who essentially control the nomination/confirmation process for political executives, choose to give a department or agency's constituencies a key role in the selecting of the men and women who will run the departments and agencies that affect their lives. The ultimate result, of course, is one more loyalty to be factored into the political executive's decision-making calculus.

It is almost impossible to say how any given political executive will sort out these various loyalties. At a minimum that sorting process will be affected by the executive's personal background, the particular agency or agencies under his or her purview, and the specific issue at hand. As we shall see in the next chapter, loyalty to Congress—its committees, of course—agency or agencies, and constituencies may all end up pointing in one direction. That would be an easy choice if it weren't for the fact that loyalty to the President might well be pointing in exactly the opposite direction. In any event, even though we can't sort out all of the factors that will determine which loyalty or loyalties prevail in any given situation, this much we can say. With a few exceptions, political executives are anything but robots programmed to carry out the President's every wish.

How Much Managing Can They Actually Do?

How much managing can political executives do? More than the President can, but less than the President would like.

On one level, of course, it is ridiculous to compare the office of President of the United States with the office of Assistant Secretary of Labor for Employment Standards. The range and scope of duties, the time pressures, the political demands, everything about the Assistant Secretary's job literally seems to pale by comparison with that of the President. But on another level, or maybe in another sense, the Assistant Secretary's job is the President's job writ small. Well, writ very small, perhaps, but you get the idea. Every one of those 4,000 plus political executives faces a downsized version of the President's main problems. To be sure, the "downsized Presidency" that faces the Assistant Secretary for Employment Standards is a whole lot more downsized than is the "downsized Presidency" that faces the Secretary of Defense, the Secretary of Health and Human Services, or even the Secretary of Labor. But the point remains the same, no matter how much the problems have been downsized. That is, just like the President, political executives lack the motivation and resources to become deeply involved in the management of the organizations they have been selected to, well, manage.

The farther down the hierarchical ladder you go, the greater the motivation to try your hand at management. After all, if you have responsibility for only a handful of agencies, you will be expected to take a more active role in managing them, so while the President's future may not ride on anything that happens at your agencies, your future just might. But even at this bottom level, things are going to be happening that don't appear to be likely to have much impact on any of the goals one would expect a political executive at this level to bring to the table. As soon as we start ascending the organization, the likelihood of motivation to spend all of one's time managing the organization is going to drop, with the drop accelerating as we continue the climb.

But it isn't so much the lack of motivation as it is the lack of resources that seems to get in the way of serious efforts at management by most political executives. Where are the time, the knowledge, and the interest? The job of Assistant Secretary of Interior for Land and Minerals Management can hardly be compared to the job of President of the United States, but that Assistant Secretary somehow has to find the time to oversee the work of three large agencies, most of whose employees work 2,000 miles or more from Washington. And he or she is going to have to muster enough knowledge about surface-mining issues to know what's going on at the Office of Surface Mining Reclamation and Enforcement, deep-shaft-mining issues to know what is going on at the Minerals Management Service, and a whole range of issues including mining but also including grazing, timber cutting, recreation, and more, at the Bureau of Land Management. Then, of course, there is the question of who would be interested in all of those issues.

Though they were originally put to paper more than thirty years ago and meant primarily to refer to the men and women who occupied the top echelon of executive-branch jobs, these words of scholar/practitioner Harold Seidman still ring true and, even though in varying degrees from one job to another, describe the world and the mindset of virtually all political executives:

> A department head's job is akin to that of a major university president and subject to the same frustrations. His [her] principal duties involve matters which are unrelated to the internal administration and management of the institution. So far as his [her] subordinates are concerned, he [she] is the institution's ceremonial head, chief fund raiser, and protector of institutional values and territory. An informal check reveals that a department head may spend 25 percent or more of his [her] time in meetings with members of the Congress and appearances before congressional committees, and probably an equivalent amount of time in public relations work such as speech making and cultivating agency constituencies. Another block of time is devoted to White House conferences and meetings of interagency and advisory committees. Minimal time is left for managing the department, even if a secretary is one of the rare political executives with a taste for administration.[20]

But It Still Matters Who Gets These Jobs

As we've seen, a President who hopes to put together a team of political executives who will extend his or her presence into the far corners of the executive domain, fearlessly and flawlessly guiding policy just as the chief would if only he or she could be there to do it, is going to be more than a bit disappointed. The flame-out of a Les Aspin, the implosion of a Linda Chavez, or the almost-coerced choice of a William Ruckelshaus may be rare, but divided loyalties and serious barriers to effective management go with the territory the political executive is expected to occupy. In the process, of course, they undermine the President's ability to use those political executives to serve his or her purposes. They undermine it, but they don't destroy it.

First of all, the men and women who occupy these jobs as political executives can set a tone for the agencies and departments they lead. In a very real sense these men and women, especially those at or near the top of the so-called bureaucratic pyramid, are symbols, not just racial, ethnic, or gender symbols but symbols of the kinds of ideas and policies that will be well received in this particular administration. That can make a real difference to the policy specialists working at the agency level. Consider just two examples.

The Assistant Secretary of Labor for Occupational Safety and Health has direct responsibility for the Occupational Safety and Health Administration (OSHA). In the Carter administration, the Assistant Secretary's job was held by Dr. Eula Bingham, a highly respected scholar of occupational health issues. When Ronald Reagan took over from President Carter in January 1981, Dr. Bingham was replaced by a man named Thorne Auchter. Mr. Auchter was the son of the owner of a Florida construction company, a company that held the record for the most fines issued by OSHA in the decade of the 1970s. It is hard to imagine clearer messages being sent, to the professionals at OSHA or to the industries they worked with, than were sent by those two appointments.

Now go up the hierarchical ladder at the Department of Labor. And fast forward two decades. Bill Clinton's final Secretary of Labor was Alexis Herman.

Ms. Herman had started her career as a social worker specializing in helping workers find new jobs in her native Mississippi. From there she moved on to specialize in labor-force issues involving women, a stint as head of the Women's Bureau in the Labor Department, and in the 1980s founded her own consulting firm designed to help corporations with recruitment and retention issues. Then came the assignment to manage the 1992 Democratic National Convention, a turn as a staff member in the Clinton White House, and eventually the job as Labor Secretary. Ms. Herman's successor, President George W. Bush's first Labor Secretary, was Elaine Chao. Ms. Chao had received an MBA from the Harvard Business School and had moved back and forth between the public and private sectors. Her public service career included a tour as Director of the Peace Corps, as well as some time spent in administrative positions at the Transportation Department and at the Federal Maritime Administration. In the private sector, she served as a Vice President at Bank of America and as President and CEO of the United Way of America. She left that post to become a Senior Fellow at the Heritage Foundation, and from Heritage she took over the Labor Department. While the difference between Ms. Herman and Ms. Chao may not be of the snap-your-neck variety seen in the difference between a respected academic with years of experience in her agency's field and a construction-company executive whose only experience with his agency is to see its name on a citation for violating the agency's rules, it is substantial nonetheless. Whether you are a professional in the middle reaches of OSHA or at the Employment Standards Administration, or someone who represents one of the Labor Department's normal constituencies, the difference is enormous and you know what direction things are going to go.

Differences in tone don't always mean huge differences in policy, but they can. When Thorne Auchter replaced Eula Bingham, one of his first acts was to inform OSHA's professional staff that all future rule-making decisions would be subject to cost benefit analysis. That would include rules about workplace exposure to suspected carcinogens. This despite the fact that the U.S. Supreme Court had ruled less than a year earlier that the Occupational Safety and Health Act did not require such analyses in cases involving possible workplace-related cancers.[21] Given the amount of time and expenditure of scarce resources involved in doing a cost benefit analysis, not to mention the difficulty often found in quantifying the health benefits of lower cancer risks, there was no doubt that Mr. Auchter was changing the rules in such a way that industry was bound to benefit. That was precisely his—and by extension President Reagan's—intention. We can just as easily see President Clinton's vision, if not his direct participation, in Alexis Herman's 1999 decision to push hard for new rules that would force more attention to the prevention of ergonomic-related injuries, and we can see President George W. Bush's views, again even if not his direct participation, in Elaine Chao's 2003 decision to go ahead with new overtime pay rules despite strong opposition from organized labor and from a good many congressional Democrats.[22]

There can be no doubt that within the limits imposed by the politics of the nomination/confirmation process and the obligatory nod to expertise required as we descend closer and closer to operating agencies, a President can use the appointments of political executives to set a tone or create an atmosphere in an agency or department, and that tone or atmosphere can sometimes find its way into important policy decisions. But on a day-to-day basis, such appointments almost always provide a more effective way to slow down bureaucratic activity than to speed it up.

When Ronald Reagan took office, he appointed a man by the name of Ford B. Ford to oversee the relatively new Mine Safety and Health Administration (MSHA). Mr. Ford quickly informed his team of mine inspectors that they should "no longer be perceived in your minds...as MSHA's chief enforcement officers. Instead you are to be MSHA's chief health and safety managers in the field."[23] And how were the inspectors to do it? Stop coming up with recommended punishments and simply offer advice. The predictable result: fewer inspections, fewer citations, and at least in the eyes of the United Mine Workers, less-safe mines.[24] I am not suggesting that Ronald Reagan wanted less-safe mines. But he did want fewer rules and fewer inspectors and fewer inspections. He got them. Had the President wanted the opposite, Ford B. Ford would have had to push for the money to hire the new inspectors, see that they were trained, and convince them that they would be backed up if they did issue citations. He would have had to prepare to fight the inevitable political and legal pressure from the mine owners. He might even have had to beat back challenges from inside the Congress. It was just easier to get MSHA to do less than it would have been to get it to do more.

It is distinctly possible that President Reagan hadn't met former Indiana legislator James R. Harris when he appointed him to head the Office of Surface Mining Reclamation and Enforcement, but the President had met James Watt, and James Watt had met James Harris and he liked Mr. Harris and his ideas. So, despite some questions about some of his dealings with the Peabody Coal Company, Mr. Harris got the job, brought a number of like-minded individuals—many suggested by his boss, Interior Secretary James Watt—on board, and proceeded to bring the office's enforcement activities nearly to a halt.[25] Again, had Mr. Harris's goal been to make the office's enforcement activities more wide ranging and vigorous, he would have faced a tougher task, this time not only involving more money and more inspectors, but involving moving state governments, never an easy job.

Examples from the Reagan administration abound, as do examples from the six years that Richard Nixon spent as President. It is possible to see some of the same in George W. Bush's years in office as well. The point here is not to criticize conservative Presidents. They want their views implemented, and as President, one of the ways they are entitled to do that is through the appointments they make. All that is being said here is this: a President who wants to slow or stop the process of writing and enforcing rules generally has an effective tool in his or her team of political executives. A President who wants to put his or her hand on the fast-forward button in bureaucracy will find that team of political executives a far less potent weapon.

In Summary

On a December night in 1968, I sat with a group of fellow teaching assistants in my apartment in Ann Arbor, Michigan, and watched as President-elect Richard Nixon introduced the men he would nominate to run the various departments of the cabinet. To the group in that room—a group that included more votes for comedian and activist Dick Gregory than for Mr. Nixon—the program looked for all the world like a parody of a very popular show aired every winter back then in which legendary comedian Bob Hope would introduce that year's All America football team. Except, instead of watching the introduction of Mike Garret, USC, halfback, Terry Baker, Oregon State University, quarterback, and Dick Butkus, Illinois, linebacker, we saw Melvin Laird, Wisconsin, Defense, William Rogers, New York, State, and John Mitchell, New York, Justice. But the look and feel were eerily the same.

Even though the show made particularly bad television, it did illustrate the way that Presidents generally think about the appointments they are called upon to make. Presidents inevitably have a great deal of faith in the notion of leadership, that is, in the idea that strong and competent individuals can take on a task and, through their intelligence, hard work, and most importantly leadership skills, can get that task accomplished. So they inevitably have a great deal of faith in the capacity of the teams of political executives they pick to get hold of the bureaucratic monster and, if not tame it, at least bring its worst tendencies under control. Besides, if Presidents don't believe in the ability of their political executives to make a substantial difference, how can they believe that they can create a presidency—an administration, if you will—that works? No matter how strong the ego, no President believes that he or she can do it alone.

So Presidents have to go into the political executive selection business with some considerable hope for, and expectation of, success. The alternative is too bleak. But the reality of the selection process itself combines with the reality of the world in which those political executives must work, to keep that hoped-for success from ever being fully within the President's grasp.

I don't know if any of the twelve men the President-elect introduced that night were "second choices" for the posts they had agreed to accept, but sooner or later every President finds that somebody he or she really wants says no, or that somebody who says yes is prevented from actually taking the job. The chief may even find out that circumstances dictate nominating someone he or she would just as soon not work with.

No matter how many of the jobs he or she has to fill are filled by people the President is thrilled to have there, every President eventually learns that there are some immense pressures on these men and women and that those pressures will move them away from the role of presidential emissary and toward the far more complicated role of political executive in the American governing system.

First of all, with the possible exception of a handful of top cabinet appointees, political executives in our system cannot give their exclusive loyalty to the President. The chief will get first call on that loyalty to be sure, but first call is not exclusive call. There is Congress, with a real constitutional prerogative to assert and plenty of political weapons to make sure its cry for adherence to the Constitution's separation of powers and co-equal branches of government philosophy is heard in the ranks of the political executives. Then there are the policy specialists at the agencies these executives oversee. Political executives may not have to "win the hearts and minds" of those careerists, but if they ignore them and create a climate of distrust and hostility, those executives are going to find themselves less than effective in leading their organizations. Finally, of course, the agencies and departments of our government have constituencies in the public, and those constituencies expect—and get—some considerable role in the selection of the political executives who will work with "their" agencies and departments, and they use that role plus their working relationships with congressional committees and the agencies and departments themselves to make sure that the political executives working on "their" turf know it is "their" turf.

Beyond that, the President's team of political executives is not really in a position to do as much managing of the agencies and departments they were sent to manage as they and their President might hope. Many lack the motivation, but even those who have motivation in abundance don't have the time, knowledge, or interest to act on it.

As we saw just a couple of pages ago, the selections a President makes for the ranks of the political executives really can make a difference. The Labor Department is a different place to work under a woman with a Harvard MBA, no significant experience with labor issues, and who is fresh from a year at the conservative Heritage Foundation than it was under a woman trained in social work, with a lifetime spent working on workforce-related issues, and experience running one of the department's constituent bureaus. The difference shows, just as the difference between an occupational health specialist and a construction-company executive showed at OSHA, or the difference between a Wall Street reformer and a trial lawyer who represented accounting and brokerage firms showed at the Securities and Exchange Commission.

Still, on balance, a President has to realize that while the men and women he or she taps for the political executive corps may well become active participants in the policy-making environments of the agencies they are sent to oversee, they will be less active than the chief might have expected, and that activity will not be guided strictly and exclusively by the President's preferences. Everybody else realizes it soon enough.

The Institutionalized Presidency

Just as the President relies on the White House staff and the corps of political executives to extend his or her presence into the bureaucracy, he or she can rely on the Executive Office of the President (EOP), the various special commissions and advisory panels that Presidents create to address—or duck—specific issues, and the career civil servants who agree to enter the Senior Executive Service (SES) and thereby serve as the President's extra hands, to make the executive branch a more receptive place to his or her leadership. As with the White House staff and the political executives, there are some significant limitations on just how much the Executive Office organizations, the commissions and panels, and the SES careerists can do. But, again, as with the White House staff and the political executives, all three of these elements of the institutionalized Presidency will give the chief at least some increased leverage in executive-branch policy making.

The Executive Office of the President

We will start with the Executive Office of the President because it is in the EOP that Presidents and those that advise them—and for that matter, those who study both Presidents and those who advise them—have generally placed the greatest hope for increasing presidential influence in the executive branch.

In a sense, the EOP, like the bureaucracy the President hopes to use it to influence, has grown more or less like a coral reef, a little at a time and never too noticeably. It was created in 1939, in large part in response to a report prepared under the direction of University of Chicago political scientist Louis Brownlow, a report which began with a sentence that has become legendary in that small circle of people who actually do study Presidents and bureaucrats and their interactions. That sentence: "The President needs help."[26] Brownlow and his colleagues had concluded that the executive branch was out of control, going its own way with little if any influence from the chief executive. More to the point, they didn't like that state of affairs. They felt it defied management orthodoxy—somebody's got to be in charge around here—and to their credit, they were very worried about what it meant for democratic responsibility in an increasingly large and active government. So Brownlow and company proposed a move of the Bureau of the Budget from the Treasury Department to the Executive Office, the creation of a new Office of Personnel Management to give the chief some influence over the policies that governed hiring and firing in the rest of the government, and the creation of a special corps of managers who would be chosen out of the ranks of the career civil service but would commit themselves to the President and his or her policies. These last two didn't happen for another four decades—they were in the Civil Service Reform Act of 1978—but the Bureau of the Budget was moved, five other units were combined with it, and the Executive Office of the President was born. By 1992, the EOP had become thirteen units, growing to fourteen the following year when President Clinton split the Office of Policy Development into the National Economic Council and the Domestic Council.[27] On July 11, 2003, sixteen units were listed as parts of the EOP on the White House website.[28]

The question, of course, is not so much how many units are there, or even what those units are called. The question is whether the President can use them to increase his or her influence over policy choices being made in the departments and agencies. As usual, the answer is hardly a clear-cut yes or no.

For a substantial number of those units, we can say that the answer is like the answer from the junior executive in the old Hertz commercials—"Not exactly." Units such as the Office of Faith-Based and Community Initiatives, the Office of National AIDS Policy, the Office of National Drug Control Policy, or the Office of Science and Technology Policy are pretty much designed to offer occasional advice to the President, and probably to provide some sort of symbols of White House concern with particular issues or problems. Once the information and advice are given, the jobs of these units are more or less done. They may try to communicate with operating agencies in their respective fields, but with virtually no statutory authority, limited budgets and personnel, and in reality located farther from the President than they appear on paper, they are not likely to be terribly effective in influencing agency policy making. This doesn't make such units worthless. Information and advice are always useful, and just reminding operating agencies that someone at least in the proximity of the White House is interested in an issue might have some limited impact. But overall, these units, and some of the others, really can't be said to do much to extend the President's presence in the policy process at the agency or even at the departmental level.

Other units, such as the Council of Economic Advisors (CEA), its cousin the National Economic Council (NEC), and the Council on Environmental Quality (CEQ) are in some senses in the same boat as the organizations who watch AIDS, drugs, or science and technology. They keep track of important issues and provide information and advice. But despite the seemingly high profiles of issues like AIDS and drug control, Presidents know that the economy and the environment are going to attract more attention come election time, so they may listen a bit more carefully when being briefed by the chair of the Council of Economic Advisors, the National Economic Council, or the Council on Environmental Quality. That's no guarantee of followup by the President, and it's hard to say how much influence the Council of Economic Advisors would have as the Departments of Commerce, Labor, or Treasury play their respective roles in the day-to-day operation of economic policy. Still, again, more presidential attention to the issues they deal with has to put CEA, CEQ, and NEC on a somewhat different footing than much of the rest of the Executive Office.

In effect, most of the sixteen units in the EOP are called on—are able—to do little more than offer some information and advice, provide an organizational presence to cover the chief in case of charges that he or she is neglecting an issue, and nip at the heels of the folks with "real responsibility" for the questions at hand. That doesn't appear to enhance presidential influence a great deal. But there are the two heavyweights of the Executive Office, the National Security Council and the Office of Management and Budget. I won't talk about the former, since it tends to operate more or less in secret, and more to the point, it tends to confine itself to a single policy area that we all expect Presidents to be involved with on a routine basis. But the Office of Management and Budget, the fabled OMB, is quite a different matter. In theory, at least, its scope is virtually unlimited, and its power would appear to be considerable. We'll talk about the B part shortly. For now let's concentrate on M.

As I noted earlier, the Bureau of the Budget was the lead organization in the newly created Executive Office in 1939. It plied its budgetary trade in a highly organized and systematic way for the next thirty years, but in 1970, Richard Nixon decided that the President needed management assistance as much as he needed budgetary assistance. So he changed the name of the Bureau of the Budget to the Office of Management and Budget, put businessman Roy Ash in charge of the renamed unit, and waited for things managerial to happen. The changes at OMB may have been a little slower than President Nixon had hoped they would be, but they came.

It began innocently enough with something called the Paperwork Reduction Act, passed late in the Carter administration.[29] The idea behind the statute was to reduce the burden on American citizens—and especially the businesses they run—of filling out all those forms and answering all those questions from the bureaucrats in Washington. Under the law, no agency under the President's direct authority could request information it hadn't already been requesting when the law was passed, unless it either got explicit approval from the Office of Management and Budget or adopted the new information request through the agency's standard rule-making process. The statute probably slowed down the information gathering activities of some agencies, but its real importance wasn't felt until Ronald Reagan had won the 1980 election, taken office, and issued Executive Order 12291.

EO 12291 required that all proposed rules with an anticipated impact on the economy of $100 million or more be submitted to the Office of Management and Budget, where said rules would be subjected to a cost benefit analysis. The executive order did not grant OMB the authority to block the promulgation of rules it found to be too costly in terms of the benefits generated, but there was no question in anybody's mind while Ronald Reagan was President that he wanted fewer rules imposed on business, and a no from OMB was assumed to be tantamount to a no from the President himself. The President can't necessarily block a rule from going into effect himself or herself either, for that matter, but the President can almost certainly fire any administrator who issues a rule he or she doesn't like, so OMB opposition to an agency's rule is going to be a serious enough business that any agency is going to have to accommodate to that opposition. OMB influence over agency rule making hit a bump in the road in 1990 when the U.S. Supreme Court held that the agency lacked the statutory authority to block the issuance of rules that agencies wished to issue.[30] The bump was smoothed out by the newly elected Republican Congress in 1995 with a new version of the Paperwork Reduction Act.

George H. W. Bush used Executive Order 12291 and the 1980 Paperwork Reduction Act on occasion, but President Clinton wasn't all that interested in slowing or stopping the rule-making process, so he tended not to use OMB in the way his two immediate predecessors had. He did, however, sign the 1995 statute that restored to OMB all of the power claimed for it by Presidents George H. W. Bush and Ronald Reagan.[31] George W. Bush, however, was very interested in using OMB to put his personal mark on the rule-making process, and he did. In fact, new ground was broken in OMB influence in the rule-making process when the agency announced in June 2002 that it would work alongside officials from the Environmental Protection Agency to come up with a mutually acceptable draft of new regulations governing the soot emissions of off-road diesel engines.[32] Clearly, having OMB representatives at the table with EPA representatives extends the President's presence into the rule-making process in ways most agencies aren't used to. Whether it is precedent for EPA or precedent for all agencies under the President's umbrella remains to be seen.

In short, most of the Executive Office of the President doesn't do all that much to make the President more of a managerial presence throughout the executive branch. Most of the Executive Office wasn't designed to. But the Bureau of the Budget was designed to make the chief a budgetary presence, and when the Bureau of the Budget became the Office of Management and Budget, it was almost certainly only a matter of time until some President decided to get more serious about managing, at least at some agencies on some issues. It has worked. That is not to say that OMB means a presidential presence everywhere in the bureaucracy. But it does mean a greater presidential presence some places in the bureaucracy, and the OMB, with a lot of input from the White House, gets to pick those places.

A Look From Outsiders: Presidential Advisory Commissions

In one sense, it might seem odd to include presidential advisory commissions in the notion of the institutionalized presidency as a means of increasing the chief executive's managerial presence in bureaucracy. Such commissions are generally issue—occasionally agency—specific, of fairly short duration, and don't do much that would appear managerial. But in a broader sense, such commissions are supposed to be, in some cases even can be, a way of dealing with two of the most significant problems Presidents face in leading the executive branch.

First of all, as we have said repeatedly, the President just doesn't have the time, knowledge, or interest to take a serious look at more than a handful of issues at a time. Finding a group of citizens with the time and interest, and giving them a budget that will allow them to hire a staff with the knowledge, can go a long ways toward alleviating that particular presidential problem.

Second, the President can become what almost amounts to a captive of what Hugh Heclo called the "mutually familiar rhetoric of argumentation" that tends to dominate the way an agency—and its traditional supporters—define and discuss the issues they deal with and the solutions they propose.[33] A different perspective may well require an entirely different set of eyes, and a presidential advisory commission may be the best way to get that different set of eyes. The institutionalized presidency itself, remember, was largely born out of the work of a special presidential advisory commission, and there can be no doubt at all that a commission headed by three political scientists from outside the bureaucracy was a lot more likely to come up with the idea of expanding the President's influence inside that bureaucracy by giving him more staff, institutions specifically geared to watching bureaucracy, and even a hand in personnel policy than any group of professionals drawn from the inside would have been.

A great many special presidential advisory commissions, of course, are not appointed to expand the President's time, knowledge, and interest about something he or she was vaguely aware might be a problem, or even to look for creative ways to address questions outside of the normal patterns of bureaucratic thinking. These commissions, instead, come into being because something happens and the chief has to respond. The presidential commission is a natural enough response. Lyndon Johnson had to appoint some sort of special commission to investigate the assassination of John F. Kennedy. He felt similarly compelled to address the issues of urban violence after the terrifying summers of 1965 through 1967. Ronald Reagan believed that a special commission was needed to investigate the causes of the explosion of the space shuttle *Challenger*, just as George W. Bush felt he needed to appoint a similar commission to investigate the loss of *Columbia*. Likewise, both Reagan and Bush came reluctantly to the need for commissions to investigate the Iran-Contra affair and the September 11, 2001, attacks, respectively.

But a good many special presidential advisory commissions really are aimed at learning more about an issue that has somehow made the White House radar screen even without massive tragedy, and at "shaking up" thinking as usual in a policy area. Quite frequently, as we will see in the three examples below, that "shaking up" is aimed at shaping a policy debate more to the liking of a President and/or some of his or her people.

In early 1987, Gary Bauer, then head of President Reagan's White House Office of Policy Development, approached the President with the idea of appointing a special presidential commission on AIDS. No one could doubt the significance of the issue, but that wasn't really what motivated Gary Bauer. An evangelical Christian with deeply conservative social values, Bauer considered homosexuality "an abomination."[34] He wanted the commission because he was very unhappy with the direction in which AIDS policy appeared to be headed and the way—and places—in which it was being made. He had already challenged Surgeon General C. Everett Koop over Koop's advocacy of condoms as a partial solution to the spread of the disease, but Bauer felt more needed to be done. A presidential commission, particularly one with the right make-up, could be used to shift the framework of debate from AIDS as public health crisis, to AIDS as moral crisis. President Reagan bought the idea, and the AIDS commission was born. The commission itself was delayed several months as Bauer fought the appointment of even a single gay member to the panel. The public health community inside the government rebelled, and the ultimate compromise was the appointment of a gay cancer surgeon from New York City.[35] There is no simple historical scoreboard to use to judge the success of Bauer's efforts. The AIDS commission clearly was a place that was friendly to the goal of debating AIDS as moral crisis, and that may well have influenced some aspects of AIDS policy over the next few years. But no presidential commission could dislodge the public health community from its view of the crisis as a public health crisis, so in whatever ways this community could shape AIDS policy, the direction of that policy was very different from what Mr. Bauer had hoped.[36]

The events of September 11, huge budget deficits, and war with Iraq and its aftermath shoved its recommendations to Washington's back burner, but President George W. Bush's special commission to study the Social Security program has to fall into the category of attempting to change the terms of debate surrounding an issue. There is no question that the idea of "privatizing" part of the Social Security system by diverting some of the taxes paid by individuals and then creating accounts that those individuals could invest in on their own had been discussed in a variety of places before George W. Bush took over as President. It was a staple at conservative think tanks. But it hadn't gotten much favorable discussion inside the government, and it certainly hadn't been given the status in the policy-making community that the President tried to give it by creating a special commission and making sure that that commission had members clearly identified with the idea.[37]

On occasion, Presidents even reach out to try to use one or two of the myriad of special advisory committees and commissions that are a routine part of the way many agencies formulate policy. Most of us—quite possibly including President George W. Bush himself—have probably never heard of the Advisory Committee on Childhood Lead Poisoning Prevention. But it exists, and in mid 2002 it was preparing to review a Centers for Disease Control staff recommendation to lower the allowable level of lead exposure for children. A few weeks before the meeting at which the initial discussion of the proposal was to take place, CDC staff scientists made a number of recommendations for individuals to fill some vacancies on the committee. Secretary of Health and Human Services Tommy Thompson took the unusual step of rejecting the names of several of those nominees. Perhaps more to the point, Thompson's own nominees included five people closely identified with the lead industry. Indeed, three of these nominees subsequently admitted that they had been contacted by a representative of the industry to ask if they would mind having their names submitted to the department for service on the committee. A similar pattern—without Secretary Thompson tossing out recommendations from the agency's scientists—appears to have been followed with respect to another CDC panel, when scientists tied to the petroleum industry were appointed to the CDC's environmental health advisory committee.[38]

No one would put special presidential advisory committees or commissions on a par with the institutions of the Executive Office of the President as a mechanism for asserting presidential influence at the agency level. But then, these committees or commissions aren't really intended for that job. They are intended to respond—or appear to be responding—to problems, to focus policy-making attention on an issue by focusing the attention of the presidency on that issue without actually tying up the President himself or herself, and changing the terms under which an issue or problem is debated. Some commissions have been successful at one or all of these. Many have not. Presidents will almost certainly continue to use them in the hope that the next one will accomplish the objective that that particular President has in mind for it.

The Senior Executive Service

The Senior Executive Service was created in the Civil Service Reform Act of 1978, though the idea was included as a key recommendation of the second Hoover Commission more than twenty years earlier. Viewed through the prism of management orthodoxy and admiration for the British Civil Service that was so widespread among executive-branch reformers from the Brownlow Committee, on through both Hoover Commissions, to the men and women who advised the Carter administration as it prepared the 1978 statute, the Senior Executive Service was seen as an excellent vehicle for helping the President manage his or her vast administrative empire.[39] Viewed from the perspective of those of us in the study of public administration who took our lead from the work of men like Emmette Redford, Roscoe Martin, and most especially Frederick Mosher, the Senior Executive Service looked like another group of proud subject-matter experts who just happened to have "risen through the ranks," and would be less than enthusiastic about carrying the flag of each new administration idea. As Mosher himself reported, "I have talked with a number of members of the Senior Executive Service who said that they had never thought of themselves as executives. They were engineers, biologists, lawyers, economists. They did not consider themselves managers or executives although they have made or participated in decisions affecting thousands of subordinates, millions of citizens, and sometimes billions of dollars."[40]

For a variety of reasons, it appears that the men and women of the Senior Executive Service did not turn into a cadre of presidentially directed managers extending the chief's influence into the agencies to which they were assigned. To begin with, as Frederick Mosher suggested, the career civil servants who traded in their GS rating for a spot in the SES were proud policy specialists. Ties to their specialties couldn't simply be put in the closet to be trotted out at the next meeting of their own particular professional society. Then add to that the fact that the SES pay system was a chaotic mess for the first few years.[41] Now bring in the fact that only two years into the experiment, the folks who had originated the idea—the Carter administration—made a constitutionally mandated exit to be replaced by the Reagan administration, complete with a chief executive, recall, who had identified government as the problem, not the solution, and run by a set of political executives who were, in the delightfully understated words of Patricia Ingraham and James Thompson, "highly ideological and opposed to the permanent bureaucracy on philosophic grounds."[42] Under such circumstances, it's hard to see how a cadre of career civil servants could have been turned into managerial shock troops for the administration just by changing the label attached to their status in the government.

Again, from the viewpoint of those who came up with the idea, it is easy to see the appeal of the idea. There was a bright and dedicated corps of senior managers who could have been added to the President's team of political executives to make a formidable force for presidential leadership. And, again, from the viewpoint of those more attuned to thinking about the federal bureaucracy with a framework derived from the work of Redford, Martin, Mosher, and others, it seemed an idea that just couldn't work. Given the circumstances in which the idea of the Senior Executive Service was implemented, we will never know if either of those viewpoints was more prescient than the other. From either viewpoint, however, it is fair to say that "the Senior Executive Service is an experiment that never happened."[43] From the viewpoint of a President who wanted to use that Senior Executive Service as part of his or her management team, it probably seems more like "an opportunity lost."[44]

In Summary

An executive, even a chief executive, even *the* chief executive, has to do some managing. That is, he or she has to provide some direction for the enterprise and has to follow up to make sure that is the direction the enterprise is going. No executive can do it alone, of course. So they get help. The President of the United States gets help in the form of a White House staff he or she can count on for a thousand tasks. The President also gets a set of organizations collected into something called the Executive Office of the President and instructed to put his or her personal stamp on the actions of the rest of the executive branch, the power to name advisory committees to study anything that attracts his or her interest, and a cadre of career managers called the Senior Executive Service who are, theoretically anyway, willing and able to put their experience and management skills at the President's disposal. And, most of all, the President gets a corps of political executives he or she can assign to the key leadership posts around the bureaucracy. But the question remains: does all this help help?

The White House staff clearly helps. The President knows that this set of people will do his or her bidding, and that they really do hope everything they do on the chief's behalf works. But Presidents eventually come to learn that even the most loyal and dedicated White House staff can only do so much to advance the President's interests. There are so few of them—relative to the immense task— and they are not viewed as particularly credible on policy questions. Their job (and their perspective) is presumed to be almost exclusively political. On top of that, they are seen as credible representatives of the President only if they are believed to be close enough to the chief to really be speaking for him or her. Obviously, that can't be the entire staff.

The institutionalized presidency—defined here in terms of the Executive Office of the President, presidential advisory committees, and the Senior Executive Service—can also help the President extend his or her reach into the bureaucracy, but only so far. Much of the EOP consists of purely advisory organizations with staffs, budgets, and mandates that simply don't allow them to be very effective representatives of the chief. The Office of Management and Budget is a clear exception, and there is no doubt that it has taken on more and more responsibility in the three decades since Richard Nixon shook up the old Bureau of the Budget by giving it added management responsibilities. Still, even OMB can't be everywhere and do everything. It can be involved in the rule-making process but must stay out of the rule-enforcement process, and it doesn't have the staff or the time to become a major force in every rule-making proceeding. Like the President it serves, OMB has to pick and choose. Presidential advisory committees can provide a means for a chief executive to get an in-depth study of an issue or, more often, to change the terms of debate about an important issue and, in the process, loosen an agency's grip on that issue and the process of addressing it. But many such committees accomplish little, and even one begun with the fanfare of President George W. Bush's Social Security commission can end up producing "much sound and fury, signifying nothing." Finally, we may never know if the Senior Executive Service would have expanded the President's ability to manage the executive branch. Given the way in which the idea was implemented, it never had a chance.

But important as White House staff, presidential commissions, the Senior Executive Service, and the Office of Management and Budget may be to a President's efforts to influence agency-level policy making, it has to be the political executives on which the President bets his or her administration. These are the people who take the spots that show up on the organization charts that tell us who has the authority to make the key decisions at the Department of Defense, the Environmental Protection Agency, the Bureau of Land Management, or the Employment Standards Administration. They help the President. They definitely help the President. But that corps of political executives isn't always composed of exactly the folks the President would like to see in those jobs, and even when the chief does get his or her "dream" candidate for Assistant Secretary of Labor for Employment Standards, Assistant Secretary of Interior for Fish and Wildlife and Parks, or Assistant Attorney General for Civil Rights, the dream may turn into a nightmare. Beyond that, nearly every one of these political executives owes loyalty—or at least responsiveness—to people other than the President, and sometimes those other loyalties will win out. Finally, there is only so much management these political executives can do. There is only so much managing they are likely to try, given the other demands on their time and interest, but even when they try, there is only so much they can do.

Brownlow and colleagues were right. The President needs help. And, thanks in part to Brownlow and colleagues, as well as to generations of other scholars and practitioners of government, the President has help. And all of this help helps him or her do the job of chief executive. But in the end, when it comes to setting the direction for the enterprise called the United States government, and especially when it comes to following up to make sure that enterprise is going in the chief's preferred direction, the President inevitably falls short of what he or she and his or her supporters hope for and expect. The help just can't help that much.

Influencing the Organizational Environment II: A Matter of Structure

Harold Seidman, the respected administrator turned insightful academic I have quoted from so often in this book, began each of the four editions of his widely read *Politics, Position, and Power* with this observation: "Reorganization has become almost a religion in Washington."[45] As we noted earlier, the modern presidency more or less began when the Brownlow Committee recommended a variety of reorganizations of the executive branch, and once World War II was over, we began almost a decade of careful and detailed study of how we went about organizing our government. Entrusting oversight of these studies to former President Herbert Hoover—the resulting products were, as you might guess, known as the Reports of the First and Second Hoover Commissions—we were offered an incredible number of recommendations about how we might better structure that government according to sound organizational and management principles. Far-reaching proposals to restructure the federal government came from Presidents as fundamentally different as Richard Nixon—who claimed that the primary cause of governmental ineffectiveness was "a matter of machinery" and proposed a reorganization more sweeping than anything seen before—and Jimmy Carter—who told the Democratic Platform Committee in 1976 that "We must give top priority to a drastic and thorough reorganization of the Federal bureaucracy."[46] Neither President followed through on this commitment to reorganizing the government, but we'll get to that shortly.

I must admit that I tend to doubt that the primary cause of governmental ineffectiveness is "a matter of machinery," but that certainly doesn't mean that the way we structure the government doesn't matter. I won't force you to go back to read parts of chapter 3, but it's worth recalling that structure really does matter.

First, let's glance back at the concept of structure itself. We defined structure, remember, in terms of the rules of the organization and its paper structure. The rule that seems to be the most important in any organization is the rule that spells out who makes the rest of the rules, and that, recall, is what we called the principle of hierarchy. The paper structure, we said, could be thought of in terms of the answers to three questions, specifically, (1) what organizational unit will get responsibility for a particular function? (2) what will be the relationship between that organizational unit and the rest of the government? and (3) whose signature will be required to make a particular decision binding on the rest of the organization and, by extension, on the citizenry?

Now, let's reconsider the importance of structure. In terms of the principle of hierarchy, we noted that that principle imposed on organizations an authority structure in which the authority to make—review and reverse in practice, but make in theory—any decision in the organization belonged to a single individual or group and was parceled out to others in the organization in a manner that was both partial and conditional. We also noted that if the principle of hierarchy were unchecked in an organization, that organization's decision-making system would suffer, as its ability to communicate ideas upward to those responsible for making decisions would be compromised, and many of its decisions would be made by people lacking in the expertise needed to make them. In terms of the paper structure, we said that it matters so much where programs or functions are placed and how the homes of those programs are related to the rest of the government because organizations are so very different in terms of their internal organizational cultures, and in terms of what we called in chapter 4 their political environments. Different kinds of political executives will be sent to lead different agencies. Different congressional committees will oversee their activities and write their laws and budgets. Different interest groups and professional associations will monitor their performance.

So, in short, structure matters. But we still have to ask ourselves if the President can use his or her powers to change the structure of bureaucracy in such a way that policy outcomes will be more to the chief's liking.

Let's start with the President and the principle of hierarchy. The political executives the President sends into bureaucracy are literally the embodiment of the principle of hierarchy. They occupy positions of authority and use their management knowledge, their "big picture vision," etc., to get done what they have been sent to get done. But, as we said in the previous section, these political executives meet a suspicious group of policy specialists who may not do exactly as they are told. For the authority one is given on paper to actually work in practice requires two things that don't automatically come with the authority. It requires power and legitimacy. The law supplies some of both, at least at the top of the bureaucracy. But it is understood that the President is expected to supply the rest. That is, the President is the elected one, the constitutional chief executive. His or her power and authority are genuine and legitimate. As a political executive, you mostly derive yours from his or hers.

But recall the words of Thomas Cronin I quoted early in the chapter. "There is a great residual of respect toward the Presidency both in Washington and in the federal agencies throughout the country. But this respect for what the President can do [and probably respect for his or her right to do it] is predicated on the fact that the Presidential voice can be heard and believed as authentic."[47] For political executives to get the power and legitimacy that make their paper authority real, their career subordinates have to believe that those political executives really do represent the President and his or her viewpoints. And remember, these policy specialists are predisposed not to believe—indeed, are even a little suspicious of the President himself or herself. Can/will the President provide the "back-up" needed by his or her team of political executives? It seems almost certain that, most of the time anyway, the barriers of motivation, time, knowledge, and interest that we discussed earlier in the chapter are going to come into play and keep the President from using his or her own power and legitimacy to strengthen the power and legitimacy of these political executives. In other words, the President is not going to be able to exercise much influence over that side of organizational structure we call hierarchy.

But what about the paper structure? That, after all, is what Richard Nixon meant by "the machinery of government," and it is what Jimmy Carter meant when he called for "a drastic and thorough reorganization of the Federal bureaucracy." Indeed, at some time or other during his presidency, every chief has given some thought to questions involving the assignment of programs or the placement of agencies. Some Presidents have even done something about them. But any President is going to face two rather formidable barriers to effectively addressing problems in the paper structure of government.

To no one's surprise, the first barrier is the President himself or herself. In the end, questions of how the government organizes to do something always take a back seat to questions of what it is that the government is doing. With presidential time, knowledge, and interest in such short supply, very little of it can be expended on trying to change policy outcomes by reorganizing the institutions that make that policy. No matter how much lip service has been paid to questions of organization, if the goal is policy change, then the President is almost certainly going to end up emphasizing the policy and not the machinery.

Jimmy Carter's "drastic and thorough reorganization" produced two new cabinet departments—Education, which the teachers' unions wanted, and Energy, which was clearly a response to a crisis—and a Reorganization Project which produced a series of comprehensive plans, none of which the President ever even talked about after their publication.[48] Richard Nixon's plan for reform was even more drastic than President Carter's, going so far as to recommend the abolition of the Department of Agriculture. In the end, however, the President withdrew that recommendation, withdrew it on the day that his Under Secretary of Agriculture, one J. Phil Campbell, was trying to sell the plan to a very skeptical House Agriculture Committee.[49] Ronald Reagan had marked Jimmy Carter's new Departments of Education and Energy for extinction during the campaign of 1980, and he mentioned the idea occasionally during his first term, but the perfunctory introduction of legislation to do so by friendly members of the Senate was as far as the effort ever went. President Reagan's idea of reorganization turned out to be to privatize whatever could be privatized, and tie the hands of the government agencies left behind. The first President Bush paid little attention to matters organizational, except to propose creation of a Department of Veterans Affairs, a reorganization that amounted to giving cabinet status to an already functioning entity, the old Veterans Administration. President Clinton wasn't much interested in organizational questions either, and the second President Bush showed only marginal interest until it became clear that a Department of Homeland Security would be a politically—maybe even organizationally—useful response to the terrorist attacks of September 11, 2001, and their aftermath.

In the end, it can sometimes be hard to see how fixing a problem in the paper structure of bureaucracy will fix a policy problem at the same time. With limited time and resources, Presidents are prone just to work on the policy problem directly and leave the question of the structure that might be the root cause of that problem for another day.

Again to no one's surprise, a President who did decide that he or she wanted to do something about the paper structure of the government would face a rather substantial barrier to success in the Congress. Congress—its committees, really, but that's a story for the next chapter—it turns out, is far more interested in the machinery of government than is the President. Far more interested, and they make that interest felt.

Subunits of the government—agencies, bureaus, administrations, etc.—can be created, abolished, combined, or moved, and program assignments can be changed in either of two ways. First, of course, any of these things can be accomplished by statute. The Occupational Safety and Health Administration was created by the Occupational Safety and Health Act of 1970, just as the National Aeronautics and Space Administration (NASA) was created by the National Aeronautics and Space Act of 1958, the Small Business Administration was created by the Small Business Act of 1953, and the United States Geological Survey was created by the Organic Act of March 3, 1879.[50] Second, any of these things can be done by what is known as a reorganization plan. The Interior Department's Minerals Management Service was created in 1982 by order of the Secretary of the Interior under authority granted by Reorganization Plan No. 3 of 1950 (that one appears a lot in the U.S. Government Manual). The Secretary of Health and Human Services was busy on October 31, 1995, signing documents creating the Agency for Health Care Policy and Research, the Agency for Toxic Substances and Disease Registry, and the Health Resources and Services Administration. On that same busy day, the Secretary "established the Food and Drug Administration (FDA) as an operating division of the Public Health Service within the U.S. Department of Health and Human Services," even though the FDA name went back to 1931 and its independent existence went back to the turn of the century.[51]

From the point of view of people being regulated by, or receiving services from, these various governmental subunits, the precise circumstances of their organizational birth and the origins of their particular assignments probably don't matter very much. From the point of view of a President who might want to move one of these subunits—including the ultimate move, kill it—or a President who might want to strip some subunit of one of its key assignments in order to shift that assignment elsewhere in the government, those birth circumstances mean a great deal.

Reorganizing units that were created and directly empowered by statute, of course, requires another statute. Reorganizing units that were created and empowered by executive reorganization plan requires another executive reorganization plan. The latter is obviously an easier path for a President to walk. Easier, but not necessarily easy. Let's start with the difficult path, the one that goes directly through Congress.

If the reorganization the President wants requires a statute, he or she has to get Congress to pass that statute, and as I noted earlier, congressional committees, the place where such legislation will get the most thorough review, care very deeply about these organizational questions. They care so very much, as we will see in the next chapter, because they have established working relationships with the agencies under their jurisdiction, and they just don't want anything to upset those relationships. Indeed, as observers have been noting from inside and outside of government for decades, these committees are particularly resistant to plans to reorganize the paper structure of what they consider "their" corner of the bureaucracy. Though he spoke them more than thirty years ago, these words of onetime Secretary of the old Department of Health, Education, and Welfare, John Gardner, remain the best statement of the fierceness of congressional committee resistance to White House efforts at reorganization.

> Some elements in Congress and some special interest lobbies have never really wanted the departmental Secretaries to be strong. As everyone in this room knows but few people outside of Washington understand, questions of public policy nominally lodged with the Secretary are often decided far beyond the Secretary's reach by a trinity—not exactly a holy trinity—consisting of (1) representatives of an outside lobby, (2) middle-level bureaucrats, and (3) selected Members of Congress. . . .
>
> Participants in such durable alliances do not want the departmental Secretaries strengthened. And they oppose even more vigorously *any reorganization that might shake up the alliance* [italics mine]. If the subject matter is shifted to another congressional committee, the congressional leg of the trinity may be broken. If the departments are reorganized, a stranger may appear on the bureaucratic leg of the triangle. The outside special interests are particularly resistant to such change. It took them years to dig their particular tunnel into the public vault, and they don't want the vault moved.[52]

There can be no doubt that some things have changed in the relationships between congressional committees and executive-branch agencies in the decade since the Republicans took control of the Congress. But there can also be no doubt that those committees are still willing and able to fight presidential reorganization plans when they believe those plans to be a serious threat to their own power. In the late spring of 2002, President George W. Bush came around to the position that we needed a Department of Homeland Security. Billing it as the most sweeping reorganization since the creation of the Department of Defense more than half a century earlier, the Bush administration prepared the necessary legislation and the strategy to defend it. In a series of votes in House committees as varied as Judiciary, Transportation, Appropriations, Ways and Means, and Science, the President's plan was changed, each change designed to protect that committee's power and/or its relationship with some agency slated for some sort of dramatic change under the President's plan.[53] Not all of these assertions of committee power succeeded. But an indication of how seriously they were taken by the President and by the Republican leadership in the House can be found in the fact that that leadership created a special committee to review all of the revisions made elsewhere and made sure they dominated that committee.[54] And remember, this battle was taking place despite the fact that the department being created would address—or at least appear to address—an issue of concern to a large number of Americans and was being offered by an extremely popular President. Still Congress fought, and some of the most intense fighting was being led by Republican committee chairs.[55]

In the end, if the Congress created an agency, only the Congress can abolish it. If the Congress put an agency in a particular department, only the Congress can move it. If the Congress assigned a particular program to a particular agency, only the Congress can assign it elsewhere. The President can have an impact on what Congress does about these questions. But it will be a very limited impact, as Congress has the motivation and the tools to resist his pleas.

But there are agencies Congress didn't create. There are agencies Congress didn't place in their current relationship to the rest of government. There are even program assignments Congress didn't make. And when it comes to agencies not created by statute, not located by statute, and/or whose program assignments don't come by statute, the President is playing with a very different hand. So is Congress.

The President's hand is much stronger, of course, and it is stronger precisely because he or she need not seek statutory authority to move programs, relocate agencies, combine previously disconnected agencies into entirely new bureaucratic units, or presumably, even to abolish agencies. But don't count Congress out of the executive-branch reorganization business, even in those areas of that executive branch the Congress didn't directly create or structure. Two reasons.

First of all, the President's authority to reorganize even those pieces of bureaucracy not originally organized by act of Congress comes in the form of a statute. The first such statute was passed in 1939 at the urging of Franklin D. Roosevelt. It turned out to be a good bit different from the bill originally pushed by President Roosevelt, but it was a start.[56] FDR got far less reorganizing authority than he had asked for, but the authority he got from Congress turned out to be the high-water mark for the presidential right to restructure the executive branch he had been elected to lead. The statute had to be reauthorized periodically, and every time Congress got another crack at it, the members demanded more and more restrictions on the President's reorganization activities. You certainly don't need the whole story, but just a few of the highlights will give you an indication of how Congress has worked to assert its authority over the structure of the entire executive branch, not just over those pieces that it specifically created. The original statute had permitted Congress to disapprove of any presidential reorganization plan, but that disapproval had to be voted by both houses. In 1949 that provision was replaced with a one-house veto. Beyond that, three different times between the early 1960s and the mid 1980s, Congress refused to reauthorize the reorganization statute. Each time, of course, the authority was restored, but each time Congress got the President's attention. Finally, and maybe most important of all, it was in the reauthorization of this statute that Congress spelled out the prohibition against including agencies created by statute in any presidential reorganization plan.[57]

Second, just because an agency wasn't created by Congress, or didn't get its own special place in the executive branch from Congress, doesn't mean that it doesn't have any friends in Congress. And those friends are almost certainly going to be gathered together on a particular subcommittee related to that agency's activities. Given the power of subcommittees, including the power they derive from the kind of reciprocity that so often exists between subcommittees, these men and women could make an awful lot of trouble for the President should he or she seek to reorganize one of "their" agencies. Then, of course, the members of any subcommittee have political supporters of their own, and it is very likely that those supporters are also supporters of the agencies within the orbit of that subcommittee, so here comes more political trouble for a President engaged in a reorganization effort. As so often happens, from the President's point of view, the stakes are low, but from the point of view of that handful of members of Congress, those stakes are so very high. In the end, that difference in stakes just might be enough for that handful to "win." Jimmy Carter learned that lesson the hard way early in his administration when he took on the Bureau of Reclamation and its western supporters in the Senate.[58]

Please don't read me as saying that it is time to count the President out of the executive-branch reorganization business. As a matter of fact, it's probably not a good idea to count the President out of anything he or she cares enough about. But influencing the structure of the executive branch is a very difficult task for any President.

The President's team of political executives needs the kind of power and legitimacy that only the chief can provide if they are to make their paper authority more than just "on paper," but no President has the time, knowledge, or interest to provide that kind of power and authority to more than a handful of those political executives at any one time. That leaves the rest of them more or less to fend for themselves.

The President's luck isn't a great deal better when it comes to influencing bureaucracy's paper structure. He or she isn't going to put an enormous amount of time or energy into the task anyway, but Congress, again, in the form of its committees, is going to be there with its own very clearly defined agenda, and that agenda essentially demands that the paper structure be left just as it is. The congressional response to President Bush's version of the Department of Homeland Security suggests that things have changed only marginally since California Democrat Chet Holifield informed the Nixon administration "If by this organization you affect in a major way the powers of the various committees in the Congress, you might as well forget it. The only way I know of to get one or more of these departments through is to allow the committees that now have the programs within their jurisdiction to follow their programs, just as they are followed now, and authorize those programs wherever those programs are distributed. If you don't do that, we are in practical trouble on Capitol Hill."[59]

Again, don't count the President out of the reorganization business. But don't bet that he or she is going to get into that business very often, and if you find out the chief has gotten in, don't bet too much on his or her success.

Influencing the Budgetary Environment: Agencies Need Money

I have always enjoyed the opening lines from Neil Diamond's "Forever in Blue Jeans," where he says that money talks, but "it don't sing and dance." I have been particularly fond of that second line ever since I became a grandfather. It helps to explain why I am so much sadder when my granddaughter goes home than when I have just written the mortgage check. In any event, money does talk, and not just in popular songs. More to the point, it is through money—the budget in the terms of this section of the chapter—that the constitutional government talks to the bureaucracy and through the bureaucracy to the nation's citizens.

No one can doubt the importance of money to any agency, indeed to any activity conducted by government. When the fiscal year 1982 budget for the Mine Safety and Health Administration was cut by $10 million, it meant that not all of the safety inspectors who left the agency could be replaced. Beyond that, of course, it meant that travel budgets had to be reduced, so inspectors were forced to spend fewer days on the road. Fewer inspectors spending fewer days on the road obviously meant fewer—or at least shorter and almost certainly less thorough— inspections of the mines. Whether the reduction in inspections played a role in the increase in mine fatalities recorded that year was a matter of dispute between the agency and the United Mine Workers, but we do know that more inspectors were added in the second half of that fiscal year, and the number of fatalities did drop, at least a little.[60] Please don't read any implication here that Ronald Reagan—or for that matter, his predecessor Jimmy Carter, who played a role in the workforce and budgetary reductions at MSHA—was indifferent to the fate of American miners. Both Presidents believed—each for his own reasons—that less money ought to be spent on the Mine Safety and Health Administration, and that inevitably translated into fewer and/or less thorough inspections. Money talks, and this time it said fewer dollars for this.

The question, then, is not whether the fiscal or budgetary climate in which an agency has to do business matters. Obviously it does. The question, instead, is whether the President has much influence on any given agency's budgetary climate. More precisely, the question is how much influence a President can have on an agency's budgetary climate and how he or she would go about exercising that influence. As always, we will see that the President does have some influence over an agency's budgetary climate, but that influence is distinctly limited. This time let's start with the limitations. Three come readily to mind.

First of all, just over three-quarters of the budget is in a fundamental sense outside the reach of the budget makers. That is, it is composed of expenditures that flow pretty much automatically out of program choices made years—in some cases perhaps decades—earlier and which can only be changed by changing those fundamental program choices. Most of the money that gets spent, then, is going to get spent, and we know what it is going to get spent on, and the President can't do much to change it, save, of course, to convince the Congress to dump the programs that are driving the spending. He or she can try, but as we will see shortly, it is never going to be an easy task. Interestingly enough, even when the President and Congress agree that a program and its resulting expenditures do deserve to die, constituencies supporting those programs—and the agencies that spend the money that comes with them—will join with members of Congress and manage to keep the programs/expenditures alive. In 1996, President Clinton and the Republican-controlled Congress agreed that it was time for American farmers to have "the freedom to farm." In congressional parlance that meant it was time to end crop subsidies. So those subsidies were ended. Except they weren't quite. Every year from 1996 through 2002, there was an emergency appropriation to pay for such subsidies, with the appropriation for fiscal 2002 ($20 billion) larger than any such appropriation when the program was still an automatic part of the budget. In the summer of 2002, President Bush joined Congress in creating a new—one presumes non-emergency—program of crop subsidies expected to cost in the neighborhood of $100 billion over the next six years.[61]

Seventy-five percent of the federal government's expenditures in any given year may be effectively beyond the reach of the President—and Congress, for that matter—when drafting that year's budget, but that leaves 25 percent, and that 25 percent is extremely important. To begin with, 25 percent of a budget the size of that of the federal government is a very substantial sum of money. More important, however, is the fact that it is by looking within that 25 percent that the Mine Safety and Health Administration finds out how many inspectors it can hire, how many miles they can travel, and how many nights they can spend on the road. It is within that 25 percent that the National Park Service finds out how many Park Rangers it can put on the payroll, how many hours major attractions can be open each day, and even how many toilets it can put in its campgrounds. And it is within that 25 percent that the Securities and Exchange Commission finds out how many accountants can be brought on board to review the books of the nation's hundreds of publicly traded corporations. So even if the President can do no more than sign off on that part of the budget that sends checks to federal government retirees and Social Security recipients, and pays the interest on the national debt, there is still a chance at influencing the budgetary environment of any given agency of the federal government. At least there is if the chief can have a significant impact on that remaining 25 percent of the budget. Here, of course, is where limitations two and three come into play.

The second major limitation on the President's ability to influence the budgetary environment of a given agency is found in the fact that the federal budget is clearly an institutional and not an individual document. This certainly comes as no surprise to anyone. The first significant institutional help the President got, after all, was in the form of the Bureau of the Budget, whose job it was, of course, to help put together the budget. But the budget that goes to Congress every January with the President's name on it is an institutional document in a way that goes beyond some Office of Management and Budget help in "crunching" some numbers.

First of all, the budget process starts a year or more in advance, with requests from the various agencies. There are guidelines from the departments these agencies are part of—if an agency is part of a department—and there are guidelines from OMB, but the agencies have to come up with requests. As Aaron Wildavsky pointed out nearly forty years ago, no agency wants to make a budget request that is "way out of line" with the expectations of the departmental and OMB officials who will review those requests, but neither does any agency want to shortchange itself.[62] All of them want to be able to do their jobs, and they feel they have a pretty good idea of what it would take to do that. They compromise with whatever political reality confronts them, but they aren't ready to abandon their own professional judgment when it comes to figuring out how much money they are going to need to do what they believe they have been told to do.

If an agency is part of a larger entity called a department, its requests are going to go to some of the political executives of that department for review before being sent to OMB. Department review is a delicate business, especially for the political executives who have to conduct such a review. Indeed, budget review time may well be the time at which the divided loyalties of these political executives create the greatest strain for them. This is the President's budget, and budgets are the language through which their President most clearly expresses his or her policy priorities. In sharp contrast, of course, these are agency requests, and given the importance of budget numbers to agencies, this is the time and place at which those agencies most expect a political executive to fight for the people who do the "real work" of this department. In the end, through all four editions of *The Politics of the Budgetary Process*, Aaron Wildavsky concluded that "The department often finds it wise to temper its preferences with a strong dose of calculations as to what would be acceptable to the other participants."[63]

Of course, if an agency stands alone in the executive branch, its requests won't be reviewed by a set of departmental political executives. Instead those requests will go straight to the Office of Management and Budget to join those sent over by the various departments on behalf of their constituent agencies. Whether an agency's requests came over as part of a departmentally constructed package or on its own, OMB does its examination of those requests on an agency by agency basis. Budget examiners, who happen to be career civil servants, then review these requests with an eye toward what they think the President might want to recommend for this program and agency—if he or she had the time and inclination to look into the matter—tempered by what Congress might be willing to appropriate, and leavened, perhaps, with what they think that agency really needs to accomplish its objectives. Exactly how these three considerations blend together undoubtedly varies from budget examiner to budget examiner and even changes from year to year. The point remains: OMB, through its career budget examiners, remains another important institutional stop on the road to the creation of the President's budget.

Finally, the President's budget has to make it to the President. He or she has to sign it. Presidents do more than sign the budget, of course, but there may be no other assignment given to the chief executive for which the limitations of time, knowledge, and interest create greater barriers to effective presidential participation than preparation of the budget. The President never has much more than a month or two to review the massive document that comes over from OMB, and reviewing thousands of pages of numbers is a daunting task for anyone, even if he or she doesn't have fund raisers to attend, legislation to push—or veto, state dinners to give, and quite possibly troop movements to watch. I realize that not a single one of you thought that the President of the United States sat hunched over a laptop computer at Camp David for a long weekend and emerged with the federal budget ready for submission to the Congress. It has to be an institutional document. But the fact that it is an institutional document means that the President has only a very limited opportunity to become a direct and forceful participant in shaping the budget that will ultimately bear his or her name. Even if the President could become such a participant, however, there would still be one final barrier to him or her becoming a direct influence on the budgetary environments of the various agencies that make up the federal government—Congress.

That institutional budget, composed of agency requests that have been reviewed at the department level, carefully examined by the Office of Management and Budget, and signed off on by the President, ends up in the Congress, where it is sent to the Appropriations Committees of the House and Senate, broken into pieces—pieces now assigned to various subcommittees of those appropriations committees—and reviewed once more by the men and women who feel it is their role to decide how much money these various agencies will "really" get. The President has two more shots at the budget—impoundment and the veto, both to be considered shortly—but for most agencies most of the time, the amount of money they can spend and what they can spend it on will be decided in Congress. The executive-branch recommendations will count. They will count a great deal. But, as members of Congress were once so fond of saying, the President proposes and the Congress disposes, and in budgetary terms those dispositions are almost always the final word.

Very nearly 75 percent of the budget is effectively out of the President's reach in any given year. Agencies know that. But they also know that 25 percent is within the reach of this year's budget, and for most agencies that 25 percent is very close to a matter of programmatic life and death. But when thinking about that 25 percent, agencies are well aware that the two-stage process of presidential recommendation and congressional appropriation is really a process of institutional recommendation in which the President has a very limited direct role and congressional appropriation in which the chief's direct role is even more limited. In all but the most unusual circumstances, the President will not play much of a direct role in shaping the budgetary environment of any given agency. But, as we saw when we looked at the President's ability to manage the executive branch, the real action for a President is almost certain to be indirect.

So, does the President have a chance to exercise indirect influence over the budgetary environments of executive-branch agencies? Yes. He or she has two, and they can, and sometimes do, work.

First, though we often forget it—this section of the chapter has ignored the fact completely up to now, for example—the federal budget is a two-sided coin. There is the revenue side. A President who can drastically reduce—drastically slow the growth, actually, but let's use reduce even though we have to use it advisedly—the revenue stream can eventually have a significant impact on the budgetary environment of just about every agency of government.

Ronald Reagan in 1981 and George W. Bush in 2001 and again in 2003 managed to convince the Congress to reduce tax rates. We aren't very far into the budgetary era created by the Bush tax cuts of 2001 and 2003, but it is already clear that those cuts have returned us to a time of extremely large deficits last visited in the aftermath of the Reagan tax cuts. While both Presidents argued that their cuts would actually bring in more revenue as the economy grew in response to those cuts, when those revenues did not materialize right away, the "unintended" consequence of the cuts—the proverbial "sea of red ink"—provided the opportunity for members of Congress to demand appropriate spending restraint. Neither President seemed to mind. Citing "budgetary realities," for example, President Bush proposed to spend only $1.9 billion of the $15 billion he had said in his 2003 State of the Union Address would be spent over a five-year period to fight AIDS in Africa.[64] As I said, the full impact of the Bush tax cuts on agency budgets won't be known for a while, but the decade between 1982 and 1992 was a decade of retrenchment—in real dollar terms—for a wide range of agencies, and the mantra of the era seemed to be "we can't afford it." For Ronald Reagan, a President whose own personal mantra seemed to be "we shouldn't do it," "we can't afford it" was a pretty good substitute. The same may one day be said for George W. Bush.

Apart from a frontal assault on the revenue side of the budget, a President can create a climate for everybody else in the budget-making game. On one level, everyone else in the game will ignore that climate. But on another level, they will not be able to escape it.

If the climate is one of cutting, that is, the "we can't afford it" climate, everyone who wants to expand an agency's budget is immediately put on the defensive. Instead of fighting for increases, they end up fighting against decreases, or at least fighting to hold onto what they had before. Beyond that, the climate creates a set of expectations that everyone has to factor into their calculations. Agencies themselves are least likely to have much respect for the President's views, but they know that what they request is going to be reviewed by political executives who will have to represent those views to some extent, and then head off to the OMB, an outfit that works for the President. Even if the budget examiners themselves are career civil servants with their own ideas about what the budget ought to look like, they work in the Executive Office of the President, and if the President is trying to create a climate of budget cutting, they will have to respect that climate and its purposes even as they try to mitigate what they consider its excesses. Besides, as we shall see in just a moment, there is the outside chance that the President will actually look at a particular agency's budget, and if it does not appear to be responsive to the climate he or she is trying to create, the President's own pen just might come into play. It probably won't happen that way, but if it did, the results could be devastating.

If the President wanted to create a climate of expansion, he or she could probably do that quite successfully inside the executive branch. Congress would be quite a different matter. We have seen only two Presidents since Lyndon Johnson who might have been expected to try to create such a climate, and Jimmy Carter ended up focusing more of his attention on cutting than expanding, and Bill Clinton talked of reinventing government and ran into the Republican buzz saw of 1994 and beyond. He more than held his own over the next couple of budget cycles, but his own meant avoiding retrenchment, letting government expand in a few areas, and ultimately fending off—in the end probably only delaying—big tax cuts. Like using the revenue system, creating a climate of expectations that ripples through budget making at all levels seems to work better for a President who wants to cut.

This climate, or set of expectations, provides no hard and fast guidelines to budget makers in the executive branch, let alone those in Congress. The latter, of course, are even more resistant to presidential leadership. Still, if a President trumpets the need for spending restraint, talks frequently of the need to do more with less, and maybe even to privatize parts of what the government is doing, everyone gets the message. Even if no one accepts it in its entirety, the President will have left some sort of mark on the budgetary environment of the entire government and, as a consequence, on the budgetary environment of its parts.

As I have said throughout this section, the odds of direct presidential influence over the budgetary environment of most agencies are extremely small. But small is not non-existent, so before we wrap up our consideration of Presidents, budgets, and bureaucratic activity, we need to take a look at the ways a truly determined President could become a direct and active player in the process of deciding exactly how many dollars a particular agency is going to be able to spend and what they will be permitted to spend it for.

First, of course, as I suggested a couple of paragraphs ago, the President can change the budget numbers for an agency before those numbers are submitted to Congress. It is unlikely the President will choose to do it, and even in the rare case in which he or she does make that choice, only a handful of agencies will likely be subject to his or her personal scrutiny, and the resulting presidential number will still go to Congress for final approval. Still, like the probability of being struck by lightning, the probability of the President changing your budget may be remote, but it is terrifying.

Even after the Congress is done with the budget, however, the President still has two avenues to try to make his or her preferences felt. One is grounded in Article II of the Constitution. The other is grounded in a statute passed amid the turmoil of the last year of the Nixon administration. Let's start with the Constitution.

The President is empowered to veto legislation, and the budget comes as legislation. But each appropriations bill contains money for dozens of agencies, and there is no way the chief can single out one of those agencies for his or her veto pen. The Constitution does not grant what is generally known as the line item or partial veto power to the President, and the Supreme Court held that Congress couldn't hand the chief that power through legislation, so an appropriations veto is an all or nothing game for the budgets of the collection of agencies/departments contained in that particular bill. Rarely would any one agency's budget be so offensive to the President that he or she would veto an entire appropriations bill to get at it. Further undermining the veto as a presidential weapon in the budgetary wars is the fact that the budget eventually has to pass and Congress knows it. When a President vetoes a piece of substantive legislation, his or her goal may be to stop that legislation. Period. But not even Ronald Reagan wanted to stop the budget and prevent its ultimate passage. So Congress feels far more confident simply returning the vetoed budget in more or less the same form a few weeks later to see if the President will get out the veto pen once more. This doesn't stop the President from using the veto power in a budget showdown or, probably more often, from threatening to use that power in a budget showdown. It just undermines his or her long-term chances of success.

The Constitution tells us that "No Money shall be drawn from the Treasury, but in Consequence of Appropriations made by law" (Article I, section 9, paragraph 7). The President can't spend money Congress hasn't authorized him or her to spend by passing a law. But does the President have to spend all that Congress appropriates? Presidents from Thomas Jefferson on argued that they could refuse to spend some of the money Congress had appropriated, and they backed up their argument with action. Called impoundment, the process was more or less like a stick behind the door. The President got it out once in a great while and hit an agency with it, but it happened seldom, and Congress usually got angry enough that some compromise was worked out to stitch up the agency's wound before much bleeding had occurred. But then came Richard Nixon, and impoundment became a front-burner issue. You don't need the whole story. This much will do: President Nixon impounded more money, more often, than any previous President, and in 1974 Congress drastically limited a President's ability to impound money it had appropriated.[65] But at the same time, of course, Congress recognized the President's power to refuse to spend money under certain statutorily defined circumstances. So a President can refuse to spend some of the money appropriated to an agency, and that is about as direct an impact on that agency's budgetary environment as anybody can have. Of course, if what a President wants is for an agency to be able to spend more money than Congress appropriated for it, the authority to impound money isn't going to be any help.

Money definitely does talk. But from the point of view of any agency, it doesn't talk with an exclusively presidential voice. Rather, the chorus of voices it will hear in its budget will include the agency's own plus that of the political executives assigned to oversee its activities, career budget examiners—and the political leadership—at the Office of Management and Budget, members of House and Senate Appropriations subcommittees, and that of the President. Rarely will the President's voice be the dominant one. The executive-branch document submitted in his or her name is far too much the institutional product for a President's voice to stand out from the chorus routinely, and as far as the Congress is concerned, that executive-branch document is an out-of-town tryout for a Broadway show. It needs a pretty thorough rewrite and some new stage directions, and Congress is more than happy to take on the role of writer/director in getting it ready to open.

But there are some things a President can do to make his or her voice stand out a little. Slowing the revenue stream and creating a climate that seems to say that money is scarce, so don't bother to ask, will leave its mark on almost every agency's budget, even if the President doesn't pay attention to the exact figures for any of them. The veto is a cumbersome business, and it might not work anyway. But it will get Congress's attention and sometimes, as it did for Bill Clinton, get the public's attention and almost force a reluctant Congress to at least compromise with the President. Impoundment is a far more precise presidential weapon, and when it is used, the President's voice is the only one being heard. But the only word the President can speak with impoundment is no, and sometimes a President doesn't want to say no.

In the end, the President does have a voice in the structuring of the budgetary environments of the various agencies of the federal government. It isn't a voice that is automatically heeded. But neither is it a voice that can be automatically ignored.

Influencing the Legal Environment: Agencies Need Authority

Agencies can't do things they can't pay for. That's why on July 16, 2003, the House Appropriations Committee voted to deny to the Federal Communications Commission the money to implement its controversial new rule that would permit a single company to own TV stations that would reach 45 percent of American households.[66]

But just as they can't do things they can't pay for, agencies can't do things they don't have the authority to do. In its slightly more than a half-century of existence, the Office of Safety Inspection (OSI), a division of the old Bureau of Mines, Department of the Interior, did not have the authority to issue citations for violations of mine safety rules. It could order a mine closed, or it could post a notice at the mine entrance warning miners of the unsafe conditions. But it could not issue a citation and order a fine.[67] Since not even the miners wanted the mines closed—how else were they to make a living?—and everyone who knew anything about mining, especially, of course, the miners themselves, knew how unsafe it was in those mines, the Office of Safety Inspection was effectively neutered as an enforcement entity. It didn't have the authority it needed to attack the problems it saw. The OSI's successor agency, the Mine Safety and Health Administration, located in the Department of Labor, was given the authority to issue citations and levy fines, and it did plenty of both.

An agency's authority, just like its budget, is a two-sided coin. An agency can't do what it can't pay for or doesn't have the authority to do, and it can and almost certainly will try to do what it can pay for and what it does have the authority to do. A good many of the men and women who took over the task of inspecting mines at the newly created Mine Safety and Health Administration came over from the old Office of Safety Inspection, yet they didn't miss a beat in aggressively pursuing their new mandate. Likewise, the Occupational Safety and Health Administration (OSHA) had a core of professionals whose only authority before the 1970 statute creating their agency had been the authority to keep statistics and publish pamphlets, yet that core was more than ready to use OSHA's newly minted authority to write and enforce workplace safety rules.[68]

Authority clearly matters to what an agency does. But we are still left with the question of how much impact the President can have on an agency's authority and how he or she would go about trying to have that impact. An agency's authority is created, defined, and limited by statute, by executive order, and by court decision—and, of course, by the interpretation of those statutes, executive orders, and court decisions. So our question comes down to this. How can a President go about trying to shape the set of statutes, executive orders, and court decisions— along with their interpretations—that constitute an agency's authority? Let's start with the statutes.

Starting with the statutes, of course, means getting the President tangled up with the Congress again, and as we saw with the confirmation of appointments, control over the paper structure, and especially the budget, tangling the President up with Congress always gives the chief some sort of headache. Leaving aside the idiosyncratic dimensions of the President's own respect in Congress, skills as a negotiator—or schmoozer—or personal popularity with the public, the size of the President's headache, and the likelihood that he or she will be able to make that headache go away will depend very much on one thing. What is it that the President wants to have happen to an agency's statutory authority?

If the President wants to see an agency's statutory authority remain just as it is, that is, not expanded and not contracted, he or she can almost certainly do it. Changes in statutory authority, of course, can only be made by statute, and when it comes to blocking statutes, the President sits on two pretty substantial powers.

First there is a process called central clearance. It is hardly the stuff of legend. It is hardly the stuff of page-four newspaper articles. But it counts. Shortening the story quite a bit, if an agency believes it wants a change in its own statutory authority, it is obligated to submit its version of that statutory change to an outfit called the Legislative Reference Division at the Office of Management and Budget (OMB). There it will be reviewed by career staff who will compare it with the President's stated goals or positions in this particular area of policy. If the career staff feels the proposal conflicts with presidential priorities, the agency will be informed and the matter is supposed to be dropped. If the career staff is unsure, the political leadership of OMB will be consulted, and the White House staff might even be asked to weigh in. An agency could conceivably engage in what might be called an "end run," that is, have the legislation introduced by a friendly member of Congress anyway, but such a course of action will attract attention at OMB, and that attention might be a real problem down the road. If the bill ends up passed, it is OMB's Legislative Reference Division that will be the first folks to consider the question of a presidential veto, and they are very likely to make precisely that recommendation. Obviously a member of Congress might introduce a piece of legislation on his or her own—without any collusion with the agency in question—but even if that is the case, the likelihood of a veto recommendation out of Legislative Reference remains high. In short, efforts to expand or contract the statutory authority of an agency by passing a new law almost certainly won't get out of the executive branch if those efforts are at odds with the President's preferences.[69]

If a change in an agency's statutory authority that the President would rather not see does get through Congress, there is always the veto. Vetoes, of course, are higher profile and higher risk than central clearance. Vetoes can be overridden. It doesn't happen often, but it happens, and that not only means the agency in question has gained or lost authority contrary to presidential preferences, but the President has also suffered the kind of defeat that Presidents don't suffer often. It will be embarrassing at best, dangerous for the chief's power on other issues at worst. Still, most vetoes are sustained, so if the President really is unhappy with changes made to an agency's statutory authority, he or she can veto those changes and almost certainly make it stick.

On the other hand, if it is the President who wants to expand or contract an agency's statutory authority, the situation looks very different. Now, of course, instead of keeping changes from being introduced in the first place, or if that fails and the stakes are high enough, pulling out all the stops and vetoing the changes Congress has tried to make, the chief has to persuade Congress to act. This is never an easy task for a President. Congress's system of subcommittees and committees—in a two-house legislature—means that any action the President wants that body to take must clear at least six hurdles before he or she can get what was asked for. That's a lot of chances for someone in Congress to say no, or if you want to look at it from the President's vantage point, a lot of places where he or she is going to have to convince some members of Congress to say yes. And, of course, the answers from those members of Congress aren't confined to yes and no. There is always "yes but," or "no unless," and that means the President is going to have to be prepared to see a change in an agency's statutory authority that isn't exactly the one he or she proposed.

In sum, a President who feels that most agencies have all the statutory authority they need, and that not too many have statutory authority he or she would prefer they weren't using, is in a pretty good position to keep things that way. Central clearance and the veto make such a President a very powerful figure. Standing in stark contrast is the President who wants to make sweeping changes to the statutory authority of some agency or agencies. Whether his or her goal is to expand that authority or scale it back, the problem is the same. Congress has to act, and getting Congress to act—more properly, getting it to act as he or she wants it to act—is always a daunting task, no matter who that President may be.

Presidents can't exactly grant—or revoke a grant of—authority to a particular agency. Even when President Richard Nixon took the surprising step of creating the Environmental Protection Agency, the authority EPA exercised was the authority that had been granted by statute to the various pieces of the bureaucracy that Nixon had brought together to create the new agency. But Presidents can issue formal executive orders, and through those orders effectively expand or contract an agency's authority. Executive Order 12291, discussed earlier in the chapter, for example, didn't give the Environmental Protection Agency new authority to regulate air quality, nor did it remove from that agency any of the authority it already had. But it clearly changed the way in which that authority was to be exercised, and in the process can be said to have reduced that authority, in practice even if not in the statute books.

But not all executive orders will be as easy to enforce as 12291 has been. Under the Administrative Procedure Act—much on that in chapter 8—agencies engaged in rule making are almost always obligated to publicize that fact, to solicit comments from the public, and generally to operate in a more or less open manner—at least open to those who know where to look. So trying to evade 12291, that is, trying to keep OMB from finding out about proposed rules, would be a violation not only of that executive order but of the Administrative Procedure Act. It just wouldn't happen. But President Kennedy's order to dismantle some Jupiter missiles based in Turkey and aimed at the Soviet Union was ignored not once, but twice, in the process becoming the stuff of legend among students of public administration, and President Clinton's famous "Don't Ask, Don't Tell" order to the uniformed services had almost no impact on the way in which those services exercised their authority over the men and women who wore their uniforms.[70] Executive orders, in other words, have to be enforced, and the primary mechanism for enforcing any rule, voluntary compliance, seems to be a somewhat weaker force when it comes to executive orders than it does when it comes to statutes.

In the end, a President can try to reshape an agency's authority by issuing an executive order. It might work. It might not. Of course, from a President's point of view, that's not so very different from what might happen if he or she tried to accomplish the same end by going to Congress and trying to change an agency's authority by statute.

Finally, an agency's authority can be expanded or contracted by the decision of a court. Chapter 9 is going to be devoted to the process of judicial review of administrative action. Our concern here, rather, is with how the President might affect an agency's authority by affecting what happens in court. Two ways.

First, the President can keep an agency out of court in the first place. Well, the President and the Solicitor General can do it, and they can really only keep an agency out of court in the second place, but the impact is the same. If an agency is sued and it loses, it can only appeal that decision with the authorization of the Solicitor General.[71] Not every decision of the Solicitor General is going to be thoroughly discussed with the President, of course, but if the chief has more than a passing interest in an area of policy and an agency's actions in that area of policy, the Solicitor General is going to know it and he or she is going to consult the White House before agreeing to an appeal. So, if an agency's authority has been weakened by a lower court decision and the President is happy with that outcome, there will be no appeal, and that means the President has, in effect, taken away some piece of that agency's authority to act. This is precisely what the Agriculture Department and the Solicitor General decided to do in early 2003 when they decided not to defend the so-called "roadless rule" left over from the last days of the Clinton administration.[72]

More controversial, and probably more effective, is the power of the President—through attorneys at the various departments operating under the watchful eye, once more, of the Solicitor General—to settle cases filed against agencies. Obviously, what the President would want to do is to settle these suits on terms that move the chief's agenda forward, regardless of how that agenda is viewed at the agency level. The year 2003 was a busy one for such activity, as the Agriculture and Interior Departments were sued all over the western United States and managed to settle nearly every suit in a fairly short space of time, always in ways that reduced restrictions on the use of western land and timber and mineral resources.[73]

The examples I have used here are clearly about specific policy questions, that is, questions about the use of natural resources, particularly in the western part of the country, where the U.S. government is the number one landlord. In that sense they aren't really about the authority of the Forest Service, the Bureau of Land Management, or the Fish and Wildlife Service. But the President's concerns are always policy concerns. He or she isn't going to worry about an agency's authority as an intellectual exercise. The concern is about what those agencies do with their authority. So the use of the Solicitor General's power to block appeals when agencies lose at the District Court level—or the decision to settle cases filed against various agencies on terms that all agree are favorable to those who want to use western land and its resources—is a policy choice, but in effect it reduces the authority of the Forest Service and the other agencies, since now certain rules are no longer there to be enforced, and certain areas no longer designated for agency protection.[74]

Even if an agency's authority doesn't change on paper, it can change in practice. In other words, it can be reinterpreted. The President isn't likely to do that reinterpreting himself or herself. It will be done by officials closer to the agency action. But it may well be done with the President's views in mind, especially if it is done by one of the political executives the President has sent to leave his or her stamp on the executive branch and its policies. Nowhere would this be more clearly on view than in the reasons given by Interior Secretary Gayle Norton for her April 2003 decision to rescind the temporary wilderness designation given to 2.6 million acres of Utah by her predecessor, Bruce Babbitt. Her statement: the authority under which Secretary Babbitt had granted that designation had expired years before. She simply didn't have the legal authority to act.[75]

Money talks. But unless it talks with, or perhaps more accurately, from, authority, nobody feels obligated to listen. Such authority—the recognized right to make decisions binding on the citizenry—comes to bureaucracy, of course, from the constitutional government. Primarily it comes in the form of statutes, but executive orders and court decisions play an important role in shaping the practical meaning of these statutory grants. For that matter, so does the interpretation given to statutes by those who occupy key positions in the executive branch.

The President is a player in all aspects of this process of granting authority to the departments and agencies under his or her ostensible command. Exactly how big a player varies from one situation to another, but a player he or she will be.

When it comes to the backbone of bureaucratic authority, the statute or statutes that create and set the boundaries of that authority in the first place, the President finds himself or herself occupying two distinctly different positions. If the chief wants to make sure that a particular agency has at its disposal next year precisely the same authority it had this year, that is, is authorized to do no more and no less than it was before, he or she can almost certainly pull it off. Agencies are expected to submit any proposals for legislation involving their domain to the Office of Management and Budget for its analysis, and they do. The Legislative Reference Division does its best to watch those proposals to make sure nothing goes forward to Congress that doesn't fit with the President's agenda— and between that division, the political leadership at OMB, and the White House staff, few pieces of legislation the President and his or her people define as inconsistent with the President's vision slip through the cracks. For those that do, or just for those that surface in Congress without some "disloyal" agency as their instigators, there is always the veto threat and, if necessary, the veto itself. If, on the other hand, the President wants to change an agency's grant of statutory authority, whether to expand or contract it, he or she must begin a long and often quite frustrating process of negotiating with various members of Congress trying to nurse the needed legislation along.

When it comes to executive orders, of course, the President can just issue them. He or she can't expect them to be obeyed, at least not automatically, but the chief can issue them. Some, like Ronald Reagan's order that all rules be submitted to the Office of Management and Budget before being issued, accomplish the President's objective. It helped President Reagan implement his anti-regulation agenda, and while how much that rule helped Bill Clinton is unclear, there can be no doubt of its importance to George W. Bush, who, as we said earlier, has even gotten the Environmental Protection Agency to allow OMB participation in the earliest stages of the rule-making process. At the other extreme would be the fate of John F. Kennedy's orders to dismantle the Jupiter missiles in Turkey, and somewhere in between would be Bill Clinton's order known as "Don't Ask, Don't Tell." Almost every executive order has some impact, but the President clearly has no guarantee that his or her efforts to use this tool to affect the authority of any given agency is going to work.

The President isn't going to appear in court, and Presidents can't call judges to suggest how they would like those judges to decide a particular case the way they can call anybody in Congress to try to move his or her vote on any issue anywhere in the legislative process. But courts make important decisions about agency authority, and the President is anything but powerless to affect the impact that those courts and their decisions have on what agencies can or cannot do. Agencies are sued all the time, sometimes by citizens who think the agency isn't doing something it ought to be doing but more often by citizens who think it is doing something it ought not to be doing. If an agency loses at the lowest (District) level, it can only appeal that loss with the approval of the attorneys of its home department as well as that of the Solicitor General. Obviously the President can have some impact there, should he or she choose to have it. A newer but maybe even more effective tactic surfaced in the early years of the George W. Bush administration when lawyers in the Agriculture and Interior Departments began to settle suits brought against some of their constituent agencies by western land user groups. The settlements were reached and filed quickly, and several of them seriously limited the authority of the agencies in question. The President didn't design those settlements, or even approve their details. But there can be no doubt his policies and preferences were reflected in every settlement filed.

Finally, almost no grant of statutory authority is unambiguous. There is room for interpretation. If the interpreting is done at the agency level by career professionals, the President's hand is weak. But if it is done at the department level by one of his or her hand-picked political executives, things change drastically. No one can be certain how the Park Service, the Bureau of Land Management, or any of the other units at the Interior Department would have responded to a request to redefine their own authority concerning the power to designate wilderness areas. But we do know what Secretary of Interior Gale Norton said about it in the spring of 2003. She said that authority didn't exist.

So, through it all, the President has a role to play in shaping the authority that agencies have available to them as they try to keep the promises they have been assigned to keep. The roles can vary all the way from the virtual one-person show of the veto to what is almost a cameo appearance in many legislative struggles, with plenty of room in between for considerable—if definitely indirect—influence over central clearance and the decisions not to appeal some cases even when the government has "lost" or to settle cases without even putting up a legal fight. There is even the hard to characterize land of the executive order, which appears to be another one-person show but which ends up being anything but, as Bill Clinton saw when he was told in no uncertain terms that the original draft of his executive order permitting gays to serve openly in the military was unacceptable—to the military and the Congress—and saw again when his compromise "Don't Ask, Don't Tell" order ended up meaning something very different from what he had intended when the military began to implement it. In the end, as with the budget or management, the President's battles are fought one at a time; his or her victories—or losses—added up exactly the same way.

SUMMARY AND CONCLUSION

Getting elected President earns a person the title chief executive. Unfortunately, the job comes with it. Armed with the constitutionally granted powers to sign (or veto) legislation—including, of course, the legislation that determines how much money the government will spend and what it will spend that money for—and to "nominate, and by and with the Advice and Consent of the Senate, ... appoint ... all other Officers of the United States, whose Appointments are not herein otherwise provided for," and buttressed by the occasional grant of power from the Congress, the chief tries his or her best to take care that the laws be "faithfully executed."

The President starts off at something of a disadvantage, a disadvantage driven in part by his or her own lack of motivation and resources and in part by the distrust with which the chief and his or her policies and preferences are generally greeted by the career professionals who do most of the execution of the laws. Presidents rarely rise or fall on the kinds of issues that occupy the time and energy of most executive branch agencies, and there is so little time, knowledge, or even interest in so many of these issues that no President is going to try to be an active participant in the processes by which those issues are resolved. Responding to that lack of time and interest and especially to that lack of knowledge, the policy specialists who gather and process information at the lower and middle levels of bureaucracy go their own way, responding to presidential leadership only when they are truly convinced that leadership really does come from the President and that it will not result in permanent damage to the agency or its policies and its supporters.

Daunting as these barriers may be, the President still has to try to be some sort of force in what happens in the executive branch he or she was elected to preside over. So the President tries to shape the organizational, budgetary, and legal climates in which the agencies of that executive branch carry out their duties.

The key elements on the organizational side of things, recall, are people and structure, and the President has a hand in both. Presidents don't choose policy specialists, of course, but they do choose managers and they choose other people to help the managers manage, and they do play a role in how the executive branch is put together.

The political executives constitute the President's main corps of managers and they do help to carry presidential priorities over to the agencies under their purview. But that corps isn't always composed of the men and women the President would most like to see representing his or her priorities—its members inevitably represent other viewpoints besides that of the chief—and they cannot always do as much managing as the President would hope they could. The White House staff is there to help the managers manage—and to help the President manage the managers, but that staff, too, has problems. Too small and considered too political, it simply cannot extend the President's influence as far as he or she might wish. The organizations of the institutionalized presidency, special presidential commissions, and the Senior Executive Service are all aimed at providing some more help to the President. They do. Some help, anyway. But the Senior Executive Service experiment went sour from the beginning, and presidential commissions are a decidedly mixed bag. The institutionalized presidency has its lions—the Office of Management and Budget and the National Security Council—and its mice—the Office of Science and Technology Policy and the President's Critical Infrastructure Protection Board, and on balance the lions provide a fair amount of help and the mice were designed to be mice. In the end, the President is a management presence in the executive branch, but that presence is one of many, much of the time only barely first among equals.

Structure is a two-part game, and the President is not all that powerful a force in either part. When it comes to providing the power to back up the paper authority of his or her political executives, the President is anything but the "Energizer Bunny." He or she simply can't/won't just keep on going. The President's role in designing the paper structure gives him or her a better chance at influencing what is happening in the rest of the executive branch, but only a little better chance. Congress guards its power over the paper structure of the executive branch most jealously, and the President is likely to lose interest in a question of structure if he or she can win at least some concessions on the policy question that drove the interest in structure in the first place.

When it comes to influencing the budgetary climate of an agency, the President faces a number of obstacles. The barriers of time, knowledge, and interest are almost certainly at their most formidable, the document that will go to the Congress with the chief's signature is an institutional document reflecting a lot of factors besides presidential preferences, and Congress takes budgeting very seriously. Very seriously indeed. The veto and impoundment offer openings after Congress is done, but they are not well suited to getting money for agencies, just to keeping it away from them, and in any event, they can use up a lot of political capital in a fight that probably won't end up a clear presidential victory. That's true, of course, unless you are Bill Clinton staring down Newt Gingrich over shutting the government down. Then victory really turned out to be possible. But, as we said, the President may be able to affect every agency's budget. He or she may be able to do it by engineering a significant change in the revenue system, creating a climate of budgetary restraint, or both.

Finally, agencies need authority. Without it they can do nothing. The President is in an excellent position from which to deny any agency new authority—or to prevent any agency from having authority stripped from it—but not such an advantageous position from which to make a change in any agency's authority, whether that change would add or subtract from that authority. Executive orders can have a significant impact on how authority is exercised, even on what that authority is in some cases, but Presidents always have to face the fact that even an executive order may not be fully and automatically obeyed. And, in rare instances, they may even find that they cannot issue precisely the order they had intended to issue.

Presidents can even affect what happens in court by using their influence with the Solicitor General—a high-profile presidential appointment likely to have been carefully screened—and with the attorneys working in a particular department, to fail to appeal decisions that go against agencies but in a direction the President likes—or more likely, perhaps, by settling cases on terms that seem to reflect or represent that President's priorities, even if they don't represent those of the agency being sued.

So, can the President be the chief executive? Yes, just clearly not a dominant or dominating chief executive. But maybe, as Louis Koenig argued in his highly respected *The Chief Executive*, that fact "is good for democracy."[76]

NOTES

1. Robert Sherrill, *Why They Call It Politics*, 2nd ed. (New York: Harcourt Brace Jovanovich, 1974), 4.

2. Quoted in Harold Seidman, *Politics, Position, and Power*, 2nd ed. (New York: Oxford University Press, 1975), 123.

3. Richard E. Neustadt, *Presidential Power* (New York: John Wiley and Sons, 1960). I used the New American Library Signet edition. The quote is found on p. 22.

4. You can find this inaugural address by using any search engine of your preference. Just be sure to specify Ronald Reagan and inaugural address. I used my favorite search engine. I called my wife and she found it while I kept working on the rest of the paragraph.

5. You can read a little about this in Dennis D. Riley, *Public Personnel Administration*, 2nd ed. (New York: Longman, 2002), 133.

6. Paul C. Light, *The True Size of Government* (Washington, D.C.: Brookings Institution, 1999). For a little more on the National Performance Review and the whole business of privatization and revitalization of government, see Riley, *Public Personnel Administration*, 16–19.

7. Hugh Heclo, "Issue Networks and the Executive Establishment," in *The New American Political System*, ed. Anthony King (Washington, D.C.: American Enterprise Institute, 1978), 117.

8. Quoted in Neustadt, *Presidential Power*, 22.

9. That marvelous phrase "And he doesn't know the territory" is borrowed from the opening scene of Meredith Willson's classic musical *The Music Man*, and captures the feeling that policy specialists inevitably have toward the President when it comes to thinking about his or her policy prescriptions.

10. Louis W. Koenig, *The Chief Executive*, 5th ed. (New York: Harcourt Brace Jovanovich, 1986), 180.

11. James P. Pfiffner, *The Modern Presidency* (New York: St. Martin's Press, 1994), 52.

12. Koenig, *The Chief Executive*, 180.

13. Thomas E. Cronin, "Presidents as Chief Executives," in *The Presidency Reappraised*, ed. Rexford G. Tugwell and Thomas E. Cronin (New York: Praeger, 1974), 241.

14. Quoted in Neustadt, *Presidential Power*, 22.

15. "Right From the Start," *Newsweek*, January 22, 2001, 21–27.

16. Hannah Rosin, "Educating Feddie," *New Republic*, February 3, 1997, 12.

17. Terry M. Moe, "Control and Feedback in Economic Regulation: The Case of the NLRB," *American Political Science Review* 79 (December 1985), 1094–1116.

18. This account is drawn largely from Fred Barnes, "White House Watch: You're Fired," *New Republic*, January 10, 1994.

19. If you are interested in a full version, complete with names long since departed from the national stage, see Dennis D. Riley, *Controlling the Federal Bureaucracy* (Philadelphia: Temple University Press, 1987), 21–26. Your library might have one of the 1,000 or so ever sold.

20. Harold Seidman, *Politics, Position, and Power: The Dynamics of Federal Organization* (New York: Oxford University Press, 1970), 134.

21. *American Textile Manufacturer's Institute v. Donovan* 452 U.S. 490 (1981).

22. The ergonomics rules made news in a wide range of media outlets, so finding out more about them should be easy enough. The preliminary version of the rules was announced on November 22, 1999. And we are far from done with the overtime pay rules. I relied mostly on a short piece, Steven Greenhouse, "Democrats Protest Changes to Overtime Rules," *New York Times* (electronic edition), July 1, 2003, but you could find the information in lots of other places.

23. Quoted in Susan J. Tolchin and Martin Tolchin, *Dismantling America: The Rush to Deregulate* (New York: Oxford University Press, 1983), 95.

24. Tolchin and Tolchin, *Dismantling America*, 95.

25. Tolchin and Tolchin, *Dismantling America*, 98–100.

26. The President's Committee on Administrative Management, *Report of the Committee with Special Studies* (Washington, D.C.: U.S. Government Printing Office, 1937).

27. Pfiffner, *The Modern Presidency*, 96.

28. Not surprisingly, that site address is www.whitehouse.gov.

29. Most of this discussion is based on Steven J. Cann, *Administrative Law*, 2nd ed. (Thousand Oaks, CA: Sage, 1998), ch. 2, 19–50.

30. *Dole v. United Steelworkers of America* 110 S.Ct. 929 (1990).

31. Cann, *Administrative Law*, 21.

32. Andrew Revkin, "E.P.A. and Budget Office to Work Jointly on Diesel Soot Rules," *New York Times* (electronic edition), June 8, 2002.

33. Heclo, "Issue Networks and the Executive Establishment," 117.

34. John B. Judis, "The Mouse That Roars," *New Republic*, August 3, 1987, 25.

35. Judis, "The Mouse That Roars," 23–25.

36. John B. Judis, "An Officer and a Gentleman," *New Republic*, January 23, 1989, 17–19; and "Koop De Grace," *New Republic*, October 23, 1989, 7–9.

37. For an excellent summary of the President's goals for and instructions to the commission, along with a reasoned analysis of its work, check out the interview with Susan Dentzer of the Kaiser Family Foundation conducted by Margaret Werner for the Lehrer *NewsHour* on PBS. I found the transcript on the PBS website, www.pbs.org//newshour. The date of the interview was December 11, 2001.

38. Jonathan Cohn, "Toxic," *New Republic*, December 23, 2002, 17–18.

39. For an excellent short summary on the goals and perspectives of those who put the SES together, as well as an excellent short summary on what befell these "best laid plans," see Patricia W. Ingraham and James R. Thompson, "The Civil Service Reform Act of 1978 and its Progeny: The Promise and the Dilemma," in *Public Personnel Administration: Problems and Prospects*, 3rd ed., ed. Steven W. Hayes and Richard C. Kearney (Englewood Cliffs, N.J.: Prentice Hall, 1995), 54–69. See especially 57–60.

40. Frederick C. Mosher, *Democracy and the Public Service*, 2nd ed. (New York: Oxford University Press, 1982), 110.

41. Riley, *Public Personnel Administration*, 265–266.

42. Ingraham and Thompson, "The Civil Service Reform Act of 1978," 59.

43. Ingraham and Thompson, "The Civil Service Reform Act of 1978," 60.

44. Ingraham and Thompson, "The Civil Service Reform Act of 1978," 60.

45. Seidman, *Politics, Position, and Power*, p. 3 of any edition.

46. Quoted in Riley, *Controlling the Federal Bureaucracy*, 42.

47. Cronin, "Presidents as Chief Executives," 241.

48. Riley, *Controlling the Federal Bureaucracy*, 42.

49. Riley, *Controlling the Federal Bureaucracy*, 42.

50. You can look up any of these and hundreds more in *The United States Government Manual 1998/99* (Washington, D.C.: U.S. Government Printing Office, 1998).

51. *The United States Government Manual*, 279.

52. This passage is quoted in every book that includes a section on executive-branch reorganization. If you want the original, go to U.S. Senate, Committee on Government Operations, *Executive Reorganization Proposals: Hearings* (Washington, D.C.: U.S. Government Printing Office, 1971), 57–58.

53. See the following two articles by *New York Times* reporter David Firestone to get an idea of the kinds of specific issues involved. David Firestone, "Congressional Panels Recast Homeland Security Department," *New York Times* (electronic edition), July 11, 2002; and David Firestone, "Top Bush Aides Urge No Change in Security Plan," *New York Times* (electronic edition), July 12, 2002.

54. Firestone, "Congressional Panels Recast Homeland Security Department"; Firestone, "Top Bush Aides Urge No Change in Security Plan."

55. Firestone, "Congressional Panels Recast Homeland Security Department"; Firestone, "Top Bush Aides Urge No Change in Security Plan."

56. For the history, see Richard Polenberg, *Reorganizing Roosevelt's Government: The Controversy Over Executive Reorganization, 1936–1939* (Cambridge, Mass.: Harvard University Press, 1966).

57. Lawrence C. Dodd and Richard L. Schott, *Congress and the Administrative State* (New York: John Wiley and Sons, 1979), 334–335.

58. For a full story of the carnage, see Marc Reisner, *Cadillac Desert* (New York: Penguin Books, 1987), ch. 9, 317–343.

59. Quoted in Dodd and Schott, *Congress and the Administrative State*, 343.

60. Tolchin and Tolchin, *Dismantling America*, 95–96.

61. Elizabeth Becker, "Accord Reached on Bill Raising Farm Subsidies," *New York Times* (electronic edition), April 27, 2002.

62. Aaron Wildavsky, *The Politics of the Budgetary Process* (Boston: Little, Brown, 1964). He made the same point in three succeeding editions.

63. Wildavsky, *The Politics of the Budgetary Process*, 33. At least it is p. 33 in the 4th ed.

64. "Talk Is Cheap," *New Republic*, July 21, 2003, 7.

65. James P. Pfiffner, *The President, The Budget, and Congress: Impoundment and the 1974 Budget Act* (Boulder, Colo.: Westview Press, 1979), 40–44.

66. Associated Press, "Committee Votes to Block FCC Media Rule," July 16, 2003.

67. Florence Heffron, *The Administrative Regulatory Process* (New York: Longman, 1983), 102.

68. Steven Kelman, "Occupational Safety and Health Administration," in *The Politics of Regulation*, ed. James Q. Wilson (New York: Basic Books, 1980), 238–243.

69. If for some reason you need the long version, try Stephen J. Wayne, *The Legislative Presidency* (New York: Harper and Row, 1978), 71–100. The examples will be a bit dated, but the description and analysis have definitely not gone out of date.

70. On the Turkish missiles, see Graham T. Allison, *Essence of Decision* (Boston: Little, Brown, 1971), 141–143.

71. Heffron, *The Administrative Regulatory Process*, 126.

72. CBS News, "New Anti-Environment Tack by Bush?" April 19, 2003. The text was reprinted at Truthout.org on April 21, 2003.

73. CBS News, "New Anti-Environment Tack by Bush?"

74. Editorial, *New York Times* (electronic edition), June 21, 2003.

75. Editorial, *New York Times* (electronic edition), May 4, 2003.

76. Koenig, *The Chief Executive*, 174.

6

Bureaucracy and the Congress

The Committees You Shall Always Have With You—Unless They End Up Being Against You

The executive power has been "vested" in the President. We call the President the chief executive. Just under 400 pages of executive-branch agencies are collected together into departments, departments complete with organization charts purporting to show how each individual reports to someone who reports to someone who reports to a member of the President's cabinet—who, of course, reports to the President.

So where is Congress in this "executive" branch? Smack in the middle, as a matter of fact, and that is what this chapter is all about. The executive power may belong to the President, but as we saw in the previous chapter, the executive branch over which the chief presides can't function without money and authority. Congress can be quite secure in the knowledge that no money can be spent unless Congress decides to spend it, and equally secure that in the final analysis authority always derives from the law, and the law is congressional business. So, the Constitution clearly gives Congress the right to put itself smack in the middle of the executive branch. The question, then, is how does it do so and what are the consequences of its being able to do so? To explore that question, however, you need a bit of background on the institution, its members, and its organization.

CONGRESS: MEMBERS, COMMITTEES, AND THE EXERCISE OF CONGRESSIONAL POWER

Most of us don't think about Congress very often. When we do, we are prone to think first of Congress the institution, the place where issues great—and perhaps not so great—get debated and decided, by men and women we have elected to "represent us." For the historians among us there may be the mental images of James Madison introducing the first ten amendments to the Constitution into the very first session of Congress, or of Abraham Lincoln rising to oppose the Mexican War, Arthur Vandenberg adding his enormous prestige—and conservative credentials—to the effort to pass the Marshall Plan for the recovery of Europe after World War II, or Hubert Humphrey arguing with his almost boundless passion for the passage of the Civil Rights Act of 1964. For me, somewhere in this office there is even a page torn from the *Congressional Record*, a page that records forever the unanimous decision of the U.S. House of Representatives to congratulate Mr. Al Kaline of the Detroit Tigers on the occasion of his 3,000th major league hit.

But, important as the institution's great—and maybe not so great—debates may be, an awful lot of what Congress does, and more to the point, most of what it does that has a substantial impact on executive-branch decision making, is done not by the institution but by its individual members. Sometimes they are acting simply as individuals, but most of the time they are acting as committees or, even more likely, subcommittees. So, to understand Congress and its impact on the executive branch and its decision-making processes, we need to understand a little more about these committees.

Start with the question of why Congress—more properly, each house of Congress—operates by handing over so much power to small aggregations of individual members called committees, and why these committees, in turn, hand over so much power to even smaller aggregations called subcommittees.

From the point of view of the institution itself, there just doesn't seem to be much alternative. The House of Representatives, for example, is a body of 435 men and women who face an incredible range of issues. Has the Justice Department gone too far in its use of provisions of the Patriot Act? Has the Federal Communications Commission endangered diversity in media voices by allowing major networks to own enough local channels to reach 45 percent of American homes rather than "only" 35 percent? Is security at America's ports sufficient to protect us from a terrorist attack using cargo ships rather than airliners? How could the information needed to make intelligent assessments of those issues— and so very many more—be gathered and understood by each of the 435? The need for adequate time, not to mention the need for at least some semblance of specialization, would make an organizational scheme in which each member tried to do everything a disaster. Assign each issue—each issue area, really—to a smaller subset of the body and then "trust" that subset to come up with reasonable answers which can be reviewed and refined by the whole body later on.

Powerful committees and subcommittees make just as much sense, maybe more sense, from the point of view of the individual member. Though every individual elected to Congress brings his or her own perspective to the job, all of them seem to share three basic goals, and as we'll see in the next couple of pages, each of these goals can best be advanced through a system of powerful committees and subcommittees.

For the individual members of Congress, everything starts with ambition. Some want to move from the House to the Senate, some from the Senate—or the House, for that matter—to the other end of Pennsylvania Avenue, and for all we know, some long to star in a long-running TV sitcom, become president of Harvard, or end up as Commissioner of Baseball. But the ambition that drives most of them is the simple ambition to keep getting elected to the seat they have now until they decide, on their very own terms, that it is time to move on. Consequently, there is nothing they do that is done without at least some concern for its potential fallout for that primary goal.

Intimately connected to reelection for just about every member is the notion of local representation and constituent service. Everyone in Congress represents a geographically defined constituency, and if that constituency is unhappy, it doesn't matter how popular a member is with his or her colleagues, the White House, or the "national" press. As a result, local people have to be represented in every aspect of a member's activities. That means staying attuned to local viewpoints on the questions that come to the floor for a vote—how do my constituents stand on cutting taxes or congratulating Al Kaline? But most of all it means protecting the interests—the economic interests first and foremost—of the geographic area that sent that member to Congress. This intense commitment to local representation and service is often reinforced by the widespread acceptance of the notion that the job of a representative in Congress is a local and not a national job, and the fact that a great many members of Congress have deep and long-standing ties to the areas they represent.

Finally, anyone elected to Congress has some interest in public policy, that is, a set of issues in which he or she is interested, and some pretty strong feelings about what government ought to be doing about those issues. Generally there are two sets of such issues, one national and one constituency. Once they get to Congress, a third set of issues often surfaces, namely, issues that don't seem to have much visible impact on a member's constituents and clearly don't move large numbers of people at the polls—or anywhere else—but that are of intense interest to some specific industry or sector of the economy. Interest in the first two types of issues—national and constituency—comes quite naturally, of course. They may be the reason this particular individual got into politics in the first place, and it would seem to be pretty difficult to get reelected or to consider oneself to have served and represented the local people without getting involved in the issues that matter most to them. Interest in that third category of issues, on the other hand, will have to be developed, but the motivation to develop such interest is clear enough. Much of what Congress does is to deal with these kinds of issues, and more to the point, the groups intensely interested in these issues are able—and most willing—to contribute substantial sums of money to individuals in a position to influence policy on the issues they care so much about.

So how do the drive for reelection, the goal of local representation and service, and the desire to influence policy on a certain set of issues convince the individual members of Congress of the need for an internal decision-making system centering its power in a set of issue-specific committees and subcommittees? As the saying *should* go, do the arithmetic. There are 435 voting members in the House, 100 in the Senate. When things finally reach a vote, a House member has only one vote out of that entire 435, a Senator only one out of that 100. Not particularly good odds. Things don't look much better from an individual perspective before the vote, that is, during the time when a member might try to influence the votes of others. That's a lot of people to try to bring around to your point of view. Move decision making down to the level of the committee, or better yet, the subcommittee, however, and the numbers—and hence, the odds—change dramatically.

The precise numbers change from session to session, but fairly typical of a House committee would be the Resources Committee, a group of 45 representatives who do the bulk of their work in five subcommittees ranging in membership from 12 on Native American and Insular Affairs, to twenty five on National Parks, Forests, and Lands. Now a single vote carries far more weight, of course, but even more important than the additional heft of one member's vote is the additional reach of one member's voice. It is going to be a lot easier to move a group of twelve in the direction you want it to go than it will be to move a group of 435. Ultimately, of course, the group of 435 is going to have to agree with the group of 12—or at least to acquiesce in what it has done—but if the rules and norms of the institution create an expectation of agreement/acquiescence, the real action will almost always be in the group of 12. In fact, in the increasingly partisan House, the numbers are quite often even smaller, as winning may well be simply a matter of bringing along your fellow partisans on the subcommittee. It is hard to say whether a majority of the House of Representatives, acting in the absence of any subcommittee recommendation, would have voted to cut the Land and Water Conservation fund appropriation from $900 million to $198 million. But once Representative Charles Taylor (R-NC) had convinced his seven Republican colleagues on the Interior Subcommittee of the House Appropriations Committee to do so, it was a very good bet that the whole House would follow suit.[1]

The purpose of committee power, then, is to enhance individual power. The purpose of individual power, in turn, is to advance the goals of the individual, that is, to help him or her get reelected, represent and serve his or her constituency, and have some influence over a selected set of issues. Obviously committee power is going to enhance the individual power of the committee's members over the issues within that committee's orbit. But whether that increased individual power over those particular issues can be translated into greater chances of reelection and a real opportunity to represent and serve the individual's constituents will depend. The individual power that flows from committee power can be used to represent and serve a member's constituents if that committee's jurisdiction includes the issues of greatest concern to that constituency. That power can be used to better a member's chances of reelection, of course, if it can somehow be translated into votes. Let's examine both of those briefly.

No one can doubt that members of Congress understand the connection between committee power and their ability to serve and represent their particular constituency. That means, of course, that they understand that such a connection can exist only if they serve on committees that directly affect the issues their constituents care most deeply about, and those are precisely the committee assignments they seek. That's why Pat Roberts, back when he was still representing the First District of Kansas, sought a seat on the House Agriculture Committee when he was first elected in 1980. Seeing himself in the words of *The Almanac of American Politics* as "the protector of Great Plains farm communities from ignorant outsiders who would upset the basis of their lives," he never stopped defending wheat subsidy programs even in the face of the huge outlays for those programs that were part of the motivation for the ill-fated Freedom to Farm Act of 1996, discussed in the previous chapter.[2] In 1995, he even vowed that while others—Senate Agriculture Committee Chair Richard Lugar (R-IN)— were debating the theoretical advantages of changing farm programs, he (Roberts) would "be holding hearings out in the field to see what farmers and ranchers want."[3]

Not everyone in Kansas farms, of course, and that's why for many years former Fourth District Representative Dan Glickman (D-KS) sat on the Space and Aeronautics subcommittee. Wichita is the heart of the Fourth, and when Representative Glickman first won election to the House, Wichita was home to the largest Boeing plant outside of the Seattle metropolitan area, and was the nation's leading producer of small planes. From that committee slot, and with the help of then Kansas Senator Nancy Kassebaum, Glickman managed to convince Congress to enact a statute reducing the product liability of general aviation manufacturers. When, despite all of this effort and considerable success on behalf of Wichita's dominant industry, Representative Glickman was unable to survive the Republican earthquake of 1994, his successor, conservative Republican Todd Thiart, slipped right into Dan Glickman's vacated seat on Space and Aeronautics without missing a beat. After all, Boeing is still there—Representative Thiart used to work for the company—and Cessna, Beechcraft, and Learjet are all located there as well.[4]

Even if you find that you "aren't in Kansas anymore," you will find that things are pretty much the same. Just pick a state, go to the website of a member of that state's delegation, and see how well you can match major district concerns with that member's subcommittee assignments. One of the biggest upsets of the year of the upsets—1994—came when George Nethercutt defeated Speaker of the House Tom Foley in Washington's Fifth District. Nethercutt was soon assigned to the Appropriations Committee and, more to the point, to the Agriculture, Interior, and Defense subcommittees. His eastern Washington district includes Fairchild Air Force Base, one of the world's richest wheat-growing districts known as the Palouse Country, the large—and magnificent—Kaniksu National Forest, and the city of Spokane. Now head down the coast to the Riverside, California, area. Here you will find another Republican, Representative Ken Calvert. Representative Calvert serves on the Armed Services Committee—March Air Force Base and the Naval Warfare Assessment Center are within the district's boundaries—and has been named Chair of the Subcommittee on Water and Power of the House Resources Committee. It is hard to imagine an issue of greater importance in Southern California than water.

In sum, every member of the House can identify the issues that are central to his or her constituents and the committees and subcommittees that will handle those issues. Given their commitment to local representation and service, it comes as no surprise, then, that every member will do all within his or her power to secure a seat on those committees and subcommittees and use that seat—those seats—to represent his or her constituents and their interests as those issues are addressed. You will find the same in the Senate, though that kind of narrowly focused representation is harder to do if you represent a large and heterogeneous state. In short, every member of the House and Senate knows that if there is a dominant economic interest in his or her constituency to represent, there is a committee—committees in some cases—from which to represent it, and that is the best place for a member to use committee power to give him or her the individual power to serve and represent his or her constituents.

That leaves us, of course, with reelection. In part, of course, that is what all that constituent representation and service is aimed at. And it seems to work. Pat Roberts won eight straight elections in his Kansas First District, and the string was only broken because he decided to seek a seat in the U.S. Senate. He won. No one would doubt the contribution of his dedicated representation of First District farm interests to his continued electoral success. Nothing short of the shifting political tectonics of 1994 could have derailed Dan Glickman, the man who had represented aviation and agriculture interests in the Kansas Fourth District for almost two decades prior to that defeat. Before becoming Majority Leader and then Speaker, Tom Foley had used his seat on the Agriculture Committee to represent Washington's Fifth District, and it had allowed him to keep winning in that increasingly Republican district. His successor, George Nethercutt, has been so successful in taking care of the wheat-growing, distribution, and processing interests that are such an important part of the district that in 2000 he won the Wheat Leader of the Year Award from the National Association of Wheat Growers, and the Golden Plow from the American Farm Bureau Federation.[5] He didn't win them by voting to impeach Bill Clinton.

Committee and subcommittee power provides another, less brightly lit path to reelection, of course. It costs money to run for a seat in the House of Representatives, and even more money to run for a seat in the Senate. Some candidates have very deep pockets, but some have to rely on others to finance their campaigns, and the many industries that believe their interests are at stake in the Congress on an almost daily basis have long since learned how to become the sources of much of that money. Those industries—the money has to come from individuals within those industries, but the point remains the same—target their money toward individuals who serve on the committees and subcommittees that deal with their particular issues and interests. In more specific terms, the energy industry is going to find ways to help fund the campaigns of the members of the Energy and Air Quality Subcommittee of the House Committee on Energy and Commerce—at least of those whom the industry feels have represented its interests "fairly"—just as the financial services industry is going to be looking for ways to help with the campaigns of members of the Financial Institutions and Consumer Credit Subcommittee of the House Committee on Financial Services. This targeted pattern of giving would extend to every subcommittee of every committee of the House and Senate. Given the power of committees and subcommittees and the cost of campaigns, how could it be any different? The point here is not that something evil is going on. The point is simply this: money can help win elections, and money can and does flow to members of subcommittees from the groups directly affected by the decisions of those subcommittees. So committee and subcommittee power enhances individual power, and individual power can be translated into votes even if the issues dealt with by the subcommittee barely make the radar screen of most of the voters in a particular subcommittee member's district. Just follow the money.

So, if Congress is going to put itself smack in the middle of the executive branch, it is going to do it through the activities of the various committees and subcommittees of its two houses. Like the President, these committees and subcommittees will try to shape the organizational, budgetary, and legal environments of the many agencies that make up the executive branch. Unlike the President, these committees and subcommittees will have an impact that is substantial and that will reach to the farthest corners of what we so often think of as the President's domain. To understand why, we have to start, as we did with the President, with questions of committee and subcommittee effort and agency response. Do committees and subcommittees have the motivation and resources to try to become a major force in agency decision making, and if they do, how do the subject matter experts at those agencies respond?

MOTIVATION, RESOURCES, AND SUBCOMMITTEE ATTENTION TO BUREAUCRACY: THESE FOLKS COME TO PLAY

In the last chapter I said that the President "leaves all agencies alone some of the time, and some agencies alone all of the time." What would be the corresponding bottom line for subcommittees? Subcommittees leave almost all agencies alone all of the time, and leave "their" agencies alone almost none of the time. Again, the reasons won't surprise you very much.

Motivation and Plenty of It

As we saw in the previous section, virtually every subcommittee of the House and Senate is composed of members with a direct stake—reelection and/or constituent representation and service—in the issues that come before that particular subcommittee. That provides plenty of motivation for paying careful attention to those issues, and subcommittee members, and their staffs, do just that. Interest in a particular set of issues, of course, gets translated into interest in—and subsequent attention to—the agency or agencies dealing with those issues. It is that agency, or those agencies, recall, that will write and enforce the rules that will determine the real impact of a law on specific industries, specific firms, specific groups, and eventually, specific individuals.

When it passed the Occupational Safety and Health Act back in 1970, Congress fully intended to protect the health of the men and women who worked in textile mills, and it is almost certainly true that most of the representatives and senators who voted on the act had a pretty good idea that the biggest threat to the health of those workers was found in the impact on their lungs of prolonged exposure to cotton dust. Still, Congress was not about to tackle the question of whether the lungs of textile workers were best protected by rules requiring reduced exposure to cotton dust or by rules requiring the use of personal protective equipment such as masks or, more likely, breathing equipment much like that used by scuba divers. It was even less likely to tackle the question of a compliance schedule for a particular textile mill in a particular town. Those were questions to be left to OSHA.

Fair enough, at least fair enough from the point of view of Congress as an institution. Handing questions like those over to bureaucracy is what legislation does. But from the point of view of those members of Congress who represent districts in which the textile industry is an important part of the economic land-scape, those issues can't be handed over to OSHA and forgotten about. The dif-ference between a rule requiring less exposure to cotton dust and a rule requiring a personal breathing apparatus for each worker is enormous. Two reasons. First, the cost of providing each worker with a personal breathing apparatus would be dwarfed by the cost of the filtration systems required to eliminate the requisite amount of cotton dust from the air of a mill. Second, from the point of view of any individual worker, getting the dust out of the air by filtering that air allows an individual to work in a more or less normal fashion, talking to co-workers, breathing in a normal way, and carrying nothing on his or her back. From that same worker point of view, however, things are very different with a personal breathing apparatus. That, obviously, a worker does carry on his or her back. Be-yond that, air has to get into the lungs and the point is to avoid breathing the dust-laden air of the mill floor, so an individual has to breathe as he or she would under water, that is, hook tubes into his or her mouth and breathe through those tubes. Not a very appealing thought eight hours a day, five days a week.

Now consider the position of the House or Senate member representing a tex-tile producing area. If he or she really wants to represent his or her constituency, whether that constituency's interests are defined in terms of the human costs of requiring an individual breathing apparatus for each worker or the economic costs of requiring the kind of air filtration that would reduce exposure levels, the member is going to have to have some influence over which rule OSHA chooses to adopt and, once that decision is made, over how the rule is interpreted with respect to the mills in his or her constituency. No one can have influence over something without paying attention to it. Consequently, the desire for influence over these kinds of policy implementation decisions provides more than enough incentive to members of the House and Senate to pay close attention to the activ-ities of the agencies that directly affect their constituencies. The subcommittee provides the vehicle.

The same keen and attentive eye will be turned on any agency that deals with issues of concern to the organized groups that provide much of the financing for a particular member's campaigns. Representative W. J. "Billy" Tauzin (R-LA) al-ways took some interest in telecommunications issues, but he tended to do most of his work on behalf of his southern Louisiana constituency from his seats on the Energy and Power Subcommittee of the House Commerce Committee and the En-ergy and Mineral Resources and Fisheries, Wildlife, and Oceans Subcommittees of the Resources Committee.[6] Representative Tauzin was a Democrat in those days, but his switch to the Republican Party and his advancement toward the chair-manship of the House Energy and Commerce Committee attracted considerable interest from telecommunications companies and, interestingly enough, from ac-countants, both of which began to funnel campaign dollars his way. Indeed, no House member received more money from the accounting industry during the decade of the 1990s than did Representative Tauzin.[7] "Billy" took a keen interest in the Securities and Exchange Commission (SEC) even before taking over the Energy and Commerce Committee chairmanship, sending three strongly worded letters to then SEC Chair Arthur Levitt opposing Levitt's efforts to enact a rule that would have barred accounting firms from doing consulting work.[8] When he did take over the chairmanship, Representative Tauzin continued the fight against increasing the agency's workforce begun by his predecessor as committee chair, Representative Thomas J. Blily Jr. (R-VA).[9] By the summer of 2003, Tauzin was leading the fight against efforts in the House to overturn the Federal Communications Commission decision to allow television networks to own individual stations reaching 45 percent of American homes rather than the 35 percent in the FCC's pre-2003 rule. Indeed, it was Representative Tauzin's staunch opposition to any such action that led the House Appropriations Committee—and ultimately the full House—to use a spending restriction to at least prevent enforcement of the new rule even if that rule could not be tossed out.[10] In Representative Tauzin's case, the subcommittee wasn't the primary vehicle for his efforts on behalf of his campaign contributors, but then, if you chair the full committee, you have, in effect, traded in your Ford Explorer for a Humvee. Complete with turret and gun.

Senators have more committee assignments, more subcommittee assignments, and more constituency interests to watch, but that doesn't mean they will ignore the interests of the groups that have helped them maintain the kinds of campaign war chests that scare off serious competitors. Senator Christopher Dodd (D-CT), for example, used his spot as ranking minority member of the Senate Banking, Housing, and Urban Affairs Committee's Securities Subcommittee to shepherd a bill making it more difficult for investors to sue businesses and accounting firms for fraud through the Senate, and when President Clinton vetoed the bill, Senator Dodd managed to organize an override. Five years later, with the subcommittee renamed Securities and Investments, Senator Dodd put immense pressure on Securities and Exchange Commission Chair Arthur Levitt to drop the proposed accounting rule that had so angered "Billy" Tauzin. In the end, the rule was in fact dropped. Senator Dodd remains, as he has for the past thirteen years, the Senate's number one fund raiser among accountants.[11]

Whether to keep the campaign dollars flowing or to serve and represent his or her constituents—both are expected to contribute to reelection, remember—any member of the House or Senate is going to pay attention to a particular set of issues. Since both houses have deputized specific committees and subcommittees do work on those issues, a member seeks out assignments to those subcommittees—the process can work in reverse as it did for "Billy" Tauzin and the telecommunications industry, but it still works—and through those assignments is positioned to meet the goals of service and representation. But to fully meet those goals, he or she is going to have to pay attention to a particular set of agencies as well, namely, the ones that deal with the issues he or she finds so important.

Of course, motivation isn't everything. I had plenty of motivation to do the repairs to the back of my beautiful old Tudor house this summer. At last count somewhere around $20,000 worth. What I lacked, of course, were the resources. I wanted to devote my time to this book, and I've never taken much of an interest in carpentry, masonry, window installation, and the like. But most of all, I don't know a blasted thing about how to do the jobs those two guys seemed to do without a second thought. So, members of the House and Senate have plenty of motivation to pay attention to the agencies dealing with the issues those members care deeply about. Do they also have the resources?

An Abiding Interest and Time to Follow It

Given what we said in the previous section, there can't be much doubt that the members of the various House and Senate subcommittees are interested in the work of the agencies implementing the policies within those subcommittees' specific jurisdictions. A President may well know that he or she will not rise or fall on the actions of any specific agency, but members of Congress know equally well that they just might. Besides, when it comes to real constituency-driven concerns, reelection is most likely married to a sincere desire to protect local interests and local people. Pat Roberts might have been made a bit uncomfortable by the specific words chosen by *The Almanac of American Politics*, that is, by the suggestion that he saw himself as "the protector of Great Plains farm communities from ignorant outsiders who would upset the basis of their lives," but I bet that he would agree with the underlying sentiment. He really did see his job in terms of the needs of "his people," and he made sure that the Department of Agriculture and its constituent agencies understood that those needs had to be met. The same can be said for Washington's Fifth District Representative George Nethercutt. He won the Wheat Leader of the Year in 2000 in large part by making sure that the wheat price-support program was adequately funded and by working with the USDA to make sure that Palouse Country wheat farmers got their share of that money. He hasn't lost his focus. In the summer of 2003, he helped Washington State University to secure a $4.4 million grant from the Agriculture Department for a new agriculture research facility.[12]

It is hard to say if Senator Christopher Dodd or Representative "Billy" Tauzin got the same feeling of satisfaction from helping the accounting profession stave off greater regulation by the Securities and Exchange Commission (SEC). I'm not sure if they have the same feeling about accountants that Pat Roberts and George Nethercutt have about farmers. But we can certainly say that both Senator Dodd and Representative Tauzin took great interest in what the SEC was thinking about requiring of accountants and felt compelled to try to help them, even if they didn't feel those accountants to be "their" people. It is, however, a pretty safe bet that both men were more than willing to spend the resulting campaign contributions.

Members of Congress are clearly busy men and women. Senator Dodd, for example, serves on four separate committees, with a total of eight subcommittee assignments. He served as the General Chair of the Democratic National Committee in 1995 and, like all members of Congress, has a wide range of political and ceremonial duties to which he must attend. House members generally serve on fewer committees and subcommittees—usually about half the number, actually—but are expected to spend more time at home than are senators, so may end up just as busy.

But there is presidential busy and there is congressional busy. No one could reasonably suggest that any individual member of the House or Senate faces the same kind of time pressures that are faced by the President of the United States.

No one has. Beyond that, and maybe more to the point, people—even, maybe especially, elected officials—decide where to put the time they do have. Members of Congress choose to put as much of their time as they can into the issues before their respective subcommittees, and as we have said repeatedly in this chapter so far, that means spending a good bit of that time paying attention to what is going on at the agencies working on those very same issues. Most members would probably like to find a little more time to spend watching "their" agencies, but all in all, they know that they are devoting a considerable amount of their time to paying attention to the agencies working on the policies those members care most deeply about.

Of course, just as the motivation to do something doesn't guarantee the resources to do it, having the interest and time to pay attention to an agency and its activities doesn't necessarily guarantee the ability to understand what is being seen. So that's our next question. Do the members of Congress have the knowledge to make that motivation, interest, and time really effective?

Subcommittee Knowledge: Informed Amateurs and the Process Called Oversight

As we noted when talking about the President's difficulties in becoming a direct participant in agency-level policy making, when we think of the knowledge needed to play that kind of role at any given agency, we are really thinking of two separate though obviously complementary things, namely, information and the expertise to make sense of that information. If the question at hand is whether to place a particular bird on the endangered species list, there are a number of pieces of information we need to know. I wouldn't pretend to be able to give you the whole list of questions we would need answers to, but obviously we would need to know how many nesting pairs exist and where they are, not just to locate them on a map in the office but to know about the habitat in which they are currently trying to survive. But that information would do absolutely no good if we didn't know, again, at a minimum, how many nesting pairs are necessary for the survival of the species and what sort of habitat these birds need in order to make it. No matter what the question, all the information in the world won't do much good without the background and expertise to apply that information to the question, and all the background and expertise in the world won't do much good without the information. So our question is simple enough. Do the subcommittees of the House and Senate have the information they need to know what to pay attention to at the agencies under their jurisdiction, and do they have the background and expertise to know what the information they do have really means? As always, of course, the question is simple. It is the answer that gets a little complicated.

So, Are These People Experts?

No, they are not really experts. At least they are certainly not experts in the sense that the men and women who make up the ranks of the people we have called the policy specialists are experts.

Consider, for a moment, the House Fisheries Conservation, Wildlife, and Oceans Subcommittee.[13] In late July 2003, the subcommittee presented its recommendations on renewal of the Marine Mammal Protection Act to the full House Resources Committee. The chair of the subcommittee, Wayne Gilchrest (R-MD), is a former high school history teacher. The chair of the full committee is a Tracy, California, cattle rancher by the name of Richard Pombo. Neither man has any real scientific background in marine biology or wildlife protection. For that matter, a quick glance at the websites of all of the members of the subcommittee doesn't reveal a single individual trained in either subject. I don't have a list of all of the individuals at the U.S. Fish and Wildlife Service or the National Marine Fisheries Service who are responsible for administering the Marine Mammal Protection Act, but I know that on that list there would be very few individuals with backgrounds teaching high school history or running a cattle ranch, and a great many with advanced degrees in marine biology or wildlife management.

There is nothing wrong with this picture. We don't elect experts to focus on a single question. We elect individuals to handle a wide range of tasks, only one of which will be to delve into highly specialized questions for which they have little background. The point is simply the one I made in the first sentence of the section. No, subcommittees are not composed of real experts.

But they are composed of relatively informed amateurs. Wayne Gilchrest certainly isn't a marine biologist. But representing a district that contains the Chesapeake Bay and its environs, he took an immediate interest in the kinds of issues that come before the Fisheries Conservation, Wildlife, and Oceans Subcommittee, sought a seat on the subcommittee, and has worked to familiarize himself with the issues and agencies under the subcommittee's jurisdiction throughout his thirteen-year career in the House. So has the subcommittee's ranking minority member, Frank Pallone (D-NJ). Though the precise number of years for training themselves to become informed amateurs would vary from member to member, Democrats Neil Abercrombie of Hawaii and Solomon Ortiz of Texas—whose district includes Corpus Christi, Texas, and the longest stretch of Texas Gulf coastline—have availed themselves of the same opportunities as did Representatives Gilchrest and Pallone. So have Republicans Walter Jones (R-NC), whose North Carolina district includes the outer banks, and James Saxton (R-NJ), a former chair who continues to serve on the subcommittee, though he has shifted some of his attention to two House Armed Services Committee subcommittees, one of which he chaired in 2001–2002 and a second he chaired in 2003–2004.

Take any subcommittee you wish and you will find the same pattern. Individuals, armed with a keen interest grounded in some sort of constituent concerns, try to overcome their own lack of expert background by making a real effort to become informed amateurs on the issues and agencies related to those concerns. How far they get on the quest will vary from one member to another as well as from one subject matter to another. But they will try, and most will have enough time—time both in the sense of a few hours each day and in the more important sense of days melting into years—and enough motivation to have at least some success in the endeavor. That is, sooner or later they should know enough to make some sort of sense of the information they will gather about the agencies and policies they work with.

Before we look at that information gathering, however, there must be an important caveat about all of this effort at achieving informed amateur status. Actually, there must be two caveats.

First, recall from chapter 4 that the very notion of expertise itself gets short shrift in some policy areas. If there is no such thing as an expert, then there is no such thing as an amateur, informed or otherwise. Consequently, in such policy areas, no member is expected to spend years trying to learn the issues. He or she simply "knows" them by virtue of his or her common sense and moral values.

Second, and probably more to the point, since it affects the operation of almost all subcommittees rather than just a few, these men and women are elected officials. They are politicians. Their informal educations are largely self-directed, and some of that direction is going to come from strongly held viewpoints on the very issues they are trying to educate themselves on. House Resource Committee Chair Richard Pombo, the fourth-generation Tracy, California, cattle rancher, proudly displays in the middle of the biography page of his website the fact that he is a co-founder of the San Joaquin County Citizen's Land Alliance, which the website then goes on to describe as "a coalition of farmers and other property owners who advocate private property rights, and fight attempts by government to strip those rights away from citizens." The predecessor to the Resources Committee—known at various times as Natural Resources and even Interior and Insular Affairs—was chaired from 1991 to 1995 by George Miller (D-CA), a man who once described the policies of the Bureau of Reclamation discussed earlier as "the biggest Western stage coach robbery of the public since Jesse James."[14] Representative Miller's informal education on the issues that came before the committee was driven by a very different ethos than was the informal education of Representative Pombo.

Still, even though it is clear enough that strongly held viewpoints will leave their marks on the efforts that members of Congress make to learn about the issues and agencies dealt with by the subcommittees they serve on, that does not negate the fact that these men and women become something we can reasonably call informed amateurs. After all, the formal education engaged in by the policy specialists at the various agencies is also informed in part by strongly held views—theirs and those of their professors—and, perhaps more to the point, there are often times when strong differences between members can melt away under the influence of common constituent interests. Remember Ken Calvert, the California Republican of a few pages ago, the one who chairs the House Resources Committee's Subcommittee on Water and Power? In a July 25, 2003, Resources Committee press release, Representative Calvert informed the release's readers that "Yesterday we took the first step toward passing practical legislation that will help solidify water policy in the West and throughout the country. I appreciate Senator Dianne Feinstein (D-CA) for testifying and, more importantly, *for emphasizing the need for compromise and cooperation to pass legislation*"[15] (italics mine). Representative Calvert's words of praise for Senator Feinstein came less than a month after Representative Don Young (R-AK), Chair of the House Transportation and Infrastructure Committee and a man known for his partisan combativeness, commended his committee colleagues on the passage of the Water

Resources Development Act of 2003 with these words: "I congratulate everyone involved in creating this bill on their outstanding job of working together on a bi-partisan basis."[16]

So, recognizing that some subcommittees operate in a world in which the notion of informed amateurism doesn't exist, and more important, recognizing that where it does exist this informed amateurism is informed by strongly held views as well as by careful study, we can still say that most subcommittees are composed of men and women with enough knowledge to at least make sense out of the information they get from the agencies they work with. That is, they can make sense out of it if they can get it. Now it's time to find out if they can.

What's Going on at the Agencies? Oversight, or at Least Half of It

Drawing on the work of a number of scholars, Lawrence Dodd and Richard Schott defined oversight as "attempts by Congress to review and control policy implementation by the agencies and officials of the executive branch."[17] Since I don't think anybody has improved on that definition in the intervening quarter-century, I still use it. As you could imply from the title, this section is going to deal only with half of the Dodd and Schott notion of oversight, and I don't imagine it took you very long to figure out which half. So let's see how Congress goes about trying to gather information about what is happening at the agencies they have created, empowered, and funded.

Congress has always paid some attention to what was going on in the bureaucracy, but what systematic inquiry into agency-level activities there was was conducted almost exclusively by the subcommittees of the House and Senate Appropriations Committees. At least that was the case until the passage of the Legislative Reorganization Act of 1946 and Congress's grudging admission that it was going to have to take a whole different approach to the task of keeping track of what all those agencies were doing with all that money and all that authority.

The Legislative Reorganization Act recognized three different types of oversight and, in keeping with the well-established tradition of committee power, assigned each of the three to a different committee. The Appropriations Committees naturally kept what had been theirs all along, the right to make sure that money is spent in the ways that Congress wants it spent. The statute created new committees in each chamber, the Government Operations Committees, and assigned to those committees the seemingly open-ended mandate for "wide ranging inquiry into government economy, efficiency, and effectiveness."[18] It is hard to say if rechristening the committees the Governmental Affairs (Senate) and Government Reform (House) Committees has made the task any easier. Finally, there is the question of whether agencies are administering programs in accordance with congressional mandates, and maybe even more important, the question of whether those programs are accomplishing their objectives and what sorts of changes might need to be made to those programs if they are not. These questions, of course, were assigned to the various legislative or authorizing committees. So how much do they find out, and how do they do it?

Program Oversight

Program oversight is the responsibility of the various legislative committees of the House and Senate, and like most of the other responsibilities taken on by those committees, it is quickly delegated down to the subcommittees. Each subcommittee, in turn, knows which agencies it is expected to pay attention to, namely, the agencies that are administering the programs that fall under the jurisdiction of that subcommittee. Lest anyone be confused on the matter, some committees follow the lead of the House Resources Committee and offer a menu pick on the committee home page that allows someone to find out just which agencies fall under the committee's jurisdiction. For House Resources the list includes sixteen agencies housed in five different cabinet departments, three more subunits of the Environmental Protection Agency, three pieces of the Executive Office of the President, a piece of the National Science Foundation, and seventeen miscellaneous outfits referred to as boards and commissions. Of course, a good number of those agencies report to other committees and subcommittees as well, but you get the idea. Subcommittees know which agencies are expected to answer to them. The question is: how do they get their answers?

Before we consider that, however, we need to take a moment to spell out exactly who "they" are when it comes to oversight. Six House committees have created subcommittees whose primary charge is oversight of agency activity, though two of them, Agriculture and Small Business, have chosen to combine the formally designated oversight responsibility and title with a specific legislative responsibility and title, so it is hard to say in those two cases if oversight is the primary activity from the members' point of view. Only one Senate committee has followed suit and created a subcommittee with oversight in its title. That is the Finance Committee, and the subcommittee is called Taxation and Internal Revenue Service Oversight, so it is not exactly handed wide-ranging oversight responsibilities.

As you probably guessed, the men and women who serve on the six House subcommittees, or on that one Senate subcommittee, with oversight in the title are not the only people in Congress seeking to find out what various agencies are up to. In fact, they are not the only people engaging in activities specifically labeled oversight. The House Judiciary Committee's Subcommittee on Immigration, Border Security, and Claims held eleven hearings between January and August 2003. They labeled nine of those hearings oversight hearings. More to the point, of course, labels matter less than content. When the Coast Guard and Maritime Transportation Subcommittee of the House Transportation and Infrastructure Committee met on July 22, 2003, to hear Coast Guard Commandant Admiral Thomas Collins and Coast Guard Director of Port Security Rear Admiral Larry Kereth discuss new port security regulations, the word oversight was never used. But it was clear enough to all that the subcommittee was informing itself on what the Coast Guard had done up to this point and what it was planning to do in the future. So, in the end, "they" are the members of any subcommittee of the House or Senate. Now let's return to the question of how they get answers to their questions.

First of all, they get some of those answers informally. Specifically, they hear from the agencies themselves and they hear from organized groups of citizens interested in what those agencies are up to. Let's start with the agencies.

At first blush it may seem a little odd to think of agencies serving as informal suppliers of information about what they are doing, but they do. In his classic study of a half-dozen federal bureau chiefs, Herbert Kaufman found one bureau to be so receptive to this kind of informal contact with key legislators that, in response to a Senate committee request to know more about a particular aspect of agency operations, it literally invited committee staffers to move in and watch.[19] I doubt that the Commandant of the Coast Guard invited the staff—or the members—of the House Coast Guard and Maritime Transportation Subcommittee to his quarters, or even his office, but he and his staff obviously did consult with the subcommittee and with others close to the subcommittee when drafting the interim port security regulations called for under the Maritime Transportation Safety Act of 2002. At least something that Commandant Collins and his people had done pleased subcommittee chair Frank LoBiondo (R-NJ). Representative LoBiondo opened the subcommittee hearings at which Admiral Collins was to explain those interim regulations by praising the admiral and the Coast Guard for preparing those regulations "in a timely manner while thoughtfully considering input from the maritime community via public meetings, written comments, and partnership efforts. I commend the Coast Guard for their collaborative approach."[20]

Agencies themselves are not the only informal source of information about their own performance, of course. Interest groups provide a constant source of feedback on agency activity. Some of this communication is formalized through testimony at subcommittee hearings, but a good bit remains informal and behind the scenes as a normal part of the ongoing relationship between congressional subcommittees and the groups active within their areas of responsibility. It is almost certain that if the Coast Guard had ignored the views of "the maritime community" in drafting those interim regulations, they would have heard a very different tune coming from Chairman LoBiondo the moment those subcommittee hearings began. Communications from interest groups to congressional subcommittees may well be biased, but the ties between the two are firmly established, and listening to such complaints and taking the offending agency to task are part of the job the subcommittee has assumed as its part of the bargain.

Not all of the information about an agency's activities that flows to a particular subcommittee flows informally. Subcommittees have two important formal sources of information, and they use them. In fact, it is very likely that the existence of these formal channels of communication tends to provide a certain amount of incentive for the informal flow of communication from agencies to subcommittees. As Aaron Wildavsky reported many years ago, Representative John Rooney (D-NY), a man who struck terror into the hearts of more than one agency administrator in his long career, took time out from a hearing his subcommittee was conducting to compliment an agency head on his consistent policy of keeping the subcommittee informed of his agency's activities "between hearings."[21] The implication that the information could always be obtained at the next hearing wasn't far beneath the surface, and even though Representative Rooney is long since dead and his name is not exactly the stuff of legend in the contemporary bureaucracy, his philosophy lives on.

As suggested by the reference to John Rooney in the previous paragraph, hearings are a subcommittee's preferred formal avenue for getting information from the agencies under their jurisdiction. Recall from an earlier paragraph, the Subcommittee on Immigration, Border Security, and Claims held eleven hearings during the first half of 2003. In that same span of time, the Subcommittee on Commercial and Administrative Law, also a subcommittee of the House Judiciary Committee, held eight hearings, while over at the House Transportation and Infrastructure Committee, the Coast Guard and Maritime Transportation Subcommittee was holding seven hearings and the Economic Development, Public Buildings, and Emergency Management Subcommittee was holding five. Some subcommittees were more active than these four, while others were less active. The point is not the numbers of hearings, any more than the point is the label put on the subcommittee conducting the hearing or the hearing itself. The point is what goes on at the hearing, that is, who testifies and about what.

Twenty years ago, Herbert Kaufman reported that representatives of the Food and Drug Administration made eighty-five separate appearances at subcommittee and full committee hearings during a period of just under two years.[22] Perhaps even more telling is Kaufman's description of the preparation engaged in by these FDA representatives—and representatives of other agencies he studied—before these committee and subcommittee appearances. "Bureau experts in the matters under consideration assembled briefing books covering every topic that might arise at hearings. Just before the appearance, the functional specialists and the chief held briefing sessions, each specialist going over his part of the bureau's responsibilities. The chief followed along in the briefing book, asking questions to make sure he was in command of the subject."[23] Even that much preparation was not always deemed sufficient, for as Kaufman goes on to say, "when a chief appeared, he was usually accompanied by specialists who either furnished him with the information needed to answer committee inquiries or were permitted to answer directly."[24]

The 108th Congress is clearly very different from the 95th in some important ways. But if you take a look at the websites of just a couple of House committees/subcommittees, some things don't appear to be all that different. If you had looked at the website of the House Transportation and Infrastructure Subcommittee on August 5, 2003, for example, you would have seen not one but two pictures of Ms. Mary Peters, Administrator of the Federal Highway Administration. In both she was testifying, once before the full committee on ways to combat "waste, fraud, and abuse," and once before the Highways, Transit, and Pipelines Subcommittee on the Bush administration's transit and highway budget. Also in that second picture was Ms. Peters's boss, Transportation Secretary Norman Mineta. Pictures don't always tell the story, however, so let's take a closer look at two subcommittees and two hearings.

Start with the aforementioned Subcommittee on Immigration, Border Security, and Claims and its June 24, 2003, hearing on "The Deadly Consequences of Illegal Alien Smuggling." Earlier that spring, nineteen people, all trying to enter the country illegally, had been found suffocated in a railroad car in Victoria, Texas. The subcommittee heard from four people that day: Jose Garza, Tom Homan, Peter Nunez, and Maria Jimenez. Ms. Jimenez was chair of a committee advising the mayor of Houston, Texas, on immigrant and refugee problems. Mr. Nunez was a former federal prosecutor from San Diego, California. Mr. Homan and Mr. Garza represented the Bureau of Immigration and Customs Enforcement and the Bureau of Customs and Border Protection, respectively. At the time of his testimony, Special Agent Homan was in charge of the San Antonio, Texas, field office of the bureau he referred to as BICE, and he took great pains to praise his newly created bureau and its new home, the Department of Homeland Security. But he also provided pages of detailed testimony, first about the nature of the problem, then about what his agency had done and would soon be doing to address it. Mr. Garza, who served his agency as Chief Patrol Agent, McAllen Sector Border Patrol, did much the same, going into considerable detail about the problem as he—his agency—saw it, and the steps being taken to combat it. All in all, a long day in which subcommittee members willing to make the effort got a crash course in what two government agencies under its jurisdiction were doing about a significant problem.

Now consider the Coast Guard and Maritime Transportation Subcommittee—joined this time by the Water Resources and Environment Subcommittee, also a piece of the House Transportation and Infrastructure Committee—and its hearing into the "Interpretation of Existing Ownership Requirements for U.S. Flag Dredges." This was a story definitely not designed for the evening news, but it seems that in 1906 the Congress got worried about the possibility of dredging of U.S. harbors being done by foreign-owned vessels and wrote into law a requirement that at least 75 percent of the ownership of any dredging vessel be in American hands. Except one category of dredging vessels was exempted. In 1992 Congress sought to end that exemption but, as it so often does, put a sort of grandfather clause into the amendment to the 1906 statute. The story could go on a very long time, but it needn't. All you really need to know is this. The Dredging Contractors of America—pushed by one particular dredging firm—complained to the subcommittee that the interpretation of the statute made by the then U.S. Customs Service in the late 1990s was inappropriate, and the subcommittee decided to find out for itself. An invited witness list of six appeared before the two subcommittees on April 30, 2003. Three of these individuals represented the complainants, that is, the Dredging Contractors of America, and two companies who believed the grandfather clause for one particular vessel and—and herein lies the rub—other vessels owned or leased by the Dutch company that owned it ought to be reinterpreted, if not repealed outright. One of the remaining three represented the American Association of Port Authorities, and the other two, the U.S. government. Mr. Barry W. Holliday, Chief, Navigation and Operations Branch of the U.S. Army Corps of Engineers, delivered a straightforward recitation of the importance of ports and harbors to American commerce, the importance of the Corps to ports and harbors, and the importance of dredging to both. Then he stopped. Mr. Larry Burton, Director, International Trade Compliance Division, Bureau of Customs and Border Protection, briefly explained his division's mandate and proceeded to tell the subcommittee what they already knew, namely, that the division and its predecessors had been asked to interpret the exemption four times and four times had said that the vessels in question—chartered to the owners of a ship called the *Stuyvesant*, which was specifically named in the 1992 amendment to the 1906 statute—met the exemption and could be used to dredge American harbors. Then he invited questions. There were many, and Mr. Burton did not budge from his division's interpretation of the exemption. As of this writing, it is too early to tell what, if anything, the subcommittee plans to do about the division and its interpretation of that particular piece of the law. But it is not too early to know that the subcommittee did try to find out what two agencies were doing about a question in their jurisdiction and why.

Some subcommittee hearings clearly aren't aimed at finding out what a particular agency is doing or proposing to do about an issue. When the Subcommittee on the Constitution of the House Judiciary Committee holds hearings on a balanced budget amendment (March 6, 2003) or a flag protection amendment (May 7, 2003), it isn't that likely that it is seeking information from the Treasury Department or Office of Management and Budget on the former, or the Justice Department on the latter. Nor was the Subcommittee on Workforce Protections seeking a greater knowledge of the Occupational Safety and Health Administration's activities when it convened its November 1, 2001, hearings on "The Role of Consensus Standard Setting Organizations With OSHA," or its July 16, 2002, hearings on the question "Can a Consensus Be Reached to Update OSHA's Permissible Exposure Levels?" No one from OSHA testified at either hearing. Still, there are hundreds of subcommittee hearings held every year, and most of the time the relevant agency, or at least department, officials are invited to testify, and they take that invitation seriously. Any subcommittee that wants to know more about what its agencies are up to has a powerful tool to find out in the hearing process.

Subcommittees have a second formal mechanism for gathering information about agency activities. They can ask for reports. There are annual reports, issue or problem-specific reports, and even some management reports. Unfortunately, at least from the point of view of a subcommittee that really wants to know more about an agency's thoughts—or actions—on a particular subject, reports suffer from a couple of pretty serious drawbacks.

First of all, they don't always get read. That was Morris Ogul's conclusion twenty-five years ago and it still holds.[25] In fact, it may be even more true now than it was then. There are more agencies doing more things, and the demands on the time of subcommittee members seem to be even greater now than they were in the 1960s, 1970s, and 1980s. It is always possible that a committee staffer will skim the reports coming from agencies he or she finds interesting, and given the idiosyncratic nature of an awful lot of subcommittee activity, that skimming might just start something. But all in all, reports simply don't attract the attention of subcommittee members the way hearings do.

Beyond that, reports are agency documents, carefully edited, often by more than one staff member. In my twelve years as a department chair, I never let a single report go out without "running it by" one or two of my colleagues to make sure it put us in the best possible light. Testimony at hearings can be rehearsed and edited, but it is hard to edit as one is speaking, especially when trying to do so under oath and on congressional turf. It is just so very much easier to do it over a familiar desk, writing one more report that you aren't sure will ever be read.

Subcommittees can get information formally by asking for reports or, more likely, by holding hearings. They can get information informally, through communications from organized interests. It was, after all, complaints from a couple of dredging companies and their association that proved to be the impetus for the Coast Guard and Maritime Transportation Subcommittee to try to find out more about how a subunit of the Bureau of Customs and Border Protection was interpreting a particular amendment to a century-old statute. And subcommittees can get information directly, and quite informally, from the agencies themselves. We can't be sure how often subcommittees avail themselves of the informal opportunities, and we can't even be sure how much they actually learn through the formal ones. Still, it seems safe to say that program oversight can, and frequently does, work. Subcommittees know an awful lot about what "their" agencies are doing. We'll have to wait until later in the chapter to see what they do with all of that information.

Fiscal Oversight

As I suggested earlier, in a sense, the whole idea of congressional oversight of administration more or less began with fiscal oversight, that is, with the efforts of the House and Senate Appropriations subcommittees to follow the money. These subcommittees have available to them precisely the same informal and formal means of finding out what they want to know, and there is ample evidence that they use them.

On the informal side, agencies do keep their appropriations subcommittees informed of budgetary and policy developments in between their annual appropriations hearings. Remember the tale of Representative Rooney interrupting a hearing to praise an agency administrator for keeping the subcommittee informed "between hearings"? That subcommittee was an appropriations subcommittee that handled spending by agencies of the Commerce, Justice, and State Departments. Many agency careerists probably feel they have little choice in the matter. Indeed, it is likely that a significant percentage of them would agree with Aaron Wildavsky's expression of the consensus among the agency officials he had interviewed that the House Appropriations subcommittees "can do you a world of good and they can cut your throat."[26]

Interest groups, too, try to keep these subcommittees informed of their thoughts on matters concerning agency budgets. There was a time—roughly the 1940s to the 1970s—when these interest-group communications might have found a cooler reception in the appropriations subcommittees than in the legislative subcommittees. During that time, it seems, the full Appropriations Committee made a distinct effort to keep individuals from serving on subcommittees in which their districts had a clear stake. The goal, of course, was to make sure that the subcommittees could perform their roles as "guardians of the treasury" without feeling the pull of constituency interests.[27] A quick glance at the districts of the members of the 108th Congress's version of the Appropriations Subcommittee on Agriculture, Rural Development, the Food and Drug Administration, and

Related Agencies suggests that at least for this subcommittee, that pattern has been thoroughly shattered. Nearly everyone on the subcommittee comes from a district in which agriculture is a key component of the economy. So, interest groups will make their preferences known about agency budgets—make them bigger—and the subcommittees will listen, but as far as real information of the type that the subcommittee might want to get, these communications are probably of very little value.

Moving to the formal side of the information-gathering process, appropriations subcommittees hold hearings. In fact, they hold hearings legendary for their thoroughness and their toughness. The six bureau chiefs of Herbert Kaufman's definitive study all agreed on one thing. The level of preparation needed for an appropriations subcommittee hearing was considerably greater than that needed for any legislative committee hearing.[28] The subject—the money to get things done— was crucial, and the atmosphere seemed to be best described by this comment made by an Appropriations Committee member to Richard Fenno: "The Appropriations Committee is the only committee where you never hear two sides of the question. The witnesses always defend their appropriation. So you have to be the prosecutor and not the judge. You have to look at [the witness] with a jaundiced eye. He is trying to protect his domain. It's just you and him."[29] The Congress is clearly a different place than it was when Richard Fenno interviewed members of the Appropriations Committees in the early 1960s or when Herbert Kaufman interviewed bureau chiefs in the late 1970s. But appropriations subcommittees still hold hearings. The Subcommittee on Labor, Health and Human Services, Education, and Related Agencies, for example, held twenty hearings between early March and mid-May 2003, even taking time out for the three-week Easter recess, and the various other subcommittees generally held hearings twice a week during that same period. And Wisconsin's Seventh District Representative David Obey (D), a thirty-four-year veteran of the House and longtime member of the Appropriations Committee, maintains that except for the drastically increased partisanship, those hearings are much like the hearings he helped to conduct two decades ago and that he had been told had been conducted two decades before that.[30]

Finally, the reports that come to the appropriations subcommittees are of the same value as those that come to the legislative subcommittees. So, like the legislative subcommittees, appropriations subcommittees get information informally from the agencies themselves and from interest groups. They get a lot of information through hearings, and they get a little through reports. In the end, it seems reasonable to say that these subcommittees can follow the money. As we will see later in the chapter, they can also direct it.

Investigative Oversight

The Legislative Reorganization Act of 1946 didn't use the term investigative oversight, but the mandate of the original Government Operations Committees (GOCs) created in response to the act itself included the responsibility to review "the operations of Government activities at all levels with a view toward determining their economy and efficiency."[31]

From the very beginning, the Government Operations Committees of both the House and Senate were severely handicapped in their efforts to become the independent watchdogs their creators at least said they were trying to add to a Congress that seemed to be a little too friendly to executive-branch agencies, and especially to the clientele groups that supported those agencies.[32] First of all, the original GOCs had no program authorization authority. They could investigate the administration of any program in the government, but they could not make a single change in how any program was run. That job belonged exclusively to the authorizing committees. Enter problem number two. There was a good bit of animosity between the Government Operations Committees and the various authorizing committees, with the GOC members often seeing the authorizing committees as agency partisans unwilling and/or unable to see problems and potential solutions, and the authorizing committee members seeing the GOCs as dilettantes, unfamiliar with program and policy details, just doing a little "headline hunting" at the expense of agencies trying to do a job. The GOCs won very very few of the resulting shootouts.[33] That brings problem number three into the equation. Knowing that the Government Operations Committees could not change their programs or their budgets, and seeing that those committees were often at war with their own authorizing committees, agency officials were reluctant to establish informal channels of communication and influence with the GOCs. That, of course, meant that the GOCs could not count on a lot of inside help when trying to find out what was happening in the executive branch.

This is not to say the Government Operations Committees accomplished nothing. These are the folks who found the Navy buying $500 toilet seats, the Air Force plan to purchase some $2,000 coffee pots, and the activities of the woman who eventually became known as Robin HUD for her ability to get money out of that department and never seem to spend it for the purposes for which HUD had granted it to her. But it is to say that thirty years after their creation, in the words of Lawrence Dodd and Richard Schott, "the GOCs simply have not proved to be aggressive oversight agents of Congress."[34]

The decade and a half that passed between those assessments of the Government Operations Committees and their success as overseers of the executive branch and the Republican takeover of Congress in the 1994 election saw no real change in the committees themselves, or in their activities. In power in the House for the first time in four decades—and convinced that the government needed a heavy dose of "reform"—the Republicans renamed the Government Affairs Committee the Committee on Government Reform. In the process, they also abolished two other committees—Post Office and Civil Service, and District of Columbia—and assigned those functions to the newly named Committee on Government Reform. It turns out that the Senate had done much the same under the Democrats in 1978, renaming the committee the Governmental Affairs Committee and giving it jurisdiction over the District of Columbia, the Post Office, and the civil service system. The question remains, however, with new names and revised charters, are the contemporary custodians of the old mandate to study "the operations of government activities with a view toward determining their economy and efficiency" any better at the job now than they used to be?

With respect to the programs they now authorize, these committees—and their various subcommittees—are almost certainly able to establish the kinds of relationships with their agencies that encourage those agencies to provide the subcommittees with plenty of information. But when it comes to all of the agencies authorized by other committees and subcommittees, things almost certainly haven't changed very much. The incentive structure that worked against information sharing from the 1950s through the 1970s—and beyond, in the case of the House Government Operations Committee—remains intact. These committees still don't have jurisdiction over most program legislation, they neither authorize nor appropriate funds for most agencies, and they are often at odds with the committees that do. Interest-group complaints aren't likely to flow through these subcommittees either, given the fact that interest groups are pretty good at figuring out who in Congress can actually get something done, and anyway, these groups have established relationships with the various authorizing committees, so that is where they will go. In short, name changes or no name changes, these committees just won't get much information about most agencies in an informal way.

On the formal side there are still hearings, and both the House and Senate committees are active when it comes to the hearing process. The Senate Governmental Affairs Committee, for example, held forty-three hearings between January and August 2003. About one-quarter of them were confirmation hearings—the Office of Management and Budget and the Department of Homeland Security—and the rest had quite an interesting range, covering abuse of prescription medications, the financing of terrorist activities, SARS, Great Lakes restoration efforts, and more, much more. Of course, that very range raises an interesting question that has always plagued the investigative oversight process. How can anybody be expected to know something about all of those questions? Jurisdiction over everything may mean knowledge of nothing. Still, forty-three hearings in eight months indicate an effort, even if the results of that effort are inevitably diluted by the size of the territory the committee is expected to cover.

According to its website, the House Committee on Government Reform held a remarkable 252 hearings during the 1997–1998 session of Congress. Deducting the roughly eight weeks of "district work periods" the House sets aside each year, that's an average of about three hearings a week while the body was in session. The 2003 schedule seems to have slowed a bit, the committee's Subcommittee on National Security, Emerging Threats, and International Relations leading the way with fifteen hearings between March and August. That's about one a week. The Energy Policy, Natural Resources, and Regulatory Affairs Subcommittee held eight hearings over that same period, while the Subcommittee on Efficiency and Financial Management held one. The other four subcommittees show no hearings during that time, but that may be a result of poor webpage management rather than lethargy on the part of the subcommittees. The committee's website reveals an ambitious twenty-five-page, two-year oversight plan, including subjects within its limited authorizing jurisdiction—a review of the latest Volcker Commission report on how the federal government might improve its operations—and subjects in its vast oversight jurisdiction, subjects like the every-other-year General

Accounting Office "high risk" list of underperforming federal agencies. Those twenty-five programs identified by the GAO can expect something from the Government Reform Committee.

If it sounds as if I am trying to hold these successors to the old Government Operations Committees up to ridicule, I am not. It is just that their problems are the same as those of their predecessors, and it is hard to see how those problems can be successfully addressed. Given the other responsibilities of the senators involved, how can the Governmental Affairs Committee be expected to hold more than forty-three hearings in eight months? How can forty-three hearings be expected to cover the range of the committee's jurisdiction? How could any one senator master all of these various subject matters? The same can obviously be said for the House Government Reform Committee. Beyond that, there is no more incentive for agency personnel to cooperate informally with these contemporary incarnations of the investigative spirit than there was to cooperate with the incarnations of the 1950s and 1960s. These committees can hurt an agency—embarrass it mostly—but they can't help, and anyway, who is going to trust somebody whose mandate is to find out if you are doing your job "economically and efficiently"?

So, in the end, there will be a lot of hearings, a few reports, an occasional informal communication, and not much in the way of real and productive investigative oversight. The odds of changing that situation are not very good.

An Overview of Subcommittee Oversight

Congress wants to know three things. So it sets committees and subcommittees to the task of finding them out. Most of all it wants to know if programs are being carried out the way Congress wants them to be carried out and if those programs are working. That job it assigns to the committees who authorize those programs in the first place, and they are eager for the assignment. Staying in communication with the agencies administering "their" programs and the groups affected by those programs, the subcommittees have a pretty good idea of how things are going at any particular time. Then there are hearings. Some of those hearings come up because a program needs to be reauthorized. Others are called for the purpose of finding something out. Either way, they provide an effective arena for asking congressional questions. Finally there are reports. They are not nearly as effective at getting information to members of the subcommittees, but they can't simply be written off as worthless. In the end, authorizing subcommittees are pretty well informed about what is going on in their programs. They could know more. Many people feel they should know more. But by any reasonable standard, they know quite a bit.

Congress also wants to know what is happening to the money it gives agencies to spend, and the appropriations subcommittees have been looking into that question since the beginning, so they naturally took it upon themselves to just keep on doing what they saw as their job. Using the same informal and formal mechanisms available to the authorizing subcommittees, the appropriations subcommittees, too, find out what they want to know.

Finally, congress wants to know—or at least claims it wants to know—if programs are run in a manner that is economical and efficient. This job has been assigned to the Government Operations Committees and their successors, but the nature of the task and the nature of the committees themselves have conspired to make it pretty much impossible for them to do their job.

Non-committee Oversight

Though most of what Congress knows about any particular agency is known because one of its subcommittees took the time to find it out, there are non-subcommittee avenues for congressional information gathering about agency activities. One of them actually works.

The General Accounting Office was created in 1921 at the same time that Congress created the Bureau of the Budget. Originally conceived as a kind of auditing firm with Congress as its only client, the GAO—which is now the General Accountability Office—has slowly but surely responded to Congress's need to, in the words of the agency's own condensed version of its mission statement, "improve the performance and ensure the accountability of the federal government for the American people."[35] Back in the 1970s, when Congress first tried to push the GAO to take on greater program evaluation and oversight responsibilities, the agency balked, believing that such responsibilities would take away from its primary mission as the Congress's independent auditor.[36] Congress's desire—need—for more help in program evaluation eventually prevailed and that job is now listed right alongside auditing as the core of the agency's mission.

The GAO is organized into thirteen teams. Some are specialized by subject matter—the Natural Resources and the Environment Team or the Financial Markets and Community Investment Teams, for example—while others—the Information Technology and Applied Research and Methods Teams—are obviously organized by function. These teams then conduct studies of various programs or agencies at the request of someone in the Congress. The results of those studies then find the light of day in three different ways. Some studies land an agency or program on the GAO's "high risk" list. That kind of "honor" any agency could do without. Other studies are simply issued as reports. The agency website has a link called GAO reports. That link, it says, is updated daily. The member or subcommittee that requested the report doesn't have to read about it on the agency website. He/she/it will get a copy. But the reports are there for any member interested in finding out what they say. Finally, and perhaps most important, GAO staff testify at subcommittee hearings. In fact, in FY 2002, the agency's people testified a total of 263 times before 104 separate committees or subcommittees. That's an average of six GAO appearances a week.

The fact that much of the GAO's work product ends up being presented as testimony to House and Senate subcommittees is telling. To be sure, this testimony is almost certainly grounded in an agency report, and the report itself will be issued except in the most unusual of circumstances. Still, all of that testimony reminds us of one basic fact of congressional life. If what the GAO has found is going to have much effect on what happens in Congress or at some federal agency, the subcommittee with responsibility for that policy area and that agency is going to have to take notice of those GAO findings and decide that they warrant action. The GAO may provide a mechanism for non-committee oversight, but the impact of that oversight will inevitably pass through a subcommittee filter before it is translated into action.

In Summary

The President just isn't able to become a direct force in agency policy making in any but the most unusual of circumstances. The chief isn't all that motivated and doesn't have the resources of time, knowledge, and interest to sustain the effort should he or she want to.

But things are different for Congress. Organized into committees and subcommittees, each with a specialized jurisdiction and a set of programs to authorize or appropriate for, and each of those programs with an agency to administer them, Congress is set up to overcome those barriers of motivation and resources and to actually become an important player in agency-level decision making.

The motivation barrier falls as subcommittees turn out to be populated primarily by individuals with a real stake in the programs under the subcommittee's jurisdiction. Constituency interests are central to any representative, in part to protect that representative's career and in part to protect his or her people. Even if there is no direct constituency interest, there will almost certainly be groups of people with money to finance campaigns and a clearly articulated concern about what government does in this particular little corner of American society.

The resource barriers fall one at a time, mostly to the same concerns of reelection—whether directly through a representative's own voters, or indirectly through campaign contributions—and constituency representation and service. Why would any representative not be interested in the issues that might affect those two central goals, and how could any representative not make the time to follow that interest? Knowledge is a trickier business, a two-part business at that. But subcommittee members are generally able to become informed amateurs in the issues under their jurisdiction, and they have available to them the means to gather a great deal of information about what the agencies who deal with those issues are doing about them. Informal communications with the agencies themselves, as well as with interest groups active in the subcommittee's areas of concern, backed up by hearings and even the occasional report, provide subcommittee members with a steady supply of information. They may not process it all, and they may not understand everything they try to process. But every subcommittee has access to quite a bit of information and most of the subcommittees make a serious effort to take it in and make sense of it.

The question for the rest of the chapter, of course, is this: how do they use what they know to shape the organizational, budgetary, and legal environments of the specialized agencies of the executive branch? Before we go there, however, one last preliminary. Agency policy specialists are wary of presidential influence. How do they feel about the Congress?

FEAR, RESPECT, COMMUNITY, POWER, AND LEGITIMACY: A RECIPE FOR COOPERATION

Of course, like any recipe, this one doesn't always work out. All the ingredients have to be there or the final product just won't look, feel, or taste like cooperation. More to the point, even when all of these ingredients are present—as they generally are—every agency/subcommittee pairing has those ingredients in somewhat different proportions from every other agency/subcommittee pairing, and if that isn't confusing enough, the amount of any specific ingredient in any particular agency/subcommittee pairing might change over time. Still, in most cases most of the time, an agency is likely to view its subcommittee—subcommittees—with a mixture of fear, respect, and empathy, and when that mixture is leavened with that agency's need for power and legitimacy, the result is almost always a strong predisposition toward cooperation.

The Human Side of the Equation: Fear, Respect, and a Sense of Community

I don't think anybody can really say which of these ingredients goes into the mix first, or even which is "the most important." On that latter score, as I suggested above, it is likely that the importance of any one of these ingredients will vary from one agency/subcommittee pairing to another or even vary over time with a particular pairing. But we have to start somewhere, so let's start with fear.

In his study of federal bureau chiefs, the one I have referred to so often in this chapter, Herbert Kaufman, observed that these chiefs were constantly "looking over their shoulders . . . at the elements of the legislative establishment relevant to their agencies—taking stock of moods and attitudes, estimating reactions to contemplated decisions and actions, trying to prevent misunderstandings and avoidable conflicts, and planning responses when storm warnings appeared on the horizon."[37] On more than one occasion, I have looked over my shoulder trying to find my wife at a party. It wasn't motivated by fear. But, generally speaking, when somebody uses the phrase "looking over their shoulders," and then closes with concern about "storm warnings," that person is talking about fear. So was the anonymous agency official quoted by Aaron Wildavsky way back in 1964. He was the one, remember, who said of his agency's House Appropriations subcommittee, "[They] can do you a world of good and they can cut your throat."[38] The basis of that fear will become ever so clear as we discuss all of the ways that House and Senate subcommittees can exercise influence over the organizational, budgetary, and legal environments of the agencies under their authority. Suffice it to say here, Mr. Wildavsky's interviewee was absolutely right. These subcommittees deserve to be feared, and agency officials know it.

Fear alone, of course, would induce only the most grudging kind of cooperation, a kind of cooperation that depends on the ability of the one who is feared to constantly monitor the behavior of the one who fears. Take away the surveillance, and the cooperation disappears. Add in some respect, however, and things change drastically. Agency policy specialists do in fact respect the subcommittees with jurisdiction over their programs. Subcommittees are composed of individual members, obviously, and not every member will get the same level of respect from agency professionals. Still, in general, there will be considerable respect for a subcommittee and many, if not most, of its members. That respect will rest on three foundations. Think back to why these same policy specialists were so suspicious of presidential leadership.

First, recall, Presidents have spent most of the past twenty-five years attacking bureaucracy, and the attack has often been a sort of blanket charge that all of bureaucracy is a wasteful, inefficient, and largely unnecessary entity. Individual members of Congress may make the very same charges, but almost never about the agencies under the purview of their own subcommittees. Nobody on the Coast Guard and Maritime Transportation Subcommittee fires broadsides at the Coast Guard, the Army Corps of Engineers, or any of the other agencies that subcommittee oversees. They may well fire the occasional warning shot. They may even fire a well-aimed shell at a particular agency decision. But never the kind of broadside that Presidents have fired routinely ever since Mr. Reagan's inaugural address. In short, subcommittees have never poisoned the water the way Presidents have, so subcommittees have never forfeited the automatic respect that careerists think they ought to feel for members of the constitutional government.

Second, agencies and Presidents have very different time perspectives. Agencies and subcommittees rarely do. Both groups view the making of public policy as a continuous evolutionary process requiring constant effort and attention. Despite some post-1994 predictions—and a lot of candidate rhetoric—to the contrary, members of Congress still seem to see their service as a career: 401 of the 435 House members, for example, sought reelection in 1998. Only seven were involuntarily retired.[39] Policy specialists at the agency level, of course, also see their service as a career. Naturally enough, these specialists are going to be drawn to the government's other careerists, the members of Congress. Here is somebody else that can understand the need and desirability of a long-term time frame for the policy-making process.

Finally, and, once again, most important, agency-level policy specialists can have some respect for the knowledge of the informed amateurs who make up the subcommittees with authority over them. Clearly, as I said earlier, we are not talking agency-level expertise. No one at the U.S. Fish and Wildlife Service (USFWS) is ready to put Subcommittee on Fisheries Conservation, Wildlife, and Oceans Chair Wayne Gilchrest in charge of a study of the Sockeye Salmon, or even of enforcement of the Endangered Species Act. Neither is anybody at the Coast Guard about to recommend replacing Rear Admiral Larry Kereth—he's the man in charge of port security for the Coast Guard—with Representative Frank LoBiondo, Chair of the Coast Guard and Maritime Transportation Subcommittee. But both the Fish and Wildlife Service and the Coast Guard know that Representatives Gilchrest (USFWS) and LoBiondo (Coast Guard) have at least a working familiarity with the issues those agencies deal with, and that's enough to generate a certain amount of respect. Remember as we add in ingredients, especially the ingredient called legitimacy, that subcommittees are always being put in a picture that includes the President and his or her political executives. Some things look better when compared with others.

Finally comes, for lack of a more precise term, a sense of community, that is, a sense that they—the agencies and subcommittees—are engaged in a common enterprise and that in the long run there is more to unite than to divide them. This sense of community tends to develop from one or the other—or both—of two sources.

For some agency/subcommittee pairings, this sense of community springs readily out of common background. The various agencies of the Department of Agriculture, for example, tend to be dominated by men and women from states in which agriculture is a key sector of the economy. What, after all, would attract someone to a career in an agriculture-related field except some sort of personal connection? Patterns of appointment to the subcommittees that deal with agriculture programs, as we said, will guarantee that most of the men and women on those committees will represent the very same states and districts in which those agriculture agency policy specialists grew up. The same was traditionally true for agencies in the Interior Department and the subcommittees that dealt with those agencies, though there has been some broadening of the regional base of those subcommittees as the House and Senate have redrawn some committee jurisdictions in the past decade. Still, Don Young of Alaska was reluctant to surrender his chairmanship of the Resources Committee, and only his chance to take over Transportation and Infrastructure—the Coast Guard is important to Alaska, too—eased the sting of losing Resources. That common origin, or common experience, may not generate a sense of community, but it certainly means that there will be enough of an affinity between agency-level policy specialists and subcommittee members and staff to provide the kind of climate in which that sense of community might develop.

Even if that sense of "having grown up together" isn't present, there is still something of a common background for any agency/subcommittee pairing. They are working on the same issues and working with the same groups. They were working on those same issues and with those same groups last year and they will be working on those same issues and with those same groups next year. And the policy specialists at the agency and the members on the subcommittee discuss those issues using a shared vocabulary and set of concepts—what Hugh Heclo called their shared "analytic repertoire for coping with the issues."[40] That shared analytic repertoire definitely separates those who do share it from those who don't, even as it creates in the minds of those who do a sense of being that small group that is truly "in the know" about the policies in their realm of responsibility. That may not exactly breed something that deserves to be called a sense of community, but the bonds of expertise combined with the bonds of longevity can create a pretty powerful feeling that agency staff and subcommittee members are in some sense "in this together" and that cooperation probably makes a lot more sense than conflict.

In the end, then, agency-level policy specialists are likely to conclude that the subcommittees with jurisdiction over them are the only other people in government who know anything—indeed, who even care at all—about the issues those policy specialists work on every day of their careers. Combine that with a certain amount of respect for the knowledge of and interest in these issues that subcommittee members often display, and with the fear those subcommittee members can engender in agency specialists when they start flexing their institutional muscles, and the stage is very definitely set for agency/subcommittee cooperation.

How much cooperation, of course, will vary from one agency/subcommittee pairing to another, and will depend, logically enough, on how much fear, how much respect, and how great a sense of community characterizes a particular pairing. Still, fear, respect, and that sense of community are powerful human incentives to cooperation. And they are not alone. So now let's turn to the institutional incentives.

The Institutional Side of the Equation: Power and Legitimacy

Agencies need power. They also need legitimacy. Subcommittees have a supply of both, and in the right circumstances might be convinced to "loan them out" to their agencies.

Agencies have a measure of power on their own, of course. First, they have the power that derives from knowledge. As we said very early in the book, all policy decisions are driven in part by knowledge and in part by politics, and the informed amateur status of the subcommittees of Congress notwithstanding, when the constitutional government needs to know about something, it has to go to the bureaucrats who are the government's primary repository of that particular piece of knowledge. That knowledge, then, will structure the vocabulary and frame the concepts that will in turn shape the debate. That is obviously a form of power. Second, agencies have the power that derives from formal authority. The constitutional government has given the Environmental Protection Agency the authority to write rules about particulate emissions from off-road diesel vehicles, as well as the authority to enforce rules already written to control the smokestack emissions of coal-fired power plants. In a society with pretty powerful expectations of obedience to the law, authority is a real source of power.

Knowledge and authority are indeed important sources of power, but no agency would feel secure if its power came exclusively from what it knows and from the authority granted to it by the constitutional government in years gone by. Knowledge—usually in the form of advice—can always be ignored, and what the constitutional government has given, the constitutional government can take away.

The advice of the U.S. Fish and Wildlife Service as well as that of the National Marine Fisheries Service was no doubt sought by the Fisheries Conservation, Wildlife, and Oceans Subcommittee while it was considering the Marine Mammal Protection Act of 2003. But some of that advice was ignored. That's what it means to say that decisions are in part the product of knowledge and in part the product of politics—that and the fact that both of those agencies probably framed their advice with an eye toward the reaction of subcommittee members to what they were advising. There isn't an agency in the government that hasn't had the same experience, that is, that hasn't been asked to turn its knowledge of a subject into advice about what to do about a question only to see that advice twisted around or ignored altogether when the question finally gets answered.

Even more serious to agency policy specialists than seeing their advice ignored, of course, would be to see their agency's authority diminished, or even just to see an agency decision overturned. The Federal Trade Commission reacted to the Surgeon General's 1964 report on smoking and health by proposing a set of rules strictly regulating tobacco advertising. At the request of the House Commerce Committee, the commission delayed implementation of the rules until after Congress could consider the issue. The result was the limited warning put on cigarette packages beginning January 1, 1966, and a statutory provision forbidding the FTC from adopting "any rules requiring either a tougher warning on cigarette packs or any warning at all in cigarette advertising."[41] As noted earlier, the Federal Communications Commission decision to change the rules for ownership of television stations brought immediate efforts to overturn the rule in both houses of Congress, and when Representative "Billy" Tauzin of Louisiana used his position as Chair of the Energy and Commerce Committee to bottle up the House version of the repeal, the Appropriations Committee and then the full House voted to forbid the use of any money to put the rule into effect. In the thirty-seven years in between these attacks on the Federal Trade Commission and the Federal Communications Commission, countless federal agencies had to watch Congress reduce their power by reducing their authority.

So, if the power that comes to bureaucracy from knowledge and authority can be trumped by the power of politicians, then what an agency needs is political power. As we will see in the next chapter, some of that political power comes from the support of groups of citizens directly affected by—and therefore interested in—what that agency is up to. But some of it comes instead from the subcommittees with authority over that agency. Satisfied subcommittees, as we'll see shortly, can almost always make sure that an agency's advice is taken, and its authority left intact. Beyond that, they can almost always make sure that budgets are protected, that the political executives appointed to positions of authority over those agencies are if not predisposed to support those agencies at least not their sworn enemies, and even that new grants of authority can be obtained when needed and will be shaped with agency viewpoints in mind.

But satisfied subcommittees have to be satisfied by something, and that something is going to be cooperation on the part of agencies, that is, an opportunity for subcommittee members to have some say in the decisions those agencies make. That's why Representative LoBiondo heaped so much praise on Admiral Collins and Rear Admiral Kereth concerning the first draft of the Coast Guard's proposed port security rules. That's also why Representative LoBiondo put both officers on notice that there were still some "maritime community" concerns to be addressed.

That same pattern is played out in agency/subcommittee pairing after agency/subcommittee pairing. With so much at stake, cooperation seems a reasonable price to pay. Besides, it isn't being paid to strangers and it isn't being paid strictly out of fear. It is being paid to members of a policy-making community and it is being paid in part out of respect.

Agencies need power. But they also need legitimacy. In other words, agencies have to be able to demonstrate a rightful claim to the possession and use of power. The authority agencies exercise, of course, comes from the constitutional government, and that gives it a powerful dose of legitimacy. But it isn't always enough. All grants of authority given to agencies are open to interpretation, and should an agency interpret its authority in ways that offend enough people—or just the right, maybe wrong, people—that agency doesn't have an automatic reservoir of legitimacy to fall back on. But if that agency has a pattern of working closely and cooperatively with one or more subcommittees of Congress, then agency staff can say, in effect, "These policies were formulated with congressional (obviously legitimate) participation. Members of Congress approve of our policies and they approve of us and, should that approval cease, they can and will take corrective action."

Legitimacy enters into agency decisions to cooperate with their subcommittees in a second way, a way that has nothing to do with the agency's need for anything. Recall back to chapter 2. The policy specialists who work in the various agencies of the federal government believe in the notion of self-government. That means that they know they must be responsive to someone. The problem, as we saw back in that early discussion, lay in the fact that these specialists wanted to be responsive without compromising their primary commitment to the use of their own knowledge in the policy process. Legitimacy—the democratic legitimacy of the whole governing enterprise, that is—demands that every agency be responsive to the constitutional government. The goal of addressing issues and problems by applying the best available knowledge demands that knowledgeable people make decisions. Being responsive to congressional subcommittees seems to be just about the only way to come close to meeting both of those demands.

Congressional subcommittees have power and legitimacy. Agencies need both. It is hardly a surprise that those agencies would figure out what was needed to "borrow" the power and legitimacy of the subcommittees that supply them with the authority and the money they need to do the jobs they want to do. Cooperate. Given how important it is to the agencies to get that power and legitimacy, and given the fact that the subcommittees who possess both are viewed with a combination of fear, respect, and a sense that a particular agency/subcommittee pairing constitutes a sort of community, it hardly seems a surprise that they decide to do it.

In Summary

Agencies aren't exactly receptive to presidential direction and leadership. They will follow if they believe it really is the President speaking and that he or she really means what is being said. But they will follow reluctantly. The attitude toward congressional direction and leadership is very different.

The reason, of course: it isn't really congressional direction and leadership. It is subcommittee direction and leadership. That means it deserves a certain amount of respect, since it isn't coming from people who have been attacking the agency for a decade or two, it isn't coming from people who feel the need to move now in some bold new direction they don't fully understand, and most of all, it isn't coming from people with only a passing knowledge of the subject at hand. Beyond that, subcommittee direction and leadership come from people that agency staff generally tend to think of as part of a community of interested and knowledgeable people trying to work toward sound and rational policy. Finally, alas, subcommittee direction and leadership come from people capable of inspiring a bit of fear in agency personnel. In addition, the fact that this is subcommittee direction and leadership means that it can be turned into power and legitimacy, two things that every agency absolutely needs.

So, fear and respect and a sense of community and the need for power and the need for legitimacy all blend together to generate cooperation. It is clear that just exactly how much cooperation emerges from this blend depends on the amount of each ingredient in the blend itself, and that, in turn, is going to depend on all sorts of things. Some of those things are quite idiosyncratic. When the Republicans retook control of the U.S. Senate in January 2003, James Jeffords (I-VT) was replaced as Chair of the Committee on Environment and Public Works by James Inhofe (R-OK). Senator Inhofe once compared then EPA Administrator Carol Browner to Tokyo Rose, and the EPA itself to the Gestapo.[42] A little more fear, a little less respect into the EPA/Environment and Public Works Committee mix. The nature of the subject matter itself can also play a role. The EPA will always have more trouble cooperating with its subcommittees, as will the Occupational Safety and Health Administration. The Army Corps of Engineers and the various agencies of the Department of Veterans Affairs will always have an easier time. The point remains, however, that despite the fact that the level of cooperation varies from agency/subcommittee pairing to agency/subcommittee pairing, the drive is always toward some sort of cooperative relationship, however tenuous it may be at times. Fear, respect, a sense of community, and the need for power and legitimacy just create too much incentive not to try.

HOW DOES THE CONGRESS INFLUENCE THE BUREAUCRACY?

So far we've seen that the Congress—through its subcommittees—is in a very different position vis-à-vis the bureaucracy than is the President. These subcommittees have far better means of finding out about agency activities and a far greater ability to understand what it is that they find. They even face agencies at least receptive to the idea that subcommittee influence would rarely do serious harm to their decision-making processes and, in fact, might even help an agency to become a more effective force on behalf of its own policy preferences. At least subcommittees would be a real help if an agency is willing to define its own preferences with subcommittee viewpoints in mind.

As we noted in the previous section, most agencies are willing to take account of the preferences of their subcommittees when exercising their own policy-making responsibilities, and as we also noted, the mix of reasons is varied and complex. But underlying all of this is the unspoken understanding on both sides that subcommittees have the tools to make their preferences felt whenever they believe those preferences have been ignored. Let's take a look at how they would do it.

Influencing the Organizational Environment I: Managing From Outside the Box(es)

The boxes of the title, of course, are the boxes on the charts that are supposed to describe the management structures of the various organizations that make up the executive branch of the government. You won't find a box labeled Subcommittee on Highways, Transit, and Pipelines anywhere on the chart describing the structure of the Department of Transportation any more than you will find a box labeled Subcommittee on Parks, Recreation, and Public Lands on the Interior Department chart. Of course, you won't find a box labeled President of the United States on either of those departmental charts either, but there is a not-so-implicit assumption that right above the box labeled Secretary of Transportation and right above the box labeled Secretary of Interior—indeed, right above the box at the top of any organization chart in the federal government—is a box labeled President of the United States. He or she, after all, is the chief executive, and he or she, after all, is the one all of those other folks who do occupy boxes that are on the page are supposed to "report" to.

Subcommittees, however, aren't assumed to be occupying some special box not on the printed page but in everybody's mind and, therefore, are not part of the "chain of command" of the departments that contain the agencies they want to influence. So, quite literally, if these subcommittees want to manage, they must manage from outside the box(es). And manage they do.

First of all, as we saw in the last chapter, Congress has some definite say over who occupies the boxes that are printed on the pages that describe the various entities of the federal government, and as it has with everything else it considers important, Congress has assigned most of the responsibility for having that say to its various subcommittees. It is the advice and consent of the Senate that a President must secure to put someone in a particular organizational box, so it is Senate subcommittees who have the greatest impact on who gets confirmed, and therefore allowed to occupy that particular box, but key members of House subcommittees who will have to work with these "box occupiers" will often have some influence over the construction of the list of names the President sends over for consideration. This will be particularly true as we move down any departmental hierarchy toward the offices a specific subcommittee would be most interested in. The House Coast Guard and Maritime Transportation Subcommittee is interested in who gets the job of Secretary of Transportation, but it is going to be a lot more interested in who runs the Maritime Administration and who ends up as Commandant of the Coast Guard. The President's interest travels an exactly opposite path, as it turns out, so as we move from Secretary of Transportation—already far less interesting than Secretary of State, Secretary of Defense, or Secretary of the Treasury—down toward Coast Guard Commandant or Administrator of the Maritime Administration, he or she is going to be less and less concerned about who puts one of those titles on his or her resume.

Second, as we also saw in chapter 5, the men and women who slide into the boxes on the organization charts of all those pieces of government are loyal not just to the President who nominated them but to the Congress—pieces of the Congress, of course—who might have had some say in getting them nominated in the first place and who definitely had some say in getting them confirmed in the second. Then, recall, there were the loyalties to the agencies and departments they were expected to manage and to the constituencies so important to those agencies and departments. Any loyalty other than the loyalty to the President tends to play into the hands of subcommittees hoping to influence the way in which the men and women sent to manage the departments and agencies of the government do their jobs. As a practical matter, loyalty to—or at least a grudging respect for—Congress ends up meaning responsiveness to committees or subcommittees, and loyalty to agencies and departments and their various constituencies means loyalty to organizations and individuals likely to be well connected to those same subcommittees.

In short, subcommittees have some definite influence over how agencies are managed by those ostensibly sent to manage them on behalf of the President. Congress has too much say over who those managers are—and too great a claim on their loyalty—to be ignored. To be sure, these men and women know they must manage with an eye toward the President's response to what they do and how they do it. That is the first expectation for their performance. But, as we saw, often as not when they cast that eye toward the President, their glance is not met by his or hers, and other loyalties, other concerns, are free to enter their management equation, just so long as they remain ready to return to the President's path should he or she define one. That's plenty of opening for the subcommittees to get themselves into the management game.

But subcommittees are hardly content with the influence they might have on agency management through the influence they might have on a department's, or even an agency's, chain of command. They want a more direct kind of management presence, and they will try to get it. Specifically, they want the kind of management presence that helps to set goals and priorities and provides guidance and direction for an organization's activities. Enter once more the process of oversight.

Oversight hearings are aimed at finding out what is going on at a particular agency, usually what is going on about a particular issue or question. But they are also aimed at expressing subcommittee views on what is going on, in particular if the subcommittee thinks it isn't terribly happy with what is going on. Let's return to two hearings conducted by the House Subcommittee on the Coast Guard and Maritime Administration talked about earlier.

When the subcommittee heard from Admiral Collins and Rear Admiral Kereth, remember, the chair, Frank LoBiondo of New Jersey, went out of his way to praise both men for the careful and consultative way they had gone about the process of drafting the interim rules for port security they had been instructed to draft as a consequence of the Maritime Transportation Security Act of 2002. But he also went out of his way to express his belief that there were "maritime community" concerns yet to be addressed. Representative LoBiondo then went on to follow Admiral Collins's testimony with that of eight representatives of that "maritime community," giving them ample time to make their points to the admiral. Most followed the lead of Cornel Martin, Vice President of the Passenger Vehicle Association, praising some elements of the interim rules, and harshly condemning others.[43] The subcommittee didn't explicitly endorse all of these objections, but the fact that they were presented, put into the record, and received the occasional favorable comment from one subcommittee member or another had to leave some sort of impression on Admiral Collins and on his chief deputy for port security, Rear Admiral Kereth. No doubt that was part of the purpose for the hearing.

Instructing an agency as well as informing itself was also the purpose of the subcommittee's hearing on Interpretations of Existing Ownership Requirements for U.S. Flag Dredges. This time only four people, representing four organizations concerned with the question of the ownership rules for a particular type of dredge, were given the opportunity to speak their piece, but it was pretty clear from what they said that they were speaking not so much to the subcommittee, but to Mr. Larry Burton, Director of the International Trade Compliance Division, Office of Regulations and Rulings, of the Bureau of Customs and Border Protection. And it was very clear from their testimony that they wanted Mr. Burton to know how angry they were at his agency's interpretation of the statutory requirements behind that agency's rules. Since the nature of their concerns—and the depth of their anger with the agency—could hardly have come as any surprise to Subcommittee Chair Frank LoBiondo or any of the members of his subcommittee, it seems clear enough that this particular group of representatives wanted the message to get through.

All of this instruction and guidance wouldn't have as much impact as the subcommittee might hope, of course, if it couldn't be backed up with somewhat more direct actions. It can, in the budget and in the law. But before we go there, a brief note on subcommittees and bureaucratic structure.

Influencing the Organizational Environment II: Subcommittees and Bureaucratic Structure

Much of what needs to be said in this section has already been previewed—maybe even already been said—in the previous chapter. Here is a quick overview of the ground we've already covered, plus a look at a couple of things we haven't.

First of all, recall our conclusion from chapter 5 that the President wasn't in a position to provide his or her political executives with the kind of political power needed to supplement their grants of organizational authority. Now think back a couple of sections in this chapter. Subcommittees are quite able—and generally willing—to provide the political power necessary to back up the legal authority of their subcommittees. They are able and willing to provide that power even—perhaps especially—when said power will be used to undermine the authority of the President's team of political executives. As political scientists have been pointing out for more than a half century, it is the political support that agency careerists get from congressional subcommittees, every bit as much as those careerists' superior knowledge and greater time and attention to detail, that provides agencies with their substantial autonomy in the American governing system.[44]

The tale of the paper structure was told in all the detail it needs in the previous chapter. Just remind yourselves of this. Congressional subcommittees, more than anyone else in government except the agency careerists themselves, care about the paper structure of the federal government. That, remember, was why the Republican leadership of the House of Representatives created a special—leadership dominated—committee to review all of the various actions coming out of the various House standing committees concerning the creation of a Department of Homeland Security. They felt they had to protect the President and his proposal from a host of angry subcommittees. They did, for the most part, even turning a deaf ear to a plea by Don Young (R-AK) to keep the Coast Guard in the Department of Transportation rather than transferring it to Homeland Security. Representative Young's primary concern, however, was to make sure his Transportation and Infrastructure Committee's Subcommittee on the Coast Guard and Maritime Transportation kept its jurisdiction over the Coast Guard despite the Guard's new organizational home. On that one, Representative Young succeeded.

In sum, subcommittees can provide the power that generates the organizational autonomy that most agencies secretly—or not so secretly—crave. They can also have a huge impact on the paper structure that determines where programs and agencies are located and who has authority over them. They do share that latter authority with the President and even with the various departmental secretaries, but the subcommittee members know that only in extraordinary circumstances will their share of the power to reorganize the government be anything but the lion's share.

Influencing the Budgetary Environment: Authorizing, Appropriating, and Instructing

Much of the story of Congress and the budgetary environment of federal government agencies has been told. Part of it was told in the previous chapter, in our discussion of the limitations on the President's ability to mold most agency budgets, and part of it in this chapter, in our discussion of fiscal oversight. But one piece of that story bears a brief retelling, and two other parts have yet to be told at all. Let's start with one of the as-yet-untold parts, the part about subcommittees and the process of authorizing agencies and their budgets.

No money can be spent until it has been appropriated, but no money is going to be appropriated until an agency has been authorized to spend it. So, when the Subcommittee on Transportation, Treasury, and Independent Agencies of the House Appropriations Committee meets in the spring of 2004 to decide how much money the Federal Aviation Administration will be allowed to spend on "weather safety research" in the fiscal year to begin in October 2004, the subcommittee's members know that back in 2003 the House and Senate agreed—after some considerable negotiation in conference committee—to authorize the FAA to spend $24,260,000 for that purpose in that year. That number—a slightly larger one, actually—was originally the product of the House Transportation and Infrastructure Committee's Subcommittee on Aviation, an outfit that held five separate hearings in the spring of 2003 on what was eventually known as "Flight 100—Century of Aviation Reauthorization Act."

The subcommittee wasn't reauthorizing aviation—or the Wright Brothers, for that matter—of course. It was reauthorizing the Federal Aviation Administration. That is, it was saying that we think the Federal Aviation Administration ought to continue, and that it ought to do the following kinds of things: it ought to conduct research toward improving aviation safety, promote the construction of new runways at congested airports, allot more landing slots at Reagan International Airport in Washington, D.C., to planes coming from outside a 1,250-mile radius, and—this one for the Transportation Security Administration—make sure that not later than forty-five days after the final passage of the act, federal screeners would be "deployed" to the airports at Kenai, Homer, and Valdez, Alaska. Indeed, this charge to the Federal Aviation Administration contained nine separate titles, with Title I alone containing ninety distinct provisions. More to the point in terms of this section of the chapter, the subcommittee went on to say that in order to accomplish all of these tasks, the FAA ought to get $3.4 billion for fiscal year 2004, and $3.5 billion for 2005. That figure would be increased by another $100 million in each of the next two years. Then, come early 2007, the subcommittee would ask itself again, Should we keep the FAA, what should it be doing, and how much money should we say it can spend doing it?

The Aviation Subcommittee was busy in the authorizing business in 2003. It was also called upon to reauthorize the National Transportation Safety Board (NTSB). That process took fewer hearings, produced a far shorter list of recommendations/demands on the agency, and authorized a far smaller amount of money. But from the NTSB's point of view, what was happening was exactly the same as what was happening for—or to—the Federal Aviation Administration, namely, a subcommittee of the House of Representatives was sitting down to tell NTSB what it ought to do and how much money that subcommittee thought it would need to do the job. That same spring, the Subcommittee on Economic Development, Public Buildings, and Emergency Management was preparing to reauthorize the Economic Development Administration, altering its duties and responsibilities somewhat, and authorizing it to spend sums from $400 million in fiscal year 2004 to $500 million in fiscal year 2008. The year 2003 was a busy time in all of the subcommittees of the Transportation and Infrastructure Committee, as its Highways, Transit, and Pipelines Subcommittee was asked by the Bush administration to reauthorize a wide range of highway, transit, and transportation safety programs in a single package. They called in the administrators of the various programs—and their departmental boss, Transportation Secretary Norman Mineta—holding a series of hearings at which subcommittee members took turns complaining about how little money these various political executives were seeking for their agencies and programs. Taking their cues from the President, the political executives asked for $247 billion. Taking their cues from constituents, organized interests, and much of the rest of the House of Representatives, the subcommittee was insisting that the more appropriate figure was $375 billion.[45]

This list of subcommittees working on authorization legislation for the agencies and programs of the federal government could, of course, go on for what would seem like forever. It needn't. The point is, as noted above, every agency has to present to subcommittees of the House and Senate its ideas for how much money it needs to do the things it thinks it needs to do. Those subcommittees are the very same subcommittees who will have the greatest say on the legal environment in which agencies operate—we'll get to that shortly—so what they say about money cannot be ignored. Besides, these subcommittees often provide the most sympathetic ear a set of policy specialists will find for their budget needs. The members, recall, almost certainly have a real stake in the programs run by these agencies. Therefore, they are going to be more receptive to agency arguments for money than the President, and everyone in government knows that the appropriations subcommittees never hand out all of the money that the authorizing committees have said was needed.

In short, the congressional budgeting process is really a two-stage process, and stage one is the authorization stage. The subcommittees that create agencies, write the laws that empower those agencies, and conduct the program oversight that is supposed to find out how well those agencies and laws are working also get the first crack at deciding how much money agencies will get to try to make things work. Those subcommittees even get the first crack at deciding what the money they are suggesting should be spent should be spent doing. Remember, the Aviation Subcommittee said $24,260,000 for "weather safety research." They also said $27,800,000 for "human factors and aeromedical research," and $10 million for "the Airport Cooperative Research Program." Only rarely are these numbers increased by much as they move through the rest of the congressional authorization process, and as I suggested above, the numbers that come out of the appropriations process will almost inevitably be smaller than those that come out of the authorization process.

In the end, then, it doesn't take policy specialists long to figure out that just as they are key players in shaping the organizational environment of their agencies, these subcommittees are key players in shaping those agencies' budgetary environments. We will see shortly that the subcommittees who authorize and oversee a particular agency will also be a major force in determining the shape of that agency's legal environment. But first, we need a word or two on the other tools by which Congress shapes an agency's budgetary environment: appropriations and instructions.

The appropriations process has gotten just about all of the discussion it needs. The days of unchallenged subcommittee power are likely gone, but the enormity of the task of going line by line over a budget of the size and complexity of the one that doles out money to all of the agencies in the federal government, coupled with the fact that most members of Congress care about only a fraction of the items in that massive budget, are bound to result in a great deal of autonomy for appropriations subcommittees as they go about their jobs. They will play an absolutely central role in deciding exactly how much agencies have to spend in a given year, and they will give some general direction as to what that money will be spent doing. They have to take account of the Office of Management and Budget's recommendations for that particular fiscal year, and they have to take account of the amounts authorized by the full Congress some time in the recent past. But remember the comment made to Aaron Wildavsky by that agency official. "They [the appropriations subcommittees] can do you a world of good and they can cut your throat."[46] No participant in government will ever underestimate the power of the appropriations part of the budgeting process in shaping the budgetary environment of federal government agencies.

That brings us to the last congressional tool for shaping that budgetary environment, the business of giving what are called spending instructions. The instruction is almost always a variation on the theme of "thou shalt not." That is, except in the rarest of circumstances, what an appropriations subcommittee wants to do is to prevent an agency from spending any money to do whatever it is that the subcommittee doesn't think should be done.

Spending instructions have a fairly long history. In his 1969 study of the appropriations process, Michael Kirst found that the appropriations bills of the 1960s generally contained five formal statutory restrictions on agency spending and the reports accompanying each appropriations act were likely to contain thirty or more informal provisions relating to the use of the dollars appropriated.[47] Congressional leaders expressed strong criticism of the process during the 1970s— legislating by appropriating, they often called it—but that didn't stop the full Appropriations Committee from instructing the Food and Drug Administration in both 1979 and 1980 "not to promulgate regulations prohibiting the addition of antibiotics to animal feed."[48] The tactic is hardly dead, as witnessed by the Appropriations Committee's 2003 instruction to the Federal Communications Commission not to spend any of its fiscal 2004 appropriation on the process of enforcing the new media ownership rules it adopted in the spring of 2003.[49]

Administrators often complain about having their hands tied by these spending instructions. It turns out from their behavior that they are using the right metaphor. To be more direct, agency-level administrators live with those instructions, no matter how much they may detest being tied up, or how much they may want to do what the instructions forbid them to do. No one can be sure if a chair of the Federal Communications Commission who is armed with the full backing of the President of the United States, as Michael Powell had been, will act differently from most of his or her predecessors, but the men and women who ran hundreds of agencies subject to spending instructions in the past forty years seemed to think that the best course of action was to grit their teeth and do as they had been "instructed."[50]

In the final analysis, then, agency-level policy specialists all realize that their budgetary environment is shaped far more by a handful of congressional subcommittees than by any other single force. Authorizing committees will be sympathetic—to a point—to agency requests for money, and their role of taking the first congressional look at what a given agency might need to do its job should not be underestimated. But the money can't come from the Treasury without an appropriation—the precise words of the provision of the Constitution grace the House Appropriations Committee website lest anyone forget—so everyone understands the importance of appropriations subcommittees in deciding how many dollars will actually flow an agency's way. Everyone also understands that appropriations subcommittees can and will issue "instructions" about where money ought not to be spent, and that agency administrators will take those instructions seriously. High-profile instructions, like those involving the FCC media ownership rules, will generate enough interest to bring about high-profile votes, but most spending instructions, like most appropriations themselves, are really the province and the product of the appropriations subcommittees who drafted them.

Influencing the Legal Environment: Remember, They Do Call Them Lawmakers

As we saw in the previous chapter, an agency's legal environment boils down to its authority, and the primary source of that authority is found in the statute books. The Federal Aviation Administration has the legal authority to regulate aircraft design, determine the number of landing slots at a particular airport, grant money to local communities to improve airports, control the flow of air traffic, and a whole lot more, and the agency has all of that authority under "Subtitle VII, Aviation Programs, of Title 49, United States Code." It was Congress that passed Subtitle VII of Title 49 in 1958, and it was Congress that revised Subtitle VII of Title 49 in 2003. It will be Congress that revises Subtitle VII of Title 49 in 2007. But, as we also saw in the previous chapter, the language of any statute leaves some room for interpretation. It is easy enough to figure out what it means to increase from twelve to twenty-four the number of slot exemptions for scheduled carriers coming into Reagan National Airport in Washington, D.C., from a distance greater than 1,250 miles. But what exactly does it mean to do so in a way that makes sure to increase "service to cities that can serve as gateways to additional western states that have only limited service to Reagan National Airport"? That injunction will be interpreted by the Federal Aviation Administration, and that interpretation will become part of the agency's legal environment. Also part of its environment, as we saw in chapter 5, would be executive orders issued by the President of the United States and decisions reached by the courts.

An agency's legal environment, then, is shaped by statutes, agency interpretations of those statutes, executive orders, and court decisions. The question for the rest of this section, of course, is how can Congress—its committees and subcommittees primarily—try to shape an agency's legal environment, and how much success is it likely to have? Let's start where the legal environment starts, with the basic statute that creates and empowers an agency.

Statutory Authority Itself

To revisit chapter 5 one more time, we know how important its basic grant of statutory authority is to any agency. It has to try to live within that grant of authority, and it has to try to live up to it. That is, it can't do things it doesn't have the authority to do, and it is expected to make a good faith effort to do things it does have the authority to do. In the end, that basic grant of statutory authority has to pass both houses of Congress and it has to be signed by the President. But at every step along the way, the most important players in the process of deciding exactly what will go into the grant of authority given to any specific agency will be the members of the subcommittee and committee with jurisdiction over that agency. Three reasons.

First of all, subcommittees and committees pretty much control the process by which such grants of bureaucratic authority are written. It was almost certainly a member of the committee or subcommittee—maybe even with a little help from the policy professionals at an agency—who came up with the original idea for changing that agency's authority in the first place, and it will be the appropriate subcommittee that will hold the hearings and make any changes in that bill that its members see fit. If the subcommittee just doesn't like the bill, it is dead. If it does come up with a version enough of the members can agree on, that version goes to the full committee for its consideration. More changes are likely, and if the full committee can't agree to support the subcommittee recommendation, the bill dies, but if the committee does agree, the bill will go to the floor, except in the rare circumstance in which that bill runs into the opposition of the majority party leadership in that chamber. Floor votes don't automatically go the way the committee has recommended, but in a great many areas of policy, the odds that such a recommendation will be defeated are slim indeed.

Second, the very nature of the product provides subcommittees and committees a tremendous advantage over everyone else involved, that is, over the rest of the House, the rest of the Senate, and especially over the President. Specifically, a bill like "Flight 100—A Century of Aviation Reauthorization Act of 2003" is long and complex, composed quite literally of hundreds of separate if more or less connected pieces. And, since it is the reauthorization—a reaffirmation with substantive changes—of the existence and authority of a particular agency, the following would be fairly typical language. "Subchapter II of chapter 417 is amended by adding at the end the following: (a) ALTERNATE ESSENTIAL AIR SERVICE PILOT PROGRAM—(1) ESTABLISHMENT—The Secretary of Transportation shall establish an alternate essential air service pilot program in accordance with the requirements of this section." If you haven't looked at Subchapter II of chapter 417 of Subtitle VII of Title 49 of the United States Code lately, that might be a little tough to decipher. The Community Flexibility Pilot Program that is to be added as subsection b following subsection a is a little easier to follow, but subsection c, the one on Fractionally Owned Aircraft, left me a bit confused. On the other hand, it was easy enough to understand the directive to the Administrator of the Transportation Security Administration to get federal baggage screeners to three airports in Alaska within forty-five days. You get the idea. Hundreds of individual provisions, adding up to a pretty substantial grant of authority to—and a pretty substantial set of instructions for—a federal agency, make tough reading, even for the most dedicated of non-committee members.

Finally, and most important of all, remember the resources these subcommittee and committee members bring to the process. First, of course, they have a level of interest in what their agencies are empowered and/or instructed to do that is matched by no one else. Constituency interests, interest-group concerns, even their own personal viewpoints all point to continued attention to the details of agency activity, and that means to the details of agency authority. Second, they have the time. The members of a subcommittee are never too busy to spend a little more time working to make sure that what happens to the agencies under their jurisdiction is what those members want to have happen. Nothing more and nothing less. Third, they have the knowledge. They are accepted as their chamber's experts on the subjects involved—most other members don't care, they have their own areas of concern—and, and here recall the previous paragraph, some of their superior knowledge is just knowing what was in subsection 2c before it was amended by the proposed language, or even having a rough idea of what is meant by a fractionally owned aircraft. Fourth, they operate in a context bounded by institutional expectations, that is, a context in which everybody agrees, however grudgingly, that most issues ought to be left in the hands of subcommittees and committees. Finally, they are determined. In their own eyes, their power in the institution and the interests of the people—constituents and interest groups—that they have chosen to represent are at stake as decisions about the authority of one of their agencies is being decided, and they are not going to back down if they do run into a fight.

Let's return for a moment to the Federal Aviation Administration reauthorization bill. Consider a single two-line provision from the point of view of the subcommittee and committee, as well as from the point of view of anybody else who might want to challenge them.

Section 613, as I noted a couple of times, instructs the Administrator of the Transportation Security Administration to "deploy Federal screeners at Kenai, Homer, and Valdez, Alaska." That provision is in the bill, to no one's surprise, because House Transportation and Infrastructure Committee Chair Don Young (R-AK) put it there. Any member of the House or Senate could have raised an objection, but none did. Respect for committees, fear of Don Young's power over other issues, and the desire to protect the possibility of trying to get a similar home-district provision into some other bill later on, among other things, provided plenty of motivation to leave the provision alone. And what about the President? If the government is spending too much money, is this one of the places? Should he veto the bill? As we said in chapter 5, the President has to veto the whole bill, and that's quite unlikely over something so small. A veto threat is no better, since the threat is only credible if members believe it will be acted on, and it is not at all likely that anyone would believe that a President would veto the reauthorization of the FAA over something that small.

Subcommittees don't win all of their battles by default because the issues seem too insignificant for anyone to challenge. The President and the Republican leadership in the House of Representatives wanted to leave baggage screening in the hands of the private companies who handled it before September 11, 2001, but the House and Senate Aviation Subcommittees sent to the floor legislation to lodge authority for that function in the Transportation Security Administration, and then fought long and hard to make sure their view prevailed. It did.

Even congressional subcommittees can't win all of the time, of course. For example, those same Aviation Subcommittees were forced to compromise a bit with the President over Section 230 of the FAA reauthorization bill. The original version of Section 230 forbid the Secretary of Transportation from authorizing the transfer of the "air traffic separation and control functions operated by the Federal Aviation Administration . . . to a private entity or a public entity other than the United States Government." President Bush was very much interested in doing exactly that as part of his effort to privatize as much of the federal government's operations as possible, so he was quite unhappy with the subcommittee language. This time the President did threaten a veto, as well as instruct FAA Administrator Marion Blakey to assure everyone that the administration had no such intentions. In the end, the conference committee handling the final version of Flight 100 left the offending language in, but added a couple of exceptions that permitted the FAA to add to its "contract program" towers in airports that had already been suggested as good candidates for that program by the Transportation Department's Inspector General three years earlier. Privatization will not come to any large airport before October 1, 2007, but it might come to a few more small airports. The subcommittee wasn't exactly beaten, but it didn't get all it sought, and that, in itself, is news.

In sum, at least as far as the most important element in an agency's legal environment—its statutory grant of authority—congressional subcommittees and committees are assigned the lead role and are in a good position to play that role successfully. First, they produce a document that makes it hard to challenge them. Second, they have the resources to cause most of the other participants to back away from any sort of challenge. And if that fails, those same resources can be used very effectively to defend the subcommittee's decisions. They will lose now and then, but when they lose, it surprises everybody.

Statutory Interpretation

As we noted several times, provisions of statutes have to be interpreted. Sending federal screeners to these three airports doesn't leave a lot of room for interpretation, to be sure, and to the insider, fractionally owned aircraft probably isn't all that much of a mystery either. But what exactly does it mean for the FAA Administrator to "take action to encourage the construction of airport capacity enhancement projects at congested airports"? I don't mean to suggest that the words provide no guidance, only that they leave open more than one clearly defined course of action. Congressional subcommittees are more than ready to step in with suggestions as to which course of action they would prefer when more than one appears to be open.

Recall our earlier discussion of the Coast Guard and Maritime Transportation and Water Resources and Environment Subcommittees' joint hearings on "The Interpretation of Existing Ownership Requirements for U.S. Flag Dredges." Though the word interpretation may not make the title of the hearing every time, it is clear enough that whenever a subcommittee is concerned about how a particular agency is interpreting a particular provision in its statute, that subcommittee will raise the question at the next hearing, whatever the title or subject of that hearing might be. In fact, the subcommittee might not wait until the next hearing.

Once again, the position from which congressional subcommittees approach the question of agency interpretation of statutory provisions is one of immense strength. Just look at the title of that joint subcommittee hearing in the previous paragraph. Would the President know or care enough to raise that issue with the agencies in question? Would anyone outside the subcommittees that did hold the hearing? There are exceptions. Secretary of Interior Gale Norton's interpretation of her legal mandate, the one that says the Secretary does not have the authority to designate public lands off limits to some kinds of uses if states want to open them, probably interests all kinds of people outside of the orbit of the House Resources Committee. Still, most of the time, the only individuals in the constitutional government who will pay much attention to how the Secretary of Transportation, or the Secretary of Housing and Urban Development, or the Administrator of the Transportation Security Administration interpret provisions of dozens of statutes they are called upon to administer will be the members of the subcommittees who wrote those statutes and who oversee those agencies and departments.

Executive Orders

Congress obviously doesn't issue executive orders. That, of course, means that Congress's impact on this element in the legal environment of federal agencies is going to be limited. It is going to be limited, all right, but not eliminated.

First of all, of course, a statute trumps an executive order. That turns out to put Congress back in the game in two interrelated ways. To begin with, if Congress actually does pass a statute that in effect repeals an executive order, that order is no longer an element in the legal environments of the agency or agencies it was aimed at. Beyond that, since no President wants to see Congress overturning his or her executive orders, the chief may end up issuing an executive order that is far different from the one that he or she would have preferred to issue. Recall the story of "Don't Ask, Don't Tell" from the previous chapter. President Clinton entered office in January 1993 after a campaign that promised gays something very different from "Don't Ask, Don't Tell." But the issue of gays in the military took media front-burner status within weeks of the inauguration, and it wasn't long before the President was informed in no uncertain terms by his Defense Secretary Les Aspin and key members of the House and Senate Armed Services Committees that if he issued the order as he had originally envisioned it, he would face trouble in the uniformed services and outright rebellion in Congress. The President, in short, was forced to remember that a statute trumps an executive order and, more to the point, to recognize that to issue an executive order that would so obviously invite Congress to play its trump card would mean a loss on the specific issue in question and the inevitable loss of informal presidential power that accompanies any high-profile defeat at the hands of the legislative branch. Then came summer, and "Don't Ask, Don't Tell."

Congress's second weapon in attempting to influence that corner of an agency's legal environment occupied by executive orders is far less visible than the process of overturning an order by statute or reminding a President that discretion really is the better part of valor sometimes. Less visible, perhaps, but just as effective. As we noted in the previous chapter, executive orders can be just as open to interpretation as are statutes, and policy specialists at the agency level, suspicious as they are of the chief's motives and expertise, are often reluctant to look for an interpretation that is most consistent with the wishes of the President who wrote the order. Congressional subcommittees will provide plenty of encouragement for that approach as well as the political power to make it possible.

Congress doesn't use its legislative powers to overturn all that many executive orders. The President doesn't end up being "scared off" from issuing such orders all that often, either. But, however seldom, both can and do happen, and they attract plenty of attention when they do. Below the radar screen, however, subcommittees encourage their agencies to interpret executive orders in a manner consistent with the shared interests of subcommittee members and agency staff, and provide the political back-up to make sure that those agencies can get away with those kinds of interpretations.

Courts and Their Decisions

Just as Congress doesn't issue executive orders, Congress doesn't tell Interior Department attorneys when and on what terms to settle a lawsuit against one of its decisions nor when to appeal an adverse decision from a Federal District or Circuit Court. Still, once again, Congress is not exactly powerless when it comes to court decisions and the role they play in shaping an agency's legal environment.

Once more, Congress's main weapon is its power to legislate. In 1989 the U.S. Supreme Court made a series of three decisions—*Patterson v. McLean Credit Union, Martin v. Wilks,* and *Wards Cove Packing Co. v. Atonio*—that a good many members of Congress felt tipped the balance in employment discrimination law too far in favor of the interests of the employer.[51] Their response was the Civil Rights Act of 1990. That was vetoed by President George H. W. Bush, but when Congress passed very similar legislation again in 1991, a number of factors—not the least of which was the furor over the Clarence Thomas confirmation hearings—convinced the President to sign this version in order to bury the issue before the 1992 presidential election.[52] Congress could do the same to court interpretations of the Endangered Species Act, the Clean Air Act, or even to Subtitle VII of Title 49 of the U.S. Code, should it choose to. As a matter of fact, of course, it has.

Beyond that, court decisions, like statutes and executive orders, are subject to interpretation, and some of that interpretation is going to be done at the agency level. Enter the subcommittees once more, encouraging and rewarding interpretations consistent with the shared interests of subcommittee members and agency staff.

If you are thinking that subcommittees of Congress rarely concern themselves with the details of the decisions or the nature of the actions of federal courts, consider this conversation between Representative Chris Cannon (R-UT), Chair of the Subcommittee on Commercial and Administrative Law of the House Judiciary Committee, Representative Thomas Feeney (R-FL), a member of the subcommittee, Thomas Saronsetti, Assistant Attorney General, Environment and Natural Resources Division of the Department of Justice, and Stuart Schiffer, Deputy Assistant Attorney General, Civil Division, Department of Justice, which took place at a hearing of Representative Cannon's subcommittee on April 8, 2003.[53] The subject was a set of lawsuits filed by Native American tribes over the handling of trust funds set up by the Interior Department to handle money belonging to the tribes and, in particular, the actions of a particular judge hearing one of those cases.

After opening testimony by Mr. Saronsetti, Mr. Schiffer, and one other Justice Department representative, Chairman Cannon began the questioning, turning immediately to the lawsuits. The department was asking for a substantial increase in funding to defend the government against these suits, but that line of questioning was soon dropped in favor of a discussion of one particular judge. Representative Cannon got things started by asking both Mr. Saronsetti and Mr. Schiffer, "Can you give us counsel on what this branch should do to oversee what this judge is doing in this process?" Both demurred, but Mr. Schiffer concluded his remarks by saying, "There may well have to be a legislative solution to the case itself at a certain point." Enter Representative Feeney: "And it seems to me that at a minimum that Congress has the right to set the jurisdiction of Federal judges." Representative Feeney then went on to say, "It does seem to me that we have got a significant portion of our Justice Department paralyzed by one Federal judge that somebody, somewhere has got to answer as to whether or not the judge has behaved appropriately."

I don't imagine Judge Lambert of the D.C. District Court read this exchange, or that, if he did, he felt the hot breath of the subcommittee and changed his tune. But there can be little question from that subcommittee hearing that the subcommittee chair, at least, was aware of what was going on in court, angry about what was going on in court, and casting about for some way to insert the subcommittee's views into the process of resolving the issues involved. He may yet find it.

In Summary

Subcommittees care deeply about what happens at the agencies under their jurisdiction. Constituency interests, interest-group concerns, even their own personal predilections all lead the members of any subcommittee to want to have influence at those agencies, and they will use the tools available to them to exercise that influence by shaping the organizational, budgetary, and legal environments of the agencies that are the object of all of that interest. And those tools will work.

Think about the organizational environment.

It starts with the President's own political executives. They aren't entirely the President's own. Congress, through its subcommittees and committees, has a real say in who occupies all of those jobs, and the men and women who end up in that corps of political executives inevitably exhibit a certain amount of loyalty to those committees and subcommittees, even if their primary loyalty does remain to the President who nominated them.

But the subcommittee role in management doesn't end with the selection of the managers. It doesn't even end when those managers show that they are loyal to both ends of Pennsylvania Avenue. Subcommittees want to be involved in providing the kind of direction and guidance that some see as the essence of management, and they take every opportunity provided by the oversight process to monitor their agencies and tell those agencies when they have somehow chosen the wrong path.

Now think about the budgetary environment.

Before money can be spent it has to be appropriated. But before it can be appropriated, it has to be authorized. Subcommittees discuss spending plans—and that, of course, means policy plans—for all of their agencies, eventually deciding the outer limits of what will be devoted to bringing to life the provisions of the Endangered Species Act, the Marine Mammal Protection Act of 2003, or Flight 100.

But money does have to be appropriated, so the subcommittees the House and Senate have created for that purpose go into action, going over every request line by line, asking all sorts of questions and listening pretty carefully to the answers. Then they hand out that money, determining to a very substantial degree exactly how much really will be done by the Fish and Wildlife Service, the National Marine Fisheries Service, or the Federal Aviation Administration.

Not content with doling out the money, the appropriations subcommittees have taken to telling agencies where not to spend it. Agencies listen, and when an agency listens, the contours of its budgetary environment are that much clearer and that much more defined—clarified and defined by a congressional subcommittee.

Finally, think about the legal environment.

Laws are the basic building blocks of any agency's legal environment. Congress passes laws, and subcommittees play the lead role in the process of passing them. Working in an environment in which they have an overwhelming advantage in terms of time, interest, and knowledge, and backed up by an institutional reality that exaggerates those advantages, subcommittees turn out an incredibly detailed and complex product that only the initiated seem to be able to make any sense out of. Of course, the subcommittee that wrote the law and the agency staff who will try to keep its promises are the initiated, so the subcommittee has already gone a long way toward structuring that agency's legal environment and structuring it to the subcommittee's liking.

In addition, laws have to be interpreted, and agency personnel do most of the interpreting. Subcommittees offer them plenty of help in doing that interpreting.

An executive order can become part of the legal environment of any agency, and that order becomes part of that environment without any direct input from Congress or one of its subcommittees. But executive orders can be overturned by statutes, and Presidents who can read that overturning handwriting on the wall will almost always compromise rather than run the risk of embarrassment and frustration. Beyond that, executive orders, too, have to be interpreted, and once again, subcommittees are there to support some kinds of interpretations and challenge others. They are also there to provide the political power to interpret such orders in ways the President might not exactly approve of.

Last of all, courts, or at least court decisions, can become part of an agency's legal environment, and again, they do so without any direct input by Congress. Once more, however, Congress can act to overturn a court decision, and its subcommittees will be there to suggest interpretations of those decisions that reflect the interests the members of that subcommittee feel should be represented, interests those members feel are shared by the staff of this particular agency.

In the end, there can be no doubt of the ability of Congress to shape the environment in which the agencies of the executive branch make policy. Most of that ability—power, if you prefer—is lodged with committees and then further delegated down to subcommittees. These are the folks who write the laws, authorize expenditures, appropriate money, and work closely with agency staff to make sure that what both sides often come to see as common interests are effectively represented. Whatever any agency does, you can be almost certain that somewhere on it you can see the stamp of one or more subcommittees.

SUMMARY AND CONCLUSION

The President has a hard time playing the role of chief executive in a way that lives up to expectations. The lack of real motivation is a handicap from the start, but the lack of resources—that is, the lack of the time, interest, and knowledge—to really get involved in what is happening at most agencies is what makes it almost impossible for the President to become a direct participant, or even a direct force, in most agency policy making. We can add to that the fact that the chief faces a suspicious set of agencies, with personnel who are frustrated by what they perceive as years of attacks on what they do and who they are, and wary of suggestions that come from someone they feel marches to a drummer playing much too fast and operates from a base of knowledge that is almost non-existent. But no President can completely ignore the rest of the executive branch, so he or she tries to use the tools of management—managers mostly—and budgets, and even the law to try to move agencies in the direction the chief would like them to go.

But there always seem to be roadblocks, and first among those roadblocks is the Congress. Congress, it seems, has assigned its role in dealing with the agencies of the executive branch to a host of subcommittees, and these subcommittees don't face those same kinds of roadblocks that so frustrated the President.

First of all, these subcommittees have all the motivation they need to make sure that they know what is going on at their agencies. Their constituents—or the groups who finance their campaigns—have something at stake when those agencies make decisions, and stakes for the people a member of Congress has been chosen—or has chosen—to represent mean stakes for the member himself or herself. That's plenty to provide the motivation.

Subcommittees have the resources to become involved in agency policy making as well as the motivation. The interest, of course, flows out of the stakes that provide them with the motivation, and the time flows almost as naturally out of the interest. That leaves the knowledge, and while subcommittee members may not be considered real experts in the subject matters assigned to their subcommittees, they can reasonably be considered informed amateurs, and with respect to those issues, that may well make them the second most informed folks in government.

Subcommittees put all of this motivation and all of these resources to work. They ask questions. They ask some of them informally. They ask some of them formally. The point remains the same. The process, called oversight, tends to give these subcommittees a real opportunity to become informed about what the agencies within their jurisdiction are doing about the issues that matter so much to them. The oversight process also gives them a real opportunity to turn the information tables—that is, not to just ask agencies what they are doing, but to tell agencies what the subcommittees think they ought to be doing.

It is obvious that these subcommittees have substantial advantages over the President in terms of motivation and resources, and equally obvious that they put those advantages to work in the oversight process. And they have yet another advantage over the chief, the advantage of working with agencies at least willing to listen. In part out of fear of the power these subcommittees can exercise, in part out of respect for the time they put in and the knowledge and interest they exhibit about the issues at hand, in part out of a sense of something almost like community, in part out of sheer self-interest, and in part out of a desire for legitimacy, agency careerists are willing at least to hear what subcommittee members have to say. They are even willing to work with those subcommittee members to try to move policy in an agreed upon direction. Most of all, they can even agree on that direction, at least some of the time.

In such a setting—that is, with plenty of motivation, substantial resources, access to information, and working with a reasonably receptive bureaucracy—congressional subcommittees are able to make their mark on agency policies. They do it the same way the President tries to do it, by trying to shape the organizational, budgetary, and legal environments in which those agencies operate.

Subcommittees get involved in the organizational environment of their agencies through both management and structure. With some say over who serves as political executives and with some loyalty from those executives, subcommittees become kind of indirect managers. But that's not enough, so they do some guidance and direction managing at every opportunity they get. Then there is structure. Subcommittees provide the political support that makes it possible for agencies to assert their independence from the departments in which they are nominally housed, and subcommittees are the primary players in deciding on the formal structure that spells out where those agencies are housed and which programs they will administer in the first place.

Subcommittees get involved in the budgetary environment of their agencies through authorization, appropriation, and even through the almost infamous spending instructions. It is two different sets of subcommittees now, but both are active in doing what they are meant to do. The legislative committees have to authorize spending, and that means they set the outer limits for spending, often becoming advocates for more than the appropriations committees want to hand out. Indeed, the authorizing subcommittees often become advocates for more than the President would like to hand out. The appropriations subcommittees do the actual handing out of the money, and they hand out instructions with that money. Both of those activities obviously have a significant effect on what agencies can and cannot do.

Finally, subcommittees get involved in shaping the legal environments of their agencies. They play the lead role in designing the basic charter for each of the agencies under their jurisdiction, and that charter is the primary element in any agency's legal environment. Then come the questions of interpretation of that basic charter, and subcommittees take a keen interest in how agencies read what they have written. Subcommittees don't write executive orders or decide about settlement of lawsuits or appeals of court decisions. But they can take the lead role in trying to overturn executive orders and/or court decisions, and they can offer their own interpretations of those orders as well as of court decisions. And they can offer those interpretations in a context in which they will be heard.

In the end, subcommittees don't run bureaucracy. But a subcommittee can have a great deal of influence on the decisions reached at one or two agencies under its purview, and that, after all, is their goal.

NOTES

1. "Environmental Carnage," editorial, *New York Times* (electronic edition), July 29, 2003.

2. Michael Barone and Grant Ujifusa, *The Almanac of American Politics 1996* (Washington, D.C.: National Journal, 1995), 530–531.

3. Barone and Ujifusa, *The Almanac of American Politics 1996*, 530–531.

4. Barone and Ujifusa, *The Almanac of American Politics 1996*, 537.

5. Just go to the House of Representatives website at www.house.gov, and go to the individual member drop-down box, and you can reach Mr. Nethercutt's very well maintained website where he proudly tells you of both awards.

6. Barone and Ujifusa, *The Almanac of American Politics 1996*, 577–578.

7. "Corporate Fraud Hypocrisy Watch," *New Republic*, July 22, 2002, 8.

8. "Corporate Fraud Hypocrisy Watch," 8.

9. Stephen Labaton, "S.E.C. Suffers From Legacy of Nonbenign Neglect," *New York Times* (electronic edition), July 20, 2002.

10. Associated Press, "Committee Votes to Block FCC Rule," July 16, 2003.

11. "Corporate Fraud Hypocrisy Watch," 8.

12. This was announced on Representative Nethercutt's website on June 14, 2003.

13. To check any of this out, or to do your own search related to some other subcommittee and some other set of issues, just go to www.house.gov, and use the drop-down boxes. Pick a committee, go to its home page, find the subcommittee you are interested in, get the roster, and go back to the drop-down box for individual members. Their websites will always contain a pick called biography, and you can almost always find out about their educational background there.

14. "Senate Water-Use Bill Pits Big Firms Against Small Farms," *Congressional Quarterly Weekly Report* 37, no. 39 (September 29, 1979), 2123.

15. I found the press release on the Resources Committee website on Sunday morning, August 3, 2003. I'm not sure if you could track it down by the time you read this book.

16. This quote is from another committee press release from mid-June, 2003. Again, it probably won't be there by the time you read this, but I got to it from www.house.gov using the drop-down box under house committees. The committee, again, is Transportation and Infrastructure.

17. Lawrence C. Dodd and Richard L. Schott, *Congress and the Administrative State* (New York: John Wiley and Sons, 1979), 156.

18. Dodd and Schott, *Congress and the Administrative State*, 157.

19. Herbert Kaufman, *The Administrative Behavior of Federal Bureau Chiefs* (Washington, D.C.: Brookings Institution, 1981), 55.

20. Press release, House Committee on Transportation and Infrastructure, July 22, 2003.

21. Aaron Wildavsky, *The Politics of the Budgetary Process*, 4th ed. (Boston: Little, Brown, 1984), 78–79.

22. Kaufman, *The Administrative Behavior of Federal Bureau Chiefs*, 48.

23. Kaufman, *The Administrative Behavior of Federal Bureau Chiefs*, 51.

24. Kaufman, *The Administrative Behavior of Federal Bureau Chiefs*, 50.

25. Morris S. Ogul, *Congress Oversees the Bureaucracy* (Pittsburgh, Pa.: University of Pittsburgh Press, 1976).

26. Wildavsky, *The Politics of the Budgetary Process*, 53–54.

27. Richard F. Fenno Jr., *The Power of the Purse: Appropriations Politics in Congress* (Boston: Little, Brown, 1966), 141–143.

28. Kaufman, *The Administrative Behavior of Federal Bureau Chiefs*, 51.

29. Fenno, *The Power of the Purse*, 326.

30. This was in a question and answer session here on campus. I can't remember the date.

31. This can be found on the website of the House Committee on Government Reform. Just click on history.

32. For a brief history of the hope for these committees, see Dodd and Schott, *Congress and the Administrative State*, 165–168.

33. Thomas A. Henderson, *Congressional Oversight of Executive Agencies: A Study of the House Committee on Government Operations* (Gainesville: University of Florida Press, 1970).

34. Dodd and Schott, *Congress and the Administrative State*, 168.

35. This is likely to still be at the GAO website when you read this. I got there by clicking on other government links on the House of Representatives home page. Or, www.gao.gov will do just fine.

36. Joseph Pois, "The General Accounting Office as a Congressional Resource," in *Congressional Support Agencies: Papers Prepared for the Commission on the Operation of the Senate* (Washington, D.C.: U.S. Government Printing Office, 1976), 40–41.

37. Kaufman, *The Administrative Behavior of Federal Bureau Chiefs*, 47.

38. Wildavsky, *The Politics of the Budgetary Process*, 53–54.

39. Gary C. Jacobson, *The Politics of Congressional Elections*, 5th ed. (New York: Addison, Wesley, Longman, 2001), 23.

40. Hugh Heclo, "Issue Networks and the Executive Establishment," in *The New American Political System*, ed. Anthony King (Washington, D.C.: American Enterprise Institute, 1978), 117.

41. Louis M. Kohlmeier Jr., *The Regulators: Watchdog Agencies and the Public Interest* (New York: Harper and Row, 1969), 56.

42. Drake Bennett and Alex Gourevitch, "Put a Face on Your Fears," *American Prospect*, December 30, 2002, 21.

43. It is said that nothing ever dies in cyberspace, and the Transportation and Infrastructure Committee does archive its hearings and that of its subcommittees, so you should be able to get a feel for the testimony of all of these "maritime community" representatives by going to the subcommittee website and following the prompts. The site is www.house.gov/transportation, if you want to do it that way. I always go to the House website and use the committee drop-down box.

44. See, for example, ch. 4 of any edition of Francis E. Rourke's *Bureaucracy, Politics, and Public Policy*, and the work of the scholars he cites in that chapter.

45. Press release, Committee on Transportation and Infrastructure, May 22, 2003.

46. Wildavsky, *The Politics of the Budgetary Process*, 53–54.

47. Michael Kirst, *Government Without Passing Laws* (Chapel Hill: University of North Carolina Press, 1969), especially 115–116.

48. Florence Heffron, *The Administrative Regulatory Process* (New York: Longman, 1983), 109.

49. Associated Press, "Committee Votes to Block FCC Rule," July 16, 2003.

50. This is certainly the conclusion of Kirst (see note 47 above), Heffron (see note 48 above), and Alan Murray—see his "House Funding Bill Riders Become Potent Policy Force," *Congressional Quarterly Weekly Report* 38, no. 44 (November 1, 1980), 3255.

51. *Patterson v. McLean Credit Union* 491 U.S. 164 (1989); *Martin v. Wilks* 490 U.S. 755 (1989); and *Wards Cove Packing Co. v. Atonio* 490 U.S. 642 (1989).

52. This is discussed in much further length in Dennis D. Riley, *Public Personnel Administration* (New York: HarperCollins, 1993), 99–101.

53. Everything here comes from the transcript of that hearing. I got it from the subcommittee website, but printed copies would be available. All you would need is the name of the subcommittee and the date of the hearing, both of which you have.

7

Bureaucracy and the Public

Supporters, Critics, and Hey, Where's the Rest of Us?

Bureaucrats, like politicians and political scientists, know there is no such thing as the public. But there are people, and some of these people feel they ought to have some influence over bureaucratic policy making. Actually, of course, nobody wants to have some influence over "bureaucratic policy making." Specific groups and individuals want to have some say over the policies of specific agencies. Some of them actually do.

From the point of view of any particular agency, "the people" can be divided into three very different sets of citizens, each with very different viewpoints and very different relationships with that agency. First, every agency has a set of supporters, that is, groups of people who believe in what the agency is doing and who, occasional family disagreements aside, are relatively satisfied with agency personnel and policies. Second, these days it seems that almost every agency has its critics, groups of people convinced that the agency is not doing what it ought to be doing, and each group is even more convinced that it (the group) has a far better prescription for policy in this agency's area of responsibility than the agency itself has ever come up with. Finally, there is the ever elusive but always talked about "general public," the mass of the citizenry that "everybody" knows ought to be heard, but whose voice almost never seems to rise above the din.

Every agency, then, establishes some sort of relationship with these three sets of citizens, that is, with its supporters, its critics, and the general public. Every one of these agency/group relationships is, by definition, of course, unique. Some are, in the words of Francis Rourke, "so close that it is difficult to know where the group leaves off and the agency begins."[1] Others, however, as Herbert Kaufman observed, seem to be "thrust on the bureaus rather than eagerly seized or initiated and cultivated by them."[2] Whether a particular agency/group relationship will produce the kind of closeness and cooperation Rourke was talking about, or the uneasy—and not always peaceful—coexistence that Kaufman witnessed, will depend on what that particular relationship is built on. Close and cooperative relationships, the kind that agencies do eagerly seize or initiate and cultivate and that groups of citizens hope to be able to use to influence agency policy, center on three dimensions.

The first, of course, is knowledge. This is bureaucracy. The whole purpose of the enterprise is to gather information and apply expert knowledge to that information to handle complex policy questions. Any relationship between a specific agency and some group of citizens that did not rest on a commonly shared set of concepts and ideas discussed in a common language—a language we outsiders could not possibly fathom—simply wouldn't feel right to agency personnel.

But all of this gathering of information and applying of expert knowledge is taking place in something called government, and that inevitably means politics is going to be the second foundation stone of any relationship between an agency and a group of citizens. As we saw in chapter 2, agency careerists know they cannot escape politics as they make decisions, and as we also saw, they have no desire to escape it completely, as that would mean denying the whole idea of self-government, and that they are not yet ready to do.

Finally, the relationship between an agency and a group of citizens will almost always have some sort of personal foundation to it. Recall from the previous chapter our discussion of the view that agency personnel often take of congressional subcommittees. Part of the incentive toward agency cooperation with these sub-committees arose out of what I referred to as almost a sense of community—a sort of personal bond developing out of common background and knowledge and leavened with years of working together that pointed toward a feeling that both the agency staff and the subcommittee members were engaged in a common enterprise with more to unite than divide them. That same feeling can become a strong foundation for an agency/group relationship.

So off we go to examine the relationships that agencies establish with their supporters, their critics, and the general public. For what kinds of agency/group pairings are the bonds of knowledge, politics, and a sense of community powerful enough to make it hard for us to tell where one leaves off and the other begins? For what kinds of agency/group pairings are those bonds so weak that each side views the other with anything from extreme caution to downright hostility, working with each other whenever they really have to, but always wary that the other side is trying to get away with something? And finally, for what kinds of agency/group pairings do we find these bonds somewhere in between, leaving each side open to the possibility of cooperation, alert to the possibility of conflict, and never entirely sure from one issue to the next which of the two it will be?

AGENCIES AND THEIR SUPPORTERS

Every agency makes a definite effort to secure the support of three sets of people. First comes that agency's clientele. Every agency does something to or for somebody. That's what agencies are for. The people who receive a valuable service or commodity from an agency, those who have to march to that agency's rulebook, or as is so often the case, those who receive an agency's services and march to its rulebook, are almost certain to organize and try to establish some sort of relationship with the government entity that has so much impact on their lives. Beyond its clientele, an agency can almost always expect to be able to obtain

the support of, in the words of Herbert Kaufman, "the professions strongly represented in its work force."[3] Whether it be veterinarians and schools of veterinary
medicine and the Animal and Plant Health Inspection Service, associations of
professional foresters and schools of forestry and the Forest Service, or even "associations and schools for accountants, lawyers, and other tax preparers" and the
Internal Revenue Service, Kaufman concluded that any agency would find fellow
professionals right alongside clientele groups as that agency's most consistent
supporters.[4] Finally, an agency can look to the ranks of individual citizens who
have somehow become duly certified as policy experts in its area of policy. Many
of these individuals come from the ranks of former government officials, but increasingly they also come from academic life and from the expanding number of
non-profit research organizations we often refer to as "think tanks."

Clientele groups, professional associations, and individual policy experts all
share the bonds of knowledge, politics, and community with the agencies that
affect their lives and livelihoods. We are about to see how and why.

Agencies and Their Clientele Groups I: Normally, We Is Us

Political scientists have been writing about the close relationship between agencies and their clientele groups for well over half a century. The purpose of this
section of the chapter is to try to understand how and why those relationships
become so close. Before we do that, however, we need to get a little more specific
about just who these clientele groups are.

Our working definition, recall, was quite simple. A group of people who are
directly and substantially affected by the decisions of a particular agency and who
make an organized effort to try to influence those decisions is a clientele group.
Some, like the American Wood Preservers Institute, were created expressly for
the purpose of influencing government policy. In its own words, conveyed to
Congressional Quarterly in 1995, the Institute exists to monitor "legislation and
regulations that affect the industry" and to act "as a liaison between the industry and federal agencies."[5] Other groups, like the American Hardwood Export
Council, exist in part for other purposes—aiding its members "in developing
and expanding export capabilities in new and existing markets," in the hardwood
council's case—but the council's office on Washington, D.C.'s, 19th Street N.W.—
at the same address as the American Forest and Paper Association—indicates that
some of that aid "in developing and expanding export capabilities" might come
in the form of working with someone in the U.S. government.[6] Some groups
are pretty clearly in the business of influencing government on behalf of their
economic interests, that is, on behalf of their desire to make money doing whatever it is that they do. Both the American Wood Preservers Institute and the
American Hardwood Export Council fit that bill nicely. So do the American Forest and Paper Association and the American Pulpwood Association. Or, if you
are tired of all that wood, so does the U.S. Tuna Foundation. On the other hand,
some groups seem to be about interests pretty far removed from enhancing the
economic livelihood of the people represented. Groups like Self-Help for Hard
of Hearing People, the National Multiple Sclerosis Society, the Autism Society
of America, or Goodwill Industries, International, may well occasionally seek to

advance the economic interests of the people they represent, or even those of the professionals who work with those people, but for the most part, they seem to be advocating a chance for a better life for people who have a hard time advocating it for themselves.

In short, clientele groups advance a wide range of interests. Some are formed specifically to try to influence government. Others take on that task because it seems a natural outgrowth of something else they do. One thing remains the same. Clientele groups are groups of people directly affected by the actions of government and determined to have some impact on those actions. A relationship with the agency or agencies that make or implement those government decisions is a path they all must take. It is finally time to examine those relationships.

It Does Matter What You Know

I am certain that by now you are getting tired of being reminded of the role of knowledge in everything that happens at the agency level of the federal government, but alas, once more, that role cannot be overestimated. The policy specialists at the Forest Service, the Bureau of Land Management, the Administration for Children and Families, or the Rehabilitation Services Administration simply could not establish a close working relationship with any group unless that relationship was grounded to a substantial degree in knowledge.

Clientele groups supply their agencies with two very different kinds of knowledge. Those agencies need both. First comes what might be called political intelligence. Clientele groups know how agency decisions are being received by the people who know and care about those decisions—the clientele groups themselves, of course—and they know whether those decisions are likely to be challenged in court, or even more likely in Congress. Herbert Kaufman was talking about congressional subcommittees when he said that bureau chiefs were frequently "looking over their shoulders . . . taking stock of moods and attitudes, estimating reactions to contemplated decisions and actions, trying to prevent misunderstandings and avoidable conflicts, and planning responses when storm warnings appeared on the horizon."[7] It was Congress he was talking about, but a lot of those storms start pretty far west of the Potomac. To head them off before they get that far east is almost certainly a wise course of action, but no agency can head off a storm it doesn't know is coming, and since, as we'll see in the next section, clientele groups are in the best position to stir up such storms, they are in the best position to provide their agencies with an early warning system. It may not exactly be knowledge as we have used it most of the time in this book, but it is knowledge that no agency would want to be without.

More in line with the kind of knowledge policy specialists normally work with comes the practical knowledge that clientele groups have because they are the ones "who actually have to get out there and do it day after day." This kind of knowledge is extremely important to agencies for a couple of reasons.

First, Americans have a profound respect for the knowledge that comes with "practical experience." Unfortunately, they also often have a profound distrust of those whose knowledge of, and experience with, a subject is primarily "academic." It is no accident that the very word academic is used by sportscasters when more appropriate word choices might be moot, irrelevant, or unimportant. Policy specialists operating at most agencies are, by definition, people with extensive academic training in their specialties. Sooner or later they will also have extensive experience at their agencies. What they will almost certainly never have is extensive "practical experience" in the "real world" of the industries they serve and/or regulate. A close working relationship with clientele groups, one that brings that kind of knowledge grounded in years of experience in "the business," can go a long way toward neutralizing the charge that a particular agency is nothing but a bunch of academics who don't know how anything works out in the "real world."

Second, despite my obvious frustration and that of almost any career bureaucrat or college professor with the misuse of the word academic, the tendency to assume that what we do is disconnected from some real world, and its attendant, if implicit, assumption that we work in a world that is not real—and the underlying ethos of it all, that implies that you can't understand anything about regulating banks or insurance companies if you've never run a bank or an insurance company—the practical knowledge that comes from clientele groups to agencies really is useful to those agencies. You see, despite my obvious frustration with all of that, I know that there is a kernel of truth to it and that kernel of truth deserves some respect. I have taught personnel administration for twenty-five years and I have even written a fairly good textbook in the field, one that has just gone into its second edition. But were I made Personnel Director of Portage County, Wisconsin, tomorrow, the results would not be pretty. There are some "practical" things I just don't know, and it would take a while for me to learn them. Most agency policy specialists are a lot like me, that is, they know there are "practical" things that they don't know but that it would be good for them to know to do their jobs right. If clientele groups will supply that kind of knowledge, so much the better for the policy process.

Like any good relationship, when it comes to knowledge, the agency/clientele group relationship is a two-way street, and if the knowledge street is going to run both ways, agencies are going to have to supply some information to clientele groups. They do.

First comes what amounts to advance information about what agencies are thinking about doing. This, of course, helps both sides, as clientele are given an opportunity to think about proposed actions and prepare their responses to those actions—with an idea toward shaping the final agency decision, of course—and agencies get an idea of how their ideas will play out with those clientele groups before too much time and energy has been devoted to an idea or too many people have dug their positions so deep that they cannot compromise.

Second, agencies provide their clientele groups with substantive information, information that might help those groups advance the goals that are the reason for the group's existence. Forest Service researchers really do know a great deal about tree "harvesting methods," and they are charged with sharing that information. Some of the people they decide to share it with are no doubt members of the American Forest and Paper Association, the American Hardwood Export Council, or the American Pulpwood Association. For that matter, the American Hardwood Export Council might find very useful information on how to expand the export capabilities of the organization's member firms among those people at the State Department who specialize in the international commodities trade.

Clientele groups provide agencies with political intelligence and practical knowledge, while agencies provide clientele groups with a heads up on what might be coming their way in terms of new policies or programs and some research that just might supplement all that practical knowledge and make those clientele groups even more effective in achieving the goals that led them to organize to influence government in the first place. The exchange meets the needs of both sides, and it is an exchange that is so natural most of the time that neither side thinks of it as part of a relationship that is grounded every bit as much in politics as it is in the knowledge that is so freely exchanged. But it is, so it is to politics that we go next.

It Also Matters Whom You Know

Knowledge may have to be first, but politics always has to be second, and a close second at that. Remember, part of the flow of information/knowledge between agencies and their clientele groups was as much political as it was substantive. But the importance of politics to the agency/clientele group relationship goes far beyond some political intelligence from clientele to agency, and a heads up about possible policy directions from agency to clientele. On the agency side of the street, we are talking about power and legitimacy. On the clientele group side, we are talking about an advocate inside the executive branch, an advocate with a great deal of influence at the crucial stage of writing and enforcing the rules that bring statutes to life. Let's start on the agency side of the street.

Agencies need power, and as Francis Rourke pointed out more than thirty years ago, one of most consistently employed and consistently successful strategies for getting that power was to "[build] strength with 'attentive' publics— groups that have a salient interest in the agency—usually because it has either the capacity to provide them with some significant benefit, or the power to exercise regulatory authority in ways that may be of critical importance to the groups concerned."[8] In fact, as generations of political scientists have argued, clientele groups make an almost ideal source of power, since they are around for the long haul, always interested in the subject at hand, and, perhaps most important of all, have power where it counts, at the level of the congressional subcommittee.[9] As we saw in the previous chapter, agency administrators generally believe that congressional subcommittees can "do you a world of good and they can cut your throat."[10] A subcommittee's urge to do an agency a world of good—or the urge to cut its throat—often originates with that agency's clientele groups, and every bit as important, when that urge originates somewhere else, clientele groups are in an excellent position to reinforce it, or to head it off. Agencies know that the backing of their clientele groups is a key element in putting together the kind of power they need to do the jobs they want to do.

Agencies also need legitimacy, and once again, clientele groups can supply it. It may seem strange to think of the American Forest and Paper Association, the American Pulpwood Association, or the American Hardwood Export Council as suppliers of legitimacy to the U.S. Forest Service. By most reasonable reckonings, after all, they are interest groups, and interest groups are hardly anybody's poster children for political or governmental legitimacy. But factor in a couple of things and it begins to make sense. First of all, agencies cannot do their work in isolation from the people and still be considered legitimate. Some people have to be involved, and clientele groups are—or at least represent—people. Now add to that the fact that these clientele groups represent people directly affected by the policies these agencies are involved in making. For reasons I talked about clear back in the first chapter, that strikes a responsive chord with Americans. Beyond that, remember our discussion in the previous section. Americans have great respect for the practical knowledge of the men and women actively engaged in a particular endeavor, so their participation in formulating government policy with respect to that endeavor provides a kind of legitimacy to the resulting decisions. The dreaded special interests or not, clientele groups can and do provide an agency and its policies with a real dose of legitimacy, and just like power, legitimacy is a key to being able to do the jobs they believe they are supposed to do.

The agency need for power and legitimacy may make it seem as if the political side of the agency/clientele group relationship is pretty one sided. It's not. Agencies can become advocates on behalf of clientele interests, pushing those interests within the executive branch—at the departmental level mostly, but on occasions even at the White House—and sometimes pushing them in the very subcommittees in which these groups already have so much influence. Beyond that, of course, rules are frequently written and almost always enforced at the agency level. It is these rule-making and enforcement decisions, recall, that really bring a policy home to the members—or member organizations—of a clientele group. Clientele groups unhappy with the direction taken by an agency in making such decisions can use their power with congressional subcommittees, but that is not a path those groups want to tread every day. Power, even the power of these kinds of groups, is a finite commodity and only so much can be spent before the account is depleted. In addition, while subcommittees are very responsive to these groups, the members don't want to be seen exclusively as water carriers for what can easily enough be labeled special interests. In more straightforward terms, clientele groups can probably fight agencies and win more than they lose, but they would rather not have to fight all that often, so what they hope for is a more peaceful environment, an environment of cooperation.

So, in the end, agencies have a great deal to offer to clientele groups, just as clientele groups have a great deal to offer agencies. In fact, in the very end, this political side of the relationship may be very even indeed.

Sometimes It Even Matters How You Feel

Just as we saw with agencies and their subcommittees, a sense of something like community can develop between agencies and their clientele groups. Once again, if it develops, it will develop out of common background, shared expertise, and years of working together.

As we noted earlier, some agencies end up with a professional staff that is relatively homogeneous in terms of their personal and professional background.

Westerners interested in government careers have always gravitated toward the Bureau of Reclamation and the Bureau of Land Management, just as midwesterners, southerners, and even westerners with farm or small-town backgrounds have always thought that a career in government was really a career in some agency of the Department of Agriculture. When that happens, these agency personnel very often find themselves dealing with clientele group representatives with very similar personal histories, and these similar personal histories can sometimes produce similar personal outlooks. Similar personal outlooks, in turn, may help to create that kind of sense of a common enterprise that can cement attachments already nurtured by knowledge and politics. In addition, shared expertise can also help to generate that sense of community that is often felt between agencies and clientele groups. To be sure, clientele representatives are not always experts. But more often than not, when dealing with their agencies, these groups do put their most expert foot forward—remember the knowledge dimension to the relationship—and that shared expertise, too, can provide some more glue for a relationship both sides want to last. Finally, even where common background and shared expertise are absent, there is a sense of community that can develop just from all those years of working together on the same set of issues.

In Summary

Agencies and their clientele groups will have their disagreements. When they do, as with most family fights, the result can be a real donnybrook. Still, most of the time, agencies and their clientele groups really do know that there is far far more to unite them than to divide them. And they act on that knowledge.

Agencies need the political intelligence that only their clientele groups can provide them. They also need that practical knowledge that Americans praise so highly. They really need it some of the time, and they need it to legitimize their own policies almost all of the time. Of course, on the other side of the relationship, clientele groups need to know what might be coming their way in terms of agency policy choices, and they can certainly use a lot of that technical knowledge that only agencies have and that clientele groups can use to advance the goals that made them agency clientele groups in the first place.

Politics will find its way into every aspect of agency activities, of course, and the agency/clientele group relationship is one of those places it is bound to be most prominent. Agencies need power and legitimacy, and working with their clientele can give them access to both. Once again, clientele groups get at least as much as they give. An advocate inside the government is a big help to any group who wants to influence that government. More to the point, agencies have a great deal of say over rules and rule enforcement, and clientele groups care deeply about both. Working cooperatively with their agencies seems a better way to have some impact on those decisions than does trying to browbeat the agencies by constantly running to Congress.

Finally, sometimes agencies and clientele groups work together just because they see themselves as part of a common enterprise. Common background, shared professional expertise, and a long time together can provide powerful reinforcers for the knowledge- and politics-driven cooperation they are already engaged in.

Agencies and Clientele Groups II: Sometimes, We Is Us and Them

Up to now I have painted a picture of a bureaucratic Camelot in which every agency has a close and comfortable working relationship with its clientele groups. In the real bureaucratic world, of course, for most agencies, these relationships have their ups and downs, and as I suggested earlier, when a fight does break out, it is a family fight, and family fights are often the loudest and messiest. Still, most agencies, most of the time, can count on the support of their clientele.

But some agencies know that clientele support is not going to be their key to exercising the kind of influence they believe they should exercise when policy decisions are being made. In general, two kinds of agencies have trouble establishing close working relationships with their clientele groups. First come the bulk of the social service agencies. The men and women who run prisons, mental health clinics, vocational rehabilitation programs, drug and alcohol rehabilitation centers, or what we once called the "welfare" agencies always have some real difficulty working closely with their clients. In addition to these social service agencies, a good many regulatory agencies also have difficulty putting together the kinds of relationships that traditionally exist in most of the bureaucracy. Other regulatory agencies, of course, have no trouble at all establishing such relationships with their clientele, and we will soon address the question of which regulators are close to those they regulate and which ones are not, and why. But first let's take a brief look at the world of social service agencies.

Social Service Agencies and Their Clientele Groups: Not Much to Build On

It won't surprise you a bit, I suspect, to find that social service agencies do not find their clientele groups to be knowledgeable suppliers of information who provide plenty of power and legitimacy even as they generate a real sense of community with the agency administrators and policy specialists. It flows pretty naturally out of who they are and what they have.

Start with knowledge. It isn't that prisoners don't know anything about prisons, mental health patients anything about mental illness, vocational rehabilitation clients anything about preparing for and finding a job despite their physical, mental, or emotional difficulties, or welfare recipients anything about welfare. These clientele groups do know these things in ways the rest of us almost certainly never can. But nobody has much respect for what they know about their respective policy areas, so the Bureau of Prisons doesn't look to prisoner organizations to warn them of potential political problems or to give them an insider's look at the problems associated with being on their side of the prison system, and the Rehabilitation Services Administration doesn't look to organizations of the physically and/or emotionally disabled for help in designing new vocational rehabilitation programs. To no one's surprise, of course, that means that the Rehabilitation Services Administration looks that much more closely at information provided to it by the American Rehabilitation Counseling Association and the Council of State Administrators of Vocational Rehabilitation, and the Bureau of Prisons looks that much more carefully at what it hears from the American

Correctional Association and the Correctional Education Association. If clientele groups can't provide much in the way of information and expertise, professional associations become that much more important.

Now consider politics. The Bureau of Prisons and the Rehabilitation Services Administration need power and legitimacy every bit as much as the Forest Service and the Fish and Wildlife Service need them. But the former two agencies can hardly look to their clientele groups to get them. Those groups simply don't have any to offer. The clients of most social service agencies don't have the political currency needed to establish themselves as key players in the relevant congressional subcommittees, and for most such groups, their standing in the community precludes using their support to legitimize an agency or its policies. How could the Bureau of Prisons Director argue that a particular policy initiative was legitimate because it emerged from a joint committee of agency specialists and inmates who had worked on it for months? Such an argument doesn't look as if it would be dramatically more successful if the Rehabilitation Services Commissioner made it about vocational rehabilitation policy or the Assistant Secretary of Health and Human Services in charge of the Administration for Children and Families made it concerning those families still on public assistance. Power and legitimacy simply have to be sought elsewhere. Social service clients are rarely attuned to the idea of gaining the benefit of increased political power by working with their agencies either. In fact, they are only rarely attuned to the notion of political power at all.

Finally, social service agencies and their clientele groups are rarely cut from similar enough cloth to develop anything that would resemble a sense of community. They certainly don't have the common background or shared values that grow out of a particular type of education. Most prisoners don't have degrees in corrections, and most families on public assistance don't have anyone who majored in social work. They also aren't that likely to develop a sense of community through their years of working together. In fact, the more time they spend working together, the more likely the agency specialists are to feel they are failing at their jobs. Anyway, the point seems obvious enough. It is almost impossible to see how the professional staff of a social service agency could begin to identify with its clientele groups strongly enough to think of agency and groups as one big us.

In sum, no information, no expertise, no power, no legitimacy, and no sense of community add up to some pretty strong barriers to a close working relationship between social service agencies and their clientele groups.

Regulatory Agencies and Their Clientele: From Capture to Conflict

At various times in the nation's history, our government has decided that it needed to write and enforce rules about the conduct of the railroad business, the trucking business, the airline business, the mining industry, the meatpacking industry, the radio and television industries—eventually branching into cable television and the "telecommunications" industry—the various stock and commodity exchanges, the pharmaceutical industry, and literally hundreds of others. In fact, in 1914 it decided to regulate all of industry, at least with respect to "fair trade practices," and in 1970 all of industry with respect to the safety and health of its workers.[11]

One can hardly make a case that these industries have no information, no expertise, no power, and no legitimacy to offer those agencies charged with regulating them, nor that a sense of community between regulated and regulators could not possibly develop. Most industries have what it takes to establish themselves in American politics, and the leading figures in those industries get more than enough respect as "practical experts" in whatever it is that they do to be able to make the claim that they have much to offer in the way of information and expertise about this particular corner of government. The sense of community that developed between the old Civil Aeronautics Board (CAB) and the airline industry was so powerful by the mid-1960s that Representative John Moss (D-CA) sued the board, demanding that it consider some interests other than those of the airline industry itself.[12] Not a whole lot of change was forthcoming, and the CAB itself was abolished in 1978 amid charges from conservatives and liberals alike that it had become simply an arm of the industry.

So it is clear enough that the ingredients for a close and cooperative relationship between a regulated industry and the agency that regulates it are present. Indeed, in 1955 Professor Marver Bernstein argued that a close and cooperative working relationship between regulator and regulated had become the norm in the world of government regulation of business.[13] In fact, Bernstein was so convinced that such a relationship would develop that he referred to it as the capture of a regulatory agency by the regulated industry and even asserted that it was a natural stage in the life cycle of such commissions. The last half-century has proven that Bernstein was wrong, but wrong only some of the time. The task now, of course, is to figure out under what circumstances regulatory agencies are ripe for capture, or more properly, given the purpose of this section of the chapter, under what circumstances they are not.

To do that, we need to look at four aspects of a particular regulatory agency. First, who is being regulated? Second, does the agency's regulatory mandate include promotion of the economic health of the industry or industries in question? Third, what is being regulated? That is, is the agency charged with regulating the economics of an industry—the prices it can charge and/or services it can deliver— or the health and safety of that industry's workers, customers, or the general public? Last, who is doing the regulating? Has the task been assigned primarily to attorneys, or is it done by a more or less clearly defined set of subject-matter experts whose careers lie in this sort of regulation? Let's take them in that order.

If a single industry is being regulated, regulators soon learn two things. From a political viewpoint, there is only one game in this regulatory town. No one outside the regulated industry is going to pay careful attention to the intricacies of the rules that govern that industry. Keep the industry happy and political support is pretty much guaranteed. Anger that industry and trouble is almost certain to arise, and there is no other possible power source to fall back on. Beyond that, on a personal level, regulators soon learn that they interact exclusively with the same set of executives from the same firms. Things have a tendency to become personalized. Both of these lead toward a close relationship between regulator and regulated. On the other hand, if more than one industry is being regulated, the world of the regulator changes. Now there are alternative sources of political support, and the coziness of a single set of executives representing a single set of firms is replaced by a more formal atmosphere with a changing cast of characters, depending on which industry is on today's regulatory hot seat. A more distant relationship is the almost inevitable outcome.

Now let's add in the nature of the regulatory mandate. Specifically, as Louis Kohlmeier pointed out a long time ago, a regulatory body charged with both the regulation and the economic promotion of a particular industry is faced with a frustrating ambiguity.[14] Such regulatory bodies are expected to protect the public from poor service at unfair prices, but they are simultaneously expected to get or keep an industry on its economic feet. The ambiguity is most often resolved in favor of the promotion part of the mandate. That is what the industry is pushing for, and after all, if the agency "regulates the industry out of existence," how exactly has the public been served? In effect, by telling regulators that they can and should take account of the impact of their decisions on the economic health of the industry they regulate, political leaders have guaranteed that they will, and that, in turn, pushes toward a more cooperative relationship between regulators and regulated. Remove the promotion mandate, however, and regulators can—and probably will—focus more on an abstract notion of protecting the public, and that will bring conflict with the industry their agency is charged with regulating. In fact, as we will see when we consider the impact of court decisions on agency policy making, an agency that doesn't have an economic promotion mandate can find itself in trouble with a judge if it tries to act as if it did. We'll be considering the case of the National Highway Traffic Safety Administration (NHTSA) and its on-again, off-again, air-bag rule later, but when NHTSA leadership did try to change its own rule concerning air bags on economic grounds, a federal judge told it to go back and read its own enabling statute.[15]

An agency charged with economic regulation, that is, something like the old Civil Aeronautics Board, which regulated airline routes and fares, or the Securities and Exchange Commission, which writes rules about the listing and selling of stocks on the various exchanges in the country—and, by extension, rules about what companies can say about themselves and their stocks—is working in a realm in which compromise—splitting the difference, if you like—is a way of life. The stakes are money, and money can be divided. Besides, in such situations the money almost always comes from a large and undifferentiated mass like consumers, passengers, utility rate payers, or stock purchasers, and flows toward a small and clearly identifiable set of economic players like utility companies, airlines, trucking or barge companies, or brokerage firms who do the trading on the various exchanges. Add to that the fact that no passenger, rate payer, or consumer ever pays very much at once, and top it off with the realization that the resulting piles that go to the regulated businesses are quite substantial, and you can begin to see how there might be a drift toward policy that serves the interests of those businesses.

In sharp contrast would be the typical situation of regulation to protect health and safety. The stakes may still be money on the industry side of the equation, but on the other side—worker, customer, or general public—the stakes are very different. Once we begin to talk about the possibility of injury, illness, or even death, things change. How exactly does one put a price tag on such things? But regulated industries are more than happy to put a price tag on complying with health and safety rules. They are even more willing to show that these costs will come up front, and that they may not even prevent the evil they are aimed at preventing. How much money should be spent protecting the lungs of a chain smoker or the hearing of a worker who plays weekends in a rock band? But how comfortable would any health and safety regulator be in saying that the dollar value of preventing this kind of cancer in 20 percent of the workers in this plant is $X and the cost of that prevention is $X plus a lot more, so we aren't going to do it? Who condemns one out of five workers to cancer? The stage is set for a battle between health and safety regulators and those they regulate.

Finally, some regulation is done by lawyers. Some isn't. When lawyers dominate the regulatory process, two things come into play. First, lawyers involved in regulation may well be hoping to land a job in the regulated industry. The so-called "revolving door" between government and industry—a door that lawyers are particularly adept at walking through, it seems—has been seen as such a problem that we have tried to legislate it closed four times in the last twenty years. It sticks a little now, but it still opens.[16] But the fact that lawyers might not want to bite the hand that might someday feed them turns out to be less important than does the fact that the norms of the legal profession are essentially procedural—and that, too, slides regulation in a direction that creates close and cooperative working relationships between regulators and regulated. If the process is more important than the outcome, and if the process is supposed to be one that models the courtroom—representation for both sides, agreed upon rules for argument and evidence, etc.—a regulated industry is in a pretty good position to take care of its own interests. Add to that the lawyer's tendency to look for a settlement before the first gavel pounds down, and the fact that most settlements fall somewhere between the original demands of both sides, and you have a real recipe for cooperative regulation.

Things are quite different when regulation is the province of subject-matter experts who think of this kind of regulation as what they do. Their job networks rarely include the industries they regulate, but more to the point, their norms are anything but procedural. They focus on outcomes, and some outcomes seem right while others seem wrong. The occupational safety profession may represent the extreme case, but it is an instructive case nonetheless. Their approach is nicely summarized by Steven Kelman when he says, "The textbooks imply that relying on personal protective equipment is seen as a confession of failure, a betrayal of the can-do approach of the engineer. . . . As much as it may be unpleasant to the workers, *personal protective equipment is insulting to the engineer.*"[17] That's not an attitude likely to lead toward cooperation with the industry that wants personal protective equipment because it is cheaper.

Now pull the four together. If a group of subject-matter experts with clear substantive standards and a career orientation is given a mandate to regulate several industries—all of industry maybe—to protect the health and safety of workers, consumers, or the general public, it is impossible to imagine a close and cooperative relationship as the outcome. Think OSHA or the Environmental Protection

Agency. If, on the other hand, a group of lawyers is given the responsibility of regulating prices and services in a given industry along with the responsibility to make sure that the industry is economically healthy and competitive, it seems only a bit of a stretch to dust off Marver Bernstein's notion of capture. Think in terms of the Civil Aeronautics Board, the Interstate Commerce Commission, any state utility regulation board, or quite possibly the Securities and Exchange Commission. Of course, some regulatory agencies don't fit either of these profiles. The Nuclear Regulatory Commission (NRC) deals with a single industry and it is charged with promoting the economic viability of that industry. On the other hand, the lead professionals are engineers, and they are expected to evaluate license applications and reactor operation procedures in terms of their potential impact on the public health and safety. Perhaps that's why the NRC and its predecessor agency the Atomic Energy Commission were criticized by the industry for heavy-handed regulation and by just about everyone else for being too close to the people who build and run the reactors and those who sell us the resulting electricity.[18]

In the end, some regulatory agencies get along fine with the industries they regulate. Some don't. The ones that don't tend to be the ones responsible for regulating a wide range of industries are dominated by subject-matter experts and are generally dealing with questions involving the health and safety of Americans whether those Americans work in the regulated industries, buy products from those industries, or just have to live with the impact those industries can have on the natural environment.

Agencies and Professional Associations

Agency/professional association relationships may have spent less time in the political science spotlight over the years, but that definitely doesn't mean they have gotten no attention at all. As I noted earlier, in his wide-ranging study of federal bureau chiefs, Herbert Kaufman found that "the professions strongly represented in its work force" constitute one of the two most consistent sets of supporters an agency possesses.[19] In fact, Kaufman first called our attention to the close interaction between professional associations and federal agencies more than four decades ago in his classic study of the U.S. Forest Service, *The Forest Ranger*.[20] He was not alone. Just as Francis Rourke observed that agencies and their clientele groups can become so closely identified that "it is difficult to tell where the group leaves off and the agency begins," Frederick Mosher argued that "in a good many cases, the goals and standards of public agencies, as seen by their officers and employees, are identical with the goals and standards of the professions as they are seen by their members."[21]

Just as the purpose of the previous section was to understand how agency/ clientele group relationships could become so close, the purpose of this one is to understand how agency/professional association relationships can come to the same point. And just as we needed to get a little more specific about just who clientele groups were before we started the last section, we need to get more specific about who these professional associations are before we start this one.

Most of us have at least heard of the American Medical Association and the American Bar Association, and students in my Introduction to Public

Administration course, many of them majors in the various programs in our nationally known College of Natural Resources, have more than heard of the American Fisheries Society, the Wildlife Society, the International Association of Fish and Wildlife Agencies, the Society of American Foresters, and the National Association of State Foresters. Those students already run highly successful student chapters of all of those organizations. Choose any policy area you can think of, pick up a copy of Congressional Quarterly's *Washington Information Directory*, and scan down the page. You will find listed on that page more than one organization composed of experts in some subject matter directly related to that policy area who are working in public and private organizations around the country and around the world and who have joined together to form that organization.

Most of these professional societies were not formed for the purpose of influencing government policy, and most are not really about protecting the economic interests of their members. To be sure, professionals are not always that good at separating their own economic interests from some broader interest they claim to be representing. Still, while the Society of American Foresters may take positions that protect the economic interests of professional foresters—mostly by trying to protect the jobs of those foresters—its primary purposes are really not economic and it is a very different kind of organization than is the American Forest and Paper Association or the American Pulpwood Association. Its relationship with the U.S. Forest Service clearly reflects that difference. But, different as agency/professional association relationships may be from agency/clientele group relationships, they are still built on the same three foundations. It's time to see how.

It Matters a Lot What You Know

One part of the U.S. Fish and Wildlife Service "Develops, manages, and protects interstate and international fisheries, including fisheries on the Great Lakes, fisheries on federal lands, endangered species of fish, and anadromous species."[22] The American Fisheries Society "Promotes the advancement of fisheries science, and conservation of renewable aquatic resources."[23] In pursuing that goal, the American Fisheries Society has decided it needs to "monitor legislation and regulations."[24] It is impossible to imagine that the two would never meet, and just as impossible to imagine that if they did, their shared knowledge would play no role in the resulting conversations. The agency/professional association relationship is grounded first and foremost in knowledge, but not exclusively in the kind of knowledge you would expect.

First of all, professional associations provide information that is analogous to the political intelligence provided to agencies by their clientele groups. The American Fisheries Society doesn't warn the Fish and Wildlife Service that if it goes forward with a particular policy there will be a revolt in the provinces that will soon spread to Washington and the appropriate subcommittee conference room any more than the Society of American Foresters provides that kind of warning to the Forest Service. Instead they warn their agencies of how a particular policy initiative or program change will be received in the community of fellow professionals. A negative reaction to a proposed Forest Service decision among the professional forestry community would hardly create the kind of political fallout in the relevant subcommittees that would almost certainly follow a negative reaction to that same proposal from the American Pulpwood Association or the American Forest and Paper Association. But, as we shall see shortly, that doesn't mean there would be no political fallout at all. It isn't the political fallout that would give the Forest Service pause, of course. It is the personal/professional fallout, and it would be considerable.

The men and women of the Forest Service, the Fish and Wildlife Service, or any agency of the government consider themselves experts. The policies they advocate are the product of the application of that expertise to the facts at hand. There is some politics to be accounted for, to be sure, but policies have to pass expert muster or they just aren't acceptable. To learn that a proposal will not pass muster within their own profession—they are, after all, almost certainly members of these professional associations themselves—is a serious blow to their personal and professional pride. Advance knowledge that such a blow might be in the offing is of great value to the staff of any agency.

Second, of course, is the knowledge and information we would expect a professional association to share with the agency or agencies working in its area of public policy, that is, the latest research in that area. It isn't so much that professional associations are in the business of doing research, though they may do some; it is more that these associations are structures that link together men and women who are doing this kind of research. These associations have meetings, meetings at which the results of research are shared with the rest of the profession. Agency staff often attend these meetings, since they are often members of the associations themselves. And it is all so very comfortable, given the fact that these agency policy specialists did this kind of research as part of their undergraduate or graduate programs and may well continue to do it as part of their jobs. Agencies need and want this information, they are getting it from people they have known a long time, and they are getting it in a comfortable and familiar setting. How could that do anything but strengthen an already natural relationship?

Agencies provide information and expert knowledge to the professional associations in turn. Much of what the members of these associations do is conduct research on the issues that interest them—and that interest the agencies the associations are linked with—and some of that research is done with at least a small hope that it will be used to guide public policy decisions in this area. Agency professionals can provide some feedback on how the research has helped to guide policy, and more to the point perhaps, on whether the policy seems to be working. Beyond that, some of these agency professionals are doing some pretty interesting research themselves, and here is an opportunity for the men and women of a particular professional association to find out about that research.

In sum, knowledge and information are bound to be at the heart of a relationship between two sets of people, each of which identifies intensely with its role in gathering that information and using that knowledge. In fact, this information sharing is such an important part of the agency/professional association relationship that both sides have a tendency to forget that the relationship has any other dimensions. But it does, and it's time to discuss the politics of what often seems to be a strictly knowledge-based business.

It Matters Some Whom You Know

It is clear that politics plays a lesser role in the agency/professional association relationship than it does in the agency/clientele group relationship. But it is also clear that politics enters into the relationship for more or less the same reasons and in more or less the same ways. That is, agencies need power and legitimacy if they are to play their role in the policy-making process, and professional associations see some definite advantages for their members in working closely with their agencies as that policy-making process unfolds. Each side can offer the other some of what it wants and needs. Once again, let's start on the agency side.

As I suggested above, the political power the American Fisheries Society or the Society of American Foresters could muster for—or even against—the Fish and Wildlife Service or the Forest Service would not flow out of the ability of those two professional associations to call in political IOUs created through years of working with House and Senate subcommittees in a context in which all concerned are aware of the implications of decisions for votes and campaign dollars. Nor would the legitimacy these fisheries or forestry experts could provide for their agencies come from bringing their "practical experience" to bear to help the Fish and Wildlife Service or the Forest Service connect to the "real world," or even from bringing the special democratic legitimacy that comes from working with the groups of citizens directly and substantially affected by the agency's policies. Instead, both the power they could deliver and the legitimacy they could confer would come from a single source, that is, their credibility.

These professional associations see themselves—and for the most part are seen by others—as experts without much of an axe to grind. Agencies have experts, but those experts represent an institution with a definite stake in both the policy process and its outcomes. Clientele groups also have experts, and while Dennis Ippolito and Thomas Walker have argued that these clientele group representatives are generally among the most knowledgeable and respected participants at congressional subcommittee hearings, everyone knows that they are putting their expertise to the service of a particular set of interests.[25] Professional associations are generally seen as the servants of expert knowledge, more or less going where that knowledge leads them without a great deal of concern for any particular institutional interests. There are obvious exceptions. When the American Medical Association talks about payments to doctors under the Medicare program, or the American Trial Lawyers Association talks about any issue involving the rights of Americans to sue anybody, anytime, anywhere, we see dollar signs and institutional/professional interests rather than some sort of expert neutrality. For that matter, a certain amount of skepticism about the extent to which professional associations are engaged in the pursuit of expert knowledge, without regard to any concerns save the pursuit and the knowledge itself, is present among all the participants in the policy-making process, probably including most of the representatives of the associations themselves. Still, nobody would put the Society of American Foresters in the same camp as the American Pulpwood Association or the American Fisheries Society on a par with the U.S. Tuna Foundation. While the Society of American Foresters' or American Fisheries Society's expert conclusions might have to be taken with a grain of the salt of self-interest, the corresponding conclusions from the American Pulpwood Association or the U.S. Tuna Foundation might require more like a pound or two of that particular seasoning.

The power that agencies derive from the support of professional associations certainly doesn't rival the power they derive from the support of their clientele groups. In the subcommittees of Congress, credibility is rarely a match for campaign dollars and constituent interests. But credibility can't be ignored as a source of power. The policy process, remember, is not supposed to be exclusively about interests, that is, about doing what those with traditional political power want done. It is also supposed to be about gathering and analyzing information and applying it to complex policy problems. People who do that, and more to the point, people who do it outside of the normal confines of politics—outside of government and the normal interest-group orbit of government—and can make a reasonable claim that they do so with less regard for self-interest than do any of the other participants in the process, have a claim to be heard. Again, those whose interests are at stake and who have made that clear through normal means of political participation—clientele groups—are going to be heard first and last. But those who have "just looked at the facts" have to be heard sometime.

It is in the realm of legitimacy, of course, where we find professional associations providing the greatest help to the agencies with which they share that all important common expertise. First of all, as you probably suspected in the previous paragraph, whatever power flows to an agency from the backing of a professional association mostly comes in the form of the added legitimacy that backing brings to a policy. An agency can, in effect, argue that the proposed policy has the support of a neutral body of experts, in the process undercutting the potential charge that the policy is really just a way to serve the interests of the agency or of its clientele. Beyond that (and this you might not have suspected) from the point of view of agency policy specialists, legitimacy is not exclusively a matter of politics or even of some popularized version of democratic theory. It is also personal and it must pass some sort of expert test, precisely because everything these policy specialists do must pass some sort of expert test. A policy, the agency, even the experts themselves are only legitimate in the eyes of those experts if they can feel comfortable that that policy, that agency, and they themselves are acceptable in the eyes of their fellow experts. Professional association backing goes a long way toward creating that particular "zone of comfort."

Despite its own admission that it exists in part to "promote the fisheries profession," the American Fisheries Society certainly doesn't approach any policy question on the agenda of the Fish and Wildlife Service or the National Fisheries Service with the kind of economic stakes that would be present in that decision for the National Fisheries Institute, or the U.S. Tuna Foundation. But that hardly means there are no stakes at all. Promoting the "fisheries profession," after all, is more than a matter of increasing salaries, or even of increasing the number of jobs available within the profession. There is the status of the profession itself, and an influential role inside the process of making policy about issues of importance to the profession is bound to build that status. Some of that is simple visibility, but much more comes from the fact that an association's knowledge is being counted on as complex questions are debated and decided. This is not to suggest that the American Fisheries Society or the Society of American Foresters don't care how many people can make a living in the fisheries or forestry professions and how good that living is going to be. Of course they do. Because a great many of the most active members in professional associations are affiliated with research universities, they also want internships for graduate students, research opportunities for those students and their faculty mentors, and even the occasional appointment to an advisory board or commission. But underlying all of that, the number of jobs, the salaries, the internships, and the research grants, is the status of the profession, and there can be little doubt that that status can be enhanced by working closely with the agency or agencies active on the issues that touch the association's expertise.

Professional associations may be no more likely to pursue "science for the sake of science" than Louis B. Mayer pursued "art for the sake of art," despite the delightful *Ars Gratia Artis* wrapped around the roaring lion in the MGM studio logo. Well, probably a little more. Professional associations are hardly seen as completely disinterested observers of the policy process, and they shouldn't be. But they are generally seen as about as unattached as anybody can be when it comes to making public policy, and that perception is the primary source of the power and legitimacy they can convey to the agencies they work with. It helps those agencies. The increment of power may not be all that much, and it can be overwhelmed by traditional political power, especially in the semi-closed arenas created by most House and Senate subcommittees. But the added legitimacy is critical to the agency and its policy experts. Without it they could not feel that they had done their jobs of seeking out policy choices that really were grounded in expert knowledge and only then leavened those policies somewhat with politics. In exchange for such a valuable commodity, professional associations increase their stature, both in the eyes of the community at large and in their own. Though neither side would likely characterize it as such, I suspect, a good trade for both.

It Matters How You Feel

That sense of community that can and does develop between agencies and their clientele groups is even more likely to develop between agencies and the organized groups of fellow professionals. In fact, this sense of community is likely to be even stronger when it comes to the relationship between an agency and the association of "professions strongly represented in its work force" than in the relationship between an agency and its clientele groups. That sense of community originates in exactly the same way in both relationships. It's just that in the agency/professional association relationship there is nothing to undermine it.

As I noted a moment ago, agencies and professional associations develop something like a sense of community for the same reasons that agencies and clientele groups develop that sense, that is, common background, shared values, and years of working together. It would probably be unlikely that a professional association would find that its membership came primarily from a single region of the country, but even if the common background and shared values generated by "growing up together" might be missing, the often more important common background and shared values born out of "being educated together" are more than strong enough to make up for it.

Professional education, as was suggested in the second chapter, is a blend of learning a specialized vocabulary and a set of skills and concepts, and being socialized into the profession. A heavy dose of that socialization, recall, is aimed at convincing the budding young professional that that specialized vocabulary and set of skills and concepts are absolutely essential to producing intelligent answers to the questions the profession addresses. In the process, of course, that socialization integrates the profession even as it sets that profession apart from the rest of society. What better way to create a real feeling of community? Then, of course, comes the powerful reinforcement of working on the same kinds of problems, seeing each other at regional and national meetings of the association, and just generally getting comfortable with each other.

Interestingly enough, the bonds of community between agencies and professional associations may well be stronger than the analogous bonds between agencies and clientele groups. One small part of that might come from the fact that not all clientele group representatives that an agency must deal with will be fellow professionals. In more concrete terms, the American Pulpwood Association and the American Forest and Paper Association may be represented by lawyers who have a solid layperson's understanding of forestry issues as well as by professional foresters. The Society of American Foresters will not. Those people are foresters, professional foresters. Probably more important in generating a greater sense of community between agencies and professional associations than between agencies and clientele groups is the very nature of clientele groups themselves. Their primary reason for existence in most cases, remember, is political, that is, to use government to advance their interests. That's expected and accepted by the agency policy specialists. But it still creates just a little crack in that feeling of community. We—the agency staff and the clientele representatives—aren't really one exactly, at least not in the way that we—the agency staff and the professional association leadership and membership—are one.

In sum, it is little wonder that an agency would find a powerful common bond with a group of men and women who, like themselves, have channeled a powerful interest in a set of issues into a career dealing with those issues. Talking about those issues together—often at meetings of a professional association to which agency personnel belong—strengthens the bond, and there is no obvious hint of the political to cast any sort of pall over the resulting close relationship. The fact that these professional associations have a kind of credibility that can provide a small increment of power and a far larger dose of legitimacy for the agency, its policies, and its staff may not get much open discussion, but everyone involved is well aware it is happening, and everyone involved is happy that it is.

In Summary

I'm not sure in how many instances "the goals and standards of public agencies, as seen by their officers and employees, are identical with the goals and standards of the professions as they are seen by their members," but I am sure that it would be a rare agency indeed that would not establish a close working relationship with the professional association or associations working in its particular field.[26] They share information on an almost constant basis. Professional associations provide agencies with advance warning if agency policies will not be well received in the wider profession and provide a vehicle for the sharing of research on the issues of common concern. Agencies, in turn, provide professional association members with the results of their research and, beyond that, with information on how the latest research has been used in the world of policy making. Beyond sharing information, they really do share knowledge, that is, the concepts and theories that make all that information have some sort of meaning.

Though neither side might describe the relationship as partly political, it is. Agencies still need power and legitimacy, and it feels awfully good to the agency's policy specialists when a little of that power and a lot of that legitimacy come from fellow experts. The credibility those experts bring to the game of politics is a real help to agencies sometimes struggling to create some of their own. Agencies give as well as get, of course. They provide the seemingly mundane in the form of research grants, internships, consultantships, etc., and they provide the increased stature that comes from insider status in the policy process. The importance of all of this is not lost on the professional association's members or leaders.

Finally, people who have similar educations and work in the same or very closely related fields are bound to feel a sort of bond with each other. The number of interactions between them only strengthens that bond.

Agencies and Individual Policy Experts (IPEs)

Last, and for once probably least, among agency supporters come the individual policy experts. Generally speaking, these individual experts come from the ranks of former officials, of academics, or increasingly of those who conduct research about particular issues at organizations like the Brookings Institution, the Heritage Foundation, or the American Enterprise Institute, or perhaps at the more specialized research institutions such as the RAND Corporation (defense) or the Women's Research and Education Institute (a range of women's issues). The one thing they have in common, of course, is an established reputation as an expert on a particular issue or set of related issues. The relationship between an individual policy expert and an agency dealing with the issues in which that individual has earned his or her reputation as an expert turns out to be almost a carbon copy of the agency/professional association relationship we just discussed, so this section can be kept mercifully short.

It Certainly Matters What You Know

Once more, these experts are part of the process because of their knowledge, so the exchange of information is central to the relationship. These individual experts will provide an agency with a heads up if they find that they will personally oppose some sort of agency initiative, but it is the results of the research done by these men and women that agencies are really interested in getting. In fact, it is not at all uncommon for some of this research—especially that done by the academics—to have been supported, at least in part, by grants or contracts from these very agencies. Agencies, in turn, supply these individual experts with the results of research being done by agency staff, as well as with the often more important—to the experts, anyway—results of the use of their previous research in the decision-making process.

It Matters a Great Deal Who Knows You

As we've seen throughout this chapter as well as the previous one, agencies need power and legitimacy. Individual policy experts can provide some of both, and the currency, as it was with the professional associations, is credibility. But some of these individual experts add a little something to that credibility, a little something that differentiates them from the professional associations and can make them important supporters of their agencies. That little something: star power.

Imagine yourself at a congressional subcommittee hearing on a proposed Forest Service policy change. The chief testifies, as do representatives from the American Pulpwood Association, the American Forest and Paper Association, and the American Hardwood Export Council. Then comes the current President of the Society of American Foresters. Last on the crowded agenda is a man named Jay Cravens. Half of the committee members instantly recognize Dr. Cravens from his years with the Forest Service, and they know he has kept his hand in as head of the forestry program somewhere in the Midwest.[27] He still does a lot of research, and it wasn't that long ago that he was President of the Society of American Foresters. He has an instant credibility that comes not just from the multiple roles he plays/has played in forest policy, but from the recognition, from the experience that these members of Congress have had with him over the years. They have heard him before and they have trusted him before. It isn't so much that he knows the members of the subcommittee as that they know him and they are comfortable with him. He has developed a reputation for expertise, but also a reputation as a "straight shooter," the kind of guy the subcommittee can trust. Every policy area has some of these people, and if an agency can get their support, that agency has added a definite increment of power and legitimacy. Any agency that can't secure the cooperation of these experts committees have come to rely on can find itself in serious trouble. It has been a long time now, and all of the principals are long gone, but when the Social Security Administration (SSA) tried to make some major policy changes in the late 1970s, they found themselves facing their recently retired commissioner in front of a key congressional subcommittee. SSA lost the ensuing confrontation.[28]

Once again, these individual experts are happy to reap the rewards, both personal and professional, that go along with a close relationship with the agencies working in the policy areas of their expertise. Jay Cravens helped a lot of UWSP (University of Wisconsin, Stevens Point) students find internships and jobs with the Forest Service and got a couple of his junior colleagues on advisory panels to the service. Others certainly have done the same. Also, I know from brief conversations with Jay that he had a mild case of what is often referred to as Potomac Fever. He very much wanted to retire from the Forest Service all those years ago, but he sure didn't want to retire from forest policy making. So he did exactly that, that is, left the service but kept right on working on the issues. His former job, his current job, and his reputation allowed him to do it.

It Matters How You Feel

That sense of community may well be strongest between the individual policy experts who are former agency officials and the agencies they have left, but it can be felt between agency staff and their academic and think-tank supporters as well. Just rewind back to our discussion of the agency/professional association relationship to see the dimensions of the one between agencies and individual policy experts. They are fellow professionals, with similar educations, similar outlooks on the world of this particular policy area, and a long time together.

In Summary

Agencies need support. That means they need supporters. There are people willing to provide that support. Some are clientele groups—organized groups of citizens directly affected by an agency's policies—some are professional associations, and some are individual experts in that agency's area of policy responsibility. Not surprisingly, these three sets of people find their agencies. Not surprisingly, the agencies aren't really hiding. The resulting relationship is generally close and cooperative, though there are a couple of glaring exceptions.

These relationships are, of course, political. Clientele groups provide classic political power where and when it counts—in congressional subcommittees—while professional associations provide credibility that can add a bit to the political power that comes from the clientele. Individual experts will use their star power to add another increment of credibility and with it another increment of power. Similarly, all three sets of supporters provide an agency with legitimacy for itself and for its policies. Working with clientele groups means working with the directly affected citizens who know how things really work, while working with professional associations and individual experts means working with knowledgeable people with no personal or economic stake in the outcomes of the agency's deliberations. All three sets of supporters, of course, take something out of the relationship as well as put something into it. Clientele will get the kind of policy they want—or at least a real chance to influence the kind of policy they do end up having to live with—and professional associations and policy experts take away status, prestige, and maybe an opportunity to be involved in seeing what happens when their knowledge is used to shape public policy.

But these relationships couldn't survive if they were solely political. Knowledge has to enter into the equation, and it does. Clientele groups provide political intelligence and a practitioner's take on what Americans love to call the "real world." Professional associations provide their own unique brand of professional/political intelligence along with the latest research and the expert framework from which to view that research. Individual experts provide much the same. Agencies, in turn, provide all three with the results of their own research and an advance indication of their thinking about new policy directions.

Finally, all agencies and their supporters really do have a sense of community, a feeling that they are all in the same boat, and that they are members of the crew, at that. Common background, whether personal or educational, combines with shared expertise, shared values, and years of working together to create a kind of cooperation that in some cases probably borders on intimacy.

Not all agencies, however, live in this world of constant support. Some agencies don't get along with their clientele groups. Social service agencies can't get from those groups what they need and clearly don't feel a real sense of community, so they have to look elsewhere, mostly to the professional associations active in their policy areas. Regulatory agencies that are assigned the task of regulating several industries, that are given little if any responsibility for gauging the impact of their decisions on the economic health of the industries they regulate, and that are engaged in health- and safety-oriented regulation done by subject-matter experts inevitably end up at odds with their clientele groups, and like social service agencies, they have to look elsewhere for support. In the end, it isn't always all that easy to find.

AGENCIES AND THEIR CRITICS

Even for agencies that have established close and cooperative working relationships with their supporters, the waters of the policy process are not always calm. The consistent support of clientele groups, professional associations, and individual experts notwithstanding, the evening news, the morning paper, the afternoon mail, or the fax machine anytime, day or night, still might contain a broadside fired at agency policies or even agency personnel. For some agencies these attacks come as something of a surprise, but for a good many others—most especially for those whose operations touch even a little on some aspect of the relationship between Americans and their natural environment—such criticism seems as natural and predictable as the prevailing westerly winds on the Oregon coast. As Herbert Kaufman put it more than twenty years ago, the Forest Service faces "some organizations against all man induced change in vast areas of the public domain [which] were apt to fight every measure for development of the resources in those properties and to denounce any public official and agency not similarly inclined."[29] The Bureau of Land Management's career leadership would recognize the situation. For that matter, the odds are they would also recognize the names of the organizations and individuals on the letters, faxes, and press releases. So would the key people at the Fish and Wildlife Service, the Environmental Protection Agency, the Natural Resources Conservation Service (that one is in the Department of Agriculture and used to be called the Soil Conservation Service), and the National Oceanic and Atmospheric Administration.

Kaufman may have stretched things a wee bit with the phrase "against all man induced change," but there can be no doubt that groups like the Sierra Club, Friends of the Earth, the Natural Resources Defense Council, and the Union of Concerned Scientists feel very strongly that most public policy dealing with questions of the use of the world's resources is seriously misguided, and that it has been seriously misguided by those very agencies and their various support groups. There can also be no doubt that they voice their complaints in a vigorous and very public way. The Union of Concerned Scientists voices its dismay with government policy in a variety of substantive areas, some such as sustainable agriculture and alternative energy sources, which are clearly resource related, and others, such as foreign policy, arms control, and disarmament, which are not. The United States Public Interest Research Group and Public Citizen, through its various spin-offs such as Critical Mass (nuclear energy) and Health Research Group (health issues), do as well, while others, like the Center for Science in the Public Interest, concentrate on a single set of related issues. In the case of the Center for Science in the Public Interest, it is issues involving policy regarding food and nutrition, especially policies involving food safety. Individuals can even get in on the act, as John Banzhaff did in the area of smoking and health before he formed the critical group Action on Smoking and Health, or as Jeremy Rifkin did with respect to a variety of food and nutrition issues before forming the Pure Food Campaign to oppose the continued development and marketing of genetically engineered food.

Whether it be in the form of the single voice of the pre–Pure Food Jeremy Rifkin, or the Greek Chorus of the Center for Science in the Public Interest, the Community Nutrition Institute, and the Health Research Group, every agency knows there is the possibility of criticism of that agency and its policies at any time, and many agencies know that such criticism is a reality all of the time. The critics are out there, and as Herbert Kaufman noted, no agency can simply assume that eventually they will tire and go away.[30] Some relationship between an agency and its critics is, in other words, inevitable. The question is: what will that relationship look like?

First of all, that relationship is almost certain to be characterized by a loud, public, and almost constant fight. It turns out that both sides need that fight.

Agencies need the fight because nothing keeps an alliance together like a common enemy, especially an enemy right outside the gate. If the Forest Service can show the American Forest and Paper Association and the American Pulpwood Association that it is engaged in a continuous struggle with the Sierra Club and the Wilderness Society over one forest management plan after another, it can show those organizations that it is out defending commonly held values. In fact, it can even make that case of defending common ground to the Society of American Foresters. Its members, you see, manage timber resources. They don't save trees. Shift the locus to the Bureau of Land Management, and a fight with the Natural Resources Defense Council over grazing rights on bureau-managed land could be quite reassuring to the Public Lands Council, whose cattle and sheep rancher membership sometimes seems to see that bureau-managed land as its very own.

Critics need the fight every bit as much as do the agencies. Credibility is at stake. First of all, of course, there is the issue of credibility with the citizens who belong to or, more likely, support those groups. They join or contribute to such organizations largely because they, too, are unhappy with what government is doing in a particular area of policy. Membership, along with financial and other support, in all likelihood hinges in large measure on stoking the fires of that unhappiness. What better way than by keeping up the fight against the agencies who are the villains of the piece? Second, there is the issue of credibility with themselves. These men and women are critics because they are deeply dissatisfied with something. In addition, many of them have adopted the personal style of the critic, always questioning and rarely satisfied with the answers. If they suddenly stopped fighting with the agencies they so sincerely believe are doing the wrong thing, they would have to explain to themselves why the fight has ended. Such explanations would not be all that easy to come by or, worse yet, would not be all that flattering.

Second, most of these agency/critical group fights are going to be won by the agencies. There will be some compromises, but most of the time the agency is going to adopt a policy far closer to the one it originally advanced than to the one offered in opposition by its critics. Most of the time, but definitely not all of the time. Though it may surprise you at first glance, once again, both sides want it this way.

Agencies expect to win most of these fights because they believe deeply in their own expertise—tempered by a well-developed sense of politics—and they often find the demands of their critics to be untenable, both in terms of the science and the politics. But agencies need to lose some of these confrontations, and they do. Don't get me wrong. This is not like a fighter "going in the tank" because he or she was bought off or scared off. Agencies carefully pick the fights they will lose, and they pick them because they believe that this time their critics have a point. But they do need to lose some. As with the critics' need for the fight itself, the issue is credibility. If the Forest Service never found any merit in any argument put forth by the Sierra Club or the Wilderness Society, it would leave itself wide open to the charge of being nothing more than the servant of its clientele groups. That would hurt. It might hurt politically if the issue ever got out of the congressional subcommittee arena. More to the point, however, it would hurt personally. The policy specialists at the Forest Service, like their counterparts in every agency of government, really do believe themselves to be experts going where sound forestry practice—seasoned with enough politics to keep the agency afloat—tells them to go. Could that really always be just where the interests of the American Pulpwood Association or the American Forest and Paper Association seem to lie? When the Forest Service responds to the Sierra Club, the Bureau of Land Management responds to the Friends of the Earth, or the Food and Drug Administration responds to the Center for Science in the Public Interest, the agency buys a little credibility in the outside political world, and a good bit of credibility at home.

Critics, too, expect, and in a way even want, agencies to win most of the time. Once more, most, not all. It's easy enough to see why the critics need to win a few of their confrontations with bureaucracy. Nobody likes to lose all of the time. Without an occasional victory, it would be pretty hard to sustain the battle day after day, year after year. Beyond that, of course, it would be difficult to keep attracting the resources necessary to sustain the battle if the battle was never successful. But hard as it may seem to believe at first, critics would not want to win a large percentage of the battles they fight with the agencies they constantly attack. It's that credibility business again. These critical groups are supposed to be the one set of participants in the American political process who push the envelope. These people do battle with politics and policy as usual, and they do it on behalf of a very different vision of how things ought to be. How would they explain to their supporters, and most of all to themselves, the fact that they were now winning more often than they were losing? The first thought, I suspect, would be the thought that they had somehow begun picking the easy fights, that they had lost their edge and their aggressiveness. That would not be a comfortable or comforting thought for any of them.

In short, neither side is all that fond of the other, and each needs a loud public fight to prove to itself and others that it is doing what it is supposed to be doing. So the battle is on. Critics need to win some of these fights if they are to keep going, but they can't afford to win too many, as winning too many would challenge their image—both their image with the public and their image with themselves—as society's real watchdogs, the ones who bark and bark and bark until the family wakes up. This suits the agencies just fine, as they need to win most of these fights to keep their support, and they need to lose a few to keep their credibility, especially their credibility with themselves.

Back in 1987, I gave this relationship a name, "contentious accommodation."[31] That name never caught on. Maybe this time.

AGENCIES AND THE GENERAL PUBLIC

Agencies establish relationships with their supporters and their critics. The former they cultivate eagerly, the latter they accept grudgingly, but in both cases, relationships exist and both sides understand and accept the boundaries and the dynamics of those relationships. But what about the "general public"? Now things get more than a little confusing. On the one hand, as I suggested in the very first sentence of the chapter, there doesn't seem to be any such thing as the general public, at least not in the concrete political or organizational sense in which clientele groups, professional associations, individual experts, and critics exist. On the other hand, however, the notion of a "general public interest" is a fixture in the American governmental landscape. Indeed, it is supposed to provide the standard by which all public policy is ultimately to be judged. In such a context, how can an agency/general public relationship emerge, and maybe more to the point, what could it look like?

We can be fairly certain that it won't emerge in the manner of the relationships between an agency and its supporters or critics. We can be just as certain that it won't look like those relationships either.

Agency/support group relationships, recall, arise out of common interests and common values and are carefully nurtured by both sides. The boundaries are set by shared knowledge, political interdependence, and a sense of community, and the resulting relationship revolves around those three key elements. Obviously none of that could happen in the context of the general public and any government agency. To begin with, the general public knows almost nothing about any agency. It could hardly warn about approaching political storms or offer its practical wisdom about the issues that face the agency. In addition, the general public almost never feels that the actions of any agency are of such import that that public will put pressure on the institutions of the constitutional government to get those institutions to ride herd on that particular agency. Finally, no real sense of community is going to develop between an agency's policy specialists and a set of people with no real interest in, or knowledge of, the issues that structure the days and define the careers of those specialists.

The relationship of contentious accommodation that exists between agencies and their critics provides no better model for an agency/general public relationship. Contentiousness or no contentiousness, expert knowledge of and passionate interest in the issues the agency deals with are still at the heart of the relationship. With respect to any agency, the general public simply has neither, and all agencies know it.

So direct relationships like those agencies establish with their supporters and their critics are out of the question, but what about indirect relationships? We operate a representative government, after all, so couldn't agencies relate to the general public through those who are chosen to represent that public?

As we have seen so far, the President may well be the symbol of representation of a general public interest, but from the point of view of any particular agency, he or she doesn't spend a great deal of time or energy articulating that general public interest with respect to that agency's issues or concerns. Besides, the chief doesn't always know what he or she is talking about with respect to those issues, and operates from a time perspective that doesn't make much sense to an agency's policy specialists. Even with the help that he or she might get from a team of political executives, it is pretty hard to think of the President as the conduit through which an agency/general public relationship could develop.

Congress doesn't offer much hope for an indirect agency/general public relationship either. Subcommittees, as we saw, are the ones that relate directly with agencies, and those subcommittees, as we also saw, tend to be responsive almost exclusively to the very support groups with which agencies have long-standing and comfortable ties. Not exactly fertile ground for the development of a concept of the public interest other than one defined in terms of the interests of a set of directly and substantially affected citizens, and an organized set at that.

In the end, then, it is clear that no agency is going to establish a direct working relationship with the general public. The glue isn't there for a relationship that would parallel the agency/clientele group relationship, and the focused anger isn't there to fuel a relationship to parallel the agency/critic relationship. It doesn't appear much more likely that any agency is going to establish an indirect relationship with the general public by listening to that public's voice as channeled through the President or the Congress. The President isn't actually all that much more concerned about what happens at most agencies than is the general public, and Congress has long since decided that its institutional interests—and especially the interests of its individual members—are best met by a committee and subcommittee centered decision-making system that rarely, if ever, provides a forum in which a general public interest might be defined and applied.

Still, two questions remain. First, in the absence of any meaningful relationship between the general public and the agencies of its government, is it fair to say that the general public is being ignored by those agencies? Second, if agencies do ignore the general public, how do they square that fact with the pervasive rhetoric about the general public interest as the guiding light for all public policy?

As far as the first question is concerned, most agencies do ignore the general public, but not necessarily in the way in which most people mean that phrase when they throw it around. That is, if most agencies don't hear the general public, it's not because they are too busy listening to their supporters. They don't hear the general public because that general public isn't talking.

The second question, however, is a bit trickier. On one level, agency policy specialists could finesse the question by simply concluding that if the general public has not spoken to an issue, then it has no interest—both in the sense of a concern and a stake—in that issue, and consequently, to ignore the general public is a perfectly acceptable course of action. What else to do? But if an agency's decisions were ever to be challenged outside of the narrow agency/subcommittee/clientele/professional association/individual expert world in which most such decisions get made, that answer simply wouldn't hold up. As a matter of fact, strange as it sounds, it wouldn't hold up to most policy specialists either. They are supposed to pursue "the public interest," not define it out of existence.

So if concluding that there is no such thing as the general public existence won't get an agency's policy specialists out of this particular box, what will? Two things, it turns out.

First, as Herbert Kaufman pointed out, "The administrators heard from self-selected, interested parties, not the general public, though all the special groups in the congressional, executive, nongovernmental, and other sets of interests claimed at various times to speak for 'it.'"[32] Inside an agency's orbit, no one ever says: "Look, we know that what we are asking goes against the interest of the general public, but we expect you to ignore that interest and protect ours." Everyone, clientele, professional associations, individual experts, critics, subcommittee members, everyone, just wants to advance the "public interest." Immersed in such rhetoric it can get pretty easy to lose sight of the fact that the word general doesn't always appear in front of public interest. Besides, these different groups have a tendency to lay out somewhat different views of where the public interest lies on a particular question, and while that may muddy the waters a bit, that very muddiness suggests that wherever the agency decides to go, it is going toward the public interest.

Second, and probably even more important than rhetoric that seems to beg the question of the general public interest almost as effectively as simply saying that that interest doesn't exist, is the fact that a great many of the mechanisms by which agencies develop and legitimize policy appear to provide numerous opportunities for public input. We are going to consider those mechanisms in detail, both in the next section of this chapter and in the next chapter. All we need say here is this. The various agencies of the federal government get advice from more than 1,500 specially formed committees. Each of these committees must be structured under the terms of the Federal Advisory Committee Act of 1972, which requires that some members of the committee be "representative of the general public," and that "Committee meetings shall be open to the public and fairly balanced in terms of points of view and the functions to be performed."[33] Beyond that, agency rule making almost always requires a "public" comment period or a "public" hearing. Throw all of that together, and you can see how an agency's policy specialists might come to believe that they have done all that they can to search for the public interest, and that what has eventually emerged from this process probably deserves that name as much as anything else that happens in government.

I don't want to make all of this sound like some sort of con game. Agencies do know that they are expected to be guided by some notion called the public interest and they know it is supposed to be defined in a manner that includes more than just the interests of their traditional clientele groups. But those agencies also know that something that deserves to be called the general public interest will not be all that easy to decipher. They hear from all sorts of people who claim that they have figured out where that elusive public interest lies, and if those agencies can put together a decision-making system that appears to grant all sorts of folks access in all sorts of ways, it begins to seem reasonable enough from their point of view to conclude that they have done all they can to seek out that public interest and act on it.

Conditions are all wrong for the development of direct agency/general public relationships. They aren't all that right for the development of indirect agency/general public relationships either. But the general public interest must be given its due, and that can't be done simply by giving up on it. In a world in which everybody claims to represent that general public interest—especially a world in which not all of those who claim to represent that interest define it the same way—there is room to create a set of opportunities for public input into the policy-making process that can help to convince agency policy specialists that they have made a good faith effort to find that public interest and to let it guide their decisions. With a little luck, they'll convince the rest of us, too.

HOW DOES THE PUBLIC INFLUENCE BUREAUCRACY?

Unlike the President and the Congress, the public doesn't write budgets, assign programs, move agencies from one department to another, or structure an agency's legal mandate. But, as I hope has been made clear in this chapter as well as in the previous two, that does not mean that the public has no influence over such decisions or, even more to the point, over the resulting agency policy choices that are a product of the environment created by those decisions. First of all, the public—whether dressed as clientele groups, professional associations, individual experts, critics, or even, on the rarest of occasions, the general public—can exercise influence over bureaucracy indirectly. That is, the public can exercise influence over Congress and the President as they try to influence the outcomes of agency deliberations by structuring the organizational, budgetary, and legal environments in which those decisions are made. Second, the public, again in any of its many disguises, can also exercise influence over agency decision making in a more direct way, informally by what amounts to lobbying of agency personnel and formally, through service on agency advisory committees, presentation of testimony at public hearings, and submission of information during the notice and comment period that is normally part of the agency rule-making process. Finally, there are one or two circumstances in which the public—almost always dressed as a clientele group—has been given what amounts to a formal role in the implementation of an agency's programs.

Indirect Public Influence

There is very little more to be said about indirect public influence over policy making at the agency level. We have already seen that the public can work through the President and the Congress, and we have seen that the latter is far more successful than the former. We'll consider using the courts in chapter 9, so for now, hold that in abeyance.

With minimal incentive and facing a serious lack of time and knowledge, the President rarely becomes directly involved in policy decisions at the agency level. Some effort is made—through cabinet and subcabinet appointments, efforts to rearrange bureaucratic structure, decisions about the budget, and the chief's involvement in efforts to change the legal authority of agencies—to make up for the lack of direct effort to influence agency policy, but those efforts, too, seem doomed to only the most limited success. The tools the President has just don't seem to be enough to overcome agency suspicion of his or her motives and capabilities, and the Congress is rarely willing to get out of the way and let the President become a major force in what agencies do. In short, it is clear enough to the public—in particular, of course, to that segment of the public most concerned with a specific area of public policy—that trying to use the President to influence what is happening at the agency or agencies operating in that area of policy is, if not a lost cause, at least a lousy bet. Why make a lousy bet when a good bet is just a short walk down Pennsylvania Avenue?

That good bet, of course, would be the bet placed on the House and Senate sub-committees with jurisdiction over the agencies the public—this segment of the public—wants to influence. Segments of the public—organized interest groups—willing and able to supply a particular subcommittee's members with votes, campaign contributions, or both, will eventually be able to establish a close working relationship with that subcommittee. Since the Congress has pretty much handed over its keys to the agency to these subcommittees, that relationship can, in turn, be used to exercise indirect influence over the agency or agencies in that subcommittee's orbit.

In short, the public can indeed exercise indirect influence over agency decision making, but almost all of that influence is exercised through subcommittees of the House and Senate, and that means that almost all of it is exercised by the organized interest groups who are the public—or at least the voice of the public—as far as those subcommittees are concerned. If any other version of the public wants to exercise influence over bureaucracy, it will have to try a more direct route.

Direct Public Influence

Citizens do hope to exercise some direct influence over agencies and the decisions they make. They try to do it both informally and formally.

The Informal Side

Nearly all observers of bureaucracy have noted that informal communications channels between agencies and their supporters are always open.[34] Though both sides would no doubt be quite uncomfortable pinning the label "lobbying" on any of this informal communication, no one can reasonably doubt that when an agency's supporters supply that agency with information, they hope that information will find its way into the agency's policy deliberations. In turn, there can be no reasonable doubt that agencies know that, and actually seek out such information for precisely that purpose. Whatever they choose to call it, direct face to face contacts, in which group representatives present lots of information and agency officials pay close attention to what they hear, are part of the daily world of most executive branch units. Given the relationships that most agencies have established with their supporters, it seems a small jump indeed to conclude that these informal contacts provide a real opportunity for those supporters to influence the decisions of their agencies. Of course, as we noted earlier, agencies have critics as well as supporters, but those critics frequently find that the reception on these informal channels isn't so good, and they switch to the more formal channels we'll talk about in a moment.

Informal influence does have its limits, however, even for the most powerful of clientele groups. In the first place, there are situations in which the law demands that informal communications channels be shut down. We will talk about these situations in far more detail in the next chapter, but the Administrative Procedure Act rules that govern what is called the "on the record" decision-making process expressly forbid any contacts between an agency and any "interested party" in a decision unless the agency shares all information about that contact with all other "interested parties."[35] Agencies have plenty of opportunity for decisions made not "on the record," but even then, most rule-making proceedings require a public notice and comment period, and comments outside that channel could raise credibility problems for the final decision should they surface later. Then there is the Freedom of Information Act, which can help to bring lots of things to the surface if some critical group is angry enough to stir the waters. All of this is not to say that clientele and other supporters cannot or do not use the informal communications channels to make their positions known. They do. But "lobbying" the bureaucracy is a far cry from "lobbying" the Congress. The former, it seems, has a lot more rules.

The Formal Side

The public has three formal opportunities for direct influence over agency decision making. Specifically, there are chances to serve on agency advisory committees, to submit comments during the rule-making notice and comment hearing, and to testify at public hearings that agencies may hold as part of a rule-making proceeding or just to gather information about some issue before that agency.

As I noted earlier, there are more than 1,500 agency advisory committees. Some are no doubt for show, and some are no doubt for cover, but a great many are real, that is, there to provide real advice on tough public policy questions.

Service on such committees is clearly a way to be heard, and as I also suggested a bit earlier, a way to be heard in a forum that won't be obviously susceptible to the challenge of being a back channel available only to the privileged few. In fact, many advisory committees really are open primarily to an agency's supporters, but increasingly agency critics find a spot or two on these committees and the "general public" must be represented as well. As a practical matter, the "general public" members may well be drowned in a sea of jargon, but if critics find their way onto a committee, they will not only be able to swim, they may well swamp an agency/clientele boat or two in the process. In the end, the point is this: agencies create committees to advise them and they tend to stack those committees with people from their own support groups. It isn't just a matter of an "old boy's network" at work. These are the groups an agency thinks ought to be represented on the committees because these are the groups who know and care the most about the subjects the committee is going to tackle. Add in the requisite general public members and some agency critics and the result will look like—maybe sometimes even be—a reasoned and expert look at a difficult issue. The result: a formal channel for direct influence for those who make the committee roster.

When rules are to be written, agencies are expected to seek public input. As we'll see in the next chapter, that input can take the form of written comments submitted during what is known as the notice and comment period, or it can take the form of testimony—both written and oral—at public hearings. The latter provides a far more complete opportunity for real and meaningful public input and influence, but that's a story for the next chapter. The story for this chapter is much simpler. The door is open to a formal opportunity to make your case to the men and women who will make a decision you believe is important to your life. There is no guarantee, of course, that the case you make in your written comments or your written or oral testimony will be taken seriously. Critics can't be cut out of these processes, but ideas, information, and viewpoints offered by supporters with whom an agency has established a long and satisfactory working relationship are bound to get a more sympathetic hearing than will ideas, information, and viewpoints offered by an individual or group dedicated to the proposition that the agency in question has never made a right decision. A never-before-heard-of outsider claiming to represent the general public interest might well find himself or herself getting an even less even-handed hearing, particularly if his or her comments or testimony weren't presented in an appropriately expert way. The point remains the same. The door marked "formal channel of public influence" is open every time an agency calls for public input. In fact, it is more open than it is when an agency forms a new advisory committee or looks for likely recruits for an existing one.

The Rare Case of Direct Program Responsibility

Though it is rare and getting rarer, groups of citizens have been given a direct role in program administration. Under the commodity price support system as it operated from its inception in the 1930s until the passage of the Freedom to Farm Act in 1996, each of the approximately 2,800 agriculture counties in the United

States had a Stabilization and Conservation Committee elected by the farmers of that particular county and delegated the legal authority to "make new allotments, work out adjustments and review complaints regarding allotments, determine whether quotas have been complied with, inspect and approve storage facilities, and perform as the court of original jurisdiction on violations of price support rules and on eligibility for parity payments."[36] From the point of view of an individual farmer, it's hard to see what role was left for the Agricultural Stabilization and Conservation Service's professional staff. The Bureau of Land Management still uses a similar set of committees composed of ranchers in a given county who graze livestock on BLM-managed land to handle a good bit of what might be considered the day-to-day administration of the grazing program, including the question of the number of head a particular rancher will be permitted to graze on his or her share of that county's BLM-managed land.[37]

SUMMARY AND CONCLUSION

The men and women who run the hundreds of federal agencies know that they must establish some sort of relationship with the American people. The very notion of self-government demands it, both in a political sense and in a philosophical sense. But the American people do not come dressed in a single costume, speaking in a single voice. So the leadership of any particular agency has to sort things out, that is, has to figure out what sort of relationship it will have with the various sets of people it encounters.

It is fairly easy for most agencies to figure out how to relate to the first three of these sets of people. The pull of shared knowledge, politics, and a sense of community says, "Work with them in a close and cooperative manner, and good things will happen."

Clientele groups—organized groups representing the people most directly and substantially affected by an agency's policies—bring political intelligence and "practical" experience, and agencies need both. Of course, clientele groups need to know what agencies are planning and even need to know the latest in agency research, so the information flow is definitely going both ways. In addition, agencies need power and legitimacy, and clientele groups can provide both. They can provide power because of their connections to the congressional subcommittees with so much influence over every aspect of an agency's activities, and they can provide legitimacy because they are the people who know and care the most about the policies in question. Clientele groups, of course, want/need to exercise influence over the decisions these agencies make, since those decisions affect their lives in what they see as such a direct and substantial way. So, once more, both sides are benefiting from a close and cooperative relationship. Finally, there is a real sense of community that develops between agencies and their clientele groups as they spend years working together and eventually begin to identify closely with one another. There are, as we said, exceptions to this agency/clientele group pattern of cooperation, exceptions we find in areas of social service administration, and in some areas of regulation, namely, those characterized by regulation of more than one industry, with no economic promotion mandate, concentrating on questions involving the health and/or safety of workers or the general public, and largely conducted by subject-matter professionals.

Agencies generally establish much the same sort of close working relationship with the organizations of professionals active in their particular field of expertise as they do with clientele groups. These associations also bring a sort of political intelligence—what sort of reaction there will be in the professional community to a particular agency initiative—and the very latest in expert thinking in the field. In turn, they walk away knowing how their ideas have fit into the world of policy making as well as what sort of research is being conducted by their agencies. Once more, these associations can add an increment of power and legitimacy to that which comes to an agency from its clientele groups. The source of that power and legitimacy is the credibility that comes from the support of supposedly neutral experts, and while it certainly won't carry the day if it is ever pitted against the raw political power of clientele groups, it can be a big help to an agency, especially when the agency's own policy specialists try to justify their decisions, to outsiders and to themselves. The associations have the satisfaction of seeing their expertise respected in policy debates and even get a few goodies for themselves. Finally, the sense of community that develops in the agency/professional association relationship is often more powerful than the sense of community in the agency/clientele relationship. After all, it doesn't feel like it might be tainted by politics. It is shared knowledge, shared values, and years of working together.

Finally, an agency may find that certain individuals have established reputations as significant experts in that agency's field, and once more, a close working relationship is likely to develop. It displays the same dimensions as the relationship between agencies and professional associations, with the sometimes important addition of the star power of some of these experts. In a world in which credibility is often driven almost as much by personality as by knowledge, star power can be a real asset, for the expert himself or herself and for the agency he or she is supporting.

But the public doesn't always come in the guise of agency supporter. Sometimes it comes as agency critic. Then the relationship changes dramatically. Critics think they bring more knowledge to the table than any other participant, but agencies don't—can't—agree. Beyond that, these critics often have some political power, but they are rarely a match for an agency's normal supporters, particularly not if the battle can be confined to the usual subcommittee arenas. Finally, no sense of community is going to develop between two groups of people who see the world so very differently. But these critical groups are not going away, so agencies have to figure out what sort of relationship to establish with them.

Contentious accommodation seems to work well for both sides. A loud public fight gives each side some of what it wants, that is, visibility and solidarity with its supporters. The fight also allows each to believe it is fighting for what it is supposed to be fighting for. Once the fight is over, it is necessary, again for both sides, that the critics win some of these battles. Some, but not too many. From the agency perspective, losing too many would mean not fighting hard enough for the common values that bind that agency to its clientele and professional supporters, but winning them all would mean that they were not the independent experts they believe themselves to be. From the critical group perspective, never winning would mean they were nothing but Don Quixote–like characters tilting at so many bureaucratic windmills, but winning too many would mean having gone soft, having lost the edge that makes them society's true watchdogs. So the fight is always on, the results almost always predictable.

Finally, there may be no general public, but as a nation we have talked so long and so hard and so often about the general public interest that no agency could possibly step forward and say, "We've thought about it and there is no general public interest, so we are going to take care of our supporters and their interests." Caught between the reality of knowing that the general public really isn't out there in a form in which its interests can be recognized and acted on, and the rhetoric of the need to find that general public interest and pursue it, agencies need an answer, and the answer seems to lie in two places. To a small degree, it lies in giving some credence to the fact that everybody who does communicate with them claims to be representing "the public interest." To a much larger degree, however, the answer to their dilemma lies in creating a decision-making system that gives every possible appearance of being as open as possible and which gives supporters—and critics, if grudgingly—a chance to bring their public-interest rhetoric to the table and express it. Lots of advisory committees, tons of paper during the public comment period, and public hearings can go a long way toward convincing agency policy specialists that they have done what they could to seek out, understand, and protect the public interest.

Some of the influence exercised by supporters, as well as some of the influence exercised by critics, is exercised indirectly. Power at the subcommittee level can be used to capture the attention of the agencies under that subcommittee's jurisdiction. Power at the White House can also be used, of course, but power at the White House is harder to come by and, in the end, harder to use.

But indirect influence can never be the whole story. Anyone who really wants to exercise influence over a particular agency has to work directly with that agency. Indirect influence, by definition, comes through politicians, and that always leaves it open to suspicion, especially to suspicion among the agency policy specialists. So clientele groups that may have a long and successful history of working with a particular subcommittee still have to take seats on advisory committees, submit written comments on proposed rules, and testify at public hearings. Knowledge has to be brought back into the policy-making picture, and the decision-making process has to at least appear to be more open and unbiased than the process we normally find at the level of a congressional subcommittee.

In the end, the problem is not that agencies of the federal government are captured and held against their will by a cabal of interest groups, professional associations, and individual experts. The problem is not even that those agencies are willing co-conspirators with the other three in a shell game in which they all try to hide the pea from the general public. What we face instead is a set of people, agencies and their supporters who have come to see the world in such similar ways that the policies they agree on seem the natural product of the best available minds applying the best available knowledge—including political knowledge—to the process of governing ourselves in a complex world.

NOTES

1. Francis E. Rourke, *Bureaucracy, Politics, and Public Policy*, 2nd ed. (Boston: Little, Brown, 1976), 46.

2. Herbert Kaufman, *The Administrative Behavior of Federal Bureau Chiefs* (Washington, D.C.: Brookings Institution, 1981), 69–70.

3. Kaufman, *The Administrative Behavior of Federal Bureau Chiefs*, 68.

4. Kaufman, *The Administrative Behavior of Federal Bureau Chiefs*, 70.

5. *Washington Information Directory* (Washington, D.C.: Congressional Quarterly, 1995), 645.

6. *Washington Information Directory*, 644.

7. Kaufman, *The Administrative Behavior of Federal Bureau Chiefs*, 47.

8. Rourke, *Bureaucracy, Politics, and Public Policy*, 44.

9. For a longer version of this discussion, see Dennis D. Riley, *Controlling the Federal Bureaucracy* (Philadelphia: Temple University Press, 1987), 104–106. Also see the works cited in the chapter (ch. 4) of which that discussion is a part.

10. Aaron Wildavsky, *The Politics of the Budgetary Process* (Boston: Little, Brown, 1964), 53–54. Wildavsky left that quote as is in every edition of the book. In fact, it is on pp. 53–54 in every edition.

11. The year 1914 saw the passage of the Federal Trade Commission Act and the establishment of the Federal Trade Commission, an agency responsible for guaranteeing fair trade practices, and 1970 saw the passage of the Occupational Safety and Health Act and the creation of the Occupational Safety and Health Administration.

12. *Moss v. Civil Aeronautics Board* 430 F2d 891 (1970).

13. Marver H. Bernstein, *Regulating Business by Independent Commission* (Princeton, N.J.: Princeton University Press, 1955).

14. Louis Kohlmeier, *The Regulators: Watchdog Agencies and the Public Interest* (New York: Harper and Row, 1969), 105–128.

15. *Motor Vehicle Manufacturers of the United States v. State Farm Mutual Automobile Insurance Company* 463 U.S. 29 (1983).

16. If you want to read more about this, see Dennis D. Riley, *Public Personnel Administration*, 2nd ed. (New York: Longman, 2002), 186–188.

17. Steven Kelman, "Occupational Safety and Health Administration," in *The Politics of Regulation*, ed. James Q. Wilson (New York: Basic Books, 1980), 251.

18. Susan J. Tolchin and Martin Tolchin, *Dismantling America: The Rush to Deregulate* (New York: Oxford University Press, 1983), ch. 6.

19. Kaufman, *The Administrative Behavior of Federal Bureau Chiefs*, 68.

20. Herbert Kaufman, *The Forest Ranger* (Baltimore: Johns Hopkins University Press, 1960).

21. The Rourke quote, of course, comes from Rourke, *Bureaucracy, Politics, and Public Policy*, 46. Mosher's comes from Frederick C. Mosher, *Democracy and the Public Service*, 2nd ed. (New York: Oxford University Press, 1982), 128.

22. *Washington Information Directory*, 642.

23. *Washington Information Directory*, 643.

24. *Washington Information Directory*, 643.

25. Dennis S. Ippolito and Thomas G. Walker, *Political Parties, Interest Groups and Public Policy: Group Influence in American Politics* (Englewood Cliffs, N.J.: Prentice-Hall, 1980), 373–374.

26. That quote, of course, is the one from Frederick Mosher that appeared in the first paragraph of this section. See note 21, above.

27. That was here, of course, or I wouldn't know anything about it. Jay has since retired, and I'm not sure what he is doing, but he remained a force in forest policy long after his twenty-five-year career at the Forest Service ended.

28. Kaufman, *The Administrative Behavior of Federal Bureau Chiefs*, 151.

29. Kaufman, *The Administrative Behavior of Federal Bureau Chiefs*, 69.

30. Kaufman, *The Administrative Behavior of Federal Bureau Chiefs*, 69–71.

31. Riley, *Controlling the Federal Bureaucracy*, 117–120.

32. Kaufman, *The Administrative Behavior of Federal Bureau Chiefs*, 76.

33. Quoted in Harold Seidman, *Politics, Position, and Power*, 3rd ed. (New York: Oxford University Press, 1980), 284.

34. See, for example, Kaufman, *The Administrative Behavior of Federal Bureau Chiefs*, especially pp. 68–69.

35. This is found in section 556 of the Administrative Procedure Act as amended. You can find it in the back of any administrative law textbook.

36. Theodore J. Lowi, "How the Farmers Get What They Want," in *Legislative Politics U.S.A.*, 3rd ed., ed. Theodore J. Lowi and Randall B. Ripley (Boston: Little, Brown, 1973), 187.

37. Phillip O. Foss, *Politics and Grass* (Seattle: University of Washington Press, 1960).

8

Bureaucracy and the Law

Sworn to Uphold

We've talked about the individual policy specialists and political executives, the perspectives they bring to their respective roles in the bureaucratic decision-making process, and how those perspectives would shape that process should either set of individuals gain the upper hand. We've talked about organizational structure and how it affects how and how much the policy specialists and the political executives can leave their respective marks on what government does about the problems these men and women have been asked to solve. We've talked about how the nature of the policy area in which a particular agency operates helps to structure the political environment its people must contend with as they gather and use information. We've talked about how the President, the Congress, and the people become part of an agency's political environment, and how they work to try to shape that agency's organizational, budgetary, and legal environments in the hope of influencing its policy choices.

But there is far more to an agency's legal environment than we have talked about up to now. Specifically, there is the ultimate law of the land, the Constitution. Beyond that, there is something called administrative law, a complex body of law that tells agencies how they ought to structure their decision-making processes in the hope that those processes can better help us achieve the goals of responsiveness, respect for the rights of individuals, and accountability. Then there is the law of individual and governmental liability, the law that says that government and its officers, like corporations and their officers, can be held to account for harm that they do to individual citizens. Finally, there is the law that contains the promise that an agency is struggling to keep. Where there is law, of course, there are courts to help figure out exactly what that law means and to make sure that it is obeyed. Citizens routinely ask courts to rule on the constitutionality, legality, or simply the wisdom of what agencies have done, and courts are willing to do so. Some of the time. That, however, is the subject of the next chapter.

So let's be off to the Constitution and how it becomes an important part of the legal environment of every agency of government.

EVERYONE SWEARS TO UPHOLD THE CONSTITUTION

The Constitution doesn't mention the Federal Aviation Administration. It doesn't mention the Fish and Wildlife Service, the Occupational Safety and Health Administration, or the Food and Drug Administration either. But every official at each of those agencies—and at all of the rest, of course—knows that he or she must live within the boundaries established by that Constitution. Even if very few of them can say with great confidence that the Fourth Amendment says "The right of the people to be secure in their persons, houses, papers, and effects against unreasonable searches and seizures shall not be infringed," or that the Fifth says "No person . . . shall be deprived of life, liberty, or property without due process of law," and even if even fewer can cite the most recent Supreme Court ruling on either the Fourth or Fifth Amendments, they do respect their obligation to the document that establishes our governing system and defines our rights as citizens.

Agency Information Gathering and the Fourth Amendment

Agencies need information. The Occupational Safety and Health Administration can't be sure that the Harley Davidson plant in Tomahawk, Wisconsin, is properly protecting the health and safety of its workers without looking at a lot of records compiled by the plant's management. For that matter, OSHA can't be sure that Harley Davidson is protecting those workers if it doesn't look at the plant itself. Similarly, the Food and Drug Administration can't be sure that Eli Lilly's latest entry into the anti-cholesterol drug market is safe and effective without a careful examination of all of the company's research testing the drug, nor can it be sure that that drug remains safe and effective without an equally careful examination of the plants at which Lilly produces and packages it. The list could go on. The point would remain the same. Every agency needs access to information, and an awful lot of that information is in the hands of individual citizens and corporations. But, as we know, individual citizens and corporations believe that much of the information they possess is theirs, that is, is something that they share only with those they wish to share it with. That list, it turns out, doesn't always include the government. That's why we have the Fourth Amendment, with its guarantee against "unreasonable searches and seizures," and even though the amendment was drafted with the sheriff and the tax collector in mind, there can be no doubt that American citizens—and especially American businesses—very much want those words to apply to anyone who wears a government hat, even if that hat looks nothing like the hat on the Sheriff of Nottingham.

If you expect to open a small business—or to become the CEO of a very very large business—one of these days, rest assured that OSHA is bound by the Fourth Amendment and its protection against unreasonable searches and seizures. So are the Environmental Protection Agency, the Food and Drug Administration, the Federal Aviation Administration, and the Wages and Hours Division of the Employment Standards Administration. The Fourth Amendment applies to administrative searches all right, but it applies in a very different way than it applies to traditional law enforcement searches. To be specific, administrators are on a far longer Fourth Amendment leash than are police. First we need to talk about why. Then we'll look at how.

Why Do We Lengthen That Fourth Amendment Leash for Administrators?

To understand why we have concluded that it is safe to allow administrators to conduct their information-gathering activities under a far looser set of Fourth Amendment–driven restrictions than those that govern the information gathering of their counterparts in traditional law enforcement agencies, we have to go back to the purposes of the Fourth Amendment itself. Those purposes are three.

First, we are concerned that corrupt or more likely simply overzealous law enforcement officials will be tempted to plant evidence. That's why the amendment itself tells us that: "no [search] warrants shall issue, but upon probable cause, supported by Oath or affirmation, and particularly describing the place to be searched and the persons or things to be seized." If police have to convince a judge that a specific item is a piece of evidence in a crime and that there is a strong probability that that item is located in a particular place, they will simply have fewer opportunities to bring their own evidence with them in order to increase their chances of a conviction and rid the community of some sort of "menace."

Second, the Fourth Amendment is designed to protect privacy. Our homes, the things we own, and we ourselves are off limits to government intrusion unless that government can make a pretty good case that we have done something that warrants such an intrusion.

Finally, the Fourth Amendment tries to strike a balance between the need to protect the individual from arbitrary government action and the need to protect the society from individuals who refuse to play by the rules of that society. When the Fourth Amendment tells us that we are to be secure against unreasonable searches and seizures, it obviously implies that some searches are reasonable and government can, by definition, conduct those reasonable searches as part of its obligation to protect some citizens from others. Likewise, when the amendment talks of warrants and the need to make sure that those warrants are issued only if probable cause has been established and if the warrant itself is limited in scope, it is saying as clearly as it can that government is going to have to be allowed to search the "persons, houses, papers, and effects" of its citizens if it is to guarantee the protection of the law to all of those citizens, but that its right to search must be carefully circumscribed lest it abuse that right and in the process oppress an individual citizen in the name of some vague protection of the needs of all citizens.

In the light of these three purposes, the courts have consistently concluded that administrative searches are fundamentally different from traditional law enforcement searches. Specifically, they have said that when compared with police searches, administrative searches present far less danger of planted evidence, constitute far less of a threat to individual privacy, and take place in a context in which we can tip the Fourth Amendment balancing act in favor of society without much risk of doing irreparable damage to the lives of those who must now subject themselves to a search. Let's look at each of these in more detail.

It is generally assumed that administrators have both less motivation and less opportunity to plant evidence than do police officers. Even police who escape the so-called "streetsweeper mentality" that pervades many big-city departments can, and do, see it as their jobs to get certain kinds of people off the streets, and must be tempted at times to cut corners just a little bit to make it happen. Would it really be such a miscarriage of justice to find a murder weapon in one place and then somehow "find" it again right where it fits your theory of the crime, especially if you had plenty of other evidence pointing to a particular individual? It is hard to imagine someone from the Employment Standards Administration's Wage and Hour Division going over the pay records of the Stevens Point, Wisconsin, Pizza Hut determined to find that one entry that will "get that crook out of this community." Beyond motivation, of course, is opportunity. Finding a bloody knife and then finding it again where you really wanted it to be is a whole lot easier than constructing a fake set of pay records for Pizza Hut, or a fake set of maintenance records for Alaska Airways, let alone hauling an unsafe piece of machinery into a Ford plant, or generating an unsafe level of noise on the floor of a tire factory. In short, it seems reasonable enough to conclude that when it comes to planted evidence, we have far less to fear from administrators than from police officers.

Reassuring as it is to think we have little reason to fear administrators planting evidence, far more central to our decision to place fewer restrictions on administrative than on police searches is the fact that administrative searches just don't seem to threaten our privacy in the way that police searches do. It's a matter of who does the searching—and of where they search.

Obviously not every police officer is Clint Eastwood, and not every OSHA inspector is Woody Allen. But a police officer coming to search may be in a uniform, and even if he or she is not, the officer is almost certainly carrying a loaded gun that he or she is trained and prepared to use, wearing—or carrying—a badge, and quite clearly capable of using force if the situation demands it. No matter how often we were told as little kids that police officers are our friends, there is a certain amount of intimidation that goes along with their presence. In a sense, it is supposed to be that way. An OSHA inspector—or FDA inspector, or Wages and Hours inspector, or any other kind of inspector—on the other hand, is not in uniform, carries identification that looks like a driver's license, is definitely not armed, and even if he looks like Superman or she looks like Wonderwoman, you know that their training did not include practice on how to "subdue a suspect." I don't mean to make light of this. It is just a very different experience to be confronted by a police officer or two asking for a chance to look around and an OSHA inspector or two asking exactly the same question. The difference, of course, is the fear factor, and we believe that that fear factor ought to count for something in deciding what sort of restrictions should be placed on the process of "looking around."

Even more important to the question of privacy than who looks, of course, is the question of where they look. Police officers search all sorts of places, but they often want to search your home, your car, or even your person. For most of us, it doesn't get much more private than that, or if you prefer more judicial language, it is there that you have the highest expectation of privacy. Administrators, on the other hand, generally search far less private places. Most, in fact, search places of business during business hours. How much privacy do the owners—or, for that matter, the plant manager—of the Harley plant up in Tomahawk expect on the floor where dozens of people lovingly assemble America's own motorcycle? More to the point, how much privacy do they have a right to expect, and how much ought we to recognize? Some, to be sure, but most of us would agree that we ought to recognize a great deal less than we recognize for that Harley plant manager's house or, for that matter, the saddlebags on his or her own classic hog.

Finally, the Fourth Amendment is a balancing act between the society's need for order and safety, and the individual's right to freedom and privacy. There are some important differences between the typical police search and the typical administrative search, it turns out, that allow us to put a great deal of emphasis on the former without feeling we have done much real damage to the latter.

First of all, as I noted a moment ago, there is a lot less privacy to be threatened in the typical administrative search than in the typical police search. Less intimidating people are conducting a search in what is essentially a public place.

Second, in the typical administrative search there is almost no chance of "fingering" the wrong person. When an OSHA inspector shows up at the Harley plant in Tomahawk—or Golden County Foods or the Del Monte processing plant here in Stevens Point—he or she has no idea if a crime has been committed. But if he or she discovers that some sort of crime—violation would likely be the term of choice—has been committed, it is clear enough who is the "guilty party." Responsibility lies with the owners.

Third, administrators have a much easier time than police protecting society from the "criminal element" each is responsible for controlling. If police are trying to catch a serial rapist and they have some leads—say a police artist's sketch and a physical description of the rapist and a set of victims who had something obvious in common—how are they to protect society while they gather the evidence they need? They cannot arrest everyone who matches up with their sketch/description of the rapist, nor can they put everyone who meets the profile of the victims into protective custody. On the other hand, an administrator can take quick and decisive protective action. Consider the situation of a restaurant inspector. If, on a routine inspection, he or she discovers practices that would lead to *e-coli* bacteria finding their way into the food that is to be served, he or she simply shuts the place down, trains the staff how to prevent the problem, allows the restaurant to reopen, and then inspects more often until he or she feels confident the problem really is solved. Would most of us feel sorry for the restaurant owner? Would most of us feel sorry for all of the men arrested so that the rapist might be caught? How about the women detained?

Finally, think about the penalties likely to be meted out to those cited by administrators versus those likely to be meted out to those arrested by police. You can get a good head start just by comparing the word *cited* with the word *arrested*. Clearly, the owner of a small restaurant cited for violations of the sanitation rules, particularly if those violations had led to an *e-coli* outbreak, might suffer serious economic consequences. But most of the time, administrators work first to help businesses fix the problem at hand, and when that fails, the penalties are almost always economic and almost always levied against the business and not against the individual. If a police search turns up evidence of a crime, the penalties are nearly always individual and they involve far more than money. In the end, we judge the consequences of a mistake to be so much greater if that mistake is made by the police than if it is made by an administrator.

In sum, administrators don't seem to constitute much of a threat to plant evidence to try to nail that _____. They don't generally think in those kinds of terms, and anyway, the opportunities to plant evidence seem to be drastically limited by the nature of their jobs. Beyond that, administrators don't seem to generate much of a threat to privacy. They normally aren't that frightening to begin with, but more to the point, they almost never search places that most of us really consider private. Now add in the fact that administrators are most unlikely to accuse the wrong person of a crime, that they can protect society from "their criminals" with relatively unobtrusive measures, and that the punishments that flow out of the violations they discover rarely rise to the level of those routinely associated with those discovered by police, and you can begin to see why the courts would be so consistent in saying that the Fourth Amendment needs to apply to administrators as well as to police, but that allowing that amendment to apply to administrators in a very different—much looser—way than it does to police can be said to protect society with little, if any, damage to the rights of that society's individual members.

How Do We Lengthen the Fourth Amendment Leash for Administrators?

It is, of course, the courts that decide exactly how long that Fourth Amendment leash will be, and as always, the courts make the many decisions that cumulate into "that" decision, one case at a time. That, in turn, means that there are dozens, perhaps hundreds, of ways that the administrator's Fourth Amendment leash is different from/longer than that of the police officer. But this isn't a constitutional law text, or even a text on the Constitution and the world of administration. So we will confine ourselves to the two most obvious and important ways in which the courts have given administrators an expansive notion of what it means to conduct a reasonable search.

First of all, the courts have made it much easier for administrators than for police officers to obtain the warrants necessary to search the places they want to search. Administrators must obtain warrants. That was decided once and for all in *See v. Seattle* and *Camara v. Municipal Court of San Francisco* in 1967.[1] But in both of those cases, and even more forcefully in striking down the warrant-less search provisions that Congress had included in the Occupational Safety and Health Act, the Supreme Court told administrators that they would not be held to the strict requirements imposed on police requests for search warrants by the Fourth Amendment. Specifically, in *Marshall v. Barlow's*, the Supreme Court told administrators that they could obtain search warrants so long as the search they wanted to conduct was (1) authorized by statute; (2) consistent with legislative standards and goals; (3) the selection of this establishment was based in some general administrative plan needed to enforce the law; and (4) carried out at the business named in the warrant.[2] That's a step or two removed from probable cause that a crime has been committed and that evidence of that crime is in a particular place.

Second, there is the question of searching without a warrant. Police officers can do so if they see the crime being committed (the plain view doctrine), if they see what they believe will be evidence while they are executing a legal arrest warrant, or if they see what they believe will be evidence within arm's length of an individual they have legally detained. There are other such exceptions, but you get the idea. The courts tailor the exceptions to fit circumstances in which a warrant would almost certainly be obtainable, but obtaining it would be more than a little impractical. Administrators, too, have the power to search without warrants, but in their case that power tends to be a little more wide open. Specifically, in a series of decisions beginning in 1970, the courts have held that businesses or industries with a history of "close" or "pervasive" regulation can be searched without the need for a warrant. This string of cases began when the Court upheld the right of agents of the Bureau of Alcohol, Tobacco, and Firearms (BATF) to conduct a warrantless search of the Colonnade Catering Corporation.[3] Colonnade, it seems, sold liquor, and Congress had granted BATF the authority to conduct warrantless searches of liquor establishments. The Court upheld that authority, "because the liquor business had historically been a heavily regulated industry in order 'to meet the evils at hand.' "[4] Over the next two decades the courts held that a business selling guns, operating a stone quarry, selling used auto parts, or racing horses also had to accept the fact that the administrators who regulated their respective industries had the right to search their businesses without first obtaining a warrant.[5] The Third Circuit Court of Appeals carried the pervasively regulated industries doctrine a step further in 1986 when it held that the New Jersey Racing Commission had not violated the Fourth Amendment search and seizure provisions by requiring random breath and urine tests for jockeys. As a result, legendary jockey Willie Shoemaker can find his name in administrative law textbooks as well as in every book ever written about the sport of horse racing.[6]

Administrators don't get a pass when it comes to the Fourth Amendment. If they want to search, they are expected to get a warrant. But administrators can get such warrants far more easily than can police officers. If the administrator can demonstrate that the search is authorized by Congress and is part of a routine administrative plan, the warrant is almost certain to be issued. Beyond that, businesses and industries with a history of close regulation can be searched without a warrant. That's a very different set of rules than those we impose on traditional law enforcement officers when they want to look for evidence of a crime. But, as we saw earlier, that's a deliberate and justifiable choice. We put administrators on a longer Fourth Amendment leash because we are just less afraid that they are going to bite.

Administrative Information Gathering and the Fifth Amendment

When trying to find out what Americans are up to, administrators may not get a pass on the Fourth Amendment, but they get what comes perilously close to a pass on the Fifth.[7] The Fifth contains a provision that is famous to people of my generation—born 1943—as we learned about it in the 1950s when "organized crime figures" took the Fifth to avoid answering the questions of Senator Estes

Kefauver and his committee, and Senator Joseph McCarthy coined the term "Fifth Amendment Communists" to refer to people who wouldn't answer his. The Fifth has many provisions, of course. The one in play here is the provision that states that "[no person] shall be compelled in any criminal case to be a witness against himself." With respect to that provision, the courts have adopted a number of rules that give administrators a pretty free hand when it comes to asking Americans to hand over pieces of paper that very well might, in the words of all those people I saw on television in the Kefauver and McCarthy hearings, "tend to incriminate me."

First of all, the Court has consistently rejected the notion of Fifth Amendment protections for corporations, partnerships, and associations.[8] Their records have been fair game to administrative inspection since 1906, and those records remain fair game even if they might incriminate specific individuals and even if the penalties specified in the law are to be imposed on the individual and not the corporation.

Second, ever since 1948 and the case of *Shapiro v. United States*, the Court has informed individuals engaged in businesses they own and run themselves that if the government requires them to keep certain records and if inspection of those records is necessary to carrying out the law, then no Fifth Amendment privilege protects those records.[9] In 1990 that same reasoning was applied to a Baltimore woman receiving payments under the then existing program called Aid to Families with Dependent Children (AFDC). The Baltimore City Department of Social Services suspected that her child was being abused, and as a consequence asked the woman to produce the child. Their argument: the child was a record that the woman was required to keep and surrender for inspection. The Court agreed.[10]

Third, of considerable importance to businesses of all sizes, the Court decided in *Fisher v. United States* that records in someone else's possession are not protected by the Fifth Amendment.[11] In *Fisher* the records were accountants' working papers which had been subpoenaed by the Internal Revenue Service from Fisher's accountants, transferred to his lawyers, and then subpoenaed again. They still had to be produced. In *Matter of Grand Jury Empaneled*, the Third Circuit held that Marion DeMato, bookkeeper and office manager for a business owned and operated by one man, Mr. Dominick Coluccio, had to produce Mr. Coluccio's records precisely because they were in her possession rather than his.[12] They were, it seems, in a safe in the company office, and Ms. DeMato had a key. Finally, in *United States v. Payner*, Mr. Payner's records were actually lifted from the briefcase of a Swiss banker who was traveling in the Bahamas.[13] The district and circuit courts had concluded that the act of stealing the records was so egregious that it could not be condoned, even given the general principle that records in someone else's possession did not receive Fifth Amendment protections. The Supreme Court disagreed.

Last, in 1976, the Court held in *Andresen v. Maryland* that records found during a legal search could be used despite the fact that they obviously incriminated a particular individual.[14] There was a good bit of scholarly criticism of the decision, and both Justices William Brennan and Thurgood Marshall produced stinging dissents.[15] Brennan was particularly unhappy, arguing that the Court was abandoning sound reasoning from its own past in holding, first, that there was a difference between a subpoena for incriminating records (unacceptable under the Fifth Amendment) and finding those same records in the context of a legal search (now acceptable), and second, that the fact that the search was legitimate under the Fourth Amendment made using the records legitimate under the Fifth. A majority of his colleagues disagreed, and Mr. Andresen's records became evidence in the proceedings against him.

In the end, the words of the Fifth Amendment haven't changed. No one is to be compelled to be a witness against himself or herself in a criminal proceeding. But "compelled" has been interpreted to mean forced to take an action, and that interpretation of the amendment has played a significant role in most of the decisions cited above. Perhaps more to the point, administrators deal mostly with businesses, and when it comes to the Fifth Amendment self-incrimination provision, we can almost certainly take our lead from the title of Professor Kenneth Warren's section on that subject in his leading text *Administrative Law in the Political System*. That title: "Toward the Virtual Elimination of the Fifth's Privilege Against Self-Incrimination for Business."[16]

A Note on the Exclusionary Rule

Everyone who is involved in enforcing the law, whether they do it in uniform with badge and gun, or in khaki pants and blue shirt with picture ID and clipboard, swears to uphold the Constitution. That means that they swear not to conduct unreasonable searches and seizures and not to compel anyone to be a witness against himself or herself in any criminal proceeding. We believe that the honesty and integrity of the vast majority of those law enforcers will lead them to make every effort to keep that promise. But we are not willing to entrust our Fourth and Fifth Amendment protections to that honesty and integrity alone. Rather we feel that we need some external reinforcement for those internal virtues, and probably more to the point, a way to make sure that these rights are protected from law enforcers when they aren't protected by them.

For much of the twentieth century, that extra incentive to law enforcers and protection for citizens was provided by something called the exclusionary rule. Put as simply as I can, evidence that a judge concluded had been obtained illegally—in an unreasonable search or as a result of compulsion of an individual to provide incriminating information—was excluded from the trial. Such a rule, it was assumed, would convince everyone in law enforcement to play by the Fourth and Fifth Amendment rules or risk losing key evidence and with it any chance of a successful prosecution. Beyond that, of course, we are far more secure against unreasonable searches and seizures if the results of those searches and seizures can't be used in any proceeding against us.

When it comes to the activities of administrators, however, the exclusionary rule is all but dead.[17] As noted earlier, the Court refused to exclude evidence the Internal Revenue Service had obtained by hiring someone to steal a briefcase from a Swiss banker, and it affirmed that ruling a decade later, concluding that a search conducted by Labor Department officials was clearly illegal, and then refusing to exclude the evidence obtained in that search anyway.[18] Then, in 1994, the Sixth

Circuit Court of Appeals refused to exclude evidence obtained against Trinity Industries by the Occupational Safety and Health Administration (OSHA) in a search conducted, in the words of Kenneth Warren, "without probable cause and in clear violation of the requirements for administrative inspections as set forth in Barlow's."[19] In fact, the Court not only admitted the search was conducted outside the rules it had laid down in *Barlow's*, but it also stated that OSHA inspections aimed at gathering evidence for the purpose of setting penalties were subject to the exclusionary rule, and it rejected OSHA's defense of its evidence.[20] Yet, as I noted a moment ago, the justices still refused to exclude the evidence. Their reason: the inspectors acted in "good faith."

In short, there is still something called the exclusionary rule. But if you are an administrator or, perhaps more important, the subject of an administrative proceeding, it is indeed "difficult to imagine when the . . . rule would apply."[21]

The Fifth and Fourteenth Amendments and Due Process of Law: Protection From Arbitrary Government

Americans fear administrators using information even more than they fear administrators gathering it. Frightening as it might be to learn that inspectors from the Occupational Safety and Health Administration are coming on Thursday to determine if the noise levels in your foundry pose a threat to the hearing of the men and women who work for you, it would be far more frightening to learn the following Tuesday that the inspectors had indeed determined that those noise levels do pose such a threat and that the agency feels compelled to "do something about it." That's why Americans who might well be pretty much ambivalent about the Fourth Amendment protection against unreasonable searches and seizures, or the Fifth Amendment protection against self-incrimination, are more than a little happy to know that the Fifth Amendment guarantees that no person "may be deprived of life, liberty or property without due process of law."

The due process clause, like the Fourth Amendment provision against unreasonable searches, or the Fifth Amendment prohibition against compelling someone to be a witness against himself or herself, is put into play one government decision at a time. If OSHA feels it needs to "do something" about the noise level in your factory, it will have to do that "something" in accordance with a prescribed set of rules, a set of rules that will have to pass the constitutional test of due process. At least OSHA will have to operate within a set of rules that meets the due process test if its decision will deprive you of life, liberty, or property. In other words, the question of administrative due process is really two questions. When is a citizen entitled to due process, and what process is he or she due? Enter the courts and their effort to define life, liberty, property, and due process of law.

When Is Due Process Due? Defining Life, Liberty, and Property

A full discussion of the efforts of the courts to come to some agreement on the meaning of the words life, liberty, and property in the context of the Fifth Amendment is beyond the scope of this book. I don't think you need it, and I'm pretty sure I can't provide it. But you do need enough of a flavor of what the courts have said to give you a feel for what administrators face when they try to figure out if the procedures they are using will pass constitutional muster, and that I can provide.

When it comes to life, the courts have been pretty consistent. It means life. It does not mean the quality of life, the meaning of life, the joy of life, or anything else. It means life, and there is very little that most government agencies can do to threaten one's life without going through the elaborate procedures of our criminal justice system, procedures we have long concluded meet the due process test.

Things get a bit trickier when we enter the realm of liberty, however. Once more, there's not much disagreement that at a minimum liberty means—in court parlance one has a liberty interest in—remaining free of physical restraint. But most of us think of liberty as encompassing more than just staying out of jail, and the Supreme Court endorsed that common-sense notion in 1923 when it held that liberty included "the right to enjoy those privileges long recognized at common law as essential to the orderly pursuit of happiness by free men."[22]

The Court didn't exactly provide a laundry list of "those privileges long recognized," but it was clear enough from the discussion that the justices felt that any such list would certainly include activities like entering into contracts, obtaining credit, or finding a job. While none of those activities—nor many of the rest one might put on such a list—depends directly on an individual's reputation in his or her community, the bulk of the litigation involving administrative threats to liberty interests has in fact revolved around the impact of agency decisions on the reputation of the individual in question.

Citizen challenges to government actions that have threatened or even harmed their reputations have ranged from the 1950s effort to force the Justice Department to adopt procedures for putting the names of organizations on the infamous Attorney General's list of "communist organizations," to a Wisconsin woman's challenge to an obscure statute that had permitted a county sheriff to post in all establishments selling liquor the names of individuals whose drinking had brought "want and deprivation" upon their families. Those two efforts were successful.[23] Not so successful were the efforts of a man whose name and picture were circulated by a county sheriff in his list of "active shoplifters," despite the fact that all shoplifting charges against him had been dropped, or those of two police officers fired from their jobs with no statement of reasons who believed they would never again find work in law enforcement with such a blot on their reputations.[24]

In short, liberty means more than freedom from physical restraint. Just exactly what more depends.

For most citizens, it isn't life or liberty they are worried about, however. It is property. The courts have long recognized a common-law notion of property that might be loosely defined as anything tangible or intangible, in your possession, that you paid for or that someone might be willing to pay you for.[25] Agencies have to walk softly whenever they might be about to step on that kind of property. Revived interest in the next clause of the Fifth Amendment, the so-called takings clause, provides agencies with incentive to soften their footsteps even more if they so much as come near this kind of property.

But there is another kind of property that government might deprive someone of. For most of us, one suspects, the most important piece of property we have is whatever generates the income that allows us to own what little traditional property we have managed to accumulate. A job, a license, an entitlement check, any one of these can form the basis of a person's relationship with the world of property, and it would be a pretty frightening thing to learn that government could threaten any or all of those without being subject to the due process restrictions of the Fifth and Fourteenth Amendments. Though it would clearly be a stretch to argue that the man who authored the Fifth Amendment intended its due process clause to guarantee a formal hearing to someone denied disability benefits by the Social Security Administration, consider these words of James Madison published in the *Philadelphia Gazette* in the summer of 1792: "That is not a just government, nor is property secure under it, where arbitrary restrictions, exemptions, and monopolies deny to part of its citizens that free use of their faculties and free choice of their occupations which not only constitute their property in the general sense of the word, but are the means of acquiring property strictly so called."

Over the last half-century, Americans have asked the courts to stretch the notion of property interests deserving of due process protections pretty far. Quite often, the courts have obliged. In 1970 the Supreme Court triggered what some have characterized as an administrative due process litigation explosion when it held in *Goldberg v. Kelly* that individuals receiving cash assistance payments under the old Aid to Families with Dependent Children (AFDC) program had a property interest in those payments sufficient to trigger due process protections.[26] Six years later, in *Mathews v. Eldridge*, the Court affirmed the status of entitlement payments—this time disability payments under the Social Security Act—as property interests entitled to due process protections. That same year (1976) the Supreme Court held that a public employee has a protected property interest in his or her job, provided that there exists a statutory provision that creates "an enforceable expectation of continued public employment."[27] Three years later, the Court required due process protections for a fifteen-day suspension of a horse trainer's license.[28] By the end of the decade of the 1970s, the Supreme Court had concluded that students facing a ten-day suspension from school for disciplinary reasons deserved due process, as did citizens of Memphis, Tennessee, about to have service by a city-owned utility terminated.[29] In 1980, however, the Court held that the forced relocation of nursing home residents did not trigger due process protections.[30]

Generalizations are hard to come by in the world of administrative due process, but this much we do know. The courts have held that life means life and that liberty means more than just staying out of jail, though how much more remains unclear. They have also held that property means what it has meant for centuries, plus government employment, entitlements, and licenses, provided the men and women on the bench at that particular moment can be convinced that some statute has made a particular job, a particular entitlement, or a particular license into a protected interest. We might like a little more certainty than that, but as long as individual citizens challenge the decisions of specific administrators in specific courts, it is pretty hard to see how we are going to get it.

What Process Is Due? A Fair Chance to Be Heard

By definition, due process is a matter of procedure. So when a citizen files a due process challenge, he or she isn't saying that the challenged action itself was unconstitutional, only that the way in which it was done was unconstitutional. Perhaps more to the point, that citizen challenge has to say what it was about the process of making that particular decision that made that process constitutionally deficient. Individual citizens have offered a rather remarkable variety of reasons for concluding that their government has not accorded them the kind of decision-making process that the Constitution demanded, but most seem to have centered around the notion of a hearing, that is, some sort of proceeding at which those affected by a decision have an opportunity to present their views on the decision, listen to the views of others—and challenge those views if they feel they are wrong—and then have the decision made by an impartial decision maker based on the arguments and evidence presented to him or her by all those interested enough to participate in the decision-making process.

The initial question in such cases, of course, is whether or not a hearing is required at all. This question was put to the Court as far back as 1915, and in an oft-cited opinion by Justice Oliver Wendell Holmes, the Court held that a hearing was required to meet the due process test only if the decision in question affected a relatively small number of people in specific and significant ways. No such hearing was required if a decision affected large numbers of people more or less equally.[31]

Even if citizen and agency agree that due process requires a hearing in a particular context, we still have to face the question of what sort of proceeding meets the definition of a hearing. Indeed, time after time, the question put before the courts in administrative due process cases was not was a hearing required, but was this a hearing? Or, more properly, was this a fair hearing?

There isn't time—or need—to go into every nook and cranny to see the remarkable variety of proceedings that agencies call hearings and the equally remarkable set of responses elicited from the courts by citizen challenges to these self-described hearing procedures. If we did, we would find the previously mentioned Supreme Court ruling that students could not be suspended from high school for ten days without a hearing sitting right alongside the Court's decision that an after-the-fact tort suit—a lawsuit asking for money damages—was hearing enough for Florida school students subjected to paddling as a form of discipline.[32] The list could go on for pages, and the inconsistencies—real and apparent—would pile up. As I noted a moment ago, and as we shall see in much more detail in the next chapter, the Court does its business case by case, and that means that it must seek to resolve a particular dispute in a fair and equitable manner even as it tries to guide bureaucrats toward some reasonable notion of due process. Even though a search of the administrative due process closet might be unnecessary—though thoroughly entertaining—we should look at two key cases from the 1970s—the already mentioned *Goldberg v. Kelly* and *Mathews v. Eldridge*—to get a feel for the guidance the Supreme Court has provided administrators making a good faith effort to provide citizens with a fair hearing without paralyzing their own operations.

As I noted in the previous section, the Supreme Court's 1970 decision in *Goldberg v. Kelly* set off what the late Circuit Judge Henry Friendly called a "due process explosion."[33] The issue to be decided was simple enough. Ms. Kelly had seen her payments under the AFDC program terminated by the city of New York. Under the city's rules, she was entitled to a hearing on the accuracy of that eligibility determination, but that hearing was to occur after the termination had taken place. Ms. Kelly sued, claiming the hearing should have been held prior to the termination of benefits rather than after. The Court agreed. But in the agreeing, Justice William Brennan laid out a set of ten ingredients that he thought should be present in a fair hearing. Specifically he argued that a fair hearing would require the following:

1. Timely and adequate notice
2. Oral presentation of argument
3. Oral presentation of evidence
4. Confronting adverse witnesses
5. Cross examination of adverse witnesses
6. Disclosure of opposing evidence
7. Right to an attorney
8. Determination on the record
9. Statement of reasons and summary of evidence
10. Impartial decision maker

These ten ingredients subsequently came to be known as the Goldberg Rules, and the Goldberg Rules set off the chain reaction that Judge Friendly described as the "due process explosion." The extent of that explosion can be seen in two numbers reported in Professor Jerry Mashaw's excellent *Due Process in the Administrative State*.[34] First, as Mashaw discovered, during the 1970s due process litigation rose by an astounding 350 percent, five times the increase in litigation overall during that same decade.[35] Second, from *Goldberg v. Kelly* (1970) to the soon-to-be discussed *Mathews v. Eldridge* (1976), the Supreme Court found in favor of 56 percent of all administrative due process claimants.[36]

By the middle of the 1970s, however, some on the Supreme Court felt that administrators were being pushed too far by the Goldberg Rules, and they looked for what they considered a more balanced approach to administrative due process. Their case came in 1976. The case itself, the aforementioned *Mathews v. Eldridge*, was, like *Goldberg v. Kelly*, about the timing of a hearing that an agency agreed it was obligated to hold. This time the Court told Mr. Eldridge that a hearing after the checks were stopped was sufficient to meet the due process test. More to the point, Justice Lewis F. Powell and those who joined him—not surprisingly that did not include Justice Brennan—told administrators and lower courts that in answering questions about administrative due process, they should engage in a deliberate balancing act. On the one side of the scale would sit the public's interest in efficient and effective government. That would normally manifest itself in the forms of time and money, but it could include other ingredients in specific circumstances.

On the other side, of course, was the interest asserted by the individual citizen. What sort of liberty or property interest was at stake here, and how much did this particular citizen have to lose? Then Justice Powell added two more questions to the judicial mix. First, what was the risk that current procedures would produce "an erroneous deprivation of the interest in question"? Second, what is the probability that stricter procedures—specifically the particular procedural change being sought by the complaining citizen—would produce a "better decision."[37] The Eldridge decision had an immediate and significant impact on administrative due process litigation. Remember the 56 percent victory rate for due process claimants that Professor Mashaw found between 1970 and 1976? That rate was cut in half between 1976 and 1980.[38]

Goldberg and *Eldridge* still provide the major guidance for administrators deciding on what it means to guarantee due process to the citizens whose fate those administrators decide and to the judges who are called upon to review the decisions those administrators reach. It is hard not to sympathize with Justice Powell's concern for effective and efficient government, and it is easy enough to wonder why we ought to spend more time and more money when the chances of reaching a more informed decision go up by a minuscule amount. But it is equally hard to look at Justice Brennan's definition of a fair hearing contained in the Goldberg Rules and decide which ones you would be willing to sacrifice if you had something important on the line. The natural administrative sympathy may be for Justice Powell's concern for resources spent for only the tiniest improvement in the decision-making process. The natural judicial sympathy may be for the model of fairness that most closely resembles the one that prevails in the courtroom. Maybe political ideology and/or personal experience may enter the equation as well. Whatever combination of factors drives a particular administrator's definition of due process or a particular judge's response to that administrator's definition, it sometimes seems as if we aren't called upon to do a balancing act in making these decisions so much as we are called upon to do a high wire act. Worse, it isn't always all that easy to see the net.

In Summary

Though it may come as a bit of a shock to many of them immersed in their daily routines, administrators do make decisions that could deprive an individual citizen of life, liberty, or property. If and when they do, they must do so while granting that citizen something we call due process. In some settings due process does not require the chance for something we have come to call a hearing, but in most settings in which agencies decide about the conduct of specific individuals or businesses, some sort of hearing is required. The Supreme Court has been quite flexible about what constitutes a hearing, and since the 1976 case of *Mathews v. Eldridge*, it has instructed us to look not just at our desire for fairer procedures, but at the likely impact of those seemingly fairer procedures. Don't make the rules for making decisions better if doing so won't make the decisions themselves better. There has been some criticism of that focus on what might be called the technical side of the decision. Robert Framton and Jerry Mashaw both wondered if such an emphasis didn't give short shrift to the goal of democratic acceptability in decision-making processes.[39] Still, the guidelines for administrators remain those of *Mathews*, with a bit of the Goldberg Rules thrown in by those administrators who feel that if one is going to err in a due process decision, it is best to err on the side of the individual citizen.

EVERYONE SWEARS TO UPHOLD THE LAW

There is no such thing as THE LAW, of course, so administrators swear to uphold the laws. Three sets of laws, to be precise.

First come what we call enabling statutes, the laws that empower an agency to make sure that the food supply is safe, that endangered species survive, that air travel is safe, or that the cholesterol drug I take is safe and effective. Second comes the body of law we lump together and call administrative law. An amalgam of statutes, executive orders, court decisions, and agency- and department-level rule writing, administrative law is our way of trying to bring the notions of responsiveness, respect for the rights of individuals, and accountability into the bureaucratic decision-making arena. Finally, there is liability law. Almost sixty years ago, we decided that our government would be far more accountable to us as citizens if it had to answer for the negligent actions of its officials in precisely the way that private businesses had to answer for the negligent actions of theirs. The result was the Tort Claims Act of 1946 and what can almost certainly be labeled a revolution in the legal relationship between the government and its individual citizens.

Let's look at these three types of laws in turn.

Enabling Statutes

In one sense, there is very little that can be said about the impact of enabling statutes on agency decision making. Such statutes are, by definition, agency, or even program, specific. Subtitle VII of Title 49 of the U.S. Code lays out some pretty ambitious goals for the Federal Aviation Administration (FAA). It also gives the FAA some substantial powers to use in trying to achieve those goals. Still, a careful study of how Subtitle VII of Title 49 affects decision processes and outcomes at the FAA wouldn't necessarily tell us much about how Title 15, Chapter 9, of that same U.S. Code affects the operations of the National Weather Service, or how Title 16 of that same chapter affects policy making at the National Marine Fisheries Service. In more straightforward terms, enabling statutes are specific, detailed, and focused on a single agency or program, and on that level best viewed through the medium of the case study.

In another sense, however, there is much that can be said about the impact of enabling statutes on agency decision making. In that other sense, of course, that is the subject of this book. It is an agency's enabling statute that makes the promise or promises that that agency is expected to keep. In that sense, everything that agency does, all of its information gathering, all of its sharing of information, all of its rule writing, and all of its rule enforcement, are shaped and guided by that enabling statute. Or, more properly, those things are shaped and guided by an agency's interpretation of that enabling statute. As we saw in earlier chapters, when it is trying to figure out exactly what its enabling statute empowers it to do in a given situation, it will get plenty of help. The President—through political executives at the agency or at the department in which the agency is housed—will offer his or her interpretations, as will the committees of Congress with jurisdiction over that agency's programs and budgets. As we will see in the next chapter, the courts will offer their interpretations, as a three-judge panel of the District of Columbia Circuit did to the Environmental Protection Agency (EPA) just before Christmas 2003, telling the agency that its interpretation of the new source review provision of the Clean Air Act was suspect enough that it could not be put into effect just then.[40] Finally, as we will see in the very next section of this chapter, the rules imposed on an agency's decision-making processes by administrative law even give citizens an opportunity to offer some help in figuring out what that agency's enabling statute obligates, forbids, or permits it to do.

So, in one sense, there isn't much that can be said, while in the other, there is a book that can be written. Either way, that is all that can—or needs to—be said in this section. So let's get on to administrative law.

Administrative Law

Our trip through the world of administrative law will not, I'm afraid, be a short one. We need to examine three pretty important questions, and the discussion of each is going to take some time. But it is time well spent, since the rules of administrative law apply to almost every agency of government, and maybe even more important, the rules of administrative law represent our way of trying to plant the seeds of responsiveness, respect for individual rights, and accountability in soil that isn't always the most hospitable.

We'll start with a quick look at why and when we need administrative law. Then we'll revisit the question of why, trying to frame that why in a way that allows us to spell out the types of rules that ought to guide administrative decision making. Once that is done, we will go on to look at the current state of administrative law, that is, what sorts of procedures do we demand of our decision makers.

Why and When Do We Need Procedures?

As I noted above, the general answer to the question of why we need procedures centers on our goal of self-government through representative institutions. Bureaucracy may not be a representative institution, but it is an inevitable part of modern government and we want it, too, to honor the values of responsiveness and respect for individual rights, and to be accountable to us. We believe that administrative law will help us to accomplish that in two interrelated ways.

First, when we impose decision-making rules on bureaucrats, it reminds them of the power they hold, and even more, of our concern for how they use that power. In effect, we remind them that they aren't so much governing us as governing for us. There is a good chance that bureaucrats reminded of our interest in what they do and how they do it will take that interest to heart. Bureaucrats, too, remember, have some sense of the obligation that goes along with the power they hold.

Second, and probably more to the point, formal procedures almost inevitably mean a paper trail. That can be important in two interrelated ways. To begin with, a paper trail acts a little like the great American journalist H. L. Mencken's concept of conscience, that is, that little voice inside that says, "Somebody might be watching." When you are told to create and keep pieces of paper, you are reminded that someday somebody might read them. Beyond that, it is the paper trail that procedures demand that will become the basis for the after-the-fact review that is the process for achieving accountability. The more pieces of paper we demand, and the more detailed those pieces of paper have to be, the easier time we will have figuring out what was done and why. It was no coincidence that it was during the unraveling of the Iran-Contra scandal in the mid-1980s that Oliver North made the paper shredder famous.

Given the immense importance we attach to the values of responsiveness, respect for the rights of individuals, and accountability, it is tempting to conclude that the answer to the question of when we need formal procedures to guide bureaucratic decision making is simple. Always. As it turns out, however, always isn't a very good answer. Three reasons: time, money, and flexibility.

Following procedures slows things down. It is supposed to. Procedures are supposed to force administrators to think more, to hear from more people, to consider more options, and to justify what they have done to outsiders. Noble things all, but if administrators do them, it will delay whatever decision they have to make. That delay, of course, like any delay, protects the status quo and, consequently, advances the interests of those who benefit from that status quo at the expense of those who desire change.

Following procedures also costs money. In part that's a function of delay. Time may not be money, but it does cost money. Specifically, staff time spent making sure procedures are followed is staff time that cannot be spent on the substance of a decision. That means either more staff—and money—to cover both the procedural and substantive aspects of a decision or, every bit as likely, the same staff trying to cover both the procedural and substantive bases and not doing either one as well as they would hope. We have pretty elaborate procedures here on campus for curriculum revision and especially for personnel decisions. Back when I was department chair, I saw my efforts to make sure those procedures were followed to the letter detract from my primary efforts to see that my students learn something.

Finally, following procedures inhibits flexibility and creativity in approaching problems. Again, in some sense that's a desired result. "Flexible" is at least a cousin to "arbitrary," and "creative" some sort of relative of "idiosyncratic." Still, when procedures become routines, it can be frustratingly easy to forget why we created the procedures in the first place. It is precisely this tendency that gives rise to the public frustration with bureaucratic "red tape," and that moved the great political scientist Wallace Sayre more than fifty years ago to refer to personnel administration as "the triumph of technique over purpose."[41]

If the answer to the question of when we need procedures is sometimes, we need to be able to figure out when those times are. That we do by looking at two things.

First, we look at stakes. What does the individual—or the society—have on the line as this decision is being made? The higher the stakes involved in a decision, the more we worry about accountability and the values of responsiveness and respect for individual rights, and the less we worry about cost, delay, or lack of flexibility. Consequently, the higher the stakes, the greater the need for strict procedures. Compare our procedures for deciding that someone must die for a crime he or she committed with our procedures for deciding if someone gets a license to drive a motor vehicle.

Second, we follow the lead of Justice Powell in *Eldridge* and look at the probability that stricter procedures will produce a better—more informed or more responsible—decision. If we conclude that that probability is high, then the time and money spent to implement stricter procedures is thought to be time and money well spent. If we conclude that that probability is low, we presume that that time and money would be better spent elsewhere.

We do look at both of these, but they are definitely not considered of equal importance in the decision as to whether we need to impose procedures. Stakes are always the more important of the two considerations. This is very clear in Justice Powell's opinion in *Mathews v. Eldridge*. Even as he was establishing this second criterion of the probability of improving the decision, Powell was careful to point out the importance of the stakes involved for the individual subject to the government decision. Eldridge had argued that, under the *Goldberg* decision, he, like Ms. Kelly, was entitled to a hearing before rather than after payments had been cut off. In informing Mr. Eldridge that his contention was wrong, Justice Powell distinguished between the decision to terminate disability payments and AFDC payments, concluding precisely that the latter was a higher-stakes decision requiring different procedures.

Defining Responsiveness, Respect for Individual Rights, and Accountability in the World of Administrative Decision Making

It is time to get specific about what a bureaucratic decision-making process that is responsive, respectful of individual rights, and accountable would look like. First, it would guarantee a meaningful opportunity for citizen input and influence. Second, it would guarantee that we could conduct an after-the-fact accounting of a decision by making sure that we can determine how and why that decision was made. Let's start with the guarantee of citizen input and influence.

Participation and Influence

No government can make a very convincing case that it is a responsive government if it doesn't provide its citizens with meaningful opportunities to participate in and exercise influence over that government's decision-making processes. At a minimum, providing citizens with such opportunities is going to require government to do two interrelated things.

First, government is going to have to make citizens aware that decisions are being made and how to participate in the process of making them. Usually referred to by the legal term "notice," this effort to make citizens aware of decisions soon to be made and how they might participate in making those decisions is an absolutely essential part of creating a responsive government. On one level, notice is a pretty mundane business. Citizens can participate only if they know when and where their participation can take place. But notice has to go to a second level to be meaningful. It has to give the citizen enough information about what the government is thinking of doing, and why, to make it possible for that citizen—or group of citizens—to prepare a case for or against that decision. To grasp the importance of notice, consider a simple personal example: the final exam in a course you are taking. You can't have much of an effect on your grade in that course if nobody tells you the date, time, and place of the final exam. Of course, you can't have much of an impact on that grade, either, if you have no idea of the content of the exam. I once walked into a final exam for my Introduction to American Politics course with a Public Personnel Administration final in my hand. Not a single student would have had a chance if I had handed that out instead of racing back to my office to get the right exam. Not a single student would have considered me a fair instructor—or anything else printable in a textbook—if I had just handed out that exam and wished them all good luck. Students who want to influence their grades in a course are entitled to an exam based on that course, in a room and at a time they have been told about beforehand. Citizens who want to influence a government decision are entitled to know that decision is going to be made and how they can weigh in on it.

A meaningful opportunity for participation and influence starts with notice, but it certainly doesn't end there. A citizen must also have a chance to speak his or her piece, and even more to the point, a guarantee that that piece will be heard and taken seriously. That, in turn, means three things.

First, it means a chance to present evidence. The presentation may be oral or written or both. The point is that any interested citizen gets a chance to submit whatever pieces of information he or she believes ought to be the basis for this particular government decision.

Second, it means a chance to counter evidence presented by others. This, too, can be done orally, in writing, or both, though it can become a cumbersome and time-consuming process if done in writing, as documents have to travel back and forth and citizens have to be given ample time to prepare their responses to the evidence submitted by other citizens. It will be difficult to do at times, but without the opportunity to, in the words of the Administrative Procedure Act, "submit rebuttal evidence, and to conduct such cross-examination as may be required for a full and true disclosure of the facts" it is hard to see how a citizen can feel that he or she had been given a real opportunity to influence a government decision.[42]

Finally, all of this oral and written punching and counterpunching has to take place in what citizens agree is a neutral arena, that is, in a place governed by agreed upon and publicized rules that guarantee a chance to be heard by someone who is actually listening and who will make his or her decision based upon the evidence presented and in accordance with those agreed-upon rules.

Accountability

Much as we might like to hope that opportunities for participation and influence will be taken advantage of by a wide range of citizens, our experience seems to suggest otherwise. That's why accountability is so important. Even if we don't participate much, the knowledge that we can ask for "a look at the books" at any time should help to remind bureaucrats of their obligations to the values that underlie our system of self-government. And, even if it doesn't, the very existence of after-the-fact accountability mechanisms mean that sometimes those mechanisms will be used, and that, too, should keep bureaucrats more aware of those obligations. After-the-fact accountability is not a perfect substitute for active citizen participation, but it is a whole lot easier to make happen.

The first key ingredient in accountability, as I noted a couple of pages back, is a paper trail. There is no better way—quite likely no other way—to reconstruct what happened and figure out who did what and how and why they did it. But figuring out what happened, or even who made it happen and why, is not the end of the accountability trail. We also want to evaluate what happened, that is, to decide if it was legal, constitutional, or on occasion, even if it was wise, and that means we have to have some sort of standard to apply to what was done to determine if it was what ought to have been done in that situation. As we saw in earlier chapters, if the accountability mechanism is political, then there is no real standard by which actions are to be judged, save whatever standard the politician in question cares to apply and/or whatever standard those who must return that politician to power wish to apply to his or her efforts to hold the bureaucracy accountable. But this is a chapter about rules and procedures and legal accountability, and that means a standard that judges are to apply when it becomes their turn to hold bureaucrats to account. Such standards do in fact exist, but it is best to postpone discussion of them until we consider the process of judicial review of administrative decision making in the next chapter.

What Kind of Procedures

As I'm sure you sensed when I was talking about when we require procedures, we do not have a generic, one-size-fits-all, procedural model. So once we have decided that procedures are needed in a particular decision-making setting, we still need to decide precisely what sorts of procedures we need. To understand how that decision is reached, we need to consider who makes the decision, the criteria on which that decision is generally based, and what sorts of procedural models those decision makers have to choose from. Let's start with the last of these.

Procedural Models

Administrative law scholars generally think in terms of two basic procedural models, one grounded in how decisions are presumed to be made in a legislative body, the other grounded in how decisions are presumed to be made in court. But it is important to note that these same scholars point out that these truly are models, that is, ways of categorizing and conceptualizing a messy reality. In a very real sense, these models represent opposite ends of a continuum of procedural formality. Every bit as important, we don't really impose either of these models in its entirety but, rather, push an agency toward one end or the other of the continuum based on factors we'll be discussing shortly.

The two models—or two ends of the procedural continuum—differ in four key respects. (1) Are there specific rules about what can be considered evidence in the decision-making process? (2) Does any citizen or group of citizens have what might be termed participation rights in the decision-making process? (3) Must the decision maker provide a written justification for the decision he or she has reached? (4) What is the mechanism by which a citizen or group of citizens can appeal the decision?

Looking first at the question of what can legitimately be considered evidence, legislators and judges find themselves in totally different worlds. A member of any legislative body can cite as the reason for his or her decision a scientific study, an ideological principle, a party platform, or a passage from holy scripture. A judge, on the other hand, must work within strict rules of evidence—an entire law school course worth at a minimum—including the all-important rule that all evidence must be submitted in such a way that those who question its validity have an opportunity to try to refute it.

When it comes to the rights of specific citizens to participate in the decision-making process under well-known rules, legislators and judges again operate in different decision-making galaxies. Legislators hold hearings, but those citizens allowed to participate—testify—are those selected by the legislators holding the hearing, and the rules for testimony are those the committee has adopted. On top of that, often as not the chair of that committee has discretion in implementing those rules that would make the average judge blush. Judges conduct trials, and certain individuals must be permitted to testify as well as to counter other testimony, and the rules for all of this citizen give and take are well known to all of the participants well ahead of time. There is discretion in applying those rules, but it is discretion bounded by commonly accepted judicial norms and, in theory anyway, subject to monitoring by other judges.

As to the third question above, no legislator is compelled to write down the reasons for his or her decision on any matter of public policy. A judge handing out a driver's license suspension may not be required to do so either, but the judge mind-set tells him or her that a written justification should be possible, and for the kinds of judicial decisions we are talking about in this and the subsequent chapter, a written justification is in fact a requirement.

Finally, short of trying to get an act of Congress declared unconstitutional, the appeal of any sort of legislative decision is exclusively political. In the end, if you were unhappy with Don Young's (R-AK) stewardship of the nation's environment while he chaired the House Resources Committee during the 1990s, you had to convince his Republican colleagues to oust him from that chairmanship or his Alaska constituents to throw him out of Congress. A judge's decision, however, can be appealed to another court and another set of judges. To be sure, you can run out of judges. But if you lose at the federal district court level, there are two levels to go, and every federal district judge knows that. He or she also has a pretty good idea of the criteria by which his or her decision will be judged at that next level, and that knowledge may well play a role in the lower court judge's decision-making process.

Remember my earlier caution. These are models, best thought of as representing the ends of a continuum of procedural formality. But they remain useful because they describe what we are going to tell bureaucrats to do. That is, we are going to say, adopt the legislative model—really a bureaucratic model grounded in that legislative model—or else adopt a judicial—judicially grounded—model and go about the business of deciding what you are supposed to decide within the confines of that model.

Criteria for Choosing a Procedural Model

When deciding whether to tell bureaucrats to assume they are legislators or judges, four considerations come into play. First we look at the type of decision being made. Bureaucrats, recall, do several different types of things, but chief among them are writing rules and deciding specific cases.

When bureaucrats write rules, the output they produce is very much like the output of a legislature. It speaks to the future and to general categories of people. Just as the Congress said through the Occupational Safety and Health Act that after July 1, 1971, no employer could subject any employee to "unsafe working conditions," so the Occupational Safety and Health Administration said through its cotton-dust rule that after January 1, 1979, no textile mill would be permitted to expose employees to concentrations of cotton dust beyond a specified level. Indeed, as I have suggested over and over, the law has little meaning without the subsequent rule, and if a textile mill is going to be penalized for violating the Occupational Safety and Health Act, it will almost certainly be one of OSHA's rules that will have tripped it up. On the other hand, when bureaucrats decide specific cases, the output is very much like that of a court. It speaks to past conduct and very likely to the past conduct of a particular individual or business firm. OSHA's decision that General Motors violated the rule about reporting work days lost to accidents looks remarkably like a federal district court's decision that GM had cheated its Oldsmobile customers when it told them they were buying cars with Oldsmobile engines when those cars were really equipped with Chevrolet engines. The fines looked a lot alike, too, though in the latter case GM also had to compensate the disgruntled customers. OSHA and the workers it was trying to protect didn't get any extra money.

The logical thing for us to do, of course, is to match outcomes with procedures, that is, legislative procedures with legislative outcomes and judicial procedures with judicial outcomes. That is precisely what we have tried to do in the Administrative Procedure Act and in the myriad of agency-generated procedural manuals. Even the courts have tried to maintain that outcome/procedure match when they have been called upon to rule on citizen complaints about agency procedures.

There are times, however, when we believe that the procedure/outcome match would not serve us well. To be specific, there are two such times, one extremely important, one far less so.

The important one, of course, comes when we conclude that the stakes involved in a particular decision—category of decisions really—are very high. Recall our earlier discussion of the importance of stakes in deciding whether or not procedures would be used at all. I feel confident that you picked up on the fact that the judicial model imposes far more restrictions on bureaucratic discretion than does the legislative model, and the higher the stakes in a particular decision or set of decisions, the more we want to limit bureaucratic discretion. These restrictions or limitations on bureaucratic discretion are simply our way of buying more participation and especially more accountability. When the stakes are high and we want more of both of those, we require judicial procedures even if the outcome of the decision or decision category in question is legislative.

The less important time in which we might question the normal rule of matching procedures to outcomes arises when an agency has to make a high volume of judicial decisions that would appear to most observers to be low-stakes decisions. Then, rather than spend the time and money required by judicial procedures, we would permit an agency to use the less restrictive legislative procedures or, more likely, procedures designed by the agency itself. The United States Grain Standards Act, for example, empowers the Department of Agriculture to license grain inspectors. It is also empowered, of course, to remove those licenses. When it does, it is not required to follow judicial procedures, though such a decision would seem to be judicial in nature, that is, individual, specific, and related to the judgment of past conduct against a standard derived from the law.[43] Apparently in the eyes of those who decide such things, there are simply too many grain inspectors and too little at stake for each one of them to treat the decision to take away a license from any one of them as a decision requiring a court-like proceeding.

Finally, there is Justice Powell and his exhortation to look at the probability that stricter procedures will improve the decision. This consideration will come into play, particularly if a citizen challenges the procedures under which a decision was reached. But it is impossible to generalize about the impact it will have on those who design procedures, precisely because it is applied one procedural requirement at a time.

In sum, bureaucrats write rules and make judgments, and we will match procedures and outcomes—legislative procedures for rules, judicial for judgments—unless there seems to be some compelling reason not to. High stakes would be the most compelling reason, and we might well impose judicial procedures on a rule-making action if we thought the stakes reached a high enough level. A high volume of decisions might cause us to opt for legislative procedures even though the decisions in question were clearly judgments. Stakes would enter here, too, as we would never abandon judicial procedures for decisions we believed to be truly high-stakes decisions. Finally, we are cognizant of Justice Powell's concern for the impact of procedures, but it is much harder to factor into the equation when it comes to deciding what sorts of procedures to require.

Who Decides Which Procedures?

Someone has to decide what sorts of procedures a particular agency must follow in making a particular category of decisions, and I can't imagine it will come as any surprise to any of you that all three branches of the constitutional government have some say in making those procedural decisions. It isn't any more likely to surprise you that bureaucrats themselves often write their own procedures.

Congress

Congress gets the first opportunity to determine what sorts of procedures an agency must follow, since it is Congress, of course, that has authorized the agency to make the decisions the procedures will apply to. Congress will generally speak to the question of what sort of procedures an agency must follow in one of three ways.

First, there is the possibility of silence. Congress just leaves it up to the bureaucrats to decide how to do whatever it is that they have been told to do. You might suspect that Congress would be reluctant to empower agencies to do much of anything without imposing some set of procedural restrictions on how it was to be done, but it is actually a fairly common occurrence. Paul Verkuil, for example, examined forty-two separate programs in his now-famous study of informal adjudication in the federal government. He found those forty-two programs in only four cabinet departments, and none of the forty-two operated under any congressionally imposed guidelines.[44]

Second, Congress may act to "trigger" the Administrative Procedure Act (APA), that is, to tell an agency that it must make its decisions in accordance with one or the other of the major procedural models contained in that statute. We will take a comprehensive look at APA-mandated procedures shortly, so just file that notion of an "APA trigger" in the back of your mind until then.

Finally, Congress can do a little custom designing of procedures. Back in the 1970s, for example, the Consumer Product Safety Commission (CPSC) was told not to write its own safety rules but to in essence contract the job out. The commission would decide which areas (products) needed new safety rules and then advertise for someone—an "offeror" was the term Congress used in the statute— to write the rule. Offerors themselves operated under some restrictions—mostly telling them whom they had to let participate—and the CPSC had a final up or down vote on the rule, but the dirty work was done outside the commission walls.[45]

The President

Presidents can get in on the procedure ordering act, too. They are in on it by virtue of their power to sign legislation, of course, but they can also get in through the route of the Executive Order.

It is hard to imagine a President deciding to veto a piece of legislation because he or she is unhappy with the procedures that Congress has spelled out for operating the program or programs contained in that particular law. It could happen, but it hardly seems likely. As we saw in chapter 5, however, presidential efforts to change how bureaucrats do things, particularly how they write rules, have a twenty-five-year history. Presidents don't get program- or agency-specific in these efforts, but rather tend to aim at the whole rule-writing business, as Ronald Reagan did with so much fanfare in 1982 and 1985, and as George H. W. Bush and Bill Clinton did in 1989 and 1993 respectively.[46] George W. Bush seems to have paid less attention to the rules for making rules than he has to the rules themselves. At least he has paid close attention to the rules coming out of the Environmental Protection Agency, as we saw back in chapter 5. While presidential motivations are more likely to stem from a desire to enhance their own influence in the rule-making process or, as in the case of President Reagan, a sincere desire to stop the regulatory state in its tracks, than from some hope for increased citizen opportunity or bureaucratic accountability, they have had some definite impact on how agencies write rules. That impact might best be characterized as considerable in specific instances, but not so considerable overall. In more straightforward terms, some specific interests got what they wanted in their dealings with specific agencies, but the process of rule writing has gone on much as before at most agencies on most issues.[47]

The Courts

The courts, too, can become involved in dictating to bureaucrats the procedures they must follow when making decisions. As we will see in the next chapter, this involvement must take the form of deciding a specific case that has resulted from a specific citizen's challenge to the procedures an agency is currently using. Such challenges will generally follow one of two tracks.

In the first place, a citizen might claim that an agency has followed procedures that violate the Administrative Procedure Act, or even violate the procedural provisions of the agency's own authorizing statute. Beyond that, of course, as we saw earlier in the chapter, a citizen might complain that an agency is using decision-making procedures that violate the Constitution. The most common of such challenges are, as we saw, grounded in the due process clauses of the Fifth and Fourteenth Amendments, but agency procedures could run afoul of the equal protection clauses of those amendments as well.

Agencies Themselves

Finally, agencies often design their own procedures. Think back to Paul Verkuil's study of informal adjudication in four departments. Congress had not specified procedures for a single one of the forty-two programs Verkuil studied, yet he found that only two had no written procedures at all. In stark contrast, Professor Verkuil found that two of these programs had imposed on themselves the full set of procedural requirements suggested by Justice Brennan in *Goldberg v. Kelly*, and another four programs had decided on their own to provide nine of the ten *Goldberg* ingredients.[48]

Bureaucrats write procedures even when not required to, for both noble and not-so-noble reasons. On the noble side, procedures help agencies to achieve a certain consistency in decision making, and they probably give the people who deal with those agencies at least a measure of confidence in their decisions, knowing that those decisions were made in accordance with specified procedures. On the not-so-noble side, however, procedures provide cover when an agency is sued and provide a way to say no. One rarely feels the need to cite a rule while saying yes.

In Summary

There will be times when the delay, the cost, and the loss of flexibility and creativity in the decision-making process that are the inevitable costs of setting up rules for making decisions will tell us that we don't want procedures at all. But there will also be times when those costs will deter us not one bit. When that happens, that is, when we know we do want procedures, we still have to ask ourselves what kind of procedures. To be specific, do we want the strict, highly formal procedures we associate with a courtroom, or the looser, less formal procedures we associate with a legislature? Sometimes one, sometimes the other, of course, but how do we decide which we want in a particular situation?

Most of the time we want to match the procedures with the output, that is, to make sure that if the outcome is a rule, we use legislative procedures, and if the outcome is an adjudication, we use judicial procedures. We do that unless. We do it unless the stakes convince us that even though the product is a rule, the administrators making that rule ought to be held to the higher accountability standards of judges. We also do it unless we feel that the number of decisions to be made is so great that we could collapse the system by requiring judicial procedures. And we match procedures and outcomes unless it is one of those rare occasions on which the courts conclude that the stricter procedural requirements of the judicial model will so improve the decision-making process that they must be imposed, even if they are being imposed in a rule-making setting.

Finally, we have to confront the question of who decides what sort of procedures will be followed by a particular agency in deciding a particular set of questions. Congress gets the first opportunity when it authorizes an agency to make this particular set of decisions, and it usually takes that opportunity. But bureaucrats themselves are not far behind, and judges are waiting around, prepared to tell both the legislators and the administrators that they have not done enough, or even that what they have done is just plain wrong. The President may even put his or her stamp on the procedures agencies follow. In most cases, the procedures finally used to make a particular type of decision will bear at least some of the stamp of the Congress, of the administrators of the agency called upon to make the decisions, and of the courts who may some day review them. There may even be trace elements of presidential directives.

The Administrative Procedure Act

Congress first passed the Administrative Procedure Act in 1946 out of a grudging recognition that the administrative state that had grown up out of the New Deal and World War II didn't seem too likely to disappear. The act has been amended numerous times since, including a major new provision passed in 1990 creating a process called negotiated rule making.[49]

The act establishes two very different sets of decision-making procedures that more or less correspond to the legislative and judicial models discussed earlier in this chapter. The conclusion that we ought to match procedures and outcomes prevailed in the initial drafting of the statute—actually, it has never really been abandoned in the APA itself—so it contains a set of procedures for rule making (Section 553) that is clearly close to the legislative end of the legislative–judicial continuum, and a set of procedures for adjudications (Section 554) very close to the judicial end. It also contains two additional sections (556 and 557) laying out the rules for conducting hearings if Congress requires them.

From the beginning, however, the APA has recognized the possibility of making rules under the stricter judicially grounded procedures of sections 556 and 557.
Subsection c of Section 553 specifically states that Sections 556 and 557 apply
"when rules are required by statute to be made on the record after opportunity
for an agency hearing." Professor Kenneth Warren has concluded that Congress
has chosen to require "formal rule making" very rarely, and a number of highly
regarded administrative law scholars have argued that it has been an almost un-
mitigated disaster every time it has been tried.[50] Still, the APA leaves the door
open to formal rule making, so we must be aware that there will be a handful
of occasions on which the "rules for making rules" won't apply to the making
of a rule. More to the point for our purposes, because the door to formal rule
making remains open—even if Congress only rarely pushes an agency through
it—I think it is best to structure the discussion of the APA not around the rule-
making adjudication distinction, but around the on-the-record, not-on-the-record
distinction.

Decision Making on the Record

Think back for a moment to our discussion of what we want from administrative
law. We want a meaningful opportunity for citizens to participate and have some
influence in the decision making process, and we want to make sure that the
officials involved in that process can be held to account for their actions. What
do the rules have to say about opportunity and accountability when Congress
exercises its power to demand that a particular decision be made "on the record
after opportunity for an agency hearing"?

Opportunity: Opportunity, we said, requires notice and a neutral forum for
citizen participation, a forum with well-known rules that give citizens a fair
chance to make a case—and to have that case heard—as well as a chance to
counter evidence and argument submitted by others, including the government
itself. Let's work on these two in reverse order.

The forum for participation, of course, is a hearing. The hearing will be conducted under the rules spelled out in Section 556 of the Administrative Procedure
Act, and those rules go a long way toward guaranteeing a neutral forum with
plenty of opportunity for citizen input and influence. First of all, 556 states that
"A party is entitled to present his case or defense by oral or documentary evidence,
to submit rebuttal evidence, and to conduct such cross-examination as may be
required for a full and true disclosure of the facts." There will be an occasional
contest over just how much cross-examination is required for a "full and true
disclosure of the facts," but overall it is pretty clear that a citizen interested in
influencing the outcome of an on-the-record decision has a serious opportunity
to be heard. Beyond that, Section 556 also makes a serious effort to eliminate the
two most serious threats to the neutrality of a decision-making process, namely,
ex-parte contacts and decision makers who are not impartial. *Ex-parte* contacts
are communications between interested parties and decision makers that are not
revealed to all interested parties, and they are strictly forbidden in on-the-record
decision making. There are all sorts of ways a decision maker can be less than
impartial, and Section 556 doesn't speak to all of them, but it speaks to the most

important, and more to the point, it guarantees a decision based exclusively on the record compiled at the hearing, so a decision maker who isn't exactly impartial is tied to a particular set of facts that leave only so much room for maneuver.

When it comes to notice, the situation is a bit more complicated. To be more precise, there is a difference between an on-the-record adjudication and an on-the-record rule making.

In an on-the-record adjudication, Section 554 of the Administrative Procedure Act requires that decision makers inform the public of "the legal authority and jurisdiction under which the hearing is to be held, and the matters of fact and law asserted." This provision has generally been interpreted to mean that an agency has to provide all of the information it has collected to this point, plus a detailed interpretation of its statutory authority to conduct the proceeding in question. A citizen who wants to support or oppose a particular adjudication should have from that notice all the information needed to prepare his or her arguments.

In an on-the-record rule-making proceeding, however, the notice rules of Section 553 apply, and those rules require decision makers to provide "reference to the legal authority under which the rule is proposed; and either the terms or substance of the proposed rule or a description of the subjects and issues involved." That provision, in turn, has been interpreted to give decision makers a lot of leeway in exactly what they put in the notice that a hearing is to be held. They have to cite the statute that gives them the authority to write the rule in question, but they don't have to provide a detailed interpretation of that statute. Perhaps more to the point, agency decision makers are not required to provide citizens with all of the information they have collected so far. They have to describe the issues and subjects involved, or even provide a rough draft of the rule, but that's not the same as laying out all of the information that has led them to the point of the hearing. In the end, I don't think we ought to make too much of the difference in notice rules, but still that difference does put a citizen wanting to challenge a proposed rule in a little less comfortable position, since he or she will hear some information for the first time at the hearing at which that information must be challenged, and that's something we might not want to do.

Accountability: When it comes to accountability, on-the-record decision-making rules require a paper trail that in some instances seems to rival the old Oregon trail, and provide a clear and for the most part understandable standard by which judges can review administrative actions.

Section 556 of the APA specifies that the record of an on-the-record proceeding shall consist of "the transcript of testimony and exhibits, together with all papers and requests filed in the proceeding." That can be a pretty formidable pile of papers, and as in the case of the 7,500-plus pages the Food and Drug Administration collected as it tried to decide if peanut butter ought to be 90 percent rather than only 87.5 percent peanuts, the pile can seem a little silly.[51] But we ought to be able to use those 7,500-plus—7,736 to be precise—pages to figure out what was on the FDA's mind as it considered the decision, and that, after all, is the point of the requirement. Maybe the silliness comes in the fact that the FDA felt that it was a decision that it needed to make. In any event, there will be a complete paper trail in any on-the-record proceeding.

Taking accountability one step further, that paper trail is, by law, the exclusive legitimate basis for an agency's decision. That requirement, in turn, leads us into the final ingredient in on-the-record decision-making accountability, namely, the standard for judicial review of such decisions. Most of that discussion has to await the next chapter. Suffice it to say here that a judge has that entire record before him or her and has been instructed by the APA to set aside any decision not supported by "substantial evidence" in that record.

I do not mean for you to read this section of the chapter to suggest that, if we could just get Congress to require on-the-record decision making in all settings, we would never again have to worry about unresponsive bureaucrats thwarting effective public participation in their decision making and escaping accountability for what they have done. As I mentioned before, there is a great deal of sentiment among administrative law scholars for getting rid of on-the-record rule making altogether. Besides, these rules are far from perfect. But they do provide a start toward opportunity and accountability. After you have compared them with what we are hoping to accomplish through administrative law, compare them with the rules for not on the record decision making. It will make them look a whole lot better.

Decision Making Not on the Record

Once more, think back to the purposes of administrative law, namely, opportunity for input and influence and after-the-fact accountability. Not-on-the-record decision making falls short of on-the-record decision making on both counts— that is, provides less opportunity and a lower standard of accountability—but, in a very real sense, that was precisely what Congress intended. Section 553 of the Administrative Procedure Act, the section that covers not-on-the-record decision making, applies only to rule making, and the procedures it contains were deliberately structured to keep bureaucrats nearer the legislative than the judicial end of the procedural continuum. Still, recognizing that Congress intended a looser and more flexible set of rules to apply to not-on-the-record decision making, it is worth a brief look at how those rules differ from the rules that apply when Congress has declared that an agency must go on the record.

Before we talk about the opportunity and accountability rules that apply to not-on-the-record decision making, however, we need to take a moment to discuss not-on-the-record—informal is the term of choice—adjudication. As we said, agencies make a number of decisions about the past conduct of specific individuals or businesses that Congress has not required be made on the record. Section 553 of the APA does not speak to the question of what sorts of rules should apply to those informal adjudications. Administrators, therefore, are on their own. As we know from the Paul Verkuil study I have cited several times already, there are numerous programs at the federal level making decisions that can reasonably be given the label informal adjudication, and more to the point, as we also know from Professor Verkuil's now classic study, these administrators left on their own have produced a remarkable variety of procedural models. As Professor Verkuil also pointed out, of course, such variety means that the answer to our central question—do the rules for informal adjudication provide citizens with an opportunity for participation and influence and a means of holding their government accountable—can only be: it depends on the agency.[52]

Section 553 may not apply to adjudications not required to be made on the record, but it does apply to most rules not required to be made on the record, so let's consider the question of just how much opportunity and accountability the rules of 553 bring to not-on-the-record rule making.

Opportunity: To provide citizens with a real opportunity, recall, we believe we need a forum that is as neutral as possible and in which those citizens can present their arguments and counter the arguments of others. In on-the-record decision making, that forum is a public hearing with the opportunity to present and rebut evidence and engage in cross-examination. Under Section 553, in contrast, the participation forum is "an opportunity to participate in the rule making through submission of written data, views, or arguments with or without opportunity for oral presentation." Now add in the difference in notice requirements. On-the-record rules, recall, require a full explanation of the "matters of fact and law asserted." Not-on-the-record rules require instead "reference to the legal authority under which the rule is proposed" and "either the terms and substance of the proposed rule or a description of the subjects and issues involved."

In effect, we have two very different situations. In an on-the-record proceeding, citizens have a fairly clear idea of what the government asserts to be true, about the law, and about the facts that have led it this far, a fairly clear idea of what other citizens have said about the government's positions, and a chance to butt heads with both the government and other groups of citizens in a forum with reasonably well understood rules. In a not-on-the-record proceeding, citizens have far less to begin with—either a rough draft of the proposed rule or a description of the subjects and issues involved—no idea of what other citizens might be thinking about the subjects, and a forum that consists of a chance to write down their thoughts and mail them in. That means no chance to challenge the validity of facts asserted by other folks or to challenge their interpretations of the law. Section 553 rule making also operates under much more ambiguous guidelines concerning *ex-parte* contacts and the impartiality of decision makers.[53]

Once more, let me caution you against the conclusion that all we need is to force all decisions on the record and we will have a fully open and participatory bureaucracy. On-the-record rule making has its distinct and substantial problems. Besides, it was Congress's choice to apply looser rules to most agency rule making, and Congress clearly has the authority to make that choice. Still, there is a pretty substantial gap between the opportunity available to citizens in on-the-record proceedings and the opportunity available to them (us) in not-on-the-record proceedings. There may well be good reasons not to require on-the-record decision making in all settings. But are there really good reasons not to close that gap?

Accountability: Just as it has chosen to impose different opportunity rules, Congress has also chosen to impose somewhat different accountability rules on not-on-the-record decision making from those imposed in on-the-record settings. Specifically, Section 553 of the APA requires that "the agency shall incorporate in the rules adopted a concise general statement of their basis and purpose." When it comes to reconstructing what happened in a particular decision-making setting—that's the purpose of a paper trail requirement, remember—a basis and purpose statement is an animal very different from the record of a formal hearing. That difference has been the subject of a great deal of debate in the courts and in the broader community of administrative law scholars over the past twenty-five years. Lower court judges complained about the inadequacy of the basis and purpose statements and began to demand more detailed records of administrative activity when citizens entered their courtrooms to challenge a particular rule. The Supreme Court weighed in once or twice, and we ended the twentieth century with some considerable confusion over just how specific and detailed a basis and purpose statement had to be in order to permit the kind of court review of an administrative action guaranteed by the Administrative Procedure Act itself.[54]

There is also a difference between the standard for setting aside an on-the-record decision and that for setting aside a not-on-the-record decision. On-the-record decisions are to be overturned if they are unsupported by "substantial evidence . . . on the record," while not-on-the-record decisions are to be overturned only if they are found to be "arbitrary, capricious, an abuse of discretion, or otherwise not in accordance with law." That is obviously a considerable difference, more or less akin to the difference between saying, "that makes sense," and saying, "that's not completely nuts." Richard Pierce, Sidney Shapiro, and Paul Verkuil are convinced that over the years judges at all levels of the federal system have done all they could to erase that difference, moving whenever and wherever they could to impose a variant of the substantial evidence test.[55]

We will consider these questions in more detail in the next chapter. At this point we can say that while it is true that the courts have moved to apply something that looks very much like the substantial evidence test in not-on-the-record decision making, just as they do in on-the-record decision making, what courts have in front of them in their search for substantial evidence is going to be different. How different is going to vary from one rule-making setting to another, but there will be a difference, and on too many occasions that difference is likely to make it harder for a court to reconstruct the process of making that decision in a way that permits it to assess that decision's wisdom and fairness.

In Summary

The Administrative Procedure Act divides bureaucratic decision making into rule making and adjudication, creates a set of rules for each, and then reserves to Congress the right to apply adjudication rules to rule-making proceedings if it so desires. Sometimes, though not that often, it does so desire.

Whether the decision be a rule or an adjudication, the rules that apply when Congress forces an agency on the record provide citizens with a better opportunity for participation and influence than do the rules that apply when it doesn't. Armed with a better idea of what an agency intends to do and why, citizens are given a chance to attack or support ideas, and beyond that, to attack or support the ideas, information, and reasoning of other citizens also involved in the process, and this give and take takes place in what at least approximates a neutral arena. To be sure, all too often the phrase "interest groups" could replace the word "citizens" in the above sentence. Still, the opportunity is there, and the fact that that opportunity ends up biased in favor of certain groups of people is the product of forces far more fundamental than the workings of administrative law.

On-the-record and not-on-the-record decision-making rules are also different in terms of accountability, but those differences are less significant to begin with, and the courts have made an effort to make them even less so. Still, one cannot completely ignore the differences in the nature of the paper trail the two sets of rules give us if and when we want to look back at a particular decision.

In the end, I remain convinced that the rules for on-the-record decision making provide more opportunity and better accountability than do the rules for not-on-the-record decision making. That does not mean, however, that we ought to apply the rules for on-the-record decision making universally. They are more time consuming, more expensive, and leave administrators with less flexibility. We want to apply them only when we are sure that we really want to bear those costs. But it is important that we always keep in mind that the cost of not applying them is a somewhat less open and somewhat less accountable decision-making process. After all, pitting one valuable thing against another is what a balancing act is all about.

Administrative Law: The Summary

We need procedures to introduce responsiveness, respect for individual rights, and accountability into bureaucratic decision making. Those procedures provide a constant reminder to bureaucrats of the fact that their power is delegated by us, and we are quite concerned to see that they use it in a reasoned fashion respectful of our most basic values and create a paper trail that helps keep us in charge. But even given such desirable results, we still don't always want to put administrators in a procedural box. Such a box, it seems, makes those administrators move more slowly, spend more money, and sometimes even keeps them from finding creative solutions to our public policy problems. So, when we think the stakes are high enough, we demand procedures. When we don't, we don't.

When we decide that we do need procedures, we still face three rather large questions. What sorts of procedures do we need—how much should we confine decision makers—who is going to make that decision, and on what basis will they make it? We have two quite distinct procedural models to choose from. One is based on how we think things work in a legislature, and it gives administrators a great deal of freedom in terms of what constitutes evidence in the decision-making process as well as who must be allowed to participate in that process and the format for their participation. The second is based on how we think courts operate, and it gives administrators far less flexibility, giving them pretty clear direction on what may constitute evidence, who must be allowed to participate, and what the forum for that participation should look like. Congress gets the first chance to decide what sorts of procedures should be required, and it may well exercise that option, either by "triggering" the Administrative Procedure Act or by custom designing procedures for a particular set of decisions. If Congress does not speak—or in some cases even if it does—an agency may choose to impose procedures on itself. Then the courts and the President can become involved in the procedure game, the courts responding to a particular citizen complaint, the

President generally trying to protect some kinds of interests in the rule-making process. Finally, we come to the question of criteria. Our general instinct is to match procedures with outcomes, that is, to tell agencies that when they are writing rules, they should work under more or less legislative style procedures, and when they are judging specific cases, they should work under more or less judicial rules. We don't always match, however. If we think the stakes are high enough, we may want the more constraining judicial model even in rule-making settings, and when we think we have too many very similar but low-stakes judging decisions to make, we opt for the looser legislative decision-making model, despite the specific and seemingly judicial nature of the outcome. Then, of course, the courts may tell us to factor into the situation the probability that different procedures will so improve the decision-making process that it will improve the product as well.

Last of all we looked at the Administrative Procedure Act and its rules for on-the-record and for not-on-the-record decision making. It is clear enough that with their call for a formal hearing at which citizens can offer evidence and argument, counter evidence and argument from other citizens or from the government, and be guaranteed a decision based solely on what happens at that hearing, the on-the-record rules provide something that at least approximates a reasonable opportunity for citizen input and influence. Likewise, the existence of such a clear and extensive record, the fact that administrators are tied to that record, and the existence of the substantial evidence test mean that agencies subject to the on-the-record requirement know that they can and will be held accountable for their decisions. In contrast, citizens interested in the outcome of a not-on-the-record decision face a few more obstacles to being effective participants in the process of making that decision. Submitting their concerns in writing without that opportunity for face-to-face interaction with other submitters and with the officials who will make the decision, combined with the inability to counter evidence and/or argument offered by others in the process, makes it harder to be heard. The lack of a detailed record to match the hearing transcript from an on-the-record proceeding and the bar set by the arbitrary and capricious test also make it harder to hold administrators responsible for a not on-the-record decision. Still, on balance, as I said several times, I would like to close the gap between on-the-record and not-on-the-record rules, but not by requiring that everything be put on the record, at least not as on-the-record is currently defined.

The Law of Government Liability

Just as they are sworn to uphold the substantive laws their agencies exist to enforce, and just as they are sworn to uphold those laws in a context defined by administrative law, administrators are also sworn to uphold substantive law in a context defined by the law of government liability. In simpler terms, they are sworn to do their very best not to act in a negligent manner that brings harm to individual citizens. As we will see in just a moment, that was not always the case. But it is now. Indeed, as David Rosenbloom and James Carroll reminded us just over a decade ago, "Today, knowledge of constitutional law is considered a matter of basic *job competence* for public administrators. Those who lack what the courts . . . deem to be 'reasonable' knowledge of the constitutional rights of their clients, their patients and inmates, their subordinates, and individuals that they encounter in other ways may be held *personally* liable in civil suits for money damages."[56] In short, whether you expect to end up a personnel administrator, a county extension agent, a social worker, or Deputy Director of the FBI, you will need to know something about the rules that govern such suits, or more properly, you will need to know what sorts of actions might put you and the unit of government you work for in the role of defendant in such a suit. More to the point in terms of this chapter, a responsible government does not bring physical, psychological, or economic harm to its citizens through its own negligent conduct, and making sure that it doesn't is one of the principal responsibilities of that responsible government's employees.

Sovereign Immunity

For about a century and a half, the government couldn't be held liable for anything it did. Well, that's not quite true. It could be held liable, but only if it first agreed to be sued, and then lost.

That rather strange set of circumstances came about with the importation of an old English common-law doctrine known as sovereign immunity. The doctrine of sovereign immunity—generally said to derive from the old adage that the king could do no wrong—is nowhere to be found in the Constitution, but in what one legal scholar described as "one of the mysteries of legal evolution," it became thoroughly embedded in American legal tradition.[57] The government could be sued only if it explicitly agreed to such a suit, and it rarely did. Recourse, such as it was, was to be found by appealing to the legislative branch, that is, by asking Congress to pass a private bill compensating you for the damages done.

In 1946 Congress passed the Tort Claims Act, granting citizens the right to sue the government for injuries caused by the negligent actions of federal government officials. Congress made that break with a 150-year-old legal tradition for three reasons.

First, many members of Congress were dissatisfied with the system of private bills as a way of compensating citizens for damage done by negligent government action. For one thing it was grossly unfair, since by no stretch of the imagination could one believe that all citizens injured had an equal opportunity for relief under the private bill system. Some political connections were obviously necessary, and not everyone had them. Beyond that, members often found the task of shepherding such a bill through Congress a real pain in the neck, with the prospect of only limited rewards for success, and of substantial penalty for failure.

Second, there was the traditional argument that underlies the tort liability system for private individuals. If you know you can be sued for damages if you act in a negligent manner, you will be less likely to do so.

Last, there was the basic question of fairness to injured citizens. Tort liability is not just a way to induce caution. It is also a system of compensation for damages. Under the pre–Tort Claims Act rules, a citizen whose car was demolished by a negligently driven beer truck could recover the cost of the car and something beyond that. A citizen whose car was hit by a negligently driven mail truck could not. It was awfully difficult to understand why one's ability to "be made whole"—economically anyway—should depend on who owned the truck.

When Is Government Liable?

The Tort Claims Act—and most of the state statutes modeled on it—states that the government "shall be liable . . . in the same manner and to the same extent as a private individual under like circumstances." In the federal context, that raises two interesting questions.

First, tort law in the United States is generally a combination of common law and state statute. An action that would be a tort in Florida might not be in California, and vice versa. Federal courts concluded that the Congress had had no intention of imposing a national standard for tort liability, and therefore that the phrase "under like circumstances" was meant to include state by state differences in tort law. If a private citizen would be liable in California but not in Florida, the same would be true for the federal government.

Second, and almost certainly more important, the goal of holding the government liable "in the same manner and to the same extent as a private individual under like circumstances" presents us with the question of what to do about functions which are exclusively or even primarily governmental. Only the government fields an army, and while there are private security forces, even private fire departments, we all recognize that they are fundamentally different in powers and responsibilities from their public counterparts, just as we realize that private social service agencies are fundamentally different from public welfare agencies, and the Better Business Bureau differs substantially from the consumer protection division of a state's Office of the Attorney General. What does "under like circumstances" mean for such governmental units?

As far as the military is concerned, the Court concluded that injuries caused by a negligently driven tank did not constitute a tort under the Tort Claims Act, and consequently that no damage suit could be filed.[58] When it comes to the rest of government—even to law enforcement—things are a bit more complicated.

The lead case in the effort to define the phrase "under like circumstances" is *Indian Towing Company, Inc. v. United States*, decided in 1955.[59] A barge belonging to Indian Towing had run aground in the Mississippi River, causing extensive damage to both the barge and its cargo. The barge had struck an island, an island on which the U.S. Coast Guard had built and maintained a small lighthouse. Unfortunately, it hadn't maintained said lighthouse particularly well, or at least that was the claim of Indian Towing. So the company filed suit under the Tort Claims Act. The government responded that the act did not apply. In the process of contesting the case, the government and the company offered the Court contrasting definitions of the statute's key phrase "under like circumstances."

Specifically, government attorneys urged the Court to conclude that circumstances could only truly be "like" if a private party *were* engaged in the particular action in question—in this case, operating a lighthouse—and *had been sued and held liable* for the challenged action—failure to maintain said lighthouse—in the state in question. Indian Towing's counsel, of course, had to offer something quite different, since if the government's definition were to prevail, the company would lose even the opportunity to present its case. So the company tried to convince the Court that circumstances would be "like" if a private party could engage in a particular activity—again, in this case operate a lighthouse—and that if it did it would be held liable in that particular state for the actions—failure to maintain said lighthouse—being challenged.

The Court sided with Indian Towing, for in the eloquent words of Justice Felix Frankfurter, "we would be attributing bizarre motives to Congress were we to hold that it was predicating liability on such a completely fortuitous circumstance—the presence or absence of identical private activity."[60] If Frankfurter's words leave you a bit confused, consider this example.

You and your new BMW are proceeding through a green light at 25 mph when a mail truck hits you broadside, causing $25,000 damage to the right fender and breaking a passenger's leg in the bargain. Under the government's definition for "under like circumstances" advanced in *Indian Towing*, your ability to collect would be predicated on what was in the truck. If it was express mail, you can collect, since Federal Express or UPS would clearly be liable. If it was junk mail, forget it. Nobody else will carry that stuff. The beer truck versus the mail truck revisited. In spades.

Exceptions to the Tort Claims Act

It would be quite unlike Congress to pass a piece of legislation without any exceptions, and the Tort Claims Act is definitely not exceptional in that regard. In fact, Congress managed to find thirteen separate sets of circumstances in which it wanted to prevent citizens from suing the government for what they believed to be negligent acts.[61] Most are technical and far beyond the scope of this book and your interest. Two, however, are not.

The Intentional Torts Exception

Sometimes government takes action that it knows will harm an individual citizen. Indeed, in a fundamental sense, harm is the purpose of the actions.

An arrest is intended to deprive you of your liberty. At least in the short run, it is. A search for evidence is part of that same intentional process. Congress and the states that have followed its lead have concluded that not every search that turns up no evidence of a crime, and not every arrest that does not lead to prosecution—or, for that matter, every prosecution that does not lead to conviction—ought to be the subject of a suit for damages. The presumption is that if they could be, the men and women involved in law enforcement would end up being far too cautious, and that was a result no legislator wanted on his or her conscience—or political record.

Some sort of intentional torts exception was definitely justified in the case of law enforcement, but critics of the Tort Claims Act feared that the exception contained in that statute was far too broad, and that government could, and would, someday use it to shield clearly inappropriate conduct. The worst fears of those critics were realized when six agents of the then Federal Bureau of Narcotics forcibly entered the home of a man named Bivens and conducted a vigorous—

some might say ruthless—search for illegal drugs. Finding none, they proceeded to arrest Bivens anyway. All this was done early in the morning, without, as it turned out, proper search warrants. It seems that the bureau's tipster had given the agents the wrong address.

Bivens sued for damages—interestingly enough while he was free on bail awaiting trial on a felony charge which would land him in a state prison—and was told by the Federal District and Circuit Courts that such a search and arrest fell under the intentional tort exception. The Supreme Court agreed. The statute was clear enough. But the Court went on to say that Mr. Bivens had the right to bring suit under the Fourth Amendment. After all, as Justice Brennan reasoned, if Bivens had been guilty of selling drugs and said drugs had been found in the search, he could have moved to have them suppressed as evidence on the grounds of an unreasonable search. Yet since he was innocent and nothing was found, he had no legal recourse. That was not acceptable to Brennan or a majority of his colleagues, and they told the District Court to rehear the complaint as a Fourth Amendment action.[62]

Finding a Fourth Amendment right to file a suit for damages was considered by many to be a bit of creative legal thinking. Still, the action of the bureau's agents was sufficiently repulsive that few challenged the decision. The revulsion was shared by Congress, which then proceeded to amend the Tort Claims Act to narrow dramatically the intentional torts exception, particularly when law enforcement officials are involved.[63]

The Discretionary Function Exception

Important—and frustrating—as the intentional torts exception may be, the most important exception in the Tort Claims Act is the one for "claims based upon the exercise or performance or the failure to exercise or perform a discretionary function or duty on the part of a federal agency or an employee of the Government, whether or not the discretion involved be abused."

Much of what government does is make hard choices among competing values. Weyerhaeuser wants a logging road and a bigger allowable harvest in a particular portion of the Kaniksu National Forest of Eastern Washington. The Sierra Club wants another backpackers-only campground and preservation of a particular stand of old-growth forest that Weyerhaeuser wants to cut. The Forest Service has to make a difficult decision. Both of these things are valuable, just to different people. We can't have both, and there are two very good reasons why we don't want to permit the loser to sue for damages once the choice is made. First of all, to permit such a suit is to say that everything really does have a price tag. All values really do come down to dollars and cents. We don't want to say that. Second, on a more pragmatic plane, we don't want government decision makers factoring into their decisions the relative difference in the size of the damage awards they would have to pay depending on which alternative they choose. This would be a particularly unhappy circumstance when one side is defending environmental or aesthetic values and the other commercial values.

But it is clear that not every choice the government makes is really an exercise in discretionary policy making or even discretionary policy implementation.

When the government entered the overnight delivery business, it expected to take some business away from Federal Express and United Parcel Service. Presumably it did. That decision was truly discretionary, and neither of the private overnight delivery services would—or should—be able to sue for the lost business. However, if the government then decides not to maintain its planes, or hires incompetent work crews, or simply has so few employees that it cannot come close to meeting its schedules, and as a result your overnight delivery takes two weeks or ends up in Lake Erie, we are looking at a very different situation. Getting into the overnight delivery business is a discretionary act. Conducting that business in such a way that promises are not kept is not. It is reasonable enough to exempt the former from tort suits. Not so with the latter.

The Supreme Court took a somewhat different position in its first attempt to give meaning to the discretionary function exception. That case, *Dalehite v. United States*, arose out of a terrible explosion and fire in Texas City, Texas.[64] As part of the plan for the post–World War II recovery of Europe and the rest of the world, the U.S. government decided to ship fertilizer to dozens of different countries. Two ships were sent to Texas City to be loaded. The fertilizer was a standard ammonium nitrate–based fertilizer, and it was being shipped in paper bags rather than in a safer alternative. Finally, it was midsummer and temperatures were reaching well into the 90s day after day. The ships blew up, and the resulting explosion and fire leveled the harbor area, killing nearly 600 people. Hundreds of plaintiffs sued under the Tort Claims Act, winning at the District Court level but losing in the Circuit. The Supreme Court upheld the Circuit Court ruling, contending that "Where there is room for policy judgment and decision there is discretion. It necessarily follows that acts of subordinates in carrying out the operations of government in accordance with official directions cannot be actionable."[65] There is no way to know if Congress agreed with the Court's interpretation of the statute. We do know, however, that the legislative branch was sympathetic enough to the plight of Texas City's survivors that it allocated nearly $17 million to compensate them for their losses.[66]

More to the point, we also know that the Court began to soften the effects of *Dalehite* only two years later. In *United States v. Union Trust Co.*, the Court held that the decision by an air traffic controller to tell two planes to land on the same air strip at the same time was not protected by the discretionary function exception. In the court's words, "discretion was exercised when it was decided to operate the tower, but the tower personnel had no discretion to operate it negligently."[67]

This is not an administrative law casebook, so it is hardly necessary to engage in a full recitation of the series of cases in which the federal courts narrowed the discretionary function exception of the Tort Claims Act. It is useful, however, to give you an indication of the primary direction of that narrowing, and perhaps more important, to give you a feel for why that narrowing was sound public policy.

Simply put, the courts have concluded that since so much of modern government is conducted by professionals and that since the concept of negligence has been applied systematically to the choices made by professionals in the private sector—medical malpractice is the headline-grabbing version, but there have been others—the discretionary function exception should not cover the choices made by professionals in implementing public policy decisions made at higher levels. Professional judgments are made in a context bounded by professional standards and values. At the very least, we ought to be able to review the conduct of government professionals to determine whether or not they have stayed within the normal canons of professional responsibility.

In moving legal doctrine in this direction, the Court of Appeals for the Third Circuit dismissed the government's claim that a decision to release a particular batch of polio vaccine despite the fact that it had "failed" one of the five tests to which such vaccines were submitted was covered by the discretionary function exception, saying, "The judgment [to release the vaccine], however, was that of a professional measuring neurovirulence. It was not that of a policy-maker promulgating regulations by balancing competing policy considerations in determining the public interest."[68] The Ninth Circuit felt much the same way about the Veterans Administration's failure to warn a woman that a man whom she—and the police—felt constituted a significant threat to her safety would not be confined to a VA mental treatment facility as she had believed he would.[69] Both cases arose, of course, because of their tragic consequences. In the first instance, a woman crippled by polio contracted from the vaccine. In the second, a woman murdered.

The more you study public administration, the more you will realize the difficulty of trying to distinguish "policy" choices from "management" or "operational" choices. A substantial amount of policy is made up of the coral reefs built by thousands and thousands of operational decisions. Still, the courts' efforts to confine the discretionary function exception to a fairly narrow range of choices involving the "balancing of competing policy considerations"[70] is a healthy development. An exception, remember, is just that, an exception. It precludes a suit. Therefore, it precludes an examination of what happened and why. That, in turn, makes responsibility, at least the kind of responsibility we believe results from an after-the-fact accounting of what government has done, much more difficult to achieve. Consequently, we want to keep the number of situations in which such an examination is precluded to a minimum. Consider just one more example.

Suppose a big city is having serious problems delivering emergency services in certain neighborhoods. The fire department and ambulance service adopt a policy telling firefighters and emergency medical technicians to terminate their response to a call if they believe that they, or their equipment, are in imminent danger. An ambulance crew is called to a housing project in one of the dangerous neighborhoods but never actually reaches the destination. A little boy dies. Should there be a lawsuit?

A wrongful death suit against the fire chief or the head of the ambulance service for adopting a policy to protect employees and equipment should certainly be precluded under a discretionary function exception. That is policy if policy has any meaning at all. Competing values—serving specific parts of the city versus serving all of the city and protecting individual employee safety—were balanced against one another and some considered more important than others.

But the policy specifically left room for choice on the part of the firefighters or EMTs. They had to decide if they or their equipment would be in imminent danger. Should that choice be protected from suit? Or would we want to look to see if there was real evidence that such danger existed? We might very well want to hold a trial and then find the government not liable. Assume that two EMTs return from an uncompleted call. Both are bloody and the ambulance windshield is shattered. There are eyewitnesses to the fact that both men and the machine were attacked by an angry crowd. That is probably enough imminence for most of us. Assume, instead, that we have no blood, no broken windows, no dents, and no eyewitnesses. Just a report that says the EMTs felt in danger. Further assume that we subsequently learn that the ambulance never came within a mile of the address to which it was called. Is that imminence?

Now you can see the importance of the notion of an exception. Grant an exception from suit and both of those situations are considered to be the same. They aren't, and we don't want the law to say that they are.

The Liability of Individual Government Officials

So far I have talked about the liability of government as government. But the "government" doesn't use unreasonable force in arresting you. A specific law enforcement officer does. The "government" doesn't run a red light and total your new car. A specific driver employed by a specific agency and driving a specific vehicle does. So, beyond the question of the liability of government is the question of the liability of specific government employees.

In general the questions and arguments are pretty much the same as they are with respect to the liability of government as government. On the one hand we have the traditional goals of tort law, that is, to induce caution and to "make whole" those who have been injured. On the other we have the worry that government will become so fearful that it cannot make the necessary decisions. But, in a sense, all of these questions become just a bit trickier when we speak of the liability of individual officials.

As I noted a moment ago, it is always real people who take the actions that cause citizens to feel they deserve compensation. When those people know that only the entity they work for—government—can be sued, their caution is of one magnitude. But when they know that they might be sued as individuals, that caution rises to new, and quite possibly inappropriate, levels. Even an official who believes that he or she will win every suit can wear down under the constant pressure of legal harassment. Caution can become paralysis. Still, if only the government—using taxpayer money—is liable, then will we get the kind of caution we want? And should a government official who has committed this sort of injury to one of his or her fellow citizens bear none of the responsibility for that action?

Absolute Immunity for Some

Some officials cannot be sued for actions taken in an official capacity. Period.

For more than a century, judges have been exempt from any suit over a decision reached while on the bench. The Supreme Court upheld that particular exemption as recently as 1978 in a case involving the sterilization of a young woman.[71] The judge accepted, read, and approved the petition all in the space of a single day.

Among the many legacies of Richard Nixon is absolute immunity from tort suits for Presidents, even when they act at the outer limits of their authority.[72] Nixon had made sure that Pentagon cost analyst Ernest Fitzgerald lost his job in a department shake-up, Fitzgerald having said some things the President did not care for in testimony before Congress. The Civil Service Commission eventually restored Fitzgerald to his job—though it did not formally endorse his claim of violation of First Amendment rights—and Nixon paid him $142,000 in an out-of-court settlement, but Fitzgerald wanted to carry the suit forward, and he and the former President established a sort of "side bet" of $28,000 to be paid by Nixon if the Court did not accept his claim of absolute immunity.[73]

The Constitution itself protects members of Congress for things they say in debate, but the Court ruled that that protection did not apply to press releases or constituent newsletters.[74] The case involved one of the then famous "Golden Fleece" awards presented by former Wisconsin Senator William Proxmire (D) for wasteful government expenditures.

Qualified Immunity for Most

Most of you will never sit on the bench or serve in Congress or as President. I'll let you decide if that makes you happy or sad. I am happy that I won't. In any event, what matters to most of you if you end up as government employees, and to most of us as citizens whether you do or don't, is the qualified immunity that exists for the vast majority of government officials.

In an effort to keep the process of post–Civil War reconstruction moving apace, the Congress passed the Civil Rights Act of 1871. Section 1983 of that act provides an opportunity for citizens to sue individual government officials for damages if the citizen believes his or her constitutional rights have been infringed upon. This has been the statutory basis for suits against individual employees at all levels of government.

Once again, there is a lot more law here than most of you will ever need to know. In essence, the Court has held that the immunity from suit normally granted to government officials is granted absolutely to Presidents, judges, and members of Congress engaged in debate, but not to anybody else. For everyone from presidential assistants to local police officers, immunity from suit is qualified, that is, sometimes it isn't there. In general, there are two "sometimeses" in which immunity disappears.

First of all, if an official is acting outside of the range of his or her normal activities and/or normal statutory authority, he or she cannot claim immunity from suit.[75] After all, when we grant immunity, what we are doing is trying to make it possible for people to perform their normal functions free of the pressure that inevitably accompanies the fear of being sued. Once an official strays from his or her normal duties, that reason for immunity disappears. It is said that back when he was Chief of Police for the City of Los Angeles, Darryl Gates would occasionally put on the full SWAT team gear and go with the team. Had he shot someone, or even done something out of the ordinary that caused someone to be shot, a wrongful death suit might well have been successful. The chief is not one of the SWAT boys.

Second, and probably more to the point in most cases, there can be no immunity if an official "knew or reasonably should have known that the action he took within his sphere of official responsibility would violate the constitutional rights of [a citizen], or if he took the action with the malicious intention to cause a deprivation of constitutional rights or other injury."[76] All federal officials are sworn to uphold the Constitution, so it hardly seems unreasonable to ask them to have some idea of the rights that document provides to the nation's citizens and, more to the point, to ask them not to deliberately violate those rights. An official who knows he or she is violating another citizen's constitutional rights and goes ahead should pay a heavy price.

Things are, of course, a bit more difficult when we ask whether or not an official "reasonably should have known" that an action would violate someone's rights. A police officer who can't remember what was in last week's Supreme Court decision might be forgiven. A police officer who doesn't know what's in the department manual can't be. There are, of course, gray areas, but in those gray areas, advice ought to be sought from those who do study the Court and its pronouncements. At least that is what the Court told then Agriculture Secretary Earl Butz in upholding a damage award against him for his violation of the rights of the owner of a commodity futures brokerage firm.[77]

Most Section 1983 suits are strictly for compensatory damages—that is, to give back some or all of what was lost—but the Court has agreed that the law permits the awarding of punitive damages as well. In upholding the award, a bitterly divided Court altered the standard used for determining liability from "malicious intent to cause a deprivation" to "reckless disregard of whether he was violating a right."[78] That was a significant change, of course, since it is far easier to prove someone was extremely careless than to prove that he or she was malicious.

In Summary

Oliver Wendell Holmes, hardly a friend of oppressive or irresponsible government, concluded that "The United States has not consented to be sued for torts, and therefore it cannot be said that in the legal sense the United States has been guilty of a tort. For a tort is a tort in a legal sense only because the law has made it so."[79] A quarter of a century later, the federal government finally gave its consent and in the process took a rather large step toward more responsible government.

The Tort Claims Act makes the government liable for its (and its employees') negligent actions if a private party would have been found liable for the same action. But, as always, there are exceptions.

The exception for intentional torts rankled many observers for twenty-five years, and as is often the case, one egregious action brought clamor for a change. The change came, and while the government still exempts itself from suit for torts it intended to commit, the hole that it creates for irresponsible government action is far smaller than it was.

The exception for torts committed in the exercise of a discretionary function has been narrowed as well. In *Dalehite*, the Court seemed to be saying that nearly any choice was an exercise in discretion. It wasn't very long, however, before the justices began to conclude that a professionalized government should be held to standards of reasonable professional conduct. The concept of liability can indeed be applied to the choices of trained professionals.

Just as government itself is liable for negligent actions, so are individual government officials. At least most are.

The President can't be sued for anything he or she does in anything remotely approaching an official capacity, and judges are protected from suit over even the most arbitrary of rulings from the bench. Members of Congress can say anything they want in floor debate but do have to take some care when they start mailing to constituents or talking to the press.

Most employees—the whole of the civil service and even the President's executive team—have only a qualified immunity, however. If an official stays within the scope of his or her legally defined duties and authority, then no suit is possible. Likewise, an official with a reasonably good knowledge of the Constitution and the good sense to ask someone with a better knowledge of same whenever he or she is in doubt about the implications of a decision for the rights of affected citizens will not be held liable for the actions he or she takes. Those who insist on pushing the outer limits of their authority or their functions and those who willfully violate the rights of their fellow citizens, will have to answer for those actions. Few doubt that they should.

SUMMARY AND CONCLUSION

Bureaucrats, whether they serve as political executives or policy specialists, are sworn to uphold the Constitution and the law. They try, and that trying leaves a real imprint on the decisions they make and the processes by which they make them.

Information gathering is one of the most important elements in the job of bureaucracy, and that means that their job is going to have to be done within constraints imposed by the Fourth and Fifth Amendments to the United States Constitution. Specifically, bureaucracy is not to gather information through "unreasonable searches," or by "compelling" testimony. No law enforcement officer is supposed to conduct an unreasonable search or compel testimony, of course, but the courts have concluded that law enforcement by OSHA is fundamentally different from law enforcement by the Detroit Police Department, and that because of those differences, the rules that apply to the information-gathering activities of OSHA can be far less restrictive than those that apply to the information-gathering activities of the Detroit—or San Francisco, Philadelphia, or any other—Police Department. So OSHA needs a warrant, but that warrant is almost automatic, and many other agencies can search without warrants at all. At least they can if they are searching pervasively regulated industries. When it comes to the Fifth Amendment and compelled testimony, bureaucrats operate under rules that, as I said earlier, are so lax that no less respected an administrative law scholar than Kenneth Warren has pronounced them nearly invisible.

Bureaucrats use information as well as gather it, and when they use it, other provisions of the Constitution come into play. Chief among them, of course, is the due process clause of the Fifth and Fourteenth Amendments. If an agency takes any action that might deprive a citizen of life, liberty, or property, it must take care to be sure that the procedure it uses to make the decision to take that action can meet the due process test. That test will almost certainly center on how the agency provided that citizen an opportunity to weigh in on the decision that will end up depriving him or her of life, liberty, or property. We will almost always use the word "hearing" in this context, and the question of what constitutes an adequate hearing fills a couple of weeks in my Administrative Law class. Suffice it to say here, if a citizen isn't happy with the hearing he or she got, a legal challenge is a possibility, and courts are generally ready to assess the constitutional adequacy of any administrative decision-making process.

Important as the Constitution obviously is, the law may be even more important, at least on a day-to-day basis. It isn't the law, of course, but the laws.

Upholding the substantive law that empowers an agency to do whatever it does is first in the minds of that agency's staff, of course, and with more than a little help from their friends—and critics—they will try to decide exactly what that statute means and how best to stay within its dictates and meet its goals.

Upholding administrative law means accepting procedural restrictions on their discretion that come from Congress, the President, and the courts. It also means creating procedures of their own and following those. All of these procedural requirements are aimed at bringing responsiveness, respect for individual rights, and accountability into bureaucratic decision making by guaranteeing citizens an opportunity for input and influence and creating a mechanism for after-the-fact accountability.

Finally comes upholding the law of government liability. On one level, that means nothing more than doing your job in a reasoned and careful manner. On another, it means accepting the fact that you—your agency, more likely—may be sued for damages, and the law of government liability will be a matter for the courts to sort out.

NOTES

1. *See v. Seattle* 387 U.S. 541 (1967); and *Camara v. Municipal Court of San Francisco* 387 U.S. 523 (1967).

2. *Marshall v. Barlow's Inc.* 436 U.S. 307 (1978).

3. *Colonnade Catering Corporation v. United States* 397 U.S. 72 (1970).

4. Kenneth F. Warren, *Administrative Law in the Political System*, 3rd ed. (Upper Saddle River, N.J.: Prentice-Hall, 1996), 527.

5. In order, the cases are: *United States v. Biswell* 406 U.S. 311 (1972); *Donovan v. Dewey* 452 U.S. 594 (1981); *Illinois v. Krull* 107 S.Ct. 1160 (1987); and *Pullin v. Louisiana State Racing Commission* 477 So.2d 683 (1985).

6. *Shoemaker v. Handel* 795 F2d 1036 (1986).

7. This section relies heavily on the work of perhaps the premier administrative law scholar of his generation, Professor Kenneth Warren of St. Louis University. See Warren, *Administrative Law in the Political System*, 535–557.

8. This began with *Hale v. Henkel* 201 U.S. 43 (1906). It is still alive and well.

9. *Shapiro v. United States* 335 U.S. 1 (1948).

10. *Baltimore City Department of Social Services v. Bouknight* 110 S.Ct. 900 (1990).

11. *Fisher v. United States* 425 U.S. 391 (1976).

12. *Matter of Grand Jury Empanelled* 597 F2d 851 (1979).

13. *United State v. Payner* 447 U.S. 727 (1980).

14. *Andresen v. Maryland* 427 U.S. 463 (1976).

15. Warren, *Administrative Law in the Political System*, 549–551.

16. Warren, *Administrative Law in the Political System*, 545.

17. Once again, I rely on Professor Kenneth Warren. See Warren, *Administrative Law in the Political System*, 554–557.

18. *United States v. Payner* 447 U.S. 727 (1980) is the IRS case; *U.S. Department of Labor v. Triplett* 110 S.Ct. 1428 (1990) obviously is the Labor Department case.

19. Warren, *Administrative Law in the Political System*, 557.

20. *Trinity Industries v. OSHRC* 16 F3d 1455 (6th Cir. 1994).

21. Warren, *Administrative Law in the Political System*, 557.

22. *Meyer v. State of Nebraska* 262 U.S. 380 (1923).

23. *Joint Anti-Fascist Refugee Committee v. McGrath* 341 U.S. 123 (1951); and *Wisconsin v. Constantineau* 400 U.S. 433 (1971).

24. The case involving the "active shoplifter" is *Paul v. Davis* 424 U.S. 393 (1976). The two cases involving the police officers are *Bishop v. Wood* 426 U.S. 341 (1976) and *Codd v. Vegler* 429 U.S. 624 (1977).

25. Richard A. Pierce Jr., Sidney A. Shapiro, and Paul R. Verkuil, *Administrative Law and Process*, 2nd ed. (Westbury, N.Y.: Foundation Press, 1992), 212–216.

26. *Goldberg v. Kelly* 397 U.S. 254 (1970). Among those to use the label "due process explosion" was the late Circuit Judge Henry Friendly, in "Some Kind of Hearing," *University of Pennsylvania Law Review* 123 (1975), 1267–1273.

27. *Bishop v. Wood*.

28. *Barry v. Barchi* 443 U.S. 55 (1979).

29. *Goss v. Lopez* 419 U.S. 565 (1975) was the school suspension case; *Memphis Light, Gas & Water Division v. Craft* 436 U.S. 1 (1978) was the utility service case.

30. *O'Bannon v. Town Court Nursing Center* 447 U.S. 773 (1980).

31. *Bi-Metallic Investment Co. v. State Board of Equalization* 239 U.S. 441 (1915).

32. The suspension case was *Goss v. Lopez*, already cited; the paddling case was *Ingraham v. Wright* 430 U.S. 651 (1977).

33. Friendly, "Some Kind of Hearing," 1264.

34. Jerry Mashaw, *Due Process in the Administrative State* (New Haven, Conn.: Yale University Press, 1985).

35. Mashaw, *Due Process in the Administrative State*, 9–10.

36. Mashaw, *Due Process in the Administrative State*, 30.

37. *Mathews v. Eldridge*.

38. Mashaw, *Due Process in the Administrative State*, 30.

39. Mashaw, *Due Process in the Administrative State*, 30.

40. Katharine Q. Seelye and Jennifer 8. Lee, "Court Blocks U.S. Effort to Relax Pollution Rule," *New York Times* (electronic edition), December 25, 2003.

41. Wallace S. Sayre, "The Triumph of Techniques over Purpose," *Public Administration Review* (Spring 1948), 134–137.

42. That passage can be found in the Administrative Procedure Act, Section 556, d.

43. Paul Verkuil, "A Study of Informal Adjudication Procedures," *University of Chicago Law Review* 43 (1976), 757–771.

44. Verkuil, "A Study of Informal Adjudication Procedures."

45. Kenneth J. Meier, *Regulation* (New York: St. Martin's Press, 1985), 103.

46. Warren, *Administrative Law in the Political System*, 278–282.

47. Warren, *Administrative Law in the Political System*, 278–280.

48. Verkuil, "A Study of Informal Adjudication Procedures."

49. Warren, *Administrative Law in the Political System*, 274.

50. Warren, *Administrative Law in the Political System*, 252.

51. Warren, *Administrative Law in the Political System*, 253.

52. Verkuil, "A Study of Informal Adjudication Procedures," 770–771.

53. Florence Heffron, *The Administrative Regulatory Process* (New York: Longman, 1983), 241–244; or Warren, *Administrative Law in the Political System*, 261–267.

54. Pierce, Shapiro, and Verkuil, *Administrative Law and Process*, 302–307.

55. Pierce, Shapiro, and Verkuil, *Administrative Law and Process*, 341–342.

56. David H. Rosenbloom and James D. Carroll, *Toward Constitutional Competence: A Casebook for Public Administrators* (Englewood Cliffs, N.J.: Prentice-Hall, 1990), 30.

57. Edwin M. Borchard, "Government Liability in Tort," *Yale Law Journal* 34 (1924), 4.

58. *Feres v. United States* 340 U.S. 135 (1950).

59. *Indian Towing Company, Inc. v. United States* 350 U.S. 61 (1955).

60. *Indian Towing v. United States*. You can find a well-edited and easily accessible version of the majority opinion in this case in Lief H. Carter and Christine B. Harrington, *Administrative Law and Politics* (New York: Addison, Wesley, Longman, 2000), 386–389. The quoted passage is on p. 388.

61. You can find the whole list in Donald D. Barry and Howard R. Whitcomb, *The Legal Foundations of Public Administration*, 2nd ed. (St. Paul, Minn.: West Publishing, 1987), 261, among other places.

62. *Bivens v. Six Unknown Named Agents of the Federal Bureau of Narcotics* 403 U.S. 388 (1971).

63. Barry and Whitcomb, *The Legal Foundations of Public Administration*, 261–262.

64. *Dalehite v. United States* 346 U.S. 15 (1953).

65. *Dalehite v. United States*. A concise description of that case, including important excerpts from the opinions, can be found in Barry and Whitcomb, *Legal Foundations of Public Administration*, 262–267. The quoted passage is on p. 265.

66. Barry and Whitcomb, *Legal Foundations of Public Administration*, 268.

67. *United States v. Union Trust Co.* 350 U.S. 907 (1955).

68. *Griffin v. United States* 500 F2d 1059 (1974). Excerpts of the opinion can be found in Carter and Harrington, *Administrative Law and Politics*, 398–391. The quoted passage is on p. 390.

69. *Jablonski by Pahls v. United States* 712 F2d 391 (1983). The essence of that opinion can be found in Barry and Whitcomb, *Legal Foundations of Public Administration*, 272–277.

70. *Griffin v. United States*.

71. *Stump v. Sparkman* 435 U.S. 349 (1978).

72. *Nixon v. Fitgerald* 457 U.S. 731 (1982).

73. Barry and Whitcomb, *Legal Foundations of Public Administration*, 293.

74. *Hutchinson v. Proxmire* 443 U.S. 111 (1979).

75. *Barr v. Mateo* 360 U.S. 564 (1959). Or at least that is Justice White's interpretation of *Barr* in *Butz v. Economou* 438 U.S. 478 (1978).

76. *Wood v. Strickland* 420 U.S. 308 (1975).

77. *Butz v. Economou*.

78. Thomas L. Horvath, "Punitive Damages Authorized in Section 1983 Action When 'Reckless Disregard' Shown," *Marquette Law Review* 67, no. 4 (Summer 1984), 759.

79. *United States v. Thompson* 257 U.S. 419 (1922).

9

Bureaucracy and the Courts

Judicial Review of Agency Action

On December 24, 2003, a three-judge panel of the District of Columbia Circuit informed the Environmental Protection Agency that the revisions to its so-called "new source review" rule announced by the agency in October and scheduled to go into effect on December 26 were to be stayed pending the outcome of a lawsuit challenging those revisions.[1] New source review was added to the Clean Air Act by Congress as part of a series of amendments to the statute in 1977, and EPA rules implementing it have been a bone of contention between industry—especially the power industry—and a coalition of states, cities, and environmental groups for the better part of a quarter-century. We needn't go into the details of that dispute here. What is important for our purposes in this chapter, of course, is the fact that New York Attorney General Eliot Spitzer was joined by his counterparts in thirteen other states, officials of several cities, and just about every major environmental group in the country in a suit to block that change in the rules. That suit serves as a reminder, if any reminder is needed, that a great many Americans feel that a lawsuit is an excellent way to challenge a public policy they find objectionable. That, of course, means that courts are going to have plenty of opportunities to exercise some influence over bureaucratic decision making.

Opportunities there will be, but as the last paragraph implies, those opportunities will be very different from the ones presented to the President and the Congress. In the first place, the Constitution and legal tradition demand that those opportunities come in the form of cases. No judge, no matter how outraged he or she may be by the action of some agency, can move to challenge that action. The challenge must come from a citizen in the form of a lawsuit. Second, as we shall see shortly, there are all sorts of rules and traditions, some imposed by Congress and the President, some by the courts themselves, that structure the way in which a judge conducts his or her review of that citizen's challenge to that particular agency action.

Since the judicial role in influencing bureaucratic policy making must be exercised in the context of specific lawsuits brought by specific individuals challenging specific actions, we must consider two questions. First, when can a citizen sue the government? Second, if a citizen does sue, under what ground rules will that challenge take place?

WHEN CAN A CITIZEN SUE HIS OR HER GOVERNMENT?

We need to begin our inquiry into the question of when a citizen can sue the government by phrasing the question in a bit more precise fashion. Specifically, we ask whether or not judicial review of a specific agency action is or is not available to a specific citizen at a specific time. The short answer to that question, to no one's particular surprise, is that judicial review is available in a particular situation if the courts say it is. Of course, all that answer provides us with is another question, namely, under what circumstances and for what reasons might a court decide that someone is not entitled to have a judge look at what an agency has done and determine whether or not that action should be allowed to stand?

It turns out that there are two sets of circumstances in which a court will deny an individual the right to challenge an agency decision. First, a court will deny review if it concludes that Congress intended to cut off access to such review of that particular action for that particular individual. Second, a court will deny review if it concludes that the traditional rules of judicial activity—as defined by the Constitution, statute, common law, judicial norms, and so on—preclude the judge from reviewing this particular decision on behalf of this particular individual. We'll start with Congress, but before we do that, we need to take a minute to think about the nature of courts.

The Nature of Courts

As Professor Kenneth Warren pointed out in *Administrative Law in the Political System*, a number of court scholars, including the highly respected John Hart Ely, have concluded that there are certain characteristics of courts themselves and of the legal system of which they are the centerpiece that make it essential that we limit the availability of judicial review of administrative action—and, when it is available, that we construct very definite rules about how that review is to be conducted.[2] Though he might not always recognize my adaptations of same, I believe Professor Warren has identified six such characteristics of courts that seem to have significance for both the availability and the nature of judicial review of agency activity.

To begin with, courts are not exactly democratic institutions, or, more properly, they are not representative institutions. Clearly courts have an important role to play in any society that values the rights of individuals and fears that the state might trample on those rights. But that role must inevitably be limited to the kinds of questions that revolve around disputes between individuals or between individuals and the government and not, in the words of former Appeals Court Justice Robert Bork, spill over into questions of "what is good for us."[3] We have representative institutions for that, and if bureaucracy has made some sort of decision we conclude isn't good for us, it is up to those representative institutions, not to the courts, to hold that bureaucracy accountable.

Second, there are very few courts and very very many agencies. If courts were to become involved in reviewing more than a fraction of what is done in the executive branch of government, they would be overwhelmed by the burden. The result, of course, would be an unacceptable delay in the functioning of government. We need to accept some limits on the availability of judicial review of bureaucratic activity just to keep the court system—and quite possibly the rest of the government—from grinding to a halt.

Third, and of at least equal importance, courts lack subject-matter expertise. No judge can possibly be expected to have the technical knowledge necessary to make an informed judgment about a Food and Drug Administration decision to approve the marketing of a new drug to reduce cholesterol, and then turn around and decide about the economic and health consequences of OSHA's requirement of expensive air filtration systems in textile factories. That doesn't mean that such decisions ought not be subject to court examination, only that the rules for conducting such an examination have to be devised so that judges are called on to make the kinds of decisions they are best equipped to make and made to defer to administrators on the kinds of decisions they cannot make. The trick, of course, is to know which decisions are which.

Fourth, courts operate in the context of what we call an adversary proceeding. Each side presents its case and then tries everything it knows to discredit the case presented by the other side. The job of the judge is to distill from all this punching and counterpunching which side is "right." There is not much room in such an atmosphere for creative problem solving. President Clinton's 1993 "Timber Summit" probably didn't have a real good chance of coming up with a plan for management of old growth Pacific Northwest forests that would satisfy very many people, but the odds were far better there than they were in a federal district court in Portland or Seattle. In fact, the "Timber Summit" came about because of the impasse created by a series of decisions made in those very district courts.

Fifth, and directly related to the point above, we see courts, and maybe more to the point, courts see themselves as places where real people argue about real injuries and real rights. Even if the dispute is actually a policy question, once it enters the courts the rhetoric is very likely to become the rhetoric of rights, and such a rhetoric tends to work against compromise. Issues often end up cast in black and white when they probably ought to be seen in shades of gray.

Finally, and more important than frequently realized, courts decide specific cases involving specific people and specific facts. That means the judge involved is not only looking for a good principle of law; he or she is also looking for a just resolution to this particular dispute. He or she wants to be fair to this particular set of people. Justice Benjamin Cardozo was almost certainly right that hard cases make bad law, and Thurgood Marshall was just as certainly right that easy cases, too, can make bad law.[4] Making it too easy for judges to correct every instance of bureaucratic injustice may create more problems for governmental responsibility than it solves.

So, as always, we face a tough balancing act. Courts have real limitations. We don't want to give them carte blanche to roam the executive-branch landscape looking for wrongs to right. But agencies do violate people's rights, and they do break the law, and they do occasionally make decisions so clearly wrong that someone has to say no. Courts can be that someone. We just have to try to devise rules to govern when they try to be that someone, and rules to govern the performance of their role as that someone, and then keep revising those rules to make sure that we haven't substituted one form of irresponsibility for another. The rest of this chapter is about the search for those rules.

Congress and Access to Judicial Review of Administrative Action

Congress speaks to the question of the right to get a court to review an agency decision precisely where you would expect it to, in the Administrative Procedure Act (APA). Specifically, Section 701 of the APA expresses the general presumption that anyone harmed by an agency action should have the right to have that action reviewed in court, unless the court finds one of two circumstances to prevail. First, the court could find, in the words of the APA, that such review is "precluded by law." Congress can—and sometimes does—include in an agency's authorizing statute what amounts to immunity from judicial review. Second, the courts could find, again in the words of the APA, that such review cannot be granted because "agency action is committed to agency discretion by law." As we shall see shortly, this is a far slipperier concept which has been controlling in only a handful of decision-making contexts. But given the importance of at least one of those contexts, we do need to consider it.

Preclusion of Review

Congress can place certain agencies, or more properly certain types of decisions made by certain agencies, off limits to judicial review. At least it can try to. Even before the passage of the Administrative Procedure Act, the courts had begun to establish a strong presumption in favor of the reviewability of administrative action, and Congress's effort to put some decisions beyond court review has been met with more than a little resistance. Over and over the courts have echoed Justice John M. Harlan's assertion that "only upon a showing of 'clear and convincing evidence' of a contrary legislative intent should the courts restrict access to judicial review."[5]

The Supreme Court has been particularly insistent on providing review of administrative action when those actions involve interpretations of statutes or of the Constitution itself. Justice John M. Harlan's conclusion that Abbott Laboratories deserved its day in court despite the claim by the old Department of Health, Education and Welfare (HEW) that Congress had intended to forbid any suit in these circumstances rested in large part on the fact that what Abbott wanted to challenge was the Secretary of HEW's statutory authority to issue a particular rule. As you might expect, the Court is even more determined to assert its right to review cases with implications for the meaning of the Constitution. There is no preclusion clause more clearly expressed or consistently respected than the one involving the administration of the various benefits available to veterans of our armed services. Yet in the case of *Johnson v. Robison*, the Supreme Court held that a decision by the Administrator of the then Veterans Administration (VA) (now Department of Veterans Affairs) to deny GI bill college-tuition benefits to a conscientious objector who had performed alternative service was subject to court review because the young man involved had raised a First Amendment question.[6] The Court found Robison's First Amendment claim invalid, but did, nonetheless, remind the VA Administrator—and the Congress, one supposes—that no one's decisions can be immunized against constitutionally based objections.

Powerful as Justice Harlan's echo may be, it is sometimes accompanied by a decision to uphold a particular preclusion of review clause. In 1984 in *Block v. Community Nutrition Institute*, in *Franklin v. Massachusetts*, and in *Reno v. Catholic Social Services* in 1993, and in *Kisser v. Cisneros* in 1994, the Court asserted its right to review administrative decisions while upholding the Congress's decision to put the particular decisions in question outside that general court prerogative.[7] In their days together on the D.C. Circuit, Antonin Scalia and Robert Bork held that the Administrator of the Veterans Administration could not be held to account in court even for his interpretation of the Administrative Procedure Act, so long as he was interpreting that act in the context of a veterans benefit decision.[8] The preclusion of review clause, according to Scalia, who wrote the opinion, was meant to cover all decisions made pursuant to the administrator's authority to decide veterans benefits cases. A compromise was worked out, and the decision was never appealed, so we will never know what the Supreme Court would have said. But it's clear enough that at least two prominent conservative justices were willing to move a long way from the old presumption that everything is reviewable in the absence of "clear and convincing evidence" to the contrary.

Agency Action Committed to Agency Discretion by Law

At first glance, it can be a little difficult for the uninitiated to figure out the difference between "precluded by law" and "committed to agency discretion by law." How else, exactly, could Congress commit an agency's action to its discretion by law than by precluding judicial review of said action? As a matter of fact, more than a few of the initiated, including Professor Kenneth Culp Davis, probably the best-known scholar of administrative law of the last half-century, seemed to think of this section of the APA as a quirky bit of language, not of much significance in the real world of administrators and judges.[9]

But quirky or not, it is there, and the Supreme Court has tried to give it some meaning. It made that effort in the case of *Citizens to Preserve Overton Park v. Volpe*, a case involving the decision of then Secretary of Transportation John Volpe to permit the city of Memphis, Tennessee, to run a stretch of Interstate 40 through Overton Park.[10] The law said that the secretary ought not to release federal funds for any highway through a public park unless he or she found "no feasible and prudent alternative." Secretary Volpe argued that his discretion on routing interstate highways was so great that his decision was precluded from review under the agency action committed to agency discretion exception of the Administrative Procedure Act. The Court said no, holding that that exception to review was applicable only "in those rare instances where . . . there is no law to apply."

The "no law to apply" standard has remained intact for thirty years, but in a pair of cases in the middle and late 1980s and a third in the early 1990s, the Supreme Court expanded the territory marked "no law" considerably. First, in 1985, the Court held that in most cases of an agency decision not to take enforcement action, there was no law to apply. The exceptions would be in those cases in which an agency's enabling statute or its own rules required action in specified circumstances.[11] Then, in 1988, the Court upheld the firing of a CIA employee, finding that Congress had made the CIA Director the virtual czar of personnel policy for the agency, and concluding that there was nothing in the statute that would guide court review of the director's decision.[12] The Court did, however, permit the fired employee to argue that his firing violated the Constitution. Finally, in 1993, the Court held that the decision of the Indian Health Service to discontinue a program designed to provide services to handicapped Indian children in the Southwest in order to reallocate the money to a similar program with nationwide reach was an action "committed to agency discretion by law," and therefore not reviewable.[13]

The "no law to apply" definition for "agency action committed to agency discretion by law" makes a certain amount of sense, especially from the perspective of judges stung by decades of criticism about their tendency to "make law" from the bench. If there is no law there, then any interpretation they give the words is new law, and that's not the court's job. Alas, on the other hand, if there is no law there for the judge to interpret, there can't be much law there for the bureaucrat to interpret. Are we better off with judge-made law or agency-made law? Maybe Kenneth Warren is right, that Theodore Lowi was right more than thirty years ago when he said it was time for Congress to stop leaving us with "no law."[14]

In Summary

Congress can tell the courts to stay out of certain types of decisions. It can do so clearly and directly by putting a preclusion of review clause in an agency's authorizing statute, or it can do so through the back door by making the grant of discretion to the agency so great that the judges have no standards by which to judge the legality of the agency's actions. The latter is less effective than the former, of course, since it still gives one judge a chance to find "some law" where another would find "no law," but less effective or not, it does work.

But no action of Congress can keep citizen challenges to the constitutionality of agency actions off the Court docket, and even when the Court does accept the validity of a particular preclusion of review clause, it always does so while reaffirming its long-standing presumption that most agency actions are reviewable and that Congress can act to prevent such review only in the clearest and most direct language.

Courts and Access to Judicial Review of Administrative Action

Even if Congress has given no indication that it would prefer not to have a particular decision or category of decisions reviewed, the courts themselves may still refuse to hear a citizen challenge to some bureaucratic decision. When the courts do refuse to permit a suit to go forward, it will be for one of two reasons: wrong person, wrong time.

Wrong Person: A Question of Standing

Before a single fact can be presented or a single argument launched, the court has to agree that in the deceptively simple words of Justice Brennan "the *particular* plaintiff then requesting review may have it."[15] In summarizing well over a century of case law, Justice Antonin Scalia wrote in *Lujan v. Defenders of Wildlife* that the right to bring a suit—known by the judge-created term "standing"— rested on three interconnected foundations. "First, the plaintiff must have suffered an 'injury in fact'—an invasion of a legally protected interest which is (a) concrete and particularlized...; and (b) 'actual or imminent,' not 'conjectural' or 'hypothetical.' Second, there must be a causal connection between the injury and conduct complained of—the injury has to be 'fairly ... trace(able) to the challenged action of the defendant.... Third, it must be 'likely' as opposed to merely 'speculative,' that the injury will be 'redressed by a favorable decision.' "[16] Let's take a more careful look at each of those three.

It is generally assumed that judges grounded the notion of standing in "concrete and particularlized" personal injury as a way of trying to be sure that they kept themselves on their own turf, that is, that they decided only real cases and controversies. Article III of the Constitution tells them that that is their only legitimate province, and judicial experience tells them that handling real disputes between real people is what they do best. Seeing themselves as the neutral arbiters in the adversary system, they want to make sure that both sides have done their homework, prepared their arguments, researched the law, and gotten their side as ready as it can be. Then the judge will decide who is "right." If one side has not prepared thoroughly enough, or, worse yet in the eyes of most judges, if both sides really want the same outcome and just want the judge's stamp of approval, the court can end up being mousetrapped into an improper decision. Courts have long since concluded that the requirement of a serious personal injury will prevent those so-called "friendly suits" aimed at getting court legitimization for a particular view of the law or the Constitution and will mean that all the relevant facts and arguments will be presented because each side will be so determined to come out on top.

In applying this first ingredient in the rules of standing, two questions come immediately to mind. First, what sorts of injuries have the courts recognized as serious enough to justify judicial review of agency actions? Second, what exactly does the court mean by "concrete and particularized," and why is that an important component in deciding if a particular individual should be allowed to sue?

To no one's surprise, the courts have long recognized economic injuries as legitimate bases for suits against the government. If you are going to lose your business or livelihood, or if the value of your property is going to drop, you have a good chance of being given the opportunity to take the offending agency to court. But economic injuries are not the only ones that have been recognized, as the courts have held that physical and psychological harm deserve recognition of their own, as do harm to a person's aesthetic values. It is through the last of these that the door has been opened to suits involving environmental damage.[17]

In order to meet the court's test that an injury be "concrete and particularized," that injury must be observable and it must "affect the plaintiff in a personal and individual way."[18] In perhaps simpler terms, the court has to be able to see the injury in question and has to conclude that said injury is happening to this particular individual in a manner and to a degree that it is not happening to others.

Concrete and particularized, like any other judge-created test, of course, is in the eye of the beholding judge or judges. In 1972, for example, the Supreme Court held that the members of the Sierra Club did not prove particularized enough injuries to sustain a lawsuit against the Interior Department over its decision to permit Walt Disney Enterprises to develop a place called Mineral King Valley.[19] A year later, however, they held that five enterprising law students could sue the Interstate Commerce Commission over an increase in freight rates because that increase could result in increased litter in a park they used for recreational purposes.[20] The students lost the suit itself, but they were allowed to carry it forward. Five years later, the Court held that thermal pollution of two small lakes constituted a concrete enough injury to sustain standing for the Carolina Environmental Study Group, but that the group's claim that the possibility of a future nuclear accident, and in particular the present apprehension generated by the fear of such an accident in the future, did not.[21] Finally, in 1990, the Court told the Defenders of Wildlife that even though it gave a careful and exhaustive listing of those of its members who would suffer if certain Interior Department–managed lands were reclassified to permit mining, and even though it gave a careful and exhaustive listing of the types of injuries they would suffer, the group still could not challenge the department's reclassification program in court.[22] A challenge to the reclassification of a specific tract of land might well have been heard, but the program itself could not be challenged on the basis of these alleged injuries.

To obtain standing you have to do more than assert an injury. You have to show some sort of connection between the injury that you claim has occurred (will occur) and the action of the government that you are challenging. In the words that Justice Scalia borrowed from Lewis Powell, a plaintiff gains standing only if the "injury can fairly be traced to the challenged action of the defendant."[23] As with the concrete and particularlized injury test, the courts have had to apply this test for the connection between alleged injury and challenged action in the always messy world of specific cases.

In 1975 a group of low-income individuals challenged the zoning ordinance in Penfield, New York—a suburban community near Rochester—claiming that the ordinance was substantially responsible for the absence of low-income housing in Penfield. The lack of such housing, they claimed, was what kept them from living in the community they wished to live in. By a 5–4 majority, the Court denied standing, ruling that plaintiffs had not demonstrated that it was the zoning ordinance that kept them out of Penfield. Instead, according to the Court, their inability to move into Penfield was a "consequence of the economics of the area housing market."[24]

The following year, the Court was presented with a case challenging an IRS change in the standards under which a hospital could qualify for tax exempt status as a charitable organization.[25] In denying standing, the Court held that while it was clear that plaintiffs had been denied medical care by hospitals in the areas in which they lived [eastern Kentucky], those hospitals were not the defendants. The defendants were officials of the U.S. Treasury Department, and those officials had not denied these plaintiffs medical care nor, more to the point, could the plaintiffs demonstrate that the IRS ruling was the cause of the hospitals' decisions to deny that care.[26]

Finally, to return once more to Justice Scalia's characterization of the rules of standing, a plaintiff will be permitted to take his or her suit forward only if "it is 'likely,' as opposed to merely 'speculative' that the injury will be 'redressed by a favorable decision.' "[27] Courts have long interpreted the case and controversy requirement of Article III to mean that their job is to resolve disputes. A decision which has no impact, that is, one which does not redress the injury, is no resolution at all, and therefore outside of the boundaries of the courts' legitimate role.

A brief revisiting of the two cases discussed above shows the Supreme Court's concern with the likely impact of the decisions that the plaintiffs in each case asked them to reach. In *Warth v. Seldin*—the case involving the Penfield zoning ordinance—the Court indicated some question about the probability that a decision to strike down the ordinance would result in much in the way of new low-income housing in the community.[28] That concern for the impact of their decision was even more directly stated in *Simon v. Eastern Kentucky Welfare Rights Organization*, when Justice Powell told plaintiffs that "It is equally speculative whether the desired exercise of the court's remedial powers in this suit would result in the availability to respondents of such services."[29]

Before we leave the question of standing, one final note is in order. To convince the court that you—"the particular plaintiff [now] requesting review"—are entitled to that review, you do not have to prove that your view of the Constitution, the law, or the facts is the correct one. What you have to prove is that if your view is the correct one, then you have suffered (will suffer) an injury that is substantial and that has not, like the rain, fallen on everyone equally, that the injury quite probably stems from the specific government action that you are challenging, and that a decision by the court will change your lot. The rules of standing are not being used to keep people from suing the government over its actions. They are being used to make sure that when the court hears a particular suit, it will be doing what we as a people have always told it to do, decide a particular case and controversy in a fair manner.

Wrong Time: You're Too Late! Or Was That Too Early?

Timing in suing the government is like timing in anything else. You could be too late, or you could be too early. Actually, you could be two different kinds of too late, and three different kinds of too early, and there are even some exceptions to those. Unless you are going to make your living suing the government—or defending it—a quick run-through of the different kinds of too late and too early should be all you need. But you do need that.

First of all, you can end up too late if the Congress has established a time frame for the filing of particular types of actions. Discrimination cases, including sexual harassment complaints, must be filed within a specified period of time if the courts are to hear them. Congress has imposed the same kinds of limitations in a variety of other situations.

Second, the courts will tell you that you are too late with your suit if they conclude that the harm has ceased, and therefore that their decision will have no practical effect. This is another angle on the case and controversy requirement. If the harm has ceased, then there is no case and controversy to decide, only a general principle to pronounce—that is, only the issuing of an advisory opinion, something the courts have forbidden themselves from doing from the beginning of our legal system.

The story of Marco DeFunis, a young man who wanted to attend the University of Washington Law School, provides a nice example of being too late—and in being too late, losing the battle and winning the war. Marco wasn't admitted to the law school, and he sued claiming reverse discrimination because the university's affirmative action program had resulted in the admission of minority candidates whose grades and LSAT scores were lower than his. Marco's attorney got a temporary injunction admitting him pending the outcome of the case, and with a couple of delaying motions combined with the crowded calendar of Seattle's Federal District Court, the case wasn't ready for final disposition until near the end of Marco's three years in school. Once the Supreme Court determined that Mr. DeFunis was going to graduate and become an attorney regardless of the outcome of the case—regardless, in other words, of whether this affirmative action plan constituted reverse discrimination—the Court refused to rule, and the country waited for Allan Bakke and the University of California to have their day in court.[30]

The Administrative Procedure Act gives the courts the right to review "final agency action," so your suit is going to be too early if the agency you want to challenge can convince the court in question that it is not finished yet. This requirement that the courts wait for agencies to finish is based on two concerns. To begin with, we are back to the effort to make sure that someone bringing suit against the government is ready to do the heavy work of making sure the best possible case is going to be made against that action. The courts want to see exactly what the impact of an action is. Who has been injured and in what ways? They can't be sure if the agency is only part way through. Beyond that, courts—and the Congress—are aware that judicial review of an administrative action not yet finished is an invitation to disaster. Judges do not have the necessary subject-matter expertise, there is no real case to be decided, and in any event, there is nothing much for a judge to review yet. The review that ultimately takes place, after all, is the review of some sort of record. Partway through the administrative process there isn't going to be the kind of record that a judge can review with confidence.

It ought to be relatively easy to figure out whether or not an agency is through with its decision, and in most cases the courts feel fairly confident that they can do just that. The judge will look at an agency's normal decision-making processes and its internal rules, and in some cases just ask the agency if in fact it is done.

But there is one situation in which courts and citizens alike have found themselves frustrated by the final agency action rule. Specifically, when the decision not to take action has exactly the same effect as a negative decision, the final action rule would seem to prevent review of that non-action decision, though it would permit review of a negative decision. Agencies used that difference to their advantage for years by casting most negative actions as inaction. In 1970 the D.C. Circuit took that issue on squarely, and the case and its resolution provide a good illustration of this one key problem with the final agency action rule.

Back in the late 1960s, the Environmental Defense Fund (EDF) asked the U.S. Department of Agriculture (USDA)—which then had jurisdiction over such questions—to review several uses of the pesticide DDT and to suspend its use in nearly all circumstances. USDA did begin to collect some data and take some very low-level steps toward restriction of DDT for some uses, but refused to begin any suspension proceeding. EDF sued, and the department replied that it had not taken any final action, so the suit was premature. The Circuit disagreed with USDA, saying in part: "When administrative inaction has precisely the same impact on the rights of the parties as denial of relief, an agency cannot preclude judicial review by casting its decision in the form of inaction rather than an order denying relief."[31]

The Seventh Circuit didn't see things the same way,[32] and neither did the newly created Environmental Protection Agency, since the Environmental Defense Fund had to take that agency to court a year later over the same issue.[33] The D.C. Circuit sided with EDF once more, but the battle continued until DDT was finally banned in all of its uses several years later.

As a practical matter, it is hard to quarrel with the D.C. Circuit when it says that when the word "no" and the words "we're not yet ready to proceed" have exactly the same effect, and when that effect is serious harm to someone, and when the word "no" is reviewable in court, it is hard to see why the words "we're not yet ready to proceed" shouldn't be as well. But as another and quite opposite practical matter, when the D.C. Circuit got into the business of reviewing "we're not yet ready to proceed," it found a real briar patch. No record, no order, administrators screaming foul, and no clear idea of what to tell USDA or EPA to do. Get the lead—or the DDT—out just doesn't seem to be much of an order for a court to issue to an agency. Why? How? How soon? All of those are questions the judges weren't in a position to answer.

On a related note, this is one of those cases I referred to earlier as one in which the search for justice for the parties involved may have gotten in the way of a sound legal principle to guide future action by agencies and courts. USDA had acted outrageously with respect to DDT, and had done so to protect its clients in the agriculture community. EPA seemed to be doing more or less the same thing. The Environmental Defense Fund couldn't seem to win anywhere else, and the judges on the D.C. Circuit concluded that they deserved to win and set about trying to find a way to make it happen. But in the end, as Richard Pierce, Sidney Shapiro, and Paul Verkuil rather clearly show, the judges created real headaches for themselves and their compatriots on the federal bench around the country, and hastened the ban on DDT only a little in the process.[34]

A court may also tell you that you have challenged an agency action too early by telling you that your case is not yet "ripe." It may take the practiced eye of a federal judge to distinguish between the doctrine of final agency action and the doctrine of ripeness, and since I am not such a judge, and since those of you reading this who will be have plenty of time and opportunity to learn how to make that distinction before you get to the bench, we will keep this discussion short and as non-technical as I can make it.

In general, the added ingredient that makes a case involving a final agency action ripe is the process of enforcement. In essence, the judges are saying let's not discuss how this rule might affect your activities, Mr. or Ms. Citizen, let's wait to see how it does affect them. Then we can talk.

Interestingly enough, the case that is usually held up as the lead case on ripeness is a case that establishes the one key exception to the notion of enforcement as a critical ingredient in making an agency action reviewable. In the mid-1960s, the Food and Drug Administration (FDA) prepared a rule that would have required all pharmaceutical manufacturers to print the generic name of any of their trademarked drugs every time they used the trade name. This would have been true in advertising, on the inserts instructing individuals how to take the medicine, and even on the packaging. Abbott Laboratories, Inc., sued, claiming the FDA didn't have the legal authority to issue such a rule. The FDA said the case wasn't ripe, since there had been no enforcement action. The Supreme Court held in favor of Abbott Labs, saying clearly and straightforwardly that if the only issue at hand is the legality of an administrative action, and if the costs of compliance with that action are substantial and probably unrecoverable—in this case Abbott Labs feared the negative publicity associated with a long hassle with the FDA—then a case is ripe for decision. There would be no purpose in waiting for the facts generated by an enforcement decision when the issue was the right of the agency even to write the rule in the first place.[35]

Nearly two decades later, the Court came to the same conclusion when Union Carbide Agricultural Products challenged the constitutionality of an arbitration scheme then in use by the Environmental Protection Agency in its enforcement of the Federal Insecticide, Fungicide, and Rodenticide Act.[36] But in 1993 the Court held that if a rule confers benefits on citizens rather than imposing burdens on them, those citizens must apply for said benefits and be denied before their cases are ripe for judicial determination.[37]

Instead of chiding you for not waiting for the agency to take final action, or bringing a case not yet ripe, the courts may say you have brought your case too early because you have failed to exhaust all of the available administrative remedies. Nearly a century ago, Oliver Wendell Holmes claimed that not requiring a citizen to follow the appeals process within the bureaucracy before approaching the courts would "create an unnecessary burden on the courts to resolve problems that should be decided by governmental agencies."[38] In 1992 the Court reminded us of another good reason to require the exhaustion of administrative remedies. An agency deserves the right "to correct its own mistakes with respect to the programs it administers before it is hauled into federal court."[39]

On the surface, exhaustion would seem to be the easiest timing test of all. If there is an administrative appeals process, and if you have not followed it step by step, your case will not be heard. But, as always, there is an "unless" or two buried beneath that surface.

If you can convince a court that the administrative appeals process you have bypassed is constitutionally deficient, you are likely to be heard. First Amendment claims, of course, have been the most successful, but a group of Alabama optometrists successfully challenged a license revocation appeals process that clearly involved conflict of interest on the part of the hearing panel.[40] The Court has also held that grievants should not be required to wait indefinitely, nor pursue an administrative appeals process in which the agency was applying a futile administrative remedy.[41] In 1986 the Supreme Court intervened because it felt that application of the exhaustion doctrine would cause "irreparable injury" to those who had brought the claim.[42] And in 1993 the Court determined that a plaintiff need not exhaust an optional administrative review process.[43]

Finally, a court might deny a plaintiff the opportunity to present his or her case on the grounds that an administrative agency has "primary jurisdiction" over this particular dispute. In a sense the court is telling such a plaintiff he or she is in the wrong place, but given the fact that when the court cites the doctrine of primary jurisdiction it is not saying that it does not have jurisdiction over such cases at any time, but rather at the present time, it is probably best to think of the primary jurisdiction doctrine as one more way of saying to a challenger: you are here at the wrong time.

The doctrine evolved largely as a way for the courts to tell people not to try to bypass the relevant administrative agencies and go straight to court for relief. Because of that, primary jurisdiction cases often involve disputes between private parties or between the government and a private party but with the government initiating the action. For example, one of the first such cases involved an argument between the Abilene Cotton Oil Company and the Texas and Pacific Railroad over what the former perceived as excessive freight charges. The Court told Abilene Cotton to take its case to the Interstate Commerce Commission, the outfit with jurisdiction over railroad freight rates.[44] The government itself got the same piece of advice from Chief Justice Warren Burger and the Court majority eighty years later in a case involving the Burlington Northern Railroad.[45]

In the early 1950s, the Justice Department went after a group called the Far Eastern Conference—a consortium of shipping companies—for a dual pricing system that the department thought violated anti-trust law. The Court told the Justice Department that it would first have to head for the Maritime Board, since that was the group who should get the first opportunity to correct the problem.[46]

Of course, the Court does sometimes feel that the primary jurisdiction belongs to the judicial branch and not the executive. In 1976, in a decision he or she no doubt regretted for a very very long time, an Allegheny Airlines gate attendant bumped a passenger with a confirmed reservation from an overbooked flight. The passenger was Ralph Nader, and in 1976 the Supreme Court reversed the ruling of the District and Circuit Courts and held that Mr. Nader was not required to take his complaint to the Civil Aeronautics Board. Since his complaint involved "fraudulent misrepresentation," the issues were well "within the conventional competence of the courts."[47]

In Summary

Just as Congress can deny you your "day in court," so can the court itself. It can do so because it has concluded that you do not have the right to bring your suit at all. Perhaps you have not suffered an injury the court finds sufficient or sufficiently different from that of others to sustain your claim. Perhaps it has concluded that the injury cannot be attributed to the particular agency action you have challenged. Or perhaps the court is convinced that the action you are asking it to take will not constitute a real remedy for your injury. Even if a court concludes that you would have standing to sue a particular agency over a particular decision, it might conclude that you have brought your suit at the wrong time. If the harm has already ceased, the court's decision will, in effect, be nothing but an advisory opinion, and no judge believes the issuing of such an opinion to be his or her prerogative. If the agency has not finished its work, if you have attempted to bypass an agency altogether, if you have not exhausted the appropriate administrative remedies, or if your case is not yet ripe, the judges will tell you to come back later. Or at least they will tell you, "not now."

When Can a Citizen Sue: The Summary

Whatever our mythology may say, there are times when an American is not entitled to his or her day in court, at least not if that day in court was to be spent challenging the action of some government agency on the grounds that that action was unconstitutional, illegal, or just plain wrongheaded. The courts may conclude that Congress has precluded that citizen's—any citizen's—day in court on this issue, or they may conclude that this particular citizen doesn't deserve a day in court over this question, or they may even conclude that this particular citizen doesn't get this particular day on this particular issue, though some other day might be just fine.

There can be little doubt that there have been instances in which a specific court used one of these doctrines—be it congressional preclusion, "no law to apply," standing, ripeness, or any of the rest—to deny an aggrieved citizen a chance to challenge some action of government that clearly deserved to be challenged. But there can also be little doubt that every one of these doctrines serves a vital purpose in dividing up the turf of government and keeping its various participants on the turf they ought to control. Congress has to be able to tell courts when to back off, or we lose an important ingredient in self-government. The courts have to be able to say, "not if it involves the Constitution, thanks," if we are to preserve the individual rights that are such an important part of our idea of what it means to be free. Courts have to make sure that they stick to the resolution of actual disputes and that their decisions will make a difference to the lives of the parties to those disputes. Administrative agencies have to be left alone to apply their expertise, interpret and apply policy, and yes, to correct their own mistakes, without judges breathing down their necks. And yet, those agencies have to know that even if the judges aren't breathing down their necks, they are on the nearby field ready to go to work if and when they are needed.

In the end, it's a little messy, but the alternative, any suit, any decision, any time, is a whole lot messier.

BEATING THE GOVERNMENT AND THE ODDS: THE SCOPE OF JUDICIAL REVIEW OF ADMINISTRATIVE ACTION

Learning that a judge has found no reason to deny you the opportunity to try to convince him or her that the government has done something it shouldn't have or hasn't done something it should have is good news. The opposite, after all, means the game is over. But to learn you can bring the suit means the game is just beginning. To complete our discussion of judicial review, we need to take a look at the rules under which that game will be played.

The rules of the judicial review game have to answer two questions. First, what are the judges supposed to review? What are they going to look at and what are they going to look for? Second, and a little more difficult to answer, what must a judge or group of judges conclude before telling an agency that it can't do what it has done, or has to do what it hasn't done?

What to Review?

The answer to our first question is deceptively simple. Judges review something called "the record." The answer is simple because there is nothing else a court could review. It is deceptive because "the record" can mean anything from the recollections of a harried administrator to a 20,000-page hearing transcript. Or it can mean lots of things in between.

If Congress has put the magic words—"on the record, after opportunity for agency hearing"—into an authorizing statute, then any judge subsequently called upon to hear a case involving a decision made under that statute will have a formal hearing transcript to review in determining whether that decision should be upheld. The transcript, like a court transcript, will include testimony given at a formal hearing plus all exhibits, written communications, and sometimes even internal agency documents relevant to the decision in question.

If Congress has decided not to require on-the-record proceedings under a particular statute, however, then the "record" that a reviewing court will have before it will consist of whatever pieces of paper the agency in question believed it was required to create and keep in the process of making this sort of decision. If the challenged agency action is a rule, then the court will be able to look at the "basis and purpose" statement administrators are required to prepare as part of their obligations under the Administrative Procedure Act. On the other hand, if the challenged action is an order or adjudication, then the record will consist of documents the agency was required to create and keep by any of three sets of people. Most often, agencies require their own paper trail as a record of the decisions they make and the reasons they make them. Occasionally, Congress will have specified what sort of paper trail it expected an agency to create when it authorized that agency to make these decisions in the first place. Finally, an agency may have been challenged on this type of decision before, and if a court demanded the creation of a particular type of record, then an agency will be expected to produce that record in any future case involving the same type of decision.

Whether the paper is stacked to the ceiling or not, the reviewing court will also hear at least some testimony and, more to the point, argument from both sides about what the stacked-up paper really says and why it says that the agency should or should not be told it has to change its ways.

When wading through the various documents before it and listening to the testimony it agrees to hear, the court is really looking at three things. First, of course, it is looking at the law or, more properly, at at least two different laws with two different questions in mind. It will be looking at substantive law, that is, at the agency's authorizing statute and the question of whether or not the agency's action is legal. Beyond that, the court will look at administrative law, that is, at the question of whether the agency made the decision illegally. Second, a reviewing court is going to look at the information the agency has collected that it claims justifies the decision it has reached. Finally, the court is going to look at the agency's reasoning process. Why does the information the agency has in its possession justify the decision it has reached? OSHA has the legal authority to regulate the noise levels to which workers are exposed, and it has collected data on the noise levels in various factories and on the connection between noise levels and hearing loss. But the big question, as always, is: does what OSHA knows about noise levels in American factories and about the connection between noise levels and hearing loss justify a rule that mandates lower noise levels? And, even trickier, does what OSHA knows about all of those things justify this particular rule specifying these particular acceptable noise levels?

So, looking at "the record"—whatever that may mean in a given context—and listening to testimony and argument, a judge tries to determine if a decision was legal and constitutional, that is, authorized by the constitutional government and made within the procedural guidelines applicable to that particular type of decision. Then he or she will look at that same record, looking for an indication of the information the agency relied on in coming to its decision and for some idea of why the agency decided the way it did. The next question, and the tougher question, is: what does the judge have to see before he or she will conclude an agency is wrong? That's the question for the next section.

When Should a Judge Say No?

Administrative law textbooks don't put the question that way. Instead, they phrase it in terms of the question of how much "deference" a reviewing court ought to show to an agency decision. The answer, it turns out, lies somewhere along a continuum with NONE at one end and ALMOST COMPLETE at the other. To be a little more precise, judges could decide to give no credence whatever to agency decisions, looking at the Constitution, the law, the evidence, and the reasoning process as if the agency had not done so already, and come to their own conclusions, overturning any decisions they didn't agree with. On the other hand, judges could look at the Constitution, the law, the evidence, and the reasoning process, assuming that the agency had done its job thoroughly and carefully, overturning only those decisions the judges found to be almost totally indefensible, that is, that were the product of obviously faulty reasoning based on facts that don't hold up to the scrutiny of even the least informed of laypersons, clearly contrary to the intent of the constitutional government, or made using procedures that violate the Constitution or the law. Then, of course, there is all that ground in between, the ground that judges normally occupy.

Judging in an Ideal Administrative World

Where we would like a judge to be on that continuum depends on the type of decision he or she is reviewing. Whether engaged in rule making or adjudication, bureaucrats make four different types of decisions, and the eye of the reviewing judge probably ought to change from one type to another.

First of all, bureaucrats sometimes interpret the Constitution. We don't normally think of that as a bureaucratic role, but whenever bureaucrats design decision-making procedures, especially procedures for making decisions about the fate of specific individuals, the phrase "due process of law" can—should—never be far from their minds. I suspect it isn't, that is, that bureaucrats do care about the Constitution and its guarantees of due process and equal protection, but when it comes to such questions, we have a long tradition of casting our lot with the judges. It is their turf and they are generally pretty familiar with it. When it comes to that continuum of deference toward bureaucrats, we feel safe letting them land near the end marked NONE.

Second, bureaucrats interpret the law. They interpret two kinds of laws, of course, the substantive laws that embody the promises they are supposed to be keeping, and the procedural laws that tell them how to make the decisions they are charged with making. Interpreting the law, too, is something we tend to believe to be judicial turf, though we tend to believe it with a bit less conviction. In part that is because there are two very different types of laws to be interpreted, and in the case of procedural laws, judges can be expected to have as much experience and expertise as do the bureaucrats. But substantive laws can be a different matter. In the first place, they are about a specific subject, a subject with which bureaucrats are, by definition, intimately familiar. Judges probably aren't. Beyond that, some people from the agency charged with administering a particular statute almost certainly helped to write it. They can be expected to have some idea of what Congress meant when it drafted specific provisions. On the other hand, substantive statutes are still statutes, drafted mostly by lawyers to be read by other lawyers, and judges are, of course, other lawyers. And, as I said earlier, judges think statutory interpretation is their job, and the rest of the government usually agrees. So we expect judges to slide a ways from NONE, but we aren't too sure—or we aren't in agreement—about how far. Judges aren't sure either, so different judges tend to slide different distances. More on that shortly.

Third, bureaucrats find facts. At least Congress, bureaucrats, and judges all say that bureaucrats do something called finding facts. There turn out to be two rather different kinds of activities that are covered by the notion of bureaucratic fact finding. To begin with, there is what most of us think of when we think of finding a fact. OSHA researchers look at every study ever done linking benzene exposure to leukemia and "find" that exposure at a particular level increases the risk of that disease by 20 percent. The National Highway Traffic Safety Administration tests two tires manufactured by different companies but given the same treadwear number under a voluntary industry testing system, only to "find" that the two tires wear very differently. But Congress, bureaucrats, and judges have also used the term "fact finding" when referring to a "finding," such as benzene being a carcinogen as defined in the Occupational Safety and Health Act, or there being no feasible alternative to routing Interstate 40 through Overton Park. We want judges to give considerable credence to these bureaucratic findings of fact, though probably more to the one type than to the other. It is one thing—a rather disturbing thing at that—for a judge to say he or she has reviewed the studies and that there is no evidence linking benzene with leukemia. It is quite another for a judge to say that there might be a feasible alternative route for Interstate 40. Whichever type of fact finding a judge is reviewing, we want deference to mean a healthy respect, not blind acceptance.

Finally comes what may be the toughest review of all, review of what the courts usually call the agency's reasoning process. What was the chain of reasoning that led the agency from these specific facts to this particular action? Or, to put it another way, why do these facts justify this action? We want judges to show deference to bureaucratic reasoning, just as we want them to show deference to bureaucratic fact finding. Just not quite as much deference. That healthy respect now has to have a bigger dose of skepticism in it. The kind of reasoning we are talking about cannot be done without some subject-matter knowledge, so we don't want judges feeling free to trash any agency decision they don't happen to agree with. On the other hand, as we saw earlier, one of the biggest problems with contemporary bureaucracy is its tendency to see everything through the very narrow field of vision typical of so many professions and the men and women in them. Looking at the reasoning process with a layperson's eye may provide at least a chance for correcting the effects of that tunnel vision that has sometimes produced ineffective and/or irresponsible policy.

In an ideal administrative world, then, we would want judges to look at the different types of decisions bureaucrats are called upon to make with different standards in mind. When bureaucrats are interpreting the Constitution, judges should feel free to arrive at their own conclusions. It's in the job description. When reviewing the interpretation of statutes, judges need to give bureaucrats a little more of the benefit of the doubt, but exactly how much will depend on the type of statute being interpreted and the situation in which the interpretation was done. When we move to fact finding, things change once more, with judges reasonably expected to give bureaucrats a wide berth on facts as pieces of information that really can be "found," while riding the agencies a good bit harder on those findings that are actually conclusions. Finally, judges need to review agency reasoning processes with the understanding that subject-matter knowledge has to be respected, but that sometimes you don't have to be an expert to see that the Emperor is wearing absolutely nothing.

Judging in the Real Administrative World

We don't live in an ideal administrative world, of course, so judges end up looking at these four kinds of decisions a little differently than we—and especially they—might wish. In part they do it for reasons of their own, but mostly they do it because Congress has chosen to structure the review process along very different lines. Specifically, if Congress has chosen to tell an agency that a particular category of decisions must be made "on the record," then we get one standard of review for that type of decision. If, on the other hand, Congress has not included the "on the record" requirement, then the review is to be conducted under a very different standard. As we'll see, the courts have done some modifying of this congressionally created dichotomy, but they have not been able—or maybe willing—to get rid of it completely.

In effect, then, the standards for reviewing different types of bureaucratic decisions are a melding of the judges' recognition that the proper division of the decision-making turf between themselves and the bureaucrats depends in large part on the type of decision being reviewed and the Congress's insistence that that proper turf division should depend on how closely the legislative branch wants the bureaucrats to be monitored by the judges. It can get a little confusing, but in the end, standards for review do exist and we can make at least some sense of them.

The Constitution and the Law

Let's start with the easy one. On-the-record requirement or not-on-the-record requirement, the courts still feel that constitutional interpretation is their job, and they look at an agency's view of what constitutes due process, equal protection, or a reasonable search, fully confident that their own judgment is the one that deserves to prevail.

The on-the-record requirement doesn't have much effect on judicial review of statutory interpretation either, since even the sketchiest of records is likely to contain some reference to the statutory authority under which the decision is being made. If it doesn't, the judge will find out how the agency interpreted the law as soon as the trial begins. Judges are a bit more circumspect about substituting their interpretation of a statute for that of an agency than they are about substituting their view of the Constitution for the one that prevailed in the bureaucracy, but that doesn't mean they are reluctant to conclude that an agency read the law wrong and should be told what the right reading is. It happens with some frequency.

The current rule for judicial review of statutory interpretation comes from the case of *Chevron U.S.A. v. Natural Resources Defense Council*, decided in 1984.[48] The 1977 amendments to the Clean Air Act required that any company planning to create a major new "source" of air pollution had to go through a new source review process conducted by the Environmental Protection Agency. During the Carter administration (1977–1981), the EPA defined "source" in very specific terms. That is, each part of a facility was considered a source in itself. When Ronald Reagan assumed the presidency in 1981, EPA redefined "source" as an entire facility. Now there would be no review requirement as long as the entire facility did not increase its emission of pollutants by more than the threshold amount set by the agency as its definition of "major" new pollution.

The Natural Resources Defense Council (NRDC) brought suit in the D.C. Circuit, arguing that the EPA could not change the meaning of the law so drastically on its own authority. The Circuit held in favor of NRDC, but the Supreme Court reversed in the process creating what it referred to as a two-part test for determining if an agency's interpretation of its own enabling statute should be upheld.

Test #1, logically enough, centered on the specificity of the language of the statute. Had Congress spoken in a clear and direct way to the question at hand? In this case, the answer was a clear-cut no. Congress had not defined source. That job did fall to the EPA. In a good many other cases, of course, the task of figuring out if Congress has given direct and concrete meaning to a particular portion of what is almost certainly a vaguely worded statute will be difficult at best. There are tools for figuring out what a statute is supposed to mean—looking at the legislative history, statements of goals, and the like—but they are imprecise tools at best, leaving judges with a good bit of room to impose their own views of what a law ought to mean.

Test #2 is even more difficult to apply. Called the "permissible construction" test, it calls upon reviewing judges to accept an agency's interpretation of its enabling statute if that interpretation is based on a "permissible construction" of the statute in question. Given the ambiguity of so many statutes, how can anyone say that any construction of a law that isn't virtually off the wall is not "permissible." Can anyone really say with conviction that we simply cannot define "source" of pollution as a single smokestack? Can anyone say we cannot define "source" as an entire factory? Both definitions work. For different purposes, to be sure, but they do both work.

Though it was decided eight years earlier, the case of *Bishop v. Wood* provides real insight into the difficulty of applying the permissible construction test. Bishop, recall from the last chapter, was a North Carolina police officer who was dismissed after his probationary period was over and who sued, claiming he had been denied due process protections in the decision to fire him. Knowing he needed to show a statutory basis for his claim that his job was a property right, Bishop's attorneys cited the city personnel ordinance of the city he had worked for. In rejecting Officer Bishop's claim that the ordinance did create for him a property interest in his job, Justice John Paul Stevens, writing for the majority, said, "On its face, the ordinance on which petitioner relies may fairly be read as conferring such a guarantee. However, such a reading is not the only possible interpretation; the ordinance may also be construed as granting no right to continued employment."[49] If a statute can reasonably be read to say yes and no to the same question, how can one give it an impermissible construction?

Difficult as the *Chevron* tests may be to apply, they may produce a more or less appropriate balance between judges and bureaucrats. The question of how to define "source" is a policy question. It takes place in the context of interpreting the law, but it is a policy decision. Courts normally aren't the places to make such decisions. So we give the agency considerable input into the interpretation of its own statute. But the notion of "permissible construction" is sufficiently vague to give a judge plenty of room for intervention if he or she feels an agency has begun making policy it isn't really empowered to make. Indeed, Professor Thomas Merrill concluded that the *Chevron* standard had left judges so much room that they were paying less deference to administrative interpretations of the law than they had before that landmark decision.[50] Interestingly enough, in that same year, Professor Michael Herz concluded just the opposite.[51] No one can be certain, but it seems as if we may have taken a less-than-direct route to someplace that looks an awful lot like where we started.

Agency Fact Finding

When reviewing agency findings of fact or reasoning processes, the courts do have to take into account Congress's effort to structure the review process around the on-the-record/not-on-the-record distinction, but as we'll see shortly, they take it into account far less than they did a decade or two ago. Still, since the Administrative Procedure Act does make the distinction and since it was a very important distinction for a fairly long period of time, it's worth taking a look at what Congress originally intended the process of reviewing agency decisions to look like.

When Congress uses the magic words "on the record, after opportunity for agency hearing," courts are instructed to set aside decisions "unsupported by substantial evidence . . . on the record." In its original definition of the substantial evidence test, the Supreme Court held that "It [substantial evidence] means such relevant evidence as a reasonable mind might accept as adequate to support a conclusion."[52] A little over a decade later, the Court came to a balancing test, that is, added to the notion of substantial evidence the idea that the reviewing court was to look at the evidence the agency said supported its decision but was also to consider "whatever in the record detracts from its weight."[53] There have been refinements of the substantial evidence test over the years, but its basic ingredients—looking at the record as a whole, not just the evidence that supports a decision, and assessing that evidence by asking if a reasonable person would reach that conclusion from that record—have survived more or less intact for more than forty years.[54]

If Congress does not impose the "on the record" requirement, however, then a reviewing court is to set aside an agency's decision only if it finds that decision to be "arbitrary, capricious, an abuse of discretion, or otherwise not in accordance with law." At first the arbitrary and capricious test was interpreted to give administrators almost unchecked authority. There wasn't much of a record to review anyway, but the courts were extraordinarily deferential in reviewing what they did find. Then, beginning in the 1960s and taking off in the wake of the Supreme Court's 1971 ruling in *Citizens to Preserve Overton Park v. Volpe*, the courts began to demand a more and more extensive record to look at, and to apply a more and more demanding standard for accepting the results of bureaucratic deliberations even in these so-called informal settings.[55]

So great have been the changes in the interpretation of these two standards in the past two decades that Richard Pierce, Sidney Shapiro, and Paul Verkuil have concluded that we are on the verge of seeing the end of the distinction itself.[56] Congress has contributed by requiring the substantial evidence test in numerous statutes that do not require on-the-record decision making, and the courts themselves have gone even further by simply redefining the arbitrary and capricious test to bring it more in line with the more familiar—and in the eyes of most judges, more reasonable—substantial evidence test.

Whether ostensibly applying the substantial evidence test or the arbitrary and capricious test, reviewing courts have been remarkably deferential to agency findings of fact. Given the rather elastic notion of "facts" and the finding of same that prevails in administrative policy making, the courts probably have little choice. Consider, for example, the Federal Communications Commission (FCC) "finding" that the marketplace rather than the FCC's own subjective judgments was the best protector of the listening public's interest in diverse entertainment.[57] What evidence would support—or refute—such a finding? More to the point, even if there is something we might call evidence on such a question, it is the kind of evidence that is best sifted through by policy makers, elected or appointed, not by judges. In fact, this is the kind of decision probably best left to policy makers, not judges, and the judges seem to recognize it. That's not to say that there should never be review of such decisions and the "evidence" on which they are based, only that, as the courts themselves have concluded, such review should be done with great respect for what the policy makers know and for their legitimate role in the governing system.

Agency Reasoning

Reviewing the agency's reasoning process can—probably should—be a somewhat different game. Even if we are willing to say that the statement that the market will protect listeners better than will the FCC is a finding of fact, there is still that final step to the conclusion that a new rule changing the standards for granting or renewing broadcast licenses is justified. That is reasoning—explaining why the facts you found led to the decision you made—and it can and should be reviewed with less deference.

In 1983 the Supreme Court heard the case of *Motor Vehicle Manufacturer's Association v. State Farm Automobile Insurance Co.*[58] The case involved the decision by the National Highway Traffic Safety Administration (NHTSA) to rescind a rule the agency had issued in the Carter administration. That rule would have required auto makers to equip all cars with some sort of passive restraint system, that is, with air bags or automatic seat belts. The Court held that an agency's action could be set aside if it "relied on factors which Congress has not intended it to consider, entirely failed to consider an important aspect of the problem, offered an explanation for its decision that runs counter to the evidence before the agency, or is so implausible that it could not be ascribed to a difference in view or the product of expertise." Looking at the recision of the passive restraint rule, the Court concluded that NHTSA had acted in a manner that was "arbitrary and capricious." Two reasons.

First, the agency had argued that most manufacturers would choose the alternative of automatic seat belts, and that would mean that the more effective air bags wouldn't be available, and so the rule as originally promulgated was counterproductive to the agency mission of saving lives and preventing serious injuries. The Court held that such reasoning didn't hold up, since the obvious alternative was to simply require air bags. If air bags are really that much better than automatic seat belts, then amend the rule to require air bags. You don't prevent people from making the wrong choice by giving them more choices, but by giving them fewer.

Second, the agency had said people would disconnect automatic seat belts and, consequently, that seat belt use would go up only 5 percent, so the rule was obviously useless. The Court reminded NHTSA that the only available data— collected and analyzed by the agency itself—showed that seat belt use doubled when cars were equipped with automatic belts, and went on to admonish all agencies not to ignore the only data it has on a subject just because that data does not support the agency's conclusions.

In Summary

If someone does end up convincing a judge to examine a particular agency action, that judge is going to ask for whatever type of record exists—or is supposed to exist—for that type of decision, determine for himself or herself the appropriate standard for review of that sort of decision, and then try to figure out if the challenged decision should be overturned. If the challenge is a constitutional one, that is, if it turns on an interpretation of some provision of the Constitution, the judge need look no further than his or her own knowledge of that document and its contemporary meaning. If the challenge is based on the law, the judge has to look at what the agency says the law means, and he or she has to consider that agency opinion as authoritative. Authoritative, but definitely not controlling. If the challenge is to an agency finding of fact, then the judge is going to be reluctant to say to that agency, "Wrong, try again". It does happen, but not very often. Finally, if the challenge is to an agency's reasoning process, the judge will land somewhere in the middle, paying careful attention to the agency's arguments and the connection between the facts it claims to have found and the decision it has reached, asking if the former justify the latter. The reasoning may have to be from pretty far out in left field to bring a judge to decide to overturn, but it probably wouldn't have to be from all the way to the left field foul pole. The warning track anywhere from left center over would probably be enough.

   In the end, the real world of judicial review of administrative actions is far from perfect. Reviewing courts can be frustratingly inconsistent, and many opinions leave administrators wondering exactly what they did wrong and how they could avoid that mistake in the future. Still, we have worked out review standards that seem to result in a sharing of power between administrators and judges that makes pretty good sense and that, in the long run anyway, gives citizens a reasonable chance to overturn clearly unreasonable decisions and administrators a reasonable chance to go on about their business in some more or less reasonable way.

Some Final Observations on Judicial Review of Policy Decisions

Judicial review does provide a check on the arbitrary use of power by bureaucracy, and consequently it helps us achieve governmental accountability. But there are some unresolved problems in the review process that tend to make it less effective than it might be in moving us toward that important goal. Four seem worthy of at least brief mention.

   First, judicial review always delays action. That is its purpose, after all: slow them down so they don't do anything illegal. But delay is never neutral. By definition, it preserves the status quo.

   Second, courts have almost never been willing to review enforcement decisions, that is, to review the penalties meted out by the various agencies. Most frustrating, at least to many people, is the refusal to entertain equal protection arguments when wildly disparate penalties are handed out for what on the surface appears to be the very same action.

Third, there is a great deal of inconsistency among reviewing courts. This, in turn, raises three very real problems. To begin with, agencies have almost universally argued that they are bound by a particular court ruling only within the geographic boundaries of that court's jurisdiction. When you add to that the fact that agencies do not consider themselves bound to seek clarification in the face of inconsistent rulings from different courts, it turns out that many agencies obey a court ruling they disagree with only in the jurisdiction in which it was made, and "obey" the friendlier ruling everywhere else. Finally, there is the question of whether or not a ruling binds an agency only in the cases decided, in all similar future cases, or in future and past cases. All three of these problems are starkly illustrated in the nearly three-year battle between the Department of Health and Human Services (HHS) and the Ninth Circuit in the early 1980s.[59]

To shorten the story a bit, HHS wanted to reduce the disability rolls, and it changed the rules for determining eligibility for such payments as a way to do so. The Ninth Circuit heard two cases and reversed HHS both times. The department proceeded to announce that the judges of the Ninth Circuit were wrong and that it would obey their ruling only in the two cases involved. The Secretary of HHS then went on to say that only a ruling of the Supreme Court would suffice to get the department to change its mind. Ninth Circuit judges were outraged, and one district judge within the circuit ordered HHS to reinstate all individuals forced off the disability rolls by the department's refusal to obey the court's ruling. The department appealed, the Ninth Circuit affirmed its district judge, and HHS still refused. It all ended when Congress changed the rules, but neither the courts nor the bureaucrats blinked, and it was a frustrating battle for both. It didn't lift the spirits of the people who felt they were wrongly denied disability benefits, either.

Fourth, last, and quite possibly most important, when an agency does lose in court, the result is what is called remanding. The agency is told to start over again and make the decision in a manner consistent with the court's opinion. Often as not, this ends up meaning that the agency can make precisely the same decision, but has to make some alterations in its procedures, or provide better reasoning, or provide evidence to counter some evidence it had ignored in the original proceeding. When that is the result, we seem to end up spending an awful lot of time and money to reach the same destination by an alternate route. Is it worth it?

SUMMARY AND CONCLUSION

Courts can, and do, review administrative actions. They can, and do, overturn those actions. But there are rules for when the courts can review what an agency has done, and there are rules for when they can overturn them. The rules for when a court can review an agency action originate both with the Congress and with the courts themselves.

Congress wants to make sure that courts don't enter the administrative decision-making process too soon, so it has made only final agency action reviewable. Congress also wants to make sure that some agency actions don't get reviewed at all, and when that is its goal, all it needs to do is insert into that agency's authorizing statute a preclusion of review clause, and unless the subsequent citizen challenge has a solid constitutional foundation, the courts will stay out.

Over the years, the courts have supplemented these congressional instructions with some rules of their own. Judges, too, know the problems that come when they enter the decision-making process too early, and they have added to the final agency action requirement the ripeness doctrine and the concept of mootness, in the hope that they will be able to stick to their specialty: real disputes between real people over real rights. Because the Constitution tells them to stick to cases—as does their training and every instinct left from their days as practicing attorneys—the courts have also demanded that both sides in every dispute be prepared to duel to the death over the issues involved. Out of that comes the notion of standing, and the requirement that an individual bringing suit be able to show a substantial personal injury, some connection between the injury and the government action being challenged, and some reason to believe that the court's decision will result in a righting of this particular wrong.

Once the courts decide to step in, there is a real temptation to consider them the 800-pound gorillas of the governing system. They decide anything they want. But they don't. There are rules for what they can decide, just as there are rules for when they can decide.

If a citizen challenges an agency action on constitutional grounds, that is judge turf. The judge can set aside what an agency has done and worry for not a moment about the fact that the administrator saw the Constitution differently. As we move from the Constitution to the statutes to the "finding of facts," of course, the situation changes, and judges begin to pay some attention to what administrators have said they believe to be the case.

All of this reviewing is done, however, within a framework created by the Congress, one that divides decisions into two categories, on the record, and not on the record. In the case of the former, the courts are supposed to set aside any agency decision "not supported by substantial evidence in the record." In the case of the latter, they are to overturn only decisions they find to be "arbitrary and capricious, an abuse of discretion." In the past decade or so, the courts have begun to merge these two standards together or, perhaps more properly, to blur the distinction between them, by demanding a more and more extensive record even for decisions not subject to the on-the-record requirement, and by reviewing what they get with a more and more careful eye.

NOTES

1. Katharine Q. Seelye and Jennifer 8. Lee, "Court Blocks U.S. Effort to Relax Pollution Rule," *New York Times* (electronic edition), December 25, 2003.

2. Kenneth F. Warren, *Administrative Law in the Political System*, 3rd ed. (Upper Saddle River, N.J.: Prentice-Hall, 1996), 421–426.

3. Robert H. Bork, *The Tempting of America: The Political Seduction of the Law* (New York: Free Press, 1990), 81.

4. *Heckler v. Chaney* 470 U.S. 821 (1985).

5. *Abbott Laboratories v. Gardner* 387 U.S. 136 (1967), quoted in Warren, *Administrative Law in the Political System*, 431.

6. *Johnson v. Robison* 415 U.S. 361 (1974).

7. Warren, *Administrative Law in the Political System*, 432. You can also find the case citations on that page, and in the table of cases.

8. *Gott v. Walters* 756 F2d 902 (D.C. Cir. 1985).

9. Kenneth Culp Davis, *Administrative Law-Cases-Text-Problems*, 6th ed. (St. Paul, Minn.: West Publishing, 1977), 63–64.

10. *Citizens to Preserve Overton Park v. Volpe* 401 U.S. 402 (1971).

11. *Heckler v. Chaney.*

12. *Webster v. Doe* 486 U.S. 592 (1988).

13. *Lincoln v. Vigil* 113 S.Ct. 2024 (1993).

14. Warren, *Administrative Law in the Political System*, 270–272. He cites Theodore J. Lowi, *The End of Liberalism* (New York: W. W. Norton, 1979), 36–38, 302–305.

15. The words are those of Justice William Brennan in *Association of Data Processing Organizations v. Camp* 397 U.S. 150 (1970), quoted in Warren, *Administrative Law in the Political System*, 433.

16. Justice Antonin Scalia summarized the law of standing in *Lujan v. Defenders of Wildlife* 112 S.Ct. 2130 (1992). I am relying on the excerpts from that opinion in Warren, *Administrative Law in the Political System*, 436–437.

17. Warren, *Administrative Law in the Political System*, 434.

18. Justice Scalia in *Lujan v. Defenders of Wildlife*, quoted in Warren, *Administrative Law in the Political System*, 437.

19. *Sierra Club v. Morton* 405 U.S. 727 (1972).

20. *United States v. Students Challenging Regulatory Agency Procedures (SCRAP)* 412 U.S. 669 (1973).

21. *Duke Power Co. v. Carolina Environmental Study Group, Inc.* 438 U.S. 59 (1978).

22. *Lujan v. Defenders of Wildlife.*

23. The words belong to Justice Louis Powell in *Simon v. Eastern Kentucky Welfare Rights Organization* 426 U.S. 26 (1976), and are borrowed by Antonin Scalia in *Lujan v. Defenders of Wildlife.*

24. *Warth v. Seldin* 422 U.S. 490 (1975).

25. *Simon v. Eastern Kentucky Welfare Rights Organization.*

26. *Simon v. Eastern Kentucky Welfare Rights Organization.*

27. Scalia in *Lujan v. Defenders of Wildlife.*

28. *Warth v. Seldin.*

29. *Simon v. Eastern Kentucky Welfare Rights Organization.*

30. *Regents of the University of California v. Bakke* 438 U.S. 265 (1978).

31. *Environmental Defense Fund v. Hardin* 428 F2d 1093 (D.C. Cir. 1970).

32. *Nor-Am Agricultural Products, Inc. v. Hardin* 439 F2d 584 (7th Cir. 1970).

33. *Environmental Defense Fund v. Ruckleshaus* 439 F2d (D.C. Cir. 1971).

34. Richard M. Pierce Jr., Sidney A. Shapiro, and Paul R. Verkuil, *Administrative Law and Process*, 2nd ed. (Westbury, N.Y.: Foundation Press, 1992), 172–174.

35. *Abbott Laboratories v. Gardner.*

36. *Thomas v. Union Carbide Agr. Products Co.* 110 S.Ct. 3325 (1990).

37. *Reno v. Catholic Social Services* 113 S.Ct. 2485 (1993).

38. *U.S. v. Sing Tuck* 194 U.S. 161 (1904).

39. *McCarthy v. Madigan* 112 S.Ct. 1081 (1992).

40. *Gibson v. Berryhill* 411 U.S. 64 (1973).

41. *Continental Can Co. v. Marshall* 603 F2d 590 (7th Cir. 1979).

42. *Bowen v. City of New York* 106 S.Ct. 2022 (1986).

43. *Darby v. Cisneros* 113 S.Ct. 2539 (1993).

44. *Texas and Pacific R.R. Co. v. Abilene Cotton Oil Co.* 204 U.S. 426 (1907).

45. *Burlington Northern, Inc v. United States* 103 S.Ct. 514 (1982).

46. *Far Eastern Conference v. United States* 342 U.S. 570 (1952).

47. *Nader v. Allegheny Airlines* 426 U.S. 290 (1976).

48. *Chevron U.S.A. v. Natural Resources Defense Council* 467 U.S. 837 (1984).

49. *Bishop v. Wood* 426 U.S. 341 (1976).

50. Thomas W. Merrill, "Judicial Deference to Executive Precedent," *Yale Law Journal* 101 (March 1992), 970.

51. Michael Herz, "Deference Running Riot," *Administrative Law Journal* 6 (Summer 1992), 187–233.

52. *Consolidated Edison Co. v. National Labor Relations Board* 305 U.S. 197 (1938).

53. *Universal Camera Corp. v. National Labor Relations Board* 340 U.S. 474 (1951).

54. Warren, *Administrative Law in the Political System*, 445–450.

55. Pierce, Shapiro, and Verkuil, *Administrative Law and Process*, 339–341.

56. Pierce, Shapiro, and Verkuil, *Administrative Law and Process*, 341–342.

57. *Federal Communications Commission v. WNCN Listeners Guild* 450 U.S. 582 (1981).

58. *Motor Vehicle Manufacturer's Association v. State Farm Automobile Insurance Co.* 463 U.S. 29 (1983).

59. Pierce, Shapiro, and Verkuil, *Administrative Law and Process*, 366–370.

⑩

The Environmental Protection Agency

Our Better Angels or Promise Breakers?

The term bureaucratic politics takes on a whole new meaning when it comes to the Environmental Protection Agency (EPA). In fact, one could argue that the central theme of this book—the competition between expert forces and political forces in shaping bureaucratic policies, procedures, and output—is epitomized by environmental policy making. While competition and differing priorities can easily be found in any other policy-making arena, the actions of the EPA affect more people in society in more ways than any other agency, and the extent of its purview could allow it to have some influence over the activities of everyone, all the time. This kind of bureaucratic reach is a panacea to some and a bane to others; it is the epitome of what government is all about or the epitome of what is so terribly wrong with government. It is alternatively conceived of as an agency advancing against an unrelenting tide of pollution, or an invasive species spreading throughout the governmental environment, taking up residence and causing destruction wherever it can find a vulnerable spot in the U.S. Code.

I have never met a self-described anti-environmentalist. Whatever role is being played—producer/consumer, business owner/laborer, developer/tourist—most people in the United States consider themselves either pro-environment or neutral (that is, they just don't think about it much). Whatever the objective destruction being wrought, few would admit to *wanting* to destroy the environment. Nobody wants to live or work or play in a polluted, dangerous, or unhealthy environment. So how could an agency dedicated to protecting and cleaning up the environment—doing something we all want to be done—be described in such radically different terms? This is the central question to be answered in this chapter. It will take some unpacking, because there are many layers to the argument, but in the end, the causes of the controversies should be clear. To get to the bottom of the mystery, we will start with a look at the general political atmosphere surrounding environmental policy making around the time of the creation of the Environmental Protection Agency (EPA). We will then move on to a review of the EPA, its creation, structure, and major policy goals. Once we have those relatively widely accepted facts down, we will move into the political realm to take a look at congressional oversight and the role interest groups play in pressuring the EPA, and in attempting to shape environmental policy. Finally, we will take a look at two EPA decisions: the 1997 decision to tighten air quality standards for two common pollutants, particulate matter and ozone, and the 2002–2003 process of restructuring another major aspect of the Clean Air Act, New Source Review guidelines. These specific examples will provide the detail needed to understand just how deeply divided the realms of politics and professionalism really are in the world of environmental policy making, but they will also show how those realms are inextricably linked.

THE SOCIAL AND POLITICAL CONTEXT

The historical setting for environmental policies is dotted with regulations about preservation, conservation, and resource exploitation. On the one hand, there was a movement at both the state and national levels to protect vast areas of undeveloped wilderness. The most recognized name associated with this perspective is John Muir, who founded an equally easily recognized group, the Sierra Club, in 1892. One of the outcomes of this movement resulted in what we now think of as the national park system. For example, the Yosemite Valley was first designated as a (California) state park (1864), and later a national park (1891). Congress created Yellowstone National Park out of the territory of three states, Wyoming, Montana, and Utah, in 1872. And the first Arbor Day, symbolizing the importance of trees and forests, was proclaimed on April 10, 1872. People in the sciences, the arts, politics, and the public in general created a relatively unified chorus about the importance of protecting nature. Yet the desire to protect did not trump all perspectives about nature; the question of how best to use the resources at hand became just as important, if not more so, as the United States developed into a bigger, more industrial nation in the late nineteenth and early twentieth centuries.

Conservation became the dominant perspective about the environment early in the twentieth century. Now, we have to keep in mind that conservation is a bit of a euphemism for "how can we use resources most efficiently to promote progress and economic growth?"—that is, the goal was not to conserve for the sake of conserving, but to conserve for future human needs. Gifford Pinchot, whose ties to the political and economic elite (for example, George W. Vanderbilt and Theodore Roosevelt) enabled him to become tremendously influential in the development of federal environmental policy, led this other camp.[1] Two of the most important policy areas that Pinchot and the conservation movement focused on were mining and water power, both of which being central to the development of the American West. In 1872, Congress passed the General Mining Law. This law gave miners free or nearly free access to mineral deposits on public land with no obligation to pay royalties to the government on what was extracted. The Reclamation Act of 1902 provided public resources for dam construction and other water projects to make farming and living on a large scale possible in the arid desert landscape of the West. We don't often reflect on the monumental impact that a few crucial decisions can have on a country, but without the mining and water laws of one hundred years ago, the United States would be a fundamentally different place to live, with a fundamentally different economy. The competition, as we can plainly see, was between appreciation for what was and appreciation for what could be: nature versus growth. Growth won.

The preservationists and the conservationists battled back and forth for decades (and still do, of course). However, after World War II and the tremendous growth in the American economy, a third perspective rose to challenge the two traditional perspectives: the general public's concerns about recreation and quality-of-life issues. This perspective was combined with a view toward government shaped by activism of the twelve-year Franklin D. Roosevelt administration. If nothing else, and to the dismay of his opponents, Roosevelt demonstrated that the government could do more than secure the country and protect against monopolies. The federal government could help you when you were down; the federal government could work to make your individual life better. The federal government was not just about system rules and large groups; it was about improving individual citizens' lives. This third perspective sowed the seeds that were to sprout in 1970 as the Environmental Protection Agency.

The briefest of overviews is enough to show us that concerns about the environment did not originate in the late 1960s; however, two main factors came together at that time to make environmental policy a leading priority in both the legislative and executive branches at the national level. The influence of science is one factor. The areas of math and science had broken out of their isolated academic shells (due in no small part to the challenges of the Cold War) and had become important to society at an obvious and daily level after World War II. The advent of nuclear weapons, the race to space, the development of intercontinental rockets, dramatic improvements in industrial and consumer technologies, and the increased use of modern chemicals to revolutionize many of the realms of life from agriculture to warfare all signaled the importance of a scientific understanding of the world. Science would help us understand the world in which we live and would help us improve upon that world. Science could make us full-bellied, comfortable, and safe; it could give us more free time and more entertaining things to do in that free time. Yet the 1960s and early 1970s showed us, too, that science, or the scientific study of social phenomena, might have a downside, or show us things we would rather not know. Rachel Carson's 1962 book *Silent Spring* brought to life some of these concerns; for example, she explained how pesticides and other chemicals and modern technologies might disrupt the natural environment and harm human health. The impact of Carson's work was reinforced by others: Murray Bookchin's 1962 offering, *Our Synthetic Environment* (published under the name Lewis Herber), Barry Commoner's 1971 *The Closing Circle*, and Paul Ehrlich's 1968 analysis in *The Population Bomb*.[2]

A second major factor in pushing the environmental agenda onto the national stage was the rise in citizen groups devoted to environmental causes. The noteworthy aspects of these groups are that they were explicitly devoted to representing the public interest, and that they comprised individuals from all aspects of society; that is to say, membership in these environmental groups was not limited to a particular occupation or industry, as was the membership in most citizen pressure groups prior to the rise of social movements in the 1960s and 1970s.[3] Membership expanded in existing groups; for example: Sierra Club membership grew tenfold from 1952 to 1969, and membership in the Wilderness Society expanded approximately 450 percent from 1960 to 1970.[4] New environmental groups took root as well: World Wildlife Fund (1961), Environmental Defense Fund (1967), Friends of the Earth (1969), Council on Economic Priorities (1969), Greenpeace (1970), and the Natural Resources Defense Council (1970).[5] These groups represented another facet of the social mobilization and activism of the 1960s, the discussion of which is usually confined to the Vietnam War, civil rights, and women's liberation movements. In fact, many of the new environmental organizations adopted some of the tactics of these more popular movements, including mass demonstrations and public protest, and university-based "teach-ins."[6]

Tying these two main factors together were the mass media. You cannot get very far analyzing politics today without focusing on the mediation of the issue in some way, and the tumultuous time of the 1960s is often looked at as the first era of television—a new actor in the world of power and persuasion. Books about the health effects of pesticides or overpopulation would not have had the impact they had without the mass mediation of these ideas. Nor would they have had the impact they had if they had not been brought to light at the same time as other large social problems and movements, problems and movements that were getting lots of coverage at the national and local levels of news. The growing impact of the mass media was based on their increased ability to bring amorphous, distant, intangible problems into peoples' living rooms with lots of color and sound. Now these problems were associated with other *people*: marching for, protesting against, learning about, and devoting their lives to. These problems were no longer just theoretical or too far away. People were being connected to other people; people were being made aware by other people; people were being activated by other people.

To review quickly: we see three trends coming together in the late 1960s. These trends are best represented as (1) a movement toward a citizen-based concern about the environment; (2) a movement toward a much more citizen-based (pluralistic) democracy, and (3) a growing acceptance, and perhaps expectation, that one of the primary roles of government was to improve the quality of life of its citizens—all the way down to the level of ensuring pleasurable places of recreation. Now, tie the three strands together and you come up with something like this: government is about improving peoples' lives; people are about improving peoples' lives—let's mix the power of the two to protect the environment.

THE AGENCY

Neither the legislative nor the executive branch of the federal government ignored these trends. Congress was active in the 1960s, passing significant laws like the Water Quality Act (1965), the Clean Water Restoration Act (1966), and the first version of the Clean Air Act (1967). The decade ended with Congress taking the lead on environmental issues: it passed the National Environmental Policy Act

(NEPA) in 1969. This law reads in part:

> It is the continuing policy of the Federal Government, in cooperation with State
> and local governments, and other concerned public and private organizations, to
> use all practicable means and measures, including financial and technical assis-
> tance, in a manner calculated to foster and promote the general welfare, to create
> and maintain conditions under which man and nature can exist in productive
> harmony, and fulfill the social, economic, and other requirements of present and
> future generations of Americans.[7]

NEPA clearly propelled a movement, already underway, to federalize an increasing
array of environmental policy issues, issues that had been largely left to the states
prior to the 1960s. One of the leading members of Congress pushing for these
changes was Senator Edmund Muskie (D-ME). It is important to mention him,
among the many members of Congress working on environmental issues, because
it was the competition between him and President Richard Nixon that fueled the
creation of the EPA. Muskie was Chair of the Senate Public Works Committee,
and according to two of the most important and prolific researchers in the field
of environmental policy, Michael Kraft and Norman Vig, he had "emerged as
the dominant policy entrepreneur for environmental protection issues."[8] Muskie
was also considered one of the leading presidential hopefuls for the Democratic
Party for the 1972 election; he was, therefore, one of Nixon's primary opponents.
Not to be outmaneuvered by Muskie or the legislative branch, Nixon signed
the National Environmental Policy Act in 1970 and declared the 1970s "the
environmental decade." Nixon had joined the race to become more in tune with
the public mood and to come up to par with the actions Congress was taking
regarding the environment. Nixon was not to be outdone. By executive order[9] in
1970, President Richard M. Nixon created the Environmental Protection Agency.
It was not created through the typical statutory process; that is, it was not a
product of legislative activity. Congress could pass all the environmental laws it
wanted to, but those laws would be implemented and administered by an agency
created by the President.

The EPA is an independent agency within the executive branch; it does not
hold cabinet-level rank. The administrator of the EPA is unique among administrators of independent agencies[10] in that the head of the EPA is presidentially
appointed (with Senate confirmation) and presidentially removable. This makes
the administrator's position particularly susceptible to political trends (again, vis-
à-vis other independent agency heads). The EPA was new, however, only in the
sense that it would become the central umbrella organization for environmental
policy at the federal level. This unification was envisioned to be the missing piece
of a comprehensive federal organization, capacity, and authority in environmental policy. It was created by a reorganization plan to bring together most (but not
all)[11] of the various components of federal environmental policy as detailed in the
history section of the agency's website:

> With Reorganization Plan Number 3, dated July 9, 1970, [Nixon] informed
> Congress of his wish to assemble the EPA from the sinews of three federal Depart-
> ments, three Bureaus, three Administrations, two Councils, one Commission,

one Service, and many diverse offices. The Interior Department would yield the Federal Water Quality Administration, as well as all of its pesticides work. The Department of Health, Education, and Welfare would contribute the National Air Pollution Control Administration, the Food and Drug Administration's pesticides research, and the Bureaus of Solid Waste Management, Water Hygiene, and (portions of) the Bureau of Radiological Health. The Agriculture Department would cede the pesticides activities undertaken by the Agricultural Research Service, while the Atomic Energy Commission and the Federal Radiation Council would vest radiation criteria and standards in the proposed agency. Finally, the Council on Environmental Quality's ecological research would be transferred to EPA.[12]

A brief amount of reflection on what you just read will give you some idea of what is coming up later in the chapter. The EPA gets into everyone's business, and everyone thinks the EPA is part of its business. This causes conflict between political forces and professional forces, but also between professional forces with different, but overlapping, agendas and priorities. Before we get into the political world, however, a bit more background on the agency is in order.

The Environmental Protection Agency's mission statement reads as follows:

The mission of the U.S. Environmental Protection Agency is to protect human health and to safeguard the natural environment—air, water and land—upon which life depends.
EPA's purpose is to ensure that

- All Americans are protected from significant risks to human health and the environment where they live, learn and work.
- National efforts to reduce environmental risk are based on the best available scientific information.
- Federal laws protecting human health and the environment are enforced fairly and effectively.
- Environmental protection is an integral consideration in U.S. policies concerning natural resources, human health, economic growth, energy, transportation, agriculture, industry, and international trade, and these factors are similarly considered in establishing environmental policy.
- All parts of society—communities, individuals, business, state and local governments, tribal governments—have access to accurate information sufficient to effectively participate in managing human health and environmental risks.
- Environmental protection contributes to making our communities and ecosystems diverse, sustainable and economically productive.
- The United States plays a leadership role in working with other nations to protect the global environment.[13]

Consider the primary elements in that statement: science, quality of life, government protection, and citizen participation—clearly the culmination of the trends mentioned earlier. Now take a second look at the mission statement and pick out as many of the areas of possible contention as you can see. I will focus on two.

First, all Americans are supposed to be protected from "significant" risks. How do we define significant? Does this mean no one gets sick or hurt, or does it mean the chances are particularly low? Does "all Americans" include children, the elderly, and the sick? How about urban dwellers or people stuck in the chemical corridor in Louisiana? We know that certain populations are more vulnerable than others to particular toxins and diseases. How do we decide to draw the value-judgment line? Moreover, how can science tell us what a significant risk really is? It is difficult (in more ways than one) to test pollution and toxins on humans, and animal tests take us only so far. We are forced to move into the world of social scientific analysis, often thought of as a much less "scientific" affair. In addition to the uncertainty, how much risk do we want to take before we find out just how harmful something might be? The scientific approach is fundamentally retrospective: gather the data and test it. Assessing potential harm to human health or natural systems is prospective: this is our best guess, within some margin of error, if we have the multivariate model right to begin with. With this very brief analysis, it is apparent that life will be difficult and uncertain for the scientists, statisticians, economists, lawyers, and policy analysts at the EPA.

One more example of just how complicated life might be for the professionals at the EPA is based on the fourth goal in the mission statement: the integral and reciprocal relationship between environmental policy and just about any other policy government might pursue at any level. Restated, the goal reads: think about the environment when thinking about doing anything else, but just as importantly, think about every imaginable impact an environmental regulation might have on any other governmental program before you implement that environmental rule. This is, perhaps, one of the best examples of, on the one hand, satisfying all stakeholders in governmental action, writ large, yet on the other hand, laying down innumerable hurdles to overcome to get anything done. It is certainly true that almost anything we do as a modern society impacts the environment; yet it is equally true that we need to come to see the *environment v. anything-else* debate as a set of negotiated trade-offs. Logging more trees, refusing to increase CAFE[14] standards, subsidizing agriculture, and viewing energy consumption as something that can continue, unabated, if we could only find a bit more oil to pump out of the ground: these are all policies or perspectives that have a negative impact on the environment. Conversely, doing the opposite in each case would harm the logging, automotive, and agribusiness industries, as well as increase the cost of living for citizens across the board. There are few examples of positive-sum (win-win) situations when it comes to the aforementioned trade-offs; most of the time it is a good old-fashioned zero-sum (win-lose) game.

Rather than simply being able to work on the science, make proclamations, and protect and clean up the environment, those who work at the EPA find themselves in the murky world of politics: competing value preferences, alternative analytic frameworks, ideological differences driving different sets of assumptions and choosing different EPA Administrators, party politics, and group politics—and we haven't even discussed the EPA and the courts! In order to deal with such a wide variety of concerns, requirements, and overseers, the EPA is organized into an equally broad and disaggregated structure.

At the top, of course, is the Office of the Administrator and Deputy Administrator. The Administrator reports directly to the President of the United States.

Within the Administrator's Office, we find the following offices:

Administrative Law Judges
Children's Health Protection
Civil Rights
Congressional and Intergovernmental Relations (Associate Administrator status)
Cooperative Environmental Management
Environmental Appeals Board
Environmental Education
Executive Secretariat
Executive Services
Homeland Security
Policy, Economics, and Innovation (Associate Administrator status)
Public Affairs (Associate Administrator status)
Science Advisory Board
Small and Disadvantaged Business Utilization.

Reporting to the Administrator/Deputy Administrator (outside of that office) are three general offices:

Office of General Counsel
Office of Inspector General
Office of the Chief Financial Officer

and ten program offices (all headed by an Assistant Administrator), with three subprogram offices nestled in:

Office of Administration and Resources Management
Office of Air and Radiation
American Indian Environmental Office
Office of Enforcement and Compliance Assurance
    (Office of Environmental Justice)
Office of Environmental Information
    (History Office)
Office of International Affairs
Office of Prevention, Pesticides, and Toxic Substances
Office of Research and Development
    (Science Policy Council)
Office of Solid Waste and Emergency Response
Office of Water.

Last but not least are the regional offices. Approximately two-thirds of the nearly 18,000 employees at the EPA work in these regional offices or in facilities outside of Washington, D.C. While all of the major decision making takes place at the national level, most of the routine implementation of environmental policy takes place at the regional level. The United States is divided geographically into these ten regions, and the EPA regional offices are located within the following major cities (by region):

EPA Regions and Regional Offices:
Region 1   Boston
Region 2   New York
Region 3   Philadelphia
Region 4   Atlanta
Region 5   Chicago
Region 6   Dallas
Region 7   Kansas City
Region 8   Denver
Region 9   San Francisco
Region 10   Seattle[15]

I did mention something about science and research, so I would be remiss if I didn't at least mention the research arm of the agency (the image of an octopus comes to mind easily). As of spring 2004, the EPA had nine ongoing research programs (from microbiology to environmental economics) and fifteen research offices scattered around the United States from Minnesota to Florida and from Rhode Island to Oregon.[16] With all of those offices and all of those workers and all of that research, we must be talking about big money, right? In typical academic fashion, the answer is: yes and no.

The Bush administration's proposed 2005 budget for the EPA is $7.76 billion.[17] The EPA's operating budget (funds used to run programs) is about half of that amount. The agency's budget has hovered between the $7 and $8 billion mark for more than a decade (in nominal dollars). The jump to nearly $8 billion occurred around 2001. This is real money, as they say, but it is instructive to put it into perspective. Of the twenty-seven agencies listed in the White House budget proposal (including the category "other agencies"), EPA ranks seventeenth in terms of allocated resources. No other substantive agency ranks below it.[18] All sixteen agencies above it have at least double-digit billions in expenditures, with the Department of Defense topping off the list, as usual, at $401.7 billion. Moreover, in constant (inflation adjusted) dollars, the EPA's operating budget has grown by just 10 percent between 1975 and 2000 (its workforce grew just under 40 percent during that same time period).[19] The EPA's budgetary situation is indicative of the total spending authorized by the federal government for all natural resource and environmental programs. Again, adjusting for inflation, spending was relatively constant from 1980 to 2000, with a drop in the 1980s and recovery in the 1990s. Spending on pollution control and clean-up actually declined over that period.[20] And as a final comparison, the budget for the EPA eats up 0.95 percent (yes, that is less than one percent) of federal discretionary spending. In sum, it is fair to say that the EPA works within relatively tight budget constraints, given its wide mandate. This situation adds to the trade-off matrix discussed above: EPA simply cannot protect or clean up everything it wants to, let alone all the projects people outside the agency want it to, nor can it enforce all of the existing rules and regulations it ought to enforce. The EPA Administrator must decide "what are the top priorities this year and how, exactly, are we going to achieve our goals?"

EXTERNAL PRESSURE

For better or for worse, the Administrator of the Environmental Protection Agency gets input from everybody. All the time. And it's not always constructive or nice. In fact, if the EPA could possibly epitomize yet another cliché, it would be: you can't please everyone all the time, and if you try, you will probably end up pleasing no one. It might be an overstatement to say that the EPA is under constant attack, but not by much. Whether it is pressure from within government, from Congress or the White House, or pressure from without, from the plethora of organized interests focused on the environment, everyone at the EPA knows that they are under the microscope—or better yet, under hundreds of microscopes!

To begin with, many congressional tentacles are wrapped around the EPA. How many congressional committees does it take to oversee EPA issues? The count for the 108th Congress is twenty-six committees and subcommittees in the House and twenty-four committees and subcommittees in the Senate. You'll find a list of these committees in table 10.1, along with a brief description of their jurisdictions.[21]

The impact of such an extensive oversight system can be measured in two distinct ways. First is the issue of time. Think back to the EPA mission statement described earlier, particularly the goal of issue reciprocity. For any given piece of legislation, environmental or otherwise, it is more than likely that some number of congressional committees greater than two will be involved in the process. When it comes to providing input to Congress through testimony or other means, executive-branch actors must be prepared to speak to many congressional actors and their staffs. It would not be unthinkable to imagine testifying before a half-dozen committees of different but overlapping jurisdictions. Preparing for this exercise, as well as the actual efforts to make all the contacts, arrange all the meetings, and follow up with any additional information for the record, takes time, and lots of it. It comes as no surprise that the EPA has an entire office devoted to congressional and intergovernmental relations.

Second is the "many masters" issue. Members of Congress specialize. They are not all generalists, taking each issue that comes up for a vote and analyzing it in depth. They specialize in areas that most affect their particular state or district, or areas they find most interesting. This tendency does not mean that the members of the House and Senate cannot vote on bills outside of their areas of expertise, but it does mean that they are likely to have a highly developed and quite conscious worldview. Members of the Agriculture Committee are going to see the world differently from those on Armed Services or Fisheries or Energy or Appropriations. How does one unite these very different worldviews? It is not impossible to unite them for a good environmental cause, but it is not easy either; one must seek to highlight a "public good" or a long-term goal that supercedes short-term, parochial interests. Officials working to interpret and implement environmental policy will focus, naturally, on the environmental side of each equation, while the members

Table 10.1.   Major Congressional Committees Overseeing EPA Issues

COMMITTEE *Subcommittee*	JURISDICTION
108th Congress–House of Representatives	
AGRICULTURE	Farm Bill; Federal Insecticide, Fungicide, and Rodenticide Act; Food Safety
Department of Operations Oversight, Nutrition, and Forestry	Pesticides; Food Safety; Forestry
Conservation, Credit, Rural Development, and Research	Soil; Water; Natural Resource Conservation; Small Watersheds
APPROPRIATIONS	EPA Appropriations
Veterans Administration, Housing and Urban Development, and Independent Agencies	EPA Appropriations
BUDGET	602 (b) Allocations for Appropriations[a]
ENERGY AND COMMERCE	Safe Drinking Water Act; Resource Conservation and Recovery Act; Superfund; Toxics; Energy Issues; Clean Air Act and Oversight
Environment and Hazardous Materials	Solid Waste; Hazardous Waste; Toxic Substances; Superfund; Resource Conservation and Recovery Act; Noise Pollution; Safe Drinking Water Act
Energy and Air Quality	Clean Air Act; Fossil Fuel Energy; Synthetic Fuels
Oversight and Investigations	General Oversight
EDUCATION AND THE WORKFORCE	Government Education Programs
Select Education	Environmental Education
GOVERNMENT REFORM	EPA
Civil Service and Agency Organization	Federal Employees
Energy Policy, Natural Resources, and Regulatory Affairs	Regulatory Reform and Paperwork Reduction
RESOURCES	Wetlands; Alaskan Federal Reserved Water Rights; Environmental Measures
Fisheries, Conservation, Wildlife, and Oceans	Coastal Zone Management; Marine Sanctuaries; Wildlife Refuges
Water and Power Resources	Federal Water Projects; Water Rights
SCIENCE	Environmental R&D; Risk Assessment; Oversight
Energy	General Energy Issues, R&D
Environment, Technology, and Standards	Environment Technology Initiative
Research	R&D
SMALL BUSINESS	Office of Small and Disadvantaged Business Utilization; Regulatory Reform and Paperwork Reduction
TRANSPORTATION AND INFRASTRUCTURE	Hazardous Materials; Clean Water Act; Superfund
Highways, Transit, and Pipelines	Hazardous Materials; Transportation Aspects of Clean Air Act
Water Resources and Environment	Clean Water Act; Groundwater; Ocean Dumping; Wetlands; Large Watersheds; Superfund
108th Congress–Senate	
AGRICULTURE, NUTRITION AND FORESTRY	Federal Insecticide, Fungicide, and Rodenticide Act; Pesticides; Food Safety; Watersheds
Forestry, Conservation, and Rural Revitalization	Watersheds and Flood Control Programs; Forestry

(Continued)

Table 10.1. *(Continued)*

COMMITTEE *Subcommittee*	JURISDICTION
Research, Nutrition, and General Legislation	Federal Insecticide, Fungicide, and Rodenticide Act; Food Safety and General Legislation
APPROPRIATIONS	EPA Appropriations
Veterans Administration, Housing and Urban Development, and Independent Agencies	EPA Appropriations
ARMED SERVICES	Federal Facilities
BUDGET	602 (b) Allocations for Appropriations[a]
COMMERCE, SCIENCE, AND TRANSPORTATION	Coastal Zone Management; Toxic Substances; CAFE; Intermodal Surface Transportation Efficiency Act; Marine Protection, Research, and Sanctuaries Act
Surface Transportation and Merchant Marine	Intermodal Surface Transportation Efficiency Act; Marine Protection, Research, and Sanctuaries Act; CAFE
Oceans, Atmosphere, and Fisheries	Coastal Zone Management; Marine Fisheries
Science, Technology, and Space	Technology R&D
ENERGY AND NATURAL RESOURCES	National Energy Policy; International Energy; Nuclear Waste; Department of Energy Cleanup
Energy	Energy Conservation; Energy; Refinery Policy; Global Climate Change; R&D Technology
Public Lands and Forests Management	Groundwater Resources and Management; Mining
Water and Power	Outer Continental Shelf
ENVIRONMENT AND PUBLIC WORKS	Air Pollution (Clean Air Act); Outer Continental Shelf; Toxic Substances; Safe Drinking Water Act; Environmental Policy; R&D; Fisheries; Flood Control; Deep Water Ports; Noise Pollution; Ocean Dumping; Solid Waste Disposal and Recycling; Clean Water Act and Water Pollution; Wetlands; Environmental Education
Transportation and Infrastructure	Water Resources; Water Pollution
Superfund and Waste Management	Superfund; Resource Conservation and Recovery Act; Recycling; Risk; Federal Facilities; Interstate Waste; Toxic Substances Control Act and R&D
Clean Air, Climate Change, and Nuclear Safety	Clean Air Act; Indoor Air; Wetlands; Private Property Rights; National Environmental Policy Act
Fisheries, Wildlife, and Water	Safe Drinking Water Act; Endangered Species; Fisheries and Wildlife Refuges
GOVERNMENTAL AFFAIRS	Regulatory Reform; New HQ Bldg. Contracts; Chief Financial Officers Act; Federal Employees Issues; Federal Managers Financial Integrity Act
Oversight of Government Management, the Federal Workforce, and the District of Columbia	New HQ Bldg. Contracts
HEALTH, EDUCATION, LABOR AND PENSIONS	Federal Food, Drug, and Cosmetic Act; Food Safety; Employee Welfare
SMALL BUSINESS AND ENTREPRENEURSHIP	Lender Liability; Office of Small and Disadvantaged Business Utilization 8(A) Firms

[a] 602(b) Allocations refer to a section of the Congressional Budget Act of 1974. It requires that total budgetary assets be allocated among relevant committees for further distribution. C-SPAN Congressional Glossary, www.c-span.org/guide/Congress/glossary/602b.htm.

of Congress sitting on the aforementioned committees will focus on the particular area under the environmental gaze. In Agriculture: the environmental question might be groundwater pollution; the rebuttal: staying competitive in a world full of commodities producers. In Armed Services: the environment = protecting species or toxic clean-up; the rebuttal: don't hamper training and national security. The list could go on. The result of this process is sometimes gridlock; nothing gets done. At other times, sweeping laws are written to protect the air or water or land or species, but those laws are written in such vague terms that implementation becomes a nightmare, and the EPA comes under fire for not following Congress's lead in the appropriate way.

This picture is even more complicated when one considers committee make-up and partisan balance. From which regions of the United States do the members of a particular committee come? If they hail from the mountain states, for example, they are going to be predisposed to resist EPA moves to strengthen environmental laws. Which party controls Congress? How close is the split? Historically, Democrats have been more supportive of strong environmental policy than Republicans, but if Republicans control Congress, the EPA does not close down shop. Its leadership might, however, be forced to rethink the most effective sales pitch. For example, should the EPA's position be more command and control, that is, more potential punishment; or should it be a more market-based solution, that is, to encourage behavioral change with increased incentives? Democrats tend to support the former and Republicans the latter, but no approach is a sure thing every time.

As if that were not enough, members of Congress put pressure on the EPA in another way, not as intra-governmental colleagues but as representatives of extra-governmental pressure groups. One of these groups is the representative's constituency. Now, this constituency is not a pressure group in itself, but there is often a decided lean for or against environmental policy in any given district or state. Partisanship is one factor. Most House districts are non-competitive; that is, these districts tend to return the same party to Congress each election. Yet party isn't the only factor that shapes environmental leanings. There are urban/rural splits, heavy industry–heavy labor/light industry–service sector splits, and regional splits, like the aforementioned mountain states region and the northeastern part of the country. These splits are the most visible manifestations of deeper conflicts, conflicts that are more clearly seen in the interest-group sector.

Organized interest groups represent a second type of pressure group to which a representative might respond. Members of Congress are interested in, among other things like public service, reelection. It's been said that members of the House of Representatives can never stop campaigning, given the short electoral cycle with which they must contend. Given that they have many other responsibilities, members of Congress need to focus their campaigning and electoral strategies on those citizens likely to vote. The long and the short of voting behavior models tells us this: people with a deep interest in an issue who have a well-developed ideology, and who also possess a high sense of self-efficacy turn out in high numbers. People who have the opposite demographic or psychological characteristics turn out in much lower numbers. If a member of Congress has a limited amount of time and money, which is the reality, then that member must focus his or her attention on the organized interests in his or her district or state. These aren't the only groups to court, but they certainly cannot be ignored. In many instances those organized interests come to be the constituency's interest, which comes to be the member's interest.

Yet members of Congress do not only advocate for their constituents, they often promote more general views about the role of government in society, or a broad view of the direction in which they feel the country should be moving. These more ideological perspectives are part of who each member of Congress is, but they are often supported by, or even enhanced by, the ideological elite in the country. What do I mean by ideological elite? The professoriate? NO. The people who fill the country's think tanks. People who work at the Heritage Foundation or the Progressive Policy Institute or the Cato Institute.[22] People whose jobs are to think and research and write and hold seminars and conferences, and who are ultimately trying to convince policy makers to adopt the "correct" view of the government's role in society or the right direction for the country.

So a member of Congress can wear many hats in front of the EPA—oversight, budgetary authority, district or state delegate, interest-group point person, or leading ideologue. Considering the EPA's structure, the legislative and executive connections to EPA, and the inherent complexity of environmental problems, is anyone up for taking the civil service exam?

While members of Congress can shift positions and move from inside the Beltway to outside, the real power of extra-governmental pressure comes from the interest groups organized to either pressure government to do more for health, safety, and the environment, or pressure government to do less of all of the above. Before I enter the world of who does what for what reason, a note of caution must be made about group influence. We know that groups matter: they inform debate, they set agendas, they lobby Congress, they fund campaigns, they challenge the government through the judicial system. Yet for all of that, it is exceedingly difficult to make definitive statements about the amount of influence they actually have.[23] Environmental groups might have some influence on a campaign, but they are not likely to be in the position of determining the winner. Environmental groups might make a national push to mobilize the public with the hopes of moving Congress, only to see an issue die in committee or be brushed aside because of other "more important" events. Group influence is also difficult to measure because of the predispositions of members of Congress and the nature of their constituencies. A quick question helps to check the logic of this: how many times do environmental groups support candidates or elected officials who didn't lean toward supporting strong environmental policies in the first place? How many times do we see a member of Congress vote for a piece of environmental legislation as an obvious quid pro quo for a group's financial or campaign support even though that vote runs contrary to what his or her constituency would want, his or her ideology, or his or her party? The answer to both questions is: rarely. The point is that group activity is so obvious and often attention-getting that we can't help but think it is making a *big* difference; the problem is we just don't have the controls in place to prove it beyond a reasonable doubt (in most cases).

Here are a few examples of the types of stories that are difficult for social scientists to unpack to find clear cases of cause and effect. A *Chicago Tribune* report on May 9, 1991, "Under Pressure, EPA Eases Wetlands Stance," described the pressure being put on then EPA Administrator William Reilly by members of Congress, the White House, farmers, homebuilders, and other business interest groups to step away from a plan to crack down on wetlands violators.[24] Clearly the combination of pressures had an impact, but the specifics are less definitive: the White House directed the Office of Management and Budget to review wetlands guidelines—hardly the kind of evidence to show that the EPA Administrator was being bullied. Moreover, who exactly said what to whom, and when, to "get the job done"? *In Motion Magazine*, December 18, 2002, reported another common story: "EPA Bows Down to Corporate Agribusiness Pressure."[25] The story goes on to talk about an "obvious" cave-in to big business, a situation where the public participated but was ignored. In a third example, Douglas M. Costle, EPA Administrator under President Jimmy Carter, related the following tidbit in an oral history interview: "EPA administrators rarely bring the President good news, but the White House is always being lobbied by everybody who is affected by the agency. When the Chairman of General Motors calls the White House, they take his call."[26]

It is not particularly revelatory that members of the economic elite have easier access to the political elite than most of us. However, that fact alone does not demonstrate that GM will always get its way. We often hear, too, about the "revolving door" in the mass media and in many policy analyses; the implication is that certain individuals have undue influence on the policy-making process because of their former ties to industry or government (depending on the side of the door the person is standing at at that time!). An example from 2003 discusses the EPA's potential changes to toxic emissions standards (to weaken them, of course!).[27] The villain in this case is Jeffrey Holmstead, EPA's Assistant Administrator for Clean Air; he worked at the law firm of Latham and Watkins before joining the EPA. This law firm had lobbied on behalf of business and industry, pushing for the change in standards. Again, raised eyebrows, but tit-for-tat behavior is much harder to uncover. With that lengthy caveat, we can move on to shine some light on the influential pressure groups in the world of environmental policy making.

In table 10.2 you will find a list of the leading environmental groups and other concerned organizations.[28] This selective listing highlights once again the broad reach that environmental policy making has, and just how diametrically opposed some groups are going to be to others. They don't have to talk to one another, but the EPA must listen to everyone. And if the EPA gives a group less time or access than that group believes it needs, well, refer back to the last section in this chapter on Congress: instead of a direct assault, the pressure group will try the indirect route, pressuring a member of Congress to force the EPA to make a change. As selective as this listing is, however, it would be wrong to lump them all together as equals in any way. Significant differences exist between the major groupings, but some differences also exist within groups.

Let's start with the organizations that get the least amount of attention of any interest groups: governmental interest groups. This is a good place to start in some ways, because they are the least one-sided of the three groupings listed in table 10.2. Governmental organizations have been created to interact with

Table 10.2. Leading Environmental Groups and Other Concerned Organizations

Environmental Groups

Alliance for Environmental Education	National Audubon Society
American Rivers	National Parks Conservation Assn.
Clean Water Action	National Wildlife Federation
Defenders of Wildlife	Natural Resources Defense Council
Environmental Defense Fund	Nature Conservancy
Friends of the Earth	Sierra Club
Greenpeace USA/International	Union of Concerned Scientists
Izaak Walton League	Wilderness Society
League of Conservation Voters	World Wildlife Fund

Non-governmental (Business and Commercial) Organizations

Alliance for Responsible CFC Policy	Hazardous Waste Treatment Council
American Farm Bureau Federation	Manufacturers of Emission Controls Association
American Gas Association	National Agricultural Chemicals Association
American Mining Congress	National Association of Manufacturers
American Petroleum Institute	National Federation of Independent Businesses
American Trucking Associations	National Coal Association
Chamber of Commerce	National Forest Products Association
Chemical Manufacturers Association	National Solid Wastes Management Association
Edison Electric Institute	Public Lands Council

Governmental Organizations

Association of Local Air Pollution Control Officials	National Association of Towns and Townships
Association of State Drinking Water Administrators	National Governors Association
Association of State and Interstate Water Pollution Control Administrators	National League of Cities
Council of State Governments	State and Territorial Air Pollution Program Administrators
National Association of Conservation Districts	State and Territorial Solid Waste Management Officials
National Association of State Foresters	United States Conference of Mayors

other governmental units for three reasons. First, open and reliable lines of communication are essential to the state and local governments—essential to foster relationships between subnational units and essential to keep an open line with Washington, D.C. As was described in the section on the EPA's organizational structure, most of the environmental policy implementation goes on at the state and local levels. These are the people with the most direct experiences with the successes and failures of policy. They need to be able to share those experiences with their colleagues and to provide feedback to the national decision-making units.

Second, these governmental organizations provide the basis for cities or coalitions of states or associations to become another set of constituencies. The political world is not simply neatly divided along state and district lines; large cities have different needs than smaller cities, the Midwest region has different needs than any one state within it, and the people in charge of the day-to-day control of pollution have yet another set of needs. If governmental organizations didn't exist, many of those needs would go unmet; traditional ways of organizing political action (again, district, state, party) do not mesh well with these non-traditional constituencies.

The third reason for governmental organizations' activities in the environmental sphere is to put a brake on federal regulation, especially unfunded federally mandated programs. As the complexity of national rule making increases, so too does the burden of local implementation. An increase in the number of rules, along with increased complexity or more stringent standards, almost always leads to an increased demand on resources. More training, more equipment, more time, more labor: these are the types of things state and local managers do not want to hear about, especially if these demands are being foisted on them by a national bureaucrat. Government organizations lobby for restraint; they lobby for increased resources commensurate with increased requirements; they lobby to be considered equals in the formation and implementation of national environmental policy.

Environmental groups and business organizations are not seeking to be equals with the hard-working people of the EPA; they want to tell EPA what to do. Business and commercial organizations (rather cumbersome, but *anti-environmental* groups would be a bit unfair) organize and lobby the legislative and executive branches of government to provide information and to protect the bottom line—or, more in line with business rhetoric, to protect the nation's overall levels of competitiveness and economic prosperity. On the one hand, miners do tend to know the most about mining, chemical manufacturers do tend to know a lot about chemicals, and so on. Bureaucratic communication with industry is important for the simple reason that gathering information is costly and time consuming; if industry has it, it would be terribly nice if they would share it. No one wants Congress or the EPA writing rules that are out of step with current business or industrial practices, or are technologically and/or financially impossible to meet. However, it doesn't take a rocket scientist to remember that economic actors have one simple goal that supercedes all others: make more money than you spend. If that goal is not met, none of the other lofty societal goals a business might entertain are possible. This leads business and commercial organizations to play the role of constant reminders: environmental policies might make us less competitive; if we are less competitive, our business shrinks; if our business shrinks . . . we all know the rest of the story. No elected official wants to be known as the person to ruin the economy of a city or a state or a region or the nation, and no policy administrator wants that label either. And everybody knows this is the situation, especially with environmental policy.

Labor is a part of business, but it deserves its own paragraph. Organized labor has had a relatively ambivalent position on environmental issues. On the one hand, organized labor has been at the forefront of occupational health and safety issues (for example, airborne particulates and toxic chemicals). Yet on the other hand, labor has often opposed pollution control and such things as species protection out of concern for job losses. Moreover, there is a not-so-subtle cultural difference between environmental activists and traditional labor. Thinking all the way back to the massive protests (50,000 people) against the World Trade

Organization (WTO) in Seattle in November 1999, one contrast stood out to me: organized labor was against the WTO because of jobs. Period. There was no mixing the message with those "radical" environmentalists or those property-destroying anarchists dressed in all black. And the environmentalists did not go out of their way to speak on behalf of those whose livelihoods could be brushed away. The environment was something that should be protected for the public good, and in fact, some jobs would probably have to be lost to do just that. A heartwarming story like that brings us to the final set of external pressure groups, the environmental organizations.

As is somewhat apparent from their names, environmental groups can be split into the categories of issue focus: single issue versus broad issue or generalist. Single-issue groups focus on such things as land conservation, property issues, wildlife/endangered species, clean water, and clean air. Many of these groups operate more or less in conjunction with state and local authorities. More broadly focused groups follow environmental policies that cover all types of issues—those already mentioned plus "big picture" issues like urban sprawl, human rights, global population problems, and global warming. Most of these issues are at either the national or international level of policy making.

Whatever their focus, environmental groups pursue different strategies to achieve their goals. One of the most important things they do is provide information. Many environmental groups spend lots of time poring over scientific research, congressional testimony, corporate activities—anything related to the topic—and then they turn around and present the most important information to the public. This function provides them the basis for developing grassroots organizations to rally for a particular cause. These grassroots organizations do not have to do all of the research groundwork to get started; they are primed into action by the pre-grassroots research of the large organization. This makes mobilizing citizens for specific causes at specific times much easier. Most people don't have the time to do all of the background work necessary to come up to speed on an environmental issue; if reliable and extensive information is available, the process is already under way. In this way, environmental organizations function as shortcuts and databanks, not unlike the roles political parties play in the United States (less so these days) in the realm of electoral politics and political issues in general.

The goal of this research and grassroots mobilization is to put pressure on elected officials or members of an executive agency. As mentioned before, members of Congress pay attention to those who take the time to voice their opinions about policies, especially if those opinions come into their offices en masse. An active, mobilized citizenry also influences bureaucrats in any agency, but particularly in an agency like the EPA. This is especially apparent when it comes to the public comment period of an agency decision or rule change.

Of course, environmental groups engage in the traditional lobbying of governmental officials, and they contribute to political campaigns in a variety of ways (voter awareness/voter guides, monetary contributions, independent advertising). However, one of the most significant strategies of the larger, national-level organizations is to challenge policy stakeholders in court—either rule violators or agencies not living up to their regulatory duties. In fact, one environmental attorney, David Sive, proclaims: "In no other political and social movement has litigation played such an important and dominant role. Not even close."[29] Without going into the specifics of the given cases, this strategy can be illustrated with a few notable examples: *Sierra Club v. Morton, Secretary of the Interior, et al.*,[30] *Chevron USA v. Natural Resources Defense Council*,[31] *Lujan v. Defenders of Wildlife*,[32] and *Friends of the Earth v. Laidlaw Environmental Services, Inc.*[33]

This focus on litigation does not sit well with all groups struggling to fight against environmental deterioration. Among the actors in the environmental arena, but often thought of as disconnected from the environmental movement, are the small groups that make up the environmental justice movement. Jacqueline Switzer, an expert on domestic and international environmental issues, recounts that the mainstream environmental organizations arose to promote resource management and clean air and water.[34] Membership in and support for those organizations was mainly supplied by the middle to upper-middle class and white citizens. These people and those issues did not overlap with the environmental concerns of the lower-middle and lower classes and non-white citizens. By the mid-1980s, African American and Latino groups were forming in cities like Los Angeles to protest the siting of hazardous waste incinerators in poor, mostly minority neighborhoods. These struggles gained momentum with the 1987 publication of *Toxic Wastes and Race in the United States* by the United Church of Christ Commission for Racial Justice.[35]

More research has been done in this area in the past ten years to bring more focus and attention to these issues.[36] However, the increased academic focus has not led to a significant uniting of the environmental and the environmental justice movements. The litigation strategy is one indicator of this discord. Working in and through the court system is a fine idea, but it takes a great deal of expertise and money. This tactic takes the power and control of the fight away from the people most affected by pollution. This does not strike many in the environmental justice movement as the proper path to take. "We shall overcome" should not become "You, very different person, shall overcome for me."

In 1994 President Bill Clinton issued an executive order (12898) instructing federal agencies to integrate environmental justice into their ongoing missions. Then EPA Administrator Carol Browner said she would make certain that environmental justice issues became an integral part of EPA's decision-making process.[37] Clinton even went so far as to order the creation of the "Interagency Working Group on Environmental Justice" to coordinate federal agencies' activities on this issue.[38] Given the environmental justice movement's non-traditional status as an environmental pressure group, President Clinton's actions represented one of the few ways they could get some national attention and one of the only instances in which they could put any kind of direct pressure on a federal executive agency. All of that having been said, neither Clinton nor Browner nor any other agency head could demonstrate over the next few years any substantive changes in policy-making procedures or outcomes. Once Clinton left office, environmental justice issues faded into the background. The executive order and the creation of the working group represent one way the President can put pressure on the Environmental Protection Agency. This White House level of influence is the final form of external pressure we will cover.

Perhaps the first thing to note is the dualistic nature of President Clinton's executive order actions: they are at once obvious to detect and can end up making no difference whatsoever in the vast machinery of an agency as large and set in its ways as the EPA. In contrast to the examples I used earlier to discuss potential interest-group influence, cause and effect are easy to identify here. The President acts and the agency either changes course or it doesn't; or perhaps more accurately, the EPA Administrator's direction or priorities change or they don't. Given the thousands of workers at EPA and the thousands of things they do on a regular basis, we should not overemphasize the magnitude of the potential change, even when we think we can measure it at the top levels of the agency. What is the purpose, then, of issuing an executive order or creating a working group? It is more likely an attempt to placate a constituency, that is, influence the public, than it is an attempt to move the EPA in a new direction, that is, a direction in which it would not otherwise have gone without the influence of the President.

Think back again to the EPA mission statement. Clearly the EPA should be pursuing environmental justice anyway. So the easy-to-identify case of cause and effect is not particularly interesting or important in trying to assess the President's influence on the EPA. Once again, we are back to the harder-to-measure, behind-the-scenes type of pressure we see with interest groups. How can we demonstrate this cause and effect? One way is to do in-depth research on every single public decision that is made by an administration about the environment. With today's technology and a few motivated citizens, that process isn't as difficult as you might imagine. BushGreenwatch represents just such a group.[39]

A look at this environmental advocacy group, along with the actions of the Bush administration, provides us with an interesting case of the combination of external pressure groups working in opposition to one another: BushGreenwatch versus President George W. Bush. BushGreenwatch is an online newsletter and environmental information database devoted to "Tracking the Bush Administration's Environmental Misdeeds." Created at the end of 2003 by Environmental Media Services, with support from another online advocacy group, MoveOn.org,[40] BushGreenwatch is a prime example of what can happen in the twenty-first century when environmentalists become extremely frustrated with an administration. Think about the work involved in creating a website and providing regular (several times per week) updates on the environmental missteps of each and every part of the Bush administration (refer back to the list of federal executive agencies connected to the environment), along with special in-depth reports on just how far the administration will go to change the environmental policy-making agendas of the Executive Office of the President. Below is a very selective review of issues BushGreenwatch has emphasized as important.[41] This review is intended to illustrate the kinds of ways a President might go about influencing the EPA, and secondarily to illustrate one of the newest forms of pressure-group strategies.

- "EPA Overrides Court Ruling Against Destructive Water Cooling Systems" (February 18, 2004). At issue are water cooling systems in power plants, whether the current standards fulfill the Clean Water Act's (CWA's) requirement to mitigate environmental damage, and whether the EPA is fulfilling its duty to properly implement and enforce a major environmental law.

In early February, a three-judge panel of the Second Circuit U.S. Court of Appeals ruled that current practices violated the CWA, and remanded the rule back to EPA. EPA then turned around and issued a rule that allowed existing plants to continue the damaging process, and to substitute restoration for mitigation. The implication is that political pressure from industry, through the White House, is restraining the bureaucratic process.

- "Congressmen Question Industry Role in EPA Mercury Rule-Making" (February 19, 2004). In this case, the issue is the degree to which the EPA Administrator (and implicitly, the President) allows external pressure groups to shape specific EPA rules (as opposed to pushing for a general policy approach). Representatives Henry A. Waxman (D-CA) and Tom Allen (D-ME) have called for an investigation to explain reports that "portions of the EPA's proposal to regulate mercury generated by electric power plants were copied verbatim from industry lobbying materials."[42]

- "EPA Misleading Public on Superfund" (March 1, 2004). The issue here is questioning the amount of pressure environmental groups believe the White House is putting on the final editors of EPA reports, pressure to the point of misrepresenting the truth. Reported by BushGreenwatch, the original investigation was done by the U.S. Public Interest Research Group (US PIRG) and the Sierra Club: "the Bush administration is cleaning up fewer toxic waste sites, underfunding the Superfund program, and forcing taxpayers to pay for more orphan toxic cleanups. EPA, however, has manipulated [the] numbers to tell a different story."[43]

- "Bush EPA Seeks Weaker Control Over Transport of Hazardous Waste" (March 15, 2004). The concern is once again about the influence of industry, specifically the nuclear industry. In this case, the pressure is evident in new transportation regulations and the redefinition of what constitutes "dangerous" toxic waste. According to the report, the nuclear industry has been pushing for a redefinition of radioactive materials, including nuclear power, nuclear weapons, and naturally occurring materials. The new definition or classification would categorize these materials as "Below Regulatory Concern." They have been seeking the redefinition in order to legally change disposal sites for nuclear waste (looking for cheaper sites) and to facilitate the deregulation of hazardous nuclear waste.[44] This is happening in the face of intense opposition from a coalition of leaders from environmental, recycling, and nuclear watchdog groups (who have also tried to influence the current Administrator, Mike Leavitt). The implication: industry pressures (or simply finds a willing collaborator in) the White House, which in turn pressures (or finds a willing collaborator in) the EPA Administrator.

In each of these examples, the influence of the President on the EPA is both direct and indirect. The direct influence can be seen in the choice of EPA Administrators and the application of the President's conservative ideology to that administrative choice, and to the direction the President would like the agency to go. The general principle at work is this: environmental problems are more easily solved and goals are more efficiently reached when the markets, or their leading representatives, lead the way. This ideological perspective is in direct opposition to the fundamental principles that created the EPA, the size and reach of the agency, and the idea that environmental issues can ever trump business issues. The current EPA Administrator, Mike Leavitt, even has a creative name for this philosophy, the Enlibra Doctrine (co-written by Leavitt and former Governor of Oregon John Kitzhaber), which he describes at the EPA Administrator's website: Enlibra, "from the Latin, means 'move toward balance.' . . . [T]he philosophy emphasizes collaboration instead of polarization, national standards and neighborhood solutions, markets instead of mandates, solutions that transcend political boundaries, and other common sense ideas that will accelerate environmental progress."[45] This direct influence then merges with the indirect: the President is also acting as a filter for a group of powerful economic actors who are generally seen as being opposed to federal environmental regulation.

Taking all of these external pressures as a whole, rolling together Congress and the President and environmental groups and their opponents, one thing is clear: no one actor determines policy at any given time. Moreover, the idea that any President or member of Congress or public pressure group can actually change the direction, focus, and momentum of an 18,000-person, $8 billion agency, in the midst of this competitive atmosphere, is invalid on its face. To get a better look at how these forces interact, we will now turn to two cases involving EPA rule making: the 1997 decision to strengthen National Ambient Air Quality Standards (NAAQS) for particulate matter and ozone,[46] and the 2003 decision to weaken provisions of the Clean Air Act (CAA), specifically with regard to New Source Review guidelines.

THE BUREAUCRATS VERSUS THE POLITICIANS

The Clean Air Act Amendments of 1970 represent some of the most significant pollution control measures introduced at the national level in the last thirty years. The Clean Air Act took environmental policy to a new, more uniform level. Its goals can be summarized as follows: (1) establish uniform federal air-quality standards—the NAAQS; (2) standards should be set at two levels: primary standards for human health, secondary standards for exposed materials, agricultural products, forests, and other non-health values; and (3) primary standards should be set at levels that would "provide an adequate margin of safety" to protect the public "from any known or anticipated adverse effects associated with such air pollutant[s] in the ambient air."[47] NAAQS were to be set for six common air pollutants: carbon monoxide, lead, nitrous oxides, ozone, particulate matter, and sulfur dioxide. Because Congress wanted to maintain standards compatible with the latest scientific understanding of health issues, the CAA requires the EPA Administrator to review each air-quality standard and the criteria on which it is based every five years and revise the standard "if the Administrator deems it necessary." This administrative flexibility is one of the continuing points of contention regarding the CAA.

On July 18, 1997, the Administrator of the EPA revised the NAAQS for particulate matter and ozone. These pollutants are both hazardous to human health at any level, so strict standards were becoming even stricter. Some estimated that compliance would cost manufacturers, and therefore citizens, hundreds of millions of dollars. As might be expected, industry was not happy about the stringent standards and attacked the EPA in the court system. Led by American Trucking Associations, Inc., the U.S. Chamber of Commerce, the National Association of Manufacturers, and the states of Michigan, Ohio, and West Virginia, industry challenged the standards as arbitrary, unconstitutional, and unreasonable. The standards were argued to be arbitrary because they were not based on a clear, scientific standard below which one could find no health effects. They were argued to be unconstitutional because the plaintiffs believed the EPA Administrator's delegated power was too vague, and that she was, in fact, legislating—something the Constitution reserves for the legislative branch alone. And they were argued to be unreasonable because they were not based at least in part on the likely cost of compliance; that is, industry wanted cost benefit analyses to become part of the process of setting NAAQS. Industry's arguments failed on all counts. In a relatively rare *unanimous* decision, the Supreme Court upheld the right of the Administrator of the EPA to set reasonable standards based on the best available evidence, and also found that cost benefit analyses were not to be used in choosing these particular CAA standards.[48]

In this case, the CAA provisions withstood the test, the head bureaucrat's ability to implement and modify relatively vague congressional orders was reaffirmed, and environmental policy was judged to be important enough to set aside concerns about the economic impact of the rules. This is quite a feat, given the opposition. Two types of external pressure groups pushed for the reinterpretation of the CAA: business/commercial organizations and loosely construed governmental organizations. Clearly, Michigan, Ohio, and West Virginia saw themselves as a unified constituency, not unlike the truckers, manufacturers, and business community. This opposition force had both the inside track, government to government communication and lobbying, and the outside economic track, major economic sector to government lobbying, under the threat of economic disaster. It might be telling that the case started under a Democratic President and a Democratically appointed EPA Administrator, and that the incoming Republican President and his head of EPA, Christine Todd Whitman, inherited the case in its final days. However, we should not make too much of the partisan power in the executive branch; liberal and conservative members of the Supreme Court alike voted in favor of the long-standing rules. This case represents a clear triumph for the professionals.

In 1977 Congress amended the 1970 Clean Air Act (as they did again in 1990). One of the most significant amendments dealt with those major air polluters (mainly power plants, oil refineries, and large-scale industrial factories) that existed before the CAA was originally passed, and that were therefore grandfathered into a situation in which they did not have to comply with the new air pollution regulations. The original act addressed new sources of pollution, meaning those businesses coming online after the passage of the CAA, but largely left preexisting polluters alone. The 1977 rules falling under the heading New Source Review (NSR) were intended to close that loophole, in essence attempting to move old plants, refineries, and factories into compliance. NSR rules required existing facilities to update their current pollution-abatement technologies to the best available technology whenever undergoing a major expansion or refurbishment that would result in significant emission increases. However, facilities' activities considered "common maintenance," "routine repairs," or "routine upgrades" were not subject to NSR. This allowed the major fixed, preexisting polluters to continue their current emission levels under the guise of "business as usual." All seemed fine for twenty years. Factories and power plants maintained that they were consistently in compliance with the rules; the EPA did its usual amount of verification, and there was no significant push to crack down on non-complying facilities (the Reagan administration has been referred to as "the first president to come to office with an avowedly anti-environmental agenda"[49]) in the years immediately following passage of the 1977 amendments. This all changed in 1999, late in the second term of the Clinton administration.

According to James M. Taylor, managing editor of *Environment and Climate News*, the Clinton EPA departed from the so-called "plain language" interpretation of NSR requirements. The administration began calculating "emissions increases" in such a way that the increases due to "common" and "routine" procedures were now significant enough to trigger NSR.[50] Traditional practices were now unlawful, and the Clinton administration had a newfound zeal for investigating non-complying facilities and referring violators to the Department of Justice for prosecution. By the end of the year, the Clinton administration had sued nine companies, saying they had modified fifty-one older facilities without adopting the required technologies.[51] This came as a shock, especially to major energy producers running coal-powered plants. If they could only get back to the status quo, life would be good again. Something had to change. The most significant thing that did change was the person sitting in the Oval Office and the introduction of his fellow travelers into the powerful positions of the Executive Office of the President.

When George W. Bush came into office, he had a problem. While his environmental stance seemed a bit weaker than Clinton's on the 2000 campaign trail, their positions were not completely dissimilar. On one rather progressive point they actually agreed: carbon dioxide emissions (the main ingredient in the mix of anthropogenic greenhouse gasses) need to be controlled and eventually curbed. This did not sit well with the energy industry, and coupled with their anger over being sued by the Clinton Department of Justice because of a new interpretation of NSR rules, they became a thundering voice for environmental policy change. It didn't hurt that energy corporations had been among the strongest contributors to Republicans and presidential candidate Bush in the 2000 campaign. In fact, there were more executives from the energy sector than from any other industry group among Bush's elite fund raisers, the "Pioneers."[52] It also didn't hurt to have people like Vice President Dick Cheney, former Republican Party chair and energy sector lobbyist Haley Barbour, future chair of the Republican National Committee and energy sector lobbyist Marc Racicot, and energy industry lobby-group head (and Yale classmate and "Pioneer") Thomas R. Kuhn all pushing for change. All of these men were influential Republicans, all with strong ties to the energy sector, all friends of President Bush, and all with easy access to the levers of power.[53] Two months after President Bush took office, he reversed his position on carbon dioxide controls. By the end of the next year, plans to make changes to the NSR rules were announced to the public.[54] The most significant change dealt with the point of contention about "common" and "routine" practices. The rule now: upgrades and maintenance are exempt from NSR if the cost of these activities is less than 20 percent of the value of the entire business. Theoretically, in five years you could have an entirely new plant and still not be forced to adopt the latest, best available technologies.

The story about NSR rule changes would not be complete without accounting for the fallout. While we cannot be so reductionist as to conclude that these specific regulatory moves resulted in the following exodus from the EPA, the argument is plausible. Most accounts of the people leaving the EPA have alluded to the fact, if they have not said outright, that the major changes in attitude about what the EPA is all about and how it is to move into the future, have driven senior people from the agency. In reality, even if many people left for a variety of reasons, the public perception, based on the media, is that they left because of the Bush/Cheney/Leavitt view of the environment, the EPA, and the kind of enforcement the EPA should be conducting. The list includes Eric V. Schaeffer, head of the Office of Regulatory Enforcement, who joined EPA during George H. W. Bush's presidency. His parting shot (to Administrator Whitman): "We seem about to snatch defeat from the jaws of victory," and the White House "seems determined to weaken the rules we are trying to enforce."[55] Christine Todd Whitman, President Bush's first EPA Administrator, lasted two years. Bruce Buckheit, who had served EPA through six presidential administrations, and his deputy, Richard Biondi, left. Biondi stated: "I just didn't feel comfortable working in that environment anymore. Certainly the direction that the agency was going over the last couple of years was different than what I'd experienced during my thirty-two years working for EPA. It was contrary to everything that I had worked for." Sylvia Lowrance, at EPA more than twenty years, also left. Overall, the number of EPA enforcement staff has fallen to its lowest level since the agency was established—a 12 percent decline from 528 to 464—since Bush took office.[56] And, by the way, the EPA has dropped investigations into fifty power plants for past violations of the Clean Air Act.[57]

The status quo (plus) seems to have returned in the NSR case, and the political forces appear to have won. I chose these two cases precisely because they provide polar opposite examples of how things come to be at the Environmental Protection Agency. In the first example, we had a challenge to a well-established rule. The challenge came from external pressure groups, but there was no institutional inclination to change. Nor were there any close relationships between the plaintiffs and the executive branch. The Supreme Court, relying on its experience and precedents in dealing with administrative procedures, sided with the established institutional process as well. A Democrat held the presidency, and therefore held, too, the tone of the leadership of the executive agencies. The EPA and its history were respected, thought of as something to build on. The second case represents a different value on every variable in the mix—and variation is key to social scientists! The challenge came from external pressure groups, and there was an institutional inclination to change. There were close personal, partisan, and financial relationships between the plaintiffs and the executive branch. The courts are involved right now, but they were not seen as the vehicle with which changes could be made; changes were sought at the source, within the EPA itself. A Republican held the presidency and therefore controlled the tone of agency leadership (Enlibra). The EPA was, and is, considered a dinosaur by the George W. Bush administration, a massive government agency to move past rather than to build upon. The differences could not be much more stark. A defender of the new NSR rules might say politics drove Clinton to go after the energy sector and to punish rule violators beyond reason. That might be true, but most of the other variables outlined above would not have turned out the same.

The Environmental Protection Agency will not disappear anytime soon, whether there is a Republican or a Democrat in the White House. The agency will constantly struggle with competing pressures from within itself, from within government, and from the many sectors of society at large. The EPA will continue to work toward cleaner air and water, toward a safer and healthier environment, toward a higher quality of life for all of us. Whatever the pressures, it will continue to do these things because one thing will not change: we, the citizens of the United States, will demand it.

NOTES

1. Jacqueline Vaughn Switzer, *Environmental Politics: Domestic and Global Dimensions*, 4th ed. (Belmont, Calif.: Wadsworth/Thomson Learning, 2004), 15.

2. Michael E. Kraft, *Environmental Policy and Politics*, 3rd ed. (New York: Pearson Education, 2004), 99.

3. Lawrence W. Rothenberg, *Environmental Choices: Policy Responses to Green Demands* (Washington, D.C.: CQ Press, 2002), 52.

4. Switzer, *Environmental Politics*, 18.

5. Switzer, *Environmental Politics*, 18; Rothenberg, *Environmental Choices*, 53.

6. Kraft, *Environmental Policy and Politics*, 99.

7. Michael E. Kraft and Norman J. Vig, "Environmental Policy From the 1970s to the Twenty-First Century," in *Environmental Policy: New Directions for the Twenty-First Century*, ed. Norman J. Vig and Michael E. Kraft (Washington, D.C.: CQ Press, 2003), 12. See also Public Law 91-90 (42 USC 4321-4347), sec. 101.

8. Kraft and Vig, "Environmental Policy From the 1970s to the Twenty-First Century," 12.

9. A presidential executive order is generally defined as a rule or regulation having the force of law, promulgated directly by the President under his or her statutory authority.

10. Examples of independent agencies include the General Services Administration, the Federal Emergency Management Agency, AMTRAK, the Equal Employment Opportunity Commission, and the Federal Trade Commission. See www.firstgov.gov/Agencies/Federal/Independent.shtml.

11. I do not want to understate the web of executive-branch offices that do have some environmental policy responsibility ("but not all"). A list of these agencies would include the Council on Environmental Quality, Office of Management and Budget, Office of Science and Technology Policy, Department of the Interior, Department of Agriculture, Department of Commerce, Department of State, Department of Justice, Department of Defense, Department of Energy, Department of Transportation, Department of Housing and Urban Development, Department of Health and Human Services, Department of Labor, the Nuclear Regulatory Commission, and the Tennessee Valley Authority. See Kraft and Vig, "Environmental Policy From the 1970s to the Twenty-First Century," 7, fig. 1-1.

12. "An Agency for the Environment," accessed at www.epa.gov/history/publications/origins6.htm.

13. "Agency Mission Statement," accessed at www.epa.gov/history/org/origins/mission.htm.

14. CAFE stands for corporate average fuel economy, the aggregate, average miles per gallon a fleet of vehicles from a given manufacturer will achieve.

15. Organizational structure information gathered from www.epa.gov/epahome/organization.htm; www.epa. gov/epahome/locate1.htm; www.epa.gov/epahome/locate2.htm.

16. Research programs and office listings can be found at www.epa.gov/epahome/program2.htm.

17. Budget of the United States Government, Fiscal Year 2005, summary tables S-3 and S-4, accessed at www.whitehouse.gov/omb/budget/fy2005/tables.htm.

18. Budget of the United States Government, Fiscal Year 2005. The agencies ranked below the EPA in terms of monies allotted to them include: Social Security Administration (just the administrative part!), "Other Agencies," Commerce, National Science Foundation, Judicial Branch, Legislative Branch, Corps of Engineers, Small Business Administration, Executive Office of the President, and General Services Administration, in that order.

19. Kraft, *Environmental Policy and Politics*, 142; Rothenberg, *Environmental Choices*, 59, fig. 3-4.

20. Kraft and Vig, "Environmental Policy From the 1970s to the Twenty-First Century," 19.

21. "Major Congressional Committees with Jurisdiction Over EPA Issues," www.epa.gov/ocirpage/leglibrary/pdf/2003_0709_108senatejuris.pdf; and www.epa.gov/ocirpage/leglibrary/pdf/108housejuris.pdf.

22. You can find more information about these different think tanks and the various views they represent by going to their websites: Heritage Foundation, www.heritage.org; Progressive Policy Institute, www.ppionline.org; Cato Institute, www.cato.org.

23. Rothenberg, *Environmental Choices*, 77. See also Frank R. Baumgartner and Beth L. Leech, *Basic Interests: The Importance of Groups in Politics and Political Science* (Princeton, N.J.: Princeton University Press, 1998).

24. Terry Atlas, "Under Pressure, EPA Eases Wetlands Stance," *Chicago Tribune*, May 9, 1991, accessed at www.rice.edu/wetlands/Newspapers/nws34.html.

25. Article accessed at www.inmotionmagazine.com/ra02/epa2002.html.

26. "Carter at EPA," Oral History Interview, accessed at www.epa.gov/history/publications/costle/07.htm.

27. Gary Polakovic, "EPA Plans to Relax Toxic Emissions Standards," *Los Angeles Times*, February 11, 2003, accessed at www.commondreams.org/headlines03/0211-05.htm.

28. This is necessarily a selective list. Groups have been culled from Kraft, *Environmental Policy and Politics*, 106–107, table 4.3; Rothenberg, *Environmental Choices*, 66–67, table 4-1; Switzer, *Environmental Politics*, 38–42.

29. Rothenberg, *Environmental Choices*, 88; Claudia Polsky and Tom Turner, "Justice on the Rampage," *Amicus Journal* 21 (1999), 34–35.

30. *Sierra Club v. Morton, Secretary of the Interior, et al.* 405 U.S. 727 (1972), the Sierra Club arguing that it had the right of "standing" in the courts because of its long-standing concern for and expertise in the conservation of national parks and forests.

31. *Chevron USA v. Natural Resources Defense Council* 467 U.S. 837 (1984), where NRDC challenged the "bubble concept" for pollution emissions from industrial groupings.

32. *Lujan v. Defenders of Wildlife* 112 U.S. 2130 (1992), another court battle about "standing," i.e., who has the right to bring suit when an environmental law is allegedly being violated.

33. *Friends of the Earth v. Laidlaw Environmental Services, Inc.* 98 U.S. 822 (2000), a case involving a citizen suitor's claim for civil penalties. Rothenberg, *Environmental Choices*, 93–94.

34. Switzer, *Environmental Politics*, 42.

35. *Toxic Wastes and Race in the United States: A National Report on the Racial and Socio-economic Characteristics of Communities With Hazardous Waste Sites*, United Church of Christ Commission for Racial Justice, 1987.

36. An excellent edited volume of some of the most recent research being done in this area is *Environmental Injustices, Political Struggles: Race, Class and the Environment*, edited by David E. Comacho (Durham, N.C.: Duke University Press, 1998).

37. Switzer, *Environmental Politics*, 43.

38. For the full text of the presidential order, see www.epa.gov/compliance/resources/policies/ej/exec_order_12898.pdf.

39. For complete information about this group and its database of information, see www.bushgreenwatch.org.

40. Environmental Media Services, www.ems.org; MoveOn.org, www.moveon.org/front/.

41. The BushGreenwatch website has all of their back issues online at this time.

42. Waxman and Allen press release, February 12, 2004. In addition, the law firm of Latham and Watkins (from an earlier example) and Jeffrey Holmstead pop up again in this example.

43. "The Truth About Toxic Waste Cleanups: How EPA Is Misleading the Public About the Superfund Program," US PIRG and Sierra Club, February 26, 2004.

44. Diane D'Arrigo, Nuclear Information and Resource Service, www.nirs.org.

45. The full doctrine can be reviewed at www.epa.gov/adminweb/leavitt/enlibra.htm.

46. NAAQS: National Ambient (outside) Air Quality Standards; particulate matter (soot), ozone (smog).

47. Paul R. Portney, "Air Pollution Policy," in *Public Policies for Environmental Protection*, 2nd ed., ed. Paul R. Portney and Robert N. Stavins (Washington, D.C.: Resources for the Future Press, 2000), 81–84. For the relevant text of the Clean Air Act, see www.epa.gov/oar/caa/caa109.txt, Title I, Part A, Section 109 (2 (b) (1) (2)).

48. *Whitman v. American Trucking Associations, Inc.* 531 U.S. 457 (2001).

49. Norman J. Vig, "Presidential Leadership and the Environment," in *Environmental Policy: New Directions for the Twenty-First Century*, ed. Vig and Kraft, 107.

50. James M. Taylor, "EPA Restores Flexibility to New Source Review," Heartland Institute, January 1, 2003.

51. Christopher Drew and Richard A. Oppel Jr., "How Industry Won the Battle of Pollution Control at E.P.A.," *New York Times*, March 6, 2004.

52. Drew and Oppel, "How Industry Won the Battle of Pollution Control at E.P.A."

53. Drew and Oppel, "How Industry Won the Battle of Pollution Control at E.P.A."

54. An in-depth investigation of these personal and monetary connections was conducted by Public Citizen's Congress Watch. "EPA's Smoke Screen: How Congress Was Given False Information While Campaign Contributions and Political Connections Gutted a Clean Air Rule," Public Citizen, 2003.

55. "EPA's Smoke Screen."

56. Amanda Griscom, "Jumping Ship at EPA," *Grist Magazine*, January 7, 2004, accessed at www.alternet.org.

57. Christopher Drew and Richard A. Oppel Jr., "Lawyers at E.P.A. Say It Will Drop Pollution Cases," *New York Times*, November 6, 2003.

Index

Central Intelligence Agency, 7, 55, 68–69, 106, 120, 338
Chao, Elaine, 158
Chavez, Linda, 151, 157
Cheney, Elizabeth, 63
Cheney, Richard, 120
Chevron U.S.A. v. Natural Resources Defense Council, 351–52, 378
Childhood Lead Poisoning Prevention, Committee on, 166
Children and Families, Florida Department of, 45
Cisneros, Henry, 150
Citizens to Preserve Overton Park v. Volpe, 337, 353
Civil Aeronautics Board, 258–59, 261, 345
Civil Rights Act of 1871, 47–48, 327
Civil Service Commission, 327
Civil Service Reform Act of 1978, 162, 167
Clamshell Alliance, 130
Clark, Wesley, 120
Clean Air Act, 9, 302, 333, 351; amendments of 1970, 363; amendments of 1977, 381; National Ambient Air Quality Standards, 381
Clean Water Restoration Act, 363
clientele groups, conflict with agencies, 256–61; regulatory agencies, 257–61; social service agencies, 256–57
clientele groups, cooperation with agencies, 250–56; role of community of feeling, 254–55; role of knowledge, 251–53; role of politics, 253–54
Clinton, William (Bill), 7, 142–43, 148, 189, 201, 335; appointments, 67, 80, 89, 106, 150–53, 157; budgets, 181, 183, 191; "Don't Ask, Don't Tell," 186, 189, 240; Environmental Protection Agency, 378, 383; privatization, 144; procedure, 310; reorganization, 172; use of Executive Order 12291, 164, 188; veto, 204
Coast Guard, U.S., 132, 210–11, 321; port security, 223–24, 226; relations with Congress, 229, 232
Collins, Thomas, 210–11, 226, 230
Colonnade Catering Corporation, 292
Coluccio, Dominick, 293
Commerce, Department of, 8, 21
Communist Party of America, 68
Community Nutrition Institute, 272
congressional committees: agency-subcommittee relations, 222–28;

efforts to influence agencies, 202–22; and executive orders, 239–40; management by, 228–31; statutory authority of agencies, 236–39; statutory interpretation, 239; structure of agencies, 231–32. *See also* oversight
Consumer Product Safety Commission, 10, 310
Consumer's Union, 119
contentious accommodation, 274–75
Corps of Engineers, U.S. Army, 91, 223, 226
Correctional Education Association, 257
Council of Economic Advisors, 163
Council of State Administrators of Vocational Rehabilitation, 256
Council on Environmental Quality, 163
Cravens, Jay, 269
Critical Infrastructure Protection Board, 191
Critical Mass, 131, 272
Cronin, Thomas, 31, 149, 171
Customs and Border Protection, Bureau of, 213–15, 231

Dalehite v. United States, 324, 328
Davis, Kenneth Culp, 337
DDT, 343
Defenders of Wildlife, 340
Defense, Department of, 106, 152–53, 169, 174
Defense Commissary Agency, 128–29, 134, 139
DeFunis, Marco, 342
DeLay, Thomas, 118
Del Monte, 290
DeMato, Marion, 293
Detroit Tigers, 75
Diamond, Neil, 176
Dodd, Christopher, 204–5
Dodd, Lawrence, 209, 217
Dole, Elizabeth, 61
Domestic Council, 162
"Don't Ask, Don't Tell," 186, 189, 240
Dreyfuss, Lee Sherman, 66
Dreyfuss, Robert, 63
due process of law, 295–301
Dulles, Allen, 68–69

Eastwood, Clint, 289
Economic Development Administration, 233
Education, Department of, 172

About the Authors

Dennis D. Riley is professor at the University of Wisconsin, Stevens Point, where he has taught since 1978. He graduated from Willamette University and earned an MPA from Syracuse and a PhD from Michigan. He is the author of *Controlling the Federal Bureaucracy* (1987) and *Public Personnel Administration* (revised edition, 2002), and has also published in the *American Political Science Review* and the *Western Political Quarterly*. He loves baseball; the beer produced by the Central Waters Brewing Co. of Junction City, Wisconsin; his wife, daughter, and stepdaughters; and his grandchildren.

Bryan E. Brophy-Baermann is visiting instructor in government at Lawrence University in Appleton, Wisconsin. He graduated from the University of Iowa, where he earned a BA and PhD. He has published in the *American Journal of Political Science* and *Comparative Political Studies*, and has also contributed to *Governments of the World: A Global Guide to Citizens Rights and Responsibilities* (2005).